Fourth Edition

REPRESENTATIVE GOVERNMENT IN MODERN EUROPE

Michael Gallagher

Michael Laver

Peter Mair

Boston   Burr Ridge, IL   Dubuque, IA   Madison, WI   New York   San Francisco   St. Louis
Bangkok   Bogotá   Caracas   Kuala Lumpur   Lisbon   London   Madrid   Mexico City
Milan   Montreal   New Delhi   Santiago   Seoul   Singapore   Sydney   Taipei   Toronto

The McGraw·Hill Companies

McGraw Hill   Higher Education

Published by McGraw-Hill, an imprint of The McGraw-Hill Companies, Inc., 1221 Avenue of the Americas, New York, NY 10020. Copyright © 2006, 2001, 1995. Previously published under the title of *Representative Government in Western Europe,* copyright © 1992 by McGraw-Hill. All rights reserved. No part of this publication may be reproduced or distributed in any form or by any means, or stored in a database or retrieval system, without the prior written consent of The McGraw-Hill Companies, Inc., including, but not limited to, in any network or other electronic storage or transmission, or broadcast for distance learning.

This book is printed on acid-free paper.

4 5 6 7 8 9 0 FGR/FGR 0 9 8 7 6

ISBN-13: 978-0-07-297706-6
ISBN-10: 0-07-297706-X

Editor in Chief: Emily Barrosse
Publisher: Lyn Uhl
Senior Sponsoring Editor: Monica Eckman
Marketing Manager: Katherine Bates
Developmental Editor: Kate Scheinman
Production Service: Matrix Productions
Manuscript Editor: Pat Herbst
Design Manager: Preston Thomas
Cover Designer: Ross Carron
Manager, Photo Research: Brian J. Pecko
Senior Production Supervisor: Richard DeVitto

Composition: 10/12 Times Roman by GTS-York
Printing: 45# New Era Matte, Quebecor, Fairfield

Cover: © Jessica Marcotte/nonstock

Library of Congress Cataloging in Publication Data

Gallagher, Michael 1951-
    Representative government in modern Europe/Michael Gallagher, Michael
    Laver, Peter Mair.—4th ed.
        p. cm.
    Includes bibliographical references and index.
    ISBN: 0-07-297706-X
    1. Representative government and representation—Europe—Case studies. 2.
Political parties—Europe—Case studies. 3. Europe—Politics and government—1945-
I. Laver, Michael, 1949-. II. Mair, Peter. III. Gallagher, Michael, Ph.D. Representative
government in Western Europe. IV. Title.

JN94.A91 G35 2005   2005047861
321.8'043'094—dc22   CIP

The Internet addresses listed in the text were accurate at the time of publication. The inclusion of a website does not indicate an endorsement by the authors or McGraw-Hill, and McGraw-Hill does not guarantee the accuracy of the information presented at these sites.

www.mhhe.com

CONTENTS

LIST OF TABLES AND FIGURES

Figures

About the Authors

MICHAEL GALLAGHER is associate professor in the Department of Political Science at Trinity College, University of Dublin; he has also been a visiting professor at New York University and at the City University of Hong Kong. He is coeditor of *Candidate Selection in Comparative Selection* (London, 1988), *The Referendum Experience in Europe* (Basingstoke, 1996), *The Politics of Electoral Systems* (Oxford, 2005), and *Politics in the Republic of Ireland,* 4th ed. (Abingdon, 2005). His current research interests include a study of the backgrounds, attitudes, and roles of members of political parties.

MICHAEL LAVER is Professor of Politics at New York University. He previously taught at Queens University, Belfast; the University of Liverpool; University College Galway; and Trinity College Dublin. He has been a visiting professor at the University of Texas at Austin; Harvard University; Duke University; SciencesPo Paris; and the University of Bologna. His books include (with Kenneth Shepsle) *Making and Breaking Governments* (New York, 1996); (with Norman Schofield) *Multiparty Government* (Ann Arbor 1998); *Estimating the Policy Positions of Political Actors* (London, 2001), and the forthcoming (with Kenneth Benoit) *Party Policy in Modern Democracies.* He is currently working on agent-based dynamic models of several aspects of party competition and on various ways of measuring the policy positions of political actors, including expert surveys and the computerized analysis of political text.

PETER MAIR is Professor of Comparative Politics at Leiden University in the Netherlands and at the European University Institute in Florence, Italy. He previously taught at the University of Limerick; the University of Strathclyde, Glasgow; and the University of Manchester. He is the author (with Stefano Bartolini) of *Identity, Competition, and Electoral Availability* (Cambridge, 1990), which was awarded the Stein Rokkan Prize, and of *Party System Change* (Oxford, 1997). Recent coedited books include *The Enlarged European Union* (London, 2002) and *Political Parties and Electoral Change* (London, 2004). He is coeditor of the journal *West European Politics* and is currently engaged in a wide-ranging study of political parties and contemporary democracy.

PREFACE

This is the fourth edition of *Representative Government in Modern Europe.* In many ways, the evolution of the book over the years since we wrote the first edition about fifteen years ago has matched the remarkable evolution of the politics of modern Europe over the same short period. We finished the first edition at a time when the end of communist rule in a group of countries that people then still thought of as the Soviet Union and its Warsaw Pact allies had occurred no more than a year or two previously. Whatever anyone might have said at the time, nobody who was being honest had any real idea whether this was a temporary blip on an essentially authoritarian trajectory for the countries involved, or a political sea change of historic proportions.

With the great luxury of hindsight we now know that these changes really were of massive proportions and that the transition from the Soviet era to democracy now seems secure in many countries. In 2004, a remarkable manifestation of this evolution was the accession in Dublin of eight eastern European postcommunist states to what had until that moment been a very "western" European Union. Shocking events in the disintegrating former Yugoslavia—at the geographic heart of Europe—have shown us a darker side of post-Soviet Europe, however. Brutal images beamed around the world have shown once again just how much blood can flow when politics fails, even in modern Europe.

The most radical change we have made in this fourth edition of the book we ourselves think of as *RGME,* therefore, has been to integrate into the mainstream of the text our treatment of the eight postcommunist states that joined the European Union (EU) in 2004. The first edition was entitled *Representative Government in Western Europe* and made no real mention of eastern Europe, treating it, as was conventional at the time, as a quite different political universe. We then retitled the book *Representative Government in Modern Europe* and, in the second and third editions, included a chapter at the end of the book on political developments in eastern Europe. We did things this way because we felt that, with eastern European states just a few years into their transitions to democracy, we were not able to see clear enough patterns in their politics to be able to integrate them into more general discussions of representative government in modern Europe. For this edition, we have bitten the bullet and integrated the eastern European EU states fully into our discussions of representative government in what we really can start thinking of as modern, as opposed to western, Europe.

In practical terms, this means that we have expanded the country coverage in this edition by adding the ten states that joined the EU in 2004. Our discussions now extend to the Baltic republics of Estonia, Latvia, and Lithuania—which in 1940 had been forcibly incorporated into the Soviet Union. We also include the central European states of Hungary, Poland, and the two parts of what had formerly been Czechoslovakia—the Czech and Slovak Republics. In addition, we have included Slovenia—the small mountain state that had been part of the former Yugoslavia but quickly became independent and escaped most of the consequences of the civil wars that wracked the rest of what had once been Yugoslavia. At the same time as these eight states, the small Mediterranean island states of Cyprus and Malta also joined the EU, and we have also incorporated these, as far as we have been able, into our country coverage. Overall, therefore, our discussions of representative government in modern Europe now cover twenty-eight countries—the twenty-five countries of the expanded EU plus Iceland, Norway, and Switzerland. The last three are part of modern Europe by any reasonable definition but, for reasons that mostly have to do with domestic politics, remain outside the EU.

While expanding our country coverage, we have been careful to retain the fundamental philosophy that has guided this book through its various editions and, to judge from the feedback we have received, is a major part of its appeal to readers. Our discussions are structured by what we see as the major substantive and intellectual themes in the study of representative government, although we have reordered three early chapters into what seems to us now to be a more logical sequence. We try as far as possible to discuss the full range of European countries, large and small, in the context of these themes, rather than organizing the book as a set of country studies. Since we feel strongly that this is the right way to do things, we are pleased to see that it has now become a much more popular approach than it was when we wrote the first edition.

Although the big change has involved bringing the eastern European EU members into the mainstream of our discussions, we have also tried to keep the book as up-to-date as possible in its discussions of ongoing theoretical and empirical work on core features of representative government in modern Europe. Reviews of the book have stressed its value in introducing readers to current debates among those who analyze European politics, and this edition sets out to keep our discussion of these debates as up-to-the-minute as possible. Naturally, we have also updated the data in most tables to make them as complete and current as possible.

Since the political science profession is nowhere near as huge as its potential subject matter, however, not everything is researched all the time. This means that there are areas for which somewhat "older" research remains the most informative, and in these cases we have tried to be careful not to replace discussions of high-quality earlier work with those of less solid recent work just because the latter has a more recent publication date. In the same vein it is a plain fact that there is still less research on the countries of eastern Europe—especially the smaller ones—covering the full range of themes discussed in this book. In effect what we have been able to do, therefore, has been to add results from new research conducted on politics in the eastern European transition states to what we have already learned about representative government in modern Europe more generally. Mundane resource constraints mean that there are inevitable gaps in the profession's coverage of eastern Europe and there will be for years to come. Notwithstanding these constraints, our ambition has been to make sure that our treatment of modern Europe is as modern and as comprehensive as possible.

We have been helped enormously while producing this fourth edition by advice and assistance from many, many friends, colleagues, and reviewers. The reviewers are: Anne Bennett, University of Nevada, Las Vegas; Gregg Bucken-Knapp, Göteborg

University; Clay Clemens, College of William and Mary; Scott Cole, Longwood University; Vincent Della Sala, Carleton University; Mark Donovan, Cardiff University; Robert Elgie, Dublin City University; Gary P. Freeman, University of Texas, Austin; Paul Hamilton, Brock University; Indriõi H. Indriõsõn, University of Iceland; Michael Kinner, University of Manitoba; Robert Klemmensen, University of Southern Denmark; Kai Lehmann, University of Liverpool; Alberto Perez, Trinity College Dublin; Richard Robyn, Kent State University; Roland Stephen, North Carolina State University; and Martin Thunert, University of Michigan.

We are also grateful for the great help given to us in keeping things up-to-date by our researcher, Ecaterina Fedoreaca, who cheerfully and efficiently broke the back of many tasks for us and who, coming originally from Moldova, gave us many useful insights into eastern Europe. We have also been mightily encouraged by reviews, comments, and feedback that we have received and by seeing the ways in which earlier editions have been cited in the professional literature.

Ultimately, however, what encouraged us to press on and produce a fourth edition is that we remain every bit as intrigued and enthused about the study of modern European politics as we were when we wrote the first edition almost fifteen years ago. What has happened in the meantime has been both exciting and humbling. It is exciting because it has shown us beyond all doubt that developing a good intellectual understanding of political processes is so very, very important. It is humbling because it has shown us—given the way that modern European politics has unfolded in a manner predicted by almost nobody—that our current intellectual understanding of these processes, though much better than nothing, is so very, very limited. We take this as a challenge for, not a criticism of, the profession—the challenge being to develop some sense now of what we might be saying about representative government in modern Europe in a future edition of this book published, say, in 2020.

Michael Gallagher
Michael Laver
Peter Mair

CHAPTER 1

INTRODUCTION

European politics is as fascinating and exciting at the beginning of the twenty-first century as at any time over the past thousand years. The long-lasting postwar division of Europe into east and west is now part of that history, with formerly communist European states having established multiparty democracy. Eight of these countries have now joined their western neighbors as part of a united Europe. On May 1, 2004, celebrations throughout the continent were held to mark the accession to the European Union of the Czech Republic, Estonia, Hungary, Latvia, Lithuania, Poland, Slovakia, and Slovenia. Also joining on the same day were the two small island states of Cyprus—the Greek part of the island only—and Malta. In 2007, the Union may well further expand to include Bulgaria and Romania. As it now stands, it now has twenty-five member states, with a population of 464 million people. Although the area over which it is spread is only roughly half the size of the United States, it stretches from the Arctic Circle in the north to the shores of the Mediterranean in the south, and from the wild Atlantic coastline of Ireland in the west to the gentle and balmy coastline of Cyprus in the east. As well as widening, the unique experiment of European integration continues to deepen: European law supersedes national law in increasingly many areas, the introduction of a single currency is creating a common means of exchange and a common monetary policy across most of the older member states of the European Union, and there is the prospect of a new Constitution before the end of 2006.

But despite the apparent erosion of traditional political and cultural boundaries in modern Europe, it is still vitally important to have a reliable feel for the national politics of European states. The transitions to democracy in postcommunist Europe were informed crucially by the western European experience. Western European states sometimes provided models for the postcommunist transitions, but they also indicated the problems that were to be avoided. And, despite all the ballyhoo about a future United States of Europe, the process of European integration is still essentially driven by political interests and demands that are shaped primarily at the national level. Member states retain important veto powers. Ultimately they can even opt out of the entire process, albeit at massive cost. They also jealously guard their autonomy in the making of foreign policy, as was seen when one group of EU member states supported the U.S. invasion of Iraq in 2003, while another group mounted quite a vehement opposition to the attack. This was not, as the then U.S. secretary of defense Donald Rumsfeld suggested, a division between "old" and "new" Europe. After all, Spain and the United Kingdom were on one side of the argument, while France and Germany were on the other side, and it is difficult to determine which is the older among that particular set of countries. What it did signal, however, was that the different national leaderships had different political outlooks, and that no new global or even European culture was going to make all of these appear the same. Politics makes strange bedfellows, and international relationships are not always faithful. In other words, the individual countries of Europe will always go their own way, and although the collapse of the Soviet Union and the process of European integration may have changed the face of modern Europe, they have not taken away from the vital importance of having a solid understanding of the comparative politics of the individual European states.

→ OUR APPROACH

We set out in this book to discuss modern European politics. We do so from a distinctive point of view. First, we concentrate on the politics of representation, focusing especially on institutions, parties, and governments. Second, our approach is wholeheartedly comparative. We organize our discussions around particular important themes in the politics of representation, not around particular important countries.

We are convinced that the benefits of our approach far exceed the costs. By restricting ourselves to the politics of representation, we give ourselves the space to take seriously the large body of comparative research and writing on this subject that can be found in the recent literature. By insisting on a comparative rather than a country-by-country approach, we give ourselves the opportunity to bring a much larger amount of evidence to bear on the problem at hand.

We feel strongly that many of the most important features of the politics of representation in modern Europe are overlooked by the still too common tendency to concentrate only on a few "important" countries. The smaller European democracies are often the sources of the most suggestive evidence on matters as diverse as the nature of party systems, the patterns in voting behavior, the importance of electoral laws, and the dynamics of coalition bargaining. If we want to find out about differences between urban and rural voters, for example, Scandinavia is one of the first places where we should start looking. If we want to find out how proportional representation electoral systems work, we do well to begin with the Netherlands. Comparing Ireland and Denmark is a good way to begin to understand what makes some minority governments stable and others not. The list could be extended indefinitely. Confining ourselves to a few big countries is not the way to come to grips with some of the most important and exciting features of the politics of representation in modern Europe.

Our way of doing things does have costs, of course, and it is as well to be aware of them. The most obvious has to do with depth. In a book of a certain size, when we broaden our coverage across a very wide range of countries, then our treatment of each is inevitably bound to be less detailed. In our view, the benefits of being comprehensive across Europe are much greater than the benefits of adding more detail on a small number of countries, but some readers may come to the opposite conclusion about this inevitable trade-off. There are plenty of other books for these people to read, so we need not feel too sorry for them, but we should remember that they do have a point. In taking several steps back to expand our field of view, we may lose sight of important detail—but we may also gain a better sense of perspective.

Another potential cost has to do with consistency. We cannot, obviously, discuss every European country in relation to every theme that we select. But if we pick and choose countries to illustrate particular points, the reader may not get a clear sense of what is going on in any particular European country. We adopt a three-pronged approach to this problem, which we hope allows us to get the best of both worlds. First, we concentrate in the text on those examples best suited to help us explore particular themes. We do this to maximize the benefits of our broadly based approach. Second, although some of our information comes from authors who studied only a limited subset of European countries, we do our best in tables summarizing particular themes to include entries for every European country with which we are concerned. We do this to ensure consistency and completeness at least at the level of basic information.

Finally, we selected a group of nine countries on which we lavish somewhat greater attention. These are France, Germany, Italy, Latvia, the Netherlands, Poland, Spain, Sweden, and the United Kingdom. We selected these countries because between them they provide considerable variation on most of the important dimensions of politics that we wish to consider. They give us a wide geographic spread, from far north to deep south. They include large and small countries; rural and urban countries; Protestant, Catholic, and "mixed-religion" countries; richer and poorer countries; countries with stable and with unstable governments; new and old democracies; postauthoritarian and postcommunist democracies; the countries with the most and the least proportional electoral systems; and so on.

✦ MODERN EUROPE

In previous editions of this book we had to make difficult decisions about how to incorporate the rapidly unfolding developments in postcommunist Europe. Although politics in these countries was increasingly comparable to politics in the west, they were still undergoing formative structuring processes of democratic development. Moreover, they obviously lacked the long history of postwar democratic experience that we frequently draw on when using west European examples to emphasize how some features of representative government remain the same while other features change. By now, however, such contrasts are no longer problematic. Despite their different experiences and their different path to democracy, eight of the postcommunist polities are now full members of the European Union, and two more are to be added in 2007. For this reason, we now integrate these countries within our general thematic approach, even though we sometimes continue to make a distinction in the questions we address to the two groups of polities. Thus, for example, while we look for evidence of electoral dealignment and change within the long-established western democracies, we tend to look for evidence of alignment and stabilization in the postcommunist world. And while we are usually concerned with how institutions adapt in the western countries, and whether political organizations survive, in the postcommunist cases we are often more concerned with how institutions are established in the first place, and whether political organizations are being built. There is now one Europe, but within it there are distinct clusters of states, each with its own set of characteristics and political processes.

We should also say a word about terminology and, to begin with, about our coverage of Europe's largest state, the Federal Republic of Germany. Before 1990, this state was familiarly referred to as West Germany, but after the absorption of the former communist East German state (the German Democratic Republic) this name ceased to be appropriate. In the following chapters, therefore, we refer to "Germany" when discussing features of the current German state, but we also occasionally use the term "West Germany" when referring to events or patterns prior to reunification. Another country for which terminology is in some sense ambiguous is the United Kingdom. Formally, the United Kingdom of Great Britain and Northern Ireland includes England, Wales, and Scotland (all three of which make up what is known as Britain or Great Britain), as well as Northern Ireland. In the tables and displays that follow, we always use the term "United Kingdom," or "UK," for the sake of consistency. In the text, for stylistic reasons, we refer sometimes to Britain and sometimes to the United Kingdom.

Finally, throughout the book as a whole, we try to deal with patterns of representative government in a total of twenty-eight countries—the twenty-five members of the European Union, plus Iceland, Norway, and Switzerland. We call this world "modern Europe," but of course the real Europe is more than this. No one would dispute that it includes the states that were once part of the former Yugoslavia, as well as Albania, Moldova, Bulgaria, and Romania. Beyond this, defining Europe requires a certain amount of subjective judgment. Geographers conventionally see the Ural Mountains and the Bosphorus (the narrow neck of water linking the Black Sea to the Mediterranean) as marking the boundaries of Europe, but that definition poses problems for political scientists since it leaves both Russia and Turkey partly in and partly out of Europe. The countries between Russia and the EU (Belarus and the Ukraine) as well as those of the Caucasus (Georgia, Armenia, Azerbaijan) are also often perceived as being part of Europe. Indeed, the European football association UEFA includes Kazakhstan, even though geographically that country is part of central Asia. Of the countries that may or may not be regarded as European, Turkey is the only one that has been invited to open negotiations with a view to possibly becoming a member of the European Union. If and when Turkey does join the EU, the Union's enlarged borders will extend to Syria, Iraq, and Iran.

➔ Plan of Campaign

In this book we describe representative government in our version of modern Europe in terms of an arena in which the hopes and fears of citizens are transformed by complex political interactions into the public policies that affect their everyday lives. At the end of this chapter we provide some basic information about modern European countries that should help set our subsequent discussions in context. In the remainder of the book, we concentrate on two basic aspects of representative government. The first concerns the institutions and "rules of the game" that create the arena for politics in modern Europe. The second concerns the political behavior that actually takes place in that arena.

Although every European country is different, the institutions of politics in most modern European states share some fundamental similarities and are collectively quite distinct from those to be found in the United States, for example, something that makes politics in Washington, D.C., a different business from politics in London, say, or in Berlin, Brussels, Stockholm, Rome, Madrid, or Prague. Modern European states are almost all run according to the principles of "parliamentary government," a set of institutions that gives a particularly important role to political parties and parliamentary elections. Constitutionally, these rules have to do with the relationship between legislature, executive, and judiciary—that is, between parliament, government, and the courts—and with the role of the head of state. In the next five chapters, therefore, we look at five different features of the institutions of representative government in modern Europe. We look in Chapter 2 at the executive and specifically at the head of state, the prime minister, and the cabinet—in a constitutional setting where the head of state is typically far less important than in the United States of America. In Chapter 3 we examine the role of the legislature, which is typically responsible not only for legislating but also for generating and maintaining a government. In Chapter 4 we look at the role of constitutions and at the role of the courts in interpreting them. Here we also draw attention to the way in which the judiciary can have an important political role, despite popular notions that it is "above" politics and despite traditional European resistance to being governed by judges. Chapters 5 and 6 present the more general context of national politics in modern Europe. In Chapter 5 we look at supranational politics and in particular at the European Union (EU), now such an important feature of the political landscape of modern Europe and such an integral part of the domestic politics of most member states. In Chapter 6 we consider both the civil service and subnational systems of local and regional administration.

Every one of the institutional features discussed in Chapters 2 through 6 has a fundamental impact on the context of representative government in modern Europe, shaping the political behavior that is the focus of the rest of the book. In Chapters 7 through 14 we move on to trace the behavior that transforms individual interests into public policies through a number of stages. We begin in Chapter 7 by looking at the party systems that determine the choices offered to voters at election time. Here we introduce the party systems in the nine countries to which we pay special attention, and we puzzle over whether we can speak of a "typical" western European party system. In Chapter 8 we present the "families" of parties that make up the cast of characters in most European elections, including communist parties, social democratic parties, liberal parties, Christian democratic parties, conservative parties, ecology parties, and the far right. We focus particular attention on the long-term patterns in the aggregate electoral development of these separate families across the past half century, and we ask whether similar patterns can be seen in the emerging postcommunist party systems. In Chapter 9, we consider the traditional cleavage structures that underpin party choice in the established democracies, as well as how these patterns might now be changing and whether, at the end of a century of mass politics, national electorates and party systems themselves are in a state of flux. We also look to see if electoral patterns in the postcommunist states are finally beginning to settle down. In Chapter 10, we step inside parties to examine some of their workings—how they organize, how they choose their leaders and candidates, and how they raise money—and we look to see how organizations are developing in the new democracies in postcommunist Europe.

Chapters 7 through 10 thus take into consideration the politics of representation from the bottom up, from the perspective of voters, elections, and parties. Chapters 12 and 13 look at politics from the top down, from the perspective of legislatures and governments. Chapter 11 examines the key institution that links the two levels—the electoral system that turns votes cast by the electorate into seats won by legislators. Many different electoral systems are used throughout Europe, which is the world's premier laboratory for all who are interested in the workings of electoral law. Having examined how European legislatures are produced, we move on in Chapter 12 to look at what they do. The most important thing that they do, as we explain in Chapters 2 and 3, is to produce and support a government. Because few European parties win a majority of seats in the legislature, forming a government typically involves forming a coalition. In Chapter 13 we explore whether the formation of different governments with different party memberships actually makes a difference in the policies that eventually emerge. If governments do not make a difference, after all, it is difficult to see why we should take an interest in the parties, the elections, the coalition bargaining, and all of the other steps in the political process by which European governments are selected. Finally, in Chapter 14 we acknowledge that the formal institutions of representative government are not the be-all and end-all of politics in modern Europe, and we look at politics outside the party system. Many political decisions—most of those having to do with the vital area of economic policy, for example—are taken by governments without recourse to the legislature. These decisions may well be strongly influenced by those who set out to apply pressure to the government, whether as part of the political establishment in an alternative institutional setting or as political outsiders using the tried-and-tested techniques of pressure politics.

Notwithstanding the trend toward European integration and the role model provided by western European states for the emerging democracies of the former eastern Europe, modern Europe remains a collection of countries with intriguingly different cultures, traditions, and political styles. There is no such thing as a "typical" European country, which is why it is so important to look at the group of European countries taken as a whole rather than at individual European countries one at a time. When we look at European politics in this way, distinct patterns do emerge. It is the search for such patterns that is the guiding purpose of this book. Before beginning the search, however, we devote the rest of this chapter to providing some basic information about the group of countries with which we are dealing. First, we provide a brief overview of the past hundred years of European history, and then we outline some of the basic facts and figures about modern Europe.

✦ A Hundred Years of European History

This is a book about the contemporary politics of Europe, not about European history. Even so, every student of the present must be aware of the impact of the past, and there is no denying that history has played a part in shaping and constraining the options facing even the most powerful political leaders and governments in the early twenty-first century. Many times in this book we make reference to aspects of the history of particular states, but here we take the opportunity to provide a very brief overview of some of the main features of Europe's rich history during the last hundred years.

Anyone examining today a map of Europe as it stood in 1914 will be struck by the mixture of stability and change in the evolution of boundaries during the twentieth century. On the western half of the continent, there has been hardly any change. The only exception is that whereas in 1914 the whole of Ireland was a part of the United Kingdom of Great Britain and Ireland (UK), in 1920 twenty-six of the thirty-two counties on the island broke away to form an independent state. The other six counties were divided between "unionists" who wanted to remain within the UK and "nationalists" who wanted to join the rest of the island in breaking the union with Britain. Since the unionists constituted a majority, these counties, now known as Northern Ireland, stayed in the UK; Northern Ireland has experienced many political difficulties, though these are now for the most part addressed through nonviolent means, in contrast to the situation in the 1970s and the 1980s. Of the twenty-eight countries that we write about in this book, nine of ten that can be found in the southwestern quadrant of the continent (Belgium, France, Ireland, Italy, Luxembourg, the Netherlands, Portugal, Spain, Switzerland, and the United Kingdom) existed in 1914; Ireland is the only subsequent addition to the list.

Scandinavia, in the north of the continent, also looks much the same. The main change here is that a century ago Finland was an autonomous grand duchy of the Russian empire, but it became fully independent in 1917. In addition, Iceland was governed by Denmark until achieving independence in 1944. Of today's five Scandinavian countries (Denmark, Finland, Iceland, Norway, and Sweden), three were independent countries in 1914, and the other two were recognizable entities even if not fully sovereign. Most of southeastern Europe falls outside the ambit of this book, but we do cover the three states that are part of the EU: Greece, Cyprus, and Malta. Of these three, Greece has a long history as an independent state, but a hundred years ago both Cyprus and Malta were ruled by Britain.

The relative stability in the borders within Scandinavia and southwestern Europe over the past hundred years should not lead us to assume that all of the various nations have a timeless history as nation states. Norway, for example, became independent from Sweden only in 1905, and Belgium came into being as an independent state in 1831 as a fusion of two linguistic groups, French-speakers and Dutch-speakers, relations between whom still dominate Belgian politics. Italy, today one of Europe's largest states, was divided into separate kingdoms and republics for many centuries, and only in 1870 was the Risorgimento (the movement for a united Italy) completed by Garibaldi, when his troops entered Rome. Still, even though some west European states were relatively new or even fragile a century ago, the configuration of 1914 changed very little subsequently.

The same is not true of central and eastern Europe. In this book we cover ten countries that belong geographically to this broad area: Austria, the Czech Republic, Estonia, Germany, Hungary, Latvia, Lithuania, Poland, Slovakia, and Slovenia. A hundred years ago, the territory now covered by these ten states was ruled by just three: the German, Austro–Hungarian, and Russian empires. Each of these empires bears the same name as one of today's states but is by no means identical to it. Germany at that time consisted not just of present-day German territory but also of a large part of today's Poland, and indeed it extended right around the Baltic coast to include what is now the Kaliningrad enclave of Russia and part of Lithuania. Despite its size and its industrial and military power, Germany, like Italy, was a relatively new creation. A unified Germany did not emerge until 1870, being forged by the Prussian leader Bismarck, who had brought together, in many cases by force, the plethora of separate kingdoms that had hitherto existed. The Russian empire covered Finland, the three states on the eastern shores of the Baltic Sea (Estonia, Latvia, and Lithuania), and much of today's Poland. The Austro–Hungarian empire was a particularly unwieldy construction that included, besides the two countries after which it was named and who jointly ruled it, much of the Balkans. Today's countries of the Czech Republic, Slovakia, and Slovenia all fell within its borders.

Borders of states, and indeed the existence of states, proved anything but durable in central and eastern Europe over many centuries. This can be illustrated by the case of Poland, which waxed and waned in dramatic fashion. A Polish state was established by around the year 1000 but by the middle of the thirteenth century had largely fallen apart. A century later, it was reunified once again, and at the start of the seventeenth century Poland was the largest country in Europe, with a territory that covered most of today's Lithuania, Belarus, and Ukraine (almost as far as the Black Sea) along with parts of Latvia and Russia. However, its position between two powerful expansionist states, Prussia and Russia, made it permanently vulnerable to invasion, and in 1795 it simply disappeared from the map for more than a hundred years as a result of the "Third Partition," under which Prussia took its western half and Russia most of the east, with Austria–Hungary receiving a slice of its southern territories.

The First World War (1914–18) led to a large-scale redrawing of the map of central and eastern Europe. The victors (Britain, France, and Italy) imposed harsh terms on the losing allies, Germany and Austria–Hungary. As well as losing significant eastern territories to Poland, which now reappeared as a state, Germany was compelled to pay heavy financial reparations to the victorious countries. The Austro–Hungarian empire disintegrated. Austria and Hungary became separate states, and two new states emerged from within its former territory: Czechoslovakia and Yugoslavia. Neither of these "successor states" was very cohesive: Both Czechoslovakia and Yugoslavia contained distinct linguistic groups, some of whom wanted independence. Russia had been an initial member of the coalition that eventually won the war, but it had pulled out in 1917 due to its internal upheavals that resulted, in October of that year, in its being taken over by the communists under the leadership of Lenin. After the war, it was forced to relinquish a lot of territory to the reborn Polish state and to grant independence to Finland, Estonia, Latvia, and Lithuania. In 1922 the communists created the Union of Soviet Socialist Republics (USSR), widely known as the Soviet Union, which came to extend over much of the Transcaucasus and central Asia as well as Belarus and the Ukraine, but ultimate power always rested in Moscow. The war was worldwide in two senses: first, in that fighting took place right across the globe in a number of the colonies of the European powers; and, second, in that troops from many other countries took part in the fighting in Europe. The entry of the United States in 1917 helped to bring the conflict to an end at a high cost in American lives, and many troops from Canada, Australia, India, New Zealand, and Africa were also killed.

After the carnage of the First World War, during which at least 7 million people were killed, many political leaders piously resolved that "this must never happen again." However, the settlement imposed on the losers has subsequently been seen by historians as having contained the seeds of the Second World War (1939–45). In particular, many Germans perceived the Versailles Treaty, which set out the terms by which postwar Germany had to abide, as a "Diktat," and nationalistic German politicians found fertile ground for their arguments that German interests had been sold out at Versailles by politicians who had been at best too accommodating to the demands of Germany's rivals and at worst traitors. These politicians represented the "Weimar Republic," established in 1919 by liberal and left-wing politicians, and although its constitution provided for a model democratic state, many vested interests on the right wing of German politics never regarded it as fully legitimate. In addition, it suffered from government instability and became further discredited by the perception that it was dominated by deal-making politicians with little interest in the people they nominally represented.

The inability of the Weimar regime to cope with the problems of economic depression in the late 1920s spelled its end. This provided the opportunity for the Nazi party (the NSDAP, or National Socialist German Workers' Party), led by Adolf Hitler, to sweep to power. The Nazis had fought three elections in the 1920s with hardly any success, but now they began to grow dramatically. Business interests, along with the self-employed and farmers, saw them as an effective way to combat the perceived communist threat; the traditional nationalist right agreed with their invective against the Versailles Diktat and the liberal democracy of the Weimar regime; many workers were receptive to their arguments that only the Nazis could provide a return to full employment; and their overt anti-Semitism also struck a chord with many Germans. As a result, the Nazis advanced from only 12 seats at the 1928 election to 107 in 1930 and 230 by July 1932. In the January 1933 election—by which time Hitler had already been appointed chancellor (prime minister)—they won 288 seats out of 647, twice as many as any other party. The institutions of liberal democracy were swiftly abolished or taken over, and by July 1933 the Nazis were the only party legally permitted to exist in Germany.

It was not just in Germany that democracy was replaced by authoritarianism. In Italy, the fascist leader Benito Mussolini came to power in 1922, and within a few years all parties except his own were banned. In Spain an unstable postwar democracy was interrupted first by a military takeover in 1923 and then, after the restoration of a parliamentary regime in 1930, by a civil war launched in 1936 by General Francisco Franco. After three years of bitter struggle in which at least half a million people were killed, Franco, who received military support from both Hitler and Mussolini, won unchallenged power, which he retained until his death in 1975, at which point a return to democracy began. In the adjoining country of Portugal, functioning democracy never got fully off the ground, and the limited democracy that existed was overthrown by the military in 1926. Portugal was dominated from 1928 until his incapacitation in the late 1960s by the conservative dictator António de Oliveira Salazar; it was not until 1974 that democratic government was established.

In eastern and central Europe, too, democracy did not flourish. In nearly all of the states established after the First World War, the initially archetypal liberal democratic regimes were either transformed into mere facade democracies or even overthrown. Leaders such as Admiral Miklós Horthy in Hungary, Marshal Josef Pilsudski in Poland, and Engelbert Dollfuss and Kurt von Schuschnigg in Austria ruled in an authoritarian manner and were not accountable to their citizens through the mechanisms of representative government that we examine in this book. In Estonia the acting head of government, Konstantin Päts, became a de facto dictator from 1934 onward. In Latvia the prime minister, Kārlis Ulmanis, staged a coup in 1934, abolishing parliament and banning parties. In the third Baltic state, Lithuania, the democratic experiment ended even earlier, as a military coup established an authoritarian regime under Antanas Smetona in 1926. In the whole region of eastern and central Europe, only Czechoslovakia remained a recognizable democracy, with regular free and fair elections, during the interwar period. The political cleavages that dominated politics in these countries in this period, and in some cases even the same parties, tended to reemerge when competitive politics was restored in the 1990s after the end of communism. Regimes in western Europe and Scandinavia, in contrast, survived as liberal democracies in the interwar period; even though in many cases significant fascist or antidemocratic forces emerged, none of these was able to come close to gaining power.

By the late 1930s Hitler was behaving in an ever more aggressive manner toward his neighbors, making demands on those parts of their territories that were occupied by ethnic Germans and implementing an extensive program of rearming in violation of the Versailles Treaty. The main western powers, Britain and France, adopted a policy of "appeasement," making concessions to him in the hope that if his immediate demands were met he would be content. Thus, in 1936 his troops were permitted to reoccupy the Rhineland (a part of Germany bordering France in which, under the terms of Versailles, Germany was not permitted to station troops); in March 1938 Austria was allowed to merge with Germany (the so-called Anschluss); and in September 1938 the western powers pressed Czechoslovakia to hand over to Germany a region, known to Germans as the Sudetenland, demanded by Hitler. However, each concession simply led to further and greater demands. In August 1939 Hitler cleared the way for war by signing, to the amazement of the rest of the world, a nonaggression pact with the Soviet Union (known as the Nazi–Soviet pact, or the Hitler–Stalin pact), thereby securing his eastern flank. Under secret protocols of the pact, the two countries would each occupy half of Poland, and the USSR would take control of Estonia, Latvia, and Lithuania.

The Nazis' invasion of Poland on September 1, 1939, marked the beginning of the Second World War. After quick successes in Poland, France, Belgium, the Netherlands, Denmark, and Norway, Germany was unsuccessful in its attempts to mount an invasion of Britain. In 1941 Hitler broke the terms of the Nazi–Soviet pact by launching an unprovoked attack on the USSR. This was spectacularly successful initially, as German armies captured vast amounts of territory and reached the outskirts of Moscow, but the tide turned after their defeat at Stalingrad in the winter of 1942–43. From the summer of 1943 Soviet armies pushed German forces back across the ground they had earlier captured, and with the entry of the United States into the war from December 1941 following the attack on Pearl Harbor and the landings of Allied forces in occupied France in 1944, the complete defeat of Germany became inevitable. With Soviet troops just a few hundred yards from his bunker in Berlin, Hitler committed suicide in April 1945, and Germany surrendered a week later. The Second World War was even more destructive of human life than the First. Noncombatants suffered greatly: Perhaps 18 million noncombatants died, including approximately 6 million Jews killed by the Nazis in fulfillment of their genocidal policy.

After the war the map of central and eastern Europe was redrawn once again. Much of what had been eastern Poland prior to 1939 was now transferred into Belarus, one of the republics in the USSR, and much of what had been eastern Germany now became part of Poland. The reduced Germany was partitioned among the four main victorious powers. The Americans, British, and French merged their zones and established the liberal-democratic Federal Republic of Germany (often known as West Germany) as a functioning democracy in the west European mode; the Soviet zone became a communist state, titled the German Democratic Republic (often known as East Germany). The USSR retained the three small Baltic states that it had captured in 1940; these were now made Soviet republics, something that the rest of the world refused to recognize de jure though it could do little about the annexation de facto. Indeed, almost all those territories from which the Soviet Union's armies had driven out the German forces remained firmly under Soviet control. The only exception was Austria, which was occupied by the USSR in 1945 but from which Soviet troops withdrew in 1955. In most cases, there was one fairly free postwar election but, whatever the result, by the end of the 1940s the country was firmly under complete communist control. The most blatant example of a communist takeover was in Czechoslovakia, where the local communist party and its supporters thwarted plans to hold an election in February 1948, and a few weeks later the non-communist foreign minister Jan Masaryk fell to his death (presumably pushed) from a window. A phrase used by Britain's wartime prime minister Winston Churchill in 1946 gained wide currency: He declared that an "iron curtain" had descended across the continent.

From the late 1940s to the late 1980s, politics took very different forms on the two sides of this divide—which is why the first edition of this book did not cover the former communist countries at all and the second and third editions dealt with them in a chapter of their own. In the western part of the continent, liberal democracy has not been seriously challenged since 1945. Learning the lessons of the Versailles Diktat, the victorious allies did not impose "victors' justice" on the defeated Germany but, rather, sought to integrate Germany fully into the west European mainstream. This approach was formalized in the creation of what has become the European Union, which we discuss in Chapter 5. Italy, too, was reintegrated into the west European core. The other countries that had had autocratic regimes in 1939 took longer to join the democratic fold. Portugal and Spain, as we have said, did not emerge from dictatorship until the 1970s. Greece, which had had periods of military rule between the wars, returned to democracy in 1946; it again fell under military rule between 1967 and 1974, but then civilian rule was restored.

In central and eastern Europe, in contrast, the institutions of representative government had little meaning, because all power lay with the communist party. Even though "elections" took place, voters had no power of choice since there was only one candidate per constituency. Parliaments, governments, and courts were all controlled by the party. Ultimate control, indeed, lay not with the national communist party but in Moscow; only in Yugoslavia, Albania, and in later years Romania were communist regimes established that were not subject to the command of the USSR. There were occasional protests against communist rule. In October 1956 the Hungarian communist party leadership, responding to popular pressure, declared that the country would revert to a multiparty system and would leave the Warsaw Pact (the military alliance among the communist countries). A week later, Soviet forces invaded and restored orthodox communist rule. Czechoslovakia experienced a very similar "Prague Spring" in 1968; again, the experiment was promptly terminated by an invasion by Warsaw Pact armed forces. In the early 1980s the Solidarity trade union mounted a challenge to the regime in Poland, posing a threat to which the government responded by imposing martial law in 1981. There were also serious risings against the regimes in East Germany in 1953 and in Poland in 1956.

Although the communist parties justified their control of these states in terms of protecting the socioeconomic rights of workers, rights that were not always well respected in the capitalist west, it was apparent that the regimes were accepted by their populations under duress. The borders between the Warsaw Pact countries and the west were heavily guarded and lined with barbed wire, and the most striking symbol of the divide between east and west was created in 1961, when the East German regime built the Berlin Wall along the border between the two sections of the divided city. This reinforcement of the borders was explained as being necessary to protect against possible invasion by the west, but few doubted that the real reason was to prevent citizens of the Warsaw Pact countries from moving, or "escaping," to the west. There were some differences between the regimes, it is true. After 1956 the Hungarian regime gradually became the most liberal and least repressive in the communist world, allowing a degree of small-scale private enterprise and some space for civil society. Similarly, the Polish regime had to confront a strongly resistant civil society and was unable ever to overcome completely the power that the Catholic Church wielded. In contrast, the regimes in Czechoslovakia, the Baltic states, and East Germany were seen as particularly hardline and orthodox. Still, the differences between the various communist regimes were minor compared with the differences between these regimes and those in the west.

The communist regimes crumbled at the end of the 1980s. In their early years they had delivered a degree of economic growth, which was at least a trade-off against the lack of personal liberty, but by the 1980s it was obvious to their citizens that economically they were falling steadily further behind the west. Change in three countries precipitated the collapse of communism. First, in Poland "opposition" forces, particularly the Solidarity movement and the Catholic Church, were able to win ever more political space for themselves, and it was clear that the communist party's grip was weakening. In June 1989, following "round-table talks" between the regime and Solidarity, semi-competitive elections were held for parliament. Although the communists were guaranteed control of a majority of the seats, Solidarity won nearly all the seats for which it was entitled to compete, thus removing all legitimacy from continued communist rule. Second, the Hungarian party leadership became convinced of the need for fundamental reform. By the spring of 1989 it had rebranded the 1956 uprising a "popular uprising" rather than the "counterrevolution" it had previously been labeled, and was moving toward a mixed economy and a multiparty system. Third, changes in Russia, with the arrival as leader of the reformist Mikhail Gorbachev, meant that reformists in other communist parties were encouraged and that everyone knew there was no longer a danger of the USSR invading if any country tried to leave the fold.

The end came once Hungary opened its borders to the west in September 1989. Many East Germans traveled to Hungary and from there made their way to the west. Unable to stop the flow, in a highly symbolic gesture on November 9 the East German regime knocked a hole in the Berlin Wall, allowing its citizens to travel to the west. There were mass protests against the communist regimes by huge crowds right across the Warsaw Pact area, and by the end of 1989 all these regimes had collapsed. Moreover, in all the countries that we cover in this book, these regime changes were achieved without violence.

The map of Europe changed yet again as a result of these developments. First, the three Baltic states that had been taken over by the USSR in 1940 reclaimed their independence in 1990. Second, Germany was reunited in October 1990 when East Germany merged with the western state. Third, the multinational republic of Yugoslavia broke up into five new states. One of these, Slovenia—which declared independence in 1991 and had to fight a ten-day "mini-war" against the Yugoslav army to secure this—is covered in this book. Fourth, in 1992 Slovakia, which like Slovenia had never previously enjoyed independent statehood, broke away from Czechoslovakia in the "velvet divorce."

Throughout this book we refer repeatedly to "postcommunist" countries, by which we mean the Czech Republic, Estonia, Hungary, Latvia, Lithuania, Poland, Slovakia, and Slovenia. Of course, there are many differences between these countries: They have different levels of economic development and linguistic homogeneity, and they have different cultures. By referring to them all as postcommunist countries we do not imply that they are all essentially the same. However, we do believe that their long experience of a common form of rule from which they all emerged at about the same time does make it sensible to look for common patterns in their contemporary politics and indeed, as this book shows, those patterns emerge in several areas of political life.

→ THE VITAL STATISTICS

The modern Europe that we deal with is divided into twenty-eight independent states, with a total population of more than 460 million—more than half again as big as that of the United States. As Table 1.1 shows, population density, on average about four times greater in the European Union area than in the United States, is—after Malta—highest in Belgium, the Netherlands, Germany, and the UK. Indeed, the area around the Netherlands and northern Germany is a very heavily populated region where the concentration of major cities and industrial infrastructure supports a population of more than 350 persons per square kilometer. In the more peripheral areas of modern Europe, by contrast, population density can be relatively low; there are only some 20 persons per square kilometer in the vast but unevenly populated country of Sweden and 62 persons per square kilometer in the harsh and inhospitable landscape of Basilicata in southern Italy. In the peripheral Irish Republic, a land area of some 70,000 square kilometers supports a population of almost 4 million; in the more centrally located Netherlands, in contrast, an area of some 41,000 square kilometers, little more than half that of Ireland, supports a population of more than 16 million, four times that of Ireland.

Modern Europe is an immensely diverse area, riven by many cultural, religious, and linguistic boundaries. Despite an overwhelmingly Christian culture, for example, a marked source of traditional diversity is created by the balance between Roman Catholics and the various Protestant denominations. Table 1.1 shows that in some places Roman Catholics are an overwhelming majority—for example, in the southern and western parts of Europe, as well as in Poland. In Greece the vast majority formally adhere to the Greek Orthodox Church, which is quite close to Catholicism. In a second group of countries Roman Catholics tend to be very thin on the ground, particularly in the Scandinavian countries—Denmark, Finland, Iceland, Norway, and Sweden—where the overwhelming proportion of the population is at least nominally affiliated to one of a variety of Protestant denominations. Indeed, it is really only in the central spine of Europe—in Germany, the Netherlands, and Switzerland, as well as in the former Czechoslovakia—that we find some sort of even balance between Catholics and Protestants, with Catholics forming a significant minority of the population. Even in these countries, Catholics often tend to cluster in areas where they constitute an overwhelming majority—in areas such as Limburg in the south of the Netherlands, or Bavaria in southern Germany. Catholics also constitute a substantial minority in Northern Ireland, which forms part of the United Kingdom, and where a virtual civil war between Catholics and Protestants persisted

TABLE 1.1

General and Demographic Data on European Democracies

Country	Capital	Total area (× 1,000 sq. km.)	Population 2004 total (× 1,000)	Population per sq. km.	Catholic (%)	Gender Empowerment Measure (GEM value), 2004[a]
Austria	Vienna	84	8,175	97	74	.770
Belgium	Brussels	31	10,348	337	75	.808
Cyprus	Nicosia	9	776	82	1	.497
Czech Republic	Prague	79	10,246	131	39	.586
Denmark	Copenhagen	43	5,413	125	1	.847
Estonia	Tallinn	45	1,342	31	0.4	.592
Finland	Helsinki	338	5,214	15	0.1	.820
France	Paris	549	60,424	107	85	—
Germany	Berlin	357	82,424	230	34	.804
Greece	Athens	132	10,647	83	0.4	.523
Hungary	Budapest	93	10,032	107	67	.529
Iceland	Reykjavik	103	294	3	2	.816
Ireland	Dublin	70	3,969	54	92	.710
Italy	Rome	301	58,057	191	97	.583
Latvia	Riga	64	3,306	37	17	.591
Lithuania	Vilnius	65	3,608	57	76	.508
Luxembourg	Luxembourg	3	463	174	87	—
Malta	Valletta	0.3	397	1,234	98	.480
Netherlands	Amsterdam	41	16,318	385	31	.817
Norway	Oslo	324	4,574	14	1	.908
Poland	Warsaw	313	38,626	123	95	.606
Portugal	Lisbon	92	10,524	113	94	.644
Slovakia	Bratislava	49	5,423	110	60	.607
Slovenia	Ljubljana	20	2,011	99	71	.584
Spain	Madrid	505	40,281	78	94	.716
Sweden	Stockholm	450	8,986	20	2	.854
Switzerland	Bern	41	7,451	176	46	.771
United Kingdom	London	245	60,271	245	8	.698
United States	Washington, D.C.	9,372	293,027	29	28	.769
EU-25	Brussels	4,016	464,269	116	—	—

[a] The higher the value of this index, the stronger the position of women in the society and in politics.

Sources: United Nations, *Human Development Report*, 2003, 2004; CIA, *World Factbook*, 2004.

for more than twenty-five years. Notice, however, that the nominal affiliations listed in Table 1.1 exaggerate the numbers of active adherents. The proportion of nonpracticing Catholics is particularly pronounced in France and southern Europe, for example.

The balance between these Christian denominations has played a major role in framing the political alternatives of many European states. As we show in Chapter 8, for example, Christian democratic parties—one of the most important party families in Europe—have always been strongest in areas where Catholics constituted a substantial minority (e.g., the Netherlands, Germany, Switzerland), or where practicing Catholics felt threatened by liberal, secular forces (e.g., Belgium, France, Italy). Non-Catholic countries, however, have tended to give rise to secular conservative rather than Christian democratic parties (e.g., Norway, Sweden, UK), although they are also often home to smaller, more fundamentalist Protestant political groupings. Historical divisions therefore often shape contemporary political alignments, and the alignments themselves survive even after their original founding divisions have faded to irrelevance. But although traditional religious divides might still seem very important in modern Europe—the Christian democrats still constitute one of the biggest party families—in practice they often count for less than those in the United States. According to recent data from the World Values study (http://www.worldvaluessurvey.org), for example, Europeans (75%) are marginally less likely than Americans (96%) to believe in God, and are substantially less likely (29% versus 75%) to believe in hell. And while close to half of all Americans attend a religious service at least once a week, only one in five Europeans does so. European culture is in this sense a much more secular culture: Only 16 percent of Europeans claim that God is important in their lives (as against 58 percent of Americans), and 12 percent agree with the idea that politicians who don't believe in God are unfit for public office, as compared with 38 percent of Americans. This is now one of the key differences between the two cultures, and it is increasing rather than diminishing in importance.

That said, religion is now reemerging as an issue in European politics through its connection to immigration. There is growing evidence of hostility between the indigenous European populations, on the one hand, and the minority Muslim community, on the other. The number of Muslim immigrants and their immediate descendants is still quite limited in Europe, of course. In the EU-15, before the accession of the ten new member states in May 2004, it was estimated that the Union included some 12 million Muslims, or just over 3 percent of the total population. This rises to 7.5 percent in France and Spain, however, and to some 6 percent in the Netherlands. Moreover, within these latter countries, the immigrant population counts are particularly high in the cities. In Madrid, the figure is now 14 percent, while in the Netherlands, more than 50 percent of school-going children in the four biggest cities—Amsterdam, Rotterdam, The Hague, and Utrecht—are of nonwestern immigrant descent, and primarily Muslim. This in itself poses a major problem for integration and cohesion within Europe's modern urban cultures, and it has become even more acute since both the attacks of September 11, 2001, and the Madrid bombings of March 11, 2004. The issue has also become widely politicized in recent years, initially by the new far-right populist parties—the National Front in France, the Danish People's Party in Denmark, the Flemish Block (now Flemish Interest) in Belgium, and the Pim Fortuyn List in the Netherlands—and then by other center–right and sometimes even center–left parties that followed in their wake. It has also led to violence and other forms of protest, such as in Sweden, where white racist gangs have become very active, and in the Netherlands, where a spate of incidents involving the burning of mosques and churches followed soon after the murder of filmmaker and anti-Islam propagandist Theo van Gogh in November 2004. Two members of the Dutch parliament, who were also very critical of Islam, received death threats at the same time and were obliged to go into hiding.

One of the issues that had concerned the critics of Islamic practices in the Netherlands, and that had initially been voiced by the radical populist Pim Fortuyn, himself later assassinated, was the attitude to women's rights, on the one hand, and to gay rights, on the other. Fortuyn's argument was that individuals who had chosen to be immigrants within a liberal state were obliged to assimilate and to respect the prevailing liberal culture—which meant, in this case, learning the indigenous language and respecting the rights of women, gays, and other minorities. Fortuyn himself was gay, and very publicly so. Indeed, one of the ironies of this burgeoning conflict is that in some of the countries in which women have been most strongly empowered, and where women's rights and hence egalitarianism seem most firmly ensconced, new far-right parties have now made quite substantial headway (Norway, the Netherlands, Belgium; see also Table 8.9). Though anti-immigrant, these parties nevertheless often couch their appeals in the form of a defense of traditional liberal values. The position of women in politics and society is noted in the final column of Table 1.1, which reports values of the Gender Empowerment Index, devised by the United Nations *Human Development Reports* (http://hdr.undp.org). This index is a composite measure of the degree of women's representation in key areas of political and economic life, and it takes account of the number of women in national parliaments (see also Chapter 11), their share of earned income, and their levels of occupancy in a range of professions. As can be seen from Table 1.1, women enjoy their strongest position in Europe in countries such as Norway, Sweden, the Netherlands, and Belgium, and they are weakest in the ten new member states as well as in southern Europe. Two factors seem to be important here, and we come across this patterning throughout our discussion of representative government: On the one hand, there is the evident difference between the newer and the older democracies, with women tending to play a stronger public role in the latter group. On the other hand, there is the difference between Catholic and Protestant Europe, and it is in the latter group that women have tended to achieve the greater success.

Cultural diversity involves much more than religious or gender differences, of course. One of the major differences between the European Union and the United States is that nearly every modern European country has its own language; the only major exceptions are Austria, a German-speaking country; Ireland, an English-speaking country; Belgium, where some 57 percent speak Dutch and some 42 percent speak French; Luxembourg, where the native language coexists with both French and German; Cyprus, or at least the southern part that is now a member of the EU, which is Greek-speaking; and Switzerland, where some 74 percent use German, some 20 percent use French, and some 5 percent use Italian. In addition, a variety of countries have linguistic minorities—including the Basque and Catalan minorities in Spain; the German-speaking minority in northeast Italy; the Swedish-speaking minority in Finland; the Hungarian minority in Slovakia; the Russian minority in the Baltic states; the Welsh in Britain; and a small number of Gaelic-speakers in both Ireland and Scotland. Across modern Europe as a whole, German is the most widely used native language, being used as a mother tongue by roughly 95 million people, followed by French (64 million) and English (63 million), then by Italian (57 million), and Polish and Spanish (both just less than 40 million). There is then a large drop to Dutch (just over 20 million). As a second language, English is increasingly popular in each of the other language groups.

TABLE 1.2

Gross Domestic Product in European Democracies

Country	Total 2003, $ billion (current exchange rates)	Per capita, 2003 $ (current exchange rates)	$ per capita PPPs (purchasing power parities)
Austria	253.1	30,960	28,800
Belgium	301.9	29,175	28,100
Cyprus	14.0	18,041	19,200
Czech Republic	85.4	8,335	15,600
Denmark	212.3	39,220	29,900
Estonia	9.0	6,706	12,300
Finland	160.8	30,840	27,200
France	1,757.5	29,086	26,900
Germany	2,401.9	29,141	26,600
Greece	172.7	16,221	17,100
Hungary	82.8	8,254	14,100
Iceland	10.6	36,054	28,800
Ireland	152.1	38,322	31,700
Italy	1,468.3	25,291	26,600
Latvia	11.2	3,388	10,200
Lithuania	20.0	5,543	11,400
Luxembourg	27.0	58,315	50,600
Malta	5.3	13,350	17,700
Netherlands	512.7	31,419	29,400
Norway	220.9	48,295	37,100
Poland	209.5	5,424	10,200
Portugal	146.8	13,949	17,800
Slovakia	32.5	5,993	12,800
Slovenia	29.3	14,570	19,000
Spain	838.6	20,819	21,800
Sweden	301.6	33,903	26,800
Switzerland	321.8	43,189	30,100
United Kingdom	1,795.0	29,782	27,100
United States	10,933.5	37,312	36,100
EU-25	11,001.4	23,697	23,400[a]

[a] EU-15.

Sources: OECD; Eurostat; CIA, *World Factbook,* 2004.

Germany also enjoys the strongest economy in modern Europe. Even before unification in 1990, West Germany's gross domestic product (GDP) was more than one-quarter again as big as that of the UK, the next biggest; now the unified Germany exceeds the UK by about one-third (see Table 1.2). In general, however, the individual European economies are dwarfed by the economy of the United States. The combined GDP of the four largest economies—Germany, France, Italy, and the United Kingdom—actually totals only to some 75 percent of that of the United States. Taking all the EU-25 countries together, however, including the poorer postcommunist countries, yields a total GDP of some $11,000 billion at 2003 exchange rates, and this is marginally greater than the U.S. figure of $10,934 billion. In effect, with the relatively weak dollar exchange rate of 2003, the two economies were identical in size.

The highest European levels for GDP per head of population, when converted into the now standard purchasing power parities (PPPs)—this is a way of adjusting and standardizing GDP per capita so that a fixed sum buys the same bundle of goods and services in every country—can be found in Luxembourg, Norway, Ireland, and Switzerland; Luxembourg and Norway exceed the comparable U.S. figure of $36,100, but the average EU-15 figure was less than two-thirds that of the United States. There is enormous variation within Europe in this regard. Levels range from highs of $50,600 in Luxembourg and $37,100 in Norway to west European lows of just $17,100 in Greece, $17,700 in Malta, and $17,800 in Portugal. Falling behind these again are most of the postcommunist countries, with Latvia, Poland, and Lithuania emerging as the poorest in the continent. There is one exception here, however. Postcommunist Slovenia, the real success story of the former Yugoslavia, emerges with a per capita income higher than Portugal's. Performances also vary over time, of course. When we prepared the original first edition of this book, using data from 1988–89, Ireland ranked as the third poorest country in western Europe, with a GDP per capita (measured in PPPs) that was little more than 40 percent of the U.S. figure. Today, a decade after the beginning of the sustained growth rates associated with the Celtic Tiger, Ireland is the third richest country in Europe, with a GDP per capita that is some 88 percent of that in the United States.

Here again, the imbalance is clearly related to different levels of economic modernization (within western Europe) and to the communist legacy (in eastern Europe). With some exceptions, it is an imbalance that also tends to be organized in terms of geographic division between richer countries in northern and central western Europe and poorer countries in the Mediterranean south and, of course, in the east. Indeed, this difference is strikingly evident in regional disparities within the boundaries of a single country, Italy. The very prosperous northern part of the country enjoys one of the highest standards of living in modern Europe, contrasting sharply with the southern part of Italy, one of western Europe's poorest regions. This social and economic tension is now also being exacerbated by a regional political divide, with the Northern League mobilizing in favor of greater political autonomy for northern Italy. Lower levels of prosperity also tend to be quite strongly associated with a continuing reliance on agriculture as a major source of employment, as in Poland, as well as with poorly developed industrial and service sectors.

Differences in sectoral development across modern Europe are less marked than was once the case. For example, as Table 1.3 shows, Estonia, Lithuania, Greece, and Iceland are the only countries in the European Union where the contribution of agriculture to GDP exceeds 5 percent. This is despite the often relatively high levels of employment in this sector. Conversely, the Czech Republic, Ireland, and Lithuania are the only three countries where the service sector contributes less than 60 percent. In all of these European states, however, without exception, it is this latter sector that contributes most to GDP, accounting for an average that now runs close to the balance in the United States. Perhaps surprisingly, in view of its conventional image as having one of the most

TABLE 1.3

Sectoral, Labor Force, and Public Sector Data

Country	Sectoral Contribution to GDP, 2002 (%)			Total General Government Expenditure, 2001 (% GDP)	Gini Index (inequality index), 2004[a]	Population Aged 65 or Over, 2004 (%)
	Agriculture	Industry	Services			
Austria	2.3	30.4	67.3	52.1	30.0	19.5
Belgium	1.2	26.1	72.6	49.4	25.0	19.5
Cyprus	—	—	—	—	—	14.9
Czech Republic	3.7	38.4	57.9	47.3	25.4	18.6
Denmark	2.4	25.5	72.2	55.3	24.7	19.2
Estonia	5.9	29.5	64.6	—	37.2	18.2
Finland	3.5	31.1	65.4	49.0	26.9	20.3
France	2.6	24.2	73.2	52.5	32.7	18.5
Germany	1.1	28.8	70.1	48.3	28.3	20.8
Greece	7.0	22.3	70.6	47.0	35.4	20.9
Hungary	3.7	30.2	66.1	—	24.4	17.4
Iceland	8.6[b]	25.7[b]	65.7[b]	43.4	—	13.5
Ireland	3.4[c]	42.1[c]	54.5[c]	34.1	35.9	13.4
Italy	2.6	27.1	70.3	48.5	36.0	22.3
Latvia	4.5	26.4	69.1	—	32.4	18.3
Lithuania	7.2	34.7	58.0	—	31.9	16.4
Luxembourg	0.6	16.7	82.7	39.4	30.8	14.4
Malta	—	—	—	—	—	18.0
Netherlands	2.5	24.9	72.7	46.4	32.6	17.4
Norway	1.6	36.8	61.5	44.6	25.8	18.0
Poland	3.1	30.0	66.9	—	31.6	14.8
Portugal	3.6	27.5	68.9	46.4	38.5	18.0
Slovakia	4.4	31.1	64.5	62.0[b]	25.8	13.6
Slovenia	—	—	—	42.8	28.4	18.5
Spain	3.2	28.5	68.2	39.3	32.5	19.2
Sweden	1.8	27.5	70.6	57.2	25.0	21.4
Switzerland	1.2[b]	26.6[b]	73.2[b]	—	33.1	22.0
United Kingdom	0.9	25.9	73.2	40.2	36.0	17.8
United States	1.6[c]	22.8[c]	75.6[c]	34.9	40.8	14.2

[a] The Gini Index measures inequality in income distribution or in consumption; 0 represents perfect equality, and 100 represents perfect inequality.

[b] Data for 2000.

[c] Data for 2001.

Sources: OECD; Eurostat; United Nations, *Human Development Report*, 2004; CIA, *World Factbook*, 2004.

traditional and unspoiled landscapes in Europe, Ireland in these figures emerges as having the single biggest industrial sector. Again, this is largely due to the enormous economic growth in the so-called Celtic Tiger period, which has led to a situation in which the only leprechauns that are still to be found are those that are made of resin and packaged up for export to gift shops around the world.

Ireland does less well when it comes to the degree of equality in the distribution of income. This is measured by the Gini Index, and ranges from 0, when there is perfect equality, and 100, when there is perfect inequality. The west European countries that score low on this index, and hence that have more egalitarian income distributions, tend to be those that also figured highly on the Gender Empowerment Index (see Table 1.1)— Denmark, Belgium, Norway, and Finland. The Czech Republic and Slovakia also emerge as having a high level of equality, while Ireland scores toward the nonegalitarian end, ranking close to Switzerland and Latvia. None of the European countries comes close to the inequality levels measured in the United States, however, and hence, despite internal variation, this is something that again marks Europe out as distinct. Through most of the postwar period, the large majority of western European countries shared a common commitment to progressive taxation and to the strengthening of social citizenship. Despite variation in the programs that were set in place to realize these goals, this commitment led most of the European polities to develop a large public sector and to build an expensive and quite all-encompassing welfare state. This also meant generous unemployment benefits, comprehensive health care, and well-funded pension schemes. It also led to less inequality and to a leveling out of lifestyles rather than simply opportunities. Today, we tend to see this outcome as having been a product of social democracy, and social democratic parties were indeed at the heart of European mass politics for most of the twentieth century. But it is important to recognize this approach as being also the product of that other powerful European party family, the Christian democrats, a group that was just as committed as the social democrats to the funding of the welfare state and to the promotion of "social capitalism."

Table 1.3 highlights the different levels of government expenditure relative to GDP in the different European countries. These figures relate to spending and employment on public welfare programs such as health, education, employment, and housing as well as the defense forces, police, administration, and publicly owned companies. The figures are not always easily comparable, however, since different state traditions use different definitions and categorizations for what are functionally equivalent activities. Moreover, the comparisons across the postcommunist countries may be particularly misleading, since in these particular cases the high expenditure levels can simply reflect lingering legacies of the predemocratic period. According to the west European figures, which apply to 2001, governments in Austria, Denmark, France, and—most notably—Sweden spend more than 50 percent of GDP, and Belgium, Finland, Germany, and Italy fall marginally below this level. The lowest levels of spending are reported by Ireland and Switzerland, both of which approximate to the more limited American figure. In general, however, over-time analysis suggests that it is toward this Irish–Swiss–U.S. level that most of the European polities are now pointing. Within a more widespread liberal consensus, and within the constraints imposed by the budgetary guidelines set by the EU, European governments are increasingly divesting themselves of public spending commitments and are attempting to reduce the government share of national income. In some cases, they have little choice. Health costs are rising throughout Europe, and the population is aging. The result is that even to maintain present welfare programs at their existing levels will cost the governments an ever-increasing share of revenue. The solution is to therefore to privatize and to divest responsibilities: encouraging more and more private health insurance, on the one hand, and demanding that citizens retire later and provide for the bulk of their own pension arrangements, on the other.

Table 1.3 also reports the percentage of the population aged 65 and above, 65 being the most common age for compulsory retirement in Europe. The contrasts with the United States are often striking, as are the internal variations. Thus some 17 to 18 percent of the population are now of retirement age in Belgium, Germany, Greece, Italy, Spain, and Sweden, and given the lower birth rates now being recorded in many of these countries, this proportion is expected to increase in the coming decade. This puts a huge burden on the developed European welfare states, particularly since the overall dependency ratio (the ratio of those working to those who are either too young or too old to work, or who are sick or unemployed) is worsening every year. Indeed, according to *The Economist* (July 17, 2003), in a comment on what it called the "population implosion," there are currently 35 persons of pensionable age for every 100 persons of working age in Europe, and, if present trends continue, this ratio will increase to 75 to every 100 by 2050. Cutting pension payments and forcing people to retire later is part of the solution to the budgetary crisis that is implied by this demographic shift; getting more people into the labor market is another, which means getting more women and older people into the workforce, and also probably more immigrants. But this, in turn, causes its own political problems—the potential mobilization of angry pensioners' parties, on the one hand, and the growth of xenophobic far-right parties, on the other.

Although policy problems such as these are common to most European countries, and although the legacy of generous social provisions that was built up during the peaceful postwar decades is now coming under strain throughout the long-established democracies, it is still evident that we cannot talk about modern Europe as though it were constituted by an homogeneous group of polities. Instead, we are talking about a collection of places with quite distinctive social, economic, and political profiles. Whether these differences are large or small depends on your point of view. As we have suggested, to travel within Italy from prosperous north to poor south is to see quite a striking social contrast. To cross the border from the newly democratized and relatively successful Hungary to the more established but politically divided Austria is to see another strong social and economic contrast. Yet even the poorer southern parts of Italy or the more impoverished parts of Hungary are in no sense whatsoever among the world's poor regions. Their levels of prosperity are far above those of almost every third-world state, whether we measure prosperity in terms of money, life expectancy, literacy, or indeed any other aspect of the quality of life. Moreover, although the differences between regions and countries in Europe can be quite pronounced, these are less striking when viewed from within the increasingly cosmopolitan and internationalized world of the major cities and towns. To the average visitor, Catania may not seem that different from Turin, nor Budapest from Vienna.

For all their diversity and commonality, the countries of Europe constitute the world's largest collection of successful capitalist democracies. Moreover, most of these European countries are tied together in an ever more powerful political union, the European Union, which we discuss in detail in Chapter 5. But the differences that we have highlighted must also be kept in mind in the comparative discussions that follow. We are, after all, talking about a collection of different countries, and that is one of the things that makes the study of modern European politics so interesting. At the same time of course, these differences must not also be exaggerated. For that reason it makes sense to analyze politics in the collection of European countries in terms of their underlying similarities as well as their distinctive features. This is the main purpose of the chapters that follow.

✦ Appendix: Using the Internet and Other Resources to Keep Up with Changes in European Politics

Representative Government in Modern Europe is as up-to-the-minute as we could make it, but, inevitably, there are details that will be overtaken by events even while the book is being printed. Fortunately, readers wanting to monitor continuing political developments in Europe have a number of sources that they can turn to.

As well as the wide range of general political science journals, there are some that specialize in European politics. The *European Journal of Political Research,* in addition to its regular issues, publishes an annual *Data Yearbook* containing the latest developments from each of the countries that we cover in this book. *West European Politics* has many articles on European politics, as its name suggests, and also carries regular reports on the latest elections in Europe—as does the journal *Electoral Studies.* There are also many more specialist journals, which you will find cited in the chapters of this book.

Increasingly, the Internet is a valuable source of political data. Nearly every government department, every parliament, every political party, every interest group, and every major newspaper in every European country maintains its own site on the Web; many individual members of parliament have their own sites, complete with photograph. We decided not to try to provide a comprehensive list of these sites. One reason, of course, is that doing so would require a huge effort on our part, but a more persuasive reason is that Web sites come and go with alarming regularity, and any such list would soon become out-of-date. Indeed, we are tempted to economize on effort even further and suggest that all any reader really needs is a search engine (such as www.google.com), because, thus armed, it is not too difficult to track down pretty much any piece of information that exists somewhere in cyberspace. Still, we list here a small number of sites that have established themselves as reliable presences on the Web, and that either contain useful information themselves or have links to other sites:

Document	Web address
1. Richard Kimber's political science resources	www.psr.keele.ac.uk
2. The Inter-Parliamentary Union	www.ipu.org
3. Welcome to Europe	www.europa.eu.int/index-en.htm
4. Elections site	www.ElectionResources.org/
5. Elections site	www.electionworld.org/
6. Elections site	www.epicproject.org/
7. Elections site	www.parties-and-elections.de
8. Project on political transformation in postcommunist Europe	www.essex.ac.uk/elections

9. International Institute for Democracy
   and Electoral Assistance (IDEA)   www.idea.int
10. Freedom House   www.freedomhouse.org
11. News and reports from 28
    postcommunist countries   www.tol.cz
12. CIA: *World Factbook*   www.cia.gov/cia/publications/factbook
13. Politics portal of the Department of Political   http://www.tcd.ie/Political_Science/
    Science, Trinity College Dublin, Ireland   courses/undergrad/bcc/portal/index.html
14. European Consortium for Political Research   www.essex.ac.uk/ecpr/
15. British Political Studies Association   www.psa.ac.uk/www/gateway.htm

Site 1 is a prize-winning site maintained by a British political scientist. Although it does not hold any information itself, it contains links to a huge number of political sites around the world and is organized very clearly so that users should have little difficulty in finding a site that is useful for their purposes. Site 2 contains some information on the Inter-Parliamentary Union and has links to all of the parliaments that are affiliated to it. In most countries, the parliament site itself contains information about its own composition and rules, as well as links to the sites of individual MPs, political parties, and governments. Site 3 is the site of the European Union, and it contains a great deal of information as well as links to all the EU institutions. Sites 4 through 7 contain details of election results around the world and, in some cases (particularly site 6), comparative and country-by-country data on election systems, laws, management, and administration. Site 8 is the University of Essex project on political transformation and electoral process in postcommunist Europe; it contains information about legislation, elections results, constituency data, and candidate data in twelve postcommunist countries of central and eastern Europe. Site 9 contains information about political participation and turnout, electoral processes, political parties, and democracy-building in the world.

Site 10 is the Web site for Freedom House, a nongovernmental organization, which regularly publishes such reports as "Freedom in the World," "Nations in Transit," and "Freedom of the Press." Site 11 is useful for finding up-to-date information and news from postcommunist countries in eastern and central Europe. Site 12 is the CIA's *World Factbook,* which contains basic data about population, government, economy, and so on, in countries worldwide. Site 13 contains links to comparative and general politics information resources. Sites 14 and 15 are the pages of two political science associations: the European Consortium for Political Research (the main Europe-wide body, which among other things holds annual workshops), and the "gateway" of the British Political Studies Association, with links to numerous official and unofficial European politics sites.

CHAPTER 2

❦

THE EXECUTIVE

↬ PRESIDENTIAL AND PARLIAMENTARY GOVERNMENT

When we think generally about representative government, one of the most important distinctions we can make is between "presidential" and "parliamentary" government systems. In presidential government systems, a powerful president is directly elected by the people to be both chief executive and head of state. There is a clear constitutional "separation of powers" between the executive, which has the president at its apex and is given the job of running the country under its constitution and laws, and the legislature, also elected by the people and given the job of making those laws. This separation of powers is most obvious in the important proviso that the executive cannot dismiss the legislature and the legislature cannot dismiss the executive. Except in the most extreme circumstances both branches of government, each democratically elected, must learn to live with each other. This creates a system of "checks and balances" on what each can do. The classic example of a "presidential government" system is the United States of America.

In parliamentary government systems, the executive in general, and the chief executive in particular, is not elected directly by the people but are instead chosen "indirectly" by the elected parliament. There is a much more fuzzy separation of powers between the government, comprising a "cabinet" of ministers with a prime minister at its apex, and the parliament elected by the people to do two main jobs—making laws, making and breaking governments. Crucially, and quite unlike the situation in a presidential system, the executive is constitutionally responsible to the legislature under parliamentary government. Parliaments not only choose the prime minister but can dismiss the prime minister at will. The system is democratic because the unelected prime minister is responsible to, and must always be able to command a majority of votes in, the elected parliament. Thus, under the parliamentary government systems, the executive changes because the outgoing government is replaced by parliament with a new one—often after a parliamentary election has changed the partisan balance of the legislature. Parliamentary government is the norm in modern Europe, and it is striking that, when the democratizing states of eastern Europe had the once-in-a-lifetime opportunity to choose a new system of government as they moved away from their old constitutions, most opted for what were fundamentally parliamentary systems of government—even if, as we shall see, some had a "presidential" twist to them.

✦ THE HEAD OF STATE

The president under a presidential system is typically also head of state. In contrast, it is rare under European-style parliamentary government for the chief executive also to be head of state. Instead the head of state is seen as someone who is "above" the cut and thrust of day-to-day politics, a lofty figurehead for the state and all its citizens. As a result, there is typically a clear separation of powers between the political executive and the constitutional head of state. This is a historical product of the evolution of many European states from traditional autocratic monarchies into the parliamentary democracies that exist today. Indeed many modern European states are still headed by monarchs. The list of constitutional monarchies embraces Belgium, Britain, Denmark, the Netherlands, Norway, Spain, and Sweden, and Luxembourg's head of state is a grand duke (see Table 2.1). Furthermore, even Europe's republics have tended to evolve a role for the president, as head of state, very much like the role of a constitutional monarch. This role is typically that of a mature public figure above the mundane, albeit vital, details of day-to-day politics, fulfilling instead the elevated functions required of any head of state in a constitutional democracy. These functions are symbolic (being a personal embodiment of the state for all to see, and for some to love and respect); procedural (presiding over major state occasions such as the opening of parliament, providing the final ratification of laws); and diplomatic (greeting other heads of state and visiting dignitaries, going on official "state visits" to other countries).

There are, however, important European exceptions to the clear-cut constitutional distinction between presidential and parliamentary systems. These combine a powerful and directly elected president with a parliament that can make or break the prime minister. Such may be the respective powers of president and prime minister that we can almost think of these states as having two executives—with an obvious potential for deadlock when these offices are controlled by different political blocs. The best known example of such "semi-presidential" systems is France, where the separation of powers between parliament and the presidency is much less clear-cut than in most other European states and, in consequence, there is a much more "politicized" presidency along U.S. lines. (For discussions of semi-presidentialism, see Elgie, "Politics.") These arrangements formed the basis for a model that was of considerable interest to the constitution-builders of the newly democratizing states of eastern Europe, facing crucial decisions on the separation of powers between legislature and executive. The first post-communist Polish constitution did indeed introduce a version of semi-presidentialism that gave both president and parliament in Poland significant independent powers. However, the new 1997 constitution removed several important powers from the Polish president and shifted Poland closer to the European norm of parliamentary government. (On the evolution of presidential politics in Poland, see Millard; Szczerbiak; Zubek). Most of the other eastern European states we are concerned with here, while flirting seriously with the semi-presidential model during the constitution-building process, went on to evolve in the mainstream European tradition of parliamentary government, leaving France still the main European example of semi-presidential government. (On the general evolution of relations between presidents and governments in eastern Europe, see Taras.)

T A B L E   2 . 1

Heads of State in Europe, 2005

Country	Constitutional Status of Head of State	Head of State (January 2005)	When Came to Office	How Came to Office
Austria	President	Heinz Fischer	2004	Direct election
Belgium	Monarch	King Albert II	1993	Heredity
Cyprus	President	Tassos Papadopoulos	2003	Direct election
Czech Republic	President	Vaclav Klaus	2003	Election by legislature
Denmark	Monarch	Queen Margrethe II	1972	Heredity
Estonia	President	Arnold Ruutel	2001	Election by legislature
Finland	President	Tarja Halonen	2000	Direct election
France	President	Jacques Chirac	1995	Direct election
Germany	President	Horst Koehler	2004	Election by legislature
Greece	President	Kostis Stephanopoulos	1995	Election by legislature
Hungary	President	Ferenc Madl	2000	Election by legislature
Iceland	President	Olafur Ragnar Grimsson	1996	Direct election
Ireland	President	Mary McAleese	1997	Direct election
Italy	President	Carlo Azeglio Ciampi	1999	Election by legislature
Latvia	President	Vaira Vike-Freiberga	1999	Election by legislature
Lithuania	President	Arturas Paulauskas	2004	Direct election
Luxembourg	Grand Duke	Grand Duke Henri	2000	Hereditary
Malta	President	Eddie Fenech Adami	2004	Election by legislature
Netherlands	Monarch	Queen Beatrix	1980	Heredity
Norway	Monarch	King Harald	1991	Heredity
Poland	President	Aleksander Kwasniewski	1995	Direct election
Portugal	President	Jorge Sampaio	1996	Direct election
Slovakia	President	Ivan Gasparovic	2004	Direct election
Slovenia	President	Janez Drnovsek	2002	Direct election
Spain[a]	Monarch	King Juan Carlos	1975	Heredity
Sweden	Monarch	King Carl XVI Gustaf	1973	Heredity
Switzerland	President	Samuel Schmid	2005	Election by legislature
United Kingdom	Monarch	Queen Elizabeth II	1952	Heredity

[a] Spain was a republic from 1931 to 1975. Juan Carlos, grandson of the king ousted in 1931, was nominated by the dictator General Franco to succeed him as head of state, and took over this position when Franco died in 1975.

Semi-Presidentialism in France

The president of France has the formal power to appoint the prime minister and to chair cabinet meetings; he or she can also dismiss the prime minister and dissolve parliament. Nobody can dismiss the president. Even so, France does not have a full-fledged presidential system along the lines of that in the United States since the French constitution clips the president's wings in several important ways. The net result is what has come to be seen as the classic semi-presidential system.

    The potential for conflict between legislature and executive in France was not manifested for some time after the introduction of the country's new semi-presidential constitution in 1958. This was because President de Gaulle's party, dominated comprehensively by de Gaulle, controlled a majority of seats in the National Assembly, so that the president's preeminence was never seriously challenged. It was not easy to tell whether what appeared at the time to be the considerable power of the French president was at least in part a product of having the same party in control of both legislature and presidency. This situation was itself a product of the semi-presidential constitution, since an incoming French president has the power to dissolve the legislature more or less immediately and call new elections—the likely result being a parliamentary election won by the same party that won the presidency just a few weeks earlier. The presidential term (seven years) was at that time longer than the parliamentary term (five years), however, meaning that there was a constitutional requirement for a parliamentary election in the midterm of the presidency. This meant that, since 1986, there have been several periods during which different parties controlled the presidency and prime ministership—a situation known in France as "*cohabitation*" and closely analogous to what is described as "divided government" in the United States. As a result, we have now learned quite a lot about the relationship between the two offices.

    Between 1986 and 1988, and between 1993 and 1995, the socialist President François Mitterrand was confronted by a legislature controlled by the parties of the right. Mitterrand came to power in 1981 and at once called parliamentary elections that predictably were won by his own socialist party. New parliamentary elections fell due in 1986, however, and were won by the right. President Mitterrand chose the right-wing leader Jacques Chirac as prime minister—he had little choice as the assembly would have voted down any other appointee—and there was an uneasy two-year period of *cohabitation* during which each leader felt constrained by the powers of the other. This came to an end after Mitterrand defeated Chirac in the 1988 presidential election. Mitterrand immediately dissolved the assembly, and the socialists won enough seats at the ensuing parliamentary elections to be able to form a government with the aid of some centrist deputies.

    Mitterrand was still in office when further parliamentary elections fell due, and the situation was repeated in 1993. The right won a sweeping victory in legislative elections and came to dominate the assembly. Mitterrand was once more forced to appoint a right-wing prime minister, this time Edouard Balladur, and to begin another period of *cohabitation*. This *cohabitation* proved more harmonious, perhaps because Mitterrand, now an old man at the end of his political career, did not see Balladur as a rival. It may also have been because Balladur, himself ambitious to run as a candidate in the 1995 presidential election but knowing he would not be contesting this with Mitterrand, adopted a less confrontational attitude. This period ended when, after a period of infighting among the Gaullists, it was Chirac not Balladur who won the presidential election for the Gaullists. Chirac appointed another Gaullist, Alain Juppé, as prime minister, and both high offices were once again in the hands of the same party.

    Already in control of parliament and deciding not to call a general election immediately after winning the presidency, Chirac had to call one on less favorable terms in 1997. The left won the elections, and Chirac was forced to appoint the socialist leader, Lionel Jospin, to the position of prime minister. Jospin immediately formed a coalition

French President Francois Mitterrand (right) and Prime Minister Jacques Chirac during their uneasy political *cohabitation.* © Orban/Corbis/Sygma

President Mitterrand and Prime Minister Balladur found *cohabitation* more congenial, despite their different political backgrounds. © Denange Francis/Liaison Agency

administration that included both Communists and Greens. Once more there was a radical divergence between partisan control of the presidency and that of the prime ministership—a new *cohabitation*. Once more, the power of a French president was seen to wane very considerably when confronted by a prime minister of a different party—and Jospin was another French prime minister with an eye on the next presidential election.

The cycle continued in 2002, when Chirac fought for reelection to the presidency and faced his own prime minister, Jospin, as the main candidate of the left. In the event, Jospin made several strategic errors campaigning in a very crowded field—the first round of the election was contested by more than 20 candidates. He did not even make it through to the second round, leaving the final race between the center–right incumbent Chirac and Jean-Marie Le Pen, leader of one of the most right-wing parties in France. All opponents of Le Pen had little choice but to vote for Chirac, a situation that saw him romping home with an unprecedented majority. He at once called a parliamentary election that was comfortably won by his own party. Control of parliament and the presidency was unified again. (For a discussion of relations between president and government in France, see Elgie, "France.")

The power of the French president is thus the product of a complex interaction between formal constitutional provisions and practical party politics. Formal powers seem to place the office of president in a class of its own in Europe. Practical politics show us that these formal powers expand considerably when both presidency and prime ministership are in the hands of the same party. However, and very significantly, the French constitution has now been changed to bring the presidential term down from seven to five years; both president and parliament will have the same terms of office, with parliamentary elections typically expected to take place shortly after those for the presidency. This greatly reduces the chances of the need for *cohabitation.* (It does not rule out this possibility altogether, since a president could in theory dissolve the legislature to call, but nonetheless lose, early elections.) On past experience, reducing the prospect of the need to share power with a prime minister from a different party should increase the de facto power of a French president, creating a situation in which the French political system looks more like a presidential than like a parliamentary government system.

Directly Elected Presidents

Many other European countries also have directly elected presidents, though none with powers equivalent to those found in France. Their number has swelled as a result of the democratization of eastern Europe; quite a few former communist states opted for a directly elected presidency, even if not for full presidential government. Besides France, we find directly elected presidents in Austria, Cyprus, Finland, Iceland, Ireland, Portugal—to which we can now add Lithuania, Poland, Slovakia, and Slovenia. Of these, Finland and, as we have seen, Poland have in the past come closest to being "semi-presidential" in nature.

For much of the postwar period, the Finnish constitution gave the president a central role in foreign policy, and the special circumstances of Finland's long land border with the former Soviet Union made this power very important throughout the Cold War. The long-serving President Kekkonen did more than anyone else to establish harmonious relations with Finland's powerful and potentially dangerous neighbor. The Finnish president was at that time also able to wield considerable influence in domestic policy, though the initiative in policy making lay with the government. Following the disintegration of the former Soviet Union and the end of the Cold War, a series of constitutional reforms in the 1990s significantly cut back the powers of the Finnish president. A two-term (twelve-year) limit was put on the tenure of any president, and the president's independent powers to dismiss a government that had not been defeated in the legislature, to dissolve parliament, and to call new elections were all removed. The result is a Finnish presidency that now has more or less the same, rather weak, powers as those found elsewhere in western Europe.

As in many other states in transition from the former Soviet bloc, Polish democracy initially operated under a set of amendments to the preexisting communist constitution. In 1992, parliament adopted the "Little Constitution," intended to operate until a comprehensive new constitution could be agreed on. Under the terms of this, the Polish president was elected by popular vote for a five-year term and accorded significant powers. He or she had the right to nominate the prime minister, but this was subject to approval by a lower house that could reject the presidential nominee and appoint its own candidate without first seeking presidential approval. Prior presidential consultation was required for appointment of ministers of defense, internal affairs, and foreign affairs, and the president had to approve all other cabinet appointments. The president also could dissolve parliament, the Sejm, in special circumstances. These included situations in which parliament was unable to approve the state budget or had passed a vote of no confidence in the prime minister without being able to agree a successor. The president also had the right to veto legislation passed by parliament, although this veto could be overturned by a two-thirds majority in the Sejm. The result was that, for most of the 1990s, Poland was marked by quite severe rivalries between prime minister and president, experiencing *cohabitation* Polish-style. The election of Lech Walesa to the presidency in 1990, for example, was followed by frequent conflicts between his office and the various fragmented coalitions that governed Poland until 1993. Many of the governing parties had emerged out of the broadly based Solidarity movement originally led by Walesa himself, but divisions within this movement widened in the years following the defeat of communism (Jasiewicz; Meer Krok-Paszowska). This *cohabitation* became even more fraught after 1993, when the former communists and their allies came to government and were obliged to share power with President Walesa, seen by many as the architect of their previous downfall. In 1995, *cohabitation* ended when the former communists also won the presidency and the two offices fell under unified partisan control.

In the event, it was 1997 by the time a new Polish constitution had been drafted by political elites and narrowly accepted by the people. This document retained core institutional features of the old constitution, albeit with some modifications (Jasiewicz and Gebethner; see also Letowska; Garlicki). The Sejm can now overrule a presidential veto with a three-fifths rather than a two-thirds majority, and the presidential veto cannot be applied at all to the budget. The president now has no special role with regard to defense, security, and foreign affairs, strengthening the prime minister's side of this dual executive. Overall, a major effect of the new constitution was to strengthen the position of cabinet and prime minister vis-à-vis both parliament and the president. According to Jasiewicz and Gebethner (p. 504), the Polish prime minister now "has a role comparable to that of the chancellor in the German system."

In Austria, Iceland, Ireland, and Portugal, less-powerful presidents are directly elected and exercise responsibilities in specified circumstances but in practice do not get involved in day-to-day politics. In Ireland, for example, the political role of the president is extensively and explicitly curtailed by the constitution. In this context it is also noteworthy that, as in October 2004 when incumbent President Mary McAleese was returned unopposed, there is not always a contest for the role of "elected" head of state in Ireland. Despite being head of state, it is remarkable that the Irish president is not permitted to leave the state "save with the consent of the government" (Article 12.9). Any "message or address" to the nation "on any matter of national or public importance" must receive the approval of the government (Article 13.7). With a very few specific exceptions, any other power of the president can be exercised "only on the advice of the Government" (Article 13.9). Even so, the Irish president does have two important powers that could be politically important in certain circumstances. The first is the power to refer bills passed by the legislature directly to the Supreme Court in order to test their constitutionality, a power that has been used on quite a few occasions, some controversial. (We return to this in Chapter 4.) The second is the power, valid only if the prime minister has lost a vote of confidence, to refuse a request for dissolution of the legislature and thereby to block new elections. This power has never formally been used in Ireland; dissolutions have always been granted on request. Nonetheless, the very existence of this explicit provision is an important constraint on the freedom of Irish prime ministers to call elections whenever they feel like it. In November 1994 Mary Robinson, who was then Irish president and a constitutional lawyer by profession, was deemed unlikely to grant a dissolution that many politicians wanted, following the collapse of the incumbent government coalition. As a result, for the first time in the history of the state and thereby changing political precedent, a new government was formed without an intervening election. This example illustrates very clearly the important general point that formal constitutional powers, including those of the president, do not actually have to be used in order to have a significant impact on events. The simple fact that such powers *might* be used can in itself be crucial, as other politicians then trim their sails in anticipation.

Indirectly Elected Presidents

In the other European republics, the president is elected indirectly, usually by members of parliament. In none of these countries is the constitutional role of the president particularly strong, although disputes between indirectly elected presidents and prime ministers have been common in eastern European states during their transitions to democracy. Despite this, it is unwise to write off any president, even one with apparently only formal powers and no history of political intervention. This is clearly demonstrated in the early 1990s by the actions of the president of Italy, during a time of turmoil in a party system rocked by a succession of massive financial scandals. In the face of these scandals and of the consequent collapse in the legitimacy and credibility of most of the established parties, President Cossiga abruptly ended a period of relative silence. He began to make regular and influential interventions in public debates, speaking directly to the nation on television for more than a hundred hours in 1991. With considerable public support, and using a series of what he described as "pickaxe blows" (*picconate*), he supported electoral and other institutional reforms, urged early elections, influenced the government formation process, and generally made his presence felt. (See Bardi for a description of this period.)

Political conflict between prime ministers and indirectly elected presidents is clearly illustrated by the situation that emerged in the Czech Republic shortly after its formation, following the dissolution of the former federal state of Czechoslovakia. The new Czech constitution, approved in 1992, provided for a president elected by a majority vote in parliament. In 1993, the leading former dissident, Vaclav Havel, who had been elected first postcommunist president of Czechoslovakia in 1990, was reelected to office, this time as first president of the new Czech Republic. A proposal for the direct election of the Czech president by the people had been rejected for fear this might lead to the accumulation of too much personal power by the incumbent. The president was given the right to dissolve the parliament under certain limited circumstances (such as when the government had been defeated in a vote of no confidence); to suspend but not veto legislation; and to appoint the prime minister and ministers, subject to the approval of the House. Although the new constitution came down firmly in favor of a parliamentary system, sharp tensions quickly emerged between President Havel and the prime minister, Vaclav Klaus, who had been Havel's former ally in the pro-democracy Civic Forum. Relations between these two leading Czech politicians had never been easy (see Kopecky), and in spring 1997, following a severe budget crisis, Havel even went so far as to suggest that Klaus's government should resign. Klaus refused and later won a confidence vote before eventually leaving office in November. At the end of that year, in his State of the Nation address, Havel attacked the social and economic record of both the parliament and the outgoing government, to which Klaus's response was that Havel simply did not understand economics. Such public disputes between a constitutionally powerful head of government and an ostensibly ceremonial head of state are nearly unknown in most long-established parliamentary democracies, even those with a president rather than a monarch at their head. In postcommunist Europe, however, including in both the Czech and the Slovak republics, they are not uncommon, reflecting a continuing uncertainty about the division of executive authority in everyday political practice.

What we see in these examples is the other side of the French coin. The French president is undeniably strong but is much stronger when formal constitutional powers are reinforced by a favorable political situation. Other presidents, such as those in Italy or the Czech Republic, are undeniably weak but may become stronger in particular political circumstances. It is thus unwise to write off the *potential* political power of any European president in times of crisis, even if it is easy to underestimate that power when things are running smoothly. (For discussions of the role of presidents, and presidential power, in modern political systems, see Shugart and Carey; Metcalf.)

Monarchs

European countries that do not have presidents retain monarchs as heads of state—although no former monarch has been restored to the throne in ex-communist eastern Europe. Many European monarchies, indeed, are very ancient institutions, and monarchs might be thought of as peculiar anachronisms in the twenty-first century. They still can have an important role to play, however, although this is typically even farther removed from the cut and thrust of party politics than the role played by presidents. In the past some monarchs succumbed to the temptation to intervene politically, using their power and position to favor some parties over others. This usually caused widespread resentment and rebounded on those who have tried it. It was the main factor behind referendums leading to the abolition of the monarchies in Greece and Italy, and the Belgian monarchy survived only narrowly in a vote in 1950. Royal houses that have remained aloof from partisan politics have managed to survive, and given the often high degree of public cynicism toward politicians, an unelected king or queen may even command more popular affection than an elected leader.

The outstanding example of a monarchy that plays an important role in society comes from Britain, where the queen sits at the apex of the social system and is even head of the established church, the Church of England. Well over a century ago, the constitutional authority Walter Bagehot identified the monarchy as a powerful force for preserving the status quo, commenting that the British working classes would never rebel against the established order because to do so would be to rebel against the queen, to whom they were intensely loyal. For much of the twentieth century, the British monarchy was so popular that the chance of any drastic change in its role seemed very slim indeed. Modern media and changing attitudes have recently subjected the British royal family to intense, uncontrolled, and increasingly "disrespectful" publicity, however. This publicity has focused not just on the glory and magnificence of the royal family in all its works and pomps, as it did to a large extent in the past, but also on the divorces, marital infidelities, and other forms of worldly behavior that have tended to portray members of the royal family as being pretty much the same as anyone else. For a monarchy that has traditionally based its popular appeal on being utterly different from everyone else, this has been a traumatic change, one that has proved very difficult to adjust to. A British monarch has never recently been involved in explicit party politics. One reason for this is that Britain's first-past-the-post electoral system typically delivers decisive election results (see Chapter 11) and removes the potential need for intervention by a head of state if government formation negotiations become impossibly deadlocked (see Chapter 12). Even in this situation the British monarchy is at least a passive participant in the political scene. One good example of this can be found in sectarian divisions of Northern Ireland, where members of the "loyalist" community profess their loyalty to the British *crown,* even when negotiations over a constitutional settlement leave them deeply at odds with the incumbent British *government.*

No other European monarchy wraps itself in as much pomp and ceremony as the British royal family, but a monarch's very existence as a symbol of the nation can be important. King Baudouin of Belgium used to describe himself as "the only Belgian," a reference to the fact that almost all others in the linguistically divided country think of themselves first and foremost as either Flemish (if they speak the Dutch language) or Walloon (if they speak French). The monarchy is one of the few symbols with which both language groups can identify.

In Spain, the monarchy exercised a vital political role in the years after the death of the dictator Franco in 1975. King Juan Carlos, designated as successor to the dictator General Franco, was expected to perpetuate the old authoritarian system. In fact, he quickly dismantled the Franco dictatorship and set up Spain's return to democracy. His intervention was also decisive in thwarting an attempted military coup in 1981. In successfully standing up to the leaders of the coup and ordering troops back to barracks, Juan Carlos played a major and widely respected role in protecting the Spanish transition to democracy. Although the Spanish monarch does also have formal powers to designate a prime minister, who then takes office subject to a majority vote in the legislature, these powers have not been significant in practice, given election results that have usually been decisive. However, the combination of moral authority and formal powers means that the Spanish monarch retains considerable potential to play an important political role in the

An attempted coup d'état in action: Spanish soldiers seize temporary control of the parliament building. This coup failed, and King Juan Carlos played a crucial role in protecting Spain's transition to democracy. © Hulton-Deutsch Collection/Corbis

event of serious failure in the mainstream political process. (See Heywood, ch. 4, for a discussion of the Spanish monarchy and its relations with the legislature and executive.)

Monarchies in other countries have deliberately shed themselves of the mystique often assumed to attach itself to royalty. Members of the Norwegian, Swedish, or Dutch royal families are as likely to be seen wearing "civilian" clothes and engaged in humdrum pursuits as dressed in the regalia of office, and the Norwegian and Swedish royal families in particular have moved away from the pomp and ceremony associated with traditional European monarchies. Nonetheless, royals are never seen by others as ordinary people. They cannot marry whomsoever they want—potential royal spouses are always subject to the most intense public scrutiny as to their suitability. Crucially, as several royal family members have found out to their cost, they cannot make the type of robust comment about social problems that is the common currency of debate both by politicians and members of the public; from the lips of a royal, such comments can lead to considerable public disapproval. Indeed the kings and queens of Europe tread on very thin ice when they make any political comment at all about the realms over which they are constitutionally sovereign, and in that sense they have oddly less freedom than ordinary citizens. The political role of constitutional monarchs is thus for the most part passive. Even so, as we saw with the case of Spain, the potential is always there for a more active role in extreme political circumstances.

Overall, despite the parliamentary government system that makes the prime minister the chief executive and the head of state a largely ceremonial role, modern Europe's monarchs and presidents cannot be dismissed as mere ciphers. Apart from the explicit powers that some of them have in the area of government formation, which we discuss later in this chapter, they can play a significant part in legitimizing the entire political system. However, it is true to say that they generally keep out of the risky business of day-to-day politics, so that real executive power in today's European states is typically in the hands of the executive branch of government rather than in those of the head of state. At the top of this political executive sits the prime minister.

✦ THE PRIME MINISTER

The political boss of most European countries is not the titular head of state but a political chief executive. This position goes under many titles in different European languages but is almost always referred to in English translations as "prime minister"—although Austrian and German chief executives are always called chancellors. A European prime minister is typically not only the chief executive of the state but also the head of one of the main legislative parties, often the largest. The combination of these roles can create a position of very considerable power—far greater than that of a U.S. president. This power arises precisely because of the lack of any separation of powers between legislature and executive. Under parliamentary government European-style, the person who can muster a legislative majority becomes head of the executive. This single person, the prime minister, thereby stands at the apex of both institutions of state. This is especially important in countries with a tradition of single-party majority government, such as Britain or Greece. Here, one person is typically leader of the party that can control the legislature and, at the same time, leader of the executive. In these countries, the only real threat to prime ministerial power comes from inside the governing party itself. Even in the more typical European coalition systems, it is usually the case that the prime minister has gained office by virtue of having a powerful bargaining position in the legislature and therefore operates from a position of strength. All of this means that, although the formal powers of the prime minister are typically laid down in the constitution, the considerable real power of almost all European prime ministers flows from practical politics as much as from explicit rules.

Perhaps the most important aspect of prime ministerial power stems from the fact that he or she is the person approved by parliament as the political head of the government. As we will see, this means that the choice of a new prime minister is the first and most important task of any new legislature after an election has been held. If the election result means that the incumbent prime minister can muster the parliamentary votes to remain in office, then, for all practical purposes, he or she has "won" the election—even if this election resulted in large losses for the prime minister's party. If the election result means that the incumbent prime minister cannot control enough parliamentary votes to remain in office, then the prime minister has "lost" the election. Changes of prime minister are thus the most obvious and dramatic changes that result from European parliamentary elections—which are much more about choosing governments than they are about choosing a group of legislators to do what they are ostensibly meant to do, which is to pass laws. It would be a gross exaggeration to say that European legislatures are no more than electoral colleges for choosing prime ministers, but being an electoral college for choosing the prime minister is certainly one of the more important jobs for the legislature under European-style parliamentary government. Thus the prominent politicians campaigning in parliamentary elections are typically party leaders. Many of these present themselves to voters, often more in hope than expectation, as candidates for the prime ministership. Crucially, *if citizens want to change their chief executive in a parliamentary government system, they do so by voting in legislative elections.* Everything else about practical politics in parliamentary government systems is ultimately less important than this simple constitutional fact. Its practical political effect is that prime ministers and potential prime ministers play a central part in the entire process of political competition.

A second important facet of the power of a typical European prime minister arises from the rather modest role of the head of state, which we have just discussed. In almost every European country with the exception of France, the prime minister is also the country's premier political figure, the most important embodiment of the government in both domestic and international affairs. Both in popular political imagination and in the eyes of the international media, a strong prime minister personifies the government of the country. The most obvious manifestations of this can be seen in the "summit conferences" that punctuate international diplomacy. Many other government members and senior civil servants are of course active in these, but the images that get into the media are of prime ministers shaking hands outside grand rooms, striking their most distinguished poses, and reading out weighty joint communiqués. This could be seen very clearly in the frenetic international diplomacy in 2003 surrounding the American-led military intervention in Iraq. European states were represented in this by *President* Chirac of France, but otherwise by *Prime Ministers* Blair, Berlusconi, and Aznar (of Britain, Italy, and Spain), *Chancellor* Schroder (of Germany), and their prime ministerial colleagues from other countries—but no other European president.

A third formal role that gives a prime minister massive practical political power arises from his or her combined position as head of both the cabinet and a major political party. A prime minister typically has the formal power to hire and fire cabinet ministers. As we will see in Chapter 12, when governments are coalitions, this power is constrained by the need to come to practical political terms with the leaders of other parties. Even in coalition cabinets, however, the prime minister typically has immense power over ministers from his or her own party. This means that he or she is a very important gatekeeper with control over the political careers of party colleagues, deciding the distribution of the most coveted set of prizes—seats at the cabinet table—in the entire political game. Obviously, this is a situation guaranteed to ensure discipline and obedience, though quite possibly neither love nor heartfelt loyalty, on the part of the PM's senior party colleagues.

A fourth element in the power of the prime minister is derived from the incredible complexity and specialization of the tasks involved in administering any modern state. It might be thought that this weakens the role of the prime minister—how can anyone be in control of all of this, or even know a fraction of what is actually happening? Of course, there is much that goes on that the prime minister does not know about, but the important thing is that he or she sits at the very center of the entire process. Whereas other members of the cabinet are given specific tasks, the prime minister's job is to coordinate these tasks and set the agenda for action. The prime minister thus has access to information about every branch of government, unlike any other politician, however senior, and this information is obviously a tremendous source of power. As guardian of the government's agenda, furthermore, the prime minister can play a large part in deciding which proposals are discussed by the government, in what order, and which of them are buried. Political scientists are paying increasing attention to the great—if often unobservable—power wielded by those who set the political agenda (Rosenthal).

There are several other sources of prime ministerial power, but it should be more than apparent by now that a typical European prime minister is a very powerful person in his or her own country. Nonetheless, it is also the case that a prime minister is by no means a dictator. An unwanted prime minister can be disposed of, sometimes ignominiously and at very short notice, by one of three basic methods.

The first requires an election. An unpopular prime minister can be thrown out of office by the voters, if his or her party loses so many seats at an election that it is no longer possible to win the nomination of the legislature. An important point here is that it is possible in almost every European country, if the prime minister loses support in the legislature for one reason or another, for his or her opponents to force an early election and hence force the prime minister out of office. In order for this to happen, the prime minister must have alienated at least some former supporters. If the original majority in favor of the prime minister is transformed into a majority against, this must mean that some of his or her original supporters have joined the ranks of the opponents who voted the prime minister out of office. When this happens, an election can result, and the prime minister's fate is then in the hands of the voters. Indeed, as we have just indicated, the decision to renew or revoke the mandate of the head of government is to a large extent what the typical European parliamentary election is about.

The second method of getting rid of an unwanted prime minister does not require an election but does require a change in the coalition of legislators that originally put the prime minister into office. Politicians controlling the votes of a majority of legislators may get together and decide to replace the incumbent prime minister. They can do this by forcing a vote of confidence in the legislature if the prime minister does not do the decent thing and resign first. In quite a few European countries—Belgium, Finland, France, and Italy are examples—it has been common in the past for the prime minister to be changed as a result of legislative politics, without an intervening election. Although Italy is best known for this phenomenon, five governments formed and fell in Belgium between April 1979 and November 1981, without an intervening election. Similarly, three different prime ministers headed French governments, again without an intervening election, between July 1988 and March 1993.

The third way of dismissing a prime minister comes from within his or her own party. We have already noted that a prime minister is typically, though not inevitably, the leader of a major political party. This means that his or her practical political position can be destroyed quickly and effectively if he or she loses the party leadership. We look in Chapter 10 at the internal politics of European political parties. For now, what is important is that parties can and do get rid of their leaders on a periodic basis, whether

Box 2.1   Executives and Heads of State

France

France has an unusual executive structure in the European context, having a president who is powerful and directly elected. Executive power is vested jointly in the president and the cabinet (Council of Ministers). Typically, the president asks a senior legislator in his or her own party to head a cabinet, which may be a single-party administration or a coalition. When a president of a different party comes into office, he or she can dissolve the legislature once in any twelve-month period. The assumption behind this is that his or her party, having just won the presidential election, will win the subsequent legislative election and then be able to form a government. On several occasions since 1986, however, French presidents have been forced to "cohabit" with prime ministers from a different party. In these situations, the power of the French president is significantly undermined. However, a recent constitutional reform has reduced the French presidential term and aligned it with the parliamentary term, making the prospect of *cohabitation* much less likely in future.

Germany

The powers of the German head of state, the federal president, are among the weakest in Europe. After a general election the president nominates a prime minister, the federal chancellor, but almost all other actions of the president must be countersigned by the chancellor. As a consequence, the role of president is largely ceremonial, although, as with the British monarch, the head of state could in theory refuse to call elections when asked to do so by the chief executive. This has never actually happened in either country. The ability of the legislature to remove the executive is constrained by the need for a constructive vote of no confidence, which requires that the legislature can bring down a government only if it can also agree on a replacement.

Italy

The Italian president is indirectly elected by an electoral college comprising both houses of the legislature and fifty-eight representatives of regional parliaments. He has some practical political power, arising from the right to dissolve the legislature and the fact that he remains in office for seven years. Given the chaotic state of the scandal-racked Italian party system during the 1990s, the stability provided by the presidency did much to enhance the role of the office and Presidents Cossiga and Scalfaro were significant political figures. In government formation, the president may nominate any legislator as prime minister, taking account of deals between parties when doing this, though is very likely to nominate the candidate who emerges from bargaining between parties. Changes to the Italian electoral system during the 1990s, however, have encouraged the formation of preelectoral coalitions—necessary to win first-past-the-post elections in multiparty systems. This has had the effect that the voters, rather than the president, have chosen the incoming prime minister.

Latvia

The role of the Latvian president is often seen as largely ceremonial. He or she acts, first of all, as the head of the Latvian state, representing the country internationally and serving as chief of the armed forces. The president is elected to a four-year term by majority secret ballot in parliament, holds the right of legislative initiative, and promulgates laws passed by the parliament. The president may also suspend promulgation of a law for a period of two months. However, parliament may then override the president by repeating its vote in favor of the bill. The position of the president is also weakened by the fact that, on the motion of at least one-half of the MPs, the parliament may initiate a vote to dismiss the president. The impeachment of the president requires a vote of not less than two-thirds of the members. However, the president of Latvia who took office in 1999, Vaira Vike-Freiberga, enjoyed wide popular support and trust; she was regarded by many as an important stabilizing factor in Latvia's path toward democracy.

Netherlands

The Dutch constitution makes no reference whatsoever to parliamentary government, vesting all executive authority in the monarch, who appoints ministers and dismisses them at will (Article 86.2). In practice the Netherlands has developed a parliamentary government system, although the monarch still plays quite an active role in government formation. After an election or a government resignation, the monarch consults all party leaders, then typically appoints an elder statesperson as *informateur* to identify the person best placed politically to lead government formation negotiations. These negotiations can be very lengthy, involving agreement to an extensive, detailed, and technical government program, a process that can take up to six months. Once a prime minister designate has agreed on a coalition deal with other parties, the monarch appoints cabinet ministers on his or her advice, although there is a strong tradition that individual parties have control over who fills their portfolios.

Poland

The powers of the Polish president have varied throughout the history of the Polish state: from presidentialism under the 1952 constitution, through semi-presidentialism under the 1992 interim constitution, to parliamentary government with some elements of semi-presidentialism under the 1997 constitution. In constitutional terms, the Polish president has lost a considerable amount of power, and the locus of power has shifted toward a prime minister accountable directly to parliament. As a result, Poland can be seen as moving away from the semi-presidential model. However, the president still retains some significant powers, such as the right to initiate legislation, refer bills to the Constitutional Tribunal, and nominate a number of key state officials. Despite a weakened constitutional position, the president continues to impose some limitations on the government. The executive's decision-making capacity is mainly constrained by the presidential veto, which becomes very significant during periods of *cohabitation* between president and prime minister of different political persuasions.

Spain

Spain's monarchy played a very important role in the country's transition to democracy, siding with those who favored democratic development and thereby reducing the probability that, following the end of the authoritarian regime under General Franco, Spanish politics would continue down the authoritarian path. That role has given the monarchy high prestige. The Spanish monarch is head of state, but under Article 97 of the 1978 constitution, executive authority is vested in a cabinet led by a prime minister. The king proposes a candidate for the office of prime minister, and the candidate is elected by an absolute majority of the legislature. Typically, however, the results of elections in Spain have been decisive enough to give the king no practical role in government formation.

Sweden

The Swedish monarchy has very little real power and since 1975 has been removed entirely from the government formation process. Instead, the speaker (chair) of the legislature nominates the prime minister, having consulted the leaders of each legislative party. If not more than half of the legislature votes against the proposal, it is approved, a procedure that allows the formation of governments that do not have the publicly expressed support of a majority of the legislature. The procedure in a vote of no confidence is similar. A new election must be held after four unsuccessful attempts to approve a prime minister. Once approved, the prime minister appoints other cabinet members, who are not subject to legislative approval.

United Kingdom

The United Kingdom is the only state in Europe without a codified constitution, so government formation is governed by custom and precedent rather than by written rules. The electoral system ensures that one-party government is nearly endemic, so that in practice the monarch asks the leader of the party with a plurality of seats in the House of Commons to form a government, even when (as in 1951 and February 1974) another party has won more votes. The leader of the largest party typically nominates a cabinet of senior party legislators, which requires no formal investiture vote in the House of Commons. Because the party almost invariably has a legislative majority, the only possibility of defeat arises from splits in the government party. If the British electoral system were ever to be changed, however, and coalition governments were to become more likely, then the need for the head of state to recognize a government *formateur* could raise important constitutional issues.

or not formal procedures are in place to do this. Losing the party leadership makes no official change in the status of the prime minister as prime minister: The constitutional seal of office handed over by the head of state cannot legally be taken away by any political party. Nonetheless, the position of a prime minister who has been stripped of the party leadership is almost always seen as untenable, forcing the person concerned to resign from office.

What is remarkable about all of this is that the prime minister of the country, the most powerful political figure in the land, can be thrown out of office on the basis of the decisions of a small number of people inside a particular political party. In 1990, for example, a few hundred members of the British Conservative parliamentary party removed Margaret Thatcher, one of postwar Europe's best-known, longest-serving, and most powerful prime ministers, and replaced her with John Major. None of the 60 million or so other members of the British public was involved in this process, although it is fair to say that her increasing unpopularity in opinion polls was an important factor in her fall. In early 2003, leading a British Labour government with an enormous parliamentary majority, Tony Blair faced a serious challenge to his position from a significant group of Labour MPs unhappy with his position on military intervention in Iraq. If Blair had lost this debate—and on this occasion he did not—then his position as British prime minister would have been irretrievably damaged, and it is almost certain he would have resigned.

Thus, although most European prime ministers are very powerful chief executives while they remain in office, their positions can be snatched from them suddenly and sometimes quite brutally. Moreover, although some of the powers of, and constraints on, the prime minister are spelled out in the formal rules of the political game, the effective position of most European prime ministers, who sit at the very heart of the political system, to a large extent depends on their practical abilities to dominate the cut and thrust of day to day politics. Anyone who has won the office of prime minister, after all, has climbed to the top of a very greasy political pole and typically has the ability to stay there—at least for a while.

✢ THE CABINET

If the prime minister is the political chief executive in a typical European parliamentary democracy, the political executive as a whole—the country's board of directors—is the cabinet. For most practical political purposes, we can think of the prime minister and the cabinet between them as being the "government" of the country. The cabinet comprises a set of ministers, and each minister plays two vital political roles. One is as the head of a government department; the other is as member of the cabinet itself, which collectively makes or at least approves most important political decisions.

The first role of a cabinet minister is to be the political head of one of the major departments of state. These departments can vary dramatically in size, both between and within countries. In Sweden, for example, the core civil service is very small because so much policy implementation and administration is decentralized. Thus it has been estimated that fewer than three thousand civil servants are directly involved in the policy process in Sweden (Larsson). This contrasts with the huge size of a number of government departments in Britain, for example. Whatever the size of the department concerned, however, its administration of the state is made politically accountable by virtue of the fact that each government department is under the jurisdiction of a cabinet minister. This minister is directly responsible to the cabinet as a whole for the affairs of his or her department, as well as being responsible for this to the legislature, and thus, via the legislature, to the electorate. If there are any problems in the department, the constitutional theory in most European states is that the buck stops with the minister, whether the minister knew about the problems or not. Indeed, a minister may even be forced to resign in response to a problem or scandal of which he or she had no knowledge. This constitutionally mandated accountability gives ministers the incentive to ensure that their departments are run properly.

However reassuring the constitutional doctrine of ministerial responsibility might look in theory, the political practice is often quite different. This is because there is increasing reluctance by cabinet ministers in almost every European country to resign in response to problems in their own department—particularly problems in which they do not see themselves as being directly involved. The real-world position is that ministers tend to be forced out of office only over major policy catastrophes or serious scandals for which they bear some direct responsibility, and not even then if they continue to enjoy the steadfast support of their cabinet colleagues. And because these colleagues are only too well aware that they too may find themselves with the sword hanging over their political careers at some time in the future, they tend to be very "understanding" about the travails of other ministers. It is probably fair to say that, these days, departmental problems can provide a very convenient excuse to get rid of an unpopular minister, but popular or powerful ministers are rarely sacked when something bad happens on their departmental watch. In this sense, the doctrine of ministerial responsibility is more a constitutional fiction than an inescapable fact of real political life. The list of cabinet ministers in modern Europe who resign because of this doctrine gets shorter every year.

The second key role for a cabinet minister is as a member of the "government," which is constitutionally defined in each European parliamentary democracy as a *collective* entity. Members of the cabinet sink or swim together, bound by a doctrine of "collective cabinet responsibility." This doctrine means that, although ministers may debate issues with great ferocity in cabinet meetings, once a cabinet decision has been taken it becomes collective cabinet policy and therefore the individual public policy position of all cabinet ministers. Every cabinet member is bound not only to *observe* the decision but also to *defend* it in public, even if he or she violently opposed it in private, and even if defending the decision is politically damaging for the minister involved. If a minister cannot publicly stand over a cabinet decision in this way, then he or she must resign or face dismissal. The constitutional principle of collective cabinet responsibility tends to go hand in hand with a principle of cabinet confidentiality. Ministers tend not to reveal the substance of political discussions within the cabinet since to do so would reveal internal divisions that would undermine the collective nature of the decision.

On balance, with a few notable exceptions, the constitutional principle of collective cabinet responsibility is diligently observed as a matter of political practice—quite unlike the doctrine of individual ministerial responsibility. This is because collective cabinet responsibility and confidentiality are usually in the political interest of all ministers—despite short-term incentives individual ministers might on occasion have to defect from them. Cabinets often have to take politically unpopular decisions, and there is comfort for ministers in the knowledge they can shelter from the fallout of these decisions under the cloak of collective cabinet responsibility. No one minister can be picked off when the going gets tough; all ministers sink or swim together. In the same way, the practical political advantages of cabinet confidentiality are very much like those of the mafia code of *omertá*. There might be short-term temptations to talk in public about debates around the cabinet table, but cabinet ministers know they are far better off holding to the principle that such things are never brought into the public domain. This means that opponents of the government have much less chance to make a play out of the cabinet's inevitable internal divisions.

Most European constitutions make general reference to the fact that the cabinet is a collective entity, and in Greece, for example, collective cabinet responsibility is enshrined in a very explicit set of cabinet bylaws. Every cabinet decision must be signed by a majority of cabinet ministers, and even though individual ministers can record their dissent, they cannot state this dissent in public once a collective decision has been made. Failure to observe this rule can lead to dismissal. A minister is obliged to sign all decisions relating to his or her own ministry, or face dismissal (Koutsoukis). Although the Greek case involves an extensive set of rules, the informal rules of the cabinet game are much the same in all European parliamentary democracies. Regardless of the formal or informal rules, one of the hard facts of political life is that members of a cabinet do pretty much sink or swim together. Sometimes an individual minister may be thrown to the sharks as punishment for a major but self-contained blunder, but for the most part when a cabinet runs into trouble it runs *collectively* into trouble. It is this, more than any written rules or cabinet procedure guidelines, that in practice forces collective responsibility upon the cabinet. (For reviews of the role of the cabinet in a number of European countries, see Blondel; Blondel and Muller-Rommel; Laver and Shepsle.)

Thus collective cabinet responsibility does tend to hold quite firm and is, indeed, one of the main causes of ministerial resignation in modern Europe. A very high-profile recent example was the resignation in 2003 of the British foreign affairs minister, Robin Cook, because he was unwilling to stay silent about his opposition to cabinet decisions on Iraq. Since such resignations typically put the government under pressure and trigger something of a political storm, the doctrine of collective cabinet responsibility forces cabinet decision making to be largely consensual. Although no single minister can formally veto a cabinet decision, any minister can threaten to resign if a particular decision is made. This threat is one that can of course be implemented only once; nonetheless, if it is indeed implemented, it can have very serious consequences for the government. This creates strong informal pressure to keep all cabinet ministers "on side" when important decisions are being made.

This role of cabinet ministers as members of the body collectively responsible for making most key political decisions on behalf of the government sharply distinguishes cabinet ministers in parliamentary democracies from those in presidential systems such as that of the United States. In presidential systems, the role of a "cabinet minister" is far more clear-cut: It is to look after a particular policy area and typically be the political head of a government department. A U.S. secretary of state typically does not make collective decisions, and responsibility for the overall political strategy of the government lies elsewhere, typically with the president and his or her staff.

The twin roles of a minister, as individually accountable head of a government department and as member of a collectively responsible cabinet, interact in a potent manner, given the vast volume and complexity of the business that any government must conduct. In Sweden, for example, it is estimated that the cabinet makes about twenty thousand collective decisions every year. Not surprisingly, most of these are waved through, by the hundreds, in formal weekly half-hour cabinet meetings (Larsson). The "real" business tends to be discussed in far more informal settings, including daily lunches that all ministers who are in Stockholm tend to eat together. Although the details may differ, this sheer weight of business can be found in most modern European cabinet systems. The bottom line is that there is a huge volume of formal business to be nodded through, accompanied by a much smaller number of urgent, complex policy problems and initiatives.

This vast volume of business means that the only effective way in which a fully developed and implementable policy proposal can be put to the government is that it be developed within one or more government departments. The cabinet does not and simply cannot sit around in a meeting and make policy in a vacuum. Real-world policy making on complex issues involves the cabinet accepting, rejecting, or amending specific and detailed policy proposals that are presented to it, based on extensive and often very technical documentation. Only the government department with responsibility for the policy area in question has the resources and expertise to generate such a proposal. Thus, only the minister in charge of the relevant department is in a position to present the policy proposal at cabinet, giving this person a privileged position in the policy area in question. An important consequence of this is that cabinet decisions on many matters are organized on departmental lines. There is in effect an intense division of labor in cabinet decision making; each cabinet minister is responsible for bringing forward policy proposals in his or her area of jurisdiction. Conversely, cabinet ministers are poorly placed to make a substantial contribution to the formation of policy in areas over which they have no jurisdiction. The minister of foreign affairs does not have access to the departmental resources and expertise to develop detailed proposals on education policy, for example. The minister for education does not have the resources to develop detailed proposals on housing policy. All of this combines to underwrite a norm that in the Dutch case, for example, is described as the "tacit rule of nonintervention," according to which it is frowned on for ministers to intervene in debates that are not directly relevant to their own portfolios. In part, this arises out of an understanding that it is not wise for a minister to give a hard time to a cabinet colleague whose future support might be critical for one of your own pet projects. In part, it also arises from a situation in which Dutch ministers do not have large teams of political advisers and therefore tend to be briefed for cabinet meetings by their own civil servants. These may not know much, or may not be inclined to tell the minister much, about the affairs of other departments (Andeweg and Bakema).

This situation in the Netherlands is fairly typical of other cabinet systems. The huge pressure of work creates a de facto division of labor that gives a cabinet minister a near monopoly on policy initiation in his or her area of departmental jurisdiction. Cabinet decisions may appear to be made collectively, both constitutionally and on the face of things. However, the practical policy decision that a cabinet typically has to make is between keeping the status quo and moving to some specific alternative policy developed by the minister and department having responsibility for the issue in question. The result is that the effective choice of policy outcomes by the cabinet is very much structured along departmental lines. Although all ministers do take collective *responsibility* for every cabinet decision, each minister does not, and indeed cannot, have equal input into the *formulation* of every decision that is taken. In this sense, cabinet ministers inevitably put themselves into one another's hands.

✦ JUNIOR MINISTERS

The power of a cabinet minister to make public policy in his or her area of jurisdiction, often away from the public gaze, is something that might worry cabinet colleagues from other parties. A potential way to assuage these fears arises from the fact that, in all European states, the political executive extends well beyond the cabinet. It extends both to what are typically known as "junior ministers" and to other crucial political offices such as that of attorney general or equivalent—the government's senior law officer and constitutional adviser. Junior ministers, sometimes known as undersecretaries or ministers of state, are not members of the cabinet—neither privy to its secrets nor subject to its disciplines. Junior ministers are typically appointed to head subsections of the major departments of state— a Department of Education might have a junior minister for higher education, for example— and thus rank unambiguously below cabinet ministers. However, junior ministers do not "report" in a strict sense to the cabinet minister in charge of their department; they too are appointed by the prime minister on behalf of the government as a whole.

In effect, parts of the cabinet minister's jurisdiction are often delegated to a junior minister, who does in fact have an independent role vis-à-vis *the minister* within his or her subjurisdiction. This delegation is part of the deal that sets up the cabinet, under which a cabinet minister is allocated particular junior ministers and cannot sack them unilaterally if they turn out to be nothing but a nuisance. This arrangement has led Michael Theis to suggest that junior ministers may tend in coalition cabinets to be appointed from parties other than that of the cabinet minister with overall jurisdiction over their department, giving these other parties the chance to monitor the behavior of the cabinet minister and ensure that he or she does not stray too far from agreed government policy (Theis). He finds systematic empirical evidence that junior ministers in modern Europe do tend to come from parties other than the party of the cabinet minister—a conclusion confirmed in more detailed recent analyses of the appointment of junior ministers in Italy (Giannetti and Laver; Mershon). Overall, therefore, although cabinet ministers can be very powerful people, there is some evidence that this power may be trimmed, when the cabinet is formed, by the appointment of junior ministers from other parties.

✦ THE MAKING AND BREAKING OF GOVERNMENTS

Parliamentary Democracy and Legislative Majorities

The fundamental principle of European parliamentary democracy, as we have seen, is that the executive is responsible to the legislature. The key constitutional devices by which this requirement is tested are legislative votes of investiture and confidence in the government. A government cannot form if it does not have the support of a majority of legislators. This support may or may not be demonstrated by a legislative vote of investiture, in which a particular government is proposed and voted on and takes office if it wins majority support. Such support may be implicit rather than explicit if legislators abstain rather than vote against a prospective government, when a vote against it would defeat the proposal. The practice of parliamentary government does not depend on the existence of a formal legislative investiture procedure, however. Even if no investiture vote is needed before a government can take office, the executive in a parliamentary government system must have the implicit support of a legislative majority. From the first moment it presents itself to the legislature, any government must be able to survive a possible challenge to its viability. Any potential government must of course take this fact of political life into account during the process of cabinet formation. The governments that actually form do tend, in the early days of their political lives, to have at least the tacit support of a majority of legislators.

The procedural device that provides the legislature with the opportunity to challenge the viability of a government is the "vote of no confidence." The opposition may propose a motion of no confidence in the incumbent government. If this vote is carried, the government is deemed to have lost the confidence of the legislature and, under almost any European constitution, must resign. Motions of no confidence thus allow the legislature to replace the executive whenever a majority of legislators choose to do so. A government that is under pressure may also propose a "vote of confidence" in itself, and it is common for the government to convert an opposition motion of no confidence into a motion of confidence. If the confidence motion is defeated, then the government also must resign. In a number of European constitutions, the main legislative vote on the government's annual budget is also treated formally as a vote of confidence. For obvious reasons, the main budget vote informally has this status everywhere.

Table 2.2 lists a range of factors that have to do with the birth and death of governments and shows that it is almost always the rule that a government defeated in a confidence vote must resign. Switzerland is the only real exception to this process: Swiss governments, once formed, do not have to face legislative confidence votes. For this reason alone, Switzerland is typically not seen as a "parliamentary government" system. Even where there is not an explicit constitutional provision for this—the main examples are Britain and Finland—there is nonetheless a very strong presumption that a government will in fact resign if defeated in a confidence vote. The requirement that executives that have lost the confidence of the legislature must resign is thus the defining characteristic of parliamentary government. If a government cannot win parliamentary confidence votes, there is no point in its forming. If it cannot keep winning them, it cannot remain in office. Table 2.2 also shows that this fundamental constitutional feature of making and breaking governments in modern Europe has been incorporated in the constitutions of all of the eastern European states with which we are concerned here, which is why they can be thought of as parliamentary rather than presidential government systems.

A major consequence of the fact that confidence votes determine the life and death of governments in parliamentary government systems, as we have seen, is that European executives do not have fixed terms of office but are liable to be replaced at any time by the legislature. Thus, although individual European legislators are not particularly

TABLE 2.2

Constitutional Factors in Government Life Cycles

Country	Does Head of State Play Active Role in Government Formation?	Is Formal Investiture Vote Needed?	Must Government Resign If It Loses Confidence Vote?	Can Government Dissolve Legislature?	Can Legislature Dissolve Legislature?	Maximum Time Between Elections
Austria	No	No	Yes	Yes	Yes	4 years
Belgium	No	Yes	Yes	Yes	No	4 years
Cyprus	Yes	No	No	No	Yes	5 years
Czech Republic	Yes	Yes	Yes	No	Yes	4 years
Denmark	No	No	Yes	Yes	No	4 years
Estonia	Yes	Yes	Yes	No	No	4 years
Finland	No	Yes	Yes[a]	Yes	No	4 years
France	Yes	No	Yes[b]	Yes[c]	No	5 years
Germany	No	No	Yes[d]	Yes	No	4 years
Greece	No	Yes	Yes	Yes	No	4 years
Hungary	No	Yes	Yes	No	Yes	4 years
Iceland	No	No	Yes	Yes	No	4 years
Ireland	No	Yes	Yes	Yes	No	5 years
Italy	Yes	Yes	Yes	Yes	No	5 years
Latvia	Yes	Yes	Yes	No	No	4 years
Lithuania	Yes	Yes	Yes	Yes	No	4 years
Luxembourg	No	No	Yes	Yes	No	5 years
Malta	No	No	Yes	Yes	No	5 years
Netherlands	Yes	No	Yes	Yes	No	4 years
Norway	No	No	Yes	No	No	4 years
Poland	Yes	Yes	Yes	No	Yes	4 years
Portugal	Yes	Yes	Yes	Yes	No	4 years
Slovakia	Yes	Yes	Yes[b]	No	No	4 years
Slovenia	Yes	No	Yes	No	Yes	4 years
Spain	Yes	Yes	Yes[e]	Yes	No	4 years
Sweden	No	Yes	Yes[b]	Yes	No	4 years
Switzerland	No	Yes	No	No	No	4 years
United Kingdom	No	No	No	Yes	No	5 years

[a] President "may" accept resignation in the event of a no-confidence vote.

[b] Absolute majority of legislature is required to pass no-confidence vote.

[c] After one year.

[d] No-confidence vote must designate new federal chancellor.

[e] Motion of no-confidence in prime minister must specify successor.

Source: Adapted from Laver and Schofield.

powerful people when it comes to passing laws and influencing specific policies, they do collectively have the power to make and break governments. (We discuss the role of legislators in modern Europe more extensively in Chapter 3.)

The fact that control over the life and death of governments is exercised through the legislative procedure of the confidence/no-confidence vote has far-reaching consequences for the degree of control that the people, via their public representatives, have over what governments actually do. Although the legislature may seem to have sweeping powers to make and break governments, these powers may often in practical terms be as useful as the power to use a sledgehammer to crack a nut. The main form of legislative control over the entire executive is to throw the executive out at will. But many small transgressions by the executive may not be sufficiently serious to warrant such extraordinary measures and may thus go unpunished. This situation can be exploited by a canny executive, which can use its power to bring matters to a head by threatening a vote of confidence in order to force an uppity opposition to back down over many minor matters. In this way an incumbent executive in a parliamentary democracy can get far more of its own way—in effect by "daring" the legislature to throw it out when there may be no viable alternative—than the formal constitutional position might suggest. (For a fascinating elaboration of this situation in the case of France, see Huber.)

Even though the vote of confidence is a standard across nearly every European system, most other constitutional rules of the game associated with the birth and death of governments vary considerably from place to place. These, too, are summarized in Table 2.2, and the overall process of building and maintaining a government is illustrated by the flowchart in Figure 2.1. The figure shows clearly that two general factors are important in the process of building and maintaining coalition cabinets in western Europe. The first has to do with the fact that no matter where you are and no matter how chaotic things might seem to be, there is always an incumbent government. The second has to do with the fact that some mechanism must be found for vesting the government formally with constitutional authority, a task usually performed by some ceremonial officer of state.

Heads of State and *Formateurs*

All governments derive their fundamental legitimacy (to put things in a rather grandiose way) and their legal recognition under the constitution (to look at the nuts and bolts of the matter) from somewhere. Thus, there is always something "above" a government, typically the constitution. In Europe there is always a person, typically the head of state, who has the job of "investing" each new government with its formal constitutional authority. As we saw, a European head of state may be a relatively powerful figure, as in France or Poland, or a much more purely ceremonial figure, as in Belgium or Germany. Even if the head of state has very little power to influence the substance of government formation, however, one job he or she must always do is participate in the formal transfer of authority from one administration to another.

This naturally raises the question of how the head of state knows which particular government should receive the seals of office when there may be several potential candidates. In other words, where do new governments actually come from? Governments do not emerge from thin air or appear under gooseberry bushes; they are formed by

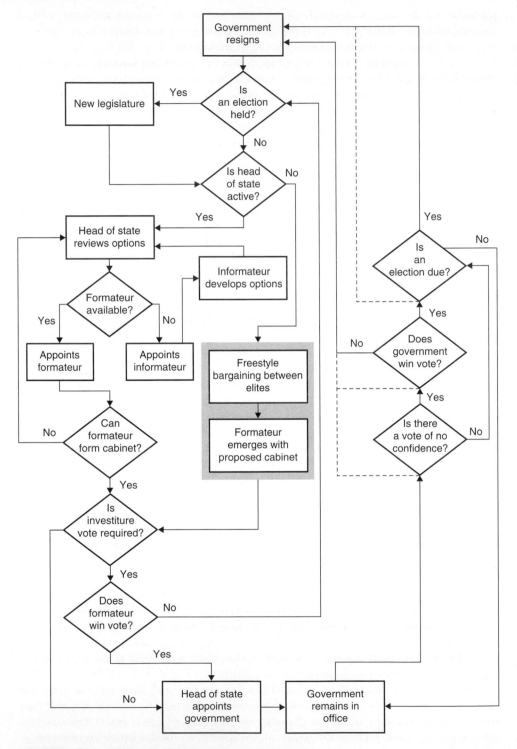

FIGURE 2.1 *Building and Maintaining a Government.*

SOURCE: Laver and Schofield, p. 63.

particular members of the political elite as a result of a very explicit and highly charged political process. Furthermore, even though the vote of every legislator may in theory be needed to determine who is entitled to a seat at the cabinet table, the tight discipline of most European political parties means that in practice the actual business of forming a government is done by a small group of senior politicians. This group typically comprises the party leaders, in consultation with potential cabinet ministers. In general, therefore, we can think of the building of a government as something that is thrashed out between party leaders and presided over by the head of state.

Table 2.2 and Figure 2.1 show that European countries can be divided into those in which the head of state plays an active role in government formation and those in which he or she has a purely formal "swearing in" function, doing little more than passing on the seals of office and shaking the hand of the incoming prime minister. Where the head of state does play an active role, this typically involves choosing a particular senior politician to initiate the process of forming a government, effectively designating this person as a potential prime minister. This designated government builder is referred to by political scientists, adopting the usage of a number of European countries, as a *formateur.*

In some countries, Greece for example, it is formally laid down that in the event no single party has a legislative majority, the head of state should first designate the leader of the largest party as *formateur.* If this person fails to form a government, the head of state must then ask the leader of the second-largest party to be *formateur,* and so on. This procedure has the interesting consequence that the process of government formation is very sensitive to election results, giving all parties a real incentive to fight elections hard in order to become the largest. This runs counter to the conventional wisdom about coalition government, which is that coalition weakens the link between voters and governments. Where this rule is rigidly applied, of course, the role of the head of state in government formation could equally well, though less congenially, be filled by a machine that identified the largest party.

In other countries, Britain and Ireland for example, the strong implicit convention is that the initiative lies with the outgoing government. Even if the government has lost support in the election that has just been held, the outgoing prime minister is still given a chance to form another administration—to be the first *formateur*—before some rival is put in the driving seat. This may often be no more than a formality; a badly beaten prime minister typically concedes defeat on election night. Nonetheless, outgoing prime minister Edward Heath held on to office in Britain for a few days after losing the February 1974 election, before conceding that he could not form a government. Similarly, in Ireland in 1989, outgoing prime minister Charles Haughey spent some days trying to form a single-party minority government before accepting the need for a coalition. In each case, the outgoing prime minister had a clear first-mover advantage in the government formation process.

In other European countries, the head of state plays a far more active role in building governments, using real discretion and judgment in selecting a *formateur.* In the Netherlands and Finland, for example, playing a part in the process of forming a government has traditionally been one of the main jobs of the head of state. Of course, even in countries where the constitution provides that the head of state should behave like a machine, a particularly intractable political stalemate may force a president or monarch to use discretion to break a deadlock. A further device may be deployed in such circumstances in order to insulate the head of state from partisan politics. This involves the nomination of an *informateur,* usually an elderly senior politician or nonpartisan public figure assumed to have no personal political ambition. Such a person may arrange formal round-table meetings between party leaders or move among politicians in an altogether more informal manner. His or her job is to investigate the range of politically feasible coalitions and identify people for the head of state to designate as coalition builders, or *formateurs.*

This system is an important part of the government formation process in the Netherlands, for example. The process begins after an election, when the queen consults senior politicians to get a sense of which governments are feasible and which individuals would be suitable *informateurs.* On the basis of these discussions, she appoints an *informateur,* who investigates practical combinations of parties that might both command a legislative majority and be able, in general terms, to agree on policy. Once the *informateur* has identified the most plausible possibility, and the *formateur* best placed to bring this about, the *formateur* is appointed and given the job of actually putting together a government. If this is successfully completed to the mutual satisfaction of all of those involved in the proposed government, and if these parties self-evidently command a legislative majority, then the *informateur* publicly announces his or her success and the queen installs the new government, without a formal legislative investiture vote. Thus the Dutch queen plays quite a significant part in the government formation process. Given this, the *informateur* system is designed to insulate her from explicit involvement in any associated political controversies, and to avoid the undignified spectacle of the head of state trailing in person from party leader to party leader, trying to do the deal that puts together a government.

Choosing Cabinet Ministers

Once the *formateur* has been officially chosen as prime minister designate, the next item of business is to choose a cabinet. If no single party has a legislative majority, then the system of parliamentary government implies that the cabinet must be acceptable to a majority of the legislature if it is to gain and retain office. Thus, the composition of the cabinet must be settled before the government first presents itself to the legislature. The identity of the cabinet ministers chosen is one of the major factors that legislators take into account when deciding whether to support the government, either explicitly in an investiture vote or implicitly by not attempting to remove it with a vote of no confidence. The group of cabinet ministers, taken as a whole, must be acceptable to the legislature and hence, indirectly, to the electorate.

The head of state, given his or her nonpolitical role, invariably appoints to the cabinet any politician who has been nominated by the prime minister for a particular portfolio and accepted (explicitly or tacitly) by the legislature. Making nominations for cabinet appointments is thus one of the most important practical sources of prime ministerial power in Europe, particularly as European cabinet nominees are not subjected to the intense process of individual scrutiny and investigation faced by their U.S. counterparts. In single-party majority cabinets, the power of the prime minister to choose cabinet ministers is limited only by the internal politics of the governing party. In coalition cabinets, however, what almost invariably happens in practice is that each party leader nominates particular ministers to the subset of portfolios that have been allocated to his or her party during government formation negotiations. The prime minister and other party leaders may veto the occasional particularly controversial nomination by another party leader, but in effect the power to choose cabinet ministers for "their" portfolios rests with the leaders of each government party.

Because of its impact on real policy outputs, therefore, the overall distribution of cabinet portfolios to senior politicians is a vital part of the process of building a government and is something that party groups take very seriously when deciding whether or not to support a proposed new cabinet. Once a particular set of cabinet ministers has been installed in office, then control over many aspects of public policy passes to them—with, as we have seen, some oversight possible by junior ministers. The legislature can reassert control only with considerable difficulty and typically only on the basis of cataclysmic threats to bring the entire government tumbling down.

Since being a cabinet minister is such a difficult and important job—one of the most vital in the country—we might expect that there would be only a limited set of particularly able politicians who are up to it. It is here that the twin roles of the cabinet minister, as political head of a government department and at the same time representing a party in the government, may well come into conflict. Politically, cabinet ministers may be chosen either for their loyalty to the party or for their ability to represent varying strands of opinion in it. The vagaries of internal party politics may well dictate that a party leader feels compelled to include some internal party opponents in the cabinet. Other leaders may choose to banish such opponents to the wilderness and reward only loyal colleagues. Whatever political considerations are taken into account, there will be a limited set of senior party politicians that the leader wishes to appoint to cabinet positions. At this point in deciding who will receive the reward of a cabinet portfolio, the leader will probably not yet have considered the administrative ability to run a major government department—an ability that need not correspond in any way to the ability to get elected to parliament.

It is clear that no party leader has an incentive to put a complete idiot in charge of a government department, since this is likely to have repercussions for the government as a whole. The person nominated must be someone judged to be at least capable of holding down the job without major scandal or disgrace. But it must be said that a party leader's room for maneuver in making cabinet nominations will already be seriously limited by the politics of the situation before administrative ability is taken into account. The process of choosing cabinet ministers, therefore, is by no means guaranteed to pick the team of people best able, in administrative terms, to run the major departments of state. This, of course, puts a premium on the administrative skills of the permanent civil service, a matter to which we return in some detail in Chapter 6.

Typically, cabinet ministers will also be parliamentarians, although this varies considerably between European states. Indeed, in some countries a minister must resign from the legislature on being appointed to the cabinet; France, Norway, and the Netherlands are examples of this. At one extreme is a small group of countries—notably Britain and Ireland—in which cabinet ministers are almost always members of parliament. At the other extreme is a group of countries in which only between one-half and about two-thirds of cabinet ministers are past or present parliamentarians;

Austria, the Netherlands, France, Finland, Norway, and Sweden are in this category. Other European countries can be found somewhere between these poles (De Winter). When cabinet ministers are not members of parliament, by far the most likely alternative occupation is civil servant. In the Netherlands, Sweden, Finland, Norway, and France, about one-quarter of all cabinet ministers are former civil servants. Elsewhere the proportion is much smaller (Thiebault).

Clearly, employing a senior civil servant as cabinet minister increases the chances of having someone who knows how to run a government department; the main factor taken into consideration in nominating a civil servant to the cabinet is thus his or her political persuasion. As we will see in Chapter 6 when we discuss the role of the bureaucracy in modern Europe, maintaining an overt political profile is acceptable in some European civil services, such as that in France, but it is more or less taboo in others, such as that of the United Kingdom. When cabinet ministers are drawn from the ranks of the civil service, however, it will obviously be necessary for those making the appointment to have a pretty good idea about the political orientations of those they are appointing. Thus, the practice of making such appointments encourages senior civil servants with designs on a cabinet seat to establish some sort of political profile and in this way politicize the civil service.

Whatever their background, however, the bottom line is that once they have been appointed to the cabinet, ministers are senior politicians charged simultaneously with running a government department, participating in the collective governance of the country, and representing the views of a particular political party in decision making at the highest level. It is this very politicization of the cabinet that ties the government to the party system and hence to the country as a whole. If a country were to be run by a powerful cabinet with no ties to the party system, it would in effect be a bureaucratic dictatorship. The other side of this coin is that cabinet ministers must be chosen from a smallish group of "possibles" with the right political credentials. Finding candidates for cabinet office who "fit" politically and at the same time will not cause administrative disasters is a delicate balancing act for any incoming prime minister. The ability to strike the right balance is an important prime ministerial skill and can often make the difference between success and failure for the government.

Investiture

Once an agreement to form a new government has been forged and a cabinet has been chosen, attention shifts to the mechanics of installing it. These vary considerably across Europe, as Table 2.2 shows. In some countries—Belgium and Italy, for example—it is necessary for a proposed incoming government to submit to an explicit formal legislative investiture vote before it can take office. In other countries—Denmark and Finland, for example—there is no formal investiture vote, though the incoming government is obviously exposed to the possibility of defeat as soon as it confronts the legislature. Governments in these countries face an "implicit" investiture vote as soon as they assume office. It is striking, as we can see from Table 2.2, that the democratizing states of eastern Europe, having been forced to consider the matter when drafting new constitutions, almost always opted for a formal investiture vote in the legislature before a new government could take office.

This distinction is important, as Kaare Strøm has demonstrated, because the absence of a strict legislative investiture test makes it easier to form minority governments, in which the government parties themselves do not have a legislative majority but must instead rely on "outside" support from other legislative parties (Strøm). Once a government has been installed, particular issues leave a minority government open to challenge; a particular piece of legislation or a particular policy may rouse the anger of sections of the opposition. As we will see, however, one strategy for minority governments, if they are not forced to face the test of putting together an overall majority on investiture, is to skip, on an issue-by-issue basis, from one legislative majority to another, with each majority made up of different parties. In such cases—Denmark is usually cited as the classic example—the government's "majority" may comprise one set of parties for one issue and quite a different set for a different issue.

In countries with a formal investiture requirement, however, this is not possible. The incoming government must present the legislature with a general policy program and a set of nominations for all cabinet positions. It must put together majority support in the legislature for the entire package and cannot rely on different majorities on different issues, because a single investiture vote must pass judgment on all of these important matters taken together. It is not surprising that this more "rational" system of forming a government in a parliamentary democracy would be selected, as in eastern Europe, when new constitutions are being designed from the bottom up.

Defeat and Resignation

Once a government has been installed in office in a typical European parliamentary democracy, it is free to govern until it is defeated in a vote of confidence or no confidence, or until an election is called. Once an election has been called, or once a government has been defeated in a confidence vote, the incumbent government remains in office to run the country as a "caretaker" administration.

In this regard it is important to remember that even if there sometimes seem to be periods when a country is "between" governments after one government has fallen and before a new government has formed, there is always a legal government, every minute of every day. To put it bluntly, somebody must always be available to sign the checks, and somebody must always have a finger on the trigger. Political life is rarely neat, and a point may well arise when the government has lost its political mandate and is legally, to use the helpful French term, *démissionné*. To avoid at all costs a situation in which there is no legal government, the *gouvernement démissionné* stays in office to fulfill key functions in what is typically referred to as a "caretaker" capacity. In some countries, such as Ireland, a caretaker government can and does use the full range of powers of any normal government; here it is not uncommon for crucial decisions to be taken, and political appointments made, in the dying days of an outgoing government. In other countries, such as Denmark, a caretaker government is very strictly constrained by constitutional conventions to do only what is absolutely necessary to keep the ship of state afloat. Laver and Shepsle (pp. 291–92) provide a comparative overview of the powers of caretaker governments in different European states. If putting together an alternative government proves to be a problem, then a "caretaker" administration can stay in power for quite some time, a situation that is not uncommon in Belgium and the Netherlands, where negotiating a new government can take weeks or even months.

Once a government has taken office, therefore, it remains in power until it can no longer win crucial votes in the legislature, and even after this it remains as a *gouvernement démissionné* until it can be replaced by some viable alternative. The loss of parliamentary support by an incumbent government typically is brought about by the return of a new legislature after an election that was "lost" by the government, or by a change in the system of alliances in an existing legislature. The system of alliances in the existing legislature obviously changes if one of the government parties resigns and joins the opposition. It also changes if one or more of the parties that are not in the government, but whose support was essential for the government's ability to win crucial legislative votes, withdraw that support.

Faced with such a situation, the government will often resign rather than play things out to the constitutionally prescribed bitter end. Although shocks and scandals do sometimes fall out of a clear blue sky to destroy individual political careers or even whole governments, prime ministers usually know when their government is going to be defeated, and they often want to avoid the additional political damage caused by an explicit and humiliating defeat. Preferring to leave office on their own terms before being defeated, they may well resign on some pretext or another. Indeed, this is the most common way in which a "beaten" government is forced from office in Europe. However, there may be circumstances—although these in practice tend to be rather rare—in which a prime minister sees an advantage in forcing opponents to show their hand in public on some issue and will therefore force the opposition to play things out according to the formal rules of the game.

There are obviously no hard and fast rules about this, but the important point to remember is that even when we do not observe governments being defeated in *actual* confidence votes, the need to win *potential* confidence votes is the fundamental criterion of the viability of any government. Once a government cannot win confidence votes, it can be defeated at will by the opposition, who will pick the most opportune moment to do this. Whatever the precise circumstances of the government's demise, its political death warrant has been signed, whether or not an actual confidence vote takes place.

✦ PUTTING IT ALL TOGETHER

The institutional theory of parliamentary government concentrates the political accountability of the entire governmental process on one key institution: the legislative vote of confidence in the executive. Parliamentary government can be said to be representative government because the legislature is held to represent the population as a whole (a matter to which we return in Chapter 11) and because the government is responsible to, and can be dismissed by, the legislature (Chapter 12). The administration of government is conducted by a civil service, overseen by ministerial masters who are themselves responsible to the cabinet and thus to the legislature.

We move in the next chapter to consider the general political role of legislatures. In the present context what is important is that, although legislatures can of course legislate, passing laws that implement policy decisions, control by the government over both the legislative agenda and the civil service—vital in the planning and drafting of effective legislation—greatly undermines the practical political effect of this theoretical legislative role. What a legislature can do in theory, and what many legislatures actually do in practice, is to eject governments from office—using either an explicit confidence vote or the threat to defeat the government in one if need be. This sweeping power can be used only in important political circumstances, giving incumbent governments considerable latitude to get their own way, even against the wishes of the majority, on many minor matters.

Nonetheless, one of the core principles of modern European parliamentary democracy is that an "unelected" government must be able to survive in the elected legislature. This, when all is really said and done, is what makes modern European politics democratic.

REFERENCES

Andeweg, Rudy, and Wilma Bakema: "The Netherlands: Ministers and Cabinet Policy," in Laver and Shepsle (eds.), pp. 56–72.

Arter, David: "Finland," in Elgie (ed.), pp. 48–66.

Bagehot, Walter: *The English Constitution,* Fontana, London, 1993 [first published 1867].

Bardi, Luciano: "Italy," *European Journal of Political Research,* vol. 22, 1993, pp. 449–60.

Blondel, Jean: "Cabinet Government and Cabinet Ministers," in Jean Blondel and J.-L. Thiebault (eds.), *The Profession of Government Minister in Western Europe,* Macmillan, London, 1991.

Blondel, Jean, and F. Muller-Rommel (eds.): *Cabinets in Western Europe,* Macmillan, London, 1988.

De Winter, Lieven.: "Parliamentary and Party Pathways to the Cabinet," in Blondel and Thiebault (eds.), *The Profession of Government Minister in Western Europe.*

Elgie, Robert: "France," in Elgie (ed.), pp. 67–85.

Elgie, Robert: "The Politics of Semi-Presidentialism," in Elgie (ed.), pp. 1–21.

Elgie, Robert (ed.): *Semi-Presidentialism in Europe,* Oxford University Press, Oxford, 1999.

Garlicki, Leszek Lech: "The Presidency in the New Polish Constitution," *East European Constitutional Review,* vol. 6, Spring/Summer 1997, pp. 81–89.

Giannetti, Daniela, and Michael Laver: "Policy Positions and Jobs in the Government," *European Journal of Political Research,* vol. 44, no. 1, 2005, pp. 1–30.

Heywood, Paul: *The Government and Politics of Spain,* Macmillan, London, 1995.

Huber, John: *Rationalizing Parliament: Legislative Institutions and Party Politics in France.* Cambridge University Press, Cambridge, 1996.

Jasiewicz, Krzysztof: "From Solidarity to Fragmentation," *Journal of Democracy,* vol. 3, no. 2, 1992, pp. 55–69.

Jasiewicz, Krzysztof, and Stanislaw Gebethner: "Poland," *European Journal of Political Research,* vol. 34, nos. 3–4 [*Political Data Yearbook*], 1998, pp. 493–506.

Kopecky, Petr: "Structures of Representation: "The New Parliaments of Central and Eastern Europe," in White, Batt, and Lewis (eds.), pp. 133–52.

Koutsoukis, Kleomenis: "Cabinet Decision-Making in the Hellenic Republic, 1974–1992," in Laver and Shepsle (eds.), *Cabinet Ministers and Parliamentary Government,* Cambridge University Press, New York, 1994, pp. 270–82.

Larsson, Torbjörn: "Cabinet Ministers and Parliamentary Government in Sweden," in Laver and Shepsle (eds.), pp. 169–86.

Laver, Michael, and Norman Schofield: *Multiparty Government: The Politics of Coalition in Europe,* University of Michigan Press, Ann Arbor, 1998.

Laver, Michael, and K. A. Shepsle (eds.): *Cabinet Ministers and Parliamentary Government,* Cambridge University Press, New York, 1994.

Letowska, Ewa: "A Constitution of Possibilities," *East European Constitutional Review,* vol. 6, Spring/Summer 1999, pp. 76–81.

Meer Krok-Paszowska, Ania van der: *Shaping the Democratic Order: The Institutionalisation of Parliament in Poland,* Ph.D. thesis, Leiden University, 2000.

Mershon, Carol A.: "Party Factions and Coalition Government: Portfolio Allocation in Italian Christian Democracy," *Electoral Studies,* vol. 20, no. 4, 2001, pp. 509–27.

Metcalf L. K.: "Measuring Presidential Power," *Comparative Political Studies,* vol. 33, no. 5, 2000, pp. 660–85.

Millard, Frances: "Poland," in White, Batt, and Lewis (eds.), pp. 23–40.

Rosenthal, Howard: "The Setter Model," in James M. Enelow and Melvin J. Hinich (eds.), *Advances in the Spatial Theory of Voting,* Cambridge University Press, Cambridge, 1990, pp. 199–235.

Shugart, M. S., and J. M. Carey: *Presidents and Assemblies: Constitutional Design and Electoral Dynamics,* Cambridge University Press, New York, 1992.

Strøm, Kaare: *Minority Government and Majority Rule,* Cambridge University Press, Cambridge, 1990.

Szczerbiak, Aleks: "Explaining Kwasniewski's Landslide: The October 2000 Polish Presidential Election." *Journal of Communist and Transition Politics,* vol. 17, no. 4, 2001, pp. 78–107.

Taras, Ray: "Executive Leadership: Presidents and Governments," in White, Batt, and Lewis (eds.), pp. 115–31.

Thiebault, J.-L.: "The Social Background of Western European Cabinet Ministers," in Blondel and Thiebault (eds.), *The Profession of Government Minister in Western Europe.*

Theis, Michael: "Keeping Tabs on Partners: The Logic of Delegation in Coalition Governments," *American Journal of Political Science*, vol. 45, no. 3, 2001, pp. 580–98.

White, Stephen, Judy Batt, and Paul G. Lewis (eds.), *Developments in Central and East European Politics 3,* Palgrave Macmillan, Basingstoke and New York, 2003.

Zubek, Radoslaw: "A Core in Check: The Transformation of the Polish Core Executive," *Journal of European Public Policy,* vol. 8, no. 6, 2001, pp. 911–32.

CHAPTER 3

PARLIAMENTS

As we have just seen in Chapter 2, European states, with only a few exceptions, are run according to the principles of parliamentary government, a set of institutions and behavior patterns that gives a particularly important role to political parties. Put simply, the decisive body in running the country is the government, but the government is answerable to, and can be dismissed from office by, the parliament elected by the voters at general elections. In classical liberal democratic theory, the government merely does the bidding of parliament; parliament makes the laws and lays down the policies, and the government, a mere "agent" of parliament, dutifully carries them out. In reality, this was never really the way things worked, and it certainly does not sum up the relationship between governments and parliaments today. In fact, many have suggested that the wheel has turned full circle and that now governments make all the decisions and parliaments merely rubber-stamp them.

There are many reasons why the initiative lies with governments rather than with parliaments, and the most important one concerns the central role played in European politics by cohesive, disciplined political parties that can ensure that all of their members in parliament vote the same way on all important issues. Before we examine the relevance of parliaments, though, we need to clarify just what we mean by "parliament," which should not be looked on either as a unitary actor or as a body that has an essentially competitive relationship with the government. Rather than ask about the extent to which parliament controls or is controlled by government, we need to examine the role of parliaments in a number of areas, including sustaining the government, lawmaking, and scrutiny of the government. After this, we consider in depth the crucial role played by political parties in determining the place of parliaments in European political systems, and then we assess the significance of the representation that is provided to Europeans by the constituency role of members of parliament. Finally, given that a number of states have a second chamber, often termed an "upper house," as well as a directly elected first chamber, often termed the "lower house," we consider whether it makes a difference whether parliaments have one chamber or two.

✦ PARLIAMENTS AND GOVERNMENTS

The question most frequently asked about parliaments is: How much power do they have vis-à-vis governments? But even though this question is very common, it is arguable that in most of modern Europe it is simply the "wrong question" or, at best, "more confusing than it is illuminating" (Andeweg and Nijzink, p. 152). When, as in almost every

European country except Switzerland, the government is elected by parliament and can be ousted from office by it, it makes little sense to envisage parliament and government as two distinct bodies vying for power. In a presidential system, when president and parliament are elected independently of each other, such a perspective does make sense, just as it used to in European countries in centuries past when the monarch appointed a government without having to consult parliament. To ask, for example, about the power of the U.S. Congress vis-à-vis the president is a perfectly reasonable question. In the parliamentary systems of government that characterize modern Europe, however, it is more realistic to see parliament as wielding power *through* the government that it has elected than to see it as seeking to *check* a government that has come into being independently of it. This is especially applicable when, as is the case in many countries, many or most members of the government are also members of parliament.

The reason why the "governments versus parliaments" framework is not particularly fruitful for analyzing European parliaments is that both of these institutions, like nearly every other aspect of political life, are dominated by political parties, and these parties are powerful and generally well disciplined (Bowler et al.). As early as 1867, the British political journalist Walter Bagehot wrote of the House of Commons that "party is inherent in it, is bone of its bone, and breath of its breath" (Bagehot, p. 160). The behavior of both MPs and ministers is likely to be conditioned more by their membership of a party than by their belonging to either parliament or government (Andeweg and Nijzink, p. 152). Of course, the rules by which any parliament operates, and the balance that these rules prescribe between the respective powers of the government and the legislature, do tell us something—yet it would be misleading to assume that the explanation as to why any given parliament is "weak" lies in the fact that the rules do not give it much leverage over government. After all, there are many more MPs than there are members of the government, and if MPs collectively wanted to change the rules so as to give parliament much more power, they could do so. The fact that they do not suggests strongly that many MPs do not want to do so, and the reason is that MPs think and act first and foremost along party lines. MPs do indeed feel that they are part of a continuous battle, but one that pitches the government against the opposition, not government against parliament. Practically all parliamentarians in Europe belong to some political party or another, and their party expects them to support the party line on all important issues when it comes to voting in parliament. If the party is in government, its parliamentarians are expected to support the government on all issues. If the parties making up the government command between them a majority of seats in parliament, they can realistically expect all their proposals to be approved by parliament.

For the most part, then, when we talk about "parliament" or "the legislature," we are not really talking either about a monolithic body or about the interaction of a large number of independent legislators; in practice we are talking about the interaction of a small number of political parties. The organization of parliament's work is usually built around the various party "groups." We can take Germany as a fairly typical example. Here, the groups are termed *Fraktionen,* and the Bundestag has been described as a *Fraktionenparlament*—in other words, a parliament dominated by the party groups. The *Fraktionen* dominate the life of the Bundestag. The leaders of the *Fraktionen* form a "Council of Elders," which prestructures all debates, allocating speaking time in such a way that there is hardly any scope for spontaneous action by individual MPs. Each

Fraktion decides which member goes onto which committee, and it can recall members from a committee (Schüttemeyer, pp. 35–39). Although the dominance of the *Fraktionen* and their leaders in Germany is perhaps more marked than in many other countries, this is only a matter of degree; everywhere, MPs are very strongly oriented to their party group, and it is the norm for the overwhelming majority of a party's MPs to vote with the party group in parliament. Parliaments all over Europe are dominated by party blocs; every parliament is to a greater or lesser degree a *Fraktionenparlament,* even if it is only in Germany that this specific term is used.

Once we view the political world in this light, we can see that any constraints imposed by parliament on government come not from a monolithic body called "parliament" but from one of three possible sources. One is that there may be rules, that are not easy to change, that allow the opposition to block or defeat government plans. This is especially likely at times of minority government, and though minority government is sometimes seen as exceptional, examination of the record shows that nearly 30 percent of postwar European governments have fallen into this category (see Table 12.2). The increased frequency of weak minority governments in Norway, for example, is seen as the main explanation for greater parliamentary activity there (Narud and Strøm, p. 183). There might, alternatively, be rules requiring certain legislative or other measures to achieve the support of a qualified majority in parliament, perhaps three-fifths or two-thirds, which means that such measures need the support of at least some of the opposition parties. The second potential source is that there may be political cultural constraints that inhibit the government from railroading its proposals through in the face of strong objections from the opposition, even if the formal rules allow this. The third is that the government may receive only conditional support from its own MPs, who may refuse to support it in some circumstances or at least may demand an input into proposals as the price of their support, and indeed this factor is of growing significance in a number of countries.

Writing thirty years ago, Anthony King suggested that parliaments could be better analyzed not in terms of relations between "parliament" and "government" but in terms of a number of "modes" in which key players might interact (King). This typology has been refined by Andeweg and Nijzink, who identify (1) an interparty mode, in which relations between different actors in parliament and government are determined primarily by their respective party affiliations; (2) a cross-party mode, in which ministers and MPs combine to interact on the basis of cross-party interests; (3) a nonparty mode, in which government and parliament interact without regard to party (Andeweg and Nijzink, pp. 153–54). The third, nonparty, mode corresponds to the "traditional" model that sees government and parliament as two separate bodies and seeks to assess the relative power of each, but in reality, given the centrality of parties to European politics, it is the interparty mode that characterizes most of the behavior of ministers and members of parliament. However, we can expect to find a degree of variation across western Europe, brought about by different institutional rules, contingent circumstances, and political cultures.

In discussing this, we can draw on Arend Lijphart's distinction between two categories of democratic regime. The first is the Westminster-type "majoritarian" model; the United Kingdom provides the clearest European example, but Greece, France, and Malta also display many of the characteristics of political systems in this category

(Lijphart, p. 248). In the archetypal majoritarian system, the government of the day has an assured majority among members of parliament (MPs) and can rely on getting all of its legislation through almost unscathed, provided it does not embark on a course of action so far removed from traditional party policy (or so unpopular in the country at large) as to alienate a significant number of its own followers, in which case it is likely to make concessions to its dissidents. The majority party or coalition is prepared, if necessary, to railroad all of its legislation through regardless of the feelings of the opposition. Effective constraints from any quarter of parliament are so low that the situation is nearly one of "cabinet dictatorship." Moreover, the opposition sees its role as criticizing the government rather than trying to influence it. The second of Lijphart's categories is the consensus model. The clearest European example is Switzerland, but Germany, the Netherlands, and Austria also are in this category. The emphasis here is, as the name suggests, on finding a broad consensus in parliament if possible rather than on merely imposing the will of the parliamentary majority. In countries in this category, as in Belgium, cabinets "tend to have a genuine 'give-and-take' relationship with parliament" (Lijphart, p. 36).

Our expectation, then, would be to find that in Lijphart's majoritarian-model countries, virtually all relationships between governments and parliaments take place in the interparty mode, with MPs and ministers having a strong party orientation that transcends any sense of "parliament" or "government" as institutions. In contrast, in consensus-model countries we would expect to encounter somewhat greater recourse to the cross-party or nonparty mode. With this in mind, we examine the record of European parliaments with respect to a number of roles in which they interact with governments.

✦ THE ROLES OF PARLIAMENTS

Later in the chapter, we look in detail at the "upper houses" of parliaments that exist in a number of countries, but it is true to say that in nearly every one of these countries, and in almost every respect, the lower house is the more significant. In most of our subsequent discussion, then, we concentrate on the activities and impact of the lower house. It can have a role to play in three areas. The first concerns the creation, sustaining, and possible termination of governments; the second is legislating; the third involves scrutinizing the behavior of governments. We examine the significance of European parliaments on each of these dimensions.

Appointing and Dismissing Governments

As we saw in Chapter 2, the government in most European countries is responsible to the legislature—typically the lower house. It often needs the approval of parliament to take office in the first place, and in nearly all countries parliament can force the resignation of the government by passing a motion of no confidence in it (for full details see Table 2.2). This in itself shows that the familiar contrast between the "powerful" U.S. Congress and the "weak" parliaments of Europe is simplistic; whatever else it can do, Congress cannot dismiss the administration, but even the humblest European parliament (with the sole exception of the Swiss parliament) has it in its power to turn the country's government out of office. If a parliament does pass such a motion of no confidence in the government, the latter usually has two options: either to resign and allow parliament to elect a new government, or to dissolve parliament and call a general election. One exception to this is Norway, where the life of a parliament is fixed at four years and "premature" general elections are not allowed. In addition, several countries—notably Belgium, Germany, Poland, and Spain—employ the "constructive vote of no confidence," which means that parliament may dismiss a government only if it simultaneously specifies a new prime minister in whom it has confidence.

It is true that European parliaments rarely use this power. For example, even in Finland and Italy, where the turnover of governments used to be extensive, government defeats in confidence motions have been rare. In Finland there have been only four since 1918, and no Italian government lost such a vote until Romano Prodi's center–left coalition lost a confidence motion by one vote in October 1998. However, parliaments use this power so rarely because usually they do not need to use it; when a government knows that it has lost the confidence of parliament and that it faces certain defeat there, it will often bow to the inevitable and resign anyway. What is important is not how often parliament has used the power but the fact that it possesses it in the first place. Because governments know that they can be dismissed from office by parliament at any time, they must be sensitive to the feelings of the key actors in parliament—which is to say, their own MPs and, if the government controls only a minority of seats, the opposition. Moreover, because most European countries use proportional representation electoral systems, which rarely give "artificial" parliamentary majorities to parties that win less than a majority of votes, most European governments depend for their existence on legislative coalitions composed of more than one party. This means that, if the legislative coalition backing the government should collapse for any reason, an executive can fall quite suddenly, without necessarily losing an actual confidence vote in parliament. Thus it is quite common in some countries—Finland and Italy used to be the classic cases, and Latvia is now a good example—to see changes in government between elections as a result of developments in legislative politics, changes on which the electorate is not asked to pass judgment. This power of parliaments, of course, is balanced by the constitutional authority of governments in most European countries to dissolve the legislature and force an election whenever they choose, as we saw earlier (see Table 2.2 for details), although, as we discuss further in Chapter 11, in many countries governments do not really have a completely free hand as to when they call an election.

Parliaments and Lawmaking

Parliaments, then, usually have the power to throw a government out of office, but this is rather a drastic measure. For the most part, MPs would be happy enough with some real degree of influence on the policy-making process. However, European governments are rarely keen to allow MPs a significant role in making laws. The very high levels of party discipline in parliament, as we have seen, mean that a government that controls a majority of seats will usually expect to be able to rely on party discipline to push its program through the legislature. In addition, the government controls the civil service, a key element in planning and implementing legislation (see Chapter 6).

This marks one of the key differences between parliamentary and presidential systems of governments: In the former, governments can expect to see the great majority of their proposals accepted by parliament. Moreover, not only do government proposals generally get adopted by European parliaments; the other side of the coin is that, in most countries, proposals not initiated by the government are usually unsuccessful. Members of parliament in Europe simply do not see themselves as American-style "legislators" with the role of initiating and piloting through pieces of legislation. Although most parliaments contain provision for a bill to be proposed by a deputy[1] or a group of deputies (termed a "private member's bill" in the United Kingdom and some other countries), such a bill, unless it is trivial in content, rarely becomes law unless the government decides not to oppose it (Mattson, pp. 478–79). In terms of the standard categorizations of legislatures, European parliaments are "reactive" rather than "active" in that they possess modest rather than strong policy-making powers (Mezey, p. 36). A common theme in studies of European politics has been the "decline of parliaments," which have everywhere, according to some perceptions, lost to the grasping hands of governments the power they supposedly possessed late in the nineteenth century. By the middle of the twentieth century, it was generally agreed that governments acted while parliaments just talked.

Having said this, the amount of variation around Europe is such that we cannot dismiss all European parliaments as mere rubber stamps. As we would expect from our earlier discussion, the variation here is related to Lijphart's distinction between majoritarian and consensus systems of governments. Three institutional features of parliaments reflect this distinction and affect the significance of parliament's role in lawmaking. The first is that in parliaments in majoritarian systems, the government tends to control the parliamentary agenda, whereas in consensual systems the agenda is decided either by consensus among the party groups or by the president of parliament after consultation with the party groups (Döring, "Time"). The second is that in consensual parliaments the most important work is done in committees, whereas in parliaments in majoritarian systems the floor of the chamber is the main arena. The third is that in parliaments in consensual systems, bills typically go to committees before they are debated by the full parliament. This increases the likelihood that bills will be amended by cross-party consensus. In majoritarian systems, in contrast, it is more common for bills to go to committees only after they have been approved by the whole house, by which stage the issues may have become highly politicized.

Although it may seem a trivial detail, one indicator of the nature of parliament may be found in the seating arrangements in the chamber (these are illustrated in Andeweg and Nijzink, p. 158). In some parliaments, government ministers and their opposition counterparts face each other across the chamber, each with their own backbench supporters ranged behind them.[2] This format might seem almost designed to engender a confrontational attitude between government and opposition and to lead to an "interparty" mode of behavior. Indeed, the parliaments that are organized like this, namely those of

---

[1]Members of parliament have many different titles across Europe. In this chapter, we use the terms "deputy," "member of parliament," "MP," and "parliamentarian" interchangeably.

[2]In this chapter, we use the term "backbencher" to denote any MP who does not hold a government position and who is not a leading opposition MP.

Britain and Ireland, tend to operate in just such a mode. At the other end of the scale, some governments (in Iceland, Switzerland, Italy, Austria, Portugal, Finland, Greece, and the Netherlands, for example) sit together facing the entire chamber of MPs, an arrangement that may be more likely to lead to some kind of collective consciousness on the part of MPs that they constitute a body that is genuinely separate from government. MPs are usually seated by party, but in Norway and Sweden they are grouped by constituency while in Iceland places are allocated by lot.

Parliaments and Lawmaking in Majoritarian Countries

As examples of government-dominated parliaments, we can look briefly at the parliaments in Greece, Britain, and Ireland. The Greek parliament (the Vouli) takes the majoritarian model to perhaps its furthest extreme. The two main parties, New Democracy and PASOK, are bitter rivals even though genuine policy differences between them are far fewer than in the past. Almost all Greek governments are single-party majority governments, and the opposition in parliament has been effectively powerless, with government taking no account of its views. Oppositions (both of PASOK and of New Democracy) have responded by being as obstructive as they could be within the rules of parliament; their approach generally takes the form of "endless lists of speakers who make repetitive speeches which add nothing to what has already been said" (Alivizatos, p. 145). Parliament operates according to "a model of spectacular confrontation," and the chamber is merely a forum for "vague, repetitive and usually outdated monologues" (Alivizatos, pp. 144, 147). Almost every bill passed by the Vouli is a government bill. Committees exist, but they are all chaired by government party members and have a majority of government supporters. Governments in two other southern European countries, Portugal and Spain, are also accustomed to expect very little trouble from their respective parliaments.

In the United Kingdom, the main nongovernment party, unlike nongovernment parties elsewhere in Europe, receives a special status—that of "Her Majesty's Opposition"— but, ironically, it has less influence than nongovernment parties in most other countries. Governments routinely command overall majorities in the House of Commons; the opposition is reduced to making speeches against the government's proposals not in the hope of bringing about a change in its plans but as part of an attempt to persuade the electorate that the opposition has alternative and better policies. For opposition MPs, speaking in the chamber, though ostensibly a contribution to the policy-making process, is no more fruitful than "heckling a steamroller," in the words of Labour MP Austin Mitchell. Critics see the Commons as a place of theater rather than a serious working body, with debates dominated not by those with most expertise but by MPs who possess "meretricious rhetorical skills" (Kingdom, p. 400). The Commons has developed a reasonably comprehensive system of committees since the early 1980s, but these play a role in overseeing the behavior of government rather than in actually making laws or policies. Even though speeches by MPs have scarcely any effect on legislation, the House of Commons spends quite a lot of its time on debates—mainly, some believe, as part of a strategy by the party leaderships to keep their restive MPs out of mischief and concentrated instead on the main interparty battle.

In Ireland, nearly all legislation consists of government bills—a private member's bill passed in 1989 was the first for over forty years. As in Britain, parliament has been strengthening its committee system in recent years, and major reforms in the 1990s greatly expanded the scope of committees both in examining legislation and in scrutinizing the work of governments, although the real power still lies firmly with the government (Gallagher, "Parliament"). In Ireland, as in Britain, the government has nearly complete control of the parliamentary agenda (Döring, "Time," p. 225). Another similarity between Ireland and Britain is that, more than anywhere else in Europe, government and parliament are almost entirely "fused"—that is, all or almost all government ministers are simultaneously members of parliament—and in such cases any idea of a clear distinction between government and parliament seems especially artificial. It is worth noting, indeed, that all over western Europe, most ministers, even if they are not MPs while in office, will have been MPs at some stage in their political career (Andeweg and Nijzink, p. 160).

Parliaments and Lawmaking in Consensus Countries

Turning to more consensual systems, we now look at the examples provided by Germany, Austria, the Netherlands, Scandinavia, and Italy. In Germany, the highly developed committee system in the Bundestag is the main focus of parliamentarians' working week. Bundestag committees concentrate on technical details of bills rather than on general principles, which are more likely to be the subject of partisan debate in which the government prevails. As long as the opposition does not obstruct the passage of bills, the government of the day is usually prepared to be flexible on the details, and there is a good deal of negotiation and compromise between government and opposition. The result is that on average over half of all bills are amended in committee, and the great majority of routine legislation is then passed unanimously by the full parliament. As a rule, the opposition does not criticize government proposals full-bloodedly; in return, the government allows the opposition almost to "cogovern"—though relations usually become more confrontational as an election approaches (Beyme, pp. 34–35; Schüttemeyer, pp. 42–44). Thus, in terms used by Andeweg and Nijzink, the Bundestag frequently adopts the "cross-party" mode, in contrast with the confrontational style of the British House of Commons, where the "interparty" mode dominates.

Committees in the Austrian parliament, the Nationalrat, are also significant; they are sometimes charged with devising legislation in a particular area, and the full parliament is virtually certain to accept their recommendations. In the Netherlands, too, committees of the lower house (the Tweede Kamer, or Second Chamber) play an important role in considering legislation. Although governments aim to ensure that their legislative proposals pass through parliament without too much trouble, parliament can set its own agenda and timetable and is not dominated by government to the same extent as legislatures in more "majoritarian" systems. A significant proportion of bills passed do so with amendments agreed between government ministers and the Second Chamber, not because the opposition is prevailing over the government but mainly due to the assertiveness of government backbenchers. The relative separation of government and parliament in the Netherlands is markedly greater than in "fused" systems such as Germany or Britain. In the Netherlands, as in France, Norway, Portugal, and Sweden, government ministers cannot according to the constitution simultaneously be MPs, although in practice most Dutch ministers are former MPs.

Scandinavian parliaments are generally thought of as relatively powerful, as "working parliaments" rather than debating societies (Arter, pp. 200–44; Damgaard, "Strong";

Petersson, pp. 77–114). Scandinavian political culture emphasizes modesty and conscientious work rather than theatrical self-advertisement, and most Scandinavian MPs are oriented toward detailed consideration of the small print of legislation in committee work rather than toward making dramatic speeches in the parliament chamber (Arter, p. 215). The sight of a group of members of, say, the Finnish Eduskunta working their way line by line through a bill regulating the water supply may make for less exciting television viewing than a British opposition MP delivering a withering rhetorical attack on the government in the chamber of the House of Commons, accompanied by a chorus of supporting or dissenting voices with a bewigged Speaker in the chair trying to keep order, but there is no doubt about which makes more impact on the shape of legislation. In all of the Scandinavian countries, committees have enabled parliament to maintain more control over and input into what governments do at EU level than is the case in other member states (Bergman and Damgaard). In both Iceland and Sweden MPs have an additional input by serving on government commissions, which are very important in formulating policies (Arter, pp. 157, 227; Kristjánsson, p. 158). In the Scandinavian countries as well as Italy and the Netherlands, furthermore, the government has relatively little power to determine parliament's agenda (Döring, "Time," p. 225).

If the Greek parliament is at one end of the scale, being totally dominated by government, then the Italian parliament, the Chamber of Deputies, is close to the other end. Until 1988 there was provision for secret ballots and, since nearly all votes were secret, party leaders were unable to ensure discipline. Before 1990, the government's agenda-setting power was exceptionally weak: The agenda was set entirely by agreement among the leaders of the various party groups. In an attempt to bring greater stability to Italian politics, the rules allowing for secret ballots in the legislature were changed and, moreover, the government was given at least some input into the parliamentary agenda. Italian legislative committees, again in contrast to the general European pattern, have explicit lawmaking powers: They can give final approval to some legislation without having to refer it to the full parliament, and they scrutinize all other legislation. Until the late 1980s, most laws were "little laws" (*leggine*), whose scope in many cases was minimal, and they were passed by committees rather than by the full parliament. It was a common diagnosis that the Italian parliament passed too many *leggine* and not enough substantive laws. Since the late 1980s the percentage of bills that is approved in committee has declined dramatically, though government bills still have a low rate of success: Only 50 percent of these passed in the 1996–2001 parliament, the same proportion as in the 1987–92 parliament (Verzichelli, p. 459; Bull, p. 558). Even after being passed, bills might take years to reach the statute books. The unusual power of the Italian parliament relative to government has not done much for its status in the eyes of the public. Its image in the past has been of an ineffective, fractious legislature whose members spent their time passing *leggine* to placate constituency interests while dragging their feet over more important decisions, which in practice are more likely to be made by agreement among the various political parties than by discussion in parliament. Consequently, when the entire Italian political system was enveloped by crisis in the first half of the 1990s, the demand was for greater system effectiveness, and the ability of parliament to block government plans came to seem part of the problem rather than part of the solution.

Most postcommunist countries are difficult to place reliably on the "majoritarian versus consensus democracy" scale, and the significance of their parliaments varies

(Kopecky, "Structures," Kopecky, "Power"). As a generalization, we can say that in the early years of the reborn democratic states, parliaments seemed quite strong, largely because governments—which under communism had been very much secondary to the communist party—were so weak. Thus, much legislation was initiated by individual MPs, on whom parliamentary parties found it difficult to impose discipline. Indeed, parliamentary parties themselves were not fixed entities, as "party-hopping" by MPs was widespread. The result was that much legislation not backed by the government was passed—and in many cases it was ill-considered and of poor quality. Further into the 1990s things began to change. Under the urging of the EU, and in preparation for membership of that body, the core executive in most countries became stronger. Parliamentary parties imposed stronger discipline on their members, and MPs who persisted in independent behavior found themselves expelled from the group. Observers no longer point to "strong" parliaments and incohesive parties but to "disciplined parties and strong government majorities" (Kopecky, "Structures," p. 146). Slovakia provides a good example. Until 1994 it was practically a case of "assembly government," with parliament opposing cabinet proposals, deputies voting down ministers from their own parties, short-lived coalition cabinets, and unclear accountability. The imposition of strong party discipline and a near end to party-hopping brought an end to this chaotic state of affairs (Malová, pp. 357–58). However, this is not the case everywhere; in Poland a significant amount of legislation is initiated by committees, and indeed some comes from individual MPs (Olson et al.; Sanford, pp. 118–21).

Parliaments and Oversight of Government

Only some parliaments, then, play a part in influencing or making the laws, but all parliaments see themselves as having the role of overseeing the work of government. This function of scrutiny or oversight is, not surprisingly, carried out with different degrees of effectiveness across Europe. Parliaments have a number of methods of carrying out this role (Döring, "Time"; Bergman et al., pp. 146–77). Needless to say, opposition MPs are far more likely than are government MPs to want to scrutinize the government by means of parliamentary mechanisms.

Nearly all European parliaments have, as part of their weekly routine, some kind of "question time" (Wiberg, "Parliamentary Questioning"). This gives members of parliament the right to submit questions in writing to ministers, and these questions must be answered within a fixed time, varying from three days in some parliaments to a month in others. In some countries there is a "question time" every day where questions are answered orally by ministers, other questions being answered in writing, and in other countries this happens less frequently. Parliamentary questions allow members of parliament to extract information from the government. In many countries, however, they are used in practice more to try to embarrass the government by asking awkward questions than to find anything out, as the questioner already has a good idea what the answer is. In response, ministers often aim to produce answers that, though not untruthful, give away as little as possible. The pattern right across Europe is of an often dramatic increase in the number of questions that MPs are asking. A study of parliamentary questions in the Nordic countries found a very consistent increase in the number of questions asked over time, with most questions coming from opposition deputies. This rise was attributed to the growth of the public sector and an increase in education levels among deputies (Wiberg, *Parliamentary Control*). Much the same pattern has been noted for many other countries. To give just two examples, between the mid-1960s and the end of the century, the number of questions asked per year rose in France from 5,500 to 12,700 and in Ireland from 4,300 to 24,000 (Safran, p. 243; Gallagher, "Parliament," p. 228). This upsurge in activity is usually seen as evidence that parliaments are wielding their oversight powers more effectively or, at least, that opposition MPs are making more noise than they used to.

A similar but somewhat weightier weapon that most parliaments can employ is the interpellation, which differs from a simple question because the reply from the minister can be debated by parliament if a sufficient proportion of deputies so request. There are far fewer interpellations than questions, but the number of interpellations too is increasing in parliaments that make provision for them.

The most effective method through which parliaments keep an eye on the behavior of governments is by means of a system of committees set up to monitor government departments; one committee oversees the performance of the Minister for Agriculture, another of the Minister for Education, and so on. Such committees usually have the power to call the relevant government minister before them to defend his or her performance in office, and civil servants can be asked to make available to the committee the information on which ministers have based their decisions.

Every parliament makes use of such committees to some extent, although, as usual, practice varies. One very distinctive case is that of the Committee on Constitutional Affairs in Sweden, which produces annual reports on the performance of each minister and has privileged access to cabinet minutes and documents (Bergman, p. 607). Scrutiny of government by committees can be quite effective in Germany, Britain, Poland, and Denmark, for example, but it is not a strong feature of parliament in Greece, France, or Spain. Committees are usually most significant when they are small and numerous as opposed to large and few as in France. Here the constitution stipulates that there can be only six committees, each of which has at least 70 members, so they operate like "mini-parliaments" and the largest have been described as "dustbins" into which the least significant business is thrown (Knapp and Wright, p. 138). When committees become significant, interest groups seek to "colonize" them, so there is a tendency for the agriculture committee to be dominated by farmers and the education committee by teachers, for example, and each committee seeks extra resources for the special interests that dominate it. This pattern has been noted in a variety of countries, including Germany and Belgium (Saalfeld, "Germany," pp. 57–61; De Winter, "Belgium," pp. 95–97). In such cases, even in majoritarian-model countries, MPs are prepared to operate in "cross-party" mode.

We should not forget that, as well as performing an oversight role, committees also offer an access point into the political system for interest groups and individual citizens, who may be given the opportunity to present their case on some issue to the relevant committee (Shaw, pp. 792–93; Gellner and Robertson, pp. 111–12). We should also acknowledge the limitations of committees, which, certainly in majoritarian countries, can highlight government errors but cannot actually change anything. In Britain, for example, committees have identified the waste of huge amounts of money without any heads rolling as a result (Budge et al., p. 468).

Box 3.1   The Role of Parliament

France

The constitution of the Fifth French Republic marked a reaction against the experience of the Fourth Republic (1946–58), in which parliament was thought to have too much power to thwart governments without being able to achieve anything very effectively itself. In consequence, the National Assembly is, by design, ineffective when it comes to overseeing the actions of the government or the president. The constitution specifies the areas in which parliament can legislate and allows the government to act by decree in all other areas, and it contains many other devices to guarantee the dominance of the government over parliament. The Assembly has only six committees, two of which have over 100 members (more than some full parliaments)—as prescribed by the 1958 constitution precisely in order to prevent the committees from becoming effective. Some governments allow the National Assembly some degree of influence when it comes to discussing and amending bills, but if there is a confrontation, the government holds all the cards. Deputies are seen by their constituents primarily as emissaries from their district to central government and have large casework loads. The Senate, with its inbuilt right-wing majority, is a minor irritant to right-wing governments and a major irritant to left-wing ones.

Germany

The lower house of the German parliament, the Bundestag, is well organized, and its members (MdBs) have better resources to assist them in their work than parliamentarians elsewhere in Europe. The main emphasis of its work is not in grand debates on general principles of legislation in plenary session but in detailed scrutiny of legislation in committees, where there tends to be a good deal of cooperation between government and opposition parties. The work of each MdB is closely overseen by the parliamentary group (*Fraktion*), leaving little scope for spontaneous parliamentary action by individual MdBs. MdBs are quite active in constituency work, on which they spend around 40 percent of their working time. The upper chamber, the Bundesrat, can act as a significant check on the government because it has significant power and moreover is often dominated by opposition parties.

Italy

The Italian parliament, the Camera dei Deputati, is less dominated by the government than most European parliaments. It can set its own agenda, and it expects as of right that the government will consult it before introducing legislative proposals. Its committees are powerful and can actually pass laws without reference to the full parliament. Much of its legislative output over the years, though, has consisted of "little laws" of benefit only to microsectional interests, which deputies have promoted in order to win favor with their constituents. The powers and (usually) the composition of the Senate are nearly identical to those of the Camera. When the Italian political system entered a state of crisis in the 1990s, the ability of parliament to block government action was widely seen as part of the problem, and steps have been taken to make it easier for the executive to govern effectively.

Latvia

In common with parliaments in other postcommunist countries, the single-chamber Latvian parliament, the Saeima, was at the center of political activity in the early years after the restoration of democracy but has since receded to the position occupied by most of its west European counterparts. This can be explained by the stabilization of the previously highly fragmented party system in Latvia, by the pattern of smoother coalition formation between parties, and by the introduction of fast-track legislative procedures in order to facilitate the country's accession to the EU and to comply with the conditions set by the European Commission.

Netherlands

The lower house, the Tweede Kamer (Second Chamber), is by no means a rubber stamp for government. It can set its own agenda and timetable, and it plays an influential role in amending bills. Because government members cannot, under the constitution, simultaneously be members of parliament, there is, at least psychologically, a greater separation between executive and legislature than is the case in most other European countries, where government ministers are usually also members of parliament. Parliamentary activity has increased greatly since the 1960s, although opinions are divided as to whether parliament is any stronger as a result. The Tweede Kamer is dominated by the parliamentary groups; individual MPs have very little freedom of action.

Poland

After 1989 Poland seemed to be developing a parliamentary-dominant system with government instability and considerable legislative activity by individual MPs, but developments in the Polish political system, such as preparation for EU entry, led to a progressive strengthening of the core executive's position vis-à-vis parliament. Even though the Sejm's star waned somewhat during the 1990s, it retained more significance as an arena than most postcommunist parliaments did. Poland's long parliamentary tradition, going back to the fifteenth century, gives the Sejm a status that not all parliaments enjoy—its committees made some impact behind the scenes even under communist rule. Polish governments have a harder job persuading MPs to pass their bills than most of their western counterparts do, and a significant proportion of legislation emanates from Sejm committees or from MPs. Turnover in the Sejm is high; a majority of MPs after each of the first four postcommunist elections were first-timers. The second chamber of the parliament, the Senate, has some minor legislative and appointive powers, but for the most part it can simply delay policies and legislation rather than block or propose them.

Spain

The Spanish parliament was suppressed during the Franco dictatorship (1939–75), and having been reinstated by the new democratic regime, its pattern of operation is still in the process of evolving. Under the majority Socialist government of 1982–93 it had a marginal position, with the prime minister, Felipe Gonzáles, rarely taking the trouble to visit it even to inform it of the government's activities, let alone to be questioned. His successor, José María Aznar, was scarcely more respectful. The Cortes is not seen as one of Europe's more significant parliaments, and the Senado is very weak and of little political significance.

Sweden

The Riksdag differs from most parliaments in that members are arranged in the chamber according to the constituency that they represent, not the party to which they belong. For example, the eleven MPs for the northerly Norrbotten county occupy the adjacent seats 339–349 in the 349-member Riksdag elected in 2002. Not surprisingly, this can lead to "log-rolling" between MPs from the same region of the country on issues of regional concern, although for the most part MPs act strongly along party rather than regional lines. Deputies can play an effective part in the policy-making process, partly through the role they play on the commissions of inquiry that are set up to consider how problems should be tackled. Although politics in Sweden has in some ways become more conflictual with the emergence of two clear-cut alternative governments, in parliamentary committees there is still a tendency to negotiate and to seek consensus.

United Kingdom

Although those who refer to a "golden age" of parliaments usually have in mind the House of Commons at some times during the nineteenth century, today's British parliament is not regarded as being among the most effective of European parliaments. A combination of single-party majority governments and a party system based on conflict between the two main parties leaves the parliamentary opposition with very little influence on legislation or on policy in general. The British tradition places great emphasis on plenary sessions in the main debating chamber—performance in debates is important, for instance, in deciding which MPs should be promoted to leadership positions— even though there are few signs that those outside "Westminster World" follow parliamentary debates with much interest or that debates have any effect on government policies. Committees, the main forum for the work of most modern parliaments, have traditionally had a much less significant role in the House of Commons, although since the early 1980s they have been increasingly effective in scrutinizing the work of government.

→ PARLIAMENTS AND PARTIES

All relations between governments and members of parliament, as we have seen, take place within a context dominated by political parties. Greater power for "parliament" therefore would really mean more power not for a unitary body called "parliament" but for the *Fraktionen* (the parliamentary party groups) or for specific actors within them. If the government controls only a minority of seats, then "more power for parliament" is in practice likely to mean "more power for the opposition." During periods of majority government, the main constraints are imposed not by the opposition but by the back-bench MPs of the governing party or parties, and it is particularly difficult to tell how much influence these members wield. If government MPs are unhappy about a government proposal, this is rarely expressed in votes or even complaints against the measure on the floor of parliament; instead, the matter will be raised behind closed doors at meetings of the *Fraktion,* and if backbench reservations are strong enough, the minister may have little choice but to amend or withdraw the proposal. What goes on at these meetings, though, is unknown both to the public and to all but the most assiduous researchers.

One problem with assessing arguments about the domination of parliament by political parties is that it is notoriously difficult to try to measure the power of any parliament. If a parliament approves every government proposal without making any amendments, we cannot be sure whether this indicates a supine parliament or whether the government, obeying the law of anticipated reactions, is taking care not to make any proposals without first making sure that parliament will approve them. Studies of European parliaments do not usually indulge in "roll-call analysis" of the bill-by-bill voting records of individual legislators, an activity that "has been viewed as the political science equivalent of stamp collecting or train spotting" (Cowley and Stuart, 2004, p. 301). One study that did take the trouble to work out precise figures found that only 0.08 percent of individual votes cast in the Danish Folketing between 1990 and 1996 broke with the party position (Skjaeveland, p. 44). Clearly, when parliamentary members of any given party vote together 99.92 percent of the time, it is obvious that the actors are the parliamentary party blocs, not individual parliamentarians. Indeed, in both the Netherlands and Portugal the official proceedings normally record the votes of parliamentary parties rather than of individual MPs, and Dutch MPs need the permission of their party group even to put down a question to a minister (Andeweg and Nijzink, p. 172; Andeweg, p. 575). In Chapter 10 we look in greater detail at the internal politics of political parties, but we can see even at a cursory glance that the leaders of these parties are far more important people, politically, than the typical rank-and-file member of parliament.

The high degree of solid party voting among parliamentarians might suggest to the uninitiated that members of parliament are mere "dumb sheep" or "lobby fodder" who must tamely vote in whatever manner the party leaders direct. That may, indeed, be the popular perception. German evidence suggests that most voters believe that MPs should be able to make up their own minds as to how to vote on each issue in parliament and should be open to persuasion by speeches by other MPs. The reason MPs do not behave like this, in the opinion of most Germans, is that "party bosses" and whips compel them to vote along party lines (Patzelt, pp. 45–46). Constitutions sometimes help to propagate this point of view by proclaiming that MPs are entirely autonomous and that no one has the right to tell an MP which way to vote on an issue, thus disregarding the central role of political parties in modern politics. However, this perspective is, as Patzelt puts it, "pure fiction" and shows "little understanding of collective action as a result of rational adaptation to team-building strategic premises." To put it simply, it makes sense for individual MPs to band together into parties that operate as cohesive entities, and it certainly makes for better policy outcomes compared with the chaotic policy making that would ensue if all MPs acted as independent agents and took an ad hoc approach to each issue (we discuss the importance of parties in Chapter 10).

Although it is true that unpleasant punishments await those deputies who are disloyal to the party, as we discuss further on, the relationship between parties and individual members of parliament is not fundamentally due to the imposition of discipline. Government backbenchers are not cowed by the government, as publics might think, but broadly supportive of it. For one thing, members of parliament belonging to the same party have a natural sense of identity; their instincts are always to vote with their party out of a sense of loyalty, solidarity, and common purpose, and for the most part they are glad to keep in line and do not need to be threatened. Moreover, decision making within each parliamentary party may be fairly democratic, so even those members who dislike a particular decision will go along with it if it represents a majority view. They are much more likely to do this, of course, if they know that other members of the group will do the same when the majority decision goes against *them*. For that reason, the success of nearly all government legislation in European parliaments may represent the outcome of a bargaining process in which the government takes into account the views of its own backbenchers rather than implying that those backbenchers have no significant input into public policy making. Thus governments will not in general proceed with legislation that their backbenchers have already indicated they will not support. In Germany, it is common for the chairpersons of the government *Fraktionen* to attend cabinet meetings to ensure that government proposals are acceptable to the *Fraktion* (Schüttemeyer, p. 39). In Austria, France, and the Netherlands, too, there is evidence of close consultation between members of the government and their parliamentary parties (Heidar and Koole, p. 258; Elgie, pp. 172–73; Timmermans and Andeweg, p. 383).

It is also the case in Britain that the decisive political relationships in recent years, given the huge Commons majorities that Labour has enjoyed since 1997, have been *within* parties rather than *between* parties. The rate of backbench rebellion in the 1997–2001 parliament was exceptionally low, and Labour MPs came to be spoken of dismissively as timid, gutless, sycophantic, cowardly, poodles, sheep, androids, or Daleks. However, their loyalty in the division lobbies was not the result of intimidation by the party leadership but came about partly because Labour MPs were often able to gain concessions behind the scenes from ministers on issues they felt strongly about, and also because, after eighteen years in opposition, they were acutely aware of the electoral damage that an image of party disunity could do (Cowley and Stuart, "In Place"). Even so, there were limits to their loyalty, and after the 2001 election they rebelled against government attempts to install supposedly "reliable," government-friendly MPs as committee chairs. By the summer of 2003 there had been more rebellions by MPs than in any previous postwar parliament (Cowley and Stuart, "Parliament," p. 311).

However, even if governments in some countries have to work a little harder for the backing of their parliamentarians than they used to, the picture is still one of very strong party solidarity in parliament. The existence of large and disciplined voting blocs is central to the practice of European parliamentary democracy. The coherence of European parties when compared, for example, with their U.S. counterparts depends on two basic and related behavioral phenomena. The first is that voters tend to vote for parties rather than for individual candidates. The second is that individual parliamentarians think of themselves first and foremost as members of their party's parliamentary group rather than as individual members. We return to political parties several times in our subsequent discussions. However, we must explore these particular points now in order to be able to provide a comprehensive picture of European parliamentary democracy.

Voters Vote for Parties

Most Europeans, when they vote in a parliamentary election, are voting primarily for a party rather than for a person. Even in those few countries where the myth that voters choose people rather than parties is still cherished, prominent and colorful individuals who eschew parties and fight elections as independents usually come to a sticky end— often at the hands of unknown opponents wielding nothing but a party label. Most European parliamentarians have got where they are by being candidates of political parties rather than by being particularly outstanding individuals in their own right.

European voters tend to vote in legislative elections for parties rather than for people precisely because, when they vote, they feel that they are helping to choose a government. Because it is the government that has the initiative in shaping public policy, voters' main concern is with which party or parties will control the government rather than with the personal qualities of individual candidates. They therefore have strong incentives to look for a clear-cut choice between alternative governments or, at the very least, between party blocs powerful enough to change the complexion of governments during the process of coalition bargaining. Except in very finely balanced situations, a legislator who is not a member of a political party is not likely to have much of an impact on government formation and maintenance, the single most important job of European legislatures.

The primacy of parties over individual candidates in Europe is made explicit in some countries where the electoral system is such that voters simply choose a party ticket without being able to express a view on specific candidates, something that we discuss in detail in Chapter 11. Even in countries where voters do have an opportunity to vote for an individual candidate, the fact that it is parties rather than individual candidates who are ultimately important in European elections means that European legislators get a far smaller "personal vote" (that is, the vote won by a candidate because of his or her perceived merits rather than because of the party he or she represents) than do their American counterparts. This is a direct consequence of the system of parliamentary government and has a number of political effects. Three are of direct relevance here.

First, because the size of a politician's personal vote is so much less in Europe than it is in the United States, the fate of European candidates is determined much more by national political forces than it is by what particular people have done for particular local constituencies. European politicians who want to advance their careers usually face incentives to concentrate on national politics rather than on the provision of goodies for their local constituents.

A second, related, matter is that incumbent candidates have much less of a built-in advantage in Europe than they do in the United States. In the United States, the incumbent is the one who brings home the bacon, thereby building a personal vote that provides strong insulation from winds of political change at the national level. Many local incumbents in the United States are able to survive what appear to be national landslides against their party, resulting in an average reelection rate of incumbents of over 90 percent in House elections since the Second World War. In Europe, in contrast, being an incumbent gives little inherent advantage when it comes to the next election. In Britain, for example, individual MPs can do far less for their constituents than their American equivalents. As Cox puts it, "the mainstays of the U.S. Congressman's particularistic usefulness to his constituents"—civil service patronage and "local improvement" bills securing public expenditure on rivers and harbors, railways, roads, dams, canals, and so on—were all largely shut off from the influence of the backbench MP from the middle of the nineteenth century onward (Cox, pp. 133–34). In most European countries MPs simply cannot supply particularized benefits to their localities ("pork") through legislation. The main exception is Greece, where bills often end up with a whole raft of such amendments, often completely unconnected to the subject of the bill, though even here the practice has been somewhat curbed of late (Trantas et al., p. 378). Because the personal vote is so much smaller in Europe, when the political tide turns against a particular party its candidates tend to lose their seats, no matter who they are or what they have done for their constituency. It is true that under some list systems of proportional representation, parties can protect their senior politicians by placing them high on party lists (see Chapter 11) and that under other electoral systems, which pit candidates of the same party against each other, there is such a thing as a personal vote for individuals within the party fold. Even so, prominent politicians can disappear abruptly from parliament simply because their party is doing badly.

The third, and probably the most important, consequence of the fact that European voters vote for parties rather than for people is that party labels are very valuable commodities in Europe. This makes party legislators unwilling to do anything—such as voting against the party line in parliament—that might cost them the label at the next election, for if they are not picked as party candidates in the next election (a subject to which we return in Chapter 10), their political careers may well be over. That would represent the loss of a sizable investment, as most MPs have spent many years building their political career—and we use the word "career" deliberately, as MPs these days are characteristically professional politicians. In Germany, for example, the average MP is elected to parliament at the age of 42, having spent nine years in local councils and another nine years before that working toward his or her first elective office. Once individuals make it to the Bundestag, they are understandably loathe to jeopardize their pension (Patzelt, p. 41). In postcommunist states, the job of a deputy is "lucrative," making MPs reluctant to risk losing their position by excessive independence (Kopecky, "Structures," p. 144). And this, of course, is one of the main reasons why European legislative parties are so highly disciplined. The battlefields of European politics are littered with the corpses of those who defied the party line.

Parliamentarians and Party Discipline

As we have pointed out, parliamentarians usually follow the party line in parliament mainly because this is what their instincts tell them to do, not because they are being threatened with dire sanctions if they do not do so. If their instincts should happen to tell them to vote against the party line on some issue, however, they quickly discover that a range of punishments await those who stray from the fold (Heidar and Koole, p. 256). To put it another way, there are powerful incentives to vote the party line whatever an MP's private policy preferences. We have already seen that one such incentive is fear of losing the party label at the next election, given that voters choose parties rather than people because it is parties rather than individual MPs that can influence the shape of governments. Party leaders have power over rank-and-file members of parliament because the latter know that if they become habitually disloyal to the party line in parliament, the candidate selectors (usually a group of local party activists) may well deny them access to the party label at the next election and thereby cast all but the most resilient out into the political wilderness. The extreme case here is perhaps Ireland, where in July 1993 the parliamentary group of the country's largest party, Fianna Fáil, decided that in future any deputy who voted against the party line on any issue (or even abstained) would automatically be expelled from the parliamentary party. In Britain, the parliamentary parties have what are termed "whips" (the term refers to the "whipping in" of foxhounds in hunting and as such is revealing of the strength of tradition in the House of Commons) whose job it is to ensure that all MPs follow the party line in votes. The whips control access to some of the perks of being a parliamentarian, such as attractive committee assignments and trips abroad, and every MP knows that such benefits will go to loyal MPs rather than to rebels. If need be, the whips will ensure the expulsion from the parliamentary group of persistent mavericks, though this is very rare. Another approach, which is employed in Belgium, is to fine MPs who breach discipline or simply do not turn up for votes (De Winter and Dumont, p. 115).

A second source of power for party oligarchs is that if they are not already senior government members, then they are the people who will be senior government members when the party next gets into government. This means that European party leaders are the gatekeepers to political office; they can use this position to reward those who are loyal to the party and punish those who are not. In Britain's House of Commons, the most closely studied European parliament, there is clear evidence that the increase in party cohesion in parliamentary voting around the end of the nineteenth century was strongly linked to an increase in the number of MPs seeking ministerial posts and concluding that the best way of gaining preferment was to remain loyal at all times to the party leadership, and this in turn led to voters developing a strong party rather than personal orientation at elections (Cox, pp. 75–79). This now applies to nearly every European parliament. Thus, party discipline is made much stronger by the system of parliamentary government. Because the legislature is the main recruiting ground for members of the executive in most countries, those who aspire to executive office must behave themselves in the legislature. If they do not, they will displease those with the power to promote them.

✦ PARLIAMENTARIANS AND CONSTITUENCY REPRESENTATION

The formal role of parliaments in the process of representation is clear enough and, to a greater or lesser degree, may be stated in a country's constitution: The people elect their representatives, and these representatives, answerable to the people at the next election, sustain, monitor, and can ultimately oust the government. A more tangible form of representation provided by MPs to many Europeans receives little or no constitutional recognition. This takes the form of constituency representation, whereby MPs promote and defend the interests of their geographical constituency, of particular sectors within their constituency, or of individual constituents. Whether an ordinary European feels "represented" by his or her MP may depend less on the views that the MP expresses in the chamber of parliament or in a committee than on whether the MP will take up a matter of personal concern or help secure some redress of a grievance. Because this kind of behavior is not constitutionally prescribed, there is sometimes a tendency to neglect it. It is possible to read some works on certain European parliaments without realizing that, for many MPs, as much time is spent dealing with constituency work as on the formally assigned tasks of an MP, such as taking part in debates or sitting on committees.

In real life, however, constituency work looms large in the lives of many, probably most, MPs around Europe, and the picture from most countries is that it is increasing. In France, where constituency representation has always been the main role of a *député,* research produced a diary of a typical rural French MP (reproduced in Safran, pp. 223–24), which shows the MP arriving in Paris on Tuesday morning and returning to his or her constituency on Thursday evening. Friday, Saturday, Sunday, and Monday are all spent in local political activity, and even while the deputy is in Paris, some of his or her time is spent in following up constituency business. The *cumul des mandats*— meaning that most MPs also hold local office—has the added benefit that it gives deputies local implantation that makes it difficult for parties to threaten credibly to deselect them (Knapp and Wright, p. 154). In Britain, there has been a huge increase in the volume of constituency work since 1970, with MPs spending about half of their time on it (Rush, pp. 210–11, 216). In Ireland, members of parliament are likely to be buttonholed by their constituents at almost any time of the day. An MP is not safe from being approached by a constituent with a problem even when relaxing in the pub on a Sunday evening (Gallagher and Komito, p. 243). In Scandinavian countries, too, MPs tend to be strongly locally oriented (Heidar). Links between citizens and MPs can be especially close in small countries. In Malta MPs are very active constituency workers, and in Iceland over half of the voting population claims to know an MP personally (Arter, p. 211). In contrast, there are some countries, such as Portugal and the Netherlands, where performance of constituency duties is only a relatively minor role for MPs. In postcommunist countries, too, MPs devote little time to such duties, though there are signs that a constituency role is beginning to develop (Kopecky, "Structures," p. 141).

The causes and consequences of this kind of representation are a matter of some dispute. When trying to explain variations in the amount of constituency work carried out by parliamentarians in different countries, many writers identify the electoral system as important (Gallagher, "Conclusion"). For most MPs around Europe, as we have seen, just about the only way to build a personal vote is through constituency work, and electoral incentives help to explain its incidence. Under certain electoral systems, as we discuss in more detail in Chapter 11, candidates of each party are competing with each other, as well as with candidates of other parties, and thus have a strong incentive to try to build up a personal vote. Some electoral systems provide individual MPs with a much greater incentive to cultivate a personal vote than others (Carey and Shugart; Mitchell, pp. 340–44). This might help to explain why MPs operating under electoral systems giving voters a choice of candidates within parties, as in Ireland and Malta, do a great deal of constituency work, while those in countries where there is little or no incentive to cultivate a personal vote, such as Portugal, do relatively little. The electoral system does not explain everything: In some countries, such as Britain and France, there is an expectation in the political culture that MPs will perform these duties. Most MPs in Britain are not provided with any electoral incentive to undertake constituency work yet are assiduous constituency workers, like their German counterparts (Saalfeld, "Parliament," p. 56). One explanation for this is that MPs derive psychological gratification from doing constituency work, which, moreover, they believe is one of their duties as an MP (Norris, p. 47). In addition, even under a list system where MPs have no incentive to cultivate a personal vote, such as Belgium in the 1990s, MPs may well fear that they will fall out of favor with their party's candidate selectors unless they maintain a high local profile (De Winter, "Belgian MPs," pp. 96–97).

The consequences of constituency work for the political representation of Europeans are mixed. On the one hand, immersion in constituency duties, whether casework for individual constituents or activity on behalf of the constituency as a whole, may distract MPs from their purely parliamentary roles, leaving them with less time to play a part in formulating legislation and scrutinizing government activity. On the other hand, it keeps MPs in touch with people who live ordinary lives and provides a form of representation that to many people is more meaningful than the representation of opinion. In that way it builds support for the political system as a whole, as well as reducing the alienation of those who would otherwise have no ready conduit to the state. Moreover, it helps MPs discharge their oversight role in parliament, in that hearing citizens' grievances alerts them to problems with the design or implementation of government policy.

✦ EUROPEAN PARLIAMENTS: ONE CHAMBER OR TWO?

The question of whether there should be one or two legislative chambers is one of the most venerable questions of parliamentary design. The main arguments in favor of "bicameralism"—that is, having two chambers—are that a second chamber can act as a check on the possibility of an overbearing majority in the lower house, and that it may be able to discuss policy proposals in a more reflective manner than the highly politicized lower house, applying "sober second thoughts" and drawing on nonparty technical expertise (Russell, pp. 21–22). The main argument against bicameralism is summed up in the frequently quoted (if perhaps apocryphal) comment of the Abbé Sièyes, made more than two hundred years ago, to the effect that "if the second chamber agrees with the first it is superfluous, and if it does not it is pernicious." Worldwide, bicameralism is in decline. Prior to the First World War a second chamber was virtually de rigueur for a sovereign state, but now only about a third of countries have one (Massicotte, p. 282).

Since upper houses are rarely in a position to block governments or lower houses, second chambers in Europe are often seen as unimportant. Tsebelis and Money, however, argue that bicameralism can make a significant difference to a country's politics. They maintain that its impact is inherently conservative, as its effect is to protect the status quo, and they argue that the relationship between the two houses is determined not only by the formal rules about how much power each has but also by how much bargaining power each house possesses in some particular conflict. For example, if the upper house has the power to delay legislation for a year, as Britain's House of Lords does, then at times when an election is less than a year away the upper house will have greater power. The lower house will then have to decide whether to press ahead with its preferred measure, knowing that it might well end up with nothing, or reach a compromise in order to get at least part of its proposals passed into law before the election. Of course, the upper house, knowing of the "impatience" of the lower house in this situation, will be tempted to drive a particularly hard bargain. Lijphart, too, identifies "strong bicameralism" as a key feature of his model of "consensus democracy." The conditions of strong bicameralism are, first, that the upper house is not elected on the same basis as the lower house and, second, that it has real power (Lijphart, p. 39). In western Europe, he judges, only the Swiss and German systems amount to strong bicameralism (Lijphart, p. 212).

In this light, the impact of bicameralism depends primarily on the composition and the powers of a second chamber, if one exists. As Table 3.1 shows, the position varies around Europe, with only twelve of the twenty-eight states having a second chamber. The two factors that seem to have the strongest influence on whether a state is bicameral are size and centralization. The sixteen states without a second chamber are all small, unitary states. Of the twelve states with an upper house only three are both small and unitary (Czech Republic, Ireland, and the Netherlands); the rest are federal (Austria, Belgium, Switzerland), large (France, Italy, Poland, Spain, the United Kingdom), or both (Germany).

In six of these countries, the most common route to the upper house is indirect election or appointment by local or provincial councils—and since these bodies may be under the control of the parties that are in opposition at the national level, there is an inherent potential for conflict between the two houses. The First Chamber in the Netherlands is elected by members of the twelve provincial councils; members of Austria's Bundesrat are appointed by the state parliaments; and local councillors dominate the election of 43 of the 60 members of Ireland's Seanad. French senators are elected for nine-year terms by an electorate of whom 95 percent are local councillors; a third of them stand down every three years; and because the composition of the electorate is biased in favor of rural areas, the right-wing parties enjoy an almost permanent guaranteed majority in the Senate (Elgie, pp. 153–55). This majority can be almost as awkward for the right as for the left, as it is not very amenable to party discipline; its members make the French Senate an independent-minded institution or, less politely, a "conservative, curmudgeonly" one, that is unlikely to change its nature given that it has the power to veto bills to reform it (Knapp and Wright, pp. 148–49).

In Germany, the Bundesrat (also known as the Federal Council) consists of the prime ministers and certain other members of the Land (state) governments, and although these individuals often appoint substitutes to attend meetings, the substitutes are either people of their own political complexion or, very often, civil servants attending committee meetings under their direction. Bundesrat members from each Land must cast their votes en bloc, even if the Land government is a coalition. The allocation of seats to Länder (states) follows the principle of "degressive proportionality"—in other words, the smaller Länder are generously overrepresented in relation to their size. With, on average, four Land elections taking place every year, the Bundesrat's composition is constantly changing.

TABLE 3.1

Second Chambers of Parliament in Europe

Country	Name of Second Chamber	Size of Second Chamber	Comments
Austria	Bundesrat	64	Elected by state parliaments
Belgium	Senate	71	40 directly elected; 21 indirectly elected; 10 co-opted
Cyprus	—	—	
Czech Republic	Senat	81	Directly elected, one-third of membership is renewed every two years
Denmark	—	—	Upper house abolished in 1953
Estonia	—	—	
Finland	—	—	Large parliamentary committee acts as quasi–second chamber
France	Senate	321	Elected mainly by local councillors
Germany	Bundesrat	69	Composed of members of state governments or their designated substitutes
Greece	—	—	
Hungary	—	—	
Iceland	—	—	
Ireland	Senate	60	43 indirectly elected, mainly by local councillors; 11 appointed by prime minister; 6 elected by university graduates
Italy	Senate	326	315 are directly elected
Latvia	—	—	
Lithuania	—	—	
Luxembourg	—	—	21-member Council of State plays the same role as a second chamber
Malta	—	—	
Netherlands	First Chamber	75	Indirectly elected
Norway	—	—	Directly elected parliament divides into two chambers
Poland	Senat	100	Directly elected
Portugal	—	—	Large parliamentary committee acts as a quasi–second chamber
Slovakia	—	—	
Slovenia	—	—	Directly elected 40-member National Council has analogous role but is essentially an advisory organ without full lawmaking powers
Spain	Senate	257	208 directly elected; the other 49 indirectly elected
Sweden	—	—	Upper house abolished in 1970
Switzerland	Council of States	46	Nearly all directly elected
United Kingdom	House of Lords	670	Mainly appointed for life by government of the day, plus some remaining hereditary peers

Sources: Inter-Parliamentary Union Web site (www.ipu.org) and parliamentary Web sites (to which the IPU site provides links); Tsebelis and Money, pp. 48–52.

There may seem to be only a weak argument for a directly elected second chamber not designed to provide a different kind of political representation from that in the first chamber. In six countries, however, direct election plays a significant role (Massicotte). In Poland all (and in Italy almost all) of the senators are elected by the people at the same time as the lower chamber is elected. Election of the Czech Republic's senate follows the model of its U.S. counterpart; senators serve six-year terms, and a third of the body stands down every two years. In Belgium, Spain, and Switzerland most members of the upper house are directly elected; in these cases, the role of the upper house is to protect regional or cantonal interests.

The most distinctive upper house is Britain's House of Lords, where for many centuries the majority of members held their positions simply by inheriting them. Even though many hereditary peers rarely or never attended parliament, their existence was widely seen by left-wing and liberal forces in Britain as an anomaly in the democratic era. The Labour government elected in 1997 developed plans to reform the Lords fundamentally, so that the hereditary component in the Lords would first be drastically reduced and then eliminated altogether. Consequently, in 1999 the number of hereditary peers with voting rights was reduced to 92. Of the remaining members, 26 were bishops (including two archbishops) and the other 552 were "life peers," that is, individuals appointed for life by the government of the day. Many critics of the House of Lords argued, therefore, that even these plans did not bring about a second chamber that was particularly representative. The 1999 change was supposed to be the first step in a program entailing a complete overhaul, but reform plans stalled subsequently as it was impossible to secure agreement on exactly how a new upper house should be composed. The government was wary about allowing a significant number of its members to be directly elected and preferred a system of appointment, which critics said would result in a house of the prime minister's loyalists—"Tony's cronies."

Also distinctive is Luxembourg's Council of State (which is not technically a second chamber, although it plays the same role), whose twenty-one members, once appointed, hold office until the age of 72. They are nominally appointed by the head of state, the grand duke, although in practice the nominations are controlled by the three major parties.

Parliaments elsewhere have only one chamber. In some of these countries, there are devices that go some way toward creating a second chamber. For example, after each election Norway's parliament, the Storting, divides into two chambers, although about 80 percent of its work is done by the two chambers sitting together in plenary session (Rommetvedt, p. 80). In both Finland and Portugal, the parliament contains one large committee (besides a number of regular committees) that serves as a kind of "mini-parliament" or "internal second chamber" (Anckar, p. 188; Braga da Cruz and Lobo Antunes, p. 166).

Whether upper houses matter depends largely on how much power they have. Constitutional rules usually prescribe that disputes between the two houses must be resolved by means of a navette (shuttle), whereby bills on which the two chambers disagree pass back and forward between them until some conflict resolution mechanism comes into play. The mechanism might be, for example, a stipulation that the lower house prevails after the measure has shuttled back and forth a certain number of times, or provision for a committee composed of members of both houses to meet and attempt to resolve the deadlock (see Tsebelis and Money, pp. 54–70). Almost invariably, the upper house has less power than the lower house. The only exception is in Italy, where the Senate has exactly the same powers as the Chamber of Deputies, so every bill must pass both houses to become law and the cabinet is answerable to both houses equally.

Typically, the upper house is able only to delay legislation passed by the lower house, but sometimes it can veto certain types of legislation (for example, legislation changing the constitution). In Germany, the Bundesrat has a veto over legislation that affects the power of the states (the Länder), and if it defeats a bill on any other subject by a two-thirds majority, only a two-thirds majority in the lower house, the Bundestag, can overrule it. In addition, since a 1992 amendment to the constitution, the Bundesrat has had a strong voice in the formulation of the line that German ministers are to take within the Council of the European Union (which we discuss in Chapter 5). Originally it was expected that only a small proportion of legislation would require the consent of the Bundesrat, but in practice most legislation has turned out to fall into this category (Schmidt, p. 58). The Bundesrat is a particularly significant actor given that, since 1972, it has usually been dominated by the parties that are in opposition at the federal level (Schmidt, p. 81). Prior to the 1998 election, for example, the left-wing opposition controlled a majority in the Bundesrat and was able to wring concessions on a number of issues from the center–right federal government. The 1998 election brought to power an SPD–Green coalition, which for a while enjoyed a majority in both houses. In 1999, however, this government suffered a series of defeats in German Land elections and, as a result, faced an opposition majority in the Bundesrat. However, since the priorities of, say, a CDU Land government and the CDU's national leadership do not always coincide, opposition members in the Bundesrat are sometimes more willing to cooperate with the government than their counterparts in the lower house would wish. The Bundesrat is thus a particularly powerful body even though, technically, it is not actually a second chamber of parliament (Beyme, p. 34).

In Britain, the House of Lords, which in the nineteenth century could veto bills, has had its power reduced in successive reforms, so by the start of the twenty-first century it could only delay bills by a year. It is not completely irrelevant, though, since by defeating a government bill when an election is less than a year away it effectively kills the bill. In the last analysis the Commons can overrule the Lords by invoking the Parliament Act, though this is very rarely done. When the Commons did this in November 2004 to insist on the passage of a bill to abolish foxhunting, it was only the sixth time it had happened since the Commons acquired this power in 1911. The preponderance of hereditary peers before the reforms in November 1999 meant that the House of Lords was instinctively more sympathetic to Conservative governments than to Labour governments, though during the long period of Conservative rule from 1979 to 1997 it did occasionally sink government measures, such as a 1986 bill to allow Sunday trading and a 1997 attempt to increase police powers. The Irish upper house, Seanad Éireann, can do no more than delay bills for ninety days.

The French Senate has even less power than the already weak French lower house. It can refuse to pass bills coming from the lower house and has sometimes been obstructive to government plans as a result, but if it pushes its obstruction too far, the government can and does exercise its own power to call on the lower house to deliver a decisive vote on the bill (Safran, pp. 230–34). Even less significant is the Spanish Senate, which, like its Polish counterpart, has only minor delaying powers (Roller; Sanford, pp. 124–28).

✦ THE SIGNIFICANCE OF PARLIAMENTS: AN ASSESSMENT

In most discussions of parliaments in Europe, as we have noted, the phrase "decline of parliaments" crops up somewhere. It sums up a feeling, which seems to have been around since the early years of the twentieth century, that parliaments are not what they were. Once upon a time, so the feeling goes, they really ran countries and swept governments into and out of office as they pleased, whereas nowadays they have been reduced to mere rubber stamps, tamely approving whatever proposals governments place before them. Needless to say, both of these images are exaggerated. The "golden age" of parliaments never really existed in most—perhaps in all—countries. And today's parliaments, though perhaps lacking in excitement, can do useful work in improving legislation through detailed examination in committees.

Certainly, it is clear that parliaments, considered as institutions, do not play an active role in the decision-making process. In many countries, members of parliament suffer from a sense of irrelevance, certainly as far as plenary sessions are concerned. There is genuine uncertainty as to whether anyone is listening when a deputy speaks, for chambers are nearly empty and newspapers, television, and radio devote very little time or space to reporting the speeches that parliamentarians make. In Denmark, there is even a joke that an MP wishing to keep something secret should announce it in the Folketing because then it is certain that nobody will hear it. The reasons for this are not difficult to identify. The whole business of making policy is now so complex that governments spend a lot of time consulting with experts in the civil service and with the major interest groups involved, such as business interests, trade unions, and farmers' groups (see Chapters 6 and 14). If a package can be put together that satisfies all these groups, the government will be reluctant to allow parliament to tinker with it. In addition, a lot of policy is made at EU level (see Chapter 5). Moreover, when it comes to getting straight answers from government ministers, the procedural devices that parliaments have at their disposal are often less effective than questioning by journalists in the mass media, which in many cases has become the main means by which governments are forced to give an account of themselves to the general public.

Nonetheless, some factors are working in favor of parliaments. For one thing, members of parliament are becoming more professional. In a number of countries, there has been a decline in the number of MPs who combine this role with another job; the trend is toward parliaments of full-time professional politicians. Moreover, parliaments are becoming better resourced, although in no country, not even Germany, do they have anything like the personal staffs that U.S. Congress members enjoy. Parliaments are becoming more active, according to most quantifiable indicators; MPs are asking more questions, initiating more interpellations, and, it seems, spending more time in committees. Most important of all, the government remains the government only for as long as it retains the confidence of parliament. It is true that, right across Europe, parliament very rarely votes a government out of office, but this should not obscure the importance of this relationship. Governments are well aware that parliament does have this ultimate power, and so they act with this consideration always in their minds, ensuring in particular that their own MPs do not become disaffected.

We have seen that the relevance of parliaments varies from country to country, but this variation is not random. We can detect a clear pattern. In particular, as we would expect, the interparty mode of behavior dominates in those countries characterized by Lijphart as "majoritarian." Relations between MPs and government ministers, or among MPs, are determined by their respective party affiliations; there is at all times a keen sense that the government and MPs of the government party or parties are on the government "side," while the rest are on the opposition "side." If government MPs amount to a majority, governments need only retain the loyalty of their own backbenchers to ensure that all their proposals are approved by parliament. This model applies to such countries as the United Kingdom, Greece, France, Malta, and Ireland. In "consensus" systems, although the interparty mode is still the most common, cross-party or nonparty modes are also manifested. MPs of different parties may combine on some issues, and there may be a sense across party lines of "parliament" as a body that can and should scrutinize government and perhaps formulate policies with or without the full agreement of government. This model fits such countries as Switzerland, the Netherlands, Belgium, Germany, and Austria.

Any overall assessment of parliaments, however, simply cannot ignore the central role of political parties. The power of a parliament at any given time will depend to a great extent on the balance of power between parties and on the distribution of power within the government parties. It is difficult to overestimate the importance of party discipline in setting the whole tone of politics in a typical European country. The system of parliamentary government would not work without it, because the party oligarchs who comprise the political executive would never know when they would be able to retain the support of the legislature. Governments would thus be liable to fall unpredictably and would have no guarantee of being able to implement their legislative program. This scenario reads very much like a description of the political chaos that beset the European system in which party discipline was at its lowest—the French Fourth Republic (1946–58). The consequence, in a parliamentary government system, was chronic political instability. Effective government was impossible, and the outcome was not, in any real sense, more power in decision making for parliament but, rather, political chaos and the discrediting of the political class generally. This situation was brought to an end in 1958 with the establishment of the Fifth Republic and the creation of a strong, separately elected executive president. The dismal history of the Fourth Republic illustrates the fact that parliamentary government cannot exist without party discipline. Above all, it explains why political parties feature so prominently in our account of representative government in modern Europe.

References

Alivizatos, Nikos: "The Difficulties of 'Rationalization' in a Polarized Political System: The Greek Chamber of Deputies," in Liebert and Cotta (eds.), pp. 131–53.

Alivizatos, Nikos, and Pavlos Eleftheriades: "The Greek Constitutional Amendments of 2001," *South European Society and Politics,* vol. 7, no. 1, 2002, pp. 63–71.

Anckar, Dag: "Finland: Dualism and Consensual Rule," in Damgaard (ed.), pp. 151–90.

Andeweg, Rudy B.: "Parliamentary Democracy in the Netherlands," *Parliamentary Affairs,* vol. 57, no. 3, 2004, pp. 568–80.

Andeweg, Rudy B., and Lia Nijzink: "Beyond the Two-Body Image: Relations Between Ministers and MPs," in Döring (ed.), pp. 152–78.

Arter, David: *Scandinavian Politics Today,* Manchester University Press, Manchester and New York, 1999.

Bagehot, Walter: *The English Constitution,* Fontana, London, 1993 [first published 1867].

Bergman, Torbjörn: "Sweden: From Separation of Power to Parliamentary Supremacy—and Back Again?" in Strøm, Müller, and Bergman (eds.), pp. 594–619.

Bergman, Torbjörn, and Erik Damgaard (eds.): *Delegation and Accountability in European Integration: The Nordic Parliamentary Democracies and the European Union,* Frank Cass, London, 2000.

Bergman, Torbjörn, Wolfgang C. Müller, and Kaare Strøm: "Democratic Delegation and Account-ability: Cross-national Patterns," in Strøm, Müller, and Bergman (eds.), pp. 109–220.

Beyme, Klaus von: "The Bundestag—Still the Centre of Decision-Making?" in Helms (ed.), pp. 32–47.

Bowler, Shaun, David M. Farrell, and Richard S. Katz (eds.): *Party Discipline and Parliamentary Government,* Ohio State University Press, Columbus, 1999.

Braga da Cruz, Manuel, and Miguel Lobo Antunes: "Revolutionary Transition and Problems of Parliamentary Institutionalization: The Case of the Portuguese National Assembly," in Liebert and Cotta (eds.), pp. 154–83.

Budge, Ian, Ivor Crewe, David McKay, and Ken Newton: *The New British Politics,* 3rd ed., Pearson Education, Harlow, 2004.

Bull, Martin J.: "Parliamentary Democracy in Italy," *Parliamentary Affairs,* vol. 57, no. 3, 2004, pp. 550–67.

Carey, John M., and Matthew Soberg Shugart: "Incentives to Cultivate a Personal Vote: A Rank Ordering of Electoral Formulas," *Electoral Studies,* vol. 14, no. 4, 1995, pp. 417–39.

Coakley, John, and Michael Gallagher (eds.): *Politics in the Republic of Ireland,* 4th ed., Routledge and PSAI Press, Abingdon, 2005.

Conradt, David P.: *The German Polity,* 7th ed, Addison-Wesley Longman, New York, 2001.

Copeland, Gary W., and Samuel C. Patterson (eds.): *Parliaments in the Modern World: Changing Institutions,* University of Michigan Press, Ann Arbor, 1994.

Cowley, Philip, and Mark Stuart: "In Place of Strife? The PLP in Government, 1997–2001," *Political Studies,* vol. 51, no. 2, 2003, pp. 315–31.

Cowley, Philip, and Mark Stuart: "Parliament: More Bleak House than Great Expectations," *Parliamentary Affairs,* vol. 57, no. 2, 2004, pp. 301–14.

Cox, Gary W.: *The Efficient Secret: The Cabinet and the Development of Political Parties in Victorian England,* Cambridge University Press, Cambridge, 1987.

Damgaard, Erik: "The Strong Parliaments of Scandinavia: Continuity and Change of Scandinavian Parliaments," in Copeland and Patterson (eds.), pp. 85–103.

Damgaard, Erik (ed.): *Parliamentary Change in the Nordic Countries,* Scandinavian University Press, Oslo, 1992.

De Winter, Lieven: "Belgian MPs: Between Omnipotent Parties and Disenchanted Citizen–Clients," in Norton (ed.), *Parliaments and Citizens,* pp. 89–110.

De Winter, Lieven: "Belgium: Insider Pressure Groups in an Outsider Parliament," in Norton (ed.), *Parliaments and Pressure Groups,* pp. 88–109.

De Winter, Lieven, and Patrick Dumont: "PPGs in Belgium: Subjects of Partitocratic Dominion," in Knut Heidar and Ruud Koole (eds.), *Parliamentary Party Groups in European Democracies: Political Parties Behind Closed Doors,* Routledge, London and New York, 2000, pp. 106–29.

Döring, Herbert: "Time as a Scarce Resource: Government Control of the Agenda," in Döring (ed.), pp. 223–46.

Döring, Herbert (ed.): *Parliaments and Majority Rule in Western Europe,* Campus Verlag and St. Martin's Press, Frankfurt and New York, 1995.

Elgie, Robert: *Political Institutions in Contemporary France,* Oxford University Press, Oxford and New York, 2003.

Gallagher, Michael: "Conclusion," in Michael Gallagher and Paul Mitchell (eds.), *The Politics of Electoral Systems,* Oxford University Press, Oxford and New York, 2005, 535–78.

Gallagher, Michael: "Parliament," in Coakley and Gallagher (eds.), pp. 211–41.

Gallagher, Michael, and Lee Komito: "The Constituency Role of Dáil Deputies," in Coakley and Gallagher (eds.), pp. 242–71.

Gellner, Winand, and John D. Robertson: "Germany: The Continuing Dominance of Neocorporatism," in Clive S. Thomas (ed.), *Political Parties and Interest Groups: Shaping Democratic Governance,* Lynne Rienner, Boulder (CO) and London, 2001, pp. 101–17.

Heidar, Knut: "Roles, Structure and Behaviour: Norwegian Parliamentarians in the Nineties," in Wolfgang C. Müller and Thomas Saalfeld (eds.), *Members of Parliament in Western Europe: Roles and Behaviour,* Frank Cass, London, 1997, pp. 91–109.

Heidar, Knut, and Ruud Koole: "Parliamentary Party Groups Compared," in Heidar and Koole (eds.), *Parliamentary Party Groups in European Democracies: Political Parties Behind Closed Doors,* Routledge, London and New York, 2000, pp. 248–70.

Helms, Ludger (ed.): *Institutions and Institutional Change in the Federal Republic of Germany,* Macmillan, Basingstoke, 2000.

King, Anthony: "Modes of Executive–Legislative Relations: Great Britain, France, and West Germany," *Legislative Studies Quarterly,* vol. 1, no. 1, 1976, pp. 11–34.

Kingdom, John: *Government and Politics in Britain: An Introduction,* 3rd ed, Polity Press, Cambridge, 2003.

Knapp, Andrew, and Vincent Wright: *The Government and Politics of France,* 4th ed., Routledge, London and New York, 2001.

Kopecky, Petr: "Power to the Executive! The Changing Executive–Legislative Relations in Eastern Europe," *Journal of Legislative Studies,* vol. 10, no. 2–3, 2004, pp. 142–153.

Kopecky, Petr: "Structures of Representation: The New Parliaments of Central and Eastern Europe," in Stephen White, Judy Batt, and Paul G. Lewis (eds.), *Developments in Central and East European Politics 3,* Palgrave Macmillan, Basingstoke and New York, 2003, pp. 133–52.

Kristjánsson, Svanur: "Iceland: Searching for Democracy Along Three Dimensions of Citizen Control," *Scandinavian Political Studies,* vol. 27, no. 2, 2004, pp. 153–74.

Liebert, Ulrike, and Maurizio Cotta (eds.): *Parliament and Democratic Consolidation in Southern Europe: Greece, Italy, Portugal, Spain and Turkey,* Pinter, London, 1990.

Lijphart, Arend: *Patterns of Democracy: Government Forms and Performance in Thirty-Six Countries,* Yale University Press, New Haven and London, 1999.

Malová, Darine: "Slovakia: From the Ambiguous Constitution to the Dominance of Informal Rules," in Jan Zielonka (ed.), *Democratic Consolidation in eastern Europe,* vol. 1, *Institutional Engineering,* Oxford University Press, Oxford and New York, 2001, pp. 347–77.

Massicotte, Louis: "Second-Chamber Elections," in Richard Rose (ed.), *International Encyclopedia of Elections,* CQ Press, Washington DC, 2000, pp. 282–7.

Mattson, Ingvar: "Private Members' Initiatives," in Herbert Döring (ed.), 448–487.

Mattson, Ingvar, and Kaare Strøm: "Parliamentary Committees," in Döring (ed.), pp. 249–307.

Mezey, Michael L.: *Comparative Legislatures,* Duke University Press, Durham (NC), 1979.

Mitchell, Paul: "Voters and Their Representatives: Electoral Institutions and Delegation in Parliamentary Democracies," *European Journal of Political Research,* vol. 37, no. 3, 2000, pp. 335–51.

Narud, Hanne Marthe, and Kaare Strøm: "Norway: Madisonianism Reborn," *Scandinavian Political Studies,* vol. 27, no. 2, 2004, pp. 175–201.

Norris, Pippa: "The Puzzle of Constituency Service," *Journal of Legislative Studies,* vol. 3, no. 2, 1997, pp. 29–49.

Norton, Philip (ed.): *Parliaments and Citizens in Western Europe,* Frank Cass, London, 2002.

Norton, Philip (ed.): *Parliaments and Pressure Groups in Western Europe,* Frank Cass, London, 1999.

Olson, David M., Ania van der Meer-Krok-Paszkowska, Maurice D. Simon, and Irena Jackiewicz, "Committees in the Post-Communist Polish Sejm: Structure, Activity and Members," *Journal of Legislative Studies,* vol. 4, no. 1, 1998, pp. 100–23.

Patzelt, Werner J.: "What Can an Individual MP Do in German Parliamentary Politics?" in Lawrence D. Longley and Reuven Y. Hazan (eds.), *The Uneasy Relationships Between Parliamentary Members and Leaders,* Frank Cass, London, 2000, pp. 23–52.

Petersson, Olof: *The Government and Politics of the Nordic Countries,* Publica, Stockholm, 1994.

Roller, Elisa: "Reforming the Spanish Senate: Mission Impossible?" *West European Politics,* vol. 25, no. 4, 2002, 69–92.

Rommetvedt, Hilmar: "Norway: From Consensual Majority Parliamentarianism to Dissensual Minority Parliamentarianism," in Damgaard (ed.), pp. 51–97.

Rush, Michael: *The Role of the Member of Parliament Since 1868: From Gentlemen to Players,* Oxford University Press, Oxford and New York, 2001.

Russell, Meg: *Reforming the House of Lords,* Oxford University Press, Oxford and New York, 2000.

Saalfeld, Thomas: "Germany: Bundestag and Interest Groups in a 'Party Democracy,'" in Norton (ed.), *Parliaments and Pressure Groups,* pp. 43–66.

Saalfeld, Thomas: "Parliament and Citizens in Germany: Reconciling Conflicting Pressures," in Norton (ed.), *Parliaments and Citizens,* pp. 43–65.

Safran, William: *The French Polity,* 5th ed., Longman, New York and Harlow, 1998.

Sanford, George: *Democratic Government in Poland: Constitutional Politics Since 1989,* Palgrave Macmillan, Basingstoke, 2002.

Schmidt, Manfred G.: *Political Institutions in the Federal Republic of Germany,* Oxford University Press, Oxford and New York, 2003.

Schüttemeyer, Suzanne S.: "Hierarchy and Efficiency in the Bundestag: The German Answer for Institutionalizing Parliament," in Copeland and Patterson (eds.), pp. 29–58.

Shaw, Malcolm: "Legislative Committees," in George Thomas Kurian (ed.), *World Encyclopedia of Parliaments and Legislatures,* Fitzroy Dearborn, Chicago and London, 1998, pp. 786–93.

Skjaeveland, Asbjørn: "Party Cohesion in the Danish Parliament," *Journal of Legislative Studies,* vol. 7, no. 2, 2001, pp. 35–56.

Strøm, Kaare: "Parliamentary Committees in European Democracies," *Journal of Legislative Studies,* vol. 4, no. 1, 1998, pp. 21–59.

Strøm, Kaare, Wolfgang C. Müller, and Torbjörn Bergman (eds.): *Delegation and Accountability in Parliamentary Democracies,* Oxford University Press, Oxford and New York, 2003.

Timmermans, Arco, and Rudy B. Andeweg: "The Netherlands: Still the Politics of Accommodation?," in Wolfgang C. Müller and Kaare Strøm (eds.), *Coalition Governments in Western Europe,* Oxford University Press, Oxford and New York, 2000, pp. 356–98.

Trantas, Georgios, Paraskevi Zagoriti, Torbjörn Bergman, Wolfgang C. Müller, and Kaare Strøm: "Greece: 'Rationalizing' Constitutional Powers in a Post-Dictatorial Country," in Strøm, Müller, and Bergman (eds.), pp. 376–98.

Tsebelis, George, and Jeanette Money: *Bicameralism,* Cambridge University Press, Cambridge, 1997.

Verzichelli, Luca: "Italy: Delegation and Accountability in a Changing Parliamentary Democracy," in Strøm, Müller, and Bergman (eds.), pp. 445–73.

Wiberg, Matti: "Parliamentary Questioning: Control by Communication?" in Döring (ed.), pp. 179–222.

Wiberg, Matti (ed.): *Parliamentary Control in the Nordic Countries: Forms of Questioning and Behavioural Trends,* Finnish Political Science Association, Helsinki, 1994.

CHAPTER 4

CONSTITUTIONS, JUDGES, AND POLITICS

Books on U.S. government and politics invariably stress the important role of the courts and the constitution. Books on European government and politics, in contrast, often say nothing about either, something that might give students of the subject the impression that courts and constitutions make little impact on the political process in Europe. Such an impression would be quite wrong. The "rules of the game" play a large part in determining a country's government and politics, and they are generally set down in a country's constitution and laws. These rules usually impose significant constraints on actors such as political parties, parliaments, and governments. Although some of the rules may sometimes be inconvenient to politicians and political parties, and some of them may be sufficiently vague to allow politicians some leeway, in the last resort they exist to determine how things are done. European constitutions contain a number of common features but also exhibit some significant variation. In the two previous chapters, and in subsequent ones, we look in detail at the *contents* of constitutions regarding such important matters as the powers of governments, presidents, and parliaments, as well as electoral law and the decentralization of power, but in this chapter we concentrate on constitutions per se, along with the authorities who interpret and apply constitutions.

If there is some doubt or dispute as to exactly what course of action the laws or constitution spell out (or rule out) in some specific situation, there is a need for someone to act as a referee or umpire. This is where the courts come in. Although the judicial system is sometimes seen as quite separate from the political system, and many Europeans still see it as "above politics," such a view does not reflect the reality of Europe today. In recent years, there has been a clear trend toward the "judicialization" of politics and the "politicization" of the judicial system, with what has been termed "the global expansion of judicial power" (Tate and Vallinder). In this chapter, therefore, we examine European constitutions, looking at their origins and contents and discussing some European constitutional traditions.

We consider the way in which judicial review—the process by which either the regular courts or, more commonly, a special constitutional court can constrain political actors, for example, by striking down legislation that is not compatible with the constitution—has become a central fact of political life in several European countries. Once again, there is significant variation across the continent. We then look at the interaction between the judiciary and politics, examining both the politicized manner in which judges are appointed and the opportunity that judges in some countries have to *make* law as opposed to merely *applying* laws. The appointment of a set of judges to a country's constitutional court receives nothing like the public attention that a parliamentary election does, yet it may matter just as much for what the next government can do.

✦ EUROPEAN CONSTITUTIONS

The Origins of Constitutions

A constitution has been defined as "a body of rules that specifies how all other legal rules are to be produced, applied, and interpreted" (Stone Sweet, *Governing,* p. 20). Why have a constitution at all? A constitution regulates the relationship between political actors such as parliaments, governments, presidents, and courts, ensuring that the powers of each are clearly defined and are not the subject of free-form bargaining or confrontation each time an issue arises. Constitutions are sometimes seen as a device of "precommitment" (Holmes; Sunstein, pp. 96–101), whereby the people, in a state of reason, voluntarily place limits on their future freedom of action, just as the Greek hero Ulysses had his sailors bind him to the mast of his ship so that he would be unable to throw himself to his death when he heard the irresistible song of the Sirens.

The political turbulence in much of Europe in the nineteenth century and in the first half of the twentieth century means that most European countries have adopted more than one constitution during the past two hundred years (Bogdanor; Johnson, "Constitutionalism"). There have been various "waves" of constitution-making. One occurred in those countries regaining independence at the end of the Napoleonic wars, and there was a second following the 1848 revolutions. After the First World War, a number of countries, especially the successor states to the Austro-Hungarian empire, drew up new constitutions. Most of the constitutions drawn up in these first three waves failed to survive. A more durable set of constitutions was promulgated in the aftermath of the Second World War, when those countries emerging from occupation adopted new constitutions, which in some cases were modified versions of their prewar constitution. More recently, new constitutions were adopted by countries moving from autocratic to democratic forms of government: Greece, Portugal, and Spain in the 1970s, and the postcommunist regimes of central and eastern Europe in the late 1980s and early 1990s.

Constitutions, then, are often adopted as part of a fresh start—either a change of political regime or the achievement of national independence. Just as the United States drew up a new constitution in 1787, so Finland in 1919 and Ireland in 1922 had to devise a constitution when they embarked on independent statehood. Dramatic changes of regime led to new constitutions in Italy in 1948, Germany in 1949, Portugal in 1976, and Spain in 1978, and in nearly all of the postcommunist countries in the early 1990s. On other occasions, a new constitution may be adopted in order to adjust the nature of an existing liberal democratic system; examples are France in 1958, Denmark in 1973, Sweden in 1974, Belgium in 1989, and Finland in 2000. Even though there was widespread agreement in Italy that fundamental constitutional amendment was needed to recast the country's political system in the wake of the upheavals of the 1990s, however, agreement could not be reached on precisely what changes should be made.

Sometimes, major political changes do not lead to a new constitution. The German constitution (known as the "Basic Law") of 1949, which originally applied only to West Germany, envisages its own demise when the reunited German people choose a new constitution; Article 146 states that "This Basic Law ... shall cease to be in force on the day in which a constitution adopted by a free decision of the German people comes into force." In the event, the reunification of Germany in 1990 took place under the terms of Article 23 of the Basic Law, which allows new units to join the Federal Republic. The Basic Law, though originally seen as only an interim document pending reunification, is thus still in operation with no great popular demand that it be replaced. The changes made to the Basic Law following reunification proved to be minor indeed. Likewise, after the collapse of communism, Hungary extensively amended its communist-era constitution (dating from 1949) rather than adopt a new one (Seitzer, p. 43). When the Baltic states left the Soviet Union in 1990 they were keen to emphasize to the world that they were not mere sections of a country that were seceding but, rather, were independent countries forcibly brought into the USSR in 1940 under the terms of the Hitler–Stalin pact and were regaining their independence. Consequently, two of them resurrected their pre-1940 constitutions. Latvia resumed political life under the terms of its constitution of 1922, with some amendments, while in Lithuania the 1938 constitution was symbolically restored for an hour before it was superseded by a newly drawn-up "basic law" (Gelazis, "Institutional," p. 168).

If nothing dramatic happens in a country's history, there may seem to be no need for a new constitution. This is part of the reason why Britain does not have a document called "The Constitution." Britain has not been invaded for several centuries and has not experienced a regime change since 1688; the emphasis since then has been on continuity and evolution, with no "clean break" with the past. Consequently, there has never been any "constitutional moment." This not to say that no changes have taken place. On the contrary: As Anthony King puts it, "although few people seem to have noticed the fact, the truth is that the United Kingdom's constitution changed more between 1970 and 2000, and especially between 1997 and 2000, than during any comparable period since at least the middle of the 18th century" (King, p. 53). Among these changes King lists membership of the EU, the introduction of referendums as a means of deciding major constitutional questions, the increase in judicial review, devolution to Scotland and Wales, and devolution to Northern Ireland. The reason why he suggests that "few people ... have noticed" the implications of these developments for the constitution is that none of the changes has required altering articles of a codified constitution, let alone the promulgation of a new codified constitution. Thus, major changes can be made under the general impression of constitutional continuity.

Britain is unique among European democracies in having no formal codified constitution, so it is hard to be certain about what exactly makes up the British constitution, which has been seen as deriving from a number of sources (Norton, pp. 5–9). The first is statute law. Some very fundamental pieces of legislation, such as the 1707 Act of Union that brought Scotland into the United Kingdom while preserving a separate Scottish church and legal system, are part of the British constitution. These pieces of legislation could, at least in theory, be amended or repealed by parliament in just the same way as any other law, although the political fallout would be immense if any attempt were made to do this in the absence of widespread consent. The fact that statute law is part of the British constitution shows that the common view that Britain has an "unwritten constitution" is not entirely true; the constitution is at least partly written. Sartori (p. 862) comments that the British constitution is not "unwritten" but "written differently." Second, the EU treaties to which Britain has acceded, and the European Convention on Human Rights, which was incorporated into British law in 2000, also form written components of the constitution. The third source of the constitution is common law, including some customs such as the supremacy of parliament and major judicial decisions. The fourth source is convention, which dictates that certain things—such as the appointment of a prime minister who does not hold a seat in the House of Commons, or any refusal by the monarch to consent to a measure passed by parliament— cannot now be done simply because it is generally accepted by the political elite that they cannot be done, even though they happened in the past. Finally, "works of authority" written by scholars of the constitution also affect perceptions of what exactly the constitution consists of.

Despite the stress usually laid by constitutions on popular sovereignty, most new constitutions are brought into being by representative organs, following the U.S. precedent. Only in a few cases have the people of a country been given the opportunity to vote in a referendum on whether they wish to adopt a document as their country's constitution. In France, when the wartime leader of the Free French, Charles de Gaulle, was invited in 1958 to return to power, he had a constitution hastily drawn up, and this was put to and passed by the people in a referendum, thereby bringing into existence the Fifth Republic. Other examples of European constitutions being adopted by referendum are Switzerland in 1874, Ireland in 1937, Denmark in 1953, Spain in 1978, Estonia and Lithuania in 1992, and Poland in 1997. In the first three of these cases, the element of popular sovereignty is strengthened by the requirement that any subsequent change to the constitution requires the consent of the people at a referendum.

Constitutions, of course, vary from country to country, but there are certain near-universal features (Finer et al; Murphy). Constitutions regulate the organization of the government, stipulating, for example, whether government is parliamentary or presidential, what power the legislature has to constrain the executive, the role of the judiciary, and how power is divided between national organs of government and state or provincial bodies. In addition, they usually declare a number of rights, though sometimes what they say on this subject is primarily aspirational. The Polish constitution, for example, declares a whole range of socioeconomic rights such as housing, child care, consumer protection, and economic protection but, implicitly acknowledging that because of limited resources governments are unlikely to be able to guarantee all of these, allows governments to regulate the delivery of these "rights" through appropriate legislation (Sanford, pp. 94–95).

Constitutional Traditions

The fact that both the United States and most European countries possess a document called "The Constitution" should not mislead us into assuming that all constitutions enjoy the same status in the eyes of the people who live under them. Ulrich Preuss contrasts the U.S. pattern of constitutional authority with that in France. In the United States, he suggests, the constitution has priority not only over the government but also over the will of the people themselves. The constitution has a crucial place in history, in creating the United States of America: "It is the sanctity of the founding act by which the polity has been created which imputes to the constitution the authority of the supreme law. The supremacy of its authority over all other laws flows from the inherent significance and uniqueness of the act of nation building" (Preuss, pp. 20–22). Interpretation of the constitution is thus very important, leading to "the almost obsessive passion" of Americans with questions of constitutional interpretation. Regarding rights, the constitution gives the impression that government and parliament are more likely to be a source of endangerment than a defender of these, with its repeated prescription "Congress shall make no law ..."

In France, in contrast, the genuine spirit of constitutionalism is encapsulated not in the constitution but in the constituent power of the nation; this constituent power cannot be bound by any constitution (Preuss, pp. 22–24). The creation of the constitution was not the founding act for the French nation; the French nation is seen as having existed long before the first French constitution, let alone the current one. The constitution is one of the emanations of the nation, which is prior to every institution. The nation has power to "constitute and reconstitute its sovereign power and give it its appropriate institutional shape at will." This helps to account for the relatively large number of constitutions in France over the past two hundred years, and the lack of veneration for any one that is comparable to the veneration accorded to its U.S. counterpart. Political actors are seen as more important than the constitution and as the appropriate actors to rectify wrongs.

Most European countries might fall somewhere on the spectrum between France and the United States, while being much closer to the French position than to the American. It would be fair to say that no European constitution inspires the kind of reverence that many Americans feel for their own constitution. Many Europeans have never seen a copy of their country's constitution and have only the most general notion of what it contains. Europeans tend to evaluate their constitutions in pragmatic and instrumental terms, with no compunction about amending or replacing an existing constitution if it prevents a favored course of action from being followed. Partly for this reason, the relationship between constitutionalism and democracy, which has been so extensively explored in the U.S. context, has generated far less agonizing in Europe (Bellamy; Holmes). Even so, European constitutions, given vitality by constitutional courts, now impose significant constraints on governments and parliaments.

Amending a Constitution

The extent to which a constitution, promulgated by people or parliament at one point in time, binds successive generations in a manner that can be seen as "rule by the dead" depends partly on how easy it is to change it. A constitution that is very difficult to amend or replace clearly constrains a nation in a way that a less rigid document does not. No one would advocate the imposition of a totally rigid, unchangeable document, but at the same time there would be little point in having a constitution that is as easy to change as any law. Such a constitution would not constrain short-term majorities, who would be able to change the rules of the game as they saw fit. Consequently, nearly all constitutions stipulate that amending them requires the support of more than a simple parliamentary majority. Certain constitutions can be changed only by referendum; as we have already pointed out, the constitutions to which this constraint applies—those of Denmark, Ireland, and Switzerland—were brought in by referendum in the first place. In some other countries, such as Austria, Iceland, Latvia, Malta, Poland, and Spain, minor changes can be made by parliament, but major changes may require the consent of the people in a referendum. In Germany proposals for change must be passed by votes of two-thirds in both the directly elected Bundestag and the Bundesrat, which represents state (Land) governments. Thus any change needs agreement between the government and the opposition in the national parliament, as well as the consent of most of the Land governments. Moreover, certain provisions are declared unamendable, such as the federal and democratic nature of the state.

The French constitution can be amended in one of two ways (Carcassonne; Morel). Article 89 outlines a procedure under which the agreement of both houses of parliament is needed for any proposed change. Unless a joint meeting of both houses then approves the proposal by a 60 percent vote, it goes to a referendum. The French Senate is dominated by conservative rural members, which means that changes proposed by the left face an uphill struggle if they are to be passed by the parliamentarians, though several proposed by the right have been passed in this way without the need for a referendum. However, constitutional change in France has often followed a different route, by means of Article 11, under which the government may propose a change and the president can then refer it directly to the people in a referendum. (In practice, the president usually tells the government what to propose to him—de Gaulle sometimes announced the referendum before he had formally received the government's proposal.) This is not really the way the constitution seems to envisage amendment taking place, but it has become accepted that it is a valid way. The French public has shown little sign of objection, evidently feeling that it does have the right to change the constitution in this way, in line with the general attitude to the constitution identified by Preuss.

When it comes to amending the British constitution, there are no firm rules, as we would expect. There is nothing that says that those pieces of statute that are regarded as constitutional in nature cannot be changed just like any other statute. After all, these statutes came into being in the first place simply by being passed by parliament. Yet there are powerful political cultural constraints in existence; for example, it is generally felt that the House of Commons could not simply repeal the laws that preserve Scotland's separate judicial system, something guaranteed under the 1707 Act of Union, against the wishes of the Scots. Similarly, given that the devolved institutions in Scotland and Wales were brought into existence by referendums in 1999, it is questionable whether they could be abolished except by fresh referendums. Other major aspects, though, certainly can be changed by parliament, such as reductions in the powers of the House of Lords, which occurred twice in the twentieth century.

Constitutions regulate the power of political actors, in relation both to each other and to civil society. The referee or umpire whose role it is to decide whether the rules have been broken is usually the judiciary, and the power of a court to declare a law or regulation to be in conflict with the constitution of a country and hence to be invalid is one aspect of judicial review. We are focusing particularly on the power to strike down legislation on the ground that it is incompatible with the constitution, and thus the term "constitutional review" might seem to be more appropriate, especially given that in most countries it is not the ordinary courts but rather constitutional courts that wield this power.

Box 4.1   CONSTITUTIONS

France

France has had a number of constitutions in the last two hundred years. The current constitution, the Constitution of the Fifth Republic, dates from 1958, when it was approved by the people in a referendum. Some subsequent changes have been made by parliament, but others have been made by referendum, including the most important, the 1962 amendment that introduced the direct election of the president. It has been argued that French political culture values the constituent power of the nation far more highly than it values any specific constitution.

Germany

The German constitution, known as the Basic Law, dates from 1949. The constitution cannot be amended without the consent of two-thirds majorities in both houses of parliament, so in practice any change requires the consent of both the national opposition and most of the state governments. Although in 1949 it was assumed that the Basic Law would be replaced by a new constitution when German unity was achieved, unification took place within the framework of the Basic Law. The Basic Law stands high in the esteem of Germans, especially those living in former West Germany.

Italy

The Italian constitution was promulgated in 1948, and in reaction to the dictatorship of Mussolini, it provided for checks and balances to a degree that critics say has hampered the achievement of effective government in postwar Italy. The political upheavals of the 1990s led to calls for a new constitution or at least a fundamental revision of the existing one, but the political elite was unable to reach a consensus on the amendments that should be made, so not very much has been changed.

Latvia

After throwing off communist (and Russian) rule in the early 1990s, Latvia declared independence in 1991 on the basis of its 1922 democratic constitution. A number of amendments were made subsequently, some designed to smooth the way to accession to the EU. Most amendments to the constitution require the approval of two-thirds of members of Latvia's parliament, the Saeima. Major changes (concerning, for example, the form of government, territory, language, and the size of parliament) need the approval of the people in a referendum.

Netherlands

The Dutch constitution dates from 1814, though it has been subjected to a number of major overhauls, most notably in 1848 and most recently in 1983. In most countries the constitution can be seen as a "basic law," with a status superior to that of any ordinary law, but in the Netherlands the constitution scarcely has this position. It states explicitly that the courts cannot review the constitutionality of acts of parliament and, unlike most constitutions, does not provide any real constraint on the behavior of parliament.

Constitutional courts are not part of the "regular" judiciary, and indeed in some countries (such as the Czech Republic, Italy, and Poland) it has been a challenge for them to assert their authority over the regular courts. However, since "judicial review" is the more widely used phrase, we shall employ it here; likewise, when we speak of "judges" in this chapter, this term usually includes members of constitutional courts. By "judicial review" we are referring to "the authority of an institution to invalidate the acts of government—such as legislation, administrative decisions, and judicial rulings—on the grounds that these acts have violated constitutional rules" (Stone Sweet, *Governing,* p. 21). The importance of judicial review varies across Europe, according to the stipulations of different countries' constitutions and to legal traditions, and it is this variation that we now explore.

Poland

Poland's checkered constitutional history reflects its attempts to establish an independent state in the face of occupations and partitions, particularly by its neighbors, Germany and Russia, along with experience of autocratic rule. It adopted new constitutions in 1791, 1921, 1935, and 1952, as well as temporary "Little Constitutions" in 1947 and 1992. Its current constitution was drawn up in the mid-1990s after extensive discussion and bargaining and in some respects is something of a political compromise between various conceptions of the state. It is very long and—containing elements inspired by socialism, Christian democracy, liberalism, and agrarianism—occasionally inconsistent. It bestows on citizens many socioeconomic "rights" that, quite obviously, the state does not in practice have the resources to assure. It was endorsed by the people in a referendum in May 1997, by a 53 percent majority on a 43 percent turnout, and given the difficulty of securing agreement on its contents seems likely to remain the basic law of the country for the foreseeable future.

Spain

When the long Franco dictatorship ended, a new constitution was drawn up and approved by the people, with a 92 percent vote in favor, in a referendum in 1978. It provides for a constitutional monarchy and recognizes the multinational nature of Spain while simultaneously asserting the indivisibility of the country. Although it has been criticized for vagueness or ambiguity in this and other areas, it provided the framework for a successful transition to democracy.

Sweden

The current Swedish constitution was adopted in 1974 and asserts that the country is a democracy in which all public power "emanates from the people," in contrast to previous constitutions, which had stressed the importance of the monarch. It is called "The Instrument of Government" rather than "The Constitution," which signifies its limited role and status compared with the constitution in many other countries. The constitution can be amended by simple majority vote of parliament, though there must be two such votes to make any specific amendment, one before and one after a general election.

United Kingdom

Unlike every other country in Europe, the United Kingdom does not have a document called "The Constitution." It is not the case, though, that its constitution is therefore unwritten; some central elements of it are contained in acts of parliament, some of them several centuries old. The principle of parliamentary sovereignty is strong, and although in recent years there have been calls for the adoption of a formal constitution setting out the limits on the powers of government and parliament, such attempts at reform have made little headway. Dramatic changes have been made to the constitutional framework of British government and politics in recent years and, with uncertainty still in the air, Anthony King has described the current state of affairs as "a new constitutional unsettlement."

→ JUDICIAL REVIEW

Judicial review may take one or both of two forms: concrete and abstract. *Concrete* judicial review is a challenge to a law arising out of some specific case before a court. *Abstract* judicial review involves the consideration of a law without reference to any specific case. Concrete judicial review can be initiated by any defendant in a court case who feels that the law under which he or she is being prosecuted is unconstitutional or is otherwise null and void. Abstract review can usually be initiated only by a designated set of political authorities (such as the head of state, the prime minister, or a specified number of members of parliament). Abstract review itself can take two forms. In some countries, it can be initiated only for a short period (typically up to three months) after a law has been passed (this is known as *a posteriori* abstract review). In Portugal, abstract review can also be initiated *before* a bill has become law; in France and Ireland, it can be initiated *only* before a bill becomes law (this is known as *a priori* abstract review).

In some European countries judicial review does not exist, and in countries where it does exist, it may be wielded either by the regular court system or by a special constitutional court (or by both, as in Portugal). We need also to remember that, for the twenty-five countries of the European Union (EU), the Court of Justice of the European Communities, which is based in Luxembourg, can exercise the power of judicial review because it can declare any law of a member state to be invalid if it conflicts either with the constitution of the EU or with an EU law (we discuss the Court of Justice in the next chapter). Although there is a lot of variation across Europe in the details of how constitutional courts are composed and what powers they possess, there are also common patterns. Characteristically, judges are appointed by political actors in such a way that the main political parties all get a share of the nominations. In countries where judicial review is strong, the political role of judges is widely analyzed and is acknowledged to be very significant. In countries where judicial review has traditionally been seen as weak, judges are becoming more assertive. We next explore these patterns in greater detail.

Strong Judicial Review

First, we look at countries where there is express provision for a judicial body to strike down legislation as unconstitutional; Markku Suksi (p. 135) finds that 75 of 160 constitutions around the world contain such provision. There are two models. One employs a dedicated constitutional court, separate from the regular court system, a model designed by the Austrian jurist Hans Kelsen before the Second World War. In his scheme, the constitution was the highest order of norm (a *Grundnorm*) and legitimized lower-order norms, specifically laws. Moreover, all laws, to be valid, had to conform to the constitution, and the task of ensuring that they did so could not be left to governments or parliaments; instead, it properly belonged to a body that had this sole and specific purpose—a constitutional court. Prior to 1945, Austria, Czechoslovakia, and Germany were the only countries that had such a body (and only in Austria was it significant), but today Kelsenian ideas dominate European constitutionalism. Such constitutional courts exist in nearly all the postcommunist countries we are considering, along with Austria, Germany, Italy, Malta, Portugal, and Spain; a similar body, the Constitutional Council, fulfills this function in France. Constitutional courts are not quite part of the regular court system. Indeed, in the text of constitutions they usually have a section to themselves, sometimes symbolically placed between the section on parliament and that on the courts. In that way the power they have does not amount to "government by judges," which in a number of European countries has been seen as something to avoid at all costs.

In two countries, the ordinary court system (in Ireland) or a body attached to it (in Estonia) exercises the power of constitutional review; this is also the situation in the United States. In the other nine countries examined in this book, judicial review is weak, though in most cases growing stronger. When we examine the record of specific countries, we shall see how significant the role of the courts can be in a country's politics.

The nearest thing to an archetypal constitutional court, and one that other countries have taken as a model, is the German Federal Constitutional Court (FCC), based in Karlsruhe, which has been described as "an institution of major policy-making importance" (Kommers, *Constitutional,* p. 1). The FCC can exercise both abstract review (bills can be referred to it by a third of the members of the Bundestag or by a Land government) and concrete review (a law can be referred to it for a definitive verdict on its constitutionality by an ordinary court during the course of a case, and citizens themselves can write directly to the FCC complaining that their constitutional rights have been violated). Ordinary German courts cannot judge the constitutionality of laws; if a question of constitutionality arises, it must be referred to the FCC. The overwhelming majority of the cases reaching the FCC are "constitutional complaints" from individual citizens (although 99 percent of these complaints are not substantial enough to warrant the FCC examining them in any detail); about 2.5 percent consists of cases of concrete review and 0.1 percent abstract review (Beyme, p. 105).

Since 1951 the FCC has declared about 5 percent of the bills passed by the Bundestag to be invalid (Schmidt, p. 120; Helms, pp. 90–94). Some of its decisions have had major political overtones. In the 1950s it banned a communist and a neo-Nazi party, and in September 1990 it complicated the process of German reunification by declaring unconstitutional the electoral system originally proposed for the first all-German elections in December of that year. In 1995 it made a controversial decision in a case in which, when the parents of a child in Bavaria objected to the presence of a crucifix in the classroom, it ruled that the crucifix should be removed because its presence violated freedom of religion. This decision prompted widespread protests, especially in Bavaria, a strongly Catholic region of Germany (Kommers, *Constitutional,* pp. 472–84; Schmidt, pp. 119–20).

Perhaps most controversial of all have been FCC decisions on the subject of abortion. In 1975 the Court struck down legislation passed by the center–left majority in parliament that had made abortion legal within the first three months of pregnancy. The FCC decided that this proposed law would not give adequate protection to life, so it gave the Bundestag instead a fairly detailed (and much more restrictive) prescription as to how abortion legislation should be framed, which the Bundestag duly incorporated in revised legislation. In the early 1990s, the Court declared unconstitutional some key aspects of a new abortion law that parliament had passed to bridge the gap between the more restrictive West German law of 1976 and the more liberal East German law of the same year. The FCC rejected the new law, requested the Bundestag to enact a fresh one, and presented an interim regulation that would be valid until such a fresh law was passed (Kommers, *Constitutional,* pp. 335–56). In addition, the FCC arbitrates in disputes over the jurisdiction of various organs of government, sometimes giving judgments that protect the rights of the Land governments and parliaments against threatened encroachment by their central (federal) counterparts and on other occasions giving decisions that favor the federal government.

Generally speaking, Germans have a high regard for the FCC. Polls have found it to enjoy substantially more public trust than any other major German institution, including parliament, the churches, the trade unions, and universities, and indeed it is more highly thought of than comparable courts are in their own countries (Kommers,

Constitutional, pp. 56–57; Schmidt, p. 121; Gibson et al.). Newspapers, with a mixture of pride and sarcasm, refer to the judges on the FCC as "kings" and to their pronouncements as "divine ordinances" (Kommers, "Federal," p. 486). Although, as we shall see, the main political parties control nomination to the court, commentators do not feel that the party affiliations of individual court members have much bearing on their judgments. The FCC has sometimes been criticized by the left, however, with the argument that it serves as a brake on social change. In addition, during the 1990s it attracted more criticism than heretofore, perhaps because to some it seemed to lose touch with changing values in German society (Helms, pp. 94–95).

The Court's ultimate legitimacy in the German system "rests on its moral authority and the willingness of the political arms of government to follow its mandates" (Kommers, *Constitutional,* pp. 54–55), and the FCC has developed its own techniques to preserve this moral authority. When faced with a politically sensitive issue, it sometimes delays making a decision until the controversy has died or the matter is settled by political means. It also has the power to distinguish between laws that are null and void as a result of being in conflict with the constitution and laws that, though unconstitutional, are not actually void. In the latter case, parliament is allowed a period of grace to put matters right, and during this period the law remains in operation. Similarly, the Court may uphold a statute while warning that it could soon become unconstitutional. The danger here, however, is that even though the legislature never explicitly defies the FCC, the Court's approach allows parliament to procrastinate interminably (laws criticized by the FCC have remained in existence for over twenty years while parliament sets up committees to consider the implications of its judgment, for example) or to respond by passing a revised bill that, while different in some respects from the one censured by the Court, still contains the key features to which the Court objected (Vanberg, "Legislative"). Its former supremacy is also under threat from the European Court of Justice (see next chapter) and from Land constitutional courts, which have become much more numerous and also more active in the wake of unification (Helms, p. 98).

Overall, the FCC occupies a very powerful position in the German legislative process. Just as U.S. Chief Justice Charles Evans Hughes declared that "the Constitution is what the judges say it is," so a German law professor was able to say that "The Basic Law is now virtually identical with its interpretation by the Federal Constitutional Court" (Abraham, p. 356; Kommers, *Constitutional,* p. 55). The fact that it has struck down only about 5 percent of laws passed by the Bundestag does not give an accurate reflection of its impact. For one thing, a number of laws have received conditional approval by the Court; using the approach of "interpretation in conformity with the constitution," the Court can declare that a law is constitutional provided that it means what the Court interprets it to mean. Of course, this interpretation may not always coincide with the original intentions of parliament. For another, parliament, when drafting legislation, goes to great lengths to try to ensure that laws will not be found to be unconstitutional, including seeking the advice of legal experts as to how the FCC will react to specific laws and whose role has sometimes been compared with that of astrologers or soothsayers. The Bundestag has been seen as legislating "in the shadow" of the Court and as being excessively cautious for fear of displeasing it (Landfried, pp. 116–19; Kommers, *Constitutional,* p. 56).

The Constitutional Court of Italy is also fairly highly regarded by that country's citizens—no mean feat given the general disdain with which many Italians regard their political institutions. In its early years in the 1950s the court struck down legislation dating from the fascist era despite the claim of the government that it had no power to do so. Those were difficult years for the court because the government did not always obey its rulings and the ordinary courts, still in many cases staffed by judges appointed during the fascist regime of Mussolini, were hostile to it and refused to refer cases up to it. In the 1970s the court showed itself willing to stand up to the power of the Catholic Church at a time when most of the political parties were not. In 1971 it invalidated fascist-era laws prohibiting contraception, between 1970 and 1974 it gave six decisions affirming the constitutionality of laws that allowed divorce, and in 1975 it nullified the portion of the penal code that made a woman's consent to an abortion a criminal act (de Franciscis and Zannini, p. 74). In recent years it has become more cautious and aware of the potential economic and political implications of its decisions. For example, it created an office to estimate the financial burden that would be created were it to strike down a law (Rolla and Groppi, p. 157). Unfortunately, it is impossible to tell how many laws have been declared unconstitutional; no records are maintained on the matter "because of the disorganization of the statute books." Indeed, no one even knows how many laws there are in Italy, though there is agreement that the number is huge, perhaps between 100,000 and 150,000, compared with fewer than 10,000 in both France and Germany (Volcansek, *Constitutional,* pp. 27, 29).

The Constitutional Court of Italy has been characterized as generally a defender of civil liberties and has not slavishly followed the wishes of the government of the day, but it would be wrong to exaggerate its independence. The court collectively does not deviate too far from the sentiments of the mainstream political elite, and individual members may be receptive to the views of the party that secured their nomination, perhaps because many of them plan to enter or reenter political life after the expiration of their term on the court (de Franciscis and Zannini, p. 78). In the mid-1990s, when most of the established Italian parties collapsed, the Constitutional Court became more independent and interventionist, perhaps because the judges knew that their sponsoring parties could no longer offer them future patronage (Volcansek, *Constitutional,* p. 49). The court is not seen as completely independent of the political parties, but it is at least felt to be less controlled by them than are most other Italian institutions. It affirmed its independence in 2004 when it struck down a controversial law passed by parliament that would have given senior politicians, including Prime Minister Silvio Berlusconi, immunity from prosecution.

The almost universal implementation in postcommunist eastern and central Europe (Estonia is the only exception) of constitutional courts is striking evidence of the dominance of the Kelsenian model. There was little or no consideration of the U.S. model of leaving judicial review to the regular courts, let alone of the idea of letting governments and parliaments make whatever laws they chose (Malovà and Haughton, pp. 114–15). These courts have been significant actors given the frequency of rows between governments and presidents, for example, that are common in new democracies. One of the most significant is the Polish Constitutional Tribunal (the Trybunal Konstytucyjny, or TK) (for the TK see Garlicki; Sanford, pp. 208–14). A wide range of actors can refer questions of constitutionality to it: not only the usual bodies (president, chairs of the two houses of parliament, fifty deputies or thirty senators, any court) but also a wide variety of religious, trade union, and local government bodies along with individual citizens. Initially parliament could, with a two-thirds majority, overturn TK judgments, but since 1999 the Tribunal's decisions have been final. However, the 1997 constitution, as well as enhancing the TK's power in this way, introduces a complication by giving the Supreme Court, too, the right to pronounce on the interpretation of laws, creating the potential for conflict between the two institutions. The TK has made controversial decisions on subjects such as abortion, the vetting of individuals who collaborated with the security services during the communist period (known as "lustration"), and the rents paid by private tenants.

In other postcommunist countries, too, constitutional courts have been important. In Hungary, for example, the Constitutional Court has exceptionally wide jurisdiction and was described as "the most important political institution for the defence of the constitutional state" (Körösényi, p. 273). In 1995 it struck down government austerity measures on the grounds that they infringed welfare rights. Following the retirement of its first president in 1999, though, it became somewhat less active (Halmai). The Czech Republic's Constitutional Court struck down laws on the funding of political parties and on electoral system reform, earning criticism from some parties and indeed threats of defiance from the parliamentary majority (Pribán). The Slovenian Constitutional Court has been so active that it has been criticized for insufficient self-restraint, and its practice of basing its judgments on principles that are nowhere to be found in the constitution gives it great freedom of action (Cerar, pp. 399–400). Although we do not discuss the work of all the postcommunist bodies in detail, the picture is much the same everywhere: Constitutional courts have made decisions with major political consequences and are generally perceived as legitimate and trustworthy institutions (see Sadurski, chs. 7–17; Zielonka).

Two countries where comparable bodies have been significant constraints on government, but where a rather different model was chosen, are France and Ireland. The French Constitutional Council, as its name suggests, is not formally a judicial body in any sense and, compared with the constitutional courts we have just discussed, is much more likely to find its decisions interpreted in partisan political terms. It was established by the 1958 constitution but made little public impact until the early 1980s. In 1974, the right to refer bills to the Council, hitherto reserved for a few figures who were likely to be government supporters and thus unlikely to want to test the constitutionality of legislation, was extended; any group of sixty deputies (or sixty senators) was given the power to refer a bill to the Council. After 1981, when the Socialist Party entered government for the first time, it became routine for the parliamentary opposition to refer every budget, and nearly every major piece of legislation, to the Council. The new left-wing government drew up wide-ranging plans for the nationalization of a number of private companies, which the right-wing opposition parties referred to the Council. To the government's dismay, the Council ruled that the compensation arrangements provided for were in conflict with the constitution, and it in effect elaborated a new compensation formula, which would raise the cost of the nationalization program by about 25 percent. The government duly drew up a new law incorporating this formula, and the Council pronounced this bill constitutional (Stone Sweet, *Birth,* pp. 140–72). The Socialist government's plans fell afoul of the Council on other issues, too—most important of all, surely, on the independence of university professors—as the opposition parties, having been outvoted in parliament, achieved total or partial victories in the Constitutional Council (Knapp and Wright, p. 392).

After 1986, when the right won power in France, the roles were reversed. The Socialists began to refer many bills to the Council, and the right-wing parties complained about the power of the Council in terms even more bitter than those used by the Socialists between 1981 and 1986. Leading right-wing politicians described one ruling as "a veritable attack on national sovereignty" and an "amputation of the power of parliamentarians" (Stone Sweet, *Birth,* p. 3). Relations between the Council and politicians were relatively quiet during the next spell of Socialist government (1988–93)—from 1989 onward, a majority of Council members were Socialist nominees—but when the right returned to power after the 1993 elections, conflicts began again. In August 1993 the Council struck down some of the new government's anti-immigration legislation, and in January 1994 it declared unconstitutional the central aspects of a bill that would have led to a great increase in the amount of public money being spent on private, church-run, schools. Between 1997 and 2002, once again, a left-wing government faced a Council dominated by the right, and some of its legislation—for example, concerning devolution of power to the Corsican Assembly—was struck down (Elgie, p. 189). Like its German counterpart, the French Constitutional Council is prone, when striking down legislation, to offer an alternative wording that it says would be constitutional, and sometimes these passages are copied verbatim into the revised bill, making the Council seem like a quasi-legislature (Knapp and Wright, p. 393).

Given the important role played by the Constitutional Council, the fact that judicial review as such is explicitly prohibited in France might come as a surprise. This has been the case since the French Revolution and owes partly to the feeling that any check on parliament would be a check on the "general will" of the people. The idea that the United States has "government by judges" and that this is highly undesirable is part of political discourse in France (Provine, p. 185). The prohibition on judicial review means that the Council's power is confined to legislation in abstract form; once a bill has become law, its constitutionality cannot be challenged. Although in principle the role of the Council is "to impose stable and fundamental values" rather than be swayed by short-term political factors (Bell, p. 40), its decisions are often interpreted in political rather than in purely constitutional terms, and it has not succeeded, unlike Kelsenian constitutional courts, in being widely regarded as an impartial, nonpartisan, institution. One reason for this view is that bills go to the Council immediately after their passage through parliament. The Council is invariably judging bills that have very recently been the subject of partisan political battles on the floor of the National Assembly, so some claim it is akin to a decisive third chamber of parliament, an impression fostered by the partisan nature of appointments (see below). Even so, unlike a parliament but like a court, it must couch its arguments in terms of legal rather than political discourse ("good law" rather than "good policy").

Finally, we look at the case of Ireland, which differs from all other European countries in that judicial review is exercised not by a special constitutional court or council but by the regular court system, as in the United States. This may be because the constitution was adopted in 1937, before the merits of the Kelsenian model were widely appreciated. The High Court and the Supreme Court in Ireland—rather than every court as in the United States—are empowered to pass judgment on the constitutionality of laws, and they can exercise not just concrete review, as in the United States, but also abstract review (the a priori form only). The right of referral of bills to the courts for abstract review is, though, much more restrictive than in the other countries we have looked at. Only the president of Ireland may refer bills to the Supreme Court for this purpose. Between 1937 and 2004, only fifteen bills were so referred (eight were found by the Supreme Court to be constitutional and the other seven to be wholly or in part unconstitutional). As in other countries, the number of actual referrals understates the significance of abstract review, for the very existence of this presidential power has no doubt made parliament particularly careful not to pass legislation that might prove to be in conflict with the constitution.

More significant in Ireland has been concrete review. Again, as in other countries, the courts in Ireland have become more active since the 1960s in exercising the power of judicial review, and lawyers have been more inclined to challenge the constitutionality of statutes (Gallagher). The courts have moved from a literal approach to interpreting the constitution to what is termed a "creative" approach, which implies that the judges do not feel limited by the actual words in the constitution but move beyond them to consider what they claim to be its overall spirit and tenor. The courts have made a number of important decisions as a consequence. In 1973 the courts declared unconstitutional the existing law banning the sale or importation of contraceptives, and in 1992 the Supreme Court decided that the constitution conferred upon women, in certain circumstances, the right to have an abortion. Anti-abortionists were aggrieved by the latter decision, especially as it was based on a section of the constitution that had been added in 1983—at the behest of anti-abortionists—precisely in order to try to *prevent* any future Supreme Court finding that constitution permitted abortion. One of their leaders criticized the very concept of judicial review, declaring that "it is unacceptable and indeed a deep affront to the people of Ireland that four judges who are preserved by the constitution from accountability can radically alter the constitution and place in peril the most vulnerable section of our society" (quoted in Gallagher, p. 93). However, this criticism was unusual, for despite the fact that the government of the day appoints judges and attaches great importance when doing so to the political links of potential appointees, the courts are widely seen as "above" politics and no government has attributed political motives to a judge who has delivered a decision that it did not like.

Judicial review is very significant in Ireland; for example, the Irish courts have proved much readier to identify unenunciated rights than their American counterparts. The jurisprudence of the courts has been extensively analysed (see, for example, Hogan and Whyte, which runs to nearly 2,200 pages). As in Germany, the courts in Ireland can exercise power not merely by striking down legislation but also by imposing their own interpretation on it. The courts approach each statute with the "presumption of constitutionality"—that is, "if a statutory provision is open to differing constructions, one constitutional, the other not, the court must opt for the former" (Casey, pp. 364–67). Although this might seem to strengthen the position of parliament—it means that less of its legislation will be struck down than if there were no presumption of constitutionality—it can work to limit the power of parliament because it may mean that the court chooses the narrowest of a number of meanings that an act could have and consequently reduces the scope of the act.

We have seen from this brief survey that courts that have the power to strike down legislation can be significant political actors. Clearly, this can be frustrating for political parties and governments, amounting to a veto by a small number of unelected individuals on policies that might have had widespread support. However, there may be times when political actors welcome the intervention of the courts. For example, the Lithuanian political class faced a dilemma in the early 1990s. It knew that the country would have to abolish the death penalty in order to gain admission to the EU, but it also knew that the people strongly favored retaining capital punishment. The solution was to ask the constitutional court to state whether the laws allowing the death penalty were constitutional, and the court obligingly declared that they were not (Gelazis, "Defending," pp. 400–01). Some of the politicians who complain that the courts have prevented them from fulfilling election pledges may be secretly relieved not to have to try to implement policies in which they never really believed, or they may be thankful to be able to pass political hot potatoes to the courts for resolution.

Weak Judicial Review

We now turn to countries where the courts have limited or no power to strike down legislation on the ground of incompatibility with the constitution—though we need to emphasize at the outset that in many countries the judges are now starting to flex muscles that had been thought to be atrophied or even nonexistent. In the United Kingdom and in Scandinavia, courts can no longer be ignored by students of government.

In Britain, the absence of a formal codified constitution leads to a degree of vagueness as to what the constitution stipulates in any given situation, so the question of unconstitutionality simply has not arisen. The courts, of course, play a role in interpreting the laws, but they cannot strike down a law on grounds of nonconformity with the constitution. However, it certainly does not follow, as is sometimes assumed, that the courts are irrelevant in deciding what governments can and cannot do, and in fact from the early 1980s onward, judges in Britain have proved increasingly troublesome for governments. "English courts are increasingly willing to tell the government officials, at both national and local levels, that their action is wrong" (Kritzer, p. 156; see also Budge et al., pp. 494–510; Gordon; Johnson, "Judicial"). They have the power to prevent ministers from exercising power beyond their legal authority (*ultra vires*), although parliament may then change the laws to confer the desired power on the minister. As judges have become more willing to exercise judicial review, so individuals and organizations have been more inclined to try this route: The annual number of applications for judicial review rose from around five hundred in the early 1980s to over four thousand by the early 2000s (King, p. 60). Even if most of these applications fail, they have an impact on the way public administration works, and civil servants are now issued a booklet titled *The Judge over Your Shoulder* to advise them how to make sure their actions do not fall afoul of judicial review (Flinders, p. 63).

The incorporation into British law of the European Convention on Human Rights from 2000 has the potential to prove a significant development in this area. The courts can now refer a bill to a committee of parliament if they believe that it conflicts with the Convention. In theory parliament could still ignore a declaration by the courts that a piece of legislation is incompatible with the Convention, though in practice such parliamentary

Box 4.2   The Courts and Politics

France

Although judicial review as such does not exist in France, partly because of a fear of "government by judges," a quasi-judicial body, the Constitutional Council, can consider the constitutionality of legislation after it has been passed by parliament and before it is signed into law by the president. Appointment to the Council takes place very much on political grounds, and conflict with the government can arise when the two bodies are dominated by opposite sides. In the first half of the 1980s, the Council, which then contained a majority of right-wing appointees, made a number of rulings restricting the Socialist government's freedom of action, and the same pattern emerged between 1997 and 2002. When the right-wing parties won power in 1986, and again in 1993, the Council continued its activist approach and caused as much annoyance to the right as it had to the Socialists. Unlike corresponding bodies in the rest of Europe, the Constitutional Council has never been able to attain the status of an impartial agency because many of its decisions are perceived as springing from political considerations rather than from purely legal ones.

Germany

The Federal Constitutional Court, whose members are appointed on a cross-party basis, exerts a significant impact on policy making. It has made major political decisions, curbing the extent to which the abortion laws could be liberalized in both 1975 and 1993 and banning two political parties in the 1950s. The nonpartisan and serious manner in which it approaches its work has given it considerable national prestige, and parliament invariably defers to its judgments; indeed, parliament is sometimes criticized for being too ready to anticipate its reactions and restricting itself for fear of falling afoul of the court. German jurists ask whether the FCC has become a "parallel government"

or "counter-government" whose views count for just as much as the democratically elected one.

Italy

The postwar Italian judiciary has been highly politicized, with factions of judges linked to the major political parties. Judges and magistrates can become well known nationally through taking the initiative in tackling what they identify as problems, and although some see them as all too often motivated by a desire for publicity, the role of judges in the fight against organized crime and the corruption of Italian politics in the mid-1990s earned them respect. The Italian Constitutional Court has also been highly regarded, and over the years it has generally worked to enhance the civil liberties of citizens—for example, by declaring repressive legislation dating from the fascist era to be invalid.

Latvia

The Constitutional Court of Latvia was established in 1996. State institutions such as the president, cabinet, supreme court, local governments, and one-third of Saeima members have the right to submit an application requesting it to pronounce on the constitutionality of any law or an international treaty. Individuals or lower courts do not have such a right. Although the constitution provides some very basic principles of the Latvian judiciary, the court system is still too weak to enforce many of them. The independence of the Latvian judicial system is undermined, in the eyes of some observers, by the fact that the courts must rely on the Ministry of Justice for administrative support.

Netherlands

There is no tradition of judicial review in the Netherlands. Article 120 of the Dutch constitution declares that the courts cannot review the constitutionality of acts of parliament. Thus the courts have generally had relatively little impact on politics, although

defiance would be very surprising. The courts have found against the government in a number of cases—often involving the treatment of refugees and asylum-seekers—in which they have held that a law conflicted with the provisions of the Convention, leading the Home Secretary, David Blunkett, to declare on one occasion in 2003: "I'm personally fed up with having to deal with a situation where Parliament debates issues and the judges they are coming to play an increasing role by interpreting the meaning of laws when parliament passes rather vague legislation and by reserving the right to annul government measures that go beyond what legislation permits.

Poland

The Polish Constitutional Tribunal (the Trybunal Konstytucyjny, or TK) was established, though it did not wield effective power, under the communist regime in 1985. Its members are appointed by parliament but, unusually for a constitutional court, not on the basis of cross-party consensus; instead, the government parties virtually monopolize the appointments. The main power of the TK is to review the constitutionality of acts of parliament. Before signing a bill, the president can refer it to the TK for a judgment on its validity. After a bill has been signed into law, a wide range of actors—including fifty deputies, thirty senators, local government units, trade unions, and religious organizations—may challenge its constitutionality. In addition, if an ordinary court hearing a case has any doubts about the constitutionality of a statute, it must refer the matter to the TK. In practice, though, the TK is still struggling to assert its authority over the "regular" court system; courts sometimes refuse to apply laws, declaring them unconstitutional without consulting the TK. Like the constitutional courts as in other postcommunist countries, the TK has made its mark, most notably by striking down a liberalizing abortion bill in 1996 on the grounds that it did not sufficiently protect the right to life of the unborn.

Spain

The Spanish Constitutional Court has the power to exercise abstract review of a law if requested to do so by a group of fifty deputies or fifty senators. After the Socialist Party won power in 1982, the right-wing opposition used the court as a means of slowing the pace of radical legislation, but the court's decisions are not widely seen as politically motivated. Eight of its twelve members are appointed by the parliament by consensus among the parties; two members are appointed by the government and two by the body representing Spanish judges. Like its counterparts in other countries, it has been dragged into controversy by some of its decisions regarding abortion legislation passed by parliament. It has also given a number of judgments strengthening the autonomy of Spain's regions.

Sweden

The Swedish constitution provides for judicial review, but there is no tradition of the courts declaring laws to be unconstitutional; the left-wing parties in particular are suspicious of the idea of allowing the courts to overrule the democratically elected parliament. However, a judicial body does give advisory opinions on the constitutionality of proposed legislation, and its advice carries considerable weight. Judges are rigorously nonpartisan and in some ways see themselves as administrators with closer links to the state bureaucracy than to lawyers in private practice.

United Kingdom

Because there is no document called "The British Constitution," the possibility of legislation being declared unconstitutional does not exist in the United Kingdom. The judges, however, do have the right to declare the behavior of public authorities invalid if they deem it to go beyond those authorities' allotted powers, and their decisions in some such cases have brought them into the field of political controversy. Critics have accused the British judiciary of being implicitly sympathetic to the views of the Conservative Party and of not showing sufficient concern for civil rights.

then overturn them" (Prince, p. 297). This was not a problem that confronted most of his predecessors in office.

Some feel that British courts should have even more power. In the 1990s, a reformist group of legal academics and others drafted a written constitution for the United Kingdom, under which a supreme court would have the power to declare acts of parliament unconstitutional (Institute for Public Policy Research). Critics of the present situation argue that whatever the theoretical advantages of the constitution's largely unwritten nature, "its flexibility and adaptability are used mainly to get governments off the hook and to evade scrutiny and democratic control" (Budge et al., p. 700). However, on the left of the British political spectrum there has always been reluctance to give the judiciary more power. Even though the courts have become increasingly willing to check governments of all persuasions as we have shown, left-wing critics have often seen the judiciary as fundamentally conservative. Consequently, the Labour government has moved cautiously in this area. In a package unveiled in 2003 it proposed the establishment of a new supreme court, whose members (unlike the current leading members of the judiciary—the Law Lords—who constitute what is currently the highest court in the land) would not belong to the House of Lords, thus drawing a clear line between the judiciary and the legislature. However, the supreme court would not be given the power to strike down acts of parliament. These proposals ran into immediate judicial resistance and no timetable for their implementation has been announced.

The absence of provision for the courts to strike down laws also applies to a number of other countries. The courts of the Netherlands are expressly prohibited by Article 120 of the Dutch constitution from considering the constitutionality of laws, and until the 1960s there was little pressure for the introduction of judicial review. However, the courts can declare government measures to be *ultra vires* and can annul acts of parliament that contravene European treaties to which the Netherlands is a party. Because, perhaps, of declining respect for politicians and increased respect for the courts, Dutch courts have become more assertive and have sometimes exercised a self-conferred de facto right of judicial review. The question of explicitly enshrining judicial review in the constitution has been discussed in recent years, partly in response to trends in other European countries (Scheltma, pp. 206–07; ten Kate and van Koppen, pp. 148–49; van Koppen, pp. 83, 91). In Switzerland the highest court—the Federal Tribunal—can strike down legislation passed by the cantons but not by the federal parliament. It is obliged to apply all federal laws, even those that it considers to be unconstitutional (Rothmayr). In Belgium, judicial review can be exercised only regarding laws concerning the balance of power between different levels of government (Brewer-Carías, pp. 261–62).

Judicial review has never been a strong feature of political life in the Scandinavian countries—indeed, none of these countries has a Kelsenian constitutional court—because of the tradition that since power emanates from the people, the decisions made by the parliament elected by the people should not be open to challenge. Yet the judiciary is stirring even in Scandinavia. In Norway judicial review has roots going back to the nineteenth century, and signs of an increase in judicial activism have been apparent since the mid-1970s (Narud and Strøm, p. 194). In Denmark the Supreme Court started to throw off its habitual caution in the late 1990s, and in 1999 for the first time ever it declared a law unconstitutional (Damgaard, p. 125). Similarly, in Iceland the Supreme Court has recently made some "landmark" decisions that have had an "explosive impact" on the political system, proclaiming a "newly born constitutional authority" and in 2000 striking down an act of parliament that dealt with state financial support for the disabled (Kristjánsson, pp. 168–69). In a rather unconventional step for a Supreme Court, its president then wrote to the speaker of parliament to make it clear just what the court's objection had been (Hardarson and Kristinsson, p. 977). In Sweden a body called the Lågradet (Law Council), which is composed of judges from the Supreme Court and the Supreme Administrative Court, may give its advice on proposed legislation. Its opinion as to whether the legislation appears to be in conflict with the constitution is given "considerable weight" by the government and parliament (Board, 1988, p. 183). Indeed, government departments when preparing legislation go to some lengths to anticipate the Law Council's views and to ensure that legislation conforms with them (Holmström, p. 159). Even in Finland, there is active discussion of the idea of judicial review, and there is scope for judicial authorities to signal their attitude to proposed legislation.

✦ THE APPOINTMENT OF JUDGES

Given that judges in most European countries have significant power to constrain political actors, we need to know who appoints judges. The potential for interaction between the judiciary, the executive, and the legislature is seen clearly in this area. Although, as we would expect, practice varies from country to country, the appointment of judges is politically controlled in most countries. We look first at appointments to constitutional courts and then at the appointment of "ordinary" judges.

Constitutional Courts

Members of constitutional courts are appointed mainly by political authorities, but the spirit in which this power of appointment is exercised varies. The most common pattern is that parliament appoints some or all of the members but such appointments need a supermajority (such as 60 percent), which ensures that each of the main parties receives its proportionate share of appointments. In Germany, care is taken to balance the nominees not only among the parties but also among the Länder. In most countries, members need strong legal credentials, such as those required to become a regular judge, and many appointees are legal academics. One upshot of major party control of the nomination process is that the political views of the appointees will not be too far from the center of the political spectrum.

The main exception to this is France, where the right to appoint members of the Constitutional Council is seen as a perk of office and is monopolized by the party or parties that control the levers of power. The Constitutional Council contains nine members, each of whom serves a nine-year term. The president of France, the president of the lower house of parliament (the National Assembly), and the president of the Senate each appoint one member every three years. There are no formal legal or other qualifications for membership of the Council, and most of those appointed are former deputies or ministers, albeit in most cases with a legal background. Not surprisingly, this can lead to the Council's decisions being interpreted in partisan terms, though it also gives it "a fine-tuned political sensitivity" (Ponthoreau and Ziller, p. 127). Because the turnover of members of the Council can be slower than the turnover of governments, a new government is liable to be faced with a council dominated by appointees of its political opponents (Elgie, p. 181).

The Court System

In most countries, the government of the day has a major role in deciding on the appointment and promotion of judges, and judges can be removed from office by a majority vote in parliament. The growing interaction between the courts and politics in appointments, and other areas, is illustrated for a variety of countries by Sturgess and Chubb (pp. 122–51). However, this interaction itself does not necessarily lead to a politically biased judiciary. Even if governments do use their role in the appointment and promotion process to favor men and women of their own outlook, they are realistic enough to know that judges cannot be kept on a political leash. In some countries, notably in Scandinavia, the political culture militates strongly against any attempt to politicize the judiciary. In Sweden, for example, there is "a long and deeply engrained tradition of an independent judiciary, insulated from the pressures and vicissitudes of partisan party politics" (Board, 1988, p. 186). In Ireland, as we have said, the Supreme Court is the final arbiter on constitutional matters, as in the United States, and appointment to this body is entirely in the hands of the government of the day, although judges need to have demonstrable legal expertise. It is accepted that all governments favor lawyers of their own political persuasion when making judicial appointments, though, equally, it is generally felt that once judges are appointed they sever their political connections and behave without regard to their former allegiance.

Moreover, the option of dismissing a judge who has given decisions inconvenient to the government of the day, though legally possible, is usually politically unthinkable, for it would be regarded as unjustified interference with the judicial process by the public in most, if not all, European countries. For example, although the two houses of parliament in Britain (the House of Commons and the House of Lords) can dismiss a judge, no judge has been dismissed since early in the nineteenth century.

In Britain, party patronage in judicial appointments is felt to have died out by the end of the Second World War. In France, though, Shapiro suggests that "judges who wish to succeed professionally are likely to give the regime the kinds of decisions it wants even though the politicians apply no direct pressure" (Shapiro, *Courts,* p. 156). Belgian courts, perhaps partly because prior to 1991 appointments to the judiciary were made mainly on a political basis, have been described as "eager to reflect in their decisions mainstream opinion or contemporary legislative policy" (Verougstraete, p. 106). Courts in Greece are also widely believed, rightly or wrongly, to take account of the wishes of the government of the day when reaching decisions in cases with political overtones.

Perhaps the most overtly politicized judges are to be found in Italy—ironically, the country where judges have perhaps a higher degree of formal independence from government than anywhere else. For many years there were four political factions (*correnti*) in the judiciary—two on the left and two on the right—which in the 1980s were associated with the main Italian parties. Even though some of the parties to which they were linked disappeared, the *correnti* continued in existence, playing a decisive role in promotions within the judiciary (della Porta; Guarnieri, p. 163). Judges and magistrates belonging to the left-wing current bestow on themselves the power of judicial review; and without referring the matter to the only body qualified to judge (the Constitutional Court), they refrain from applying legal norms that they claim to be in conflict with the constitution, or they develop new constitutional "rights" themselves (di Federico and Guarnieri, pp. 175–77). All the Italian parties attempt to build up a pool of sympathetic judges by offering inducements, such as seats in parliament or well-paid positions on commissions, and the partisan ties and loyalties of investigating magistrates are "perceived as motivating or thwarting criminal investigations" (Volcansek, "Judicial," p. 127). In an attempt to "extract a more benevolent attitude" from the judiciary, Italian governments have readily met the demands of magistrates, who as a result have become the highest-paid members of the state sector and are automatically promoted to the top of their scale regardless of performance (Guarnieri, pp. 159–60; di Federico and Guarnieri, p. 179).

Magistrates may have their own political goals to achieve as well as, or instead of, purely financial goals. The term "assault judges" has been coined for judges and magistrates who use their positions to "tackle what they see as problems, which may be a person, an institution or a condition" (Volcansek, "Judicial," p. 126) and as a result often receive widespread publicity. In the mid-1990s the unearthing of the massive Tangentopoli (Bribesville) scandal, which entailed numerous links between politicians and organized crime, was initiated by magistrates from Milan, who achieved nationwide prominence. Some identified a new relationship of shared interests between judges and the media, with the growth of a media-friendly "judicial populism" (Guarnieri and Pederzoli, p. 190). The political vacuum that followed was filled by politicians, such as Silvio Berlusconi, who capitalized on the public's revulsion at the corruption of the established political class, but once in power Berlusconi himself was frequently indicted by the judiciary for alleged corruption, which he attributed to a "political conspiracy" against him by "red judges" (della Porta, pp. 11, 19).

In the 1990s, there were signs that the Spanish judiciary was starting to develop along similar lines. Politically aligned associations emerged among the judges and magistrates; some members of the judiciary readily sought to rectify what they saw as shortcomings in the political system; and there was an increasing backlog of cases due to a certain lack of efficiency in the judicial system (Heywood, pp. 117–20; Newton, p. 303).

✧ JUDGES AND LAWMAKING

Under all legal systems judges apply the law, but under some legal systems judges can also make the law. When we look at the role of the courts in making law in various countries, it is useful to adopt the conventional distinction between two general types of legal systems: the common law tradition and the civil law tradition. This distinction is less clear-cut in reality than in theory, but it is still useful for understanding the different approaches to the role of the courts across Europe. Common law systems are confined to Britain and English-speaking former British colonies. Within Europe, only Britain and Ireland are classifiable as common law countries. Outside Europe, examples of common law countries are most of the United States and Canada, as well as Australia and New Zealand. Most European countries belong instead to the civil law tradition, which originated within a continental tradition of "Roman" law that has now been transformed into a comprehensive system of legal codes. Codified legal systems of one form or another prevail in all European states other than Britain and Ireland; more generally, this group includes many former continental European colonies including Louisiana, much of Latin America, and parts of Canada.

The fundamental difference between the two is that common law systems rely less on "laws," seen as acts of parliament, and more on "the law," seen as the accumulated weight of precedent set by the decisions, definitions, and interpretations made by judges. Central to the common law tradition is the principle of *stare decisis* (let the decision stand)—in other words, a judge considers himself or herself bound by judgments in previous essentially similar cases. Many key legal principles and rules are thus established not in statutes made by the legislature but in judgments made by the judiciary. In a British, Irish, or American court, a precedent, if it applies to the case in question, *is* the law. Judges do not merely apply in a mechanistic way the laws made by parliament; they actually play a part in making the laws, by pronouncing judgments that will be drawn on by other judges when interpreting the law. The common law approach is to resolve specific disputes in a "pragmatic and improvisatory way," and statutes, particularly in England, are passed partly to build on or classify existing case law (de Cruz, p. 105).

The essential feature of a codified legal system, in contrast, is that the ultimate foundation of the law is a comprehensive and authoritative legal code. On this foundation is built a superstructure of statutes enacted by the legislature. Every legal decision, in principle, can be deduced from the legal code and subsequent enacted statutes. No reference need be made to any existing body of case law. The first and most influential of the modern legal codes is the Napoleonic Code, the *Code Napoléon,* which emerged as a part of the new order after the French Revolution. The five basic codes on which all of French law still rests are the Civil Code (1804), the Code of Civil Procedure (1806), the Code of Commerce (1808), the Code of Criminal Procedure (1811), and the Penal Code (1811). Subsequent legislation has built extensively on these, although changes have often been incorporated as amendments into the original codes. The influence of the *Code Napoléon* can be clearly seen in the legal systems of Belgium, Luxembourg, the Netherlands, Italy, Spain, and Portugal. The second major source of codified European law is the German Civil Code of 1900. Besides Germany, the five Scandinavian countries—Norway, Sweden, Denmark, Finland, and Iceland—are usually identified, for historical and cultural reasons, with this tradition. Differences between the German and French traditions are minor compared with the difference between all codified continental traditions on the one hand and the Anglo-American system of common law on the other.

In civil law countries, then, judges do not in any sense "make" law; they merely apply the law made by parliaments. Judges in France are expressly forbidden by the Civil Code from going beyond the case at hand to lay down general rules amounting to a regulation. Judges are mere legal technicians, whose decisions could in theory be made equally well by a computer into which the appropriate rules and the facts of the specific case had been fed. Because of this, judges typically have a lower standing (often significantly lower than that of law professors) than their counterparts in common law countries, where judges are usually appointed from the ranks of senior lawyers. In civil law countries, law students usually have to choose before the end of their studies whether to become a private lawyer, a prosecutor, or a judge (Holland, "Introduction," p. 8), and accordingly judges are sometimes seen as having the attitudes of bureaucrats to a much greater degree than common law judges, who acquire the outlook of the law profession in their country rather than that of the permanent civil servants. In Sweden, for example, judges "tend to see themselves as administrators"; both careers are in the bureaucracy, and there is some interchangeability between judges and administrators (Board, "Judicial," p. 185).

The role of the judiciary (and of parliament) can be expected to vary between civil law and common law countries. In civil law countries, the judiciary is, at least in theory, much less important than parliament—it merely applies the law made by the legislators. Moreover, in France, for example, and in many other continental European systems, parliamentary debates, committee reports, and other public pronouncements that are related to the passing of the legislation—the *travaux préparatoires* (preparatory works), as they are usually called—may be used as sources of a legal opinion as to what parliament had in mind when it passed a law. This is typically ruled out in a common law system such as that of Britain, in which the sum total of the work of the legislature is the text of the laws that it enacts. In common law countries, therefore, the potential for conflict between legislature and judiciary can be expected to be greater, because when judges can "make" law, the law that they make might not coincide with the preferences of legislators.

Having outlined this clear distinction between the civil law tradition and the common law tradition, we must say that there is general agreement that the lines between the two are rapidly becoming blurred. In the words of Peter de Cruz, "recent trends have indicated that the common law and civil law systems have been coming closer together in their use of cases and statutes" (de Cruz, p. 36). In Britain and Ireland, law is increasingly based on statute; the volume of legislation has expanded, and, in cases where precedent and statute point to different decisions, judges are obliged to give priority to statute. Moreover, it is not unknown for the courts in Britain to consult parliamentary debates to clarify the meaning of particular pieces of legislation (Oliver). In civil law countries, precedent is of increasing significance. Indeed, it is arguable that it always was important, and that its absence from judges' written decisions gives a misleading impression. Martin Shapiro observes that the French legal code, for example, does not really consist of detailed rules that provide the answer to every case; rather, it consists of principles that the judges must interpret. When doing this, the judge "is acknowledging the body of legal doctrine built up around the bare words of the code by previous cases"— in other words, is following precedent (Shapiro, *Courts,* pp. 134–35; Stone Sweet, *Governing,* p. 146). Although *stare decisis* is not officially recognized, hundreds of volumes of case reports are published, and lawyers in France and in other civil law countries cite precedents in their arguments in court just as British or American lawyers do (Shapiro, *Courts,* p. 147; de Cruz, p. 67). In Italy, judges are expected to take account of decisions in previous cases, and "it seems doubtful that judicial precedents are de facto less binding in the Italian judicial process than in countries where judges are formally bound by judicial precedents" (di Federico and Guarnieri, p. 175). Similarly, in Sweden judges "have always deferred somewhat to precedent, and in recent years the tendency appears to be growing" (Board, "Courts," p. 185). In the Netherlands, too, since 1919 the courts have increasingly become interpreters of the law rather than mere appliers of it, partly because parliament has been inclined to include in statutes "vague norms" that leave considerable discretion to the judges. In areas such as euthanasia and abortion, the Supreme Court has in effect produced case law where parliament was unable to pass detailed legislation (ten Kate and van Koppen, pp. 146–47; van Koppen, pp. 84–85).

Judges, then, can to some extent make law in both common law and civil law countries, and thus they can be important actors in the process of policy making. When they are required to make decisions in cases in which political parties or pressure groups have an interest, they are, whether they like it or not, part of the political process. Although judges might like to maintain that they merely hand down an impartial decision based on the application of the relevant law or precedent, it is unrealistic to imagine that the political and personal outlooks of the judges themselves play no part in determining the decisions they make. As Benjamin Cardozo, member of the U.S. Supreme Court from 1932 to 1938, put it: "The great tides and currents which engulf the rest of men do not turn aside in their course and pass the judges idly by" (quoted in Abraham, p. 357).

All of this goes to show that the judiciary can have a significant role in politics when it comes to applying and interpreting laws. In common law countries, judges can play a part in "making" the laws by delivering judgments that then become precedents to be drawn on by subsequent judges. Even in civil law countries, judges can—indeed, must—exercise more discretion than is acknowledged in some accounts that portray judges in civil law jurisdictions as mere appliers of unambiguous statutes and codes. In most countries—Italy is the most notable exception—the judiciary is not explicitly politicized, and judges are generally seen as "nonpolitical" or "above politics," but realists accept that the personal and political views of judges will have some bearing on the judgments they deliver, in both common and civil law jurisdictions.

✢ CONCLUSION: JUDGES AND REPRESENTATIVE GOVERNMENT

The courts in many European countries have increasingly found themselves compelled, or presented with the opportunity, to make decisions on the legality or constitutionality of the actions of political authorities. Pressure groups and individuals perceiving a threat to their rights or interests have turned with growing frequency to the courts for redress. Dedicated constitutional courts such as those in Germany and Italy must be counted among the political actors of those countries, in the sense that they have the power to constrain and even direct government and parliament, as must the Constitutional Council in France and the Supreme Court of Ireland. Even where courts cannot or do not strike down legislation as unconstitutional, as in Britain and the Netherlands, close examination reveals that the judiciary is not as passive and irrelevant to decision making as some used to assume.

On the one hand, many consider this a welcome development. Parliaments, as we saw in Chapter 3, usually seem unable to impose a meaningful check on governments, because they are dominated by the same political parties that are in government. If parliaments cannot control government, perhaps courts can. Government ministers in most European countries are not kept awake at nights wondering whether or not parliament will approve a bill they have drawn up. Many ministers, however, clearly do worry about whether the courts will approve their plans, and they go to some lengths to ensure that their schemes will meet with the approval of the judicial authorities. This can be seen as a good thing, on the grounds that there are rights so fundamental that not even a majority can ride roughshod over them and the courts and the constitution provide a necessary check on the exercise of power by governments. A more pragmatic defense of judicial power is that the judiciary prevents government policy in certain areas from drifting too far from the middle of the road. This has been especially apparent in France since the early 1980s, where governments of both left and right have had their wings clipped by the Constitutional Council.

On the other hand, opponents of the growing power of the judiciary make the point that it contradicts the very notion of representative government. Judicial review, according to its critics, entails giving power to a handful of unelected, unaccountable, and unrepresentative individuals to override the wishes of those who were elected by the people and on whom the people will be able to pass judgment at the next election. Judges may be informally accountable to others—such as legal scholars, their peers, and to some extent the mass media, all of whom may call attention to unexpected or politically relevant behavior—but they are not formally accountable in the way that elected politicians are. Shapiro compares judges to "junkyard dogs," ferocious beasts that patrol their allotted territory as they see fit and are out of anyone's control, even those who put them in place. Although it is usually ne'er-do-wells who feel the sharp edge of their teeth, they will inevitably bite the wrong person from time to time (Shapiro and Stone Sweet, pp. 163–64). Another writer, commenting on the argument that constitutions are a valuable precommitment device, suggests that "the dangers of a ... dogmatic constitutional court may be worse than the opportunistic behavior [that it is] set up to prevent" (Elster, p. 174). Courts and judges may be an essential check on the behavior of governments and parliaments—but who checks the judges? Opponents are also unconvinced by the argument that judicial review ensures that government policies do not drift too far from the center of the political spectrum: If the people want a radical break with centrism, should a handful of unelected figures in the judiciary be able to prevent it?

Judges, the members of France's Constitutional Council apart, are very rarely seen to be acting for blatantly partisan political motives. However, they *are* frequently seen as policy-driven power maximizers, and phrases such as "the rise of the political judge" are commonplace (for example, Guarnieri and Pederzoli, p. 4). In a number of countries their technique for increasing their power has been the same: They are "past masters at awarding immediate victory in a particular case to one party while planting doctrinal seeds that will eventually favor the other." The politicians who potentially oppose judges have horizons that are more short-term than those of the judges, so they do not try to tear up the seeds because all that matters is that they have won the immediate victory—but in the long term the seeds sprout (Shapiro, "Success," p. 212). The policies that judges seek to promote or thwart vary from country to country. In Britain and Germany they are usually accused of being too conservative; in Italy they have been accused of being too left-wing; in Ireland they have been criticized for too often placing the interests of the individual above those of the community. We would like to know more about how far judges' values affect their judgments, of course, but this is very difficult to find out because, in contrast to the U.S. Supreme Court, European constitutional courts typically give just one collective judgment, and the opinions of individual judges are not disclosed.

Quite clearly, arguments about the wisdom or otherwise of judicial review, which have been animatedly discussed in the United States for the last two centuries, will never be definitively resolved. Systematic data on the opinions of the European public on the issue of judicial power are lacking, though we may note that observers from a range of countries do not detect any popular resentment at the growing influence of the courts; indeed, in some countries the judicial authorities are more highly regarded than parliaments or political parties, the archetypal actors of representative government. What is certain is that the impact of the judiciary on politics in Europe has been growing steadily in recent years, and no account of European governance can neglect the role of courts and constitutions.

REFERENCES

Abraham, Henry J.: *The Judicial Process: An Introductory Analysis of the Courts of the United States, England and France,* 7th ed., Oxford University Press, New York and Oxford, 1998.

Bell, John: *French Constitutional Law,* Clarendon Press, Oxford, 1992.

Bellamy, Richard (ed.): *Constitutionalism, Democracy and Sovereignty: American and European Perspectives,* Avebury, Aldershot, 1996.

Beyme, Klaus von: "The German Constitutional Court in an Uneasy Triangle Between Parliament, Government and the Federal Laender," in Sadurski (ed.), pp. 101–18.

Board, Joseph B.: "The Courts in Sweden," in Waltman and Holland (eds.), pp. 181–98.

Board, Joseph B.: "Judicial Activism in Sweden," in Holland (ed.), pp. 175–88.

Bogdanor, Vernon: "Conclusion," in Vernon Bogdanor (ed.), *Constitutions in Democratic Politics.* Gower, Aldershot, 1988, pp. 380–86.

Brewer-Carías, Allan R.: *Judicial Review in Comparative Law,* Cambridge University Press, Cambridge and New York, 1989.

Budge, Ian, Ivor Crewe, David McKay, and Ken Newton: *The New British Politics,* 3rd ed., Pearson Education, Harlow, 2004.

Carcassonne, Guy: "The Constraints on Constitutional Change in France," in Hesse and Johnson (eds.), pp. 152–77.

Casey, James: *Constitutional Law in Ireland,* 3rd ed., Round Hall, Sweet and Maxwell, Dublin, 2000.

Cerar, Miro: "Slovenia: From Elite Consensus to Democratic Consolidation," in Zielonka (ed.), pp. 378–405.

Conradt, David P.: *The German Polity,* 7th ed., Addison-Wesley Longman, New York, 2001.

Damgaard, Erik: "Developments in Danish Parliamentary Democracy: Accountability, Parties and External Constraints," *Scandinavian Political Studies,* vol. 27, no. 2, 2004, pp. 115–31.

de Cruz, Peter: *Comparative Law in a Changing World,* Cavendish, London, 1995.

de Franciscis, Maria Elisabetta, and Rosella Zannini: "Judicial Policy-Making in Italy," in Volcansek (ed.), pp. 68–79.

della Porta, Donatella: "A Judges' Revolution: Political Corruption and the Judiciary in Italy," *European Journal of Political Research,* vol. 39, no. 1, 2001, pp. 1–21.

di Federico, Giuseppe, and Carlo Guarnieri: "The Courts in Italy," in Waltman and Holland (eds.), pp. 153–80.

Elgie, Robert: *Political Institutions in Contemporary France,* Oxford University Press, Oxford and New York, 2003.

Elster, Jon: *Ulysses Unbound: Studies in Rationality, Precommitment, and Constraints,* Cambridge University Press, Cambridge, 2000.

Finer, S. E., Vernon Bogdanor, and Bernard Rudden (eds.): *Comparing Constitutions,* Clarendon Press, Oxford, 1995.

Flinders, Matthew: "Mechanisms of Judicial Accountability in British Central Government," *Parliamentary Affairs,* vol. 54, no. 1, 2001, pp. 54–71.

Gallagher, Michael: "The Constitution and the Judiciary," in John Coakley and Michael Gallagher (eds.), *Politics in the Republic of Ireland,* 4th ed., Routledge and PSAI Press, Abingdon, 2005, pp. 73–101.

Garlicki, Leszek Lech: "The Experience of the Polish Constitutional Court," in Sadurski (ed.), pp. 265–82.

Gelazis, Nida: "Defending Order and Freedom: The Lithuanian Constitutional Court in its First Decade," in Sadurski (ed.), pp. 395–408.

Gelazis, Nida: "Institutional Engineering in Lithuania: Stability Through Compromise," in Zielonka (ed.), pp. 165–85.

Gibson, James L., Gregory A. Caldeira, and Vanessa A. Baird: "On the Legitimacy of National High Courts," *American Political Science Review,* vol. 92, no. 2, 1998, pp. 343–58.

Gordon, Richard: *Judicial Review: Law and Procedure,* Sweet and Maxwell, London, 1996.

Greenberg, Douglas, Stanley N. Katz, Melanie Beth Oliviero, and Steven C. Wheatley (eds.): *Constitutionalism and Democracy: Transitions in the Contemporary World,* Oxford University Press, New York and Oxford, 1993.

Guarnieri, Carlo: "The Judiciary in the Italian Political Crisis," *West European Politics,* vol. 20, no. 1, 1997, pp. 157–75.

Guarnieri, Carlo, and Patrizia Pederzoli: *The Power of Judges: A Comparative Study of Courts and Democracy,* Oxford University Press, Oxford and New York, 2002.

Halmai, Gábor: "The Hungarian Approach to Constitutional Review: The End of Activism? The First Decade of the Hungarian Constitutional Court," in Sadurski (ed.), pp. 189–211.

Hardarson, Ólafur Th., and Gunnar Helgi Kristinsson: "Iceland," *European Journal of Political Research,* vol. 41, nos. 7–8, 2002, pp. 975–77.

Helms, Ludger: "The Federal Constitutional Court: Institutionalising Judicial Review in a Semisovereign Democracy," in Ludger Helms (ed.), *Institutions and Institutional Change in the Federal Republic of Germany,* Macmillan, Basingstoke, 2000, pp. 84–104.

Hesse, Joachim Jens, and Nevil Johnson (eds.): *Constitutional Policy and Change in Europe,* Oxford University Press, Oxford and New York, 1995.

Heywood, Paul: *The Government and Politics of Spain,* Macmillan, Basingstoke, 1995.

Hogan, Gerard, and Gerry Whyte: *J. M. Kelly: The Irish Constitution,* 4th ed., LexisNexis Butterworths, Dublin, 2003.

Holland, Kenneth M.: "Introduction," in Holland (ed.), pp. 1–11.

Holland, Kenneth M. (ed.): *Judicial Activism in Comparative Perspective,* Macmillan, Basingstoke, 1991.

Holmes, Stephen: "Pre-Commitment and the Paradox of Democracy," in Jon Elster and Rune Slagstad (eds.), *Constitutionalism and Democracy,* Cambridge University Press, Cambridge, 1988, pp. 195–240.

Holmström, Barry: "The Judicialization of Politics in Sweden," *International Political Science Review,* vol. 15, no. 2, 1994, pp. 153–64.

Institute for Public Policy Research: *A Written Constitution for the United Kingdom,* Mansell, London, 1995.

Jacob, Herbert, et al.: *Courts, Law, and Politics in Comparative Perspective,* Yale University Press, New Haven and London, 1996.

Johnson, Nevil: "Constitutionalism in Europe Since 1945: Reconstruction and Reappraisal," in Greenberg et al. (eds.), pp. 26–45.

Johnson, Nevil: "The Judicial Dimension in British Politics," *West European Politics,* vol. 21, no. 1, 1998, pp. 148–66.

Kenney, Sally J., William M. Reisinger, and John C. Reitz (eds.): *Constitutional Dialogues in Comparative Perspective,* Macmillan, Basingstoke, 1999.

King, Anthony: *Does the United Kingdom Still Have a Constitution?* Sweet and Maxwell, London, 2001.

Kingdom, John: *Government and Politics in Britain: An Introduction,* 3rd ed., Polity Press, Cambridge, 2003.

Knapp, Andrew, and Vincent Wright: *The Government and Politics of France,* 4th ed., Routledge, London and New York, 2001.

Kommers, Donald P.: *The Constitutional Jurisprudence of the Federal Republic of Germany,* 2nd ed., Duke University Press, Durham (NC) and London, 1997.

Kommers, Donald P.: "The Federal Constitutional Court in the German Political System," *Comparative Political Studies,* vol. 26, no. 4, 1994, pp. 470–91.

Körösényi, András: *Government and Politics in Hungary,* Central European University Press, Budapest, 1999.

Kristjánsson, Svanur: "Iceland: Searching for Democracy Along Three Dimensions of Citizen Control," *Scandinavian Political Studies,* vol. 27, no. 2, 2004, pp. 153–74.

Kritzer, Herbert M.: "Courts, Justice, and Politics in England," in Jacob et al., pp. 81–176.

Landfried, Christine: "The Judicialization of Politics in Germany," *International Political Science Review,* vol. 15, no. 2, 1994, pp. 113–24.

Malová, Darina, and Tim Haughton: "Making Institutions in Central and Eastern Europe, and the Impact of Europe," *West European Politics,* vol. 25, no. 2, 2002, pp. 101–20.

Morel, Laurence: "France: Towards a Less Controversial Use of the Referendum?" in Michael Gallagher and Pier Vincenzo Uleri (eds.), *The Referendum Experience in Europe,* Macmillan, Basingstoke, 1996, pp. 66–85.

Murphy, Walter: "Constitutions, Constitutionalism, and Democracy," in Greenberg et al. (eds.), pp. 3–25.

Narud, Hanne Marthe, and Kaare Strøm: "Norway: Madisonianism Reborn," *Scandinavian Political Studies,* vol. 27, no. 2, 2004, pp. 175–201.

Newton, Michael T.: *Institutions of Modern Spain: A Political and Economic Guide,* Cambridge University Press, Cambridge, 1997.

Norton, Philip: *The Constitution in Flux,* Martin Robertson, Oxford, 1982.

Oliver, Dawn: "Pepper v. Hart: A Suitable Case for Reference to Hansard?" *Public Law,* Spring 1993, pp. 5–13.

Ponthoreau, Marie-Claire, and Jacques Ziller: "The Experience of the French Conseil Constitutionnel: Political and Social Context and Current Legal–Theoretical Debates," in Sadurski (ed.), pp. 119–42.

Preuss, Ulrich K.: "The Political Meaning of Constitutionalism," in Bellamy (ed.), pp. 11–27.

Pribán, Jiri: "Judicial Power vs. Democratic Representation: The Culture of Constitutionalism and Human Rights in the Czech Legal System," in Sadurski (ed.), pp. 373–94.

Prince, Sue: "The Law and Politics: Upsetting the Judicial Apple-Cart," *Parliamentary Affairs,* vol. 57, no. 2, 2004, pp. 288–300.

Provine, Doris Marie: "Courts in the Political Process in France," in Jacob et al., pp. 177–248.

Rolla, Giancarlo, and Tania Groppi: "Between Politics and the Law: The Development of Constitutional Review in Italy," in Sadurski (ed.), pp. 143–59.

Rothmayr, Christine: "Towards the Judicialisation of Swiss Politics?" *West European Politics,* vol. 24, no. 2, 2001, pp. 77–94.

Sadurski, Wojciech (ed.): *Constitutional Justice, East and West: Democratic Legitimacy and Constitutional Courts in Post-Communist Europe in a Comparative Perspective,* Kluwer Law International, The Hague, 2002.

Sanford, George: *Democratic Government in Poland: Constitutional Politics Since 1989,* Palgrave Macmillan, Basingstoke, 2002.

Sartori, Giovanni: "Constitutionalism: A Preliminary Discussion," *American Political Science Review,* vol. 56, no. 4, 1962, pp. 853–64.

Scheltma, Michiel: "Constitutional Development in the Netherlands: Towards a Weaker Parliament and Stronger Courts," in Hesse and Johnson (eds.), pp. 200–13.

Schmidt, Manfred G.: *Political Institutions in the Federal Republic of Germany,* Oxford University Press, Oxford and New York, 2003.

Seitzer, Jeffrey: "Experimental Constitutionalism: A Comparative Analysis of the Institutional Bases of Rights Enforcement in Post-Communist Hungary," in Kenney, Reisinger, and Reitz (eds.), pp. 42–61.

Shapiro, Martin: *Courts: A Comparative and Political Analysis,* University of Chicago Press, Chicago and London, 1981.

Shapiro, Martin: "The Success of Judicial Review," in Kenney, Reisinger, and Reitz (eds.), pp. 193–219.

Shapiro, Martin, and Alec Stone Sweet: *On Law, Politics, and Judicialization,* Oxford University Press, Oxford and New York, 2002.

Stone Sweet, Alec: *The Birth of Judicial Politics in France: The Constitutional Council in Comparative Perspective,* Oxford University Press, New York and Oxford, 1992.

Stone Sweet, Alec: *Governing with Judges: Constitutional Politics in Europe,* Oxford University Press, Oxford and New York, 2000.

Sturgess, Garry, and Philip Chubb: *Judging the World: Law and Politics in the World's Leading Courts,* Butterworths, Sydney, 1988.

Suksi, Markku: *Bringing in the People: A Comparison of the Constitutional Forms and Practices of the Referendum,* Martinus Nijhoff, Dordrecht, 1993.

Sunstein, Cass R.: *Designing Democracy: What Constitutions Do,* Oxford University Press, Oxford and New York, 2001.

Tate, C. Neal, and Torbjörn Vallinder (eds.): *The Global Expansion of Judicial Power,* New York University Press, New York, 1995.

ten Kate, Jan, and Peter J. van Koppen: "Judicialization of Politics in the Netherlands: Towards a Form of Judicial Review," *International Political Science Review,* vol. 15, no. 2, 1994, pp. 143–51.

Vanberg, Georg: "Abstract Judicial Review, Legislative Bargaining, and Policy Compromise," *Journal of Theoretical Politics,* vol. 10, no. 3, 1998, pp. 299–326.

Vanberg, Georg: "Legislative–Judicial Relations: A Game-Theoretic Approach to Constitutional Review," *American Journal of Political Science,* vol. 45, no. 2, 2001, pp. 346–61.

van Koppen, Peter J.: "Judicial Policy-Making in the Netherlands: The Case-by-Case Method," in Volcansek (ed.), pp. 80–92.

Verougstraete, Ivan: "Judicial Politics in Belgium," in Volcansek (ed.), pp. 93–108.

Volcansek, Mary L.: *Constitutional Politics in Italy: The Constitutional Court,* Macmillan, Basingstoke, 2000.

Volcansek, Mary L: "Judicial Activism in Italy," in Holland (ed.), pp. 117–32.

Volcansek, Mary L. (ed.): *Judicial Politics and Policy-Making in Western Europe,* Frank Cass, London, 1992.

Waltman, Jerold L., and Kenneth M. Holland (eds.): *The Political Role of Law Courts in Modern Democracies,* Macmillan, Basingstoke, 1988.

Zielonka, Jan (ed.): *Democratic Consolidation in Eastern Europe,* vol. 1, *Institutional Engineering,* Oxford University Press, Oxford and New York, 2001.

CHAPTER 5

꧁

The European Union and Representative Government

In earlier chapters of this book and in Chapters 7 to 14, we focus primarily on the politics of representation in the individual countries of Europe, identifying general patterns and broad trends as well as interesting variations and idiosyncrasies. In this chapter and the next, we turn our attention to other levels of government. In Chapter 6, we examine subnational government, looking at the division of powers within countries among central, regional, and local governments. In this chapter, we look at supranational government as we consider a new development—quite different from anything that has ever taken place in any other part of the world—that in recent years has made European politics even more intriguing than before. We are referring to the moves toward a pooling of sovereignty among many European states that is expressed in their membership in the European Union (the EU). Although some would like the EU to reach the point where it facilitates close and smooth cooperation between the governments of the member countries and then to stop, others hope that the Union is going down a road leading to a federal Europe. In this chapter, we assess the significance of the emergence of the EU as a major factor in politics in contemporary Europe.

First of all, we outline the evolution of the European Union since the dream of European unity began to be taken seriously in the 1940s. We then look at how the EU works and consider whether it has made national governments less important political actors. As in the other chapters of this book, we examine the process whereby interests and preferences are turned into policies, which entails asking who plays what role in the decision-making process and to whom the various actors are accountable. Finally, we attempt to assess the direction of the Union and the chances that a United States of Europe will one day parallel the United States of America.

Before we begin, we need to clear up one matter of terminology that may confuse—namely the distinction between the European Community (EC) and the European Union. The EC has been evolving since the 1950s as an entity with political institutions each of which has defined powers and responsibilities. The European Union, in contrast, came into existence in November 1993. It is envisaged metaphorically as a kind of building (a temple, in the eyes of enthusiasts) resting on three "pillars." One of these pillars is the EC; the other two are cooperation on foreign and security policy (the "second pillar"), and cooperation on judicial and home affairs (the "third pillar"). The EU, then, is a new body, not just another name for the EC or a revamped EC. However, for the sake of simplicity we refer to the body under discussion as the EU throughout, even though, strictly speaking, the EU did not come into existence until 1993.

✦ THE DEVELOPMENT OF EUROPEAN UNITY

Given the record of war between European countries during the first half of the twentieth century and for many centuries before that, the prospect of a united continent might not have seemed bright in the 1940s. However, the very ruthlessness and destructiveness of modern warfare contributed to a conviction among the postwar political elites in a number of countries that such conflict must never again take place on European soil. The causes of World War II were, of course, many and varied, but two of the more obvious were unbridled and sometimes rabid nationalism (manifesting itself both in xenophobia and in the persecution of internal national minorities) and the Versailles Diktat imposed on the vanquished Germany after World War I. However understandable the latter might have been from the viewpoint of the victorious allies, it served merely to fuel German resentment and was eventually seen to have contained the seeds of the 1939–45 war. For this reason, once World War II was over, the politicians of the wartime allies—such as Jean Monnet, a prominent figure in the French Fourth Republic—looked for ways to integrate Germany into the postwar European framework rather than ostracize it. They also looked for structures that would promote cooperation rather than rivalry between the countries of western Europe. The emergence of the "iron curtain" dividing Europe, following the imposition of communist regimes in the Stalinist mold on the reluctant populations of eastern and central European states, heightened a belief in the west that adherence to common democratic political values was something worth preserving.

Despite all of this, the road toward even a partial undermining of the traditional fetish of absolute national sovereignty was long and rocky (for details, see Burgess; Dinan, pp. 9–201). One of the first tangible steps was taken in April 1951 with the signing of the Treaty of Paris, which established the European Coal and Steel Community (ECSC). The treaty came into effect in July 1952. Many countries were invited to take part in the creation of this new body, but in the end only six did so: France, Germany, Italy, and the three Benelux countries (Belgium, the Netherlands, and Luxembourg). By joining the ECSC, member states ceded some of their sovereignty to a supranational body, and this factor was enough to dissuade Britain from joining. Britain's economic significance at that time was such that a number of smaller countries that felt that their fortunes depended on the British market (particularly Ireland and the Scandinavian countries) also remained aloof.

The European Coal and Steel Community worked very satisfactorily from the viewpoint of the member states, and this led to a discussion of the idea of extending the range of policy areas in which countries might agree to combine in similar organizations. In the summer of 1955, the foreign ministers of the six countries met in Messina, Sicily, and decided to work toward the establishment of a customs union that would involve the creation of a common, or single, market embracing all the countries. They invited Britain to join them in this enterprise, but the invitation was declined. The British, while keen on the idea of turning western Europe into a free-trade area, were still suspicious of any supranational political authority with the right to constrain their own government, and they remained unconvinced that their destiny lay primarily with the rest of Europe. The ideas of the six ECSC countries were fleshed out over the next two years, and in March 1957 two Treaties of Rome were signed.

Each of these two treaties established a new Community. The more important and wide-ranging in scope was the Treaty of the European Economic Community (EEC), which laid down policy aims and guidelines concerning the establishment of a common market and the creation of a common policy in areas such as agriculture and transportation. The other treaty was the Euratom Treaty, which dealt with atomic energy and covered matters such as the pooling of resources and research.

As a result, the six countries involved were now members of three different communities: the ECSC, the EEC, and Euratom. Each of the two new communities had its own set of institutions: a quasi-government (termed a Commission), a quasi-parliament (the Assembly), a Council of Ministers, and a Court of Justice. Sensibly, it was decided that only one Assembly and one Court of Justice were needed to serve all three communities. However, the Commission and the Council of Ministers continued to exist in triplicate until the mid-1960s, when the 1965 Merger Treaty, which came into effect in 1967, merged the three sets of institutions into one. Technically, there were still three communities, but after 1967 the body to which the member states belong was generally known as the "European Community" before the European Union was established in 1993. The ECSC, which had been created under a treaty giving it a fifty-year lifespan, ceased to exist in July 2002. The two founding treaties from 1957, together with subsequent treaties and acts amending the original treaties, make up what is in effect the Union's written constitution. Partly because the constitution is therefore scattered among many documents, there is pressure to adopt a new "European constitution," as we discuss later.

Since 1958, the European Union (EU), as we shall henceforth call it, has grown to twenty-five countries (see Table 5.1). There have been four phases of enlargement: a northern enlargement in the 1970s, a southern one in the 1980s, a neutral one in the

TABLE 5.1

Member Countries of the European Union

Country	Year of Joining	Country	Year of Joining
Belgium	1958	Finland	1995
France	1958	Sweden	1995
Germany	1958	Cyprus	2004
Italy	1958	Czech Republic	2004
Luxembourg	1958	Estonia	2004
Netherlands	1958	Hungary	2004
Denmark	1973	Latvia	2004
Ireland	1973	Lithuania	2004
United Kingdom	1973	Malta	2004
Greece	1981	Poland	2004
Portugal	1986	Slovakia	2004
Spain	1986	Slovenia	2004
Austria	1995		

Note: The first six countries were all founding members of the EEC and of Euratom in 1958 and were all already members of the ECSC. The next nine countries joined all three communities upon their respective accessions; the ECSC had ceased to exist by the time the last ten joined. The European Union itself came into existence in November 1993.

1990s, and a predominantly eastern one in the 2000s. The first expansion occurred in 1973, with the accession of Britain, Denmark, and Ireland. Britain, having stood aloof from the integration process in the 1950s, changed its mind in the 1960s, but French president Charles de Gaulle vetoed its admission. Once de Gaulle retired in 1969 the way was open for the membership of Britain, and three smaller countries that were then highly reliant on the British market were also invited. Two of these, Denmark and Ireland, joined along with Britain but the other, Norway, did not; the issue generated a deep division in Norwegian society, culminating in a referendum in which the people voted by a narrow majority against EU entry (Wyller). In the 1980s the Community expanded further to twelve members with the admission of Greece (in 1981) and Portugal and Spain (in 1986); all three countries were emerging from periods of dictatorship and were keen to join both to consolidate their democracy and to reap economic benefits.

In the 1990s, three countries that had maintained a policy of neutrality during the Cold War—Austria, Finland, and Sweden—joined. Norway successfully negotiated terms of entry but, once more, a referendum of its people rejected membership. In contrast to the 1980s entrants, these three new members were all wealthy countries, and in each there was a significant bloc of people, both before and after EU entry, that was fundamentally opposed to EU membership. The largest expansion took place in 2004, when ten countries joined. Eight of these were postcommunist states whose levels of wealth were well below those of the existing members (see Table 1.2); the other two were small and relatively wealthy Mediterranean islands. The economic and environmental problems of many of the 2004 entrants led to some reservations about admitting them, but these feelings were overcome by enlightened self-interest. It was in the economic and security interests of the existing fifteen members to facilitate the development of the postcommunist countries into stable, prosperous democracies, and in addition the EU has always been sensitive to accusations that it is a "rich person's club" and would therefore be uncomfortable about turning away any European democracy that wants to join. All but Cyprus of these countries made the decision by referendum. The size of the yes vote ranged from 54 percent in Malta up to 94 percent in Slovakia (Szczerbiak and Taggart, p. 560).

Enlargement has affected the nature of the EU considerably. The original six members were close to one another geographically and, with the exception of southern Italy, had very similar levels of wealth and economic development. Two languages (French and German) were enough for nearly all informal transactions between members of the political elite. Even if it did not always operate entirely harmoniously, the EU in its original form was much more of a cozy club than its expanded version proved to be. Now that it embraces nearly the whole of Europe, its diversity almost mirrors that of the continent. The process of making decisions is more complex and often more protracted than was the case when there were only six member states, and if the Union still consisted of only these six, it is likely that the process of European integration would have advanced much further than it actually has. There has been a traditional tension between widening the membership of the EU and deepening the level of integration between the member states. As a result, each enlargement of the Union has been accompanied—sooner or later—by treaty reform designed to facilitate improved decision making and to expand the range of policies dealt with at the European level.

The original treaties have been amended over time. The Single European Act of 1987 reformed the Union's decision-making process so as to facilitate the creation of a single market with no trade barriers between member states. This long-standing goal had earlier been thwarted by cumbersome decision-making procedures and by the ability of individual member states to veto proposals that they did not like. In December 1991, in the Dutch city of Maastricht, the Treaty on European Union was agreed (it was formally signed two months later and finally came into operation in November 1993). This treaty formally established the "European Union," further amended decision-making procedures, laid the foundation for monetary union and the creation of the "euro," and formalized member state cooperation in the areas of foreign policy and of justice and home affairs. It was intended that the Amsterdam Treaty of 1997 would agree on the institutional changes necessary for the enlargement of the Union. Although it brought about some streamlining of EU decision making and enhanced the position of the European Parliament, many of the toughest issues—such as voting procedures and the size of the Commission—were not resolved. These issues were taken up again in the difficult negotiations that led to the Nice Treaty agreed in 2000. It established new voting weights for the member states, eliminated national vetoes in several policy areas, agreed to reduce the size of the Commission, and established a procedure whereby some member states would be allowed to integrate even more closely than the Union as a whole. Following its ratification by the member states, it came into operation on February 1, 2003.

Up to that point, these agreements had simply amended the original set of treaties. Following the Nice Treaty, however, it was agreed that a root and branch review of the Union's legal and constitutional underpinnings was necessary, both to make the Union more effective and to make it more understandable to its own citizens. A Constitutional Convention was thus established, bringing together national parliamentarians, government representatives, and members of the European Parliament under the chairmanship of former French president Valéry Giscard d'Estaing. Within eighteen months, this "Convention on the Future of Europe" drew up a draft constitutional treaty that was submitted to national governments and—following some difficult negotiations—emerged as the draft treaty establishing a Constitution for Europe. This treaty was signed by EU governments in Rome on October 29, 2004, and submitted for ratification to the member states with a view to its coming into operation in late 2006. We discuss it further toward the end of this chapter.

✦ HOW THE EUROPEAN UNION WORKS

It is often said that because the EU is a unique body, its system of government cannot be compared with that of a country. However, as Hix (p. 2) observes, the questions that we would ask when trying to ascertain how domestic politics work in any country can also be asked about the EU, and the methods that we might use to tackle these questions can also be applied to the EU. In Chapter 3 we outlined two models of democracy identified by Lijphart—the Westminster-type majoritarian model and the consensus model. Lijphart cites the European Union as an archetypal example of the latter because of the way in which, as we shall see in the course of this chapter, power is diffused among a number of institutions, with none being dominant (Lijphart, pp. 42–47). The EU has four main institutions: the Commission, the European Parliament, the Council, and the Court of Justice. (There are also a number of others, such as the European Central Bank, which oversees the single currency, and the Court of Auditors, which has the role of checking whether the EU's money has been spent as it should have been—see Laffan, "Financial.") Outlining the powers of these institutions is made especially complicated by the fact that the power of each varies somewhat from "pillar" to "pillar." As a broad generalization, we can say that the Commission in particular has more power in policy areas that come under the first pillar (the European Community), while the national governments, acting through the Council, are relatively more powerful over issues arising under the other two pillars (cooperation on foreign and security policy, and cooperation on judicial and home affairs). Consequently, there is sometimes argument about which pillar a particular matter properly belongs with, since this will affect the ability of the national governments to block a Commission proposal.

We now look in more detail at the role played by each of these institutions (for accounts of how the EU works, see Hix; Nugent; Wallace and Wallace). We follow the flow of policies through the EC's decision-making process, from Commission to Parliament to Council. As noted above, there has been extensive amendment of the treaties since the mid-1980s, particularly in the area of decision making. Thus, as a general rule of thumb (and there are many exceptions), the cumulative effect of these amendments has been to create a system in which the Commission proposes legislation and the Council and Parliament jointly amend, pass, or reject that legislation. If the Council and parliament disagree, the fate of the proposals depends on which precise set of rules needs to be used to resolve their disagreement, because different decision-making procedures apply to different policy areas. Where there is a dispute as to which rules should apply, the Court of Justice decides. Once a proposal has been passed, the Commission is responsible for its implementation—either on its own or in partnership with national or local government. In addition, the European Council, which is made up of the heads of government of the member states, has emerged as the most powerful body of all. It is this body that provides the overall political direction of the Union and within which final decisions are made.

The Commission

The Commission looks, at least at first sight, like the "government" of the EU (for the Commission see Peterson, "College"). In reality, it is more of a hybrid between a government and a civil service, as the Council also has a governmental role. The Commission, which is headed by a president, consists of twenty-five members, one from each country, each with a specific policy jurisdiction (or "portfolio"). The formation of a Commission begins with the governments nominating a person as president; they can decide this by qualified majority vote (see details below), but in practice they operate on the basis of unanimity. The need in practice for the nominee to be acceptable to all the governments means that there is a strong chance that he or she will be a lowest-common-denominator choice, with inoffensiveness being a stronger asset than leadership qualities. The European Parliament (EP) can approve or reject this nominee. Assuming it approves him or her, then the governments, in consultation with the president, nominate their commissioners. Once a full team of commissioners has been put together, the entire proposed Commission requires the approval of the Parliament before it can take office.

The Commission president can make a big difference to the development of the EU. He or she is a significant actor, with the right to attend all meetings of the most powerful body in the EU, the European Council, which we discuss later. Under the former French finance minister Jacques Delors (president from 1985 to 1994), some major steps were taken toward integration. His successor Jacques Santer (1995–99), a former Luxembourg prime minister, was not the first choice of most heads of government and proved rather ineffective. Romano Prodi, his successor, started with the advantage of being a political heavyweight, as a former Italian prime minister. Prodi was able to be more assertive than his predecessors about the composition of his Commission, strengthened by the additional powers conferred on the president by the Amsterdam Treaty of 1997. In addition, he secured from each commissioner upon appointment an undertaking that if he asked them to resign, they would do so; previous presidents were unable to dismiss individual commissioners whose behavior was tarnishing the entire Commission. Prodi's influence, however, waned as his term proceeded, partly because of his growing reinvolvement in domestic Italian politics. To succeed him, the heads of government chose José Manuel Barroso, the Portuguese prime minister. He was a late compromise choice as president, so his capacity to direct the Union's affairs may be limited. Still, even if the president is not quite the "prime minister of Europe," a phrase used by Walter Hallstein, who was Commission president in the 1960s, he is at least coming to look more like a prime minister of the EU.

The Commission has a five-year term in office and is based in the "European quarter" in the eastern part of Brussels, the capital of Belgium. Most commissioners are former senior politicians in their home countries (MacMullen). The members of any one Commission are likely to have different party backgrounds, reflecting the compositions of the governments that nominate them. Commissioners also vary in ability. Some are chosen as the person who seems likely to be able to achieve most, either for the country or for the EU as a whole. The appointment of others results from political deals done between parties in the member states, or to free up a key position in government and thus allow a government "reshuffle" to take place. In some cases the appointment of a commissioner is used to get rid of a politician "who cannot be tolerated at home for one reason or another" (Peterson, "European," p. 562).

Once the commissioners have been nominated, the president decides which commissioner should be given which portfolio. This is a key power, one that gives the president considerable leverage over national governments when it comes to their choice of nominee. Member governments often lobby vigorously to get "their" commissioner assigned to a significant position, but such lobbying is less effective than it once was, as illustrated by the relatively junior portfolios given by Barroso in 2004 to the commissioners of some major member states. The portfolios, which more or less correspond to ministries in domestic government, include economic and financial affairs, agriculture, external economic affairs, industrial affairs, social affairs and employment, environment, regional policy, and so on. Each commissioner-designate appears before a European Parliament committee to be questioned, and finally the Commission as a whole must receive a vote of approval from the European Parliament before it can enter office. The significance of this power was illustrated forcefully in October 2004 when it became clear that the EP would reject the proposed Commission put together by Barroso because he refused to reconsider his nomination to the Justice portfolio of Rocco Buttiglione, an Italian politician whose conservative Catholic views (he described homosexuality as a "sin," for example) made him unacceptable to a majority of members of the European

Parliament (MEPs). Barroso had to withdraw his proposed Commission from the firing line and put together a new one, which did not contain either Buttiglione or several other members of the original team. This was finally approved by the EP in November 2004, nearly a month after the Commission was supposed to have taken office.

Although commissioners are nominated on national lines, they are emphatically not in the Commission to represent national interests—at least in theory. Upon taking office, each commissioner has to take an oath to the effect that he or she will serve the overall interest of the EU and will not take instructions from a national government or from any other body. After all, another Union institution, the Council, exists expressly to safeguard national interests, as we will see. Despite this, it is tacitly accepted that commissioners do not suddenly slough off their national identities the moment they are appointed and become transformed into Euromen or Eurowomen. After all, any commissioner who hopes to be reappointed has an incentive not to alienate the government that has the nomination in its control. This is not to say that any commissioner acts as a government puppet, but undoubtedly governments do expect "their" commissioner to give them advance warning of impending developments and generally to advise them as to how to maximize benefits for the country. In addition, commissioners may also harbor ambitions for a return to national politics in one form or another and so will wish to be seen as having "done their bit" for the country while working in Brussels. A commissioner from, say, Latvia might well receive representations from Latvian interest groups, which are likely to see him or her as "the Latvian commissioner."

The Commission has two main powers. First, it has the primary responsibility for initiating legislation, and it sends a steady stream of proposals and recommendations into the EU's policy-making process, though it usually tests the water first to ensure that its proposals have a realistic chance of being accepted by the other institutions, especially the Council. As a result, the Commission spends a lot of its time consulting and canvassing the twenty-five governments and major interest groups about its ideas. In addition, the Council as a whole, national governments individually, and the Parliament all attempt to use the Commission to push matters forward in areas that are important to them. Although it is true that only the Commission can actually initiate most legislation, in practice it is often heavily lobbied to table or amend draft proposals and may often act more as a mediator and broker between various interests than as a real independent initiator. The question of whether the Commission should be a "principal"—an independent actor with its own agenda—or merely an "agent" of other actors, such as the Council or national governments, was left unspecified from the start, and the issue still divides senior Commission officials (Hooghe, pp. 142–67; Pollack, pp. 75–154).

The Commission's second main responsibility lies in trying to ensure that others in the Union are behaving as they should. When EU legislation is passed, this generally imposes obligations on the twenty-five national governments or parliaments to take action, either by introducing domestic legislation or by implementing a policy. If this is to mean anything, then clearly someone has to check that these obligations are being fulfilled, and the Commission has this role. However, the Commission is grossly understaffed, with only about twenty thousand employees (many of whom are translators), and is unable to monitor Union-wide policy implementation in anything like a comprehensive fashion, so it tends to concentrate on potential major breaches. If it discovers a case where a national government has apparently failed to meet its obligations, it notifies the government and waits a specified period for a formal response. If the government in question is uncooperative, the Commission can ultimately refer the case to the Court of Justice, although this step rarely has to be taken. Partly because of the Commission's limited resources, implementation of Union law is always a major issue, as we explain later in the chapter.

The Commission, then, plays a vital role in providing an overall Union viewpoint on important matters, however attenuated or diluted this may sometimes appear, and in negotiating with and mediating between the other actors in the decision-making process. In addition, the Commission represents the Union externally in important ways: It negotiates trade issues with other international actors, and its president attends the gatherings of the heads of government of the wealthiest nations in the world, known as "G8." However, the Commission is a far cry from the engine of European integration that some would like it to be. It contains a mix of both nationalities and political views—typically containing commissioners from most of the main political tendencies in the EU apart from the extremes of left and right. The fact that the Commission is appointed in a piece-meal fashion by governments of varying political persuasions, as opposed to being made up of party representatives pledged to implement an election manifesto, has sometimes led to its having no overall goal or program of the sort that national governments usually adopt, and Commissions have sometimes seemed to lack a sense of purpose. However, a powerful and dynamic president may be able to avoid this problem by ensuring that the incoming Commission sets out a clear program and works to achieve it.

The European Parliament

The European Parliament has been steadily growing in significance in recent years. It has three main powers, which concern appointment and dismissal of the Commission, legislation, and the budget (for the EP see Hix and Scully; Kreppel).

The power of the Parliament in the appointment of the Commission has existed only since 1993. After each five-yearly EP election, the Parliament is consulted on the appointment of the next Commission president, and then the new Commission as a whole requires approval by a vote in the EP before it can take office. The EP can also dismiss a Commission. Formally, a motion to do this needs to be passed by a two-thirds majority with those voting for the motion amounting to more than half of the total number of members of the European Parliament; politically, though, it is questionable whether a Commission could survive a simple majority vote of no confidence from MEPs. Most fundamental conflicts within the EU tend to see the EP and the Commission ranged on the same side, in favor of greater European integration, with the Council on the other, defending the position of the national governments, and so the EP is unlikely to reach a position of complete disgruntlement with the Commission very often. Events in 1999, however, following evidence that there was mismanagement and corruption within the Commission bureaucracy for which commissioners were not taking appropriate responsibility, showed that this EP power has real substance. In January of that year a motion to dismiss the Commission was defeated by a margin of only 293 to 232 votes, and two months later, as EP dissatisfaction with the Commission continued to rise, the Commission preempted further steps against it by resigning en masse.

The EP's role in the legislative process, the second area where it plays a part, has been steadily expanding and is now significant. Its precise position in the legislative process can vary according to the type of legislation under discussion; its role in most areas is governed by the co-decision (Article 251) or consultation (Article 252) procedure. Under an Article 251 procedure, neither the Council of Ministers nor the European Parliament can overrule the other, and differences over legislative proposals must be resolved in a "Conciliation Committee" to the satisfaction of a majority of members in each institution. In a very few remaining cases the consultation procedure still applies. Here, the Parliament may offer its opinion and propose amendments, but the Council, if it is acting unanimously, can prevail (for details see Nugent, *Government,* pp. 197–203, 337–53; Shackleton). In a few particularly important areas, the "assent procedure" comes into play; in these areas, no change can be made by the EU without the EP's express approval. These areas include the admission of new member states, all major international agreements including association agreements between the EU and other countries, treaty change, and the role of the European Central Bank.

Finally, the EP has a significant role in deciding the EU's budget (for the budgetary procedure see Laffan and Shackleton; Jones, pp. 182–203). The EP is kept informed as the budget is being drafted, and the final outcome represents the result of negotiations between the EP and the Council on the basis of the Commission's proposals. At the final stage, the EP is entitled to make some changes in certain areas of spending. If these changes satisfy it, the president of the Parliament signs the budget into law. If the EP is still not satisfied—in other words, if it would like to make changes greater than those it is allowed to make under the terms of the treaties—then it can reject the entire budget. In order to do this, it needs a two-thirds majority, provided that those voting for rejection constitute a majority of all MEPs. Although this happened several times in the 1980s, since then the EU has committed itself to more medium-term financial planning, so the parameters of the budget are broadly settled well in advance of the detailed preparation, and the scope for disagreement between the various EU institutions is much less than in the past.

Having outlined the Parliament's powers, we turn now to its composition and operation. The Parliament contains 732 members, who come from the member states in approximate proportion to their population, although the smaller states are generously overrepresented in per capita terms—a principle that the EU, with its fondness for jargon, terms "degressive proportionality" (see Table 5.2). Direct elections to the EP have taken place at five-yearly intervals every June since 1979. The elections take place in all countries within a few days of each other; the different dates reflect different national traditions as to the day of the week (usually Thursday or Sunday) on which elections are held. No results are supposed to be released from the early-voting countries until voting is completed in every country, because of a pious belief that voters might be influenced by news of results elsewhere, though there is no evidence that voters have any interest at all in EP results in other countries (or even much interest in their own country's, in many cases). Although the EEC Treaty speaks of a uniform electoral system being used for European Parliament elections, this can happen only if all member governments acting in the Council agree on one and the EP itself approves it. Every country uses some variant of proportional representation (PR) to elect its MEPs, though not necessarily the same one that it uses in domestic elections.

TABLE 5.2

Seats in the European Parliament at the 2004 Election

Country	Population	Seats	Population per MEP	Seat Entitlements if Seats were Strictly Proportionate to Population
Germany	82,424,609	99	832,572	134
France	60,424,213	78	774,669	98
United Kingdom	60,270,708	78	772,701	98
Italy	52,057,477	78	667,403	85
Spain	40,280,780	54	745,940	65
Poland	38,626,349	54	715,303	63
Netherlands	16,318,199	27	604,378	27
Belgium	10,348,276	24	431,178	17
Czech Republic	10,246,178	24	426,924	17
Greece	10,647,529	24	443,647	17
Portugal	10,524,145	24	438,506	17
Hungary	10,032,375	24	418,016	16
Sweden	8,986,400	19	472,968	15
Austria	8,174,762	18	454,153	13
Denmark	5,413,392	14	386,671	9
Slovakia	5,423,567	14	387,398	9
Finland	5,214,512	14	372,465	8
Ireland	3,969,558	13	305,351	6
Lithuania	3,607,899	13	277,531	6
Latvia	2,306,306	9	256,256	4
Slovenia	2,011,473	7	287,353	3
Estonia	1,341,664	6	223,611	2
Cyprus	775,927	6	129,321	1
Luxembourg	462,690	6	77,115	1
Malta	396,851	5	79,370	1
Total	450,285,839	732	615,145	732

Note: Proportional allocation made by the Sainte-Laguë method, which is unbiased in that it does not favor either large or small countries.

Elections to the European Parliament are, in some senses, rather curious affairs. They are impressive in their own way, as the people of twenty-five countries, with a total electorate of over 350 million, turn out at about the same time to elect a genuinely transnational parliament, the only one of its kind in the world. But they are a far cry from being the EU equivalent of general elections at the national level. In general elections, the question of the composition of the next government is uppermost in voters' minds, even if, as we will see in Chapter 12, government formation is sometimes a

TABLE 5.3

Results of European Parliament Elections, June 2004

Country	Seats	Electorate (in millions)	Votes (in millions)	Turnout (%)	EPP-ED	PES	ALDE	Greens/ EFA	EUL/ NGL	Ind-DEM	UEN	NA
Austria	18	6.0	2.6	42.4	6	7	—	2	—	—	—	3
Belgium	24	7.6	6.9	90.8	6	7	6	2	—	—	—	3
Cyprus	6	0.5	0.4	71.2	3	—	1	—	2	—	—	—
Czech Republic	24	8.3	2.3	28.3	14	2	—	—	6	1	—	1
Denmark	14	4.0	1.9	47.9	1	5	4	1	1	1	1	—
Estonia	6	0.9	0.2	26.8	1	3	2	—	—	—	—	—
Finland	14	4.2	1.7	39.4	4	3	5	1	1	—	—	—
France	78	41.6	17.8	42.8	17	31	11	6	3	3	—	7
Germany	99	61.7	26.5	43.0	49	23	7	13	7	—	—	—
Greece	24	9.9	6.3	63.4	11	8	—	—	4	1	—	—
Hungary	24	8.0	3.1	38.5	13	9	2	—	—	—	—	—
Ireland	13	3.1	1.8	58.8	5	1	1	—	1	1	4	—
Italy	78	49.9	35.6	73.1	24	16	12	2	7	4	9	4
Latvia	9	1.4	0.6	41.3	3	—	1	1	—	—	4	—
Lithuania	13	2.7	1.3	48.4	2	2	7	—	—	—	2	—
Luxembourg	6	0.2	0.2	89.0	3	1	1	1	—	—	—	—
Malta	5	0.3	0.3	82.4	2	3	—	—	—	—	—	—
Netherlands	27	12.2	4.8	39.3	7	7	5	4	2	2	—	—
Poland	54	30.0	6.3	20.9	19	8	4	—	—	10	7	6
Portugal	24	8.8	3.4	38.6	9	12	—	—	3	—	—	—
Slovakia	14	4.2	0.7	17.0	8	3	—	—	—	—	—	3
Slovenia	7	1.6	0.5	28.3	4	1	2	—	—	—	—	—
Spain	54	34.7	15.7	45.1	24	24	2	3	1	—	—	—
Sweden	19	6.8	2.6	37.8	5	5	3	1	2	3	—	—
United Kingdom	78	44.2	17.1	38.8	28	19	12	5	1	11	—	2
Total	732	352.7	160.4	45.7	268	200	88	42	41	37	27	29

[a] The political groups are as follows: EPP ED—European People's Party and European Democrats (Christian democrats); PES—Socialists; ALDE—Liberals; Greens EFA—Greens and European Free Alliance; EUL NGL—European United Left and Nordic Green Left; Ind-DEM—Independence-Democracy (the most Eurosceptic, sometimes Europhobic, group); UEN—Union for Europe of the Nations (dominated by parties unenthusiastic about further integration); NA—Nonattached.

Source: www.elections2004.eu.int

complex process not directly brought about by the preferences expressed by voters. But in European Parliament elections, it is often hard to say exactly what is at stake. Certainly, no government is accountable to the EP or will be put together from it. Many voters undoubtedly conclude that in fact nothing much is at stake, and so only a minority actually turn out to vote (see Table 5.3). Turnout in 2004 was below 40 percent in eleven countries and below 30 percent in five of them; it was particularly low in the postcommunist countries, not reaching 50 percent in any. Overall turnout is declining steadily at EP elections, to levels well below the comparable figures for domestic general elections (Blondel et al.). If EP elections are intended to provide popular democratic legitimacy for the EU's decision-making process, they must be adjudged a failure.

This lack of clarity about the real purpose of European Parliament elections arises partly because, despite the theory, they are not fought on the basis of European issues. Indeed, few could say if pressed just what "European issues" really are. It is true that there are pan-EU political groups that correspond quite closely to the party families that we discuss in Chapter 8, the most important of which are the Party of European Socialists and the European People's Party (mainly representing Christian democratic parties), but these are essentially very loose umbrella bodies linking national parties, and the manifestos that they issue at EP elections are very bland and completely indistinguishable from each other (Irwin). EP elections are fought on the ground in each country by national parties rather than by these transnational groups, and the parties stress national issues when campaigning. Although they may be criticized for this "parochial" behavior, the parties are inclined to argue that there is no other way of generating any interest at all among the electorate. The consequence is that the performance of the current national government tends to become the main EP election issue in each individual state. When the EP election falls midway in the domestic electoral cycle, it is seen by voters, the media, and the political parties alike as a midterm test of the national government's popularity, although voters are not necessarily simply passing judgment on their government's record (Franklin; Marsh).

Once the elections have been held, the MEPs sit in the Parliament's chambers in Strasbourg and Brussels according to their political group, not according to the country they represent. The EP operates very much along party lines, like national parliaments throughout Europe. In the Parliament elected in 2004 the two main center–right groups, the EPP and the Liberals, secured nearly half the seats. Even so, the EPP reached an agreement with the Socialists on filling the prestigious position of EP president: For the first half of the parliament's term the office would go to Josep Borrell, a Spanish Socialist member, and in January 2007 he would be succeeded by Hans-Gert Poettering, a German MEP from the EPP group. The MEPs from each national party maintain a separate existence within the EP groups (thus, for example, there is a British Labour group, a French Socialist group, and so on, within the Socialist group, each with its own internal structure). Voting within each of the political groups is fairly solid; the groups are somewhat less cohesive than party groups in most domestic parliaments in Europe but more cohesive than parties in the U.S. Congress (Hix et al., pp. 317–318; Judge and Earnshaw, pp. 146–51; Hix and Lord, pp. 134–36). A group may punish mavericks by not giving them places on delegations or committees or, in extreme cases, fining them, though generally EP groups prefer to let national groups impose discipline on their own members. If a national group chooses to go its own way in a vote, there is nothing the EP group as a whole can do (Corbett et al., pp. 88–89). Research conducted in 1996 showed that, notwithstanding this group solidarity, for most MEPs the most important focus of representation was their own country rather than "Europe as a whole"; MEPs from every country except Germany felt this (Wessels, p. 216).

The EP does most of its work through committees, of which there are approximately twenty at any one time, corresponding to the main areas of EU activity. Seats on the committees are shared among the political groups in proportion to their size; within each political group, posts are shared among the various countries represented within it. Besides holding committee meetings, the Parliament meets in week-long plenary sessions twelve times a year, at which it considers reports from the committees and votes on declarations or proposed amendments to legislation. As in most national parliaments, attendance in the chamber during plenary sessions tends to be low.

The EP, as we have indicated, does not have some of the powers that belong, at least in theory, to domestic parliaments in Europe. It cannot dismiss or appoint the Council of Ministers, which plays an important governmental role, and it cannot initiate or promulgate legislation. One mark of the constraints under which the EP operates is its lack of control over its location. With both the Commission and the Council offices based in Brussels, it would seem natural for the Parliament also to be there, and most MEPs would prefer this. Instead, EP operations are scattered around three countries. Although it holds its committee meetings in Brussels, which is the seat of most of the real action in the Union, it must hold nearly all of its plenary sessions in Strasbourg, in northeastern France, and, moreover, most of its administrative staff are based in Luxembourg. Decisions on its location are in the hands of the Council, representing the national governments, and neither the French nor the Luxembourg government has been prepared to give up the prestige and such financial benefits as may arise from having the Parliament meet in its territory. Consequently, truckloads of documents are constantly on the road between Brussels, Luxembourg, and Strasbourg, at a considerable cost in time and money; it is estimated that this geographical dispersion costs around 15 percent of the EP's budget (Corbett et al., p. 28).

The low turnout at EP elections and the way they are dominated by domestic rather than European political issues suggests that the Parliament has not managed to make itself very relevant to most Europeans. This weakens claims by the EP to represent the views of the European public on European issues. The regular proceedings of the EP receive little media coverage in the member states, and when the EP does get into the news, it is because of a sudden political "crisis" or for all the wrong reasons, such as when allegations about MEPs engaging in "creative accountancy" over their expenses surface. Members of the EP are often exasperated by the media's approach to coverage of their institution, complaining that the serious work they do in committees and in the legislative process goes nearly unreported while the most minor misdemeanors, real or alleged, are blown up out of all proportion. But although they have a fair point, it remains a fact that the EP has been unable to mobilize European public opinion in its perennial quest to gain greater powers. Although in principle EU citizens want the EP to have more power, both the level of information they possess and their degree of trust are quite low, and there is little tangible sign of public demand for a more central role for the EP (Wessels and Diedrichs, p. 147).

Yet, notwithstanding all this, the EP is unquestionably growing in power and significance within the EU's decision-making process. Every reform of the EU's institutions has brought increases in the EP's powers. MEPs are able to use the powers they have, especially those in the areas of the budget or the appointment and dismissal of the Commission, in such a manner as to get their way in other matters. The EP is thus a major actor in the Union's decision making precisely because of the separation of its role from that of the executive. The EP, like the U.S. Congress but unlike parliaments in most

European countries, is able to vote against individual items of legislation or to compel changes to the budget without thereby risking bringing down a government. Moreover, its members see the job of an MEP as a worthwhile one in itself, and this attitude would apply even more if the EP were given extended powers (Katz and Wessels, p. 236). In contrast to some national parliaments, the EP is not, and is unlikely to become, a mere stepping-stone on the way to a position in a European government. It is thus likely that members in a more powerful EP will take their parliamentary role more seriously than do many deputies in national parliaments in Europe. Unconstrained by any incentive to be loyal to the executive so as not to jeopardize their promotion prospects—a factor that partly explains the solid party bloc voting among government backbenchers that we witness in national European parliaments, as we saw in Chapter 3—MEPs may in future become even more significant players within the EU's policy-making process.

The Council of the European Union

So far, the Council has been mentioned quite frequently in this chapter, and we have noted that it has considerable power, but its precise nature has not been spelled out. The Council of the European Union (also known as the Council of Ministers) represents the governments of the twenty-five member states of the EU (for the Council, see Hayes-Renshaw; Sherrington). Although there is in principle only one Council, in practice there are several "formations" (up to twenty in the past but just nine since 2002), because each national seat on the Council is filled not by the same person every time but by the national minister with responsibility for the policy area that is to be discussed. Thus, if a forthcoming meeting of the Council is going to discuss EU transport policy, each government sends its transport minister (or at least a very senior civil servant from its Transport Ministry) to the meeting; if farm prices are to be discussed, it sends its agriculture minister; and so on. The Council meets in one form or another about 80 to 100 times a year; the foreign, finance, and agriculture ministers meet most often, perhaps once a month.

At any given time, one of the member states holds what is termed the Council presidency, and meetings of the Council and its many subcommittees are chaired either by the minister or by an official from this country. At the moment, the presidency rotates among the member states in a fixed order designed to ensure something close to alternation between large and small states. Each country has the office for six months. In 2005 the schedule called for Luxembourg to be followed by the UK, and in 2006 Austria would precede Finland. The period of each country's presidency is too short to make this a very significant role. It is generally reckoned that the lead-in period for a new policy is about eighteen months, so it is clear that the country holding the presidency can rarely bring any new initiative to fruition; the most it can do is speed up or slow-pedal some of the projects already on the books and perhaps introduce initiatives that it expects might be carried forward. In recent years, there has been more coordination between adjacent presidencies in an attempt to avoid the situation where a new presidency might try to reverse the priorities of the preceding one. Multi-Council programs are now agreed, setting out policy priorities for periods of two to four years.

When the Commission sends a proposal to the Council, the Council forwards a copy to the Parliament and also begins extensive scrutiny of the proposal itself. The

Council has a complex network of around 250 working parties and committees, staffed mainly by senior national civil servants. This process, known as "comitology," is the first stage at which the acceptability or otherwise of the proposal to the twenty-five national governments is assessed. Not surprisingly, quite a few proposals are killed off at this stage if the relevant committee finds it impossible to reach an agreement and explicitly rejects or simply shelves the proposal. The best the Commission can hope for is not unanimous approval from the committee, which is unrealistic to expect, but an agreement to pass the proposal on to the next stage of the decision-making process, subject to some or all of the member states entering specific reservations about it.

From the specialist committee, the proposal goes to a body called COREPER, the Committee of Permanent Representatives, which consists of the heads of the permanent delegations maintained in Brussels by each country. These senior diplomats and their staff iron out as many as possible of the problems identified by the specialist committee, and, before Council meetings, they brief the ministers about areas where agreement has and has not been reached. All proposals pass from COREPER to a meeting of the Council itself. The Council, unlike the Commission, has no permanent presence in Brussels (though of course it has a permanent secretariat based there); indeed, it has no permanent physical existence at all. When a Council meeting is to take place, the relevant ministers arrive from the respective national capitals, and they usually go home again a day or two later. Although both the Commission and the EP maintain information offices for the public in many cities across the Union (and, indeed, outside it), the Council has none. Far from being open and transparent, it has been described as "that most opaque of EU institutions" (Hayes-Renshaw and Wallace, p. 275).

When the ministers do gather in Brussels, they are likely to be faced with a number of proposals that have come through the Union's policy-making process and perhaps with other decisions as well. In areas where COREPER has reached an agreement, the Council needs merely to give formal ratification to the proposal or decision. If COREPER has proved unable to sort out the problems, the ministers themselves will try to break the deadlock with horse trading that may cross policy areas. The kind of wheeling and dealing that goes on at Council meetings makes it easy to understand why the Council would prefer to relegate the European Parliament to the periphery of decision making, as it could in the past, rather than have to engage in fresh negotiation with the EP. Indeed, when issues have to be resolved in a Conciliation Committee, it is often the case that the Parliament's negotiators prevail over a more fractious and heterogeneous Council delegation.

The manner of Council decision making can be important in bolstering its power. The treaties provide several ways for the Council to make decisions: by unanimity, by qualified majority, and by simple majority (the last of these is hardly ever used except for minor procedural matters). Unanimity is needed when the Council wants to amend a Commission proposal against the wishes of the Commission, on major constitutional questions, and in a handful of policy areas (taxation, defense, and immigration issues, for example), but successive treaties have greatly reduced the number of other situations in which it is required. Qualified majority voting is now the standard method of decision making. When a decision is reached by qualified majority, each minister wields a number of votes corresponding approximately to his or her country's population, though,

TABLE 5.4

Votes per Country in the Council of the European Union When Decisions Are Made by Qualified Majority

Country	Population	Council Votes	Population per Council Vote	Council Votes entitlement if Votes were Strictly Proportionate to Population
Germany	82,424,609	29	2,842,228	59
France	60,424,213	29	2,083,593	43
United Kingdom	60,270,708	29	2,078,300	43
Italy	52,057,477	29	1,795,085	37
Spain	40,280,780	27	1,491,881	29
Poland	38,626,349	27	1,430,605	27
Netherlands	16,318,199	13	1,255,246	12
Greece	10,647,529	12	887,294	8
Portugal	10,524,145	12	877,012	7
Belgium	10,348,276	12	862,356	7
Czech Republic	10,246,178	12	853,848	7
Hungary	10,032,375	12	836,031	7
Sweden	8,986,400	10	898,640	6
Austria	8,174,762	10	817,476	6
Slovakia	5,423,567	7	774,795	4
Denmark	5,413,392	7	773,342	4
Finland	5,214,512	7	744,930	4
Ireland	3,969,558	7	567,080	3
Lithuania	3,607,899	7	515,414	3
Latvia	2,306,306	4	576,576	2
Slovenia	2,011,473	4	502,868	1
Estonia	1,341,664	4	335,416	1
Cyprus	775,927	4	193,982	1
Luxembourg	462,690	4	115,672	0
Malta	396,851	3	132,284	0
Total	450,285,839	321	1,402,760	321

Note: A majority requires 232 votes, and a blocking minority requires 90. Proportional allocation made by the Sainte-Laguë method.

as with the allocation of EP seats, the small countries continue to be overrepresented (see Table 5.4). The total number of votes among the twenty-five ministers is 321, and 232 (72 percent) of these are needed for a majority. Moreover, the votes in favor need also to represent at least 62 percent of the EU's population. It can be seen from the table that at least twelve countries are needed to produce a qualified majority and at least four to produce the 90 votes that make up a blocking minority.

In the past, the Council preferred to operate on the basis of unanimity so as not to overrule any state that had a strong objection to any proposal. The so-called Luxembourg Compromise of 1966 was interpreted for the next twenty years as allowing any state to veto any proposal by claiming that its "vital national interests" were at stake. The result was a very slow-moving decision-making process until, from the mid-1980s onward, the use of qualified majority voting was extended by successive treaties. However, it is true that the Council still prefers to operate on the basis of consensus, and that if a country, or a group of countries, has strong objections to a proposal that has majority support, the majority will try to find a way of accommodating the objections rather than railroad the proposal through (Hayes-Renshaw and Wallace, p. 275). This "culture of consensus" springs largely from a feeling that, in the long run, imposing policies on countries that intensely dislike them would not be good for the EU's legitimacy or for the successful implementation of its policies. At the same time, however, the fact that decisions *can* be made by a qualified majority vote—and that they have been made in the past even in the face of vigorous opposition from one or more states—means that those states in a negative minority also have an incentive to work with the majority on an acceptable compromise because they can no longer simply rely on a veto. In addition, there is a certain amount of "logrolling"—states agree to go along with proposals with which they are not entirely happy in the expectation that other countries will do the same when the roles are reversed.

The European Council

The European Council was created formally in 1974, and its first meeting was held in Dublin in March 1975 (for the European Council see de Schoutheete). It consists of the heads of government of the twenty-five member states (the foreign ministers, the president of the Commission, and another commissioner also attend European Council meetings). It meets at least twice every year, and these summit meetings attract extensive media coverage. All the major steps forward taken by the EU in recent years have been initiated either by the European Council or by the Commission, and at the very least they have needed the backing of the European Council to get going.

The Maastricht Treaty of 1992 gave its central role explicit mention, stating that the "European Council shall provide the Union with the necessary impetus for its development and shall define the general political guidelines thereof," and this position was confirmed and strengthened by the Amsterdam Treaty. Even so, the authority of the European Council is essentially political rather than legal. Its lack of legal powers is more realistically seen as a lack of constraints; its relationship with the rest of the Union's decision-making structure is that of a free-floating agent, able to intervene in any area at any time.

Some advocates of closer European integration regret the rise and central position of the European Council when it comes to major decisions. It seems to confirm the position of the member states and their governments, rather than the Union's collective institutions (the Commission and the Parliament), as the central actors in the EU, and it gives the impression that the EU is still more of an intergovernmental organization than a supranational one. On the other hand, it could be argued that the EU would be far less relevant to the member states were it not for the direct interest and involvement of the heads of government in shaping its affairs, and, moreover, that if EU initiatives and policies are to make fundamental progress, they need behind them the weight that only the heads of government can supply.

The centrality of the European Council, and the important role of the Council of the European Union in general, raise fundamental questions about democratic accountability within the EU. The Commission is accountable to Parliament (which appointed and can dismiss it), and the Parliament is accountable to the European public through the direct elections held every five years. But to whom are the Council of the EU and the European Council accountable? The short answer is: to no one. It is true that all the heads of government attending a European Council meeting, as well as all the ministers attending a Council meeting, are individually accountable to their own parliament for what they have or have not done at the meeting—though how effective parliaments are in enforcing this accountability is another question (see Chapter 3). In addition, the EP has the power to question national ministers when they hold the rotating presidency of the Council. But neither the Council of the EU nor the European Council as an institution is answerable or accountable to anyone at all, except that of course both must respect the limits of competence imposed by the treaties and by the Court of Justice. The move away from unanimity to qualified majority voting as the basis for decision making has compounded this. Whereas, when decisions required unanimity, each minister could be asked by his or her national parliament why he or she did not veto a proposal, under qualified majority voting no single minister has this power. The lack of accountability of important decision makers has led to much talk of a "democratic deficit" within the EU, a subject to which we return later in this chapter.

The Court of Justice

The Court of Justice (the ECJ) is based in Luxembourg and consists of twenty-five judges, one from each member state, appointed for a six-year term (for the ECJ see de Búrca and Weiler). The fact that each judge is appointed by a government, and is dependent on the support of that government for renomination for a further term, causes some concern about how independent the judges can afford to be (Arnull, pp. 251–52). The Court interprets and applies EU law and the Union's constitution. Its decisions are binding on all member states, citizens, and legal entities within the Union, and this marks one of the main differences between the EU and other international organizations. Under the "doctrine of direct effect," EU law confers on individuals rights that public authorities in the member states must respect (Shapiro and Stone Sweet, p. 264). Although a state may refuse to accept a judgment made by another international court (such as the International Court of Justice at The Hague or the European Court of Human Rights at Strasbourg), states belonging to the EU cannot pick and choose among the judgments of the Court of Justice. Its decisions override those of domestic courts, even though this is not explicitly stated in the treaties, and it has pronounced that EU law takes precedence over national law (the "doctrine of supremacy").

The Court of Justice is in effect the final court of appeal in the EU; there is no higher authority. In giving its judgments, the Court has not confined itself to the treaties (which are concerned mainly with economic matters); it has also looked for inspiration to the constitutions of the member states and to the European Convention on Human Rights. It has taken a creative rather than a positivist approach to its role—that is, it has supplied interpretations to fill gaps in the Union's legislation and has cited its own case law rather than feeling confined strictly to the letter of the treaties. It is sometimes seen as the "motor of integration," and one writer declares that "no other court ... has ever played so prominent a role in the creation of the basic governmental and political process of which it is a part" (Martin Shapiro, quoted in Kenney, p. 145).

One of the ECJ's functions is to determine the constitutionality of EU laws. It is thus comparable to the constitutional courts that we discussed in Chapter 4. Domestic courts frequently refer cases to the Court if a question of the interpretation of Union law is involved. In addition, governments may be taken before the Court for failing to meet their obligations. As a result of such cases, the Court has stated, to give a few examples, that it is not permissible for a member state to fund advertising campaigns designed to promote domestic products; to discriminate against workers with regard to employment, pay, or other conditions of work or employment, on the basis of nationality; to operate pension schemes with different retirement ages for men and women; or to conduct excessive checking or inspection of imported goods. The growing recourse to the Court has created problems by greatly increasing its workload. In 1989 a "Court of First Instance" was introduced to share the load and speed up the process of justice, though it still takes about two years on average from the filing of a case with the Court for a decision to emerge. At the end of 2003 there were 974 cases outstanding, a significant number given that the Court completed only 494 during that year (Court of Justice, p. 215).

As we mentioned, the ECJ is not formally stated in any treaty to be superior to domestic courts, and the relationship between the two is imprecise. After some initial difficulties, the ECJ sought actively to increase its power and was able to do so, whether by persuading national courts to defer to it through "champagne lunches at the Court of Justice in Luxembourg" or by employing various strategies that took account, for example, of the short-term horizons of political actors (Alter, pp. ix, 188; Tallberg, p. 137). Once national courts started referring cases to it on a large scale, its impact was greatly increased, because even if governments were prepared to ignore ECJ jurisprudence, "ignoring their own courts was a different matter entirely" (Alter, p. 219). However, the ECJ's position at the top of the European juridical hierarchy is not necessarily secure. Domestic courts, especially constitutional courts, have expressed concern when it seems to them that an EU law or treaty conflicts with the rights guaranteed by the country's constitution, and the judgment of Germany's Federal Constitutional Court in a challenge to the Maastricht Treaty was anything but deferential toward the ECJ. In its judgment it affirmed that it would treat as invalid any EU action that it regarded as going beyond the EU's authority (Kokott, pp. 98–107; Stone Sweet, pp. 174–78).

The key question has often been one of who decides how far the EU's competence runs. Suppose the EU makes a decision or rule that some argue goes beyond its allotted sphere. Who has the right to decide whether it has, or has not, exceeded its authority? In the eyes of the ECJ, the ECJ itself has this right; in the eyes of many constitutional courts, they do. Thus, it has been argued that the ECJ "has not established a psychic hegemony over the supreme national courts," which still give the impression that "they are making a graceful concession when they follow the line laid down by the Court in a particular matter," while Weiler refers to "a certain credibility issue" given "troubling" or "defiant" decisions by courts in Germany, Italy, Denmark, Belgium, and Spain in recent years (Allott, pp. 216–17; Weiler, pp. 220–21). National courts may avoid referring cases to the ECJ by declaring, justifiably or otherwise, that the issue is self-evident or has already been decided by the Court (Raworth, p. 137).

Even though the Court possesses political antennae, "taking care in its judgmental policy not to push the willingness of the Member States over the limit" (Hunnings, p. 132), governments are not always compliant with its judgments. They may feel that defiance could lead to a change in the law under which they have been censured, or that the political cost of compliance would be too great, or that by the time the appeal process is exhausted another government will be in office (Alter, p. 228). The Court of Justice, unlike domestic courts, has no police force or army to enforce its judgments. Until November 1993, when the Maastricht Treaty came into operation, it did not possess any formal sanctions for use against those who do not obey its decisions. Since that date, it has been able to impose fines on member states for such disobedience or for failing to implement Union laws, though this has rarely happened (Alter, p. 11). As of the end of 2002, there had been a number of cases in which these penalties were imposed; in one case, France was, on paper anyway, incurring fines at the rate of 316,500 euro per day for failing to comply with a judgment on urban water treatment (Commission of the European Communities, p. 10). The Court must rely on the law enforcement agencies of the member states and, hence, ultimately on their governments to enforce compliance. In general, it is true, "the declaratory judgment is its own sanction," and states usually seek to avoid a judgment against them (Freestone and Davidson, p. 152). However, this does not always apply, and the Court sometimes experiences great difficulty in trying to secure implementation of its judgments.

In such cases, it is confronted not by explicit refusal to comply with a Court judgment but with delaying tactics: States receiving an adverse judgment from the Court sometimes respond by saying that they will need time to consider the full implications of the verdict, a process that in some cases has apparently required several years. Moreover, certain governments seem to be little put out by receiving judgments against them. Table 5.5, which shows the position in 2003, reveals that there is significant national variation. The Scandinavian countries—ironically, some of the most Eurosceptic countries—have the best record of compliance (Sverdrup), and southern European countries the worst. Greece may have joined the EU late but it rapidly caught up with most of the other countries on this measure. In one of the cases where a state had not complied with a judgment by 2003, the original judgment had been delivered in 1989, and there were several that had been rumbling on since the mid-1990s! Generally speaking, the national governments concerned do not take such an indulgent attitude to the enforcement of judgments given by their own domestic courts, although it is probably true to say that the degrees of rigor with which domestic laws and EU laws are enforced in each country are strongly correlated.

TABLE 5.5

Actions of the European Court of Justice with Respect to the Member States

Country	Actions for Failure to Fulfill Obligations		Judgments with Which State Had Not Yet Complied as of December 31, 2002
	1953–2003	2003	
Austria	63	20	5
Belgium	281	17	12
Denmark	29	3	1
Finland	15	6	2
France	309	22	27
Germany	190	18	9
Greece	238	16	13
Ireland	147	16	9
Italy	471	20	21
Luxembourg	149	16	8
Netherlands	91	9	2
Portugal	91	10	3
Spain	130	28	7
Sweden	15	5	2
United Kingdom	85	8	8
Total	2,304	214	129

Sources: Court of Justice of the European Communities, *Annual Report 2003;* extract "Statistics of judicial activity of the Court of Justice," available at http://curia.eu.int/en/instit/presentationfr/rapport/stat/st03cr.pdf, p. 226; Commission of the European Communities, *Twentieth Annual Report on Monitoring the Application of Community Law* (2002), available at http://www.europa.eu.int/comm/secretariat_general/sgb/droit_com/pdf/rapport_annuel/20_rapport_annuel_en.htm

✦ WHAT DOES THE EUROPEAN UNION DO?

As time has passed, the range of policy areas in which the EU shows an interest has steadily increased. In recent years the emphasis has been on establishing a single market and a single currency across the Union. In addition, in an attempt to give the EU a human face and to moderate some of the effects of giving market forces fairly free rein, members of the Union have set about creating a "People's Europe" or a "Social Europe." In terms of where the EU's money is spent, the main policy area remains agriculture.

Single Market and Single Currency

For many years a prominent concern of the Union was the completion of the single internal market. The aim of creating a common European market features strongly in the EEC Treaty of 1957. A common market would mean that goods and services could be marketed and sold with equal ease all across the Union; there would be no barriers to trade within the Union. Real political will was put behind this goal from the mid-1980s onward, and the task of completing the single market was largely completed by 1992. Beyond the single market lies the possibility of a single economy. Economic and Monetary Union (EMU) is another long-standing goal of European integrationists, and after approximately twenty years of groundwork that produced little tangible, a decisive step was taken in the late 1990s with the establishment of a common European currency, termed the "euro" (the name was another common-denominator choice, since almost every other possibility had some national overtones). Of the then fifteen members, eleven joined the scheme and a twelfth, Greece, joined later. The other three—Denmark, Sweden, and the United Kingdom—each took a political decision not to enter the single currency. Most of the 2004 entrants hope to be part of the eurozone within a few years.

The currency was established under the terms of a "Stability and Growth Pact," under which member states are obliged to keep their budget deficits within certain limits. However, enforcement of the rules depends in the first instance on the other governments taking the initiative in imposing discipline against the offending government, and questions were asked about how likely it was that governments would punish "their own." The fears of the doubters were realized in November 2003, when a meeting of EU finance ministers refrained from acting against France and Germany, whose budget deficits were in excess of the permitted level (3 percent of GDP), despite the protests of both the Commission and the European Central Bank, which warned that the decision undermined the credibility of the currency. The economies of the participating countries are diverse, with a range of economic cycles, and it remains to be seen whether future governments that breach the terms of the pact by running large budget deficits will be reined in as provided in the scheme for EMU. If all countries obey the rules, certain key economic levers—control over interest rates, public spending, and some taxes—will be outside the control of national governments.

A People's Europe

There are nowadays very few policy spheres in which the EU is not concerned, at least to some degree. The EU has the aim, even if this is not precisely expressed in any of the treaties, of bringing about equality of civil and social rights, of living and working conditions, of opportunities, and of income across the Union; this goal is sometimes characterized as building a "Social Europe" or a "People's Europe." To this end it has tended to get involved in nearly all policy areas, including some not enumerated in the founding treaties. It has issued legal instruments covering such diverse subjects as the size and grading of eggs, the purity of tap water to which citizens are entitled, the length of time truck drivers can drive without a break, the safety and cleanliness of the sea at bathing beaches, the extent to which countries can reserve their coastal waters for the exclusive use of their own fishing fleets, equal pay for men and women, the rights of consumers, and aid for the third world.

In addition, the Union has the aim of reducing the significant disparities in wealth that exist within its boundaries, both between and within countries; this is known in the characteristically opaque Eurojargon as "cohesion policy." Ever since the three southern European countries joined in the 1980s, there have been large wealth differences among

TABLE 5.6

Gross Domestic Product of EU Member States, and Contributions to and Receipts from the 2003 Budget

Country	Per Capita GDP in 2003 ($)	Share of 2003 EU Budget Revenues Contributed (%)	Share of 2003 EU Budget Expenditure Received (%)	Net Gain/ Loss as % of EU Budget	Per Capita Net Gain/ Loss (euros)
Luxembourg	58,315	0.2	0.2	−0.1	−122
Denmark	39,220	2.1	1.9	−0.3	−61
Ireland	38,322	1.3	3.4	+2.1	+384
Sweden	33,903	3.0	1.8	−1.2	−119
Netherlands	31,419	5.9	2.5	−3.4	−183
Austria	30,960	2.3	2.0	−0.3	−46
Finland	30,840	1.6	1.7	+0.1	−3
United Kingdom	29,782	11.9	7.8	−4.1	−65
Belgium	29,175	4.2	2.2	−2.0	−173
Germany	29,141	23.0	13.5	−9.5	−106
France	29,086	18.1	16.9	−1.3	−34
Italy	25,291	14.1	13.5	−0.5	−21
Spain	20,819	8.9	20.4	+11.5	+209
Greece	16,221	1.8	6.2	+4.4	+310
Portugal	13,949	1.5	6.1	+4.6	+329
Total/average EU	30,430	100.0	100.0	0	—

Note: Countries are ranked in order of per capita gross domestic product.

Sources: Per capita GDP—as in Table 1.2. Share of EU budget expenditure and revenue 2003: European Commission, *Allocation of 2003 EU Operating Expenditure by Member State,* pp. 15 and 99, available at http://europa.eu.int/comm/budget/agenda2000/reports_en.htm

regions, and some feared that the moves toward a single market might be of most benefit to a "golden triangle" covering the southeastern part of England, parts of France, northern Italy, together with most of western Germany and the Benelux countries, with the rest of the Union becoming ever more peripheral.

Table 5.6 shows the degree of variation between the member states, with GDP per capita in Luxembourg over four times the corresponding figure for Greece and Portugal (and over 11 times that of the poorest 2004 entrant, Slovakia). The table shows that the budget has some redistributive effect, in that all of the three poorest countries receive more from the EU budget than they give to it. The main beneficiary per capita has been Ireland, now one of the wealthiest countries thanks to a sustained economic boom aided by the inflow of EU funds. As a result of this new wealth, Ireland is set to become a net contributor to the EU budget by 2007. Germany is a large net contributor, and with its increased financial burden after German unification there was growing unhappiness in Germany with the scale of its contribution (Laffan, *Finances,* pp. 54–56). To try to even out the fruits of economic growth, the EU has set up a number of "structural" funds, the most important of which are known as the Regional Development Fund and the Social Fund, to attempt to promote development in the less wealthy parts of the Union. Under these headings, the Union funds schemes to give job training to the unemployed throughout the EU and to combat unemployment in the peripheral regions. The size of these funds increased greatly in the 1990s, and, at least partly in consequence, wealth per capita in Ireland, and to a lesser extent in Greece, Portugal, and Spain, made notable strides toward the EU average. The accession of the eight postcommunist countries in 2004, with wealth levels well below the EU average, was projected to see the structural funds account for 39 percent of the EU budget by 2006, having made up only 9 percent of it in the 1980s (Allen, p. 244).

As to the substance of EU policies, it would be difficult to categorize these unequivocally as either basically left-wing or basically right-wing; indeed, the EU comes under attack from both left and right. Some of its decisions, such as its insistence on privatization of industries such as telecommunications, promote private enterprise and free trade, but it also adopts a very interventionist approach to agriculture and is active in defending the social rights of sections of society who suffer discrimination of one sort or another, such as women, migrant workers, and workers in general. Its policies to promote gender equality have had particular impact in countries where women have traditionally encountered discrimination. The growing steps toward a single EU economy will make it difficult for any country to pursue policies that drift very far to the right or left of the consensus, a consensus sometimes termed the "European social market" or "neoliberalism meets the social market" (Hix, pp. 269–70). This may be a concern for some governments, though, on the other hand, the claim that "the EU made us do it" (or "the EU stopped us from doing it") can be a useful excuse for a government secretly relieved at the chance to wriggle out of unwise election promises (Smith).

In order to make the EU clearly and directly relevant to its citizens and to justify the claim that a "People's Europe" is being constructed, the Union has attempted to create symbols with which Europeans can identify. The EU has its own flag, consisting of twelve gold stars arranged in a circle on a blue background, which can be seen flying from many public buildings across the Union alongside the appropriate national flag. The EU also has its own anthem (the prelude to Beethoven's "Ode to Joy"). The passports of all EU countries are now issued in a uniform size and color, and travelers from one EU country do not have to pass through customs when they visit another. Those living in the thirteen countries (the pre-2004 members, apart from Ireland and the UK) covered by the Schengen agreements do not even pass through a border control when crossing an internal EU frontier. Even if today's Europeans, especially the young ones, are not impressed by the mantra that the EU helps prevent another Franco–German war, they may be enthused by the freedom to take holidays around Europe without having to change currency at the bank or undergo passport checks at every border.

Agriculture

In the past, agriculture not only has accounted for the bulk of the EU's budget but also has been one of the areas in which it has been hardest to find agreement. In recent years, though, it has slipped down the political agenda, yet, through the Common Agricultural Policy (CAP), it still consumes a massive amount of the Union's expenditure. Although

Box 5.1   The European Union

France

France was one of the six original members of the EEC in 1958. Under General de Gaulle (President of France from 1958 to 1969), France opposed the admission of Britain, but de Gaulle's attitude toward the EU was not too different from that displayed by certain British governments after 1973. De Gaulle was in favor of the economic benefits that the Union brought but was very suspicious of any steps that might dilute the traditional sovereignty of the state. Since his departure from office, France has been more willing to contemplate closer integration among the member states, but despite the rhetoric of some of its leading politicians, it is not generally seen as being at the forefront of the integrationists. France has consistently been a strong defender of the Common Agricultural Policy, from which its inefficient agriculture sector benefits greatly. France has been accustomed to playing a leading role in the EU, often in combination with Germany, but the incorporation of ten new members in 2004, none of them a traditional ally of France, plus the lowly portfolio given to the French member of the Barroso commission later that year, led to questions as to whether France's role in future might be less central.

Germany

For Germany, one of the six founders, membership in the EU offered the prospect both of economic gains and of political rehabilitation after World War II. As the member state with the largest economy in the Union, Germany has picked up the largest share of the bill for funding the EU. In the past, most Germans have been willing to see this as a price worth paying, even in pure economic terms, for securing access to the huge EU market for their efficient industries, but in recent years there have been signs of a feeling that their country is asked to shoulder an unfairly large proportion of the contributions to the EU's budget. When the single currency was established in 1999, concern was expressed in Germany that too many countries, including some that had not shown convincingly that they were capable of adhering to disciplined economic policies, were being admitted to the scheme. Ironically, Germany soon became one of the first countries to flout the financial discipline that membership of the eurozone was supposed to impose.

Italy

Italy was one of the founders of the EU, which has brought significant economic benefits to the country, although Italy's wealth is concentrated heavily in the northern half of the country. Italy has a less than glorious record when it comes to implementing Union law and complying with judgments of the Court of Justice. Despite its size, Italy has generally been content to allow other countries, particularly France and Germany, to take the lead in shaping the future direction of the Union. When the single-currency scheme was launched in the late 1990s, it was widely assumed that Italy would be unable to meet the conditions for entry, but several years of atypically austere budgets enabled the country to (just) meet the entry terms. Among both politicians and the public, enthusiasm for moves toward a federal Europe is high, perhaps because of despair at the quality of domestic governance: EU directives have been seen as "a *deus ex machina* saving Italy from itself," as Vivien Schmidt puts it.

Latvia

The EU–Latvia relationship began in September 1991, when the EU granted Latvia trade concessions and financial assistance, and Latvia formally applied for EU membership four years later. Throughout accession negotiations, Latvia and the other two Baltic states were regarded as "favorite" candidates due to their high economic growth rates, healthy public finances, low taxes, and fast-rising productivity. Trade with EU countries dominates the Latvian economy. One of the big issues in complying with the conditionality applied by the EU was the subject of minority rights, especially the status of the sizable Russian-speaking minority in Latvia. The 1994 Law on Citizenship was interpreted by the EU as demonstrating Latvia's inability to progress on the road to European integration, and only when this was amended in the late 1990s was the deadlock broken. In its 2003 referendum Latvia voted 2 to 1 to join the EU, but, as in the other two Baltic states, some people were concerned about "escaping" from the clutches of one Union (the USSR) only to join another one.

Netherlands

The Netherlands was one of the founding members of the EU, but as a small country it has accepted that its impact on decisions will be relatively marginal. Attitudes toward the EU in general, as well as specific attitudes toward closer integration, are broadly favorable, even though the Netherlands is a significant net contributor to the EU budget. Unlike the governments of some other small countries, which fear that a supranational EU government would lead to their interests being overlooked in favor of the larger countries, Dutch governments believe that such supranational bodies, by making decisions in the broader European interest, are more likely to benefit them than a purely intergovernmental arrangement would. The Netherlands was one of the few countries to favor censuring France and Germany for breaching the rules on the size of budget deficits in 2003.

Poland

Poland is by far the largest of the ten countries that became members of the EU on May 1, 2004. After forty years of Soviet-imposed communism the Poles see EU membership as a way to reclaim their historic place at the heart of Europe. With a population of nearly 40 million, Poland accounts for over half of the newcomers' population and 41 percent of their total GDP. The Europe Agreement was signed in 1991, and Poland applied for EU membership in April 1994. The accession negotiations began in 1998 and were concluded in 2002. During this period important institutional adjustments took place in Poland, driven by EU accession criteria. Poland has done a remarkable job getting ready for entry to the EU. The economy is growing more rapidly than most analysts predicted, driven by the weak zloty and steep rises in productivity. Poland is also expected to benefit from the EU budget in the future, in the form of considerable farm subsidies, grants to encourage industrial restructuring, and other payouts. Although the accession referendum was passed by a margin greater than 3 to 1, many Poles remain to be convinced about the economic benefits that membership could bring, and there remains a strong undercurrent of anti-EU feeling rooted in traditional Catholicism.

Spain

Soon after the first democratic election in forty years was held in 1977, Spain applied for membership in the EU and, after protracted negotiations, joined on January 1, 1986. The potential economic benefits of membership were a powerful incentive, but just as important were the political implications. Under the long rule of the dictator Franco, Spain had been isolated from western European political thought and developments, and joining the EU was an ideal opportunity to join the mainstream rather than remain on the fringe. In addition, it was felt that the risk of a military coup by far-rightists attempting to restore a quasi-Francoist dictatorship would be greatly reduced if the country was part of (and was benefiting economically from its membership in) a community committed to the preservation of liberal democratic values. Spain is one of the more integrationist of the member states and favors an expansion of the role of the European Parliament. Until the 2004 expansion it was the largest net beneficiary from the EU budget. In a February 2005 referendum, Spanish voters endorsed the proposed European constitution by a large margin (over 4 to 1), but on a turnout of little more than 40 percent.

Sweden

Sweden has a long-standing policy of neutrality, which kept it out of World War II and led to its refusal for many years to consider joining the European Union. The ending of the Cold War led to a rapid reassessment of Sweden's attitude, and the country became a member of the EU in 1995, following a referendum in which 52 percent of the voters supported membership. Enthusiasm soon cooled, though, and Sweden is seen as one of the least satisfied members of the EU, a perception confirmed by its people's rejection in a 2003 referendum of the idea of joining the eurozone. As in other Scandinavian countries, support for European integration is highest in the urbanized south and lowest in the peripheral north. The Swedish parliament, like its Danish and Finnish counterparts, demands a high degree of accountability from its ministers as to what they plan to do at forthcoming Council meetings.

Continued

Box 5.1   The European Union (*Continued*)

United Kingdom

Britain did not hold a referendum on joining the EU in 1973; but in 1975, after some "renegotiation" of the entry terms, it held one on whether to withdraw, and the people voted to remain in the EU. However, Britain was sometimes perceived as having, psychologically at least, one foot inside the EU and one still outside. Under Margaret Thatcher and John Major, its minimalist attitude toward such aspects of European integration as a common currency and guaranteed protection for the rights of workers across the Union irritated many other members in the 1980s and 1990s. After 1997, when Tony Blair entered power, Britain's rhetoric changed greatly, but Blair too had to pay due heed to the strength of Euroscepticism among the British public and in the popular media, which portray EU membership as "rule by Brussels" and run frequent stories, often exaggerated or downright false, about the bizarre plans that "Brussels bureaucrats" are about to impose on the British people. The question of relationships with Europe is a major and contentious issue in British politics; it divides each of the two main parties and has led to the rise of an anti-EU party, UKIP (UK Independence Party), which won 11 seats at the 2004 EP elections. Any decision to join the eurozone, or to adopt the new EU constitution, would need the support of the people in a referendum.

the proportion of the Union's labor force working in agriculture has fallen from over 25 percent in the late 1950s to less than 6 percent, the share of Union spending going to agriculture has consistently been far in excess of this. Having exceeded 60 percent in nearly all budgets of the 1970s and 1980s, it fell to around 50 percent in the 1990s but is not projected to fall much below this in the foreseeable future.

The CAP was designed to guarantee both farm incomes and an adequate supply of food in a Europe haunted by memories of food shortages, but by the 1970s it had become notorious for resulting in massive surpluses of food products—especially beef, butter, and wine—that could not be sold on the world market because they were so expensive. Farmers regarded this as highly satisfactory, but no one else did. EU consumers had to pay well above the market price for their food, while producers in the developing world found themselves unable to gain access to the highly protected EU market and, moreover, were faced in their own countries with EU surpluses dumped at artificially low prices. Over time, the costs and contradictions of the CAP became increasingly unsustainable. Domestically, the Union could not afford to support this one sector at such cost, and pressure internationally from the Union's trading partners and from the World Trade Organization made reform a priority.

Reform took the form of decoupling farmers' income support from their production. In other words, instead of receiving inflated prices for their production, farmers now receive a direct income supplement (based on an average of their previous years' income) and are then free to produce whatever they wish for the open market without price supports. Even so, the CAP remains a very expensive feature of the EU's operations. In addition, the sheer size of the agriculture budget and the convoluted nature of many of the CAP schemes provide plenty of opportunity for fraud (anything from 1.4 percent to 10 percent of the EU's budget is used fraudulently—Laffan, "Financial," p. 236). Further reform of the CAP, in order to reduce the payments given to farmers so as to free up funds to benefit EU citizens generally, is widely agreed to be desirable, but in every country, and at EU level, farmers' interest groups are powerful and governments of all political complexions are reluctant to alienate such a well-organized lobby, as we discuss further in Chapter 14. In the words of Rieger (p. 207): "The small political costs to consumers and taxpayers, because they are spread diffusely, mean that it still pays the national politicians to woo farmers with anti-market policies, and to disregard their blatant incfficiency." Of course, farmers are able to obtain such special treatment in other polities too, such as the United States.

→ THE EUROPEAN UNION: INTERGOVERNMENTAL OR SUPRANATIONAL ORGANIZATION?

The EU contains elements of two kinds of polity. One is the intergovernmental organization, in which the governments of sovereign member states cooperate without giving up the ultimate right to make their own decisions. The second is the supranational body, in which the ultimate power rests with the common institutions and the national governments have room to maneuver only within the framework of policy decided at the collective level. Developments such as the increasing power of the European Parliament and the introduction of a common currency suggest that the EU may be moving in the direction of a supranational organization, but, at the same time, the EU still seems to bear many of the characteristics of an intergovernmental organization. We can see the continuing relevance of the intergovernmental model when we examine two of its aspects: the implementation of policy and the financing of the EU.

How fully EU legislation is implemented across the EU is unknown, in the absence of detailed study. It is generally accepted, though, that implementation is far from uniform or perfect, and "implementation deficit" is a widely used phrase (Cini; Dimitrakopoulos and Richardson). In the words of Martin Shapiro (p. 29):

> Implementation, as we all know, is in the hands of the administrations of the Member States. As to that implementation, there is a basic rule: Don't ask, don't tell. . . .
> Everyone knows it would be a miracle if all Member State administrations were implementing most EU regulations, let alone directives, in approximately the same way.[1]

There is widespread concern that at least some member states make only token efforts to secure the enforcement of EU decisions about which they happen not to feel strongly or which they never really supported in the first place (see Peters; Falkner et al.). A government that "loses" in the policy-making stage of the process might not be too concerned because it knows that when it comes to the second stage, implementation, it will determine what really happens in the country (Hans Samsem, quoted in Demmke and Unfried, p. 123). Should such states wish to behave like this, they have many strategies short of outright disobedience, such as lack of implementation, lack of enforcement, lack of application, evasion, noncompliance by the legislature, executive, or judiciary, and benign noncompliance (Snyder, p. 56). The Common Fisheries Policy, for example, has been something of a disaster, resulting in serious depletion of fish stocks because a

---

[1]Regulations and directives are different kinds of EU legislation. Regulations, once adopted at EU level, are immediately binding in every country without needing approval at the national level. Directives bind the member states to take appropriate steps, within a specified period, to achieve a stipulated end, but allow each member state to choose the methods of achieving this end.

number of governments—such as those of Belgium, France, Portugal, and Spain—lack the resources or the will (or both) to implement its restrictions fully and effectively (Lequesne, p. 361). Similarly, in environmental law, "ineffective application and enforcement remains a problem" (Demmke and Unfried, p. 81).

Even if a state is willing to implement the legislation, doing so might prove time-consuming or complicated. For one thing, EU legislation is full of complicated terminology and acronyms, so the EU has had to produce a thesaurus of this jargon, known as "Eurovoc," which runs to five volumes (Burns, p. 438). Civil servants attempting to implement legislation sometimes find themselves unable, due to its vagueness or ambiguity, to understand what obligation it imposes or what action it requires, and the Commission is seen as prone to supply unsatisfactory or tardy answers to questions seeking clarification (Bekkers et al., pp. 467–68). The structure of national administration may not be conducive to the implementation of EU policy. In the Netherlands, for example, some items of legislation require action from more than one government department, and different departments are accustomed to using different methods of issuing regulations, leading to deadlock or confusion. Matters might be improved if one department was in charge of overall coordination, but in fact three different departments are competing for this role, and none possesses the authority to impose itself (Bekkers et al., pp. 474–75).

The relatively low level of finances controlled by the Union institutions as opposed to the national governments also suggests intergovernmentalism. There is a ceiling on the size of the EU's budget relative to the total GNP of the member states for each year; this ceiling stands at 1.27 percent, illustrating the way in which the resources available to the EU institutions are dwarfed by those controlled by national governments. This is partly because some responsibilities usually shouldered by the central government in a federal state, such as defense, are handled at the national level within the EU. In 2002 the EU had a larger population than the United States, but the U.S. federal budget was over twenty times as large as the EU's budget (Sbragia, p. 115). EU expenditure in 2003 came to nearly €91 billion, about €237 per person (at prevailing exchange rates in early 2005, around $293, or £164).

The Union is financed on the basis of what are termed "own resources." This means that it does not receive a block grant from the twenty-five governments, which would give it an overtly subordinate and dependent position; instead, it has a statutory right to the revenue derived from the flow of money into and around the Union. The EU has two main sources of "own resources" revenue: It receives 0.5 percent of what national governments collect from the main indirect tax in the Union—the value-added tax (VAT)—and it also keeps the duties collected from trade with countries outside the EU. In addition, a direct levy is imposed on member states in proportion to their gross national products (GNPs); this source of revenue, which has a progressive effect on wealth distribution, is now the largest (Nugent, *Government,* pp. 370–71).

Trying to decide whether the EU is essentially supranational or essentially intergovernmental raises what Brigid Laffan (*Finances,* p. 264) refers to as "one of the great dilemmas when analysing the Union—should we see strength or weakness?" Focusing on the difficulties of uniform implementation of legislation and the small proportion of resources controlled at EU level emphasizes how far the EU has still to go before being considered a truly supranational body. Nevertheless, it is clearly more than a merely intergovernmental body and has moved closer to being a genuinely supranational polity than any entity before it. We next consider whether it will move further in this direction in the future.

✦ THE FUTURE OF THE EUROPEAN UNION

The EU is not a static organization. Perhaps it never can be. Many observers have discussed the "bicycle theory," or compared the EU to a shark: It must keep moving forward or die, because the status quo is not a stable situation (Wind, p. 103). Three separate aspects of its future are uncertain: first, the extent of its membership; second, the extent to which integration takes place; and third, its political structures and system.

EU Enlargement

Despite the addition of ten members in 2004, the enlargement process is not over. The EU has expressed its willingness to admit those states that have shown their commitment to democracy and the rule of law. Bulgaria and Romania were originally expected to join in 2004, and their entry is unlikely to be long delayed. Of the successor states to Yugoslavia, only Slovenia has so far joined; Croatia has reasonable prospects of admission before too long, but Bosnia-Herzegovina, Macedonia, and Serbia and Montenegro are not seen as close to meeting the qualifications for membership. Albania, too, is not yet a credible candidate. Switzerland (where in a December 1992 referendum the people narrowly voted against joining the "European Economic Area," a free-trade area including all the EU member states and a number of non-EU members), Iceland, and Norway are the only countries that at this stage seem unlikely to want to join the European Union. The most contentious case is that of Turkey, which has been an applicant for membership since the 1960s. It has a number of long-standing advocates within the Union, but other members are openly opposed to its admission. It is not only very poor in comparison with the EU, but it is also large (over 70 million people) and overwhelmingly Muslim—though opponents of its admission stress their concerns about its level of internal democracy rather than, at least in public, about its religious composition. Turkey's prospects were not helped when, in 2004, President Chirac announced that France would not agree to its admission without the consent of the French people as expressed in a referendum.

EU Integration

In theory we could expect enlargement and integration to be inversely related. After all, the wider the range of countries and cultural traditions that are brought within the Union, the harder it would appear to be to create a shared identity. At present, any of the twenty "official" languages in the EU can be used in any Union forum, thus creating the need for a sizable army of translators to be present whenever Union business takes place. In 2001, when there were only fifteen members, no fewer than 757,900 pages of documentation were translated within the EP alone (Corbett et al., p. 36). In informal discussions, either English or (to an ever-decreasing extent) French tends to be used, for there are few politicians or officials who are not reasonably fluent in at least one of those languages. Language is often a badge of identity, so the profusion of languages imposes a limit to the closeness of identity that can be expected to develop. One writer does indeed argue that each wave of accessions has led to a decline in the coherence of the system and speaks of the "Austro–Hungarianization" of the EU, "a story of steady progress backwards" (Allott, p. 222). Nevertheless, proposals for ever-closer integration run hand in hand with the extension of the EU's membership.

Ever since the first of the three Communities, the ECSC, was founded in the early 1950s, there have been some who have hoped, and others who have feared, that the existing Union framework would become the vehicle for a process generally termed "European integration," ending in the creation of a federal European state similar in its political structure to the United States of America. The feasibility of this idea has ebbed and flowed over the years, but given the establishment of the eurozone it could be argued that it would be illogical, inconsistent, and undemocratic not to have EU-wide political institutions to monitor economic decisions made at the EU level.

There is some variation among the member states on the question of giving more power to the Union institutions (in other words, the Commission and the Parliament) and taking power away from the national governments (in other words, the Council). Of course, there are also nuances of opinion within each country, and there may be differences between verbal positions and the action a government takes when it comes to the crunch. Even so, a certain degree of generalization is possible. Some countries are traditionally *communautaire;* in the forefront of the integrationists can be found Belgium, Italy, the Netherlands, Germany, and Spain. Others are notoriously recalcitrant when it comes to European integration. The countries that have generally led the resistance to moves toward greater unity are Britain, Denmark, and Sweden, but several other states— Austria, Finland, and probably France—would not be far behind them, even though they are usually content to let others take the lead. In 2004 there were expectations that most of the ten new members, because of their relative poverty, would be content to sit quietly while the longer-standing members made the decisions, but Poland's resistance to attempts to reduce the number of Council votes it was awarded by the Nice Treaty showed that this assumption was ill-founded.

What does the European public want? The moves toward European integration that have taken place over the past fifty years have been instigated almost entirely by political elites rather than by the public. The most important decisions have been taken by governments and ratified by parliaments, though 29 referendums, involving seventeen of the member states, took place among the member states between 1970 and 2004. Most member states held a referendum to decide whether to join in the first place, but only in Denmark and Ireland, because of the details of their constitutions, have referendums become the norm. To date, the people of these two nations have approved every treaty, though in both countries one treaty (Maastricht in Denmark and Nice in Ireland) required two votes before the people "got it right." Surveys of opinion consistently find that Catholic southern Europe is more supportive of the EU than Protestant northern Europe, and indeed individual Catholics are more supportive than individual Protestants; strong believers of each religion are more supportive than lukewarm ones (Nelsen et al.). Although the pattern can fluctuate slightly from year to year, generally, among the pre-2004 entrants, Greece, Ireland, Italy, and Spain tend to be Euro-enthusiastic while Austria,

Denmark, Finland, Sweden, and the UK display significant signs of skepticism. Voters in many of the 2004 entrants have fairly low levels of initial enthusiasm, and there is a high percentage of undecideds (for Poland see Kopecky and Mudde, pp. 310–13).

The Institutional Framework

The EU's complicated structures are not only hard to understand but are creaking under the impact of successive enlargements. Accordingly, a convention was established in February 2002 to draw up a new EU constitution, and in June 2004, under the auspices of the Irish presidency, the twenty-five heads of government reached agreement on a constitutional treaty based largely on the convention's recommendations. The constitution is intended to increase transparency and simplicity. If it is adopted there will be only one body, the European Union, with a single document as its written constitution, replacing the present unwieldy structure of a Union, Communities, and pillars, all based on a plethora of different documents.

There will be a number of changes in the institutions. The Commission will continue to consist of one member per state until 2014, after which its membership will be reduced to two-thirds of the number of member states, with equal rotation among the member states. The size of the EP will be raised to 750, with no country having fewer than 6 or more than 96 seats; smaller states will still be overrepresented. The EP's power will be increased, since 95 percent of laws will be made on the basis of co-decision between it and the Council. The EU, for the first time, will have a Minister for Foreign Affairs, thus finally answering the question attributed to Henry Kissinger in the 1970s: "If I want to find out what the EU's foreign policy is, what telephone number do I ring?" The European Council will be chaired by a full-time president with a term of two and a half years, but the various formations of the Council of Ministers will continue to be chaired by each country in turn for a six-month period.

The thorniest question concerned the balance of power within the Council. For several months in 2003–4 there was deadlock between France and Germany, on the one hand, and Poland and Spain on the other. Eventually the agreement reached was that, as of November 2009, the present system under which each minister wields a certain number of votes will end. Instead, a majority within the Council will require a "double majority": 55 percent of the member states (including at least fifteen of the members) representing at least 65 percent of the population. A blocking minority will require at least four states, with at least 35 percent of the population.

We use the word "will" in the previous two paragraphs, but the adoption of this constitution is by no means assured. A number of countries have already indicated the possibility (or in some cases certainty) of holding a referendum on it; besides serial referendum-holders such as Denmark and Ireland, these include Belgium, the Czech Republic, France, Germany, Luxembourg, Netherlands, Poland, Portugal, Spain, and the United Kingdom. The prospect of the constitution's adoption depending on a positive vote from the highly Euroskeptic British people sends a chill down the spine of integrationists, and there are also doubts about whether such a referendum could generate the 50 percent turnout that is needed to make the result valid in a number of postcommunist countries (see Chapter 11). It would therefore be surprising if the constitution were to win support from every member state. If it does not, it cannot come into existence.

❖ REPRESENTATIVE GOVERNMENT AND THE "DEMOCRATIC DEFICIT"

A recurring criticism of the EU is that it suffers from a "democratic deficit"—that its decision makers are not accountable to the European public in the way that we would expect in a democracy and that the EU as an institution suffers from a legitimacy crisis. Others, however, disagree, saying that there is neither a deficit nor a crisis.

The first school points to the inability of voters to exercise any real control over those who make decisions within the EU. Indeed, the decision-making process within the EU is so complicated that very few ordinary Europeans have more than a minimal grasp of it or could say with certainty who should be held responsible for the policies that emerge. Not only do the EU's political structures make it impossible to "throw the rascals out" if voters do not like the outputs of policy, but it is almost impossible for disgruntled voters even to identify the rascals who should be thrown out. Responsibility for some EU policy that does not work out well on the ground could be the fault mainly of government ministers acting in the Council, one or more commissioners, MEPs, or some official at either the EU or the national level working outside political control—or, in the complex polity that the Union is, quite probably some combination of these. Responsibility is diffuse, and the separation of powers could really be "a confusion of powers" (Allott, p. 218). Voters are never presented with alternative programs for the future direction of the EU, or even with alternative sets of decision makers to choose between. Parties, which as we see throughout this book are essential components of a liberal democratic regime, do not dominate the politics of the EU and do not structure the choices facing voters (Mair). There is no real European *demos* (people), with a sense of identity as such, that is willing to accept "rule by Europe" (see the essays in Auer and Flauss, especially the one by Bryde). Whereas people in one part of France, say, accept the legitimacy of decisions made by the government elected by the French people even if they do not personally support those decisions, because of a feeling that "we, the French people" expressed the will behind the decision, the people of France collectively might well not accept as legitimate a policy foisted on them in the name of "the European people." The upshot, according to critics, is that the EU can hardly claim to be a democracy, and given that the Union will admit only democracies to membership, it has been asked sarcastically whether the EU itself would be eligible for membership if it had to apply (for further discussion see Andersen and Eliassen; Harlow).

Others maintain that this criticism is wide of the mark and counter that the EU has only a limited involvement in the decisions that affect people's lives and does not (yet, anyway) wield the kind of power that might lead to people feeling that it is acting beyond its authority, so there is no legitimacy problem (Barker). The Commission employs only from five thousand to seven thousand top officials, around the size of a European city government and so is far from being a kind of unelected dictatorship, and in many respects is "extraordinarily weak" (Moravcsik, "Federalism," p. 171). It is also argued that even if there is no European *demos* at the moment, this might be brought into being by the experience of a common constitution and government, as was the case in a number of countries, such as Switzerland (Hug, p. 111). The institutional design of the EU is anything but undemocratic and can be compared to that of the United States (Crombez). Those who criticize the EU for being insufficiently democratic tend to compare it with an idealized version of a perfect democracy rather than with the imperfect reality of governance in the member states, where most of the faults supposedly displayed by the EU can also be found (Moravcsik, "In Defence"). Similarly, others argue that we should judge the EU not as a conventional nation state but rather as an entity hovering between politics and diplomacy:

> Viewed from the perspective of representative democratic government, the Union is remote and undemocratic. Yet from the perspective of traditional diplomacy and "balance of power" systems, the Union is based on law, regularised procedures, and openness. (Laffan et al., p. 193)

In addition, it is argued, all of the EU's decision makers are constrained by other actors and work under close scrutiny. The level of accountability required from political actors is higher at EU than at national level, as shown by the fate of some politicians who "got away with it" in their own country but were "found out" at EU level, indicating that the EU "is, without a doubt, more transparent than all, or nearly all, of its Member States" (Moravcsik, "Federalism," pp. 174–75).

While this second batch of arguments has merit, the fact remains that the EU does make decisions that affect citizens across Europe yet ordinary Europeans feel that they have little or no ability to affect those decisions or to hold the decision makers accountable. Scharpf, accepting that the decision-making process of the EU lacks legitimacy (the "government by the people" dimension), maintains that the EU can and does nonetheless enjoy legitimacy as "government for the people," in other words by producing policy choices "that can be justified in terms of consensual notions of the public interest" (Scharpf, p. 188). The EU's legitimacy, in this perspective, depends on its delivering good government. It may, in many ways, provide this. It is fair to say that most Europeans are not too dissatisfied with its performance, and there is evidence that the integrationist positions taken by political elites are reasonably close to the preferences of the voters (Carrubba). Even so, the EU cannot be said to amount to particularly representative government.

How could the EU's policy-making process be made more responsive and accountable to ordinary citizens? One idea is to provide for more referendums across the EU to allow the voters a direct voice on major decisions. One objection to this is the claim that when EU referendums take place, voters are more likely to express their views on the government of the day than on the EU issue at stake. Upon closer examination, though, this claim hardly stands up (Gallagher, pp. 239–40). Another objection is that whereas the introduction of EP elections in 1979 could be presented as simply the extension to the EU level of practice at the national level, the same rationale could not be offered for the introduction of EU-wide referendums, given the national variation in the use of the referendum (see Chapter 11). A second idea entails introducing direct elections for the president of the Commission, to allow Europeans to choose their chief executive just as Americans do. One such scheme would require candidates to be nominated by a set number of national MPs or MEPs, and then to compete for "presidential mandates" across the EU, with a runoff between the top two candidates if no one won an overall majority on the first round—the same system as is used for the election of French presidents (Laver et al.). However, this would be a radical step; the national governments would lose a significant element of the control that they possess at present, and the impact of a directly elected president on the functioning of the EU's political system would be unpredictable, so this idea is unlikely to be adopted in the near future.

To defend itself against charges that it is keen to accrete as much power to itself as possible, the Commission stresses that the EU should operate according to the principle of "subsidiarity"—that is, that it should perform only those tasks that cannot be performed effectively at a more immediate or local level. Thus, the EU should not take decisions or try to take care of business that domestic governments are perfectly capable of looking after. This approach is very much to the liking of the more anti-integrationist governments, which are reluctant to let more power than is absolutely necessary drift upward to the EU. The principle of subsidiarity does not mean, of course, that power should necessarily rest with national governments; if applied fully, it means that within each country as much power as possible is devolved downward, to provincial, regional, or local governments. In practice, the extent to which subsidiarity is genuinely applied as the basis of decision making, as manifested in the distribution of power between national and subnational governments, varies widely from country to country around Europe, as we shall see in the next chapter.

REFERENCES

Albi, Anneli: "EU Accession Referendums in the Baltic States," *Tilburg Foreign Law Review,* vol. 11, 2003, pp. 653–70.

Allen, David: "Cohesion and the Structural Funds," in Wallace and Wallace (eds.), pp. 243–65.

Allott, Philip: "Epilogue: Europe and the Dream of Reason," in Weiler and Wind (eds.), pp. 202–25.

Alter, Karen J.: *Establishing the Supremacy of European Law: The Making of an International Rule of Law in Europe,* Oxford University Press, Oxford and New York, 2001.

Andersen, Svein S., and Kjell A. Eliassen (eds.): *The European Union: How Democratic Is It?* Sage, London, 1996.

Arnull, Anthony: "The Rule of Law in the European Union," in Anthony Arnull and Daniel Wincott (eds.), *Accountability and Legitimacy in the European Union,* Oxford University Press, Oxford and New York, 2002, pp. 239–55.

Auer, Andreas, and Jean-François Flauss (eds.): *Le Référendum Européen,* Bruylant, Brussels, 1997.

Barker, Rodney: "Legitimacy, Legitimation, and the European Union?" in Paul Craig and Richard Rawlings (eds.), *Law and Administration in Europe: Essays in Honour of Carol Harlow,* Oxford University Press, Oxford and New York, 2003, pp. 157–74.

Bekkers, V. J. J. M., A. J. C. de Moor-Van Vught, and W. Voermans: "Going Dutch: Problems and Policies Concerning the Implementation of EU Legislation in the Netherlands," in Craig and Harlow (eds.), pp. 454–78.

Blondel, Jean, Richard Sinnott, and Palle Svensson: *People and Parliament in the European Union: Participation, Democracy and Legitimacy,* Clarendon Press, Oxford, 1998.

Bryde, Brun-Otto: "Le Peuple Européen and the European People," in Auer and Flauss (eds.), pp. 251–74.

Burgess, Michael: *Federalism and the European Union: The Building of Europe, 1950–2000,* London, Routledge, 2000.

Burns, Tom: "Better Lawmaking? An Evaluation of Lawmaking in the European Community," in Craig and Harlow (eds.), pp. 435–53.

Carrubba, Clifford J.: "The Electoral Connection in European Union Politics," *Journal of Politics,* vol. 63, no. 1, 2001, pp. 141–58.

Cini, Michelle: "Implementation," in Michelle Cini (ed.), *European Union Politics,* Oxford University Press, Oxford and New York, 2003, pp. 349–64.

Commission of the European Communities: *20th Annual Report on Monitoring the Application of Community Law (2002),* Office for Official Publications of the European Communities, Luxembourg, 2003.

Corbett, Richard, Francis Jacobs, and Michael Shackleton: *The European Parliament,* 5th ed., John Harper Publishing, London, 2003.

Court of Justice: *Statistics of Judicial Activity of the Court of Justice,* 2004. Available at http://curia.eu.int/en/instit/presentationfr/index.htm

Craig, Paul, and Carol Harlow (eds.): *Lawmaking in the European Union,* Kluwer Law International, London, 1998.

Crombez, Christophe: "The Democratic Deficit in the European Union: Much Ado About Nothing?" *European Union Politics,* vol. 4, no. 1, 2003, pp. 101–20.

de Búrca, Gráinne, and J. H. H. Weiler (eds.): *The European Court of Justice,* Oxford University Press, Oxford and New York, 2001.

Demmke, Christoph, and Martin Unfried: *European Environmental Policy: The Administrative Challenge for the Member States,* European Institute of Public Administration, Maastricht, 2001.

de Schoutheete, Philippe: "The European Council," in Peterson and Shackleton (eds.), pp. 21–46.

Dimitrakopoulos, Diontssis, and Jeremy Richardson: "Implementing EU Public Policy," in Richardson (ed.), pp. 335–56.

Dinan, Desmond: *Ever Closer Union: An Introduction to European Integration,* 2nd ed, Macmillan, Basingstoke, 1999.

Falkner, Gerda, Miriam Hartlapp, Simone Leiber, and Oliver Treib: "Non-Compliance with EU Directives in the Member States: Opposition Through the Backdoor?" *West European Politics,* vol. 27, no. 3, 2004, pp. 452–73.

Franklin, Mark: "European Elections and the European Voter," in Richardson (ed.), pp. 201–16.

Freestone, D. A. C., and J. S. Davidson: *The Institutional Framework of the European Communities,* Croom Helm, London and New York, 1988.

Gallagher, Michael: "Conclusion," in Gallagher and Uleri (eds.), pp. 226–52.

Gallagher, Michael, and Pier Vincenzo Uleri (eds.): *The Referendum Experience in Europe,* Macmillan, Basingstoke, 1996.

Harlow, Carol: *Accountability in the European Union,* Oxford University Press, Oxford and New York, 2002.

Hayes-Renshaw, Fiona: "The Council of Ministers," in Peterson and Shackleton (eds.), pp. 47–70.

Hayes-Renshaw, Fiona, and Helen Wallace: *The Council of Ministers,* Macmillan, Basingstoke, 1997.

Hix, Simon: *The Political System of the European Union,* 2nd ed., Palgrave Macmillan, Basingstoke, 2005.

Hix, Simon, Amie Kreppel, and Abdul Noury: "The Party System in the European Parliament: Collusive or Competitive?" *Journal of Common Market Studies,* vol. 41, no. 2, 2003, pp. 309–31.

Hix, Simon, and Christopher Lord: *Political Parties in the European Union,* Macmillan, Basingstoke, 1997.

Hix, Simon, and Roger Scully (eds.): "Special Issue: The European Parliament at Fifty," *Journal of Common Market Studies,* vol. 41, no. 2, 2003.

Hooghe, Liesbet: *The European Commission and the Integration of Europe: Images of Governance,* Cambridge University Press, Cambridge, 2001.

Hug, Simon: *Voices of Europe: Citizens, Referendums, and European Integration,* Rowman and Littlefield, Lanham (MD), 2002.

Hunnings, Neville March: *The European Courts,* Cartermill, London, 1996.

Irwin, Galen: "Second-Order or Third-Rate? Issues in the Campaign for the Elections for the European Parliament 1994," *Electoral Studies,* vol. 14, no. 2, 1995, pp. 183–99.

Jones, Robert A.: *The Politics and Economics of the European Union,* 2nd ed., Edward Elgar, Cheltenham, 2001.

Judge, David, and David Earnshaw: *The European Parliament,* Palgrave Macmillan, Basingstoke, 2003.

Katz, Richard S., and Bernhard Wessels: "Parliaments and Democracy in Europe in the Era of the Euro," in Richard S. Katz and Bernhard Wessels (eds.), *The European Parliament, the National Parliaments, and European Integration,* Oxford University Press, Oxford, 1999, pp. 231–47.

Kenney, Sally J.: "The Judges of the Court of Justice of the European Communities," in Sally J. Kenney, William M. Reisinger, and John C. Reitz (eds.), *Constitutional Dialogues in Comparative Perspective,* Macmillan, Basingstoke, 1999, pp. 143–71.

Kokott, Juliane: "Report on Germany," in Anne-Marie Slaughter, Alec Stone Sweet, and J. H. Weiler (eds.), *The European Court and National Courts— Doctrine and Jurisprudence: Legal Change in Its Social Context,* Hart Publishing, Oxford, 1998, pp. 77–131.

Kopecky, Petr, and Cas Mudde: "The Two Sides of Euroscepticism: Party Positions on European Integration in East Central Europe," *European Union Politics,* vol. 3, no. 3, 2002, pp. 297–326.

Kreppel, Amie: *The European Parliament and Supranational Party System: A Study in Institutional Development,* Cambridge University Press, Cambridge, 2002.

Laffan, Brigid: *The Finances of the European Union,* Macmillan, Basingstoke, 1997.

Laffan, Brigid: "Financial Control: The Court of Auditors and OLAF," in Peterson and Shackleton, (eds.), pp. 233–53.

Laffan, Brigid, Rory O'Donnell, and Michael Smith: *Europe's Experimental Union: Rethinking Integration,* Routledge, London, 1999.

Laffan, Brigid, and Michael Shackleton: "The Budget," in Wallace and Wallace (eds.), pp. 211–41.

Laver, Michael, Michael Gallagher, Michael Marsh, Robert Singh, and Ben Tonra: *Electing the President of the European Commission,* Trinity Blue Papers in Public Policy 1, Department of Political Science, University of Dublin, Dublin, 1995.

Lequesne, Christian: "The Common Fisheries Policy," in Wallace and Wallace (eds.), pp. 345–72.

Lijphart, Arend: *Patterns of Democracy: Government Forms and Performance in Thirty-Six Countries,* Yale University Press, New Haven and London, 1999.

MacMullen, Andrew: "European Commissioners: National Routes to a European Elite," in Nugent (ed.), pp. 28–50.

Mair, Peter: "The Limited Impact of Europe on National Party Systems," *West European Politics,* vol. 23, no. 4, 2000, pp. 27–51.

Marsh, Michael: "Testing the Second-Order Election Model After Four European Elections," *British Journal of Political Science,* vol. 28, no. 4, 1998, pp. 591–607.

Moravcsik, Andrew: "Federalism in the European Union: Rhetoric and Reality," in Kalypso Nicolaidis and Robert Howse (eds.), *The Federal Vision: Legitimacy and Levels of Governance in the United States and the European Union,* Oxford University Press, Oxford and New York, 2001, pp. 161–87.

Moravcsik, Andrew: "In Defence of the Democratic Deficit: Reassessing Legitimacy in the European Union," *Journal of Common Market Studies,* vol. 40, no. 4, 2002, pp. 603–24.

Nelsen, Brent F., James L. Guth, and Cleveland R. Fraser: "Does Religion Matter? Christianity and Public Support for the European Union," *European Union Politics,* vol. 2, no. 2, 2001, pp. 191–217.

Nugent, Neill: *The Government and Politics of the European Community,* 5th ed., Palgrave Macmillan, Basingstoke and New York, 2003.

Nugent, Neill (ed.): *At the Heart of the Union: Studies of the European Commission,* 2nd ed. Macmillan, Basingstoke, 2000.

Pernice, Ingolf: "Rethinking the Methods of Dividing and Controlling the Competencies of the Union," in Mads Andenas and John A. Usher (eds.), *The Treaty of Nice and Beyond,* Hart, Oxford and Portland (OR), 2003, pp. 121–45.

Peters, B. Guy: "The Commission and Implementation in the European Union: Is There an Implementation Deficit and Why?" in Nugent (ed.), pp. 190–205.

Peterson, John: "The College of Commissioners," in Peterson and Shackleton (eds.), pp. 71–94.

Peterson, John: "The European Union: Pooled Sovereignty, Divided Accountability," *Political Studies,* vol. 45, no. 3, 1997, pp. 559–78.

Peterson, John, and Michael Shackleton (eds.): *The Institutions of the European Union,* Oxford University Press, Oxford and New York, 2002.

Pollack, Mark A.: *The Engines of European Integration: Delegation, Agency, and Agenda Setting in the EU,* Oxford University Press, Oxford and New York, 2003.

Raworth, Philip: *Introduction to the Legal System of the European Union,* Oceana, Dobbs Ferry (NY), 2001.

Richardson, Jeremy (ed.): *European Union: Power and Policy-Making,* 2nd ed., Routledge, London and New York, 2001.

Rieger, Elmar: "The Common Agricultural Policy," in Wallace and Wallace (eds.), pp. 179–210.

Sbragia, Alberta: "Key Policies," in Elizabeth Bomberg and Alexander Stubb (eds.), *The European Union: How Does it Work?* Oxford University Press, Oxford and New York, 2003, pp. 111–35.

Scharpf, Fritz W.: *Governing in Europe: Effective and Democratic?* Oxford University Press, Oxford and New York, 1999.

Schmidt, Vivien A.: "National Patterns of Governance Under Siege: The Impact of European Integration," in Beate Kohler-Koch and Rainer Eising (eds.), *The Transformation of Governance in the European Union,* Routledge, London and New York, 1999.

Shackleton, Michael: "The Politics of Codecision," *Journal of Common Market Studies,* vol. 38, no. 2, 2000, pp. 325–42.

Shapiro, Martin: "Implementation, Decisions and Rules," in J. A. E. Vervaele, G. Betlem, R. de Lange, and A. G. Veldman (eds.), *Compliance and Enforcement of European Community Law,* Kluwer Law International, The Hague, 1999, pp. 27–34.

Shapiro, Martin, and Alec Stone Sweet: *On Law, Politics, and Judicialization,* Oxford University Press, Oxford and New York, 2002.

Sherrington, Philippa: *The Council of Ministers: Political Authority in the European Union,* Pinter, London and New York, 2000.

Smith, Mitchell P.: "The Commission Made Me Do It: The European Commission as a Strategic Asset in Domestic Politics," in Nugent (ed.), pp. 170–89.

Snyder, Francis: "The Effectiveness of European Community Law: Institutions, Processes, Tools and Techniques," in Terence Daintith (ed.), *Implementing EC Law in the United Kingdom: Structures for Indirect Rule,* John Wiley, Chichester, 1995, pp. 49–87.

Stone Sweet, Alec: *Governing with Judges: Constitutional Politics in Europe,* Oxford University Press, Oxford and New York, 2000.

Svensson, Palle: "Denmark: The Referendum as Minority Protection," in Gallagher and Uleri (eds.), pp. 33–51.

Sverdrup, Ulf: "Compliance and Conflict Management in the European Union: Nordic Exceptionalism," *Scandinavian Political Studies,* vol. 27, no. 1, 2004, pp. 23–43.

Szczerbiak, Aleks, and Paul Taggart: "The Politics of European Referendum Outcomes and Turnout: Two Models," *West European Politics,* vol. 27, no. 4, 2004, pp. 557–83.

Tallberg, Jonas: *European Governance and Supranational Institutions: Making States Comply,* Routledge, London and New York, 2003.

Wallace, Helen, and William Wallace (eds.): *Policy-Making in the European Union,* 4th ed., Oxford University Press, Oxford and New York, 2000.

Weiler, J. H. H.: "Epilogue: The Judicial Après Nice," in de Búrca and Weiler (eds.), pp. 215–26.

Weiler, J. H. H., and Marlene Wind (eds.): *European Constitutionalism Beyond the Nation State,* Cambridge University Press, Cambridge, 2003.

Wessels, Bernhard: "Whom to Represent? Role Orientations of Legislators in Europe," in Hermann Schmitt and Jacques Thomassen (eds.), *Political Representation and Legitimacy in the European Union,* Oxford University Press, Oxford, 1999, pp. 209–34.

Wessels, Wolfgang, and Udo Diedrichs: "The European Parliament and EU Legitimacy," in Thomas Banchoff and Mitchell P. Smith (eds.), *Legitimacy and the European Union: The Contested Polity,* Routledge, London and New York, 1999, pp. 134–52.

Wind, Marlene: "The European Union as a Polycentric Polity: Returning to a Neo-Medieval Europe?" in Weiler and Wind (eds.), pp. 103–31.

Wyller, Thomas: "Norway: Six Exceptions to the Rule," in Gallagher and Uleri (eds.), pp. 139–52.

CHAPTER 6

LEVELS OF GOVERNANCE

Elections, political parties, parliaments, and governments are the first things in most people's minds when they think about representative government in modern Europe. However, most of the key public decisions that affect what happens in the real world deal with a wide range of matters that are certainly political but lie outside the realm of front-line electoral politics. At a grand international level, for example, every government in the world had to decide in 2003 how it would respond, without an electoral mandate on the matter, to the dramatic series of events unfolding in Iraq. At a national level, key public decisions have to be made about many important aspects of macroeconomic policy, including levels of service and spending in major parts of the public sector such as health, education, or policing. At a regional level, decisions are needed on important matters such as investments in roads, public transport, and other aspects of the communications infrastructure. At a local level, public decisions may involve critical issues such as land-use planning and zoning—making trade-offs, for example, between the need to provide new housing in a particular area and the need to protect the environment and amenities of people who already live there. At the level of the individual citizen, important decisions on the practical implementation of policy must be made about matters such as whether particular individuals are deemed eligible for given health or welfare benefits.

A large part of the business of running a country, of real-life governance, is about administering the machinery of state. It is about making practical policy decisions that give expression to the general principles that might have been contested and eventually settled in the arenas of representative politics. This means that a large part of how representative government really works on the ground has to do with the relationship between politics and public administration. As we explained when looking at the role of the executive in Chapter 2, the formal link between politics and public administration in European representative democracies is provided by the two key overlapping roles of a cabinet minister—a person who is at the same time part of the political executive and head of a major administrative department. This focuses our attention on the interaction between politics and public administration at the national level, and in particular the interaction between senior politicians and senior civil servants.

Another important aspect of real-life governance concerns *where* each public decision is made—in particular, whether key decisions are made at the local, regional, national, or supranational level. The jurisdiction of any government is never all-embracing. Even in the most totalitarian of societies, "the government" does not tell people how many times to chew their food, when to breathe, or what to dream about. In these respects, at least, each person is a self-governing principality, and there is no such thing as an absolutely unitary state. As we move from the level of the individual decision maker to the level of the national government (and beyond, to supranational institutions), we find a large number of different places in which decisions are made. These range from the family, to the street, to the neighborhood, to the district, to the town, to the county, to the region, to the province, and on to the nation state. This variety reflects a reality in which different decisions bear in different ways on different geographical groups of individuals, who therefore have different interests in affecting the outcome. Thus, a decision about whether or not the national government builds a new bridge in some particular place has vastly different consequences for different people, depending on where they live. The lives of people who live right beside the bridge may be ruined by its noise and disruption. People who live in the region but not in the immediate locality of the bridge may find the bridge saves them hours each week behind the wheel of an automobile and reduces the risk of being involved in a fatal accident. Those who live elsewhere in the country but too far away ever to use the bridge may be forced to pay for part of it with their taxes while getting, as they see it, no benefits from it. The extent to which the interests of these different constituencies of individuals are represented in the eventual outcome is affected crucially by whether the ultimate decision is made at the local, regional, or national level.

The themes that we touched on here raise huge questions, each of which could occupy a lifetime's research or a fat book in its own right. In this chapter we focus on some of the key issues, since if we are interested in representative government it is important to have some sense of how and where the outputs of representative decision making are implemented. We look first at the relationship between politicians and the civil service at national level, before moving on to consider the different geographic levels at which decisions might be made.

✦ POLITICIANS AND THE CIVIL SERVICE

> Politicians in all forms of government must delegate policymaking authority to bureaucrats. Since this practical necessity can result in substantial authority by bureaucrats over society, concern about excessive influence by bureaucrats has a long history. (Huber and Shipan, p. 17)

A typical modern European government, as we have seen, comprises a cabinet chaired by a prime minister and composed of a set of ministers who are usually senior party politicians. Most ministers not only are members of the cabinet as a collective entity but also are individually responsible as the political heads of important government departments. When we look at the relationship between minister, as politician, and the bureaucrats in his or her department from the top down, we see that the doctrine of individual ministerial responsibility means that it is the minister's job to make sure that the bureaucrats actually do implement government policy. This job is particularly important when government policy changes. The minister must ensure that the department does not just blithely go on with its day-to-day routine, doing things exactly as it has always done them. If this role is not fulfilled, then official government *policy* may change at the level of the cabinet, but nothing may actually change in the real world.

Looking at the relationship between minister and department from the bottom up, we see that the doctrine of individual ministerial responsibility means that the buck stops with the minister for bureaucratic mistakes and misjudgments in his or her department. The *theory* is certainly that the minister must resign, or at least offer to resign, in the face of serious civil service blunders, even when he or she had no personal dealings with the matter. Indeed, the convention that a minister may have to resign in such circumstances is what gives all ministers an incentive to police their departments with vigilance. In *practice,* however, as noted in Chapter 2, not all ministers do offer to resign as a result of blunders in their departments in which they had no close hands-on involvement. Indeed, recent examples of this happening are actually quite hard to come by. The tendency for ministers to unload the blame for such problems onto their civil servants appears to be growing, thereby undermining the constitutional doctrine of individual ministerial responsibility. (See Woodhouse for a more detailed discussion of this matter.)

The relationship between a European cabinet minister and the state bureaucracy under his or her jurisdiction has long been a topic of heated debate. There are very different civil service traditions in this regard, both in western Europe and in the former communist states of eastern Europe—while radical reform of the civil service has been an important project for all countries experiencing a transition to democracy. In the former communist states, the entire civil service was systematically politicized in what was known as the *nomenklatura* system. In order to ensure that the civil service implemented the wishes and decisions of the communist party, almost all civil service appointments were under the patronage of the party. Only individuals vetted and approved by the party—the *nomenklatura*—could hold civil service positions, and promotion and advancement depended at least as much on political as on administrative criteria. Under the *nomenklatura* system, therefore, the problem of ensuring civil service responsiveness to political decisions was addressed by politicizing the civil service.

The evolving western European bureaucratic tradition has seen the civil service as an independent "corps" of professional administrators rather than as a "cadre" of partisan functionaries. This view leaves open the matter of how independent administrators can be made responsive to political decisions arising from the process of representative government. The formal position—typically promoted by the civil service itself—is that the civil service is no more than a loyal and efficient administrative apparatus, a neutral policy implementation machine that has no political opinions of its own but merely puts into practice political decisions made by democratically elected public representatives. According to this ideal, policing the bureaucracy is simply a technical administrative problem of designing the appropriate monitoring systems, because the interests of politicians and bureaucrats will never conflict. Of course, a complicated modern world may need a complicated bureaucracy to administer it, so this monitoring is not a trivial problem. Essentially, however, it remains a technical problem of designing an administrative system that works, rather than a political problem of controlling a complex system of administrators, all trying to promote their private political agendas.

In practice few people, even civil servants, regard the civil service as an automatic implementation machine. This raises the vital issue of political, as opposed to purely administrative, control of the state bureaucracy. Here we focus on two important factors that affect the political relationship between ministers and senior bureaucrats. The first concerns the political culture of the civil service itself—in particular, the way in which the political culture derives from patterns of recruitment and training. The second concerns the extent to which ministers can select their senior civil service advisers and thereby feel more confident in political terms that they are being advised by people who are not pursuing conflicting policy objectives.

Civil Service Cultures

Looking first at the culture of the national civil service, we find that, as with legal systems, western European bureaucracies can rather easily be divided into two broad types. To these types as we have just seen, we can add the highly politicized *nomenklatura* system that was the initial bureaucratic inheritance of the eastern European countries considered here. Once more we will see that, although these broad differences are helpful in providing a way to think about things, the differences are often much smaller in practice than they might seem at first sight.

On the one hand, there is a style of civil service in the British mold. Supporters would describe this as "generalist," opponents as "dilettante." This type of bureaucracy is characterized by a heavy reliance on civil servants who succeed or fail on the basis of their general administrative and managerial skills, as opposed to any particular areas of technical expertise. The administrative system tends to reproduce itself on the basis of a very heavy emphasis on peer group pressure and socialization into a particular decision-making culture, as opposed to technical training in particular skills.

The archetypal case of a generalist civil service can be found in Britain, a generalist civil service was inherited on independence by Ireland, and strong tendencies in this direction can also be seen in Italy, Spain, and Portugal. The image, and to some extent the reality in Britain, is of a civil service staffed at senior levels by classics scholars from prestigious private secondary schools and universities (Hennessy). Although various commissions of inquiry into the British civil service have commented on this situation and recommended a variety of reforms, it is extraordinarily difficult to reorient an entire civil service culture. Perhaps most important, there are still separate career tracks for individuals—be they statisticians, engineers, or scientists—who are recruited on the basis of specific technical expertise and for those who are recruited as generalist administrators. Those attempting to make the transition from (more junior) specialist to (more senior) generalist still face many obstacles. Those recruited as fast-track general administrators, imbued with the culture that these positions tend to imply, still have a clear head start over their more technocratic rivals.

The main European alternative to the generalist civil service culture epitomized by Britain has a far more technocratic ethos, characterized by much greater reliance on specialists and technical training, either in administrative skills or in specialized roles such as economist, engineer, or lawyer. The French civil service, for example, is divided into a series of administrative "*corps,*" known as the Grand Corps de l'État, membership in which is absolutely essential for a successful career in the civil service. These *corps* recruit, train, and socialize members on the basis of what is effectively an alternative higher education system outside the university sector. They have a series of dedicated schools, in particular the École Polytechnique, which specialize

in technical education and recruit students on the basis of intensely competitive exam-
inations. A specialized administrative education is given by the École Nationale
d'Administration, which recruits students who have an undergraduate degree, once
more on the basis of a very competitive examination that candidates spend a long
time preparing for. Despite periodic attempts to liberalize this process and open up
other methods of entry, almost all entrants to the senior civil service in France follow
one of these routes.

Although it might seem as if this pattern of civil service education in France would
produce an administrative elite with a high degree of technical expertise, French civil
servants may find themselves doing jobs that bear little concrete relationship to their technical training. As with most forms of education almost everywhere, however, what is of
primary importance is the process by which students are socialized into a particular culture. The most relevant aspect of this process in the present context is the technocratic
approach to problem solving by administrative elites, rather than any specific area of substantive expertise, which in all civil services (in common with most other careers) is most
effectively learned on the job.

The German civil service is also generally felt to have a technocratic ethos,
though the emphasis in this case is on legal training, and a very high proportion of
German civil servants have a legal background. Recruitment to the senior civil service
takes place after undergraduate university education. It is intensely competitive and
based on a general state examination consisting largely of law and political science—
making these subjects preferred choices for undergraduates hoping to enter the civil
service. In common with France, however, and unlike Britain, Germany has a civil
service whose recruitment and socialization process is education oriented and subject
focused; as result German civil servants tend to think of themselves as technocratic
public administrators.

Although much is made of differences in civil service cultures by scholars whose
primary intellectual concern is with the internal workings of the bureaucracy, the impact
of cultural differences on the interface between the partisan political system and the
civil service may not be as great as some suggest. It is more or less the received wisdom these days, both among more traditional institutional theorists in the tradition of
Wildavsky, for example, and among economic modelers in the tradition of Niskanen,
that all bureaucracies can be seen as groups of people concerned to advance their own
interests, typically by increasing the size of their agencies and maximizing their budgets.
A variation on this argument has been put forward by Dunleavy, who argues that civil
servants are interested not so much in maximizing budgets as in making their jobs more
congenial. This tendency results in what he calls "bureau shaping" by public administrators. Thus civil servants in the department of finance may advise against wholesale
tax reform, for example, not because of any impact it might have on the size of their
empire but because such reform may promise to upset a well-oiled administrative system
and even threaten established intradepartmental power structures. Thus, other things
being equal, there is a general tendency for bureaucracies to resist political change that
runs counter to bureaucratic interests.

Such tendencies are likely to affect all civil services, regardless of their
administrative cultures. To the extent that they do, arguments about the different civil
service cultures that prevail in different European states may tend to exaggerate the

practical differences we find on the ground. This view also suggests that control of the bureaucracy is a political as well as a technical administrative problem, the matter to which we now turn.

The Politicization of Senior Bureaucrats

The need for political as well as administrative control of the bureaucracy explains why the issue of the politicization of parts of the senior civil service is so important. Even if the civil service were nothing more than a well-oiled and unfeeling machine to which politicians could issue orders that would be carried out to the letter, ministers would still need to be able to rely on people who shared their own political viewpoints for help with developing new policy proposals. If the civil service does indeed have an agenda of its own, furthermore, then ministers are likely to want to have in key positions people they can trust politically, to make sure that what politicians decide is carried out when policy implementation passes down the line. The more complex and technical policy areas become, the less transparent is the implementation process, and the greater is the need for ministers to have policy specialists from their own political camps, either in the senior echelons of their departments or at least with an overview of them.

At the same time the civil service does need to provide a comprehensive source of independent expertise from which political decision makers can draw. In an increasingly technical world, this expertise is likely to extend far beyond the knowledge and competence of senior elected politicians, who will inevitably need to rely on the independent advice of their civil servants if they are to make wise decisions in the public interest. Such independent advice is unlikely to be provided by bureaucrats who are no more than the political lackeys of the parties in power.

There is thus a delicate balancing act to be performed in designing a system that guarantees ministers genuinely independent technical advice yet at the same time reassures ministers that their political preferences—preferences that after all have recently been endorsed by the voters—are also respected by the senior administrators who have the job of implementing them. Intriguingly, since the collapse of the former Soviet Union, we can observe European countries following two quite distinct trajectories in this regard.

For the former communist states of eastern Europe, the key bureaucratic issue has been the depoliticization of their inherited *nomenklatura* systems. Depoliticization poses some surprisingly difficult problems and is much easier said than done. For forty or fifty years, nearly all of the individuals appointed to civil service positions in eastern Europe were politically vetted and approved; the civil services in these countries—the entire group of people with practical experience of running the machinery of state—were appointed by the communist party. Obviously it was impossible in practical terms to replace this entire administrative cohort overnight. Thus the newly democratizing states had to rely, for their initial public administration, on civil services whose personnel and bureaucratic cultures were rooted in the Soviet era.

Although pressure for economic and political reforms tended to push those matters ahead of bureaucratic reform as priorities for urgent action, the selection of a civil service "model" for the transition states was clearly an important issue. On the one hand, there was an understandable desire among elected politicians in the postcommunist era to ensure that "their" people, rather than functionaries of the old one-party state, were running the civil service. This desire led to high levels of turnover in the senior civil service, the personnel of which changed as governments changed. Such turnover tends to undermine the development of an "independent" professional civil service capable of serving governments of many different political stripes. On the other hand, there is a desire to move away from the highly politicized state bureaucracy of the Soviet era, which will require the evolution over time of mutual trust between politicians and public servants. Because such trust derives from deeply rooted civil service traditions of professionalism and meritocracy, depoliticization will require a period of stability in the corps of senior civil servants in each country. Stability can occur only if incoming ministers forbear from parachuting all of their own people into the top civil service positions as soon as they take office. Given the time it takes for any civil service culture to develop—for the most senior bureaucrats to be drawn from the ranks of those who were socialized into the culture as young administrators—it will be a while before the final shape of the relationship between politicians and civil servants in eastern Europe will stabilize. (For a review of eastern European civil services, see Verheijen.)

In western Europe, the trend if anything has been toward the politicization of the civil service, although nowhere in the west do we find the highly politicized system of appointments to the senior civil service that exists in the United States. When a U.S. president changes, so does a high proportion of the most senior bureaucrats in the main federal departments and agencies. A large group of lawyers, academics, and other professionals known to be sympathetic to the president's views are brought in, typically from outside the government system as a whole, to take over the levers of power. A vestige of a spoils system designed to reward individuals who helped the president get elected, this system is now used far more to ensure that the president can take effective political control of the senior bureaucracy.

Starting from a position at the opposite extreme to this are Britain and Ireland, where official civil service culture has traditionally been strenuously nonpartisan. When a new minister takes office and walks into his or her department for the first time, this is very much a voyage into the unknown. The minister will be greeted by the civil service head of the department, most likely a total stranger who has been in the same department for thirty years or more and knows every nook and cranny of it. All of the papers of the former minister typically will have been removed, and the new minister will have to become familiar with the new job on the basis of briefings by senior civil servants. If the political "master" and his or her civil "servants" do not get along, there is not much to be done about it; this is the hand the minister has been dealt, and the minister must play it. A new minister who is particularly powerful may be able to get the department head moved, but even then there will be a very limited choice of candidates from which to pick a successor.

On the other side of this coin, most senior British and Irish civil servants take a positive pride in being able to serve different political masters and have been thoroughly socialized over a long career into the need to do their very best for the minister of the day. A very striking example of this could be seen in late 1999, with the formation of the cabinet to take over a range of executive functions in Northern Ireland. Martin McGuinness, a high-profile Sinn Féin politician seen as having had close associations with the outlawed paramilitary IRA, was appointed as the new Northern Ireland Minister

Well-known republican activist Martin McGuinness, following his appointment as Northern Ireland Minister of Education in 1999, meets the head of his civil service department for the first time. © United Kingdom PA Photos Limited

of Education—one of the big-budget departments in the new administration. No matter how surprised senior civil servants might have been at the identity of their controversial new ministerial boss, top bureaucrats took care to be photographed smiling and greeting him warmly as he arrived for his first day of work. This, indeed, was one of the enduring public images of the dramatic installation of a new executive in Northern Ireland.

In general, while they typically pride themselves on being nonpartisan, it is not the case that senior civil servants are indifferent to the identity of their political masters. If they do have a preference for one minister over another, however, it is typically based not on particular policies but rather on the desire to have a strong political boss rather than a weak one. What senior civil servants most like tends to be a really powerful minister, a "big beast of the jungle," in the words of Anthony King, who can fight and win the department's case in cabinet and who will not be forced into embarrassing public climbdowns. (For a lengthy but outstanding treatment of the British civil service in these terms, see Hennessy.)

Even in Britain, however, recent trends are toward the creation of a new political cadre within the senior civil service. When Labour Party leader Harold Wilson first became British prime minister in 1964, after a long period of Conservative rule, he feared that the civil service would not cooperate in a series of major policy changes he wished to implement. He therefore appointed a number of "outsiders" with well-known Labour credentials to specially created positions as personal advisers. For the most part, the career civil servants resented what they saw as interlopers and were able in a passive but nonetheless very effective manner to freeze them out of the decision-making process. Margaret Thatcher distrusted the senior civil service as much as Harold Wilson and also appointed her own personal advisers from outside the government system, fearing that public servants might not cooperate in the massive cutbacks of the public service that she wished to implement. When Labour returned to power under Tony Blair in 1997, and again in 2001, political advisers to key ministers continued to be very important players in the policy-making process. For many ministers, key advisers came to be seen as gatekeepers in the system. Many of them were policy specialists with solid Labour credentials. Thus, in addition to providing technical advice, they were able to be the eyes, ears, and sometimes even voice of the minister in the policy process. The net result was a system in which the policy-making role of the senior civil service was "supplemented," at the very least, by a more politicized cadre of ministerial advisers.

On continental Europe, there is a higher level of politicization of the senior civil service in countries such as Belgium, France, and Germany. In France, politicization has been quite explicitly institutionalized into a system of ministerial *cabinets,* teams of trusted ministerial advisers. The head of the team, the *directeur de cabinet,* may indeed be endowed with the authority of the minister. (The term *cabinet* when used in this context is always pronounced as a French word, as if spelled "cabinay," to distinguish it from the cabinet of ministers, with a "t," that forms the government.)

These *cabinets* are teams of about twenty to thirty policy professionals on whom the ministers can rely for two important forms of support that might otherwise be missing. The first is to ensure that ministerial policies are actually carried out on the ground; members of the *cabinet* in effect are the minister's eyes and ears within the department. The second is to advise the minister on developments outside the department that are likely to have a bearing on the minister's departmental responsibilities. As we have noted, in the complex environment in which any modern cabinet minister must work, ministers are for the most part forced to concentrate on their own departmental briefs. A department's career civil servants also may be preoccupied with rather specific departmental responsibilities. As a result, there is a danger that developments outside the department may catch the minister by surprise, because a real-world policy problem is likely to have an impact on a range of government departments even if one department has ultimate responsibility for dealing with it. The *cabinet* will keep track of events outside the minister's department, reporting on external developments that the minister needs to be aware of and acting as a point of contact with other government departments.

Although in theory the *cabinet* system gives French ministers the opportunity to appoint outside policy advisers to guard against being railroaded by the civil service, in practice the vast majority of members of a typical ministerial *cabinet* are civil servants. As we mentioned in Chapter 2 when discussing the executive, however, many French ministers are themselves former civil servants, and the political affiliations of civil servants in France are often more explicit than those elsewhere in Europe. This makes it easier for an incoming minister to select for the *cabinet* a team of civil servants who can be relied on to share his or her general political approach.

The system of French ministerial *cabinets* also can be found in Belgium, where there is also a substantial turnover in the minister's senior civil service team when political power changes hands. It cannot be found in quite such an explicit and institutionalized form in any other European country, although the trend is running strongly in the direction of having more people involved as part of a personal team of advisers tied to a particular minister.

In the Netherlands, for example, ministers seek advice from a wide range of policy professionals, commissioning studies and policy reviews that are conducted outside the career civil service by people whose political affiliations are often quite explicit. This occurs in the context of a system in which only the very top positions in a government department are open to any political input in the nomination process, and those appointed to these top positions stay in post after the minister leaves office. This may well lead ministers to feel that the political loyalties of senior civil servants differ from their own. In recent years several incidents in which the loyalty of senior civil servants has been discussed have led to a revival of interest in the doctrine of ministerial responsibility.

In part, of course, the trend toward more explicitly political ministerial *cabinets* is probably no more than an explicit recognition in an increasingly technocratic world of something that has always been there—namely the need for ministers to have access to expert advice that they feel comes from an ideologically sympathetic perspective and that is based outside the civil service department of which they are the political head.

Conclusion: The Increasing Accountability of Public Servants?

Overall, there can be no doubt that, regardless of its culture and style, public administration is political and that public bureaucrats are in many senses politicians in their own right. Senior civil servants make important decisions about policy implementation, albeit under the auspices of political bosses. These decisions have important implications for the allocation of resources among different social actors—something that is of the very essence of politics. Civil servants are also responsible for much of the preliminary work that goes into the development of new policy initiatives—and thus leave their fingerprints all over the making of public policy in many subtle ways. Indeed, for a young person leaving university in almost any European country with the ambition to have a real impact on public life, joining the civil service is an option at least as likely to be effective as becoming a rank-and-file elected politician. The interaction between the senior civil service and the political executive is thus a vital one to understand for all who are interested not only in the implementation but also in the shaping and making, of important public policy decisions.

At the purely administrative level, furthermore, increasing skepticism about the management style associated with the traditional "big government" public sector has led to a growing influence of the ideas of "new public management." These stress the need for a clear sense of mission in each public sector department, the need for a strategic plan for how to realize this vision, the need for a client-centered approach to service delivery, and the need for the public sector to be held clearly accountable for any failure to deliver. These managerial developments, combined with a situation in which cabinet ministers seem less and less inclined to take the rap for everything in their jurisdiction, are likely to make the public accountability of senior civil servants a matter of increasing public concern.

✦ LEVELS OF GOVERNANCE

Despite their many similarities, modern European states vary hugely in the territorial organization of decision making. Traditionally, for example, Britain and Ireland have been highly centralized states in which most important decisions are made at the national level. In other countries, especially Switzerland but also Germany and Austria, decision making has traditionally been far more decentralized. Taking European countries as a whole, however, we notice that the trend for important decisions to be taken at the EU rather than at the national level, discussed in Chapter 5, has been combined with a strong tendency within individual countries toward greater decentralization, which involves the shifting of important policy *decisions,* not just policy *implementation,* to more local or regional arenas. This trend has been evident even in countries such as Britain and France, noted for much of their recent history as having very centralized decision-making regimes (Batley; Stoker). In countries that already have well-established institutions for local decision making—for example, Sweden and Denmark—even more powers are being handed over to local authorities. For east European countries undergoing a transition to democratic governance, furthermore, it is easy to see that decisions on the decentralization of decision making are very significant indeed. Under their former communist administrations, municipalities and regions were to a large extent part of a top-down system of local administration, with decisions made nationally being implemented at the local level. A fundamental part of the democratization process in eastern Europe, therefore, was settling on the extent of decision-making autonomy for local government units. This was the subject of extended debate in Poland, for example, resulting in provisions in the 1997 constitution that entrenched the principle of "subsidiarity" discussed in Chapter 5—which in this context essentially means that policy decisions should be taken at the lowest level of government that is practically feasible.

There are two different, though related, features of the decentralization of decision making in modern Europe. The first has to do with the distinction between "federal" and "unitary" states (although, as we will see, this distinction is becoming blurred by the increasing powers of the regional tier of government in a number of European countries). The second has to do with the system of local government. It is possible for unitary states to have strong systems of local government. And it is also possible for federal states to have weak local government systems.

✦ FEDERAL GOVERNMENT IN MODERN EUROPE

Although most people feel that they know a federal state when they see one, it is actually quite difficult to produce an abstract definition of a federal state. In the European context the problem is complicated by the fact that the main examples of federal states—Switzerland, Germany, Austria, and, since 1993, Belgium—not only are very diverse institutionally but also differ in striking respects from non-European federal states such as the United States, Canada, and Australia. It is further complicated by the fact that countries such as Spain and Britain, once bastions of centralized governance, have moved strikingly toward the establishment of strong regional administrations and assemblies with substantial powers. In doing so they now look far more "federal" than they once did.

This text, however, is not the place to luxuriate in the theoretical nuances of various definitions of federation, confederation, and federalism (see Burgess; Elazar; P. King). We merely pause to note that most authors agree that "federation" implies an irrevocable entrenchment of some level of regional (state) government within the national decision-making process, with significant powers that are protected by the constitution.

In the remainder of this section, we explore federal government in modern Europe in a more empirical manner. We leave to one side the post-1993 Belgian case, which is an attempt at a constitutional solution to the country's long-standing problem of incorporating deeply entrenched language communities into national governance rather than an exemplar of federalism European-style. It involves a unique and complex inter-action between three geographical units—Brussels, Flanders, and Wallonia—and three language communities: Dutch, French, and German. To further complicate matters, Brussels, the "bilingual" capital of Belgium, in practice has a huge majority of French-speakers yet is geographically located within Dutch-speaking Flanders. (See Fitzmaurice for a discussion of post-1993 Belgian federalism.) In what follows, therefore, we outline the territorial distribution of decision making in Switzerland and Germany, which almost all observers take to be federal states, whatever definition they use. (The remaining major example of federalism in Europe, Austria, can be seen as being much closer to Germany than to Switzerland.) We also discuss the decisions *not* to adopt federalist arrangements by eastern European states making the transition from communist rule.

Federal Government in Switzerland

There is some difference between the romantic image and the practical reality of federal government in Switzerland. The romantic image dates the Swiss confederation back to 1291 and portrays it as a loose union of ancient provinces, called cantons, that arouse intense loyalties among their citizens and only grudgingly cede very limited powers to the Swiss central government. The practical reality of the modern Swiss state is that it is governed according to a federal constitution that dates from 1875 and was framed on the basis of European observations of, among other things, the experience of federalism in the United States. Nonetheless, twenty-five of the twenty-six cantons that form the constituent parts of the union are indeed very old, although Jura was formed from a part of Berne in 1980. Earlier Swiss federations had united three of these cantons (from 1315 to 1515), thirteen of them (from 1515 to 1798), and all twenty-five (from 1815 to 1875). (For a discussion of the evolution of the Swiss federation, see Hughes.) As Hughes points out, none of these cantons was ever really a fully autonomous state as we would now understand the term—another parallel with the constituent states of what is now the United States. Furthermore, when we actually look at what the cantons have the power to do, this turns out to be quite limited, on a par with the power of typical local author-ities in many European countries.

What underpins Swiss federalism has as much to do with the social structure as with the constitution. In the first place, a canton does evoke strong feelings of traditional loyalty among many of its citizens, to the extent that the canton is often their primary focus of political affiliation, as opposed to the Swiss state itself. Probably more important than historical loyalties are two significant sources of social division in Switzerland—language and religion. The population consists of French-, German-, and Italian-speakers.

The population also is divided between Protestants and Roman Catholics. Although those two broad cleavages cut across one another so that not all members of the same language group have the same religion, and vice versa, language and religious frontiers nonetheless do follow the borders of cantons rather closely.

Almost all cantons comprise an overwhelming majority of one or the other language group, for example, and are strictly unilingual. The different language groups keep very much to themselves at the local level, and only at the federal level does social and political life become bilingual or even trilingual. Because language defines the communication structure of any society, the distribution of language groups in Switzerland is almost bound to impede any process of centralization.

Religious groups are also sorted between cantons in a very structured manner. Individual cantons are either mostly Protestant or mostly Roman Catholic, reflecting the historical role of the cantons in assimilating or resisting the Reformation. Because organized religion provides almost as powerful a cultural network as language, this geographical pattern of religious affiliation also serves to establish the canton as a focus of social and political life. (See Linder, pp. 1–37, for a discussion of the political impact of religious and linguistic diversity in Switzerland.)

Despite these obvious sources of individual loyalty to the canton, there is more or less general agreement that the trend in Switzerland has been toward greater centralization. The list of functions formally allocated to the federal government is long and growing longer; local councils in "unitary" systems such as Sweden and Denmark typically have more functions than Swiss cantons. (Linder, pp. 40–44, sets out the relative powers of the federation and the cantons in Switzerland.)

Nonetheless, Swiss cantons do have substantial powers and are responsible for the administration of much of the welfare state, overall policy for which is set at the federal level. They have power to set local taxes, including income taxes, and above all their autonomy is deeply entrenched in the constitution. One very important manifestation of this autonomy is Article 3 of the federal constitution, which vests all future powers in the cantons. New powers can be given to the federal authority only with agreement by the cantons and by the people in a referendum. This restriction clearly limits the growth of federal government. As a result, the share of both taxes and spending under the control of the federal government in Switzerland is much lower, for example, than the share controlled by the federal government in the United States, and very much lower than in unitary government systems such as the Netherlands or Spain (Linder, p. 43). The power of central government in Switzerland is further weakened by the long-standing custom that the presidency of the Swiss Federation rotates between senior politicians on an annual basis, resulting in a situation that means the vast majority of Swiss citizens do not know who their president is. In general, the particular character of Swiss federalism means that the visibility of Swiss national politicians is lower than that of national politicians in most other modern European states.

A second important manifestation of the constitutional entrenchment of the autonomy of the canton can be seen in the relationship between the two chambers of the Swiss legislature. As in most federal systems, the lower house (the National Council) is elected on a one-person-one-vote basis to represent the population as a whole, and the upper house (the Council of States) is designed to represent the interest of the constituent states of the federation, the cantons. The Council of States thus has two representatives from every full canton. The cantons themselves determine how these representatives are selected, although they are now for the most part directly elected, often by majority rule. If both upper and lower houses do not pass legislation, then it cannot be passed; there is no provision for one house to overturn the vote of the other by special majority. This means that the autonomy of the cantons vis-à-vis the central government is entrenched somewhat more deeply than that of the constituent parts of the German federal state, to which we now turn.

Federal Government in Germany

The historical and cultural context of the German federal state is quite different. The current German constitution, or Basic Law, was effectively framed for what was then West Germany by the victorious western Allies in 1949. It was an explicit piece of constitutional engineering, using a federal structure to prevent the emergence of the type of powerful centralized state seen in Bismarck's Prussia and Hitler's Third Reich. Indeed, so concerned were the Allies to decentralize the German state that the implementation of an extensive system of local government was already well under way by the end of 1945. Although some of the constituent states (Länder) of West Germany—Bavaria, for example—had long historical traditions, many were formed from scratch from the areas that the three western occupying powers, Britain, France, and the United States, happened to control. There was a huge variation in the sizes of the states. Some are no more than medium-sized cities; others, especially North Rhine–Westphalia, are bigger than many European countries.

Not surprisingly given this context, the German federal arrangements set out in the Basic Law borrowed heavily from U.S. experience. Furthermore, given the fears of the Allies at the time, the federal structure is given an "eternal guarantee" in Articles 20 and 79 of the Basic Law: Abolishing the federal system in Germany would in effect require a revolution that overthrew the constitution as a whole. As we saw in Chapter 4, however, citizens in a number of countries have introduced completely new constitutions on the basis of the consent of a majority of the population. Thus constitutional guarantees such as these, however "eternal" they might purport to be, are never really absolute. The reunification of Germany in October 1990 resulted in the assimilation of 16 million people living in five Länder from the former East Germany. In addition, with the unification of Berlin, this city became a Land in its own right, so there are sixteen Länder in the united Germany. The postunification system of Länder, therefore, seems likely to persist. Obviously, some adjustments were necessary, but the essential structure of the West German federal state, as laid down in the Basic Law, remained the constitutional basis of the new Germany. (For a discussion of postunification federalism in Germany, see Bräuninger and König.)

The division of responsibilities between the Länder and the German federal government (the Bund) gives a list of designated powers to either the central government or the Länder; the powers of the Länder were been strengthened somewhat in 1994. In addition, there are quite a large number of "concurrent" areas in which both the federal government and the Länder may pass laws, although federal law takes precedence over Land law in concurrent areas. The federal government deals with matters such as defense, foreign trade, and major instruments of macroeconomic policy. Powers explicitly reserved to the Länder include control over education and the mass media, but Article 30 of the Basic Law permits Länder to legislate on any matter that is not explicitly stated to be the preserve of the federal government.

Politically, the Länder are represented at the federal level in the upper house of the federal parliament, the Bundesrat. As you saw in Chapter 3, Land members of the Bundesrat are not elected directly (in contrast, for example, to members of the U.S. Senate). Rather, they are delegations from the Land governments, the number of delegates being related, though by no means proportionally, to the population of the Land in question. Thus, the Bundesrat is sometimes referred to as a "conclave of states." Each delegation—the members of which are typically members of the Land cabinet—votes as a bloc under the instructions of the Land government. The Bundesrat has considerable powers to block the passage of bills passed by the lower house, the Bundestag, all of which must be submitted to it. If a bill is defeated in the Bundesrat by an ordinary majority, then this veto can be overturned by the lower house with an ordinary majority. If a bill is defeated with a two-thirds majority, then a two-thirds majority in the Bundestag is needed to overturn the veto. And if a bill affects the constitutional position of the Länder or the balance of taxes between the federal government and the Länder (this includes a lot of bills), then the Bundesrat has an absolute veto.

When the two houses are controlled by different party groupings, this division of powers leads to potential confrontation and the clear possibility of legislative gridlock, so that the presence of the Länder is definitely felt in federal politics. The two houses, furthermore, can quite easily have different patterns of political control, because Land elections do not take place at the same time as federal elections and voting patterns at the Land level may differ from those at the federal level. Recent research by Bräuninger and König, however, has shown that in many actual policy areas the power of the federal government to set the agenda may give it more power in practice than formal rules might otherwise indicate.

The legal balance of power between the federal and the Land governments is adjudicated by the Federal Constitutional Court, discussed in Chapter 4. The economic balance of power—so vital in practical politics, whatever the legal position—is guaranteed by the fact that the Länder have significant sources of tax revenue from both indirect taxes and a guaranteed proportion of federal income tax revenues. Thus the federal government has not traditionally been able to use the power of the purse strings to bring Länder governments to heel, though this situation changed somewhat with the addition of the far poorer eastern Länder to the German federation.

The extent to which the Länder come into open conflict with the federal government and the extent to which each Land pursues policies without regard to what goes on elsewhere are mediated by a very extensive system of ad hoc committees. These are designed both to resolve potential conflicts before they become explicit and to coordinate the activities of different Länder, creating a coherent development of public policy across the Länder as a whole.

Overall, therefore, German federalism is underwritten by an explicit and powerful constitutional structure and appears to operate effectively despite the fact that many of the Länder are not entities to which citizens have strong traditional affiliations. Furthermore, with the exception of staunchly Roman Catholic Bavaria, Länder boundaries do not closely follow the boundaries of ethnic, religious, or language groups. Essentially, German federalism is a political and constitutional, rather than a cultural, phenomenon.

One implication of this is that German federalism may change as the political environment changes. As Burgess and Gress have pointed out, both reunification and membership in the European Union (EU) may have fundamental implications for German federalism. Reunification, as we said, added five Länder from the former East Germany, all much poorer than those of the former West Germany. The policy of bringing public and personal services in these new Länder toward the standard enjoyed by people in the west generates a need for huge cash transfers, from western Länder through the federal government to the eastern Länder, and clearly increases the role of the federal government. The impact of the EU is more complex, for the concentration of powers in Brussels has been accompanied by strong support for regions within EU member states. This support has the potential to enhance the role of German Länder if they become actors in their own right on the European political stage.

Both reunification and European integration have generated lively debates between the Länder and the federal authorities in Germany. The fact that they have indicates that the federal ideal is now deeply rooted in the German political system. And the fact that this was achieved in the relatively short period of time since the introduction of the new Basic Law in 1949 suggests that, notwithstanding some spectacular failures around the world, constitutional engineering can sometimes fulfill its basic objectives.

Decisions Against Federalism in Eastern Europe

Confronted with the need for a root and branch review of their fundamental constitutional arrangements, the democratizing states of eastern Europe had a clear opportunity to opt for federal structures, following in the footsteps of post-Nazi Germany. A strikingly different pattern has emerged, however. None of the postcommunist states of central and eastern Europe opted for a federal system. They all are unitary states, notwithstanding what is often considerable ethnic and cultural internal diversity and a significant history of federalism in the region. The establishment of a federal Czechoslovakia in 1918 was the modern founding act of statehood for the nations of Slovakia and Bohemia/Moravia. The Yugoslav federation was largely based on the nineteenth-century vision for a south-Slav federation; and the formation of the Soviet Union following the Bolshevik revolution also can be linked to pan-Slavic movements of nineteenth-century nationalists.

To a large extent, however, the historical experience of federalism in eastern Europe was one that its modern citizens were not anxious to repeat, for three main reasons (for overviews see Heinemann-Grüder; Schlesinger). First, previous federations in eastern Europe tended to dominated by one of the constituent states. The Soviet Union was dominated by Russia; Czechs were dominant over Slovaks in Czechoslovakia; Serbs dominated the Yugoslav federation. This led to what was widely felt to be second-class citizenship for the nondominant members of the federations concerned. Second, the republics of the socialist federations were also ethnic territories with distinctive cultures, histories, and languages; each constituent part of the federation could typically lay claim to independent sovereignty and the right to secede. Third, one-party communist rule, with its governing principle of "democratic centralism," mandated strict discipline and loyalty to the center among the ostensible leaders of the republics and required validation of any regional policy or reform by central party leaders. As a result, opposition to communist rule in federal systems was largely centered in the constituent republics. Putting all of this together, we can see why there were so few defenders of the federal idea after the collapse of the communist regimes. Federalism in eastern Europe came to be associated with the communist past.

Thus the transition from communism in eastern Europe was marked by the rapid *dismantling* of federations on a remarkable scale, a process that affected six of the eight eastern European states joining the European Union in 2004. The independence of Estonia, Latvia, and Lithuania arose as part of the collapse of the "federal" Soviet Union. The Czech Republic and Slovakia emerged out of the dissolution of federal Czechoslovakia. Slovenia quickly and successfully declared itself independent from the former Yugoslav federation. In a handful of years, the map of eastern Europe was completely redrawn as a result of the collapse of the communist federations. Only Hungary and Poland entered the EU as states that had existed in the Cold War era. In these circumstances it is easy to see why citizens of the eastern European transition states saw federalism as something to leave behind, rather than as a way forward for the future.

→ THE GROWING IMPORTANCE OF REGIONAL GOVERNMENT

Regional Government in Spain

Despite the powerfully centralist system of governance in Spain, imposed under the dictatorship of General Franco, which ended with Franco's death in 1975, many Spanish regions have powerful local traditions and have long demanded autonomy. The province of Catalonia has been at the forefront, even receiving limited autonomy between 1913 and 1923 before the imposition of military governments, first under General Primo de Rivera and then under General Franco, that were deeply committed to turning Spain into a strong unitary state. When the Spanish constitution was rewritten at the end of the Franco era, the relative power of regional and central governments was a major bone of contention between left and right. The left wanted Spain to be a federal state; the right was utterly opposed to this. The result was a compromise. The new constitution recognized a series of "autonomous communities," and some communities with strong historical traditions were granted more autonomy than others.

There are seventeen autonomous communities, in effect regional governments, in Spain. Each of them has many of the political and administrative trappings of a ministate: a legislature, an executive, and a president, as well as a civil service and a high court. Certain important powers are reserved by the constitution to the national government— for example, defense, foreign policy, macroeconomic policy, and certain major aspects of the social welfare system. Regional powers, which the autonomous communities must exercise in a way that does not conflict with the national constitution, include important areas such as education and health care. The ability of the regions to raise taxes independently, obviously crucial to the possibility of making truly autonomous decisions on many aspects of public policy, depends on the national government ceding specific powers of taxation to specific autonomous communities. The reality, for nearly all communities, is that the national government retains most of the important powers of taxation. This means that the communities' main source of funds is grants from the central state.

A few communities, such as the Basque Country and Navarra, have powers to collect a wide range of taxes locally and pass a large share of this revenue on to the central government—but in practice they must set these taxes at the same rate as the rate in the rest of the country.

Despite their relatively limited powers to vary national tax rates, some of the autonomous communities in Spain have maintained a strongly independent local line on many nonfinancial aspects of public policy. Perhaps the most striking of these is Catalonia, with a distinctive language, a long history, and Barcelona, one of Europe's major cities, as its capital. The "government" of Catalonia presents itself in many ways as being on a par with the national government, and in 1992, the year of the Barcelona Olympics, the Catalan president created the position of Foreign Minister. Furthermore, the Catalan rather than the Spanish national anthem has been played on state visits abroad by the Catalan president. Although Catalonia is ahead of the other communities in presenting itself as having potent features of an independent state, several other of Spain's autonomous communities do have "foreign relations" departments, mostly used to promote regional interests within the EU.

Overall, there can be no doubt that the evolution of regional government in post-Franco Spain challenges the traditional neat separation of countries into those that have a federal system of governance and those that are unitary states. Formally, Spain remains a unitary state in which any power at the disposal of the regions has been ceded by the central government. Constraints on the central government's taking back these powers—which has indeed happened in Spain—depend more on practical politics than on the letter of the constitution. Despite its formal unitary status, however, the practical political autonomy of a Spanish regional state such as Catalonia is probably far greater than the political autonomy of a typical Land or canton in "federal" Germany or Switzerland. (For a discussion of the system of government in post-Franco Spain, see Heywood.)

The "Devolution" of Power in the United Kingdom

The very name "United Kingdom of Great Britain and Northern Ireland" hints strongly at the regional diversity underlying a union of what can be seen as four separate units. Great Britain comprises the countries of England, Wales, and Scotland; how, precisely, to describe Northern Ireland is in itself an intensely political matter. Each of these units has very strong regional traditions.

Although the English conquest of Wales dates from 1282, there remains a strong Welsh nationalist movement, and the Welsh language—utterly different from English—remains in widespread everyday use in parts of Wales. English unity with Scotland came much later, with the succession of a Scottish king to the English throne in 1603, consolidated by the Act of Union in 1707. Many Scottish institutions—the legal and educational systems, for example—have remained quite distinct from those in England and Wales. Although Scots Gaelic is very much less current than Welsh as an everyday language, Scottish national identity has remained very strong and has formed the basis for a very successful and effective Scottish nationalist movement. Scottish nationalism was given a huge boost by the discovery of major offshore oil reserves in Scottish waters, which allowed a plausible case to be made that Scotland could be financially self-sufficient. After a long and troubled history of relations between Britain and Ireland, the current province of Northern Ireland came into being with British withdrawal in 1921 from the twenty-six counties of what was later to become the Republic of Ireland. The remaining six counties of Northern Ireland remained under the control of the British State, and the United Kingdom of Great Britain and Northern Ireland (UK) came into being.

The postwar emergence of strong nationalist movements in Wales and Scotland—together with continuing sectarian strife between "unionist" and "nationalist" communities in Northern Ireland—kept the issue of regional governance very firmly on the UK political agenda from the late 1960s on. Although there were a number of unsuccessful attempts to find a constitutional settlement for Northern Ireland, little was done about the constitutional position of Wales and Scotland during the long period of Conservative government that ran from 1979 to 1997. Immediately on taking office in 1997, however, Labour prime minister Tony Blair announced referendums on the creation of regional parliaments for Scotland and Wales—in the case of Scotland, with an executive that would have certain tax-varying powers. These referendums were held in September 1997 and resulted in the subsequent creation and election (using a proportional mixed-member electoral system that was in itself a great innovation for Britain) of Scottish and Welsh regional assemblies. The first elections to the new Scottish Parliament and Welsh Senedd took place in May 1999, and powers that devolved to these bodies took effect on July 1, 1999.

There is a separate Scottish cabinet—the Scottish Executive—with its own first minister filling a role that could almost be described as that of "the prime minister of Scotland." Because of the strong element of proportional representation in the new electoral system that was used, the result of the first election was the formation of a coalition Executive combining Labour and the Liberal Democrats—another first for Britain. Following the second Scottish Assembly elections in 2003, this coalition arrangement was renegotiated and a second Executive comprising Labour and the Liberal Democrats took office for a further four-year term. Scotland is thus establishing itself as a coalition system, a further clear illustration of the fact that most single-party majority governments are manufactured by electoral systems rather than chosen by voters. The powers devolved to Scotland are considerably more than those devolved to Wales. Very significantly, the Scottish Parliament, based in Edinburgh, has the right to vary the rate of income tax levied in Scotland (by up to three pence per pound). It also has powers over education, health, environment, economic development, local government, transport, sports, and agriculture, among other things. Powers reserved to the British parliament in Westminster include defense, foreign policy, large-scale economic management, and the social security system. Powers devolved to Wales are rather fewer. There is no Welsh executive, there is no right to vary income tax, and fewer functions can be performed locally, leading some to decry the Welsh Senedd as no more than a talking shop. (For a discussion of regional government in Britain, see Kingdom, "England").

As part of the Northern Ireland peace process, the "Good Friday Agreement" of April 1998 and consequent legislation created a new provincial assembly for Northern Ireland. It is based in Belfast, with substantial powers to be devolved to a Northern Ireland Executive with a cabinet and a First and Deputy First Minister, consequent upon the successful implementation of all aspects of the agreement. The rights of both nationalist and unionist communities are protected by a complicated system of qualified majorities needed to pass resolutions in the Assembly, and by a requirement that parties be represented in the "power-sharing" Executive in strict proportion to their representation in the Assembly. Elections to the Assembly were held in 1998. After much delay resulting from protracted negotiations over the "decommissioning" of IRA weapons, power was devolved to the Northern Ireland Assembly and Executive in December 1999. However, following unionist pressure over the lack of progress on the decommissioning issue, the British government suspended the Northern Ireland Executive in January 2000, even though it had been in operation for no more than a few weeks. De facto "direct rule" over Northern Ireland was thereby restored to Westminster, before being returned to Belfast again in June 2000. The continued stalling of negotiations between all sides led to a further suspension of the Assembly and Executive in October 2002 followed, in an unusual development, by new elections to the suspended Assembly in November 2003. (For a discussion of Northern Ireland politics leading up to the peace process, see McGarry and O'Leary. More generally on recent Northern Ireland politics, see Tonge.)

In the short space of two years, therefore, very significant steps were taken to shift power in the United Kingdom away from London and toward regional capitals. The term used to describe this is "devolution": the granting of power from the center to some local region. The constitutional implication of "devolved" as opposed to "federal" government is that what has been given away could in theory be taken back by another new government with popular support and a huge parliamentary majority. This did indeed happen when the British government reimposed direct rule on Northern Ireland in 1972 in response to the intense communal violence in the province, setting aside a regional assembly at Stormont that had wielded considerable local power without intervention from Westminster over a fifty-year period. Furthermore, the difference between devolved and federal government is highlighted in the clearest possible way by events in Northern Ireland in January 2000 and October 2002. That which the British government had "given" to Northern Ireland, it could also take away by rushing legislation through the Westminster parliament in a matter of hours, motivated by the political exigencies of the time. However pressing those political exigencies might have been, such action would have been utterly unthinkable in a federal system.

Notwithstanding the Northern Ireland experience, the practical politics of abolishing the Scottish and Welsh assemblies and the Scottish Executive, now that they have been created, might make abolishing them a very unattractive prospect in the short to medium term. Indeed, there is nothing in theory to prevent the Scottish Executive from organizing a referendum on the total independence of Scotland from the United Kingdom and thereby provoking a serious constitutional crisis, although the current composition of the Executive makes such action unlikely. The Northern Ireland experience shows that it will take some time before devolution arrangements become deeply enough entrenched to be regarded as an irrevocable move toward a British variant of strong regional government that comes quite close to federalism. But these changes are nonetheless very significant.

→ LOCAL GOVERNMENT

Many of the services that governments provide, such as health care and education, are delivered to end users at a local level—in schools, hospitals, and the like. Much of the regulatory activity of government, such as land-use planning or pollution control, operates on the ground at the local level. It is thus inevitable in practice that at least some of the machinery for delivering public policy outputs will be "decentralized" in the sense that it is located at the local level near end users. Whatever the political system, local government, in the sense of local public administration, is inevitable in the real world.

There are also sound theoretical and philosophical reasons for a decentralization of decision making. Aside from the argument about practical efficiency that we have just discussed, there is the argument that a division of powers helps to avoid a single monolithic state machine. There is also the argument that increasing the possibilities for ordinary citizens to get involved in the state's everyday workings enhances the legitimacy of the political system. It is no accident that strongly authoritarian regimes, such as Franco's Spain or Salazar's Portugal, have relied on highly centralized structures of governance. It would be very difficult to run an authoritarian regime if real political power were highly decentralized. An entrenched decentralized system of governance provides a check on the excessive accumulation of power in the hands of a tiny elite. From the perspective of the ordinary citizen, the probability of having any real impact on decision making declines as the decision-making unit gets larger and more remote. A highly centralized state offers little possibility for ordinary citizens to make any impact, either real or imaginary, and may result in citizens coming to feel powerless and alienated, which in turn may undermine the popular legitimacy of the state. A more decentralized regime may offer more opportunities for citizen participation and hence encourage more of a sense that the regime is legitimate and worthy of popular loyalty.

Notwithstanding these general arguments, which apply to all countries, the precise form that local government takes, together with the extent to which it is locally politically accountable, varies considerably from country to country in modern Europe, although all modern European countries have some form of elected local government. The key variables are these: the structure of the system of local government, together with the size and number of local government units; the policy areas in which local government has real power; the financial basis of the local government system; and the relative powers of local and national governments in the event of a conflict. Despite the diversity of European local government systems, we can develop some generalizations about these key variables.

The Structure of Local Government

Almost every European country has more than one level of local government; most have two levels, and some have three. The basic unit of local government in nearly every European country—often called a commune or municipality—is typically small and ancient in its origins. (As recently as the mid-1990s, for example, one Slovakian municipality comprised no more than sixteen citizens.) However, nearly all communes or municipalities did undergo major reorganization at some stage during the nineteenth century, when the foundations for most modern European systems of local government were laid. As Spence notes for Italy, "it is not uncommon for historians to trace the development of the commune as an almost unbroken process beginning in the twelfth century and continuing into the present day" (Spence, p. 74). He goes on to argue, however, that the current structure of Italian local government can be dated to Italian unification in 1861. Similarly, although the English system of parishes and boroughs is very old, the current system of local government can be traced more directly back to a series of major reforms beginning in 1835, and the parish no longer has any political significance. In Ireland, the division of the country into the counties that remain today as the basic local administrative units began with the Norman conquest and was more or less complete by the end of the seventeenth century (Coakley). France's communes, not surprisingly, can be traced to the Napoleonic era. The Swedish system of local government established in 1863 created municipalities based on administrative units that were already several hundred years old (Wallin). In Denmark, the communes were created in 1841 to take over many of the functions formerly fulfilled by parishes. German local government also has a long tradition, as shown by the extensive set of rights enjoyed by its medieval cities. This tradition was broken under Hitler's strongly centralist Third Reich, however, and the current system of municipalities (*Gemeinde*) derives from the arrangements put in place by the Allies in the immediate aftermath of World War II. Most eastern European states have had a long tradition of local government, with systems of municipalities often dating back to the Middle Ages. World wars and the period of communist rule disrupted these, however, and the "democratic centralist" traditions of twentieth-century communism resulted in local government systems designed to ensure that local authorities did not defy national policy makers.

In almost every European country there is at least one additional tier of local government between the basic unit of the commune or municipality and the national government. (For an overview of European local government structures, see Norton.) These are typically described as provinces or counties, and there are obviously far fewer of them. There are nineteen in Norway, for example; fourteen in Denmark; and twelve in the Netherlands. In some countries, especially those with very large numbers of communes or municipalities, the number of provincial areas is larger. There are over ninety departments in France, over ninety provinces in Italy, and over three hundred *powiats* drawing together over 2,500 municipalities in Poland, for example. In these cases, there is then an additional, regional level at the top of the local government pyramid and below the national government. There are seventeen regions in Spain, fifteen in Italy, and sixteen in Poland. In countries such as Spain and Britain, as we have seen, the power of provincial governments is now such as to have created a system of governance that lies somewhere between traditional "federal" and "unitary" models. In other countries, such as the Netherlands, the powers of the regions are weaker.

Thus most modern European states, one way or another, have a system of local government that starts with the commune or municipality and ends with a set of regional or provincial administrations that number somewhere between twelve and twenty-five. Typically, although there are obviously fewer units at each "higher" level of local government, the relationship between levels is not strictly hierarchical in the sense of one level reporting to, and needing sanction from, the next. Rather, between levels of local government there tends to be a division of labor that is defined either in the constitution or in the national legislation that underpins the local government system. (An exception to this rule is Germany, where the system of municipal government is effectively under the jurisdiction of the regional Länder governments.) Indeed, it is sometimes the case that "lower" levels of local government are considerably "more important" than "higher" ones, if we define importance in terms of the range and significance of the public functions for which they have responsibility. Middle-level agencies are often responsible for strategic planning and coordination, whereas lower-level agencies actually produce and deliver services on the ground.

This relationship between levels of local government has been extensively debated and thought through, for example, in postcommunist Poland. As we have already explained, rather than muddling along with traditional political structures—a luxury always open to long-established western democracies—citizens of eastern European countries have had to confront a series of crucial governance issues over a short period of time. Although reforming the system of local government may seem less exciting than reforming the national political system or setting up massive privatizations of state assets, it is of course a crucial part of any constitution-building process. Furthermore, in countries that moved rapidly away from a highly centralized state system under communism, the decentralization of political power is clearly an important issue. Thus the new Polish constitution of 1997 begins with a preamble stating the principle of "subsidiarity." Interpreted literally, subsidiarity implies quite radical decentralization. In the Polish context, the constitutional theory is that the local municipality (*gmina*) deals with matters beyond the scope of the individual, the region (*powiat*) deals with matters beyond the scope of the municipality, and the province (*voivodship*) deals with matters beyond the scope of the region. The result is "a kind of reverse hierarchy. 'Superstructures' are added to institutions in those places where smaller organizations, situated closer to citizens, are not able to perform more complex tasks" (Regulski, p. 205). The theoretical implication is that the state itself will do only the things that cannot be done at the sub national level, but this system is not something that we in practice can observe anywhere. As Regulski says in a wide-ranging discussion of local government reform in Poland, "This principle is of fundamental importance. But it was, and still is, very difficult to introduce into practice" (Regulski, p. 205).

This Polish debate shows clearly that there are two quite distinct philosophies of local government. On the one hand the subsidiarity principle implies that decisions should be taken at the lowest level possible, with higher tiers of government handling only problems that lower tiers cannot handle. On the other hand there is the "devolution" principle seen most clearly in Britain and Ireland, under which local government has only such powers as are conferred on it by the national government. In practice, in modern Europe, the subsidiarity principle for local government is never observed in its purest form, and the crux of the issue when we evaluate any real-world system of local government is the practical significance of the role it fulfills and the degree of autonomy it has to fulfill that role.

The Functions, Finances, and Autonomy of Local Government

Although discussions of the functions, finances, and autonomy of local government might seem to raise quite different issues, they are in practice so intimately interrelated as to be inseparable because, as we have noted, a very wide range of government policy outputs must be delivered at a local level. Of course, to administer these policies, the central government may set up locally based agencies responsible directly to the central bureaucracy. This was traditionally the preferred solution in Italy, where, before a series of reforms in the mid-1970s, it was estimated that there were about sixty thousand such agencies (Spence). More commonly, however, the central government mandates local government to administer particular policy areas on its behalf. In these cases, it is vital to know the extent to which the local government bureaucracy is forced to implement a national policy slavishly and the extent to which local government agencies are free to modify national policies on their own initiative.

Although the range of public services administered locally is actually rather similar in many European countries, the level of local autonomy varies considerably. Because it is usually safe to assume that real political power follows the purse strings, the level of de facto autonomy of particular local governments depends to a crucial extent on their ability to raise and spend money independently of the national government. Intimately related to this matter is the extent to which local people have a real input into local government decision making. Traditionally such input was seen in terms of conventional voting in local elections. Recently, however, and in the wake of worries about popular alienation from public decision making at all levels, local government agencies in a number of countries have set up a number of interesting experiments in innovative ways to involve local people in local decision making.

It would be an immense task, quite beyond the scope of this book, to run through all of the powers of the different levels of local government in each European country. (Much of this information can be found in Norton.) There are, however, some general patterns. Almost all local councils, even those with relatively fewer powers, play an important role in land use planning and environmental control: the zoning of development, the processing of individual applications for new development, the issuing of certain licenses and permits, and the monitoring of noxious land uses. Most local councils also have a duty to provide a range of services to local property: fire protection, garbage collection, public utilities, and possibly also police. (There is, however, considerable variation in the organization of European police forces—several are organized nationally.) Other important aspects of the local infrastructure that are often the responsibility of local councils are local public transport and the local road system, as well as one or more of three important aspects of the welfare state: the school system, personal health care and social services, and public housing.

Even though almost no European local council is responsible for every one of these functions, many councils oversee a number of them. Even in "centralist" France, it typically falls to local communes to build and maintain local roads, schools, libraries, and tourist offices; to dispose of refuse; and to take care of other aspects of minor local infrastructure. In Italy, this list must be expanded to include local government provision of health care, personal social services, housing, land use planning, pollution control, and local public transport. In Poland, almost the entire primary education system was taken over in the late 1990s by the municipalities. In Scandinavia, at the other end of the scale, most aspects of a comprehensive welfare state are supplied on the ground by the local government system. In Sweden in the late 1980s, for example, 32 percent of the entire workforce was employed by the public sector, 7 percent by the national government, 15 percent by municipal governments, and 10 percent by regional governments (Wallin, p. 99). The vast bulk of the day-to-day activity of the Swedish welfare state, therefore, was conducted within the local government system. The pattern is similar in other Scandinavian countries.

To what extent is the activity of local councils "mere" policy implementation at the behest of the national government, a role that could in many ways be performed just as well by a local branch of the central bureaucracy? Here we need to look at

The difference that local land-use planning can make: a tranquil canalscape in Amsterdam . . . © Alessandra Quaranta/Black Star

. . . and a depressing housing environment in the former East Germany. © Rainer Unkel/SABA Press Photos

both the formal legal position and the power of the purse. But in doing so, we must always remember that in all European countries it is almost undoubtedly true that the powers of local government are, or can be, constrained in important ways at the national level.

From a constitutional point of view, an interesting illustration of this constraint can be found in the "free commune" or "deregulated local government" experiments that have been tried in a number of Scandinavian countries (for descriptions of them, see Gustafsson; Lodden; Rose). These experiments started in Sweden but quickly extended to Denmark, Norway, and Finland. They allowed certain municipalities to be designated as free communes. These were then allowed to make proposals that would allow them to opt out of national laws in certain specified policy areas that did not affect individual rights, health, and well-being in order to be able to develop more effective local arrangements. Areas specifically indicated included land use planning, the organization of local administration, fees and service charges (in Norway), and education (in Denmark).

The first thing that is striking about this, of course, is that such a policy was needed in the first place. That it was indicates that, despite the size of Scandinavian local government systems, on most matters local councils were implementing national policies rather than deviating from them on the basis of local initiative. The most important thing to note, however, is that the central government in each country orchestrated the entire experiment. Only certain municipalities were approved by the central governments for these experiments. And all proposals for local initiatives had to be approved by the national government before they could come into effect; by no means were all of them approved (Rose).

The key feature of the Scandinavian free commune experiments, shared by every other European system of local government, is that change could take place only with the approval of the national authorities. In this sense, the constitutions of European unitary states put the boot very firmly on the national, rather than the local, government foot. Unlike federal arrangements that are typically deeply entrenched in the constitution and these cannot be changed by the government of the day, the precise system of local government is more typically determined by legislation. This arrangement makes it easier to reform the local government system and also constrains the ability of local councils to defy the national government in any systematic manner.

Very clear examples of the cavalier treatment of the local government system by national governments can be seen in both Britain and Ireland, neither of which has traditionally provided any constitutional protection whatsoever for local government. One round of British local government reorganization in 1974, for example, casually swept away counties that had been in existence for many centuries, creating new areas with invented names. In 1985, the powerful, Labour-controlled Greater London Council, which had become a thorn in the side of Margaret Thatcher's Conservative government, was simply abolished, and its powers were redistributed between unelected authorities and smaller local councils. The change of government from Conservative to Labour in 1997 heralded equally dramatic changes in the opposite direction. In addition to the creation, previously discussed, of new regional assemblies and administrations for Scotland, Wales, and Northern Ireland, the Labour government under Tony Blair engaged in some radical new thinking about local government, expressing a clear preference for creating stronger local executives. A first step toward this goal was the creation of the very high-profile position of elected mayor of London, the first election for which was held in 2000 and the second in 2004. Taken together with other local government reforms, this development gave considerable extra power to the London region. A striking example of the use of this power was the introduction in February 2003 by Ken Livingston, the elected mayor of London, of a "congestion charge" to address the city's chronic traffic problems. In an experiment closely watched throughout Europe, London motorists were forced to pay a £5 fee to drive their cars into the city between 7a.m. and 6:30p.m., Monday to Friday. The result of this highly controversial initiative was a considerable improvement in traffic flow. Notwithstanding these recent developments, however, the lack of any entrenched constitutional position for local government in Britain, taken together with a long tradition of centralist government, means that any recent reforms must be seen as a "devolution" of power from central or local government. Functions that are devolved by central government can also be taken back again in a minute. If Tony Blair had chosen to do so, he could easily have rushed legislation through Westminster banning London's congestion charge and abolishing the mayoralty occupied by Ken Livingstone.

In Ireland, the system of domestic rates (local property taxes), which was a vital part of the revenue base of local councils, was abolished by the central government, without even the need for legislation, in 1978. Irish governments have traditionally had little compunction about postponing scheduled local council elections when they seemed likely to prove politically embarrassing. Only in 1999 was a constitutional amendment passed that specifically referred to the local government system and mandated the holding of local elections every five years. The desire to attract European Union regional funding prompted attempts in 1999 to establish a new tier of government in Ireland. The result was a new system of "regions" bearing virtually no relationship to existing geographical or cultural boundaries. Many Irish people have not the slightest idea that such regions exist, and many others do not know which region they live in. Thus local government in Ireland remains weak and ineffective, and attempts to restructure its finances have so far proved unsuccessful. There is an inherently top-down approach to local governance, and debate tends to be about which particular powers can safely be devolved to local authorities without threat to the unitary system, rather about which functions can be fulfilled only by national governments.

It is, of course, inconceivable that the national government could behave in ways such as these toward states in a federal system, in which intergovernmental relations are embedded in the constitution. In a very real sense, therefore, local governments in almost every European country ultimately can do only what their central government allows them to do. Powers that are given can be, and sometimes have been, taken away.

Despite this ultimate constitutional reality, there is very wide variation between countries in the level of autonomy that local councils are allowed by central government, and nowhere is this more evident than in the system of local government funding. Everywhere in Europe, there are three basic sources of local government financing. These are local taxes on property, business, or income; local service charges; and transfers from higher levels of government. One of the best measures of differences between countries in the degree of local autonomy has to do with how much freedom local councils have to raise money from these various sources as they please, and then to spend this money as they see fit.

At one extreme we find Denmark, where the commune is the main tax-gathering agency for the state as a whole, remitting the appropriate funds to the central government. The communes are the government agencies that collect the information on which the tax and welfare system is based. Danish communes finance their very extensive activities on the basis of local income taxes, the rates of which can be set locally by the commune and vary from about 13 percent to about 32 percent. In addition, both counties and communes may raise a local land value tax, the level of which the communes also have freedom to determine. There are also transfers of funds from the central government in the form of block grants, which can be used to compensate for the unequal revenue-gathering abilities of different communes in a country in which the same welfare system applies to all. Overall, even though much of the expenditure by Danish communes is on the administration of a welfare state effectively determined at national level, the high level of local discretion in revenue raising does provide considerable scope for local policy making.

At the opposite extreme we find countries such as Ireland and Italy, in which local councils have very little scope for independent revenue raising. In Ireland, one of the main sources of local revenue was domestic property taxes and rates, abolished at a stroke in 1978. These revenues were replaced by a block grant from the central government that puts it overwhelmingly in control of the local government system. A rather similar situation arose in Italy in 1982, when fiscal reforms "effectively denied the communes the power to finance their services through local taxation, by abolishing a number of taxes on housing, families, goods, services, and businesses. These changes robbed the communes of something in the region of 92 percent of their income. . . . The result of the transfer of financial responsibility from the periphery to the centre was that Italy had one of the largest systems of transfer finances in the western world" (Spence, p. 85). Since then, against a background of massive local authority indebtedness, the Italian central government has played an ever more dominant role in local government finances.

Britain, too, has seen major central government attacks on the financial independence of local government. As a result of a series of reforms during the 1980s, local councils were first prohibited from setting rates for local property taxes at will, while both spending and revenue raising had to comply with strict central government guidelines. Councillors who defied the central government were threatened with the suspension of the council and its replacement with a government-appointed commissioner, and even with imprisonment. Subsequently, domestic rates were abolished and replaced with a local "poll tax," so called because every adult on the electoral register was liable to pay a fixed charge. This innovation proved massively unpopular, provoking widespread violent demonstrations and contributing in no small way to Margaret Thatcher's downfall. After her departure, the poll tax was replaced with a "council tax," a modified system of the old property tax but one that remains firmly under the control of the central government. (For a discussion of local government financing in Britain, see Kingdom, "England"; Kingdom, *Government*).

Most other European countries fall somewhere between these extremes. In the Netherlands, for example, less than 10 percent of local expenditure is raised locally; the remainder comes from central government grants, many of them already earmarked for particular projects and programs. Similarly, most of the high-profile regional governments in Spain, including the Catalan government, derive up to 80 percent of their income from

Poll tax riots: The reform of British local government finance turns ugly. © AP/Wide World Photos

central government grants. In Poland, despite the considerable range of functions fulfilled by the local municipalities, they raise relatively little local revenue. The fundamental source of tax revenue is the national government, which allocates a fixed share of national revenues directly to local authorities (Regulski, p. 147).

In France and Belgium, in contrast, a far higher proportion of local spending is funded from local taxes, especially on land, property, and businesses (Hunt and Chandler). Germany cleaves more closely to the Scandinavian pattern, with the funding to local government coming from income taxes, business, and property taxes. In the German case, however, the local councils receive a fixed proportion, currently 15 percent, of all national income tax raised in their local area. Local taxes on business are also shared on a rigid basis with higher levels of government, with municipal councils retaining 60 percent and passing the remainder on to the regional and federal governments.

Popular Participation in Local Decisions

Central government control over the local purse strings is obviously one key indicator of the autonomy of local decision making in modern Europe. Another is the nature and extent of popular participation in local decisions. One distinctive approach to local participation can be found in Switzerland. Here, local participation can take the form of "direct" rather than representative democracy, with many local referendums and even a tradition of *Landsgemeinde* (popular assemblies held in the open) for making decisions in several small cantons. Rates of participation in local referendums are often very low, however, and since 1997 a number of cantons have abolished the system of *Landsgemeinde.* The largest open assembly in Switzerland (to which women had been admitted only since 1991) was abolished in Appenzell in September 1997, and similar abolitions have occurred or are being considered elsewhere.

In most of modern Europe, the traditional method of involving citizens in local decision making has been through a system of elections to local councils—in effect, viewing local politics as a microcosm of politics at the national level. There are very wide variations in levels of participation in local government elections across Europe. The highest levels are found in Scandinavia, Luxembourg, Belgium, and Italy, and the lowest in Britain, Greece, Portugal, and the Netherlands (Hoffmann-Martinot et al.). The general trend across Europe, however, has been for turnout in local elections to decline. Combined with what appear to be steady declines in turnout at national elections, and relatively low levels of turnout at European Parliament elections, the local decline has led to a concern that European voters may be getting increasingly alienated from politics.

Concern among political elites at declining levels of popular participation in traditional models of representation in local decision making has been accompanied by increased interest at the grassroots level in alternative forms of political expression. As you will see in Chapter 14, a wide range of formal and informal social groups in what we can generally think of as civil society can all play a part in the process of making decisions. Popular participation in such groups, which may deal with either single "pet" issues or matters of more general concern, can be an important way of bringing people into the decision-making process.

This combination of elite concern at declining turnout in local elections and increasing popular awareness of alternative forms of participation has resulted in increasing interest in experimental methods of involving ordinary people in public decision making, especially at the local level. A common theme in these experiments has been a desire to make decision making more interactive and "deliberative." These approaches set out to go beyond the mere aggregation of individual preferences that is typical of elections and referendums. Reasoned discussion, dialogue, and debate at the local level are intended to allow a range of options to be developed, examined, challenged, and evaluated. Proponents claim the following benefits of this approach: an improvement in citizen awareness and information; an increased sense of local involvement; a general willingness of citizens to take account of the views of others; and an increase in the level of popular acceptance of the decisions that are eventually taken. (See both Elster and Fishkin for a discussion of the ideas of deliberative democracy.)

At a practical level, recent experiments in places such as Denmark and the Netherlands have attempted to put these ideas into practice. In the county of Funen in Denmark, for example, a series of decisions about the future of county hospitals was made on the basis of local deliberative techniques. In particular, a traditional survey of one thousand individuals was supplemented with a day long "deliberative hearing" of the issue by seventy-five representative local citizens. Experts were brought in and interrogated, policy makers made presentations, and the eventual policy emerged as a result of intense interactive discussion among what might be thought of as a "citizens' jury."

Similarly, in the Netherlands, the local community of Zeewolde, with fifteen thousand inhabitants, developed a new policy on public safety out of a series of local seminars, debates, and surveys, and a photo competition, that directly involved about two hundred citizens in the policy-making process. Also in the Netherlands, the city of Enschede, with about 150,000 inhabitants, delegated responsibility for the redesign of a public square to a working group that comprised delegates of interest groups and a sample of directly involved citizens. They organized debates, public excursions to other cities, and a survey to involve citizens in the eventual decision that emerged.

Many of these experiments are at an early stage, yet they are obviously very significant for the entire concept of representative democracy, especially at the local level. In the face of declining levels of turnout in elections to traditional representative institutions, they at least hint that the way forward may not necessarily be found in attempts to force turnout up again. Rather, they suggest that the answer may be to find new ways for ordinary people to participate in the key public decisions that affect them.

✦ CONCLUSIONS

The European variations we find in patterns of local governance tell as much about national political cultures as about anything else. In Germany and Scandinavia, we see a strong decentralizing ethos. It is reflected both in the large scale of the operations of local or state governments and in their substantial sources of revenue. Elsewhere in western Europe, especially in countries with a long-standing imperial tradition that favors a strong centralized state, local government tends to be significantly weaker, both in what it can do and in how it chooses to do it. Governments in such countries seem much less willing to allow local governments to develop alternative power bases that might ultimately challenge their authority. In eastern Europe, countries that might have had a long tradition of local government found it significantly disrupted during the period of centralized communist rule. Part of the transition process in these countries has been to redesign systems of local government—a process that is still bedding down, having typically been given a lower priority than major constitutional reforms of national decision-making structures. The Polish case shows us that, although radical thinking about the subsidiarity principle can inform debate about local government reform, such thoughts are much easier to think than they are to implement on the ground in a political system that already has a national government.

The explicit redesigning of political institutions in eastern Europe is also striking in this context for the unwillingness, given their recent histories, of the new generation of constitutional engineers to take the federalist path. We can see a clear desire for decentralization following the demise of highly centralized systems of government, but the manifestation of this desire has been the fragmenting of existing federations into a larger number of smaller independent states, rather than the creation of federal arrangements within existing states. The extent to which decentralization can be achieved in practice will thus depend on the bedding in of the new local government systems in eastern Europe.

Overall, however, there can be little doubt that the trend toward shifting the powers of national governments "up" to the EU level, discussed in Chapter 5, has been combined with a trend toward decentralizing decision making "down" from national governments to subnational arenas—at least in terms of political structures and rhetoric even if not in the practices of real political power. Almost no European politician these days fights elections on the platform of gathering ever more power to the center, and decentralization is almost universally acknowledged as a "good thing." It is also clear, however, that it is very hard to decentralize real power in an already centralized state. Important in this connection is the role of the national civil service. An established civil service with a strong sense of self-worth may develop an identity that links it inextricably with the capital city—senior civil servants may consider postings to provincial locations as demotions or punishments. The doctrine of ministerial responsibility also tends to "metropolitanize" administration, as top bureaucrats work directly for cabinet ministers, who tend to be based in the seat of national power. The ultimate reality is that European states have not grown from the bottom up into the shape they now have. Their boundaries have been set by politics and war at the international level, and their administrative systems thus tend to extend from the top down. In this context, the decentralization of decision making may be seen as politically expedient—increasingly so—but it tends actually to happen only if it is seen as being expedient when viewed from the perspective of powerful national politicians.

REFERENCES

Batley, R.: "Comparisons and Lessons," in Batley and Stoker (eds.), pp. 1–20.

Batley, R., and G. Stoker (eds.): *Local Government in Europe: Trends and Developments.* Macmillan, London, 1991.

Bekke, H. A. G. M., J. Perry, and Th. A. J. Toonen (eds.): *Civil Service Systems in Comparative Perspective,* Indiana University Press, Bloomington, 1996.

Bräuninger, Thomas, and Thomas König: "The Checks and Balances of Party Federalism: German Federal Government in a Divided Legislature," *European Journal of Political Research,* vol. 36, 1999, pp. 207–34.

Burgess, Michael: "Federalism and Federation: A Reappraisal," in Burgess and Gagnon (eds.), pp. 3–14.

Burgess, Michael, and F. Gress: "The Quest for a Federal Future: German Unity and European Union," in Burgess and Gagnon (eds.), pp. 168–86.

Burgess, Michael, and A.-G. Gagnon (eds.): *Comparative Federalism and Federation: Competing Traditions and Future Directions,* Harvester Wheatsheaf, Hemel Hampstead, 1993.

Castles, Francis: "Decentralisation and the Post-war Political Economy," *European Journal of Political Research,* vol. 36, 1999, pp. 27–53.

Chandler, J. A. (ed.): *Local Government in Liberal Democracies,* Routledge, London, 1993.

Coakley, J.: "The Foundations of Statehood," in J. Coakley and M. Gallagher (eds.), *Politics in the Republic of Ireland,* 4th ed., Routledge, London, 2004.

Dunleavy, P.: *Democracy, Bureaucracy and Public Choice: Economic Explanations in Political Science,* Harvester Wheatsheaf, Hemel Hampstead, 1991.

Elazar, Daniel: "Contrasting Unitary and Federal Systems," *International Political Science Review,* vol. 18, 1997, pp. 237–51.

Elster, Jon (ed.): *Deliberative Democracy,* Cambridge University Press, Cambridge, 1998.

Fishkin, James: *The Voice of the People,* Yale University Press, New Haven, 1997.

Fitzmaurice, John: *The Politics of Belgium: A Unique Federalism,* Westview Press, Boulder (CO), 1996.

Gustafsson, A.: "The Changing Local Government and Politics of Sweden," in Batley and Stoker (eds.), pp. 170–89.

Heinemann-Grüder, Andreas (ed.): *Federalism Doomed? European Federalism Between Integration and Separation,* Berghan Books, New York, 2002.

Hennessy, P.: *Whitehall,* Secker and Warburg, London, 1989.

Heywood, Paul: *The Government and Politics of Spain,* Macmillan, London, 1995.

Hoffmann-Martinot, Vincent, Colin Rallings, and Michael Thrasher: "Comparing Local Electoral Turnout in Britain and France: More Similarities than Differences?" *European Journal of Political Research,* vol. 30, 1996, pp. 241–57.

Huber, John D., and Charles R. Shipan: *Deliberate Discretion? The Institutional Foundations of Bureaucratic Autonomy.* Cambridge University Press, Cambridge, 2002.

Hughes, C.: "Cantonalism: Federation and Confederacy in the Golden Epoch of Switzerland," in Burgess and Gagnon (eds.), pp. 154–67.

Hunt, M. C., and J. A. Chandler: "France," in Chandler (ed.), pp. 53–72.

King, A.: "Ministerial Autonomy in Britain," in M. Laver and K. A. Shepsle (eds.), *Cabinet Ministers and Parliamentary Government,* Cambridge University Press, New York, 1994.

King, P.: *Federalism and Federation,* Croom Helm, London, 1982.

Kingdom, J.: "England and Wales," in Chandler, (ed.), pp. 7–27.

Kingdom, J.: *Government and Politics in Britain: An Introduction,* 3rd ed., Polity Press, London, 2003.

Lijphart, Arend: *Patterns of Democracy: Government Forms and Performance in Thirty-Six Countries,* Yale University Press, New Haven and London, 1999.

Linder, W.: *Swiss Democracy: Possible Solutions to Conflict in Multicultural Societies,* Macmillan, London, 1994.

Lodden, P.: "The 'Free Local Government' Experiment in Norway," in Batley and Stoker (eds.), pp. 198–209.

McGarry, John, and Brendan O'Leary: *Explaining Northern Ireland: Broken Images,* Blackwell, Oxford, 1997.

Niskanen, W.: *Bureaucracy and Representative Government,* Aldine-Atherton, Chicago, 1971.

Norton, A.: *The International Handbook of Local and Regional Government Status, Structure and Resources in Advanced Democracies,* Edward Elgar, Cheltenham, 1991.

O'Halpin, Eunan: "Partnership Programme Managers in the Reynolds/Spring Coalition," *Irish Political Studies,* vol. 12, 1997, pp. 78–91.

Page, E. C.: *Political Authority and Bureaucratic Power: A Comparative Analysis,* 2nd ed., Harvester Wheatsheaf, Hemel Hampstead, 1992.

Regulski, Jerzy: *Local Government Reform in Poland,* Open Society Institute, Budapest, 2003.

Rose, L. E.: "Nordic Free-Commune Experiments: Increased Local Autonomy or Continued Central Control?" in D. S. King and J. Pierre (eds.), *Challenges to Local Government,* Sage, London, 1990, pp. 212–41.

Schlesinger, Rudolf: *Federalism in Central and Eastern Europe,* Routledge, London, 1998.

Spence, R. E.: "Italy," in Chandler (ed.), pp. 73–98.

Stoker, G.: "Introduction: Trends in European Local Government," in Batley and Stoker (eds.), pp. 1–20.

Tonge, Jonathan: *The New Northern Irish Politics?* Palgrave Macmillan, Basingstoke, 2004.

Verheijen, Tony (ed.): *Civil Service Systems in Central and Eastern Europe,* Edward Elgar, London, 1999.

Wallin, G.: "Towards the Integrated and Fragmented State: The Mixed Role of Local Government," in J.-E. Lane (ed.), *Understanding the Swedish Model,* Frank Cass, London, 1991, pp. 96–121.

Wildavsky, A.: *The Politics of the Budgetary Process,* Little, Brown, Boston, 1964.

Woodhouse, Diana: *Ministers and Parliaments: Accountability in Theory and Practice,* Clarendon Press, Oxford, 1994.

CHAPTER 7

PATTERNS IN PARTY POLITICS AND PARTY SYSTEMS

This book is about the politics of representation in modern Europe. Much of it, in some way or another, is about party politics. In this chapter we therefore look at the political parties and party systems that lay claim to representing the interests of European voters. Many of these parties, particularly in the long-standing democracies of western Europe, can be classified as belonging to one or another of a small number of party "families"—the Christian democratic family, for example, or the social democratic family, or the liberal family, and so on. We consider in detail these party families in the next chapter. In this chapter we explore the way in which the character of political competition in any given country is conditioned by a particular constellation of competing parties that together make up a national party system. We focus on the nine countries to which we return throughout this book, and we report the results of recent elections in these countries. As you will see, although each of these countries has a distinctive blend of party families, and hence a distinctive party system, there are striking similarities between their party systems, as well as between the party systems throughout modern Europe.

We in no sense claim that the countries we have selected are "typical"—it should already be clear that there is no such thing as a typical European country. We chose the nine systems discussed here and, indeed, throughout the book because, between them, they include most of the types of variation that we must use if we are to be able to describe the complex mosaic of modern European politics.

→ NINE EUROPEAN PARTY SYSTEMS

Party Politics in the United Kingdom

The British party system is often seen as one of the simplest and most clear-cut in Europe. Two large and more or less evenly matched parties confront each other. On one side is the Labour Party, a social democratic party that initially mobilized in order to promote and defend the interests of the working class. The party has always enjoyed a close relationship with the trade union movement and has traditionally seen itself as the political wing of a wider Labour movement. Despite this, Labour governments have sometimes found themselves in bitter confrontation with the trade unions over attempts to impose national income policies, notably during the long 1978–79 "winter of discontent" that led to Labour's defeat in the 1979 general election and ushered in the era of Conservative governments, led by Margaret Thatcher until 1990 and then by John Major until 1997.

The Conservative Party is Labour's main opponent. Like all traditional conservative parties in western Europe, the Conservative Party in the United Kingdom strives to defend the rights of private property, to encourage market forces, and to resist the encroachment of the state into spheres of (especially economic) activity seen as being properly the realm of unregulated private individuals. For most of its history, the party has also defended the traditional moral order, even if this has meant state involvement in regulating personal morality. The Conservatives have also been advocates of tough law-and-order policies and nationalist foreign policy stances based on a strong military profile. This has often led the party to advocate high levels of public spending on policing and national defense, and more recently it has helped push the party into a more Euroskeptic stance. In contrast to the support for Labour, the Conservatives' strongest support comes mainly from middle-class voters and the most privileged sectors of British society.

As Table 7.1 shows, the Conservatives won a majority of seats in the UK parliament following the elections of 1987 and 1992, thanks in part to a disproportional first-past-the-post electoral system (see Chapter 11). In fact, this extended period of Conservative rule began in 1979, when Margaret Thatcher won her first election victory. The period from 1979 to 1997 marked an unprecedented period of single-party dominance in British politics and, following Sartori's classification, actually transformed the United Kingdom from

TABLE 7.1

Elections in the United Kingdom Since 1987

Party	1987 % of Votes	1987 Seats	1992 % of Votes	1992 Seats	1997 % of Votes	1997 Seats	2001 % of Votes	2001 Seats	2005 % of Votes	2005 Seats
Conservatives	42.0	376	41.9	336	30.7	165	31.7	166	32.3	198
Labour	30.7	229	34.9	271	43.3	419	40.7	413	35.2	356
Liberals[a]	12.8	17	17.8	20	16.8	46	18.3	52	22.0	62
Social Democrats[a]	9.7	5	—	—	—	—	—	—	—	—
Scottish Nationalists	1.4	3	1.9	3	2.0	6	1.8	5	1.5	6
Welsh Nationalists	0.4	3	0.5	4	0.5	4	0.7	4	0.6	3
Irish Nationalists	0.8	4	0.7	4	1.1	5	1.3	7	1.1	8
Irish Unionists	1.2	13	1.2	13	1.4	13	1.5	11	1.4	10
Referendum Party	—	—	—	—	—	—	2.6	—	—	—
Others	1.1	—	1.1	—	1.6	1	1.4	1	5.9	3
All	100.0	650	100.0	651	100.0	659	100.0	659	100.0	646

Party Composition of Government

1987–97   Conservative single-party government

1997–   Labour single-party government

[a] In 1987, the Social Democrats and the Liberals formed an electoral pact and subsequently merged under the name "Liberal Democrats."

Source: The sources used for these results and all election results reported in this chapter are Mackie and Rose; *European Journal of Political Research*; *West European Politics*; and various national and international Web sites.

being a two-party system to a "predominant party system"—that is, a system in which a single party manages to win a majority across four consecutive legislative periods (King; Sartori, pp. 192–201). During this period, the Conservatives sought to weaken the power of the trade unions, to reduce the size of the state sector, and to sell off many public enterprises to the private sector (see Chapter 13). Throughout the same period, Labour offered more or less consistent opposition to this program, resisting attacks on public spending, opposing encroachments on trade union rights, and defending existing levels of public provision of a range of goods and services.

The opposition between these starkly contrasted partisan views was clearly of major importance to the people of Britain. Deciding which view was to prevail had fundamental implications for the basic concerns of almost every individual citizen. This important ideological decision was also sharply defined for voters, for only these two major parties had a realistic chance of winning an overall legislative majority. Voters were therefore in effect choosing between two alternative governments with clearly distinctive policy profiles. In the United Kingdom, the party that wins an election with a working majority has every opportunity to implement its policy program. In 1979, for example, the Conservatives held an overall majority of 43 seats in the 635-seat House of Commons; in 1983, when reelected, they enjoyed a majority of 144 seats in the newly enlarged 650-seat House; in 1987, they enjoyed a majority of 102 seats. Given such clear majorities, the Conservative governments of the 1980s had little fear of defeat and hence experienced few real difficulties in pushing through their strongly partisan program. In 1992, however, they were reduced to have a majority of just 21 seats over all the other parties taken together, and thereafter they were obliged to move a little more cautiously. By the time the 1997 election was held, defections from the Conservative Party in Westminster and a series of bruising by-election defeats had destroyed the party's overall majority, and it ended the parliamentary term as a minority government. It was then replaced by Labour, or by "New Labour" as it became known under the leadership of Tony Blair, which emerged from that election with a lead of some 250 seats over the Conservatives and with an overall majority of almost 90 seats over all the other parties taken together. Labour went on to win the 2001 election with another very substantial majority and remained in a strong position following its victory in the 2005 election. With this record in office, Blair's party has come close to equaling the succession of Conservative victories under Thatcher and Major. This might then also suggest that rather than an alternating two-party system, Britain is becoming instead a system of "alternating predominance"—one in which each of the major parties enjoys extended periods in government but then also suffers extended periods in opposition.

This image of clear-cut confrontation between two sharply distinguished parties, each hoping to form a majority government on its own, is, of course, something of a simplification. There are, for example, several small regionally based nationalist—and antinationalist—parties. There is the Scottish National Party, as well as a Welsh nationalist party (Plaid Cymru). In Northern Ireland, which remains an integral part of the United Kingdom, there are two parties that advocate breaking away from the United Kingdom and favor eventual unity with the Irish Republic: the Social Democratic and Labour Party (SDLP) and Sinn Féin, the latter being also strongly supportive of the Irish Republican Army (IRA). There are also two unionist parties that fight to preserve Northern Ireland as part of the United Kingdom: the Ulster Unionist Party and the Democratic

Unionist Party. But although often winning substantial support in their own local areas and taking some seats in the House of Commons, these parties hardly impinge at all on the British party system taken as a whole. In 2001, for example, the total number of seats won by regional parties in the House of Commons was only 28, fewer than 7 percent of the Labour total!

Of greater potential importance as a deviation from pure two-party politics in Britain is the presence of a "center" party. Now represented by the long-established Liberal Party (the official name is now the Liberal Democrats), this center alternative traditionally promoted policies that fell between the more radical alternatives of Labour and the Conservatives, and won support from both major social classes. The center received a major electoral boost in the early 1980s when the Social Democratic Party (SDP), a moderate faction of the Labour Party, split off as a result of what it saw as the unwelcome growth of the Labour left. Together, the Liberals and Social Democrats formed an alliance of the center and posed perhaps the greatest postwar challenge to the dominance of two-party politics, which itself was particularly polarized during the 1980s. In 1987 the center alliance won almost 23 percent of the vote, just 8 percent less than Labour. Indeed, in the southern part of England, this alliance actually displaced Labour as the major challenger to the Conservatives.

However, even this development had little real impact. Despite the electoral popularity of the Liberal–Social Democratic alliance, the bias against third parties in the British single-member plurality voting system (see Chapter 11) left the two allied parties with only 17 out of 650 seats for their 23 percent of the vote. When the chips were down, the alliance did little to disturb the traditional British two-party system—at least at the parliamentary level. Thereafter, the majority of members of the SDP joined the Liberals in a new but still electorally weak Liberal Democrat Party, which won almost 17 percent in 1997 and just over 18 percent in 2001. On these last two occasions, however, support for the Conservatives was so low that the Liberals were able to enjoy a tactical advantage, and although their overall share of the vote did not change very much, they managed to win 51 seats in 2001 and 62 seats in 2005.

The biggest change in 1997 was the overwhelming victory of Labour under its dynamic new leader, Tony Blair. Before the 1997 election, Labour had languished in opposition for eighteen years and had chosen initially to challenge the increasingly right-wing government of Margaret Thatcher by adopting quite a marked left-wing program. This strategy, to say the least, had proved unsuccessful. Indeed, by moving to the left, Labour had alienated many of its more moderate leaders and voters, some of whom then shifted across to the new SDP. After its 1987 defeat, however, Labour slowly began to reorganize and adapt, initially under Neil Kinnock and later under John Smith and then Tony Blair. By the time Blair had cemented his control over the party, the move toward the moderate center of the political spectrum had become unstoppable.

Blair discarded many of the older left-wing policies and campaigning styles and, partly modeling himself on the U.S. Democratic Party under Bill Clinton, made a determined effort to appeal to middle-class voters and to promote centrist policies. "New" Labour, as he insisted on referring to his party, was different from "old" Labour. A number of the existing social democratic commitments were maintained, but they were to be recast as "traditional values in a modern setting." Part of the change involved the removal of the famous "Clause IV" from the party constitution, a clause that had committed the party—in principle, if not in practice—to wholesale public ownership. New Labour was not going to advocate old-style socialism. Nor was it to convert completely to the neoliberalism of the Conservative Party, although it did insist it was pro-business and it accepted a large number of the Thatcherite reforms enacted by previous Conservative governments. Instead, New Labour was to advocate the "Third Way," an approach to policy making and to governance that owed much to the ideas then being advanced by Blair's intellectual guru, the sociologist Anthony Giddens, then director of the London School of Economics (Blair; Giddens; Marquand).

Although Labour's additional electoral gains in 1997 amounted to less than 10 percent, the translation of its higher vote total through the simple-plurality electoral system provided the party with a record majority in Westminster. Moreover, it also left the Conservatives with their smallest-ever share of seats. In parliamentary terms, this was a major landslide, and the Conservatives were left without a single parliamentary seat in either Scotland or Wales.

Since achieving office in 1997, and since being reelected in 2001, Labour has pushed forward a massive program of reform, not only in the social and economic sphere but also in constitutional terms. In its first three years of office, for example, devolved government was introduced in Scotland, Wales, and Northern Ireland; the Bank of England was given its independence; the House of Lords was reformed through the abolition of voting rights for hereditary peers; a system for the direct election of the city mayor was introduced for London and then extended to other major cities; proportional representation was introduced for elections to the regional assemblies in Scotland and Wales, as well as for the election of British representatives to the European Parliament; and a form of judicial review was introduced by means of the domestication into British law of the European Convention on Human Rights (see Chapter 4; see also both Flinders and Bogdanor).

As the traditional opponent of this active, ambitious, yet socially moderate Labour government, the Conservative Party has found itself more and more isolated and has struggled to find a new role in the system. "The government has stolen our language," complained the Conservative leader in an interview with *The Guardian* (November 17, 2004), going on to state that "it becomes very difficult for people to distinguish them from us. . . . In party political terms this is not where I want to be. I am frustrated." However, one way in which the Conservatives have tried to carve out a more distinctive profile is by increasingly emphasizing the party's stance in defense of British independence in Europe. Being significantly more skeptical than Labour toward European integration, and also more skeptical than most mainstream center–right parties across Europe, the Conservatives have increasingly taken on the image of a nationalist party. And since they remain so weak in both Scotland and Wales, this image is also one of a specifically English nationalist party. Meanwhile, the Liberals, buoyed up by their unprecedented success in winning seats, have sought to position themselves to the left of Labour, accusing the governing party of having taken over too many of the traditional Conservative economic policies. The Liberals have also become very critical of New Labour's foreign policy, urging closer engagement with Europe and voicing quite vocal opposition to Blair's support for the United States in the Iraq war. From a Liberal perspective, Labour is the new Conservative Party, and the Liberals themselves are increasingly in a position to offer a new and more radical alternative.

The United Kingdom has one of the oldest and most stable party systems in Europe, but it now seems increasingly vulnerable. Despite the economic successes of New Labour, the governing party seems unable to engage the support or commitment of the average British voter. Disillusion with politics remains high, and the 2001 election recorded the lowest level of turnout since the introduction of universal suffrage. Party membership has also fallen, and many voters and political activists from across the political spectrum have voiced their dissatisfaction with the quality of public services and with the policies being pursued by New Labour—particularly in relation to the United States and Iraq. At the same time, however, there is little real alternative to Labour. The Conservatives remain weak and isolated, and the Liberal Democrats remain small and untested. Discontent is evident, but it has few if any outlets. (On the traditional British party system, see Finer; for a more recent assessment, see Webb.)

Party Politics in Sweden

In Sweden, as in Britain, there is a major socialist party that initially mobilized in order to promote and defend the interests of the working class and forged strong links with the trade union movement. There is also a Swedish conservative party, now known as the Moderates, which sets out to defend the interests of the middle class and the more privileged sectors of the population. In this sense, Sweden is no different from Britain, with the representation of class interests taking the form of a partisan conflict between left and right. But it is here that the parallels end, for as Table 7.2 shows, the actual balance of forces on both left and right in Sweden differs sharply from that in the United Kingdom.

TABLE 7.2

Elections in Sweden Since 1991

Party	1991		1994		1998		2002	
	% of Votes	Seats	% of Votes	Seats	% of Votes	Seats	% of Votes	Seats
Social Democrats	37.7	138	45.2	161	36.6	131	39.9	144
Left Party/Communists	4.5	16	6.2	22	12.0	43	8.3	30
Ecology Party	3.4	—	5.0	18	4.5	16	4.5	17
Liberal Party	9.1	33	7.2	26	4.7	17	13.3	48
Center Party	8.5	31	7.7	27	5.1	18	6.2	22
Christian Democrats	7.1	26	4.1	15	11.8	42	9.1	33
Moderates (Conservatives)	21.9	80	22.4	80	22.7	82	15.1	55
New Democracy	6.7	25	1.2	—	—	—	—	—
Others	1.0	—	1.0	—	2.6	—	3.6	—
All	100.0	349	100.0	349	100.0	349	100.0	349

Party Composition of Government

1991–94   Coalition of Moderates, Liberals, Center, and Christian Democrats
1994–   Social Democratic single-party government

The Swedish Social Democrats have been much more successful than the British Labour Party, holding governmental power in Sweden almost without interruption from the early 1930s through the mid-1970s. Indeed, the Social Democrats in Sweden have been the most successful socialist party in western Europe and have used this success to establish one of western Europe's strongest and most egalitarian welfare states.

The second point of contrast between Sweden and the United Kingdom is that, despite their success, the Swedish Social Democrats have never monopolized the representation of the left. They have always been challenged by a small but persistent Communist Party, now renamed the Left Party, which won 8 percent of the popular vote in the most recent election, in 2002. The challenge posed to the Social Democrats by the Left Party is nevertheless a reasonably amicable one, and the smaller party has often supported its larger rival in parliament, enabling the Social Democrats to take control of the government even when they do not command a majority of seats, as was the case from 1982 to 1991 and since 1994. The Social Democrats have also sometimes had to rely on the small Green Party to remain in office as a minority government.

A third point of contrast with Britain is that unlike the British Conservatives, the Swedish Moderates fall very considerably short of monopolizing the nonsocialist opposition in parliament. On the contrary, the Swedish center and right are quite severely fragmented. In addition to the Moderates, there is a small Liberal Party, which commanded some 10 percent of parliamentary seats during the 1980s and draws support primarily from middle-class voters who are reluctant to endorse the more conservative Moderates. Although support for the Liberal Party fell back in the 1990s, Liberals recovered in the most recent election, tripling their vote with respect to that of 1998. There is also a Center Party, which initially grew as an agrarian party seeking to represent the interests of Swedish farmers and now draws support from across the social spectrum; it won around 12 percent of parliamentary seats in the 1980s but has since fallen back to around 5 or 6 percent.

Part of the reason why the Liberal and Center Parties experienced a loss of support during the 1990s was because of the sporadic but quite substantial increase in the vote for the once marginal Christian Democrats. This party had formed part of the center–right coalition in 1991–94 and grew to almost 12 percent of the vote in 1998 before falling back to 9 percent in 2002. This is a largely Protestant party that campaigns in defense of traditional values against the rise of more permissive attitudes. The Moderates, which polled an average of just over 20 percent in the 1990s but fell back to just 15 percent in 2002, have to remain content with the idea that they are just one of a group of nonsocialist parties competing on the center–right of the Swedish party system.

Although the Social Democrats have always been helped by this fragmentation on the center–right, they have not had it all their own way. The three stronger parties of the center–right cooperated to form a series of antisocialist coalitions in the late 1970s and early 1980s, and from 1991 to 1994, together with the Christian Democrats, they returned once more to government.

The overall pattern of votes in Sweden has therefore tended to be quite finely balanced between the left and center–right blocs, a two-bloc competition that had a lot of similarities with the two-party competition that characterized British politics for much of the postwar period. That said, there have been challenges to this pattern. The Greens, who were initially reluctant to define themselves in left–right terms, suddenly emerged to win more than 5 percent of the vote and 20 seats in 1988 but then fell below the 4 percent threshold in 1991 and lost their seats in parliament. Since then they have recovered and now usually poll some 5 or 6 percent of the vote. They have also aligned themselves more clearly with the left bloc, although, like the Left Party, they differ from the ruling Social Democrats in adopting a Euroskeptic position. More recently, the two-bloc divide was potentially undermined in the lead-up to the 2002 election when the Social Democrats began to make overtures to the Center Party about a possible coalition. This strategy failed to bear fruit, however, not least because the Center Party still preferred to align itself with the antisocialist camp.

Where Sweden remains distinctive, especially with respect to its Scandinavian neighbors, is in the absence of a major far-right challenge. Back in 1991, it seemed that such a challenge had emerged, in that a new protest party of the right, New Democracy, won almost 7 percent of the vote by appealing to the sense of popular dissatisfaction with politicians from the traditional parties and with traditional politics more generally. Although this party suffered severe internal conflicts and then failed to win reelection to parliament in 1994, its short-lived success did seem to indicate that there was indeed room for party growth on the far right of the Swedish party spectrum. Moreover, far-right parties have enjoyed quite substantial electoral success in neighboring Denmark and Norway. In Denmark, the far-right People's Party polled more than 12 percent of the votes in the 2001 general election, while in Norway in the same year the far-right Progress Party polled almost 15 percent of the vote. In Sweden, however, at least as yet, the far right remains quite marginal, although as in many other European democracies, immigration issues have begun to emerge within the mainstream political discourse in Sweden. It was reckoned that one of the reasons behind the success of the Liberals in 2002, for example, was the relatively hard line taken by the Liberal leader regarding the integration of immigrants. He had been the first senior political figure to advocate that all foreigners applying for Swedish citizenship should pass a Swedish language test. A similar policy has been advocated by the center–right parties in the Netherlands (see below). But despite this slight shift in the ideological consensus in Sweden, and despite the occasional challenge to the traditional two-bloc system, Sweden reflects a remarkably stable, if not traditional political image. As Madeley notes, the continued success of the Swedish Social Democrats contrasts quite sharply with that of Britain's New Labour, in that it has not necessitated any full-scale reinvention of the social democratic alternative. Rather, the Social Democrats have succeeded even though they have "stuck doggedly to the tough-minded pragmatism which has been their hallmark since the 1930s." (Madeley, p. 165). (For a classic account of the Swedish party system, as well as Scandinavian party politics in general, see Berglund and Lindstrom. For more contemporary assessments, see Arter; Sundberg.)

Party Politics in Germany

On the face of it, at least for most of the postwar period, the German party system has appeared very similar to that of Britain. Here, too, there are two main protagonists: the Social Democrats (SPD), the traditional party of the working class, and the Christian Democrats (CDU/CSU), the main representative of conservative interests (see Table 7.3). Lying strategically—if not always ideologically—between these two parties, with a small

TABLE 7.3

Elections in United Germany Since 1990

Party	1990 % of Votes	1990 Seats	1994 % of Votes	1994 Seats	1998 % of Votes	1998 Seats	2002 % of Votes	2002 Seats
Christian Democrats (CDU/CSU)	43.8	319	41.5	294	35.1	245	38.5	256
Social Democrats (SPD)	33.5	239	36.4	252	40.9	298	38.5	251
Free Democrats (FDP)	11.0	79	6.9	47	6.2	44	7.4	47
Greens	5.1	8	7.3	49	6.7	47	8.6	55
Democratic Socialists (PDS)	2.4	17	4.4	30	5.1	35	4.0	2
Republicans	2.1	—	1.9	—	1.8	—	0.6	—
German People's Union (DVU)	—	—	—	—	1.2	—	—	—
Others	2.1	—	1.6	—	3.0	—	2.0	—
All	100.0	662	100.0	672	100.0	669	100.0	611

Party Composition of Government

1990–98   Coalition of Christian Democrats and Free Democrats

1998–   Coalition of Social Democrats and Greens

but enduring presence, is a liberal party, the Free Democrats (FDP). Although the Free Democrats poll fewer votes than their British counterpart, they have always won quite a substantial representation in the Bundestag, the lower house of the German parliament, because the electoral system ensures that all parties polling 5 percent or more of the vote (or winning three seats in the single-member districts) are represented in proportion to their electoral support (see Chapter 11).

Despite superficial similarities between the British and German systems, however, there are also striking contrasts. In the first place, the relatively strong parliamentary presence of the Free Democrats has helped to ensure that neither of the two major parties was able single-handedly to command a majority of seats in the Bundestag. In Germany, therefore, in contrast to Britain, coalition government has been the norm. Indeed, the last occasion on which a single party secured an overall majority in the Bundestag was in 1957, when the Christian Democrats, under their powerful and popular leader Konrad Adenauer, won just over 50 percent of the votes and 54 percent of the seats. Even then, however, a coalition government was formed; the CDU was joined in government by the now defunct German Party, which then held 17 seats in the Bundestag. Since then, the FDP has provided necessary coalition support for each of the major parties, and (with one exception during the "grand coalition" between the CDU and the SPD in 1966–69) it served as junior partner in every government from 1961 to 1998. The FDP cooperated with the CDU from 1961 to 1966 and resumed support in 1982, and it cooperated with the SPD from 1969 through 1982.

In addition to its powerful governmental role, the FDP can be distinguished from the British Liberals in two other respects. First, it promotes an emphatically conservative liberalism. It emphasizes individual as opposed to collective rights and lays greater emphasis than even the CDU on the need to roll back the state and maximize private freedoms. Second, the FDP's roots can be found in secular opposition to Catholic politics rather than in liberal opposition to secular conservatism. Despite its brokerage role in government formation, the FDP can therefore be seen as being substantially to the right of the British center parties and more akin in many ways to the British Conservatives.

Another major point of contrast with Britain concerns the CDU. First, as its name implies, the CDU is not simply a conservative party; it is also a Christian party, a party that has traditionally placed substantial weight on the defense of religious values against the secularism of both the SPD and the FDP. Heir to the primarily Catholic Center Party of Weimar Germany, which was the major representative of the moderate right in the period prior to the mobilization of Nazism in 1930s Weimar Germany, the postwar Christian Democrats have since broadened their support base through an explicit appeal to Protestant voters. This pan-Christian strategy was encouraged by the fact that a large proportion of the Protestant electorate in Germany resided in what was to become the German Democratic Republic (East Germany), thus undermining the potential for the emergence in West Germany of distinctively Protestant parties such as those that proved so crucial in Dutch politics (see below). Second, the "Christian Democrats" are effectively two parties, the CDU proper and its permanent political ally, the Bavarian Christian Social Union (CSU). Unlike the CDU, the CSU is almost exclusively Catholic and, to the extent that it operates autonomously, is generally regarded as the most conservative party in Germany.

Germany has more in common with Britain when it comes to the socialist party, the SPD. From its origins in the late nineteenth century as the most radical and powerful socialist party in Europe, when the SPD leadership included some of the foremost Marxist intellectuals in the international socialist movement, the party has developed into one of the most moderate and centrist social democratic organization in western Europe. The SPD was effectively excluded from office in the early years of postwar West Germany, and it suffered from the reaction against political extremism that flowed in the wake of both Nazism and the communist takeover of East Germany. In 1959, in an effort to acquire a legitimate role in the new state, the party adopted what became known as the Bad Godesberg program, accepting the principle of the free-market economy and a commitment to the North Atlantic Treaty Organization (NATO) and effectively endorsing the policies then being pursued by the incumbent Christian Democratic government. This transformation was finally completed in 1966, when, as noted, the party joined in a grand coalition with the Christian Democrats. Since then, the degree of ideological conflict between the two major parties has often been quite insignificant, and the German party system was often regarded as among the most consensual in western Europe.

The traditional combination of alignments based on class (SPD versus CDU and FDP) and religion (CDU versus SPD and FDP) once led Pappi (pp. 12–14) to view the German party system as being characterized by a "triangular" rather than "unidimensional" pattern of competition. According to this view, various alliances can and do prove possible. Thus, the moderate socialism of the SPD and the residual Catholic emphases of the CDU could find common ground in a defense of the welfare state and of consensual rather than confrontational policy making. The SPD and FDP, in turn, could find common ground in rejecting the incorporation of Catholic values into public policy (on issues such as abortion and divorce, for example). And the CDU and FDP could—and most often did—find common ground in their defense of the interests of private property and capital.

In the 1980s, two factors emerged that helped to undermine this particular and often quite cozy balance. In the first place, since 1983 a new, radical Green Party managed to win sufficient electoral support to push it past the 5 percent threshold imposed by the German electoral system and to gain strong representation in the Bundestag. This expansion of the number of parties in parliament offered the possibility that party competition could develop into a confrontation between two rival blocs, with the SPD and Greens confronting the CDU and FDP. To be sure, it was always known that there would be much difficult negotiation and internal party conflict before the SPD and Greens agreed on a common program for government. Nevertheless, the presence of the Greens did have the potential to destroy the pivotal role of the FDP in German politics and create a two-bloc pattern quite similar to that which, for example, characterizes party competition in Sweden. This potential was finally to be realized in 1998.

The second and incomparably the more important development was the collapse of the East German state and the unification of the two Germanies in 1990. Greater Germany then accommodated more than 12 million new voters who had yet to be socialized into stable partisan identities and whose political behavior could therefore prove quite volatile for some time to come. In the first democratic elections in East Germany in March 1990, these new electors voted overwhelmingly for the Christian Democrats (which won 47 percent of the poll); the Social Democrats won just 22 percent, and the reformed Communist Party won 16 percent. The Christian Democratic successes were later confirmed in the first Bundestag elections of the newly unified state, which were held on December 2, 1990 (see Table 7.3). These were the first all-German elections since Hitler seized power in 1933, and once again they left the coalition of the Christian Democrats and the liberal FDP with a clear overall majority, in which they held a total of 398 seats in the newly enlarged Bundestag, as against 264 seats for the combined opposition parties. Indeed, the FDP success was even more marked than that of the CDU, and the party then polled a substantially larger share of the vote in the eastern part of the country than it did in the west.

As part of the transitional arrangements prior to complete unification, the rule whereby parties require a national minimum of 5 percent of the vote in order to win representation in the Bundestag (see Chapter 11) was modified for the purposes of these first all-German elections. Rather than treating the threshold as applying to Germany as a whole, it was agreed that a party would need 5 percent either in the area that was formerly West Germany or in the area that was formerly East Germany. Thus, although the former East German Communist Party, now reorganized as the Party of Democratic Socialism (PDS), won only 2.4 percent in the nation as a whole, it won some 10 percent of the vote in the former East Germany, double the threshold and sufficient to win the party 17 seats in 1990. The Greens, in contrast, were weakened by this rule, failing to reach the threshold in the west (they polled only 4.7 percent) and continuing to be represented in the Bundestag only under the auspices of the Bundnis '90, the alliance of East German citizens' movements that included New Forum, the popular movement that had spearheaded the 1989 protests and revolution. The two groups formally merged in November 1992.

Despite the success of the incumbent coalition, the new German party system after 1990 was to prove more fragmented than at any point in the previous thirty years. Five parties are represented in the Bundestag, including the Greens and the reformed East German Communist Party, the PDS, which increasingly plays the role of a regional party promoting the interests of the eastern Länder. Political problems also quickly began to accumulate in the new Germany. The government was already having to cope with the arrival of unprecedented numbers of immigrants, refugees, and asylum-seekers, and these numbers accelerated in the wake of the collapse of the Soviet Union. Meanwhile, unemployment continued to remain particularly high in the former East German area, and voters there were increasingly disillusioned with the lack of economic and social progress, while in the western areas voters were also increasingly discontented about having to bear the burden of the economic costs of reconstruction and resettlement. Symptomatic of this discontent has been the more or less steady support won by the former communist PDS in federal elections, as well as the ebbs and flows of support for far-right parties such as the Republicans, the German People's Union (DVU), and the neo-Nazi National Democratic Party (NPD). In eastern German Land elections in September 2004, the NPD actually polled 9 percent of the vote in Saxony, while the DVU polled 6 percent in Brandenburg. These were the best results achieved by far-right parties since unification. For some time now, German commentators have also regularly pointed toward the growth of what they call *Politikverdrossenheit,* or disillusion with politics, a syndrome that has also been increasingly noted in other advanced western democracies (Poguntke and Scarrow; Norris).

These problems are not new, of course, and disillusion with traditional alternatives was undoubtedly one of the factors leading to the success of the new alternative Red–Green coalition of the SPD and the Green Party under the leadership of Gerhard Schröder in the federal elections of 1998. In fact, this was not only the first time that the Greens had become part of a coalition in Germany, but it was also the first time that an incumbent German government had been thrown out of office in its entirety and a wholly new government installed in its place.

As in the United Kingdom, the change of government had been made easier by the increasingly moderate stance adopted by the SPD—although Schröder himself preferred to speak of the "new middle" rather than the "third way." Ironically, one of Schröder's first crises, which was prompted by the sudden resignation of the more left-wing SPD deputy leader Oskar Lafontaine, occurred precisely on the day when Schröder was intending to make a speech heralding the publication of a German translation of Giddens's book, *The Third Way.*

The agreement between the SPD and the Greens had also been forged by necessity, of course. As in the UK, both parties had become increasingly frustrated by the long tenure in office of their center–right opponents. However, relations between the two parties were not always easy in the beginning, and the change of government did little to abate the discontent in the eastern parts of Germany in particular. The new government also suffered from increasing budgetary problems at the end of its first term of office, as well as from high unemployment levels and a widespread sense of economic doom and gloom (Kitschelt and Streeck, "From Stability"). By then, however, relations between the Greens and the SPD had improved substantially, and despite the poor economic prospects and a series of small corruption scandals, the two parties narrowly managed to hold on to office in the 2002 election—the losses of the SDP being partially compensated by the narrow gains of the Greens, leaving the coalition with a very small majority in the Bundestag. Despite its electoral survival, however, the Red–Green coalition seems unable to lift Germany off the bottom of the European growth league. For this reason, voices in Germany now also call for a grand "crisis" coalition between the CDU and the SPD. This may also be the one of the only realistic options for the future, of course, since the drift of votes to the far right, on the one hand,

and to the PDS, on the other, may make it more difficult to build conventional coalitions on the center–left or center–right. (On the problems facing the German party system, see Roberts; Padgett and Saalfield; Scarrow; Kitschelt and Streeck, *Germany*).

Party Politics in the Netherlands

Like politics in Sweden and unlike politics in Britain and the former West Germany, Dutch politics is highly fragmented. Many parties compete for electoral and parliamentary support (see Table 7.4). Nor does the Netherlands have competition between two clearly distinguished parties or blocs. Rather, three large parties, none in a position to win a working majority on its own, provide the major alternatives before

TABLE 7.4

Elections in the Netherlands Since 1989

Party	1989		1994		1998		2002		2003	
	% of Votes	Seats	% of Votes	Seats	% of Votes	Seats	% of Votes	Seats	% of Votes	Seats
Socialist Party	—	—	1.3	2	3.5	5	5.9	9	6.3	9
Green Left	4.1	6	3.5	5	7.3	11	7.0	10	5.1	8
Labor Party (PvdA)	31.9	49	24.0	37	29.0	45	15.1	23	27.3	42
Democrats 66	7.9	12	15.5	24	9.0	14	5.1	7	4.1	6
Liberals (VVD)	14.6	22	19.9	31	24.7	38	15.4	24	17.9	28
Christian Democratic Appeal (CDA)	35.3	54	22.2	34	18.4	29	27.9	43	28.6	44
Reformed Political Union (GPV)	1.2	2	1.3	2	1.3	2	—	—	—	—
Christian Union (CU)[a]	—	—	—	—	—	—	2.5	4	2.1	3
Reformed Political Federation (RPF)	1.0	1	1.8	3	2.0	3	—	—	—	—
Political Reformed Party (SGP)	1.9	3	1.7	2	1.8	3	1.7	2	1.6	2
Pim Fortuyn List (LPF)	—	—	—	—	—	—	17.0	26	5.7	8
Old People's Alliance	—	—	3.6	6	0.5	—	—	—	—	—
Union 55+	—	—	0.9	1	—	—	—	—	—	—
Center Democrats	0.9	1	2.5	3	0.6	—	—	—	—	—
Others	1.2	—	1.8	—	1.9	—	2.4	2	1.3	—
All	100.0	150	100.0	150	100.0	150	100.0	150	100.0	150

Party Composition of Government
1989–94	Coalition of Christian Democrats and Labor
1994–2002	Coalition of Labor, Liberals, and Democrats 66
2002–3	Coalition of Christian Democrats, Liberals, and Pim Fortuyn List
2003–	Coalition of Christian Democrats, Liberals, and Democrats 66

[a] The Christian Union is a merger of the GPV and RPF.

voters. The various maneuverings of these parties create a shifting system of coalitions and alliances.

The first of these parties is a socialist party, the Labor Party (PvdA), which usually won between a quarter and a third of the vote but then fell back dramatically to just 15 percent in 2002 before recovering to 27 percent a year later. This is also more or less the story of its share of parliamentary seats, since the Dutch electoral system is exceptionally proportional (see Table 7.4). Both programmatically and in its electoral support, the party stands as the effective equivalent of the German, Swedish, and British social democratic parties. Indeed, it sometimes claims to be the true inventor of the "third way" or "new middle." The party based itself traditionally in the working class, and it promotes both the role of the welfare state and a more egalitarian distribution of social and economic resources. Given its relatively small size, however, it has little hope of forming a government of its own and is obliged to forge alliances with parties to its right.

The second of the large traditional parties is the Christian Democratic Appeal (CDA), which usually vied with the Labor Party over which would be the biggest single party in the Netherlands. As its name implies, and like the major nonsocialist party in Germany, the Dutch CDA is not simply a conservative party. It also seeks to represent the views of Christian voters, both Protestant and Roman Catholic. Religious divisions, reflecting conflicts between the different Christian denominations and between voters who are generally proclerical and those who are anticlerical, have always been important in Dutch politics. For much of the postwar period, indeed, Protestant and Catholic voters were represented by two separate Protestant parties and one Catholic party. Since 1977, however, and partly as a result of the general weakening of religious ties and the decreasing political salience of interdenominational divisions, those three parties have united behind one pan-Christian party, the CDA. Over and above its defense of religious values, the CDA maintains a moderate conservative position in relation to social and economic policies, drawing electoral support from all major social classes. In the late 1980s and 1990s, however, it entered into a serious electoral decline. Indeed, between 1986 and 1998 its vote fell by almost half, and whereas it (or one of its denominational predecessors) played a pivotal and often dominant role in all postwar coalitions, it was forced into opposition between 1994 and 2002. Since then it has staged an impressive recovery, increasing its support to almost 28 percent in 2002 and to almost 29 percent in 2003, and becoming once again the biggest single party in the Netherlands and the leader of the governing coalition.

The third major traditional party in the Netherlands is the Liberal Party (VVD). This party has a much more distinctively middle-class electoral profile than the CDA and usually won less than 20 percent of the vote. Most recently, however, it has been gaining support, and it polled almost 25 percent in 1998 before falling back to 15 percent in 2002 and to 18 percent in 2003. For a long time; the Liberals represented the main secular opposition to the Labor Party and proved far less willing than the CDA to compromise in the direction of Labor's social and economic concerns. At the same time, however, the VVD was also hostile to the representation of religious values in politics. In this respect it sometimes found common ground with the Labor Party in opposition to the CDA. Indeed, the Liberal Party first mobilized in Dutch politics primarily as middle-class opposition to the growing appeal of religious parties. (This links the Dutch Liberals to the German FDP and sets them apart from the British and Swedish Liberals, both of which originated as moderate middle-class alternatives to secular conservative opponents and both of which are still oriented toward more centrist policies.)

Thus, when it comes to class issues and an economic program emphasizing the need for a minimum of state intervention and a maximum reliance on market forces, the Dutch Liberals could always identify more strongly with the CDA than with Labor. In the religious–secular divide, however, the Liberals found themselves on the same side as Labor. At the same time, because the CDA's conservative appeal is more moderate than that of the Liberals, the CDA sometimes sought alliances with Labor rather than with the other right-wing party. The result, as might be expected, was—and still is—a shifting pattern of coalition government. In 1989 a CDA–Liberal coalition was replaced by a CDA–Labor coalition. This government, in turn, was replaced in 1994 by a coalition of Labor, Liberals, and Democrats 66, a small left-leaning liberal party—the "purple coalition," the first Dutch government to exclude the Christian mainstream. That coalition lasted until 2002 and was replaced by a short-lived coalition consisting of the CDA, VVD, and the new Pim Fortuyn List, and that coalition in turn was replaced in 2003 by a new coalition of CDA, VVD, and Democrats 66.

At center stage in Dutch party politics, therefore, are three key actors that go in and out of government in a shifting series of alliances. This pattern is complicated by the presence of a number of smaller parties, on both left and right and both secular and religious. These include the increasingly important Green Left and the Socialist Party, both of which have managed to attract some of Labor's more radical supporters, as well as the moderate Christian Union (CU) and the more fundamentalist Christian Political Reformed Party (SGP). In 2002, however, the traditional patterns of Dutch party politics were suddenly torn apart by the arrival of the right-wing populist Pim Fortuyn List (LPF), a new formation led by the articulate and very flamboyant Pim Fortuyn, who castigated the closed consensual culture that had been formed by the Dutch political class, and who also broke with many of the familiar taboos of Dutch politics by criticizing Islamic culture and by questioning many of the accepted policies regarding immigration, integration, and multiculturalism. This was the biggest shake-up ever experienced by Dutch politics, and Fortuyn clearly struck a chord with disillusioned voters on both left and right; opinion polls indicate that his list could win up to 20 percent of the vote. But it was not to be. In a dramatic turn of events, Fortuyn was assassinated by an animal rights activist on the eve of polling, and his then leaderless and subsequently fractured party polled 17 percent of the vote and won 26 seats (the best account and analysis is by Holsteyn and Irwin). Although not as great a success as had been anticipated, this outcome was still a record for any new party in the Netherlands, and the losses experienced by both Labor (from 29 to 15 percent) and the Liberals (from 25 to 15 percent) were also at record levels. The opposition CDA, which had refrained from criticizing Fortuyn, proved the most successful of the traditional parties and later formed a government with the VVD and the LPF. Conflicts between the parties within the cabinet, however, as well as very sharp disputes between the two leading LPF ministers, forced the government to resign after only a few months in office. In the subsequent election in 2003, the CDA maintained its leading position, the PvdA recovered, and the LPF fell back to just 6 percent of the vote. Normality seemed to have returned, even if the short-lived success of the LPF had shown that there existed a major potential for change. (For an analysis of the traditional Dutch party system, see Daalder. For more contemporary assessments, see Andeweg and Irwin; Brug and Pellikaan.)

Party Politics in Italy

Reflecting on the nationalist revolution in early-twentieth-century Ireland, the poet W. B. Yeats wrote that "things fall apart; the centre cannot hold." In contemporary Italy, where party politics has been reshaped to a degree unprecedented in any postwar European party system, the center has also been unable to hold, and the traditional system has fallen completely apart (see Table 7.5). The degree of change is such that it is still impossible to foresee what sort of alignment will emerge because it is as yet impossible to predict the future structure of Italian party politics or, indeed, of the Italian political system as a whole.

At first sight, the traditional patterns of postwar party politics in Italy did not appear to differ very markedly from those in the other countries surveyed here. In Italy, as in each of the other countries, a left–right opposition lay at the heart of party competition, reflecting the confrontation between parties promoting working-class interests and those promoting the interests of better-off social groups. As in the UK and Sweden, the traditional left, represented in Italy by both a communist and a socialist party, usually won about 40 percent of the vote. And as in West Germany and the Netherlands, there was also a religious–secular divide, although in Italy proclerical forces are exclusively Catholic.

The distinguishing feature of the Italian party system was not so much the particular interests that were represented as it was the depth of the ideological divisions between the competing parties. The major party on the traditional left was the Italian Communist Party (PCI), which in early 1991, after much agonizing and in reaction to the collapse of the communist regimes in eastern and central Europe, changed its name to the Democratic Party of the Left (PDS), and even more recently to simply Democrats of the Left (DS). Before this change, the PCI had been the strongest communist party in western Europe and averaged 29 percent of the votes during the 1980s. For most of the postwar era, the PCI retained the aura of a far-left opposition, and the strength of PCI support thus marked the Italian party system off from the party systems of many other European democracies. At the opposite end of the left–right ideological spectrum in Italy was the neofascist Italian Social Movement (MSI), which usually polled about 6 percent of the vote.

Ranged between these extremes lay five more central parties. The biggest of these was the Christian Democratic Party (DC), which usually polled about 30 percent of the popular vote. Like the Dutch CDA, this party combined a moderately conservative economic appeal with the promotion of religious values.

Two other parties mobilized on the center–right in Italy: The Liberals and the Republicans between them averaged about 7 percent of the vote. The tiny Liberal Party was the more right-wing of the two and had an ideological position similar to that of its Dutch and German counterparts. The Republicans reflected the more centrist politics characteristic of the liberal parties in both Sweden and the UK. Both were largely middle-class parties that endorsed many of the conservative economic appeals of the DC while rejecting its emphasis on religious values.

TABLE 7.5

Elections in Italy Since 1992

Party	1992 % of Votes	1992 Seats	1994 % of PR Votes[a]	1994 Seats	1996 % of PR Votes[a]	1996 Seats	2001 % of PR Votes[a]	2001 Seats
Greens	1.8	16	2.7	11	2.5	16	2.2	17
Communist Party (PCI)[b]	—	—	—	—	—	—	1.7	10
Communist Refoundation	5.6	35	6.0	39	8.6	35	5.0	11
Democratic Party of the Left (PDS)	16.1	107	20.4	109	21.1	171	16.6	137
La Rete	1.9	12	1.9	6	—	—	—	—
Socialist Party (PSI)/Dini List[c]	13.6	92	2.2	14	4.3	26	2.2	2
Social Democrats (PSDI)	2.7	16	—	—	—	—	—	—
Republicans	4.4	27	—	—	—	—	—	—
Liberal Party	2.9	17	—	—	—	—	—	—
Democratic Alliance	—	—	1.2	18	—	—	—	—
Segni Pact	—	—	4.7	13	—	—	—	—
Christian Democrats (DC)[d]	29.7	206	—	—	—	—	—	—
Christian Democratic Center/ Christian Democratic Union (1994: CCD)	—	—	—	29[e]	5.8	30	3.2	40
People's Party(PPI)/Prodi List	—	—	11.1	33	6.8	75	14.5	80
Forza Italia	—	—	21.0	99	20.6	123	29.5	189
Northern League	8.7	55	8.4	117	10.1	59	3.9	30
Social Movement (MSI)/ National Alliance	5.4	34	13.5	109	15.7	93	12.0	96
Radicals/Pannella List	1.2	7	3.5	6	1.9	—	2.3	—
Others	5.0	6	3.4	27	2.6	2	7.0	18
All	100.0	630	100.0	630	100.0	630	100.0	630

Party Composition of Government

1992–94   Coalition of Christian Democrats, Socialists, Social Democrats, and Liberals

1994   Coalition of Forza Italia, National Alliance, and Northern League

1995–96   Nonparty government

1996–01   Olive Tree Alliance, including Democratic Party of the Left, People's Party, Greens, and Dini List (Italian Renewal)

2001–   Coalition of Forza Italia, National Alliance, Northern League, and Christian Democrats (CCD–CDU)

[a] From 1994 on, "% of votes" refers only to the share of the vote in the PR (proportional representation) districts, and "Seats" refers to the total number of seats won in both the PR and single-member districts. It should also be noted that the lists competing in the PR districts since 1994 sometimes involved quite heterogeneous alliances of parties, and the overview provided in this table does not necessarily provide a wholly accurate party-by-party breakdown.

[b] The Communist Party (PCI) split in 1991. The majority of the party reorganized as the social democratic Democratic Party of the Left (PDS), later renamed "Democrats of the Left" (DS), and a minority maintained a more orthodox communist position as Communist Refoundation (RC).

[c] Although the Socialist Party did not contest the 1996 election as an independent party, an official Socialist Party list was included in the list headed by Lamberto Dini.

[d] The Christian Democrats fell apart after 1992 and were succeeded by various smaller parties including the Christian Democratic Center (CCD), Christian Democratic Union (CDU) and the People's Party (PPI); in 1996 the PPI formed part of a list headed by Romano Prodi, which also included the former Segni Pact.

[e] All of the CCD seats in 1994 were won in the single-member districts.

On the center–left of the system sat the small Social Democratic Party (PSDI), which usually polled about 4 percent of the vote. More influential on the left was the Socialist Party (PSI), which usually polled about 12 percent of the vote and shared many of the concerns of the major social democratic parties in the United Kingdom, Sweden, the Netherlands, and West Germany.

The traditional Italian party system, therefore, comprised both a more fragmented and a more polarized set of alternatives than could be found in the other countries we have considered. As a consequence, it was impossible for a clear-cut left- or right-wing bloc to present itself to voters as a realistic governing option. On the left, the combined support of the PCI, PSI, and PSDI, together with that of the smaller radical parties, might have appeared sufficient to form a government coalition. Yet, because of the perceived extremism of the PCI, this option seemed impossible to realize. There might also seem to have been a potential parliamentary majority on the right, but this option also proved impossible to realize given the far-right position of the MSI—suggestions by the Christian Democrats that they might deal with the MSI proved very unpopular with voters. The consequent exclusion of both ends of the political spectrum from government therefore left the remaining parties searching for a parliamentary majority through the creation of persistent—if unstable—governments of the center, much like the pattern that prevailed in the French Fourth Republic (see below). The participants typically ranged from the socialists to the Christian democrats to the liberals, who combined into a five-party (*pentapartito*) or four-party coalition straddling the center–left and the center right (Mershon).

As is clear from our phrasing, however, all this is now in the past, and the Italian party system has been reshaped to an extraordinary degree. Three factors are important here. In the first place, the end of the Cold War led to a decisive shift in which the new Democrats of the Left (DS) abandoned the traditional communist character of the PCI and moved toward a more conventional social democratic position (the new party is now actually a member of the European Socialist Party federation). This has forced the other parties, and the voters, to accept that the DS now has the potential to form part of a coalition government and that, unlike the old PCI, it can no longer be excluded as a matter of principle. This in itself changes the terms of reference of traditional politics.

Second, increasing discontent with the endemic corruption and clientelism that characterized Italian governments fueled support for the Northern League (Lega Nord), which won almost 9 percent of the vote in 1992 and ended up as the biggest single party in parliament in 1994 (see Table 7.5). The Northern League, a far-right populist movement based mainly in the richer northern regions of Italy, demands an end to the system whereby the taxes paid by its relatively prosperous supporters are used to fund welfare programs and public works in the poorer south and therefore help the government win support in the south. The party also advocates the creation of a federal structure in Italy.

Third, and most important, support for the traditional governing parties, the Christian Democrats (DC) and the Socialists (PSI), was more or less completely undermined by the revelations of corruption and bribery uncovered by the so-called *mani pulite* (clean hands) investigation. This was an investigation by Italian magistrates that began in Milan in February 1992 and then spread to many other parts of the country. After little more than a year, at the end of March 1993, the investigation had led to accusations of bribe taking (*tangenti*) against more than 150 members of the Italian parliament and against almost 900 local politicians. Those accused included many prominent figures in the DC and the PSI. Indeed, almost one-third of the PSI's MPs were by then under investigation, as were more than one-quarter of its party executives. The PSI leader, Bettino Craxi, fled to Tunisia.

The result was that the center of the old party system, in the form of the DC and PSI in particular, was effectively swept away. In fact, while the PSI more or less faded away, the DC broke up into disparate elements, including the more left-leaning Popolari (People's Party), on the one hand, and the more right-leaning Centro Cristiano Democratico (Christian Democratic Center) and Christian Democratic Union (CDU), on the other.

In the 1994 general election, which was the first to be held under the new electoral system (see Chapter 11)—inaugurating the "Second Republic"—and which witnessed the biggest shift in the political balance ever recorded in postwar Italy, the Northern League won just over 8 percent of the PR vote and 111 of the 475 single-member districts and emerged as the biggest single party in the new parliament; the DS was a close second with 20 percent of the proportional representation (PR) vote and 77 seats in the single-member districts (see Table 7.5). The neofacist MSI, reconstituted as the National Alliance, came in third, with 14 percent of the PR votes and 86 single-members districts. Perhaps the greatest surprise, however, was the strong showing of Forza Italia (literally "Go, Italy!"), which was formed just three months before the election by the media tycoon and owner of AC Milan soccer team, Silvio Berlusconi, and which won 21 percent of the PR vote and 67 single-member districts.

Together with the Northern League and the National Alliance, Forza Italia had formed a joint right-wing electoral alliance (the Pole of Liberty) in opposition to the DS, and this new alliance emerged from the election with a clear overall majority in the Chamber of Deputies, the lower house of parliament. The three parties later went on to form a government under the premiership of Berlusconi, which included in the cabinet five ministers drawn from the far-right National Alliance/MSI. Under the leadership of the DS, the left had also formed an electoral alliance (the Progressives), which included remnants from the old PSI as well as the more orthodox Communist Refoundation, the Greens, and other reformist movements; this bloc of parties constituted the major opposition to the new right-wing government.

Berlusconi's government proved fragile, however, not least because of tensions between the Northern League and the National Alliance, and it was quickly replaced by a "technical" nonparty government. Then, in 1996, came the second major change of the Second Republic, when the so-called Olive Tree (Ulivo) Alliance, dominated by the PDS but led by Romano Prodi, leader of the People's Party, won a narrow overall majority. The new alliance also included the Greens, as well as new groupings that had emerged from the remnants of the old socialist and liberal center, and it won grudging support from the Communist Refoundation. For the first time since 1947, former Communists had managed to win government. For the first time also, there was a complete alternation in government.

Although Prodi later went on to become president of the European Commission in 1999, the new center–left alliance remained in office until 2001. It proved internally divided, however, and had to be reconstituted on a number of occasions. A major parliamentary defeat in late 1998 led to Prodi's resignation and his replacement by DS leader Massimo D'Alema, and in April 2000, D'Alema himself was replaced by Giuliano Amato, a former PSI premier. By then, however, the alliance seemed very fragmented, and although still formally united under the Olive Tree label, it went into the 2001 contest as a varied collection of different and unlikely-sounding groups including the DS, the Daisy (Margherita—itself an alliance of several center parties), and the Sunflower (Girasole—an alliance of Greens and former Socialists). On the right, meanwhile, efforts to build a new alliance had succeeded, and in 2001 Berlusconi returned to power at the head of the House of Liberty coalition—including, once again, Forza Italia, the National Alliance, and the Northern League, as well as the Christian Democratic Center and the Christian Democratic Union. This time the alliance proved quite robust, and it went on to become the longest-serving postwar Italian government. At the same time, it also met with severe criticism both at home, in the form of protests and strikes, and abroad; in both cases increasing concern was expressed about government policy being used to help promote and protect Berlusconi's personal and business interests.

For now, at least, politics in Italy has taken the form of a bipolar confrontation of left and right, and if this persists, then the new party system will end up looking completely different from the system that prevailed in the "First Republic" under Christian Democratic centrist domination. The blocs of both left and right, however, are still fragile coalitions, and despite the pressure of the new electoral system, holding them together may prove difficult. (On the traditional Italian party system see Farneti. For an analysis of the more recent patterns of party politics, see Bardi; Bartolini et al.; Bull and Rhodes; Newell and Bull. On the Berlusconi phenomenon, see Ginsborg.)

Party Politics in France

The current French constitution dates from 1958, which marked the beginning of the French Fifth Republic. Before this, France was governed under the constitution of the Fourth Republic, dating from 1945. During the Fourth Republic the French party system bore many similarities to that of pre-1990s Italy. Politics on the left was dominated by the large pro-Moscow Communist Party (PCF), which polled on average about 27 percent of the vote. There was also a steadily weakening Socialist Party (PS), which averaged less than 19 percent of the vote. The center was occupied by a radical party, which won an average of 12 percent, and by the Catholic Popular Republican Movement (MRP), which polled over 25 percent in the 1940s but then fell back to 12 percent in the 1950s. On the right, a conservative party persisted throughout the period, with around 13 percent of the vote. In the 1950s, however, the conservatives were marginalized by two rivals on the right; the Gaullists (winning 22 percent of the vote in 1951) and the far-right Poujadists (winning 12 percent in 1956), both reflecting opposition to the constitutional arrangements of the Fourth Republic. Faced with anticonstitutional opposition from both left and right, which proved both more extremist and more powerful than in Italy, the center was unable to hold and the result was chronic political instability.

Two key changes occurred in the party system during the early decades of the Fifth Republic (Bartolini, pp. 104–15). First was the emergence of a much more clearly defined bipolar pattern of competition, much like the two-bloc model in the Swedish case, in which the left, represented by the Socialist Party (PS) and the Communist Party (PCF), competed against the right, represented by the new Gaullist party (RPR) and the coalition of forces that organized under the label Union for French Democracy (UDF). The emergence of this bipolar pattern was facilitated by the

TABLE 7.6

Presidential Elections in France Since 1988

Party	1988[a] 1st Round % of Votes	1988[a] 2nd Round % of Votes	1995[b] 1st Round % of Votes	1995[b] 2nd Round % of Votes	2002[c] 1st Round % of Votes	2002[c] 2nd Round % of Votes
Greens	3.8	—	3.3	—	5.2	—
Communist Party (PCF)	6.8	—	8.6	—	3.4	—
Socialist Party (PS)	34.1	54.0	23.3	47.4	16.2	—
Rally for the Republic (RPR)	19.9	46.0	39.5	52.6	19.9	82.2
Union for French Democracy (UDF)	16.5	—	—	—	6.8	—
National Front (NF)	14.4	—	15.0	—	16.9	17.8
Other left (various)	4.5	—	5.6	—	22.6	—
Other right (various)	—	—	4.7	—	10.4	—
Total	100.0	100.0	100.0	100.0	100.0	100.0

[a] The second-ballot contestants were outgoing President François Mitterrand (PS), the eventual winner, and Jacques Chirac (RPR).

[b] The RPR (Gaullists) ran two candidates in the first ballot, Jacques Chirac and Eduard Balladur, and the figure of 39.5 percent refers to their combined vote. There was no UDF candidate in that first ballot. Chirac, who was the higher-polling Gaullist candidate and who came in second to the eventual first-ballot leader, Lionel Jospin (PS), then went on to win the presidency in the second ballot.

[c] Jean-Marie Le Pen of the National Front narrowly beat Lionel Jospin (PS) into third place on the first round of voting and went on to contest the second round against the incumbent, Jacques Chirac. The National Front vote did not increase very much in 2002, but the PS was badly damaged by the participation of many other left candidates in the first round.

abandonment of the proportional electoral formula that had been used in the Fourth Republic and its replacement by a double-ballot majority system, which encourages competition between only two candidates in each constituency in the second round of voting (see Chapter 11). It was also encouraged by the introduction of a directly elected president in 1962, which also involves just two candidates competing in the second round of voting (see Table 7.6).

The second change that occurred during the Fifth Republic was a shift in the balance of forces within both left and right. For a variety of reasons, both ideological and institutional (Bartolini), the PCF became increasingly marginalized, and the left grew to be dominated by the Socialist Party. Already by the 1980s the PS, together with its electoral allies among the left radicals (MRG), commanded the largest share of the vote in France. The PCF had then fallen to 10 percent of the poll and was reduced to playing a supporting role for the PS. In the most recent election, in 2002, the party was reduced to less than 5 percent of the vote—a far cry from the 20 percent or more it had enjoyed in the 1960s. In 1981, for the first time ever, the PS emerged with an overall majority of seats in the lower house of the French parliament, although it initially chose to govern in coalition with the PCF. Earlier that same year, with PS candidate François Mitterrand, the left had won the presidency for the first time ever.

There was also a substantial shift in the balance of forces on the right, with the disappearance of the MRP and with the development of a more or less stable and evenly balanced alliance between the Gaullist RPR and the UDF. (The latter, like the early center–right electoral alliances in Spain (see below), combines liberal, Christian, and conservative forces.) Party competition in the Fifth Republic, therefore, not only took the form of a much better defined confrontation between left and right but was also, at least until recently, increasingly dominated by the more moderate of the forces within each bloc. The polarization of the Fourth Republic appeared a thing of the past.

This pattern came to be challenged, however, at least on the right, by the emergence of the far-right National Front. The National Front mobilizes a strongly racist and xenophobic political appeal and has clocked up some significant electoral successes in the southern parts of France in particular. The problem for the mainstream right is that future support for the National Front may be sufficient to prevent the UDF and RPR from achieving a majority in either the presidential or the parliamentary elections. If they try to come to terms with the National Front, however, and if they attempt to forge a new and more broadly defined alliance on the right, they risk losing their more moderate voters—and some of their leaders—in the center. The problem is a major one for the mainstream right. In the 1997 parliamentary elections, the National Front polled almost 15 percent of the vote, although it was denied almost any seats by the double-ballot majority voting systems (see Table 7.7). In the presidential elections of 2002, the leader and candidate of the Front, Jean-Marie Le Pen, polled 17 percent of the first-ballot vote, coming a close second to the Gaullist Jacques Chirac and knocking the PS candidate Lionel Jospin into third place. In the second ballot, however, Le Pen barely improved his position, and Chirac went on to win by a landslide. Further problems have also been precipitated on the right by conflicts over Europe, with various short-lived Euroskeptic groups emerging from among the ranks of both the UDF and Gaullists.

In an effort to contain this fragmentation, and to finally develop a more coherent anti-Socialist alternative, both major parties on the center–right have tried to merge their forces into the so-called Union for a Presidential Majority, later renamed the Union for a Popular Majority (UPM). Although it has not succeeded in gathering together all the disparate forces on the center–right—a recalcitrant UDF minority competed independently in the legislative elections of 2002, for example, but polled less than 5 percent of the vote—this is the most advanced attempt to date to build a genuine catch-all conservative party in France, and it may yet serve to bring French politics closer to the British model.

Although the right now holds power in France, the Socialists played the dominant role in French government for most of the 1980s and early 1990s. Mitterrand was reelected to the presidency for a second seven-year term of office in 1988, and the PS also maintained control of the cabinet from 1981 to 1986, a control it regained from 1988 to 1993 and again from 1997 to 2002. Initially elected on quite a radical program of social and economic reform, which included a commitment to the widespread nationalization of private sector services, the PS quickly became more centrist and, as Machin (1989, p. 68) observed, promoted a more "modernizing, moderate and managerial image." This was to some degree part of a more widespread trend in the early 1990s, whereby social democratic parties throughout western Europe began to drift toward the center. It was also a result of the weakening of the communist challenge, however, in that PS no longer needed to be so concerned about guarding its left flank. Competition on the left still exists, of course, and one of the reasons why Jospin polled so badly in the 2002 presidential elections

TABLE 7.7

Legislative Elections in France Since 1988

	1988		1993		1997		2002	
Party	% of Votes	Seats	% of Votes	Seats	% of Votes	Seats	% of Votes	Seats
Greens	0.4	0	7.6	0	6.3	8	4.5	3
Communist Party (PCF)	11.3	27	9.2	23	9.9	37	4.8	21
Socialist Party (PS)[a]	37.6	280	18.5	60	25.5	246	24.1	140
Other left	0.4	0	3.6	10	5.3	29	1.5	7
Union for French Democracy (UDF)	18.5	129	19.1	213	14.7	109	4.8	29
Rally for the Republic (RPR)/ Union for the Presidential Majority (UMP)[b]	19.2	128	20.4	247	16.8	139	33.7	357
Other right	2.9	12	5.0	24	4.7	8	—	—
National Front	9.6	1	12.4	0	14.9	1	11.3	0
Others	0.1	0	4.3	0	1.9	0	15.3	20
All	100.0	577	100.0	577	100.0	577	100.0	577

Party Composition of Government
1989–93   Coalition of Socialist Party and Left Radicals
1993–97   Coalition of Rally for the Republic and Union for French Democracy
1997–02   Coalition of Socialist Party, Left Radicals, Communist Party, Greens, and other left
2002–   Coalition of UMP and UDF

Note: Voting percentages are first-ballot results only.

[a] Includes Left Radicals.

[b] In 2002 the RPR joined with the most of the UDF in a new electoral organization, the Union for a Presidential Majority, later renamed "Union for a Popular Majority."

is that so many left-wing voters opted for various communist, Trotskyist, or Green candidates. But this was a short-lived protest, and apart from a potential further growth in Green support, the PS is now reasonably secure in its domination of the French left. Here too, then, we see a possible drift toward the mechanics of two-party politics. (The best and most recent comprehensive account of the French party system is that of Knapp.)

Party Politics in Spain

Before the collapse of communist rule in eastern Europe in 1989 and 1990, Spain was one of Europe's youngest democracies. The elections held in Spain in 1977, two years after the death of the right-wing dictator General Franco, were the first since Franco seized power after the defeat of the democratic Republican forces in the 1936–39 civil war. As in the early years of many other new democracies, the first period of Spanish democracy was characterized by the creation of many new parties and by great electoral volatility.

The early stages of the transition to democracy in Spain were dominated by the Union of the Democratic Center (UCD), a broad coalition of various center–right and center–left groups under the leadership of Adolfo Suarez, a former minister in Franco's cabinet and the first prime minister of democratic Spain. This coalition of forces, though electorally successful in 1977 and 1979, was inherently very fragile and collapsed dramatically in 1982 when its share of the vote fell from 35 percent to less than 7 percent (Hopkin, *Party*). Suarez himself had resigned as prime minister and had abandoned the party in 1981, setting up a new party, the Social and Democratic Center, which eventually disappeared in the mid-1990s.

With the collapse of the UCD, the key role in the Spanish party system passed to the Socialist Party (PSOE), which polled almost half the votes in 1982 and almost 40 percent in 1989. With the help of the bias shown toward larger parties in the Spanish electoral system, this level of support guaranteed Socialist Party government in Spain for an extended period from 1982 to 1996, although PSOE lost its overall majority in 1993.

Socialist dominance in Spain was then also facilitated by the fragmentation of the center–right opposition; indeed, even into its second decade of democracy, Spain remained among the most fragmented of the European party systems. The largest single party on the right is currently the People's Party (PP), formerly known as the People's Alliance, which initially formed the dominant group within the sporadically cohesive People's Coalition, a federation of diverse parties that embraced liberal, Christian democratic, and conservative factions, and that grew to almost 35 percent of the vote in 1993. In the following election the PP overtook the PSOE, emerging as the single biggest party in 1996 and forming a single-party minority government. The party went on to win an overall majority in 2000 but then lost again when the PSOE gained an unexpected victory in the dramatic 2004 election (see Table 7.8).

Prior to the election itself, the PP had been expected to win, notwithstanding the anticipated resignation of its long-term leader, José Maria Aznar. Nevertheless, the slow and inadequate reaction to the ecological disaster that followed from the sinking of the *Prestige* oil tanker off the northwest coast of Spain had damaged the standing of the government, and the Spanish decision to fully back the U.S. and British invasion of Iraq and to commit troops to the war was also proving widely unpopular. In the end, the crucial issue that turned the tide so dramatically was the horrific rail bombing in Madrid on March 11, 2004, which occurred precisely two-and-a-half years after 9/11, and just three days before polling, and left almost two hundred people dead in the city. The damage this caused to the pro-American PP government was then compounded when the government tried to insist that the bombing was the work of the Basque terrorist organization ETA rather than of the Islamic terrorist al-Qaida, a story that was quickly shown to be implausible. The result, three days later, was a massive swing against the government and a decisive victory for the PSOE and for its new young leader, José Luis Rodriguez Zapatero, who quickly confirmed his long-standing promise to bring Spanish troops home from Iraq (see Chapter 13).

Although the PSOE and PP now dominate Spanish politics, they are not the only relevant actors. Other forces on the center–right include the Catalan Convergence and

TABLE 7.8

Elections in Spain Since 1993

Party	1993 % of Votes	Seats	1996 % of Votes	Seats	2000 % of Votes	Seats	2004 % of Votes	Seats
United Left (IU)	9.6	18	10.5	21	5.5	8	5.0	5
Socialist Party (PSOE)	38.7	159	37.6	141	34.1	125	42.6	164
Democratic and Social Center (CDS)	1.8	—	—	—	—	—	—	—
People's Party (PP)	34.8	141	38.8	156	44.5	183	37.6	148
Convergence and Union (CiU)	5.0	17	4.6	16	4.2	15	3.2	10
Basque Nationalists (PNV)	1.2	5	1.3	5	1.5	7	1.6	7
Herri Batasuna (HB)	0.9	2	0.7	2	—	—	—	—
Others	8.0	8	6.5	9	10.2	12	9.9	16
All	100.0	350	100.0	350	100.0	350	100.0	350

Party Composition of Government

1993–96   Socialist Party single-party government
1996–2004   People's Party single-party government
2004–   Socialist Party single-party government

Union (CiU), a loose alliance of conservative, Christian, and liberal elements united in their support for greater regional autonomy for Catalonia. Though a relatively small party in Spanish terms—it now polls only around 3 to 4 percent of the vote in Spain as a whole—the CiU has proved remarkably adept at bargaining with its larger opponents in Catalan interests. In return for important economic and political concessions, it supported the minority PSOE government from 1993 to 1996, and it pursued the same strategy with the minority PP government from 1996 to 2000.

Opposition on the left of the political spectrum is focused primarily in the Spanish Communist Party (PCE), which was one of the major parties in the ill-fated Second Spanish Republic (1931–36) and constituted one of the most powerful clandestine oppositions to Francoism during the period of the dictatorship. The PCE and its leader, Santiago Carrillo, were also at the forefront of the shift toward Eurocommunism in western Europe in the late 1970s, when a number of leading communist parties sought to distance themselves from Moscow and attempted to forge a new, more consciously democratic strategy for reform (e.g., Lange and Vanicelli). But despite some early speculation that the PCE might emerge as the leading party of the left and thus occupy a position similar to that of the PCI in Italy, the party has, in fact, remained quite marginal. It was only through the recent formation of an electoral cartel—the United Left—with a number of other small parties of the left that the PCE could be seen as a serious political force, polling almost 11 percent of the vote in 1996 but falling to just over 5 percent by the time of the latest election, in 2004.

The fragmentation of the Spanish party system has also been compounded by the emergence of a plethora of regional political forces, far too many to be listed separately in Table 7.8. In addition to the Catalan coalition, parties representing the local interests of Andalusia, Galicia, Aragon, Valencia, and the Canary Islands have also won representation in the Cortes, the Spanish parliament. Regionalism is strongest in the Basque Country in northern Spain, and has supported two important parties, the Basque Nationalist Party (PNV), a pro-independence conservative party; and Herri Batasuna (Popular Unity), a radical left-wing nationalist party that endorses ETA, the Basque paramilitary organization that is engaged in an armed struggle against the Spanish state. In March 2003, Herri Batasuna was banned by the Spanish Supreme Court on the grounds that it was part of the ETA terrorist network. The Basque region is one of the most distinctive and prosperous in Spain, with a population of over 2 million and with its own language and culture. Two-thirds of Basque voters have supported one or the other of the Basque national parties, and the region has been plagued by a level of political dissension and violence almost comparable to that which prevailed in Northern Ireland until recently.

The overall picture is thus of an increasingly structured party system in which conflicts between left and right overlay and intersect conflicts between center and periphery and between church and state. At the core, there is a strong two-party contest, and beyond that, the system fragments into a host of smaller regional or more radical parties. The latter parties do little to undermine the ever more sharply defined bipolar pattern of competition, however, and the result is a pattern that makes the Spanish case look increasingly like the traditional British model. (On the Spanish party system in general see Hopkin, "Spain"; Linz and Montero; Chari.)

Party Politics in Latvia

Although probably not ranking as highly on the instability scale as the Polish case (see below), the Latvian party system would run a close second. Like many postcommunist systems, it is certainly closer to the Polish pattern than to the more consolidated and institutionalized systems of western Europe. Prior to being annexed by the Soviet Union in 1940, Latvia was an independent republic in which a democratic system with a highly fragmented party system survived until an authoritarian coup in 1934. When Latvia reacquired its independence in 1991, and when democracy was restored, some of these former party alternatives reappeared—most notably the Social Democratic Workers' Party (LSDSP) and the Latvian Farmers' Union (LZS). By then, however, they had become relatively marginal forces. The situation in Latvia had changed utterly, and the problems faced by the new regime were now specific to post-Soviet reconstruction and national reassertion. Not least among these problems was the presence of a substantial Russian-speaking minority—formerly experienced as part of the ruling order but now facing a denial of rights and threats of discrimination or even expulsion. In 1989, on the eve of independence, the Russian share of the population was some 34 percent, and the ethnic

Latvian share was just 52 percent (Sprudzs, p. 146). Since democratization, one of the persisting issues has been how or whether to integrate this minority and the conditions—such as language tests—under which resident Russians could be granted Latvian citizenship. With time, requirements for citizenship have been eased slightly, as have rules regarding the citizenship rights of children of noncitizens who were born in Latvia. By 1997, the percentage of noncitizens resident in Latvia had fallen to 28 percent, and to 22 percent in 2003 (Smith-Sivertsen, p. 103).

The new party system that emerged in Latvia after the immediate transition period was initially dominated by the center–right Latvia's Way (LW), which polled almost one-third of the vote to the Saeima (the Latvian unicameral parliament) in 1993 and then formed a minority coalition government with the LZS; and by the nationalist Latvian National Independence Movement (LNNK), which won just over 13 percent of the vote (see Table 7.9). A second nationalist party, For Fatherland and Freedom (FFF), also competed but polled only 5 percent of the vote in this first properly competitive election. Latvia's Way itself was a loose coalition of local notables and leaders of former exile organizations, and it favored a liberal and accommodating approach to the issue of the Russian minority while also pushing for a rapid transition toward a market economy. This election was also marked by the reasonably strong performance of the People's Harmony Party (TSP), which supported rights for Russians and other non-Latvians and polled more than 12 percent of the vote, emerging as the third biggest party in parliament. It later split, however, leading to the formation of a small, pro-welfarist splinter party, the Political Union of Economists (PUE). When relations between LW and the LZS broke down less than one year after the elections, the PUE joined the LW in a caretaker cabinet that held office until the elections of 1995.

Even though LW lost a substantial share of its support in the 1995 election, it emerged as the second biggest party, falling narrowly behind the center–left Democratic Party–Saimnieks (DP), a party that was itself a coalition of older and newer political groupings. Both parties eventually formed the core of a broad, multiparty coalition that brought together all of the mainstream parties from both right and left as well as the Latvian nationalist parties. The opposition was constituted by the Popular Movement for Latvia, a populist nationalist party led by a prominent German Latvian politician, Joachim Siegerist, which had emerged as one of the biggest parties in 1995, as well as by the pro-Russian Latvian Socialist Party (LSP) and the TSP. The latter two parties not only were strong advocates of full citizenship for the Russian minority but also were more welfarist and advocated greater compensation for the heavy social costs that were being incurred in the transition toward a market economy. In Latvia, as elsewhere among the postcommunist democracies, the latter issue forms the basis for an important political divide. Although the new government was cast as an administration of the broadly defined center against the margins, or the extremes, holding it together proved difficult. Allegations of corruption against several ministers, and power plays by the various parties in the grand coalition, eventually led to the resignation of the nonpartisan prime minister, Andris Skele, in 1997, and his replacement by Guntars Krasts of the FFF. Skele then went on to found the center–right People's Party (TP), which emerged as the single biggest party following the 1998 elections.

Though marked by substantial volatility, the 1998 elections also appeared to point toward a simplification and perhaps even the consolidation of the previously fragmented

TABLE 7.9

Elections in Latvia Since 1993

Party	1993 % of Votes	1993 Seats	1995 % of PR Votes	1995 Seats	1998 % of PR Votes	1998 Seats	2002 % of Votes	2002 Seats
New Era (JL)	—	—	—	—	—	—	24.0	26
People's Harmony Party (TSP)[a]	12.0	13	5.6	6	14.2	16	19.1	25
People's Party (TP)	—	—	—	—	21.2	24	16.7	20
Christian Democratic Union/ Latvia First Party (LPP)	5.0	6	6.4	8	2.3	—	9.6	10
Latvian Farmers Union (LZS)	10.7	12	6.4	8	2.5	—	9.5	12
Fatherland and Freedom (FFF)	5.4	6	12.0	14	14.7	17	5.4	7
Latvia's Way (LW)	32.4	36	14.7	17	18.4	21	4.9	—
Latvian Social Democratic Workers' Party (LSDSP)	1.6	—	4.6	—	12.8	14	4.0	—
New Party (NP)	—	—	—	—	7.3	8	—	—
People's Movement	—	—	15.0	16	1.7	—	—	—
Democratic Party–Saimnieks (DP)	4.8	5	15.2	18	1.6	—	—	—
Latvian Unity Party	0.1	—	7.2	8	0.5	—	—	—
Latvian National Independence Movement (LNNK)	13.4	15	6.3	8	—	—	—	—
Latvian Socialist Party (LSP)[a]	5.8	7	5.6	5	—	—	—	—
Latvian People's Front	2.6	—	1.2	—	—	—	—	—
Others	6.2	—	6.2	—	3.8	—	6.8	—
All	100.0	100	100.0	100	100.0	100	100.0	100

Party Composition of Government

1993–94	Coalition of Latvia's Way and Farmers Union
1994–95	Coalition of Latvia's Way, Political Union of Economists, and independents
1995–97	Coalition of DP–Saimnieks, Fatherland and Freedom, Latvia's Way, LNNK, Unity Party, and Farmers Union
Feb. 1997– Aug. 1997	Coalition of DP–Saimnieks, Fatherland and Freedom/LNNK, Latvia's Way, and Farmers Union
1997–98	Coalition of DP–Saimnieks, Fatherland and Freedom/LNNK, Latvia's Way, Christian Democrats, and Farmers Union
1998–99	Coalition of Latvia's Way, Fatherland and Freedom/LNNK, and New Party
1999–2000	Coalition of People's Party, Fatherland and Freedom/LNNK, and Latvia's Way
2000–2	Coalition of People's Party, Latvia's Way, Fatherland and Freedom/LNNK, and New Party
2002–	Coalition of the New Era, Latvia First Party, Farmers Union, Fatherland and Freedom/LNNK, Green Party, and independents

[a] The People's Harmony Party and LSP competed as the Human Rights Alliance in 2002.

party system. Both the Siegerist List and the DP fell well below the 5 percent threshold; each polled less than 2 percent of the vote and marked up a combined loss of more than 25 percent. Moreover, the coalition government that was formed in the wake of the elections was led by Latvia's Way, which had formed part of every government since 1993. In this sense, elements of continuity and stability in the party system seemed to be coming to the fore. The coalition was also joined by FFF, as well as by the smaller New Party (NP), which had competed for the first time in 1998 but later fell apart and disappeared. The new government broke up within less than a year, however, and was reorganized in July 1999 with the new People's Party (TP) taking the place of the small NP, and with Andris Skele coming back as prime minister. This government too fell into difficulties and was reorganized yet again in May 2000, this time with Andris Berzins of LW replacing Andris Skele as prime minister, and with the NP coming back into the cabinet to join the other three parties. This new coalition managed to hold on until the elections of 2002, thus setting a record for longevity in this troubled new party system— an achievement that was seen to be due to the ideological consistency among the center–right parties, on the one hand, and to the exhaustion of all other possible alternatives, on the other (Ikstens, p. 1007).

Despite its success in holding on to office, however, the coalition was internally troubled; sharp personal and political conflicts, as well as allegations of corruption and dirty tricks, soured relations between the LW and the TP in particular. Partly as a result of these problems, and in response to the sense of popular disquiet that they provoked, the 2002 election was joined by the new, reformist New Era (JL), led by the former president of the Latvian Central Bank, Einars Repse. Committed to better and more transparent governance, this new party won a massive 24 percent of the popular vote. Both the TP and the LW lost support, the latter falling narrowly below the threshold for the first time and losing its place in parliament. The FFF also lost heavily but stayed just above the threshold and won 7 seats in parliament. By contrast, the main pro-Russian parties, campaigning in a joint list called "For Human Rights in a United Latvia" and voicing the main left-wing opposition to the pro-market center–right governments, polled 19 percent of the vote—a gain of 5 percent over 1998. Two other changes of note were also registered. Latvia First, a Christian party that had formally competed as the Christian Democratic Union, polled close to 10 percent of the vote on its first electoral outing in this new guise, and another new formation, the Union of Greens and Farmers, also polled close to 10 percent. Three of the six lists to win representation in the Saeima were therefore new to Latvian politics—at least formally speaking—and were also somewhat closer in ideological profile to some of the more familiar western European party families. Together with the reduced FFF, these three parties formed the new center–right coalition government, this time under the leadership of Einars Repse of New Era. But although the parties may have seemed more conventional, their relations with one another proved no more congenial, a problem that came to the fore once again in February 2004, when Prime Minister Repse dismissed his deputy in the government, Ainars Slesers of the Latvia First Party. The result was that Latvia First pulled out of the government, causing it to collapse. A new government, Latvia's twelfth since independence in 1991, took office in March, this time being composed of the Union of Greens and Farmers, Latvia's First, and the reduced People's Party (TP). Exceptionally, it was the Green leader, Indulis Emsis, who won the position of prime minister—this being the first time that a Green became head of government in a European democracy. (On the Latvian party system see Pettai and Kreuzer; Smith-Sivertsen; Ikstens.)

Party Politics in Poland

Following a series of reforms introduced in the wake of protests against communist rule in 1956, Poland was initially allowed to pursue a distinctive path within the then all-powerful Soviet bloc. Private agricultural production was accepted, and freedom of religious practice was given to the overwhelmingly Catholic population. This distinctiveness was confirmed in 1980 when, after a series of strikes centering on the Lenin shipyards in Gdansk, the communist government agreed to recognize the existence of the independent trade union Solidarity, led by Lech Walesa, who was later to be elected as Poland's first postcommunist president. Little more than a year later, however, the tide turned: The reform policy was reversed in 1981, martial law was imposed, Solidarity was banned, and its leadership was arrested. Thereafter things eased again, with martial law being lifted in 1983. Then, in the late 1980s, fueled by a severe economic crisis, on the one hand, and by the stimulus of the reforms in the Soviet Union, on the other hand, the protest movement began to mobilize once more. This time around, the pressure for reform proved unstoppable, and eventually a series of roundtable negotiations began between the ruling communist party and Solidarity. In April 1989 these talks led to a commitment to hold relatively free parliamentary elections in which the opposition would be allowed to compete for 35 percent of the seats in the Sejm, the lower house of parliament, and for all of the seats in the Senate, the upper house. The remaining 65 percent of the seats in the Sejm were to be retained by the communist party and its allied satellite party groups, such as the United Peasant Party, Christian Democracy, and the Democratic Party.

Communist rule in eastern Europe had first been undermined in 1980 through the official recognition of Solidarity. This new agreement of 1989 was now to echo throughout the Soviet bloc and was to signal its final demise. Poland was leading the way toward democracy.

Solidarity and its allies, representing a broad anticommunist front and encompassing a wide variety of diverse strands of opinion, went on to win every single one of the contested seats in this new "managed" election to the Sejm, as well as all but one of the 100 seats in the Senate (Olson). Moreover, despite being kept to 35 percent of the seats, they also won effective control of government; the communists' ostensibly allied satellite parties suddenly switched their support to the anticommunist alliance. The result was that Poland's first noncommunist government took office on September 12, 1989, under the prime ministership of Tadeusz Mazowiecki of Solidarity. Solidarity also gained control of ten additional ministries; other parties initially involved in the broad coalition included the United Peasant Party, which was later to reorganize itself as the Polish Peasant Party (PSL), and the Democratic Party. Both were former communist satellite parties that had been allowed to exist under communist rule and had been represented in the predemocratic parliament under the aegis of the ruling communist party. The communists themselves held four ministries in this interim administration.

As part of the commitments made in the roundtable agreement, the new parliament also elected as president the communist party leader and a former prime minister, General Wojciech Jaruzelski, who had been responsible for the introduction of martial law in

1981. In September 1990, however, Jaruzelski stepped down in order to be replaced by a directly elected president. This new democratic presidential election was then organized in much the same way as presidential elections in France, with a second round of voting between the two leading candidates being required if no single candidate won an absolute majority in the first round (see Chapter 2). The divisions that were later to pull Solidarity apart had by then become apparent, however, and the principal candidates in the first presidential election included the sitting prime minister, Mazowiecki, as well as Lech Walesa, who had refused to present himself as a candidate in the partial parliamentary elections of 1989. Walesa's supporters had already formed their own political group, which was openly critical of what they regarded as the slow pace of reform under Mazowiecki's government. There was also a third candidate, Stanislaw Tyminski, a Polish-born Canadian businessman, who attempted to hold out the prospect of a miraculous transformation of the Polish economy and who was later involved in the creation of the so-called Party X. The results proved somewhat of a surprise. Walesa emerged as the strongest candidate in the first round, but without an overall majority (he polled 40 percent of the votes), and Tyminski war in second place (23 percent). The sitting prime minister, Mazowiecki, with 18 percent of the vote, was therefore eliminated (see Table 7.10).

TABLE 7.10

Presidential Elections in Poland Since 1990

Candidate (Party)	% of Votes in 1990		Candidate (Party)	% of Votes in 1995		Candidate (Party)	% of Votes in 2000
	1st Ballot	2nd Ballot		1st Ballot	2nd Ballot		1st Ballot
Lech Walesa (Solidarity)	40.0	74.3	Aleksander Kwasniewski (SLD)	35.1	51.7	Aleksander Kwasniewski (SLD)	53.9
Stanislaw Tyminski (Ind.)	23.1	25.7	Lech Walesa (Ind./Solidarity)	33.1	48.3	Andrzej Olechowski (Ind.)	17.3
Tadeusy Mazowiecki (UW)	18.1	—	Jacek Kuron (UW)	9.2	—	Marian Krzaklewski (AWS)	15.6
Wlodzimierz Cimoscewicz (SLD)	9.2	—	Jan Olszewski (Ind.)	6.9	—	Jaroslaw Kalinowski (PSL)	6.0
Roman Bartoszczcze (PSL)	7.2	—	Waldeman Pawlak (PSL)	4.3	—	Andrzej Lepper (SO)	3.1
Leszek Moczulski (KPN)	2.5	—	Tadeusz Zielinski (Ind.)	3.5	—	Jamusz Korwin-Mikke (UPR)	1.4
			Hanna Gronkiewicz-Waltz (Ind.)	2.8	—	Lech Walesa (Chr. Dem)	1.0
			Janusz Korwin-Mikke (UPR)	1.4	—	Others (N = 5)	1.8
			Others (N = 5)	3.7	—		
Total	**100.0**	**100.0**		**100.0**	**100.0**		**100.0**

In the second round of voting, Walesa went on to poll 74 percent of the vote and was duly elected. Less than a week later, the Mazowiecki government resigned. After pressure from Walesa, it was agreed that new parliamentary elections would take place in October 1991.

The results of the 1991 election revealed the exceptionally fragmented nature of the emerging party politics (see Table 7.11). A total of 111 lists were registered for the election, and 29 of them eventually won representation in the Sejm. The single most successful party, the ex-Solidarity Democratic Union (UD), won just over 12 percent of the vote and 62 (13 percent) seats. A total of nine additional ex-Solidarity parties also won representation, including Catholic Electoral Action–National Christian Union (WAK–ZChN), which won 9 percent of the vote, the Agrarian Alliance (PL), which won almost 6 percent, and the Center Alliance. Taken together, the combined vote for all of the ex-Solidarity parties totaled almost 52 percent. The former communist party and its one-time allies were represented in the Democratic Left Alliance (SLD), which emerged as the second biggest party with exactly 12 percent of the vote and 60 seats; the Polish Peasant Party (PSL), with just over 9 percent of the vote; and two smaller parties, which together polled almost 4 percent. Among the other parties in the new Sejm was the Beer-Lovers' Party (3 percent), which began as a joke party but was later backed by a number of leading Polish businessmen.

As in Spain, the first fully democratic election in Poland was the followed by a period of pronounced political instability. The new minority government that took office at the end of December 1991 under the leadership of Jan Olszewski of the Center Alliance, and that also included the National Christian Union (ZChN) and the Agrarian Alliance, lasted just six months. It was followed first by a caretaker cabinet that was backed by Walesa but failed to win support in parliament and lasted just thirty-three days, and then by yet another minority cabinet under the leadership of the first female prime minister, Hanna Suchocka, which held office until new elections were held in September 1993. Suchocka's government included her own party, UD, which was still led by Mazowiecki, as well as the ZChN and five other parties and independents, and although it survived longer than expected, it was nevertheless divided internally over long-term issues relating to the position of the Catholic Church, the question of decommunization, and the extent and pace of the transition to a market economy. This last problem proved the most crucial in the run-up to the 1993 elections (Vinton), as it was in many of the early elections in postcommunist Europe. The liberal UD was pushing for a more rapid program of privatization and marketization, and many of the opposition parties, including the reformed communist party and its former satellites, were arguing for the provision of more effective safety nets for the unemployed and the poor and for more state intervention to ease the traumas of transition. This approach also won support from some of the ex-Solidarity parties, including the Union of Labor and the Agrarian Alliance.

The results of the 1993 election indicated high levels of popular discontent with the social costs of liberalization and marketization, and they reflected a significant shift away from the former anticommunist opposition. The reformed communist SLD polled more than 20 percent of the vote and won 171 of the seats, while the former communist satellite party, the PSL, emerged as the second biggest party, with more than 15 percent of the vote and 132 seats. These two parties went on to form a majority coalition, which

TABLE 7.11

Legislative Elections in Poland Since 1991

Party	1991 % of Votes	1991 Seats	1993 % of Votes	1993 Seats	1997 % of PR Votes	1997 Seats	2001 % of PR Votes	2001 Seats
Democratic Left Alliance (SLD)[a]	12.0	60	20.4	171	27.1	164	41.0	216
Labor Union (UP)[a]	2.1	4	7.3	41	4.7	—	—	—
Civic Platform (PO)	—	—	—	—	—	—	12.7	65
Self-Defense (SO)	—	—	2.8	—	0.1	—	10.2	53
Law and Justice (PiS)	—	—	—	—	—	—	9.5	44
Polish Peasant Party (PSL)	8.7	48	15.4	132	7.3	27	9.0	42
League of Polish Families (LPR)	—	—	2.7	—	5.6	6	7.9	38
Democratic Union (UD/UW)	12.3	62	10.6	74	13.4	60	3.1	—
Solidarity Electoral Action (AWS)	—	—	—	—	33.8	201	5.6	—
National Christian Union (ZChN)	8.7	49	6.4	—	—	—	—	—
Confederation for an Independent Poland	7.5	45	5.8	22	—	—	—	—
Independent Bloc to Support the Reforms	—	—	5.4	16	—	—	—	—
Social Movement–Solidarity	5.1	27	4.9	—	—	—	—	—
Center Alliance	8.7	44	4.4	—	—	—	—	—
People's Alliance	5.5	28	2.4	—	—	—	—	—
Liberal Democratic Congress	7.5	37	4.0	—	—	—	—	—
Party of Christian Democrats/ Christian Democracy	3.5	9	6.4	—	—	—	—	—
German minority	1.2	7	0.7	4	0.6	2	0.4	2
Others	17.2	40	6.8	—	7.3	—	0.6	—
All	100.0	460	100.0	460	100.0	460	100.0	460

Party Composition of Government

1991–92   Coalition of five center–right parties, including Confederation for an Independent Poland (KPN), Center Alliance, and Liberal Democratic Congress

1992–93   Coalition of four-party Christian and Peasant Block plus Little Coalition formed around the Democratic Union (UD)

1993–97   Coalition of Democratic Left Alliance (SLD) and Polish Peasant Party (PSL)

1997–2001 Coalition of Solidarity Electoral Action (AWS) and Freedom Union (UW)

2001–3   Coalition of Democratic Left Alliance (SLD), Labor Union, and Polish Peasant Party (PSL)

2003–   Coalition of Democratic Left Alliance (SLD) and Labor Union

[a] In the 2001 elections Democratic Left Alliance (SLD) and Labor Union (UP) formed an alliance.

took office at the end of October 1993 under the prime ministership of PSL leader Waldemar Pawlak. In other words, having been ousted from power by a wave of popular mobilization at the end of the 1980s, the former communists now found themselves back in office on the basis of a clear democratic mandate. This was a crucial moment in Polish political development, and it was being echoed in Hungary, where the reformed communists had found a new lease on life as defenders of a more welfarist regime. With the exception of UD, which experienced a small decline in electoral support but an increased representation in parliament, all the other former incumbents fared badly in the 1993 election, often failing to reach the electoral threshold for representation. Indeed, the parties that polled less than the threshold and hence failed to win any representation in the Sejm accounted for a total of almost 35 percent of the vote in 1993.

Despite the fragmentation and confusion of Poland's emerging party system, however, there were signs that two broad alignments were beginning to take shape. On the one hand was the socialist (or former communist) party, the SLD, and its main ally, the PSL. This was the old left—the successor parties of the old regime. On the other hand was the loose grouping around the former Solidarity and its allies, which itself fell into two crudely defined camps—one that was liberal and secular, such as the UD, or its successor, the Freedom Union (UW), and one that was liberal in the pro-market sense but was also strongly Catholic. This crude divide between the two alignments was complicated by the tensions that existed between the two arenas in which competition took place—the presidential arena and the parliamentary arena.

By 1995, some of the tension seemed to have evaporated. PSL leader Pawlak had been replaced by Josef Olesky of the SLD as head of the government, and Walesa had been defeated by Aleksander Kwasniewski, also of the SLD, in the new contest for the presidency (see Table 7.10). By 1995, in other words, the SLD seemed to be in more or less undisputed control of democratic Poland. But the respite proved short-lived, and the parliamentary elections of 1997 heralded a new period of divided government. Solidarity Electoral Action (AWS), a freshly minted electoral coalition of the old opposition groupings, together with the UW, won a clear majority in parliament and went on to form a new government under the leadership of Jerzy Buzek, and although the SLD itself performed well in these elections, its Peasant ally lost heavily. The five parties that managed to surpass the threshold on this occasion together accounted for almost 90 percent of the total vote—thus leaving little more than 10 percent unrepresented—a sharp reduction in the very disproportionate outcome of 1993. These signs of growing consolidation proved deceptive, however, for by 2000 the governing alliance had fallen apart, with Solidarity once more fragmenting and regrouping. In 2000 Kwasniewski of the SLD was reelected president, and in 2001 the SLD also returned to power in parliament, this time winning a clear majority in alliance with the Labor Union (UP). The main opposition was now represented by more newly formed parties—Civic Platform (PO), Law and Justice (PiS), and the League of Polish Families (LPR)—all of which traced their roots back to Solidarity while also distancing themselves from the groupings that had been involved in the AWS–UW government, none of which actually reached the threshold in 2001. The 2001 election also saw the emergence of an agrarian populist Self-Defense (SO), which emerged as the third largest party in the Sejm.

In short, despite some evidence of an emerging two-bloc alignment, the Polish party "system" remains remarkably ill-defined and inchoate. Indeed, some fifteen years after democratization, the Polish party system is still less institutionalized than was the Spanish party system at the beginning of the 1980s. To be sure, some points of stability and political anchoring are evident—most notably in the organizational persistence and sporadic electoral success of the former communist SLD. Beyond that point, however, there is little sign of any institutionalization or consolidation. The legacy of Solidarity persists, and the ideological appeal of the Polish version of Christian democracy also persists, but neither tradition seems capable of finding expression in a consolidated or coherent set of party alternatives. For voters, in short—as well as for students of politics— the Polish case seems sometimes impenetrable; indeed amid all the confusions that characterize party competition at the parliamentary level, it is worth noting that voter turnout has averaged less than 50 percent across the last three elections. And in terms of our comparisons here in this volume, it is probably the least consolidated party system in the European Union (The most comprehensive analysis in English is Szczerbiak. Also see Jasiewicz; Markowski; Millard.)

✦ THE DIVERSITY OF MODERN EUROPEAN PARTY POLITICS

Each of the party systems that we have considered is characterized by a basic confrontation between left and right; each also contains one or more parties that we might think of as being at the center. Beyond this, however, differences between systems appear to be more striking than similarities. Moreover, when comparing west and east, the differences become even more pronounced.

Let us look at the complexities of the older systems first. In Sweden and the United Kingdom, liberal parties are to be found between left and right, and they reflect a more moderate class alternative than that promoted by conservative parties. In the Netherlands and Germany, in contrast, traditional liberalism has its roots in conservatism—and the liberal parties are mainly to be found on the right. In Sweden and the United Kingdom, class confrontations define the only major dimension in politics, although in Sweden the pattern is more complex given the secondary role of agrarian and religious interests. In Italy, the Netherlands, and Germany, in contrast, religion traditionally provided a major dimension of party competition.

Differences also extend to the pattern of government formation. In France, Spain, Germany, Sweden, and the United Kingdom, the left can hope to govern alone. In the Netherlands, the left has for a long time been too weak, and in Italy, except perhaps now in the so-called Second Republic, too divided, to do so; in each case the left has been obliged to forge coalitions with parties on the center and right. Finally, Germany, the Netherlands, Sweden, and Britain have strongly structured party systems, but France and, to a lesser extent, Spain have systems that include loose and often fragmented alliances that lack the cohesion and discipline normally associated with European political parties. The shape of the new Italian party system is still too uncertain to define.

Given such diversity, to speak of a "typical" western European party system is clearly unrealistic. Nonetheless, the countries in certain groups do seem quite similar to one another. The Swedish party system, for example, has been compared with the party systems in Denmark and Norway by observers who speak of a typical "Scandinavian" party system (Berglund and Lindstrom). The Netherlands has been compared with Belgium and Switzerland in an extensive literature that treats them as "consociational democracies" responding to very deep-seated social and ethnic cleavages (Lijphart; Luther and Deschouwer). The deep ideological divisions in the Italian party system before the 1990s have been compared with those in France between 1946 and 1958 and with those in Finland, as examples of "polarized pluralism" (Sartori). The southern European democracies of Greece, Spain, and Portugal have also been extensively compared in a literature that highlights the common problems experienced by parties in the consolidation of new democracies (Morlino), and it is now interesting to see in each of these three systems the possible development of a British-style two-party system. In short, although it may be far too simplistic to speak of even west European party politics as being a set of variations on a single theme, it is reasonable to think of them as reflecting variations on a relatively limited set of themes.

Left and Right

One theme that recurs in almost all western European countries concerns the role of the left–right dimension in structuring politics. The terms "left" and "right" have always been widely accepted as part of the common political currency of western Europe. To be on the left has traditionally meant supporting a communist or socialist party claiming to represent the interests of the organized working class. Every western European country, without exception, has such a party. This, more than anything else, is the common theme in the politics of representation in western Europe, and it also, incidentally, marks off the western European experience from that in the United States.

To be on the center and right has meant supporting those who stand against the communist or socialist parties. On the center–right, however, there are few features common to all the western European countries. In some countries, parties of the right have a distinctly religious basis; in others, they are secular. In some countries, parties of the right traditionally have included those reflecting rural or farming interests; in others, they include those representing a particular cultural or linguistic subculture. One of the most striking features of western European party politics is thus that although the left has been reasonably homogeneous and has traditionally been represented by at most two parties, the right has been more fragmented, including religious, secular, agrarian, nationalist, and other parties under the same broad umbrella.

Describing right and left in terms of the class interests that were traditionally represented by particular parties is only part of the story. There is also clearly a separate ideological sense in which we can speak of such parties as having programs that are on the left or right of the political spectrum. The problem here is that although it is easy to identify parties that mobilized in defense of particular social interests, it is less easy to specify who is on the left or the right in purely ideological terms.

The problem is compounded by the actual behavior of parties. In the 1970s and early 1980s, for example, the major social democratic parties in Britain, Denmark, and the Netherlands experienced splits that led to more right-wing elements within these parties setting up alternative organizations—Democratic Socialists '70 in the Netherlands, the Center Democrats in Denmark, and the Social Democratic Party in the UK. In terms of traditional interest representation, all three of these new parties might be regarded as being on the left in that all derived from the historic political alignment forged by the working class. In ideological terms, however, these parties were far from being on the left and often empathized with the traditional parties of the center–right of their respective party systems.

A similar problem arises in relation to the traditional right. In Italy, for example, a split from the traditionally right-wing Liberal Party in the mid-1950s led to the formation of the Radical Party. Although spurning alliances with the Socialist and Communist Parties, the Radical Party quickly developed ideologically into one of the most left-wing of Italian parties. A similar split occurred in the Dutch Liberal Party in the mid-1960s. The new party that formed as a result, Democrats 66, clearly aligned itself on the ideological left. In all of these cases, the "sociological" or "organizational" alignment of the new parties ran counter to their developing "ideological" positions.

Yet another confusion is of more recent origin and concerns the mobilization of environmentalist, or "green," parties in western Europe. This is a relatively new but increasingly relevant and pervasive phenomenon that has emerged from the organizational traditions of neither left nor right. Indeed, these parties are sometimes claimed to reflect a wholly "new" politics that, in both social support and organizational form, represents a genuine challenge to traditional alignments. Increasingly, however, these new parties are seen as moving toward the ideological left of the political spectrum, particularly when they demand both radical economic change and new forms of social justice. In practice, these parties now often find themselves in alliances with social democratic parties. Here, too, therefore, organizational and social definitions of the left and the right fit uneasily with more strictly ideological criteria.

When a country had two or more parties on the traditional left—a socialist and a communist party, for example—we might expect the parties to have acted in concert in an attempt to realize shared goals. In practice, however, this was often not the case. In Italy, as we have seen, the Socialist Party traditionally cast its lot with the Christian Democratic Party and smaller parties of the right and refused to consider an alliance with its communist ideological neighbor. Even though the combined vote of the Italian left sometimes exceeded 40 percent, prior to the 1990s Italian voters were never offered the prospect of a left-wing coalition government. Relations between Communists and Socialists have also often been very strained in France. Here, however, an eventual alliance of the two parties did lead to an unprecedented left-wing victory in the presidential elections of 1981. Prior to this historic breakthrough, the French Socialists had often despaired of finding common ground with their communist neighbors and had opted instead to chase alliances on the center and right of the party system.

More recently—in Italy in 1996, in France in 1997, in Germany in 1998 and again in 2002, and in Belgium in 1999—socialist parties have gained government office through alliances with the newer Green parties, and one of the more important consequences of the rise of Green parties in Europe has been to add sufficient strength to the broad bloc of the left to allow it to regain control of government after long periods of center–right dominance. Indeed, for a brief period at the turn of the new century, socialist parties—whether alone or in alliance with Greens or parties of the center—were in government in all but three (Spain, Luxembourg, and Ireland) of the then fifteen member states of the European Union, and for the first time in postwar history, the major party of the left was in government in all four of the major west European polities at the same time (France, Germany, Italy, and the UK). Needless to add, the balance shifted back to the center–right soon afterward.

Maintaining alliances on the right may now prove more problematic, particularly since the recent rise of the far right (see Chapter 8). Many of the new far-right parties—such as the National Alliance and the Northern League in Italy, the National Front in France, the Flemish Block in Belgium, or the Progress parties in Denmark and Norway, perhaps also the Pim Fortuyn List in the Netherlands—may share many concerns with their more moderate neighbors of the right. Their sheer radicalism or sometimes even the extremism of their ideological position often makes it difficult for them to form or sustain cooperative arrangements with these neighbors, however. In party systems that are ideologically polarized, indeed, it is usually easier for parties of the center–right to find common ground with parties of the center–left than it is to find common ground with some of their fellow right-wing parties. This was certainly the case for a long time in Austria, for example, where the increasingly extremist positions adopted by the right-wing Freedom Party under the leadership of Jörg Haider served to isolate his party from coalition-building in the 1990s, while at the same time strengthening his capacity to appeal to voters as an outsider seeking to challenge the control of the established parties. Haider eventually managed to break through to government, marginally outpolling the People's Party in the election of October 1999 and then joining that party in the new government that took office in February 2000. Two years later, the Pim Fortuyn List also joined a right-wing coalition in the Netherlands. In both cases, it seemed that taboos had been broken, although the experience in government proved unhappy for both parties, each of which lost quite heavily in the subsequent election (see Heinisch).

Both of these parties also reflected a growing sense of disillusion with politics, which is something that is found in almost all of the countries that have been surveyed here. One consequence of this disillusion is the greater room that is now afforded for the mobilization of protest movements and "antiparty"—or antiestablishment—parties. The sources of this protest are potentially legion. The persistence of economic problems certainly fuels dissatisfaction, as does the perceived growth in social inequalities. A rising tide of racism creates new tensions that are difficult to resolve. The integration of nation states within the European Union (see Chapter 5) and the internationalization of economies appear to leave many voters wondering about what responsibilities, if any, still remain with their own national governments. As in the United States, there is also increasing concern with political corruption and patronage and a growing sense that politicians are concerned only with looking after themselves. All of these factors help explain the increasing support for parties of the populist right, on the one hand, and for "new politics" parties of the left, on the other. They also help explain the increasing appeal of flash parties, which suddenly emerge on the campaign trail and equally suddenly disappear. As yet, of course, the antiparty parties to which we refer account for only a very small share of the popular vote in European democracies, and in this sense the traditional patterns still continue to dominate political life. At the same time, however, there is little denying the sense of vulnerability now being felt by some of the most powerful European parties on both left and right.

Although the terms "left" and "right" might seem to provide a convenient shorthand for describing party politics in different countries using broadly similar terms, superficial similarities nevertheless can be deceptive. Moreover, as the new centrist policies of the "Third Way" or "New Middle" gain ever-widening support, the use of terms such as "left" and "right" becomes less meaningful. Thus the story is told of how President Chirac of France once listened to a speech by Tony Blair of Britain about the need for more market-friendly policies and then asked him: "Let me be clear about this. I am the leader of the Right in France. You are the leader of the Left in Britain. Or is it the other way around?" (Hoggart). In this sense, and given the range of variation that can be found in the different European party systems, an alternative response might be to claim that as every country is different, we should simply look at the countries one at a time (accepting that, in reality, we will probably have time for only the big ones). Yet, as we have suggested, although each of the countries considered in this chapter is clearly distinctive, each does represent something of a pattern, with elements that can be found elsewhere. The key question is whether these patterns extend throughout Europe, or whether the patterns to be found among the long-established democracies are different from those to be found among the postcommunist democracies. There are obviously some similarities between east and west, of course, as was noted by one Latvian commentator when the country's eleventh government collapsed: "We are becoming the Italy of northern Europe," he complained (*The Economist* February 12, 2004). But there are also major differences.

Postcommunist Patterns

One of the major difficulties in determining the character of the new parties and the new party systems that are emerging in postcommunist Europe is that they are still very much in a process of formation. It takes time to settle the structure of mass politics (see Chapter 9). Nevertheless, even though we know this, it is still perhaps surprising to see how little stabilization has been evident, at least in Poland and Latvia, even after some fifteen years of democratic politics. Why might this be the case? One obvious reason is that the voters in these countries have yet to develop the sort of stable set of partisan loyalties that have helped to underpin the stabilization of politics in established party systems, and hence they are likely to prove significantly more volatile than their west European counterparts. The levels of electoral instability recorded in recent Polish and Latvian elections, for example, are still substantially higher than that recorded in most postwar west European elections and show little signs of abating (see also Table 9.12). Moreover, because many voters initially opted for parties that failed to win representation in parliament or that subsequently collapsed, and because other potential voters have yet to begin to participate in the electoral process (voter turnout in the Polish parliamentary elections is less than 50 percent), we can expect to see future elections recording quite substantial shifts in levels of party support. A second reason is that despite the efforts to clarify the rules of the game as quickly as possible, the precise shape of the institutional environment in these new democracies still remains somewhat uncertain, and demands for further changes in the electoral laws and the structures of government could well prove unsettling for both the voters and the parties. Third, there is the sheer openness of the electoral market, which implies that new parties can be formed and can make an impact with relative ease, and that existing parties can just as suddenly leave the stage. Both Latvia and Poland offer numerous examples of such entries and exits, as well as numerous examples of party fission and fusion. Moreover, given that so many of the parties are relatively new creations, and given that they lack any well-established organizational roots or identities, then we cannot expect their supporters or leaders to have developed any strong sense of discipline or loyalty, which implies that these parties will also be quite susceptible to internal splits and fractures (Biezen).

But even though the picture that emerges from the postcommunist experience is certainly complex, it is still tempting to try to indicate some of the likely sources of future division and to relate them to the traditional oppositions that have helped to structure the established party systems in western Europe, and that we have already looked at briefly. Issues revolving around the core problem of church–state relations, for example, are clearly apparent in Poland and also, to a degree, in Latvia, and both political systems have produced parties that more or less identify themselves with the sort of policies pursued by traditional Christian democratic parties in the west. Center–periphery problems are also apparent. The position of ethnic and national minorities in particular provides the basis for tensions that may yet emerge to threaten the long-term stability of many of these new democracies, including Latvia. Urban–rural divisions are also pronounced, much more so than in the west, and agrarian parties have proved to be significant political forces in both Latvia and Poland. Evidence of more conventional left–right oppositions, however, which have proved so important in the development of west European party systems, is more difficult to characterize. This is partly because the class structure that has emerged from communism is itself so unsettled, with yet little scope, or time, for the development of more typically capitalist class relationships. Nevertheless, even at this early stage, it is possible to identify the existence of a substantial conflict of interest generated by the process of transition itself, with the more liberal reformers pitted against those whose jobs and living standards are inevitably threatened by marketization. This conflict is clearly present in Latvia, where it overlaps to some degree with the division between ethnic Latvians and the Russian-speaking minority. It is also to be seen in Poland, where it has provided a base of support for the former communist party and its allies. It is even to be found in the former East Germany, where resistance to rapid reform has helped to win votes for the former East German communist party, the PDS.

In the end, however, a lot of this sort of analysis must remain somewhat speculative. The patterns in practice are both confusing and diverse, and they defy easy generalization. According to an early assessment by Kitschelt, for example, future cleavage structures in the postcommunist democracies were going to revolve around at least three overlapping sets of issues: first, the opposition between an inclusive definition of citizenship, which seeks to integrate individual citizens regardless of their ethnicity, class, or culture, and a more exclusive definition of citizenship, which emphasizes the importance of homogeneity; second, the opposition between more liberal procedures of decision making and more authoritarian procedures, an opposition that also includes the question of the role of religious authorities; and third, the opposition between those who favor a political redistribution of resources and those who prefer to rely on market forces (Kitschelt, pp. 11–14). Some of these oppositions are now clearly to be seen in both Latvia and Poland, in some cases with more sharply defined contours than in others. But precisely because the parties themselves, both as teams of leaders and as organizations, are so fragile and volatile, it is difficult to see any dimension of competition being frozen into place for some time to come. This also means that the parties have an additional source of flux, and this means, in turn, that it is even more difficult to locate them within the traditional family groups that are to be found among the west European democracies. East and west may be coming closer together, but, as shall be seen in the following chapters, the differences between the two sets of cases are still more striking than the similarities.

One of the most convenient ways of providing an overview of the combination of uniformity and diversity that characterizes the European party mosaic, both west and east, is to speak of "party families," and this is something we address in Chapter 8. Even though there are differences between "Christian democratic parties" in different countries, for example, there are also some striking family resemblances that go beyond mere name and religious affiliation. Such parties tend to be located on the center–right of the system, to be flanked by both social democratic and other right-wing parties, to be commonly found at the heart of government coalitions, and so on. Accordingly, we now move our discussion forward by looking at the main party "families" in modern Europe, as well as at how they have developed through the years. Our intention in doing this is to highlight the point that although no two parties are exactly alike, the parties in particular groups do bear striking resemblances to one another.

REFERENCES

Andeweg, Rudy B., and Galen A. Irwin: *Governance and Politics of the Netherlands,* Palgrave, Basingstoke, 2nd ed., 2005.

Arter, David: "Sweden: A Mild Case of 'Electoral Instability Syndrome?'" in Broughton and Donovan (eds.), pp. 143–62.

Bardi, Luciano: "Italian Parties: Change and Functionality," in Webb, Farrell, and Holliday (eds.), 46–76.

Bartolini, Stefano: "Institutional Constraints and Party Competition in the French Party System," *West European Politics,* vol. 7, no. 4, 1984, pp. 103–27.

Bartolini, Stefano, Allesandro Chiaramonte, and Roberto D'Alimonte: "The Italian Party System Between Parties and Coalitions," *West European Politics,* vol. 27, no. 1, 2004, pp. 1–19.

Berglund, Sten, Joakim Ekman, and Frank H. Aarebrot (eds.): *The Handbook of Political Change in Eastern Europe,* 2nd ed., Edward Elgar, Cheltenham, 2004.

Berglund, Sten, and Ulf Lindstrom: *The Scandinavian Party System(s),* Studentlitteratur, Lund, 1978.

Biezen, Ingrid van: *Political Parties in New Democracies: Party Organization in Southern and East-Central Europe,* Palgrave, London, 2003.

Blair, Tony: *The Third Way: New Politics for the New Century,* Fabian Society, London, 1998.

Bogdanor, Vernon: "Our New Constitution," *Law Quarterly Review,* vol. 120, April 2004.

Broughton, David, and Mark Donovan (eds.): *Changing Party Systems in Western Europe,* Pinter, London, 1999.

Brug, Wouter van der, and Huib Pellikaan (eds.): *Electoral Revolt or Continuity: The Dutch Parliamentary Elections 2002 and 2003,* special issue of *Acta Politica,* vol. 38, no. 1, 2003.

Bull, Martin, and Martin Rhodes (eds.): *Crisis and Transition in Italian Politics,* special issue of *West European Politics,* vol. 20, no. 1, 1997.

Chari, Raj S.: "The 2004 Spanish Election: Terrorism as a Catalyst for Change?" *West European Politics,* vol. 27, no. 5, 2004, pp. 954–63.

Daalder, Hans: "The Dutch Party System: From Segmentation to Polarization—And Then?" in Hans Daalder (ed.), *Party Systems in Denmark, Austria, Switzerland, the Netherlands, and Belgium,* Pinter, London, 1987, pp. 193–284.

Farneti, Paolo: *The Italian Party System (1945–1980),* Pinter, London, 1985.

Finer, S. E.: *The Changing British Party System, 1945–79,* American Enterprise Institute, Washington (DC), 1980.

Flinders, Matthew: "Majoritarian Democracy in Britain: Labour and the New Constitution," *West European Politics,* vol. 28, no. 1, 2005, pp. 61–93.

Giddens, Anthony: *The Third Way: The Renewal of Social Democracy,* Polity Press, Cambridge, 1998.

Ginsborg, Paul: *Silvio Berlusconi: Television, Power and Patrimony,* Verso, London, 2004.

Heinisch, Reinhard: "Success in Opposition—Failure in Government: Explaining the Performance of Right-Wing Populist Parties in Public Office," *West European Politics,* vol. 26, no. 3, 2003, pp. 91–130.

Hoggart, Simon: "A Perfect Reflection of Left and Right," *Guardian,* March 29, 1997.

Holsteyn, Joop J. M. van, and Galen A. Irwin: "Pim Fortuyn and the Dutch Election of 2002," *West European Politics,* vol. 26, no. 2, 2003, pp. 41–66.

Hopkin, Jonathan: *Party Formation and Democratic Transition in Spain: The Creation and Collapse of the Union of the Democratic Centre,* Macmillan, Basingstoke, 1999.

Hopkin, Jonathan: "Spain: Political Parties in a Young Democracy," in Broughton and Donovan (eds.), pp. 207–31.

Ikstens, Janis: "Latvia," *European Journal of Political Research,* vol. 42, no. 7–8, 2003, pp. 1003–9.

Jasiewicz, Krzysztof: "Poland: Party System by Default," in David Stansfield, Paul Webb, and Stephen White (eds.), *Political Parties in Transitional Democracies,* Oxford University Press, Oxford, 2005.

King, Anthony: "The Implication of One-Party Government," in Anthony King et al., *Britain at the Polls, 1992,* Chatham House, Chatham (NJ), 1993, pp. 223–48.

Kitschelt, Herbert: "The Formation of Party Systems in East Central Europe," *Politics and Society,* vol. 20, no. 1, 1992, pp. 7–50.

Kitschelt, Herbert, and Wolfgang Streeck: "From Stability to Stagnation: Germany at the Beginning of the Twenty-First Century," *West European Politics,* vol. 26, no. 4, 2003, pp. 1–36.

Kitschelt, Herbert, and Wolfgang Streeck (eds.): *Germany: Beyond the Stable State,* special issue of *West European Politics,* vol. 26, no. 4, 2003.

Knapp, Andrew: *Parties and the Party System in France: A Disconnected Democracy?* Palgrave, London, 2004.

Lange, Peter, and M. Vanicelli (eds.): *The Communist Parties of Italy, France and Spain,* Allen & Unwin, London, 1981.

Lijphart, Arend: *Democracy in Plural Societies,* Yale University Press, New Haven, 1977.

Linz, Juan J., and José Ramón Montero: *The Party Systems of Spain: Old Cleavages and New Challenges,* in Lauri Karvonen and Stein Kuhnle (eds.), *Party Systems and Voter Alignments Revisited,* Routledge, London, 2001, pp. 150–96.

Luther, Richard, and Kris Deschouwer: *Party Elites in Divided Societies: Political Parties in Consociational Democracy,* Routledge, London, 1999.

Machin, Howard: "Stages and Dynamics in the Evolution of the French Party System," *West European Politics,* vol. 12, no. 4, 1989, pp. 59–81.

Mackie, Thomas T., and Richard Rose: *The International Almanac of Electoral History,* 3rd ed., Macmillan, Basingstoke, 1991.

Madeley, John T. S.: "'The Swedish Model Is Dead! Long Live the Swedish Model!' The 2002 Riksdag Election," *West European Politics,* vol. 26, no. 2, 2003, pp. 165–73.

Markowski, Radoslaw: "Party System Institutionalization in New Democracies: Poland—a Trendsetter with No Followers," in Paul Lewis (ed.), *Party Development and Democratic Change in Post-communist Europe,* Cass, London, 2001.

Marquand, David: "Progressive or Populist: The Blair Paradox," in David Marquand, *The Progressive Dilemma,* 2nd ed., Phoenix Giant, London, 1999, pp. 225–46.

Mershon, Carol A.: "The Costs of Coalition: Coalition Theories and Italian Governments," *American Political Science Review,* vol. 90, no. 3, 1996, pp. 534–54.

Millard, Frances: "Poland," in Stephen White, Judy Batt, and Paul G. Lewis (eds.), *Developments in Central and East European Politics 3,* Palgrave, London, 2003, pp. 23–40.

Morlino, Leonardo: *Democracy Between Consolidation and Crisis: Parties, Groups, and Citizens in Southern Europe,* Oxford University Press, Oxford, 1998.

Newell, James L., and Martin J. Bull: "Italian Politics After the 2001 General Election," *Parliamentary Affairs,* vol. 55, no. 4, 2002, pp. 626–42.

Norris, Pippa (ed.): *Critical Citizens: Global Support for Democratic Governance,* Oxford University Press, Oxford, 1999.

Olson, David M.: "Compartmentalized Competition: The Managed Transitional Election System of Poland," *Journal of Politics,* vol. 55, no. 2, 1993, pp. 415–41.

Padgett, Stephen, and Thomas Saalfield (eds.): *Bundestagswahl '98: End of an Era?* special issue of *German Politics,* vol. 8, no. 2, 1999.

Pappi, Franz Urban: "The West German Party System," *West European Politics,* vol. 7, no. 4, 1984, pp. 7–26.

Pettai, Vello, and Marcus Kreuzer: "Party Politics in the Baltic States: Social Bases and Institutional Context," *East European Politics and Society,* vol. 13, no. 1, 1999, pp. 148–89.

Poguntke, Thomas, and Susan Scarrow (eds.): *The Politics of Anti-Party Sentiment,* special issue of the *European Journal of Political Research,* vol. 29, no. 3, 1996.

Roberts, Geoffrey K.: *Party Politics in the New Germany,* Pinter, London, 1997.

Sartori, Giovanni: *Parties and Party Systems,* Cambridge University Press, Cambridge, 1976.

Scarrow, Susan E.: "Party Decline in the Parties State? The Changing Environment of German Politics," in Webb, Farrell, and Holliday (eds.), pp. 77–106.

Smith-Sivertsen, Hermann: "Latvia," in Berglund, Ekman, and Aarebrot (eds.), pp. 95–131.

Sprudzs, Adolf: "Rebuilding Democracy in Latvia: Overcoming a Dual Legacy," in Jan Zielonka (ed.), *Democratic Consolidation in Eastern Europe,* vol. 1, *Institutional Engineering,* Oxford University Press, Oxford, 2001, pp. 139–64.

Sundberg, Jan: "The Scandinavian Model at the Crossroads," in Webb, Farrell, and Holliday (eds.), pp. 181–216.

Szczerbiak, Aleks: *Poles Together: Emergence and Development of Political Parties in Post-Communist Poland,* CEU Press, Budapest, 2001.

Vinton, Louisa: "Poland's Political Spectrum on the Eve of Elections," *RFE/RL Research Report,* vol. 2, no. 46, 1993, pp. 1–21.

Webb, Paul: *The Modern British Party System,* Sage, London, 2000.

Webb, Paul, David Farrell, and Ian Holliday (eds.): *Political Parties in Advanced Industrial Democracies,* Oxford University Press, Oxford, 2002.

CHAPTER 8

⚜

PARTY FAMILIES

As we argued in Chapter 7, although no two political parties are quite the same, the parties in particular groups may share a considerable family resemblance. Three conventional characteristics can be used to define different party families in Europe (Mair and Mudde). First, parties can be grouped according to some shared origin—parties that mobilized in similar historical circumstances or with the intention of representing similar interests can be treated as having a distinct family resemblance. On these grounds all traditional socialist or social democratic parties, for example, can be considered as belonging to the same family, as can all agrarian parties. This might be termed the genetic approach.

The second sort of family resemblance is defined by the parties themselves, in the way in which they forge links across national frontiers. Such links may take the form of transnational federations, such as the federation established by various liberal parties. It may also take the form of a membership of institutionalized multinational political groups, such as those to be found in the European Parliament (see Chapter 5), and because the EP now involves the full twenty-five member states of the European Union, it can offer a reasonably clear guide to the extent of cross-national partisan collegiality in western Europe (for an early application, see Hix and Lord). In this case we are concerned with behavior.

The final way in which party families can be identified has to do with the extent to which the policies advocated by one party in a country are similar to those professed by another party in another country. There are some problems with this, because the "same" policy may mean quite different things in the practical politics of two different countries, but to ignore professed policies altogether when looking for similarities between parties would clearly be to stick our heads in the sand. It matters what parties say.

Although no single one of these criteria—genetics, behavior, or discourse—provides a clear-cut classification, a judicious balance of the three suggests that, as far as modern Europe is concerned, we can think in terms of about nine main party families, and in this chapter we present a brief description of each of them. We also chart changes in their long-term electoral following over the past half century of democratic development in western Europe, and we contrast the changing patterns of support they enjoy in different countries. The classification into families in postcommunist Europe is more blurred than that in western Europe, however. In the first place, as we have seen, the parties and the still nascent party systems are often very fragmented, and it is sometimes difficult to find a situation that is stable enough to speak of coherent families. Second, the problems facing political actors in postcommunist Europe are often still specific to the transition from postcommunism and hence have few if any parallels with the west. Even when we can identify families, therefore, they are sometimes different and particularistic. That said, there are broad pan-European elements constituted by religion, by urban–rural divides, and even occasionally by class, and we discuss these later in the chapter. As a major first step, however, we focus on the long-established democracies of western Europe because here we are primarily concerned with how the various families have developed across more than a half century of democratic politics and hence we need to concentrate on the democracies that have experienced this extended period of party competition. Later in the chapter we look at the newer European democracies.

For the purposes of this initial longitudinal analysis, and despite many problems of definition, we have divided these different families of parties into two broad groups— families of the left, which include social democrats, communists, the new left, and the Green parties; and families of the center and right, which include Christian democrats, conservatives, liberals, agrarian or center parties, and the far right. For each family, where relevant, we include a table reporting average electoral support in each of the countries in the 1950s, 1960s, 1970s, 1980s, and 1990s. We also consider developments in the most recent twenty-first-century elections as a final point of reference. When presenting these comparative data, we concentrate mainly on those countries that have had an uninterrupted history of democratic politics since the 1950s; separate figures are provided for Cyprus, Greece, Portugal, and Spain. Later, we also discuss the relevance of these broad family distinctions to the newly emerging postcommunist party systems.

✦ FAMILIES OF THE LEFT

There are four relevant party families to be found on the left-wing side of the political spectrum in traditional western European party systems. Social democratic parties are the strongest and most enduring of western Europe's political families, not only on the left but also in European politics taken as a whole. Communist parties are a very clear-cut group, traditionally comprising parties that began as pro-Soviet splits from social democratic parties in the wake of the Russian Revolution of 1917. The third and fourth families on the left are the new left and the Greens, which represent more varied collections of more recently formed parties, often grouped together under the general label "left–libertarian parties" (Kitschelt, "Left–Libertarian"). All four families can be seen as representing the contemporary left in west European politics; however, they clearly incorporate between them some huge variations both in ideology and of interest representation.

The Social Democrats

Organized social democracy is one of the oldest surviving political forces in western Europe. Even at the beginning of the twenty-first century, the social democrats remain the single most important group in contemporary politics. The majority of the social democratic parties first entered electoral politics in the last quarter of the nineteenth century and were initially mobilized to represent the political interests of the growing working class, often acting in concert with the trade union movement. In some cases, as in the United Kingdom, a social democratic party was actually created by the trade unions in order to represent their interests in parliament. In other cases, as in the Netherlands, a political party was formed first in its own right and later established links with the trade unions (for a

TABLE 8.1

Mean Electoral Support for Social Democratic Parties, 1950–2004

Country	1950s	1960s	1970s	1980s	1990s	2000–4
Austria	43.3	45.0	50.0	45.4	37.2	36.5
Belgium	35.9	31.0	26.6	28.0	23.8	27.9
Denmark	40.2	39.1	33.6	31.9	36.0	29.1
Finland	25.9	26.9	25.1	25.4	24.4	22.9
France	25.9	18.6	22.1	35.0	24.4	26.7
Germany	30.3	39.4	44.2	39.4	36.9	38.5
Iceland	19.5	15.0	14.8	17.1	20.3	31.0
Ireland	10.9	14.8	12.7	8.9	14.9	10.8
Italy	18.0	19.4	14.4	16.4	25.7	17.6
Luxembourg	37.1	35.0	35.4	32.3	24.8	23.4
Malta	54.9	38.5	51.2	49.0	48.1	47.5
Netherlands	30.7	25.8	31.9	31.0	26.5	21.2
Norway	47.5	45.4	38.8	37.4	36.0	24.3
Sweden	45.6	48.4	43.7	44.5	39.8	39.9
Switzerland	26.0	26.0	25.7	21.2	21.0	23.3
United Kingdom	46.3	46.1	39.1	29.2	38.9	40.7
Mean (N = 16)	**33.6**	**32.1**	**31.8**	**30.7**	**29.9**	**28.8**
Cyprus				9.7	9.5	6.5
Greece				43.5	43.8	42.2
Portugal				28.7	39.4	37.8
Spain				43.5	39.4	38.4
Overall mean (N = 20)				**30.8**	**30.5**	**29.3**

Note: Since Greece, Portugal, and Spain did not become fully democratic until the mid-1970s, decade averages are reported only for the 1980s and 1990s. Cyprus is also included from the 1980s only. In the 1960s and 1970s elections were infrequent in Cyprus, and the different Greek Cypriot parties sometimes formed a broad national front.

Source and clarifications: For this and other tables in this chapter, see Table 8.10.

comprehensive account, see Bartolini). As the franchise was extended to include more and more working-class voters, the social democratic parties grew in support. In the majority of European countries they gained their first experience of government in the years immediately following World War I. By the late 1940s the position of the social democrats in European politics was well established. It was largely as a result of their intervention that most western European welfare states were expanded during the 1950s and 1960s (Flora).

As Table 8.1 shows, the strongest social democratic presence in contemporary western Europe can be found in Austria, Denmark, Germany, Malta, Norway, Sweden, and the UK, where in each case the average social democratic share of the vote was still more than 35 percent during the 1990s. Social democracy has also proved a very powerful political force in Greece, Portugal, and Spain, where democracy was reestablished in the 1970s following periods of authoritarian rule, and where social democratic parties averaged around 40 percent of the vote in the 1990s. In 2004, the socialists had been returned to office in Spain and were the major opposition party in both Greece and Portugal.

In a second group of countries—Belgium, Finland, France, Iceland, Italy (principally the former communist Democratic Party of the Left), Luxembourg, the Netherlands, and Switzerland—the social democratic share of the vote has recently averaged around 25 percent. In Cyprus and in Ireland the social democrats are weaker. In Cyprus, this weakness is understandable, given the strength of the local Communist Party (see below); Ireland is genuinely exceptional, however, in that Labour—and the left as a whole—have always polled so little in Ireland. The Irish Labour Party is in this sense the real Cinderella of European social democracy. In the Irish election in 1992, however, there was an unprecedented if temporary surge of support for the party, which almost doubled its vote to more than 19 percent.

In general, as can be seen from Table 8.1, the electoral position of social democracy declined slightly during the postwar period, from an average of almost 34 percent in the 1950s to just less than 30 percent in the 1990s. This decline was most marked in Luxembourg, the Netherlands, and Norway, while in the UK the real low point was reached in the 1980s, when support fell below 30 percent. But the steady electoral decline of social democracy is not pervasive. By comparison to the earlier decades, social democrats now poll a greater share of the vote in Germany, in Iceland, and arguably also in Italy. In addition, in Denmark, Iceland, and the UK the social democratic vote in the 1990s was higher than that recorded in the 1980s; in France it was precisely in the 1980s that the peak in support was recorded.

These data therefore offer the useful early lesson that it is difficult to generalize about patterns of party support across western Europe as a whole. Not only do the aggregate electoral strengths of the parties differ considerably from one country to the next, but their patterns of development also vary—showing growth in some countries, decline in others, and more or less trendless fluctuations in yet others.

Now that European welfare states have been established for such a long period, it is easy to forget the radicalism that was once an integral part of social democracy in western Europe. In many cases, the social democratic parties adopted an explicitly Marxist philosophy and ultimately envisaged the replacement of capitalism by a genuinely socialist order. During the period in which the franchise was being expanded to include the working class, social democratic parties sought the full extension of political rights and the introduction of social policies designed to protect the interests of workers and of the unemployed.

With time, however, the initial radical impulse of social democracy began to wane. As Michels argued, electoral imperatives implied more professional organizational techniques, which did much to blunt the parties' political purism. A further push toward moderation occurred when the Russian Revolution of 1917 precipitated splits in the socialist movement. The consequent creation of communist parties drew away many of the more radical members from the social democratic parties. The moderation of the views of the social democratic parties was also, in part, a product of their very success. The experience of participating in government, particularly in the wake of World War II, increased pressures toward ideological compromise and firmly ensconced social democratic parties at the heart of the political order they initially sought to overthrow. Finally, much of the early radicalism of the social democrats was dissipated as a result of the successful implementation of their short-term policies: Full political rights were won, and welfare states grew quickly in most European countries.

As a consequence of all this, the social democrats came to settle for a political role based on managing a mixed economy. They steadily dropped what Kirchheimer described as their "ideological baggage" and extended their electoral appeal to the middle class, particularly the middle class working in the rapidly expanding state sector, thus becoming catchall parties. This drift toward moderation became even more accentuated in the 1990s, as social democratic parties throughout Europe came to terms with the limits to state intervention set by the demands of the international global economy. Within the increasingly integrated European Union area, of course, these limits are even more pronounced (Scharpf). But although this constraint might be seen to have frustrated social democratic appeals since the 1990s, it is quite remarkable to note the extent to which social democrats have recorded recent successes, gaining access to government at the end of the 1990s in almost all west European countries, before often losing out again to conservative and center–right forces in the immediate following elections. Here again, there is a useful lesson: Even when European voters shift to the left or to the right, they rarely stay there but instead shift back again soon after.

Despite their increased moderation, the policy emphases of contemporary social democratic parties retain a commitment to welfarism and egalitarianism, even though they now tend to place less emphasis on the need to control and regulate economic life. Social democratic party manifestos no longer present a direct ideological challenge to the capitalist order in western Europe. What remains of their traditional radicalism has passed either to increasingly marginalized communist parties or to new left and Green parties that first came to prominence in the 1970s and 1980s. They tend to have become strong supporters of European integration and, more often than not, now follow the "Third Way" style of politics that was pioneered so successfully by Tony Blair in the UK. In brief, this new approach moved social democratic parties away from their commitment to public ownership and toward a greater acceptance of the market and of market solutions, seeking to establish a middle path—the "third way"—between traditional socialism and neoliberalism. The policy would no longer emphasize equality of income and resources, or "outcomes" but would instead emphasize equality of opportunity. Rather than governments providing citizens with solutions to their problems, governments could create the conditions in which citizens would find their own solutions. "Having abandoned collectivism," argues Anthony Giddens (p. 65), "third way politics looks for a new relationship between the individual and the community, a redefinition of rights and obligations." For Tony Blair, the Third Way was about placing what he called traditional Labour values within a modern setting, and about creating a new synthesis that would rise above left and right. Indeed, in a very public effort to consolidate this approach more effectively at the international level, a major conference was held in Florence, Italy, in 1999. It brought together U.S. president Bill Clinton and the leaders of some of the Europe's major social democratic parties, with a view to outlining plans for "progressive governance for the 21st century." The conference was hosted by the then leader of the Italian Democratic Socialists, Massimo D'Alema, and participants included Tony Blair of the UK, Lionel Jospin of France, and Gerhard Schröder of Germany.[1] (On social democracy in general, see Cuperus and Kandel; Kitschelt, *Transformation;* Moschonas.)

---

[1]The conference proceedings were published as *Progressive Governance for the XXI Century* (Florence: European University Institute and New York University School of Law, 1999).

The Communists

Significant communist parties could traditionally be found in fewer countries than their social democratic rivals, and, in the main, they have also proved substantially less successful at winning votes. Moreover, since the collapse of the Berlin Wall in 1989 and the breakdown of the communist regimes in eastern Europe and in the former Soviet Union, the communist parties that have remained in western Europe have been engaged in a process of reform and have sometimes either dropped their ideological label (as in Finland and Sweden) or effectively disappeared as an independent force (as in the Netherlands and Norway). Only occasionally, as in Cyprus, have they persisted while attempting to hold on to their traditional identity. Even before this, however, as can be seen from Table 8.2, communist parties commanded a substantial proportion of the vote only in Italy and Cyprus and, to a lesser extent, in Finland, France, and Iceland. Explicit communist parties were effectively nonexistent in Ireland, Malta, and the

TABLE 8.2

Mean Electoral Support for Communist Parties, 1950–2004

Country	1950s	1960s	1970s	1980s	1990s	2000–4
Austria	4.3	1.7	1.2	0.7	0.4	0.6
Belgium	3.4	3.7	2.9	1.4	0.2	—
Denmark	4.5	1.0	3.0	0.9	—	—
Finland	22.1	21.6	17.6	13.9	10.7	9.9
France	23.9	21.4	21.0	12.4	12.6	4.9
Germany	1.1	—	—	—	4.0	4.0
Iceland	16.4	16.3	23.7	15.3	9.6	—
Ireland	—	—	—	—	—	—
Italy	22.7	26.1	30.7	28.3	6.7	6.7
Luxembourg	11.6	14.0	8.2	5.1	2.8	0.9
Malta	—	—	—	—	—	—
Netherlands	4.4	3.2	3.4	1.1	—	—
Norway	4.3	1.8	1.0	0.9	—	—
Sweden	4.2	4.2	5.1	5.6	7.6	8.4
Switzerland	2.7	2.6	2.4	0.9	1.1	0.7
United Kingdom	—	—	—	—	—	—
Mean (*N* = 16)	**7.9**	**7.3**	**7.5**	**5.4**	**3.5**	**2.3**
Cyprus				30.1	31.8	34.7
Greece				12.1	9.5	5.7
Portugal				16.0	9.7	6.9
Spain				6.1	9.9	5.5
Overall mean (*N* = 20)				**7.5**	**5.8**	**4.4**

Note: Since Greece, Portugal, and Spain did not become fully democratic until the mid-1970s, decade averages are reported only for the 1980s and 1990s. Cyprus is also included from the 1980s only. In the 1960s and 1970s elections were infrequent in Cyprus, and the different Greek Cypriot parties sometimes formed a broad national front.

Source and clarifications: See Table 8.10.

United Kingdom and have now become even more marginalized in Austria, Belgium, Denmark, Norway, and Switzerland. Although they have proved more serious contenders for votes in the new southern European democracies—Greece, Portugal, and Spain— there has recently been some slippage in their vote in these countries too, and such success as they have had—as in Spain—has required the formation of electoral alliances with other left groupings. In general, across the whole postwar period, average electoral support for communist parties fell from almost 8 percent in the 1950s to less than 4 percent in the 1990s and to just 2 percent in the first elections of the new century—this most recent decline being partly accounted for by the split in the Italian Communist Party (PCI), which resulted in a relatively small party (Communist Refoundation) remaining in the communist camp, with a much larger fraction of the former communists (the DS) now being effectively located in the social democratic family. Taking all twenty democracies together, the communists polled an average of just 4.4 percent in 2000–4, as against 7.5 percent in the 1970s.

Yet even these relatively modest levels of support tend to exaggerate the importance of communist parties in those countries where they might appear on the face of things to have counted as a relevant political force. In Italy, for example, which traditionally hosted the most important of the western European communist parties, the 1980s had already witnessed a major erosion of the distinctively communist element in both party ideology and party organization. In France, in contrast, the distinctively communist identity of the French Communist Party (PCF) has been jealously guarded at substantial electoral cost. The 1980s witnessed a major electoral decline of the PCF to the benefit of its more moderate and increasingly successful socialist rival. In Iceland, the People's Alliance (PA) has largely shied away from promoting a distinctive communist identity. It includes quite a substantial social democratic component, and in the 1999 and 2003 elections it took part in a left-wing electoral alliance with the Women's Party and the social democrats. In Cyprus, the communist identity has been deliberately retained. The party had been banned in the 1930s and again in the 1950s, but it has managed to hold on to a substantial electoral following since 1960. Finally, the communist party in Finland, which used to be known as the Finnish People's Democratic Union (FPDL), banned prior to World War II, enjoyed a peculiar status owing to the country's close geographic and cultural links with the Soviet Union. Even here, however, the FPDL was an alliance that included a social democratic component. The strains in this eventually led to a split between more moderate and extreme elements in 1985 and to the creation of the more orthodox Democratic Alternative. Since the late 1990s, both sides have joined together again in the new and more moderate Left-Wing Alliance.

The European communist parties were almost all formed in the immediate wake of the Russian Revolution of 1917, espousing Leninist principles and advocating the revolutionary road to socialism. They thereby established themselves as a radical alternative to the parliamentarism of social democracy. These parties were formally aligned with and took their lead from the Soviet Communist Party. This leadership was organized initially through Comintern, the Communist (or Third) International, which lasted from 1919 to 1943. It was later organized through the less formal Cominform network, which lasted from 1947 to 1956. This alliance with Moscow, together with the parties' evident radicalism, ensured that the parties were typically regarded as antisystem oppositions, and as such they often polarized the party systems in which they operated.

Inevitably, they had little experience with government office, although, in the immediate wake of World War II, bolstered by the credibility that they had achieved as a result of their crucial role in the antifascist resistance, several communist parties were to enjoy brief periods as partners in the widely based coalition governments that sought to reestablish democratic politics in countries such as Austria, Belgium, Denmark, Finland, France, and Italy. Since then, communist parties have been involved in government only in Cyprus, Iceland, Finland, and, since the early 1980s, France. Beyond this, however, they have sometimes offered the parliamentary support necessary to sustain other parties in office while not formally joining the cabinet. In Italy, for example, the PCI helped to sustain the Christian Democrats in office in the late 1970s, and Communist Refoundation also helped to keep the DS-dominated Olive Tree Alliance in government in the late 1990s. In Sweden, the small but remarkably persistent Communist Party, now renamed the Left Party, has regularly provided the parliamentary support necessary to maintain the Social Democrats in office.

In part as a response to electoral decline or stagnation, in part as a means of ending their political isolation, many western European communist parties began to distance themselves from Moscow during the postwar period. This shift heralded the emergence of "Eurocommunism" in the 1970s, in which the Italian, French, and Spanish parties, in particular, sought to elaborate a distinctively non-Soviet strategy for achieving political power. However, this strategy of legitimation did not reap the hoped-for political rewards, and the 1980s witnessed further electoral decline.

Partly as a result of the Eurocommunist strategy, the policy emphases of communist parties ceased to be markedly different from those of their social democratic rivals, and they also began to emphasize questions of welfare, social justice, and the need for democratic decision making. Where they do still differ from the social democrats is in their emphasis on state involvement in the economy and in their greater skepticism about the free market. They stress the need for a controlled economy as well as for more public ownership, and they are much more critical about the benefits of European integration. They are also much more explicit in their claim to represent the specific interests of the traditional working class and trade unions in contrast to the more catchall electoral appeal of social democracy. (For a useful assessment of the western European communist parties in the immediate wake of the end of the Cold War, see Bull and Heywood.)

The New Left

The third party family on the left is usually described as the "new" left. As can be seen from Table 8.3, patterns of popular support for the new left make it easier to understand the general decline of social democratic and communist voting. Through to the 1980s, the trend in support for the new left ran counter to that for the traditional left, rising from just 1 percent in the 1960s in western Europe as a whole to almost 3 percent in the 1980s before falling back again—to the benefit of the Greens—since the 1990s. This suggests a reshuffling rather than a decline of the left.

The first new left parties emerged in the 1960s. These tended more toward an orthodox Marxist position, having often emerged as a result of divisions within the established communist parties. The later new left parties, in contrast, tended to be stimulated by the wave of student radicalism of the late 1960s, and they have also been spurred on by the

TABLE 8.3

Mean Electoral Support for New Left Parties, 1960–2004

Country	1960s	1970s	1980s	1990s	2000–4
Austria	—	—	—	—	—
Belgium	—	—	—	—	—
Denmark	7.7	8.3	14.4	7.7	6.4
Finland	—	—	—	—	—
France	—	—	—	—	2.7
Germany	—	—	—	—	—
Iceland	—	—	7.8	7.4	—
Ireland	—	1.4	3.9	3.2	0.8
Italy	2.2	3.3	4.0	—	—
Luxembourg	—	—	—	—	1.9
Malta	—	—	—	—	—
Netherlands	3.0	4.0	2.6	2.4	6.1
Norway	4.0	6.9	6.8	8.4	13.7
Sweden	—	—	—	—	—
Switzerland	—	0.9	2.3	0.3	—
United Kingdom	—	—	—	—	—
Mean (N = 16)	**1.1**	**1.6**	**2.6**	**1.8**	**2.0**
Cyprus			—	—	—
Greece			—	—	5.5
Portugal			—	—	2.7
Spain			—	—	—
Overall mean (N = 20)			**2.1**	**1.4**	**2.0**

Note: Since Greece, Portugal, and Spain did not become fully democratic until the mid-1970s, decade averages are reported only for the 1980s and 1990s. Cyprus is also included from the 1980s only. In the 1960s and 1970s elections were infrequent in Cyprus, and the different Greek Cypriot parties sometimes formed a broad national front.

Source and clarifications: See Table 8.10.

growing ecology movement. Indeed, it is often difficult to distinguish these new left parties from more orthodox Green parties (see below), and since the emergence of the latter, the two groups have frequently worked in concert. The Dutch Green Left, for example, is an alliance between Greens, new left parties, and the old Communist Party. (See also Kitschelt, "Left–Libertarian," who groups both types of parties under the label "left–libertarian.")

As Table 8.3 shows, new left parties have established themselves in only a scattering of the western European polities, and even where they exist, they often remain quite marginal. Only occasionally, as in Denmark in the 1980s, when two new left parties were competing, or in Norway in 2001, has the new left vote reached double figures. Outside Denmark and Norway, new left support has proved notable only in Iceland (where it has included the Women's Alliance) and Sweden. In this sense it may be regarded as a primarily Scandinavian phenomenon.

Not least as a result of their diverse origins, the policy emphases on new left parties reflect a wide-ranging set of concerns. The new left parties echo traditional communist parties in their opposition to market forces and their concern for public ownership and a controlled economy. Again like traditional communist parties, and quite unlike their Green allies, they emphasize an explicit appeal to the traditional working class. And although they stress a commitment to the welfare state, social justice, and environmental protection, in common with all left parties, they also promote a more libertarian trend of freedom and democracy. Finally, they also tend to be more skeptical about European integration.

Green Parties

Radical left politics can be seen as having developed in four distinct phases. As we have explained, the first, most important, and most enduring of these phases was the emergence of social democratic parties in the late nineteenth century. The second phase involved the spilt in social democracy in the wake of the Russian Revolution and the consequent emergence of the communist alternative. Here, too, the new parties proved reasonably enduring and, in certain limited instances, grew to a majority position on the left. The third phase was the mobilization of the new left in the 1960s and 1970s, a movement that managed to establish itself in mainstream politics in only a handful of countries, and in these largely at the expense of the traditional communist parties. Finally, in the late 1970s and 1980s came the fourth phase—the emergence of "Green," or ecology, parties. Green parties tend to poll only a small percentage of the total vote. Nevertheless, their recent growth and pervasiveness have generated substantial interest among students of the western European party mosaic.

Table 8.4 shows that by the 1990s Green parties had gained a respectable level of electoral support in the large majority of western European countries. To be sure, the Green alternative remains essentially marginal by comparison to that of its larger rivals and on the average accounted for little more than 2 percent of the vote in western Europe in the 1980s and for less than 5 percent in the 1990s. But the Greens represent a new and growing phenomenon, and average figures mask the increase in Green support that has occurred in the some recent elections. They also mask substantial variations between countries. In Belgium, for example, average Green support exceeded 10 percent in the 1990s, then fell back in the elections of 2003, when Greens polled less than 6 percent after an unhappy experience as a coalition partner in the national government. In Austria, Finland, France, Germany, and Switzerland these parties polled an average of between 6 and 9 percent and came close to 12 percent in Luxembourg in 2004. The Netherlands also comes close to this level, although the Green alternative there is one that competes as part of an electoral coalition involving also the new left and the former Communist Party.

In contrast, there is as yet no effective Green representation in Malta, Norway, or the United Kingdom. In the UK, however, the British Green party did poll almost 15 percent of the vote in the 1989 British direct elections to the European Parliament. This was the largest national vote share ever won by a Green party, but given that the British first-past-the-post electoral system was also then in operation for the British European elections, it yielded not a single seat. (Conversely, with a lower share of the

TABLE 8.4

Mean Electoral Support for Green Parties, 1980–2004

Country	1980s	1990s	2000–4
Austria	4.1	6.6	9.5
Belgium	6.0	10.9	5.5
Denmark	0.7	2.2	2.4
Finland	2.7	7.0	8.0
France	0.9	8.4	5.6
Germany	5.1	6.4	8.6
Iceland	—	3.1	8.8
Ireland	0.4	2.1	3.9
Italy	1.3	2.7	2.2
Luxembourg	6.4	9.3	11.6
Malta	—	1.5	0.7
Netherlands	1.1	5.6	6.1
Norway	0.1	0.1	—
Sweden	2.9	4.3	4.6
Switzerland	5.0	6.3	7.9
United Kingdom	0.3	0.3	—
Mean (N = 16)	**2.3**	**4.8**	**5.4**
Cyprus	—	—	2.0
Greece	0.2	0.6	—
Portugal	—	0.3	—
Spain	—	1.0	—
Overall mean (N = 20)	**1.9**	**3.9**	**4.4**

vote, the Scottish Green party did manage to win representation in the new devolved Scottish parliament in 1999.) Nor have Green parties made any significant impact in the new democracies of southern Europe, although Green MPs were elected in 1989 in Greece, in 2001 in Cyprus, and as part of the broad United Democratic Coalition in 1987 in Portugal.

Even though a major electoral breakthrough has so far eluded Green parties in Europe, in other respects they have achieved some notable political successes, entering government coalitions in Belgium, Finland, France, Germany, and Italy. Indeed, as we saw in Chapter 7, they have also notched a major success in Latvia, where Europe's first ever Green prime minister was appointed. In Luxembourg, the Netherlands, and Switzerland it is also possible that the Greens might enter government in the near future. The most important contribution of these new parties might well be that they provide the additional support necessary to allow the formation of center–left governments. Without the Greens, for example, it would have been impossible for any left-wing coalition to displace the center–right governments in France, Germany, or Italy during the latter half of the 1990s.

The policy emphases of Green parties, as might be expected, give pride of place to the need to protect the environment, promoting policies that would curb economic growth and require substantial regulation of industrial and commercial activity. Green manifestos also emphasize the need for international peace and disarmament and urge an increase in the level of development aid provided for third-world countries. They emphasize social justice, particularly the need for equal treatment of women, as well as of ethnic and racial minorities. Green parties also stress participatory democracy and even attempt to structure their own organizations in such a way as to allow maximum grassroots involvement. Finally, and like the other smaller parties of the left, they tend to question the value of further European integration—or when they accept this development, they push strongly for it to be accompanied by more democratic decision making. Bearing in mind the rapidly rising salience of the issues valued by the Green parties, we might also probably judge their success by the extent to which these issues now rank so highly on the policy agendas of all political parties on the left. (On Green parties in general, see Burchell; Delwit and de Waele; Müller-Rommel and Poguntke.)

✦ FAMILIES OF THE CENTER AND RIGHT

The party families of the right are more heterogeneous than those of the left and show much more evidence of flux in their aggregate electoral support over time. These families include the Christian democrats, made up of parties that temper mainstream conservatism with a defense of religious values; conservative parties, distinguished from the Christian democrats by a more strident antisocialist rhetoric as well as by the absence of traditional links with organized religion; and liberal parties, a heterogeneous group that includes centrist parties such as the British Liberals and quite right-wing parties such as the Dutch Liberals. There is also a group of agrarian or center parties that originally mobilized in defense of farming interests in a variety of western European countries. Finally, there is a family of far-right parties characterized by the promotion of populist and sometimes xenophobic political appeals.

The Christian Democrats

For most of the postwar period, the Christian democratic family constituted the largest single group on the center–right of western European politics. This family has a base in most established western European democracies, the main exceptions being Iceland and the United Kingdom. It has also emerged as at least a marginally relevant political force in Portugal.

The Christian democratic family contains a number of distinct strands. The first is primarily Roman Catholic in origin and includes Christian parties that began to mobilize in the mid-to-late nineteenth century and that are now among the strongest in Europe. This strand is made up of Christian democratic parties in Austria, Belgium, Italy, Luxembourg, Malta, and Switzerland, although the Swiss party now also wins support from Protestant voters.

The second strand in Christian democracy comprises two parties that draw substantial support from both Catholics and Protestants. The German Christian Democratic Union (CDU) and its Bavarian sister party, the Christian Social Union (CSU), were both formed in 1945 in the period of immediate postwar reconstruction. They built on the legacy of the former Catholic Center Party, one of the dominant parties in Germany before the Nazi regime. In 1945, however, in a deliberate effort to erode the divisions that had been so evident in the prewar period, the new CDU sought the support of both Catholics and Protestants. This cross-denominational appeal has become even more pronounced since German unification, because the eastern parts of Germany contained a high proportion of Protestant voters. The CSU, in contrast, remains almost wholly Catholic. The second biconfessional Christian democratic party is the Dutch Christian Democratic Appeal (CDA), which was originally divided into three separate parties: the Catholic People's Party and two smaller but persistent Protestant parties, the Anti-Revolutionary Party (ARP—the revolution to which it was opposed was the French Revolution of 1789) and the Christian Historical Union (CHU). These formed a federation in 1975 and then fused into a single party in 1980. Both the CDU and the CDA, with their substantial Protestant components, can be differentiated from the essentially Catholic parties in the first strand of Christian democracy. In all other respects, however, and not the least in their inheritance of a long tradition of confessional politics and in the strong bargaining positions they now enjoy in their respective party systems, these two strands of Christian democracy fill rather similar roles in party politics.

The third strand is largely Protestant and is of more recent origin—the parties involved often first contested elections only after World War II. It is also more marginal in electoral terms. It comprises the Christian Democrats of Denmark, Norway, and Sweden, together with the minor evangelical and reformed Protestant parties in the Netherlands and Switzerland. The Swedish party enjoyed a strong surge of support in the 1990s and took part in the Swedish center–right coalition government in the mid-1990s. It then lost support again in 2002, polling just over 9 percent. The Christian People's Party in Norway also did particularly well in the 1990s, polling almost 14 percent of the vote in 1997 and going on to become the senior partner in the new minority center–right coalition that displaced the minority social democratic government after that election. Although its vote also fell back in 2001, it still managed to poll more than 12 percent, almost exactly on a par with the Socialist Left.

Over and above these cases of explicit Christian parties, a Christian democratic element can also be identified in France and Ireland. The French case is the more interesting of the two because a substantial Catholic party, the Popular Republican Movement, was among the most influential parties in the French Fourth Republic (1946–58). With the shifting center–right alliances that have characterized French politics since 1958, however, the distinct Christian alternative has all but disappeared. Much of its more conservative support was eventually captured by the Gaullists, and the more moderate elements operated under the Center Social Democrat label within the loose alliance called the Union for French Democracy.

In Ireland, where the population is still almost 90 percent Catholic and where rates of church attendance are, with Poland, still among the highest in Europe, there is no tradition of organized Christian democracy. In recent years, however, one of the leading parties of the center–right, Fine Gael, has affiliated with the transnational federations of Christian democratic parties—the European People's Party and the European Union of Christian Democrats—and the party is also affiliated with the Christian democratic People's group in the European Parliament in Strasbourg. Hence, although historically

TABLE 8.5

Mean Electoral Support for Christian Democratic Parties, 1950–2004

Country	1950s	1960s	1970s	1980s	1990s	2000–4
Austria	43.8	46.9	43.2	42.2	28.7	42.3
Belgium	45.4	36.3	33.7	27.8	23.1	19.1
Denmark	—	—	3.9	2.4	2.2	2.3
Finland	—	0.6	2.9	2.8	3.4	5.3
France[a]	—	—	—	—	—	—
Germany	47.7	46.3	46.0	45.9	40.1	38.5
Iceland	—	—	—	—	0.2	—
Ireland[b]	28.1	33.4	32.8	33.9	26.3	22.5
Italy	41.3	38.6	38.5	33.6	17.8	3.2
Luxembourg	37.5	34.3	31.2	33.3	30.3	36.1
Malta	35.9	52.7	48.3	50.9	50.5	51.8
Netherlands	53.2	49.8	37.8	36.6	23.3	32.2
Norway	10.3	9.0	11.9	8.7	10.8	12.4
Sweden	—	1.1	1.6	2.4	7.7	9.1
Switzerland	24.2	24.4	23.2	22.2	18.8	17.1
United Kingdom	—	—	—	—	—	
Mean (N = 16)	**22.9**	**23.4**	**22.1**	**21.5**	**17.6**	**16.9**
Cyprus				—	—	—
Greece				—	—	—
Portugal				6.9	7.3	8.7
Spain				2.2	—	—
Overall mean (N = 20)				**18.4**	**15.1**	**14.0**

Note: Since Greece, Portugal, and Spain did not become fully democratic until the mid-1970s, decade averages are reported only for the 1980s and 1990s. Cyprus is also included from the 1980s only. In the 1960s and 1970s elections were infrequent in Cyprus, and the different Greek Cypriot parties sometimes formed a broad national front.

[a] Since the mid-1970s, the Christian democrats in France, together with conservative and liberal forces, have contested elections as part of the UDF alliance and later, in a link with the Gaullists, as part of the UMP; as such, their electoral support has been grouped together with that of the conservatives.

[b] For the purposes of this analysis, the Irish party Fine Gael is classified as Christian democratic.

outside the Christian democratic tradition, Fine Gael has proved willing to adopt this transnational organizational identity.

As Table 8.5 shows, and notwithstanding the more recent successes of the smaller Protestant parties, Christian democracy as a whole experienced substantial erosion of electoral support toward the end of the postwar era, falling from an average of almost 23 percent in the 1950s to less than 17 percent in the most recent elections. Across all twenty democracies, its average support now comes to some 14 percent. Without the exceptionally strong support for the Maltese party, which may be regarded as being close to the order of the conservative party family (see below), the decline would be even more pronounced. With Malta excluded, the Christian democrats fall to just 14 percent in 2000–4, and to just 12 percent when all nineteen other systems are taken into account.

Among the most dramatic declines was that experienced in the Netherlands, where the various Christian parties accounted for more than half the vote in the 1950s, as against less than a quarter in the 1990s. In 1994, the dominant Christian party, the CDA, recorded its worst ever result, polling just over 18 percent of the vote. Thereafter it recovered and in the elections of 2002 and 2003 emerged as the biggest single party. Nonetheless, its support remains vulnerable. There has also been a marked decline in neighboring Belgium, where the Catholic parties (one Flemish, one Walloon) have lost more than half their support and finally have also lost their presence in government.

In Italy, the Christian democratic vote has been drastically reduced; the allegations of corruption destroyed the party after 1992 and left behind a group of divided smaller parties that split between the alliances of left and right. In Austria, the People's Party lost around one-third of its support between the 1950s and the 1990s, principally to the benefit of the far-right Freedom Party. Indeed, in the crucial election of 1999 the Freedom Party narrowly managed to outpoll the People's Party. Both parties then went into government together, under the leadership of the People's Party, and in the following election the latter won back a lot of its original support. Elsewhere, particularly in Germany, Luxembourg, and Switzerland, the Christian vote has also fallen. What is striking, however, is that with the exception of the small Protestant Party in Sweden, no country has experienced a sustained increase in Christian democratic support over the postwar period. Excepting Malta, the electoral record of Christian democracy in postwar western Europe reflects the most substantial erosion experienced by any of the nine party families.

The dominant strand in western European Christian democracy was always represented by the Catholic parties in particular. Even in the case of the biconfessional parties, the Catholic heritage has been well to the fore. This particular heritage dates back to the nineteenth century, when Catholic mobilization took place in response to secularizing and anticlerical impulses from both conservatives and liberals (Kalyvas). Since then, however, the issues that first generated these conflicts between church and state have largely been settled, and the parties themselves have developed into mainstream components of the center–right. Their religious emphases surface only in response to the appearance on the political agenda of moral issues such as abortion, euthanasia, and divorce, on which the established Christian churches have strong views. The smaller Protestant parties share these positions but add a concern for reversing what they see as the general trend toward permissiveness and ungodliness. The Norwegian and Swedish parties, for example, have campaigned strongly against both alcohol and pornography.

Christian parties can be distinguished from their conservative counterparts (see below) because their popular base, their social concerns, and their reluctance to promote policies that might lead to social conflict have always inclined them (the Catholic parties in particular) toward a more centrist, pro-welfare program. Indeed, the impetus behind the development of welfare states in postwar Europe derived almost as much from Catholic pressure as it did from social democracy. This was particularly true in countries such as Belgium, the Netherlands, and Italy, where social democracy has always remained relatively weak (Kersbergen). In short, Christian democratic parties have traditionally tended to be state-oriented parties, sharing common ground with the social democrats in their opposition to neoliberal, libertarian, and individualistic policies. Apart from some of the smaller Protestant parties, these Christian parties have also been among the strongest advocates of European integration. (On Christian democracy, see Kalyvas; Gehlen and Kaiser; Hecke and Gerard.)

The Conservatives

Across western Europe in general, conservative parties have begun to poll almost as big a share of the votes as the Christian democrats. Indeed, if we exclude the small island state of Malta, where the Christian democrats are closely akin to a conservative party, the conservatives now poll more votes than the Christian democrats. This is not so much due to the conservatives' own success—they have stayed remarkably steady at an average of just over 15 percent in the 1950s and in 2000–4—but because their overall vote held firm while that of the Christian democrats sometimes came close to free-fall. For example, the Christian democrats polled half again as much as the conservatives in the 1950s, but the gap narrowed to less than 2 percent by 2000–4. Conservative parties also poll particularly well in Greece and Spain, where they constitute the principal opposition to the social democrats. Across all twenty democracies, the Conservatives now poll an average of more than 18 percent of the vote, substantially more than the Christian democrats. What is most striking about the conservative vote is that even this high level of average support is depressed by the fact that conservative parties do not compete in a number of countries. Where they do exist, conservative parties often do very well, winning around 40 percent in France, Iceland, Ireland, the UK, Greece, and Spain (Table 8.6).

As in liberal and Christian families, there are several strands within conservatism in western Europe. One increasingly important strand includes what we might think of as "national" parties, which marry a conservative socioeconomic appeal with an emphasis on the pursuit of the national interest. This strand includes the Independence Party in Iceland, Fianna Fáil in Ireland, the French Gaullists, the British Conservatives, and the Cypriot Democratic Coalition. All five parties, which also tend to be the most successful in the family, stress the importance of national shibboleths, and all decry the "antinational" character of sectional or class politics. This strand also includes some strong Euroskeptic elements, particularly in France and Britain, while in Fianna Fáil the attitude toward Europe is one of pragmatic support. Forza Italia in Italy can also be considered to belong to this "national" group, as might many of the major center–right parties in postcommunist Europe, where conservatives have emerged as one of the major political alternatives (see below). A second distinctive strand within European conservatism is made up of traditional conservative parties in Denmark, Finland, Norway, and Sweden. These are characterized by a more moderate opposition to state intervention, married to a commitment to a consensual approach to policy making. The development of these parties has also been constrained by their relatively limited support. Unlike their larger counterparts in the UK, France, and Ireland, these parties have almost always had to govern in coalition and have had to fight for dominance on the center–right.

Although the conservatives are more clearly on the right than are the Christian democrats, the two families can in many ways be viewed as functional equivalents. Both represent the major alternative to the appeal of social democracy, and, what is more telling, the two families rarely flourish within the same party system. Where secular conservatism is strong, Christian democracy tends to be weak or nonexistent (in the Scandinavian countries, Cyprus, the United Kingdom, Greece, and Spain). Where Christian

TABLE 8.6

Mean Electoral Support for Conservative Parties, 1950–2004

Country	1950s	1960s	1970s	1980s	1990s	2000–4
Austria	—	—	—	—	—	—
Belgium	—	—	—	—	—	—
Denmark	18.4	21.3	10.5	19.5	13.3	9.1
Finland	14.2	14.2	19.6	22.9	19.5	18.5
France[a]	44.2	55.6	50.3	42.7	39.7	45.0
Germany	—	—	—	—	—	—
Iceland	41.3	39.5	36.8	38.4	38.8	33.7
Ireland	46.0	45.7	49.1	45.9	39.2	41.5
Italy	—	—	—	—	13.9	29.4
Luxembourg	—	—	—	—	—	—
Malta	—	—	—	—	—	—
Netherlands	—	—	—	—	—	—
Norway	18.7	20.2	20.9	28.1	15.7	21.2
Sweden	17.0	14.4	15.4	21.1	22.3	15.3
Switzerland	—	—	—	—	1.2	1.3
United Kingdom	47.6	42.7	41.0	42.2	36.3	31.7
Mean (N = 16)	**15.4**	**15.8**	**15.2**	**16.3**	**15.0**	**15.4**
Cyprus				32.8	35.2	39.2
Greece				41.8	44.0	44.1
Portugal				—	—	—
Spain				25.9	33.3	41.1
Overall mean (N = 20)				**17.5**	**16.9**	**18.5**

Note: Since Greece, Portugal, and Spain did not become fully democratic until the mid-1970s, decade averages are reported only for the 1980s and 1990s. Cyprus is also included from the 1980s only. In the 1960s and 1970s elections were infrequent in Cyprus, and the different Greek Cypriot parties sometimes formed a broad national front.

[a] Since the mid-1970s, the UDF alliance, which is treated here as a conservative party, has brought together under one umbrella Christian democrats, conservatives, and liberals.

democracy is strong, secular conservatism tends to be weak or nonexistent (in Austria, Belgium, Germany, Malta, and the Netherlands). In Italy, it is precisely the conservative Forza Italia that has been attempting to take the place of the once powerful but now shattered Christian democrats.

The policy priorities of the conservative family are quite distinctive. Although they share some degree of commitment to welfarism with all other European party families, welfarism ranks lower in conservative party programs than in the programs of many other parties on the right. Rather, conservative parties emphasize the need to support private enterprise and to encourage fiscal austerity. They also emphasize government efficiency, as well as law and order. Moreover, in many countries they stress the importance of traditional national values, combining economic liberalism with sometimes heavy-handed social interventionism. The conservative version of the strong state is therefore one that confines itself to questions of defense, national security, and law and order but leaves the running of the economy to the market. (On conservative parties in general, see Girvin.)

The Liberals

Electoral support for liberal parties in western Europe increased in the postwar period and since the 1990s stands at an average of just over 10 percent of the total vote. The liberal presence is also pervasive. The small island states of Iceland and Malta are the only established European democracies that do not have a relevant liberal party, whereas liberal parties, broadly defined, are strong in Cyprus and Portugal. Ireland has also witnessed the emergence of a liberal party in the 1980s, the Progressive Democrats. This party polled more than 11 percent of the vote in its first electoral outing in 1987, and although its vote declined thereafter, the party has succeeded in entering government coalitions with Fianna Fáil. The fact that Ireland did not have a liberal presence before the late 1980s suggests an intriguing but probably spurious relationship between small island polities, on the one hand—Iceland, Ireland, Malta—and a rejection of liberalism, on the other! Cyprus would present a problem here, however, because the liberals poll quite a substantial vote. Finally, although a strong liberal tradition exists in France, the present liberal tendency has been largely subsumed within the loose, wide-ranging alliance of the Union for French Democracy (UDF) and is now even more diluted within the new center–right alliance, the Union for a Popular Majority (UMP).

As Table 8.7 shows, despite the fact that liberal parties are present in almost all European countries, there is substantial variation in liberal strength. During the 1990s, for example, the liberals won an average of more than 20 percent of the vote in Belgium, Luxembourg, the Netherlands, and Switzerland—all of which belong to the well-known group of consociational democracies (Lijphart; Luther and Deschouwer). The Dutch figure is truly striking, for although it now encompasses two parties, the left-leaning Democrats 66 and the more conservative Liberal Party, there was an almost fourfold growth: from just less than 10 percent in the 1950s to almost 35 percent in the 1990s. That said, the both parties suffered badly in the wake of the rise of the populist Pim Fortuyn List, falling back to an average of 21 percent in the two most recent elections. Liberals also poll reasonably well in the UK, averaging more than 17 percent in the 1990s and winning a record 52 seats in the House of Commons in 2001.

Elsewhere, liberals are quite marginal in electoral terms, failing to come even close to double figures in all other countries where they compete. The exception is Portugal, where the liberals have become the main opposition to the social democrats, and where they have risen to an average of some 40 percent of the vote. Yet even in countries where liberal support falls below 10 percent, the parties concerned often exert a political influence far exceeding that suggested by their low legislative weight. Their position, which is sometimes close to the center of the party system, allows them to take on a crucial role as junior partners in coalition governments of the center–right as well as the center–left (Keman). Indeed, liberal parties are governing parties par excellence. Ironically, in the United Kingdom, where the liberal tally has at times exceeded the liberal vote in almost every other European country, liberal parties never won office in the postwar period, although they have formed coalitions with Labour in the regional parliaments of Scotland and Wales.

TABLE 8.7

Mean Electoral Support for Liberal Parties, 1950–2004

Country	1950s	1960s	1970s	1980s	1990s	2000–4
Austria[a]	8.4	6.2	5.6	7.4	5.0	1.0
Belgium	11.5	18.3	15.4	21.1	22.6	26.8
Denmark	8.1	9.3	8.3	5.6	4.0	7.0
Finland	7.1	9.7	5.4	0.9	1.7	—
France[b]	—	—	—	—	—	—
Germany	8.6	9.4	8.2	8.9	8.0	7.4
Iceland	—	—	—	—	1.8	7.4
Ireland	—	—	—	3.5	4.7	4.0
Italy	4.8	8.1	5.4	6.9	5.8	23.0
Luxembourg	12.6	13.6	21.8	17.5	20.7	16.1
Malta	—	—	—	—	—	—
Netherlands	9.9	12.8	19.7	25.5	34.6	21.3
Norway	9.8	9.5	5.8	3.4	4.1	3.9
Sweden	22.1	16.3	11.8	10.8	7.0	13.4
Switzerland	31.4	32.9	31.1	30.1	24.8	20.0
United Kingdom[c]	5.1	9.9	14.7	23.9	17.3	18.3
Mean (N = 16)	**8.7**	**9.8**	**9.6**	**10.3**	**10.1**	**10.7**
Cyprus				23.6	20.6	17.4
Greece				—	—	—
Portugal				27.3	39.4	40.2
Spain				4.6	3.2	—
Overall mean (N = 20)				**11.1**	**11.3**	**11.4**

Note: Since Greece, Portugal, and Spain did not become fully democratic until the mid-1970s, decade averages are reported only for the 1980s and 1990s. Cyprus is also included from the 1980s only. In the 1960s and 1970s elections were infrequent in Cyprus, and the different Greek Cypriot parties sometimes formed a broad national front.

[a] The Austrian Freedom Party is considered as a liberal party through to the end of the 1980s, and as a far right party since the 1990s.

[b] Since the mid-1970s, the liberal forces in France, together with conservatives and Christian democrats, have contested elections as part of the UDF alliance; as such, their electoral support has been grouped together with that of the conservatives.

[c] Includes Liberal–SDP alliance in the 1980s.

The liberal political family is often seen as a "center" group in western European politics, but in practice liberal parties represent a diverse range of ideological concerns. Historically, they have been associated with the impulse to extend the franchise, to promote individual rights, and to resist clerical influences in political life (as a leader in the newsweekly *The Economist* emphasized immediately after the reelection of George W. Bush—see the issue of November 6, 2004, p. 14). Prior to the emergence of social democracy, liberal parties thus constituted the first real opposition to conservatism and the right. Some of these concerns have survived and are more or less common to all European liberal parties—an emphasis on individual rights and a residual (though increasingly less relevant) anticlericalism. Over time, however, other liberal concerns have mutated, and two clear strands of European liberalism can now be identified.

Within the first strand, an emphasis on individual rights has led to a concern for fiscal rectitude and opposition to all but minimal state intervention in the economy. This right-wing strand of liberalism has been particularly important in Austria, where the Freedom Party used to be regarded as the most rightwing of European liberal parties but is now better grouped with the far right (see below). The right-wing strand is also important in Belgium, Germany, Italy, Luxembourg, the Netherlands, and Switzerland, and this is the position toward which the Progressive Democrats in Ireland have gravitated. Thus, this brand of liberalism has tended to emerge in countries that are also characterized by strong Christian democratic parties and hence where the anticlerical component of liberalism was once important. Indeed, anticlericalism in these countries has two distinct forms, being represented on the left by socialist or communist parties and on the right by secular liberal parties.

The second strand of European liberalism reflects a more centrist, if not left-leaning, position in which a concern for individual rights and progressive politics has engendered an emphasis on social justice and egalitarianism. This strand has tended to emerge in countries where the main right-wing group is a conservative party that has taken over the more anti-interventionist liberal tendency and where the anticlerical component in liberalism has proved less relevant. This strand is evident in Denmark, Norway, and Britain and is also represented by Democrats 66 in the Netherlands. Sweden can also be regarded as belonging to this group, although the party there made a sharp rightward turn in the 2002 election.

Above all, European liberal parties have demonstrated a strong appetite for participation in government, and the policies implied by the different ideological strands of liberalism have not been allowed to get in the way of it. In Belgium and Luxembourg, for example, governments tend for a long time to alternate between coalitions of the center–left (Christians and social democrats) and of the center–right (Christians and liberals). In Germany, in contrast, notwithstanding their philosophy, the liberals have played the role of center parties in government formation negotiations, switching support from time to time between social democrats and Christian democrats. In Scandinavia, yet another pattern is apparent: The dominance of the social democrats encourages liberals, as well as agrarian or center parties, to join forces with the other bourgeois parties to construct a "broad-right" antisocialist coalition. In each case, however, the liberals are regular participants in the politics of government formation.

The presence of two major strands of liberal ideology and the diversity of liberal party strategies suggest that any overall depiction of liberal party policy concerns may be misleading. Although the more left-leaning British, Danish, and Norwegian liberals traditionally placed a major emphasis on the need for a controlled economy, this emphasis was largely absent from the programs of the Austrian, Dutch, and Italian liberals. In common with most other parties, however, all liberal parties share a commitment to welfarism, and, in common with the left and the agrarian parties, they also stress the need for environmental protection.

What can also be taken as reasonably characteristic of all liberal parties is an emphasis on freedom, democracy, decentralization, and social justice, reflecting a continuing and pervasive concern for individual rights and freedoms, as well as a reluctance to tolerate more authoritarian styles of governing. In a curious way, therefore, liberal parties now reflect a set of political appeals that echo elements of both the new left and the traditional right. This may well stem from the shared contemporary orientation of all three groups toward an essentially middle-class electoral constituency. (On liberal parties in general, see Kirchner.)

The Agrarian or Center parties

As can be seen from Table 8.8, although agrarian parties do not exist at all in many west European countries, where they do exist, they tend to be quite large. Agrarian parties have sometimes contested elections in both Ireland and the Netherlands, but they are essentially a Scandinavian phenomenon with a strong presence in Denmark, Finland, Iceland, Norway, and Sweden. Outside the Nordic area, an agrarian party persists only in Switzerland. Even so, the Swiss "agrarian" party is actually an alliance between a peasant party and two quite different parties and is only marginally compatible with other

TABLE 8.8

Mean Electoral Support for Agrarian/Center Parties, 1950–2004

Country	1950s	1960s	1970s	1980s	1990s	2000–4
Austria	—	—	—	—	—	—
Belgium	—	—	—	—	—	—
Denmark	22.9	20.0	15.1	11.4	21.0	31.2
Finland	23.6	23.7	24.1	25.2	24.6	26.3
France	—	—	—	—	—	—
Germany	—	—	—	—	—	—
Iceland	22.6	28.2	23.0	20.0	20.2	17.7
Ireland	2.8	0.5	—	—	—	—
Italy	—	—	—	—	—	—
Luxembourg	—	—	—	—	—	—
Malta	—	—	—	—	—	—
Netherlands	—	3.5	1.3	—	—	—
Norway	9.5	9.9	9.8	6.6	12.3	5.6
Sweden	11.0	14.2	21.8	12.2	7.0	6.2
Switzerland	12.1	11.2	10.8	11.1	16.5	26.7
United Kingdom	—	—	—	—	—	—
Mean ($N = 16$)	**6.6**	**6.9**	**6.7**	**5.4**	**6.4**	**7.1**
Cyprus				—	—	—
Greece				—	—	—
Portugal				—	—	—
Spain				—	—	—
Overall mean ($N = 20$)				**4.3**	**5.1**	**5.7**

Note: Since Greece, Portugal, and Spain did not become fully democratic until the mid-1970s, decade averages are reported only for the 1980s and 1990s. Cyprus is also included from the 1980s only. In the 1960s and 1970s elections were infrequent in Cyprus, and the different Greek Cypriot parties sometimes formed a broad national front.

members of the agrarian political family. Indeed, some observers now categorize the Swiss party as belonging to the far right, particularly since the emergence to prominence of its outspoken leader, Christoph Blocher. Outside western Europe, in turn, agrarian parties now compete in elections in a number of postcommunist democracies, but even there they are now less popular than before (see below).

As their name suggests, agrarian parties were primarily special-interest parties. They were initially mobilized in the late nineteenth and early twentieth centuries to represent the specific concerns of farmers and the agricultural sector. With the economic and demographic decline in this sector over time, agrarian parties have attempted to extend their appeal to middle-class urban voters. This shift was most clearly signaled by a change of name to Center Party in Finland, Norway, and Sweden (in 1965, 1959, and 1957, respectively). The strategy proved at least temporarily successful in Sweden, where support for the party grew to almost 22 percent of the vote in the 1970s, and, most recently, to more than 30 percent in Denmark.

One result of this process of adaptation is a curious amalgam of agrarian party policy concerns. Despite their move away from a distinctively rural base, agrarian parties continue to stress the interests of agriculture and farmers and are the only party family to do so. Two other emphases also reflect their particular heritage, one on decentralization, which harks back to their essentially peripheral roots, and the other on a form of environmental protection that, in its anti-industrial bias, is also characteristic of such parties. At the same time, however, agrarian parties also emphasize welfare provision, social justice, and the need for a controlled economy, which suggests a leftist orientation; and they favor both private enterprise and the maintenance of traditional moral values, which suggests quite a conservative impulse.

Although this mix of policy concerns allows agrarian parties to appeal to both right and left, their earlier positions in Scandinavian party systems suggested a reasonably close alignment with the social democrats. In both Norway and Sweden in the 1930s, for example, some of the most important welfare legislation was passed by social democratic governments supported by agrarian parties—a powerful if now old-fashioned version of a "Red–Green" alliance that helped lay the basis for the present advanced welfare states in these countries.

Nowadays, however, agrarian or center parties attempt to play the role of genuine center parties, bridging the gap between the social democrats and a fragmented bourgeois opposition. In this sense they can now be difficult to distinguish from more orthodox liberal parties (see above), especially when, as in Denmark, there is even confusion about the names used by the parties (the name in English of the Danish liberal party is the Social Liberals, whereas the agrarian/center party is known simply as the Liberals). Indeed, the similarities among these groups are highlighted by the fact that the strongest agrarian parties have emerged in systems where liberalism is weak (the Scandinavian countries) whereas the strongest liberal parties tend to be found in countries where there is no agrarian presence (see also Steed and Humphreys).

In general, however, agrarian parties can be regarded as having drifted from the left toward the right over time. This is particularly so in Switzerland. On the infrequent occasions when they win government office, they now tend to be the moderate allies of bourgeois coalition partners. (On the emergence and development of agrarian parties, see Arter; Urwin.)

The Far Right

The most striking development in the politics of the center–right during recent decades has been the growth of parties of the far right. Indeed, whereas such parties were to be found only in Italy, France, and marginally in Germany in the 1950s, they now compete more or less seriously in Austria, Belgium, Denmark, France, Italy, the Netherlands, Norway, and Switzerland. As yet, they have not begun to compete in a significant way in Cyprus, Iceland, Ireland, Malta, or the United Kingdom, and they also are not present in Greece, Portugal, or Spain, although in many of these countries, far-right elements exist as factions within conservative and liberal parties. Though small in European terms, they tripled their vote in the last decades, rising from an average of just over 2 percent in the 1980s to more than 6 percent in the 1990s (see Table 8.9), when they also outpolled the Greens. Though falling back since then in some cases, most notably

TABLE 8.9

Mean Electoral Support for Far-Right/Populist Parties, 1950–2004

Country	1950s	1960s	1970s	1980s	1990s	2000–4
Austria[a]	—	—	—	—	22.0	10.0
Belgium	—	—	—	1.5	9.7	13.7
Denmark	—	—	11.0	6.6	7.5	12.9
Finland	—	—	—	—	0.3	—
France	4.3	—	—	6.7	14.2	11.1
Germany	1.1	2.1	—	0.3	2.5	0.6
Iceland	—	—	—	—	—	—
Ireland	—	—	—	—	—	—
Italy	11.1	6.3	6.7	6.6	20.9	16.3
Luxembourg	—	—	—	1.2	1.2	—
Malta	—	—	—	—	—	—
Netherlands	—	—	—	0.6	1.8	11.4
Norway	—	—	3.5	7.1	10.8	14.2
Sweden	—	—	—	—	2.6	1.4
Switzerland	—	—	4.8	4.3	7.6	1.0
United Kingdom	—	—	—	—	—	—
Mean (N = 16)	**1.0**	**0.5**	**1.6**	**2.2**	**6.3**	**5.8**
Cyprus				—	—	—
Greece				—	—	1.1
Portugal				—	—	—
Spain				—	—	—
Overall mean (N = 20)				**1.8**	**5.0**	**4.7**

Note: Since Greece, Portugal, and Spain did not become fully democratic until the mid-1970s, decade averages are reported only for the 1980s and 1990s. Cyprus is also included from the 1980s only. In the 1960s and 1970s elections were infrequent in Cyprus, and the different Greek Cypriot parties sometimes formed a broad national front.

[a] The Austrian Freedom Party is classified as far right in the 1990s.

Austria, they have built significant new support in Denmark and the Netherlands. Far-right parties were also elected to two of the Land parliaments in the former East Germany in 2004.

The principal protagonists on the far right include the National Front in France, the National Alliance and the Northern League in Italy, the Freedom Party in Austria, and the Flemish Block in Belgium. In addition, their ranks have been swelled by the Progress Parties in Denmark and Norway, and also in Denmark, albeit more recently, by the Danish People's Party, which won more than 12 percent of the vote in 2001. The Progress Parties began as tax-protest parties but have since settled down quite firmly on the far right of the political spectrum. Although parties such as the German People's Union are not yet significantly relevant actors at the national level, a historical legacy and sporadic successes at the regional and local levels suggest that they might also not be discounted.

By and large, parties of the far right are small parties, although in Austria, Belgium, France, and Italy they have proved sufficiently popular to have had a major impact on the direction and pattern of party competition at the national level. In the wake of the collapse of the center in Italian politics, the former Italian Social Movement (MSI), which was reconstituted as the National Alliance, suddenly polled exceptionally well in the 1994 elections, as did the Northern League, which in many ways is similar in outlook to the Austrian Freedom Party. Both parties then entered government with Forza Italia in 1994 and again in 2001. Since then, however, they have moderated, and whether they should be classified as members of the far-right group or as conservatives is open to question (Ignazi, pp. 35–61).

Some of these parties, including the French National Front and the Belgian Vlaams Blok are extremely right-wing and highly xenophobic; some also claim to be heirs to the fascist and antisystem right-wing movements that rose to prominence in interwar Europe. In November 2004, for example, the Vlaams Blok was banned by the Belgian Supreme Court on the grounds that it incited racism. This was the culmination of a three-year lawsuit and, perhaps ironically, came just at the moment when the party itself was adopting a more moderate-sounding program. The ban has little real impact, however, in that the party has simply reconstituted itself under a new name, Vlaams Belang (Flemish Interest).

At least two appeals characterize the new far-right parties and have acquired particular force in recent years. First, almost without exception, they mobilize against immigration and against policies that are seen to promote multiculturalism. They are nationalist parties in the main, sometimes extremely so, and they have also served as a focus for the more strident opposition to European integration. Second, as "outsider" parties, they mobilize against the political establishment and what they see as the self-serving character of the political class. In this they have been bolstered by the increased allegations of political corruption that are now current in many of the west European polities (Heywood), as well as by the more generalized disillusion, indifference, and sometimes even antiparty sentiment that characterizes many European voters (Mudde, "Populist"). The latter protest is often self-sustaining. Because these parties are so extreme, there is a reluctance among the established parties to consider them as suitable coalition allies. And as long as they remain excluded from processes of government formation, they can continue to assert a populist—and often popular—antiestablishment appeal. This is certainly a large part of the reason why Jörg Haider's Freedom Party proved so successful in the Austrian elections of the 1990s. Once it was admitted to government in 2000, however, its support began to fall. The same was true of the Pim Fortuyn List in the Netherlands, even though Fortuyn himself rejected the far-right label and identified more closely with politicians such as Berlusconi rather than with Haider or Le Pen. As Heinisch has argued, although these new right-wing populist parties may be successful in opposition, they can fail in government.

More generally, the relative electoral success of these new parties can also be linked to the growth of Green and left–libertarian protest on the left of the political spectrum. Ignazi, for example, has suggested that the rise of the extreme right in recent years may reflect the other side of the "new politics" divide, in which the growing support for new left and Green parties is now being counterbalanced by a shift toward a new right—the one side representing the interests of those who have found themselves benefiting from postindustrialism, the other representing the interests of those who are being left behind (see also Müller-Rommel). In both France and Austria, for example, it is striking to see the extent to which these new parties of the right have made inroads into some of the traditional working-class constituencies of the social democratic and communist left. (On the far right in general, see Betz; Betz and Immerfall; Hainsworth: Ignazi; Mudde, *Ideology;* Taggart.)

✦ OTHER PARTIES

Although most European countries are presented as being nation states in which the boundaries of nation and state coincide, many incorporate important local minorities of distinct national, linguistic, and ethnic groups. These groups are often represented by parties that have their basis in local ethnic or regional identities, with demands that range from greater regional autonomy to full-fledged separatism. These parties, though linked to one another by their strong regional or ethnic concerns, vary immensely in their other policy positions and in their general positioning on the left–right scale.

Regional or ethnic parties can be found in one form or another in almost all western European states, as well as in a number of postcommunist states. But despite what are often quite high levels of electoral support in local power bases, these parties are relevant at the national level in only a handful of countries. Belgium, given its deep ethnic and linguistic divisions, provides the most striking examples, including various Flemish (Dutch-speaking) and Walloon (French-speaking) regional parties. Indeed, given that even all the mainstream Belgian parties have separate Flemish and Walloon organizations, and given that the Walloon organizations do not compete for Flemish votes, and vice versa, it is now almost impossible to speak of a single Belgian party system at the electoral level.

Also of some significance have been the Swedish People's Party, the political voice of the Swedish-speaking minority in Finland and a regular participant in Finnish coalition governments; the nationalist Sinn Féin Party, which offers political support to the Irish Republican Army and mobilizes both in the Irish Republic and, within the United Kingdom, in Northern Ireland; various Basque separatist parties in northern Spain, including Herri Batasuna, which supports the armed struggle of Basque paramilitary organizations and was banned by the Spanish Supreme Court in 2003; and, in the United Kingdom, the Scottish and Welsh nationalists, together with constitutional nationalists and unionists in Northern Ireland. The UK has also recently witnessed the emergence of the UK Independence Party (UKIP), which polled particularly well in the elections to the European Parliament in 2004 but has yet to make any impact on elections to Westminster. In Belgium, the Vlaams Blok (now Vlaams Belang), which we group under the far right, is a strong advocate of Flemish independence.

In general, the strongest support for these parties within the west European area is to be found in Belgium, Spain, and the United Kingdom. Although these parties remain a tiny electoral minority within most of western Europe, it is important to remember that these movements do command substantial support in their local areas. Roughly two Basque voters in three support Basque nationalist parties, for example. In Northern Ireland nearly all of the vote is won by nationalist or regional (including unionist) parties. Indeed, none of the mainland British parties is even willing to nominate candidates for elections in the province, and when the British Conservative Party tested the waters in Northern Ireland in a by-election back in 1990 it was utterly trounced by local parties. (On ethnic, nationalist, and regionalist parties in general, see Rokkan and Urwin; De Winter and Tursan.)

There are also additional parties that compete in European elections but defy simple categorization in terms of party families. These include a number of small Danish parties, including the long-standing Justice Party. Pensioners' parties have occasionally competed in Finland, Italy, Luxembourg, and the Netherlands (as well as in postcommunist Slovenia, where the pensioners' party DeSUS polled 4 percent of the vote in 2004). Europe's first "anti-Green" party, the aptly named Automobile Party, was founded in Switzerland in 1985. It is also important to note that independent candidates and loose, ill-defined alliances can from time to time be significant in a variety of countries—most notably in France, Ireland, and the United Kingdom, where electoral systems place few obstacles in the way of independent candidacies.

It is in Portugal and Spain, however, where "other" parties have been most important—at least in the early years of their democracies. As these new party systems emerged in the wake of the transition to democracy in the late 1970s, a number of temporary and shifting alliances appeared, often involving protagonists who shared little other than a desire to ensure the consolidation of democratic practices. These alliances were oriented toward particular domestic problems of democratic transition and consolidation, bearing little relationship to the interests and programs of parties in the established democracies. In Portugal, for example, a group known as the Democratic Alliance polled more than 48 percent of the vote in 1980 and then fell apart into various factions and units. Two elections later, in 1985, the Democratic Renewal Party was created; it won more than 18 percent of the vote before falling back to 5 percent in 1987. The number and size of these loose electoral alliances in 1980s Portugal and, to a lesser extent, Spain offered an ample indication of the difficulties involved in consolidating a new party system, a problem that has also proved very apparent in the newly emerging postcommunist party systems. Indeed, it is because so many of the new democratic parties in postcommunist Europe are short-lived and merging and dividing, and because so many defy easy categorization within the familiar western party families, that we treat them separately here.

✦ Party Families in Postcommunist Europe

We still have to be very cautious about predicting the future shape of the parties and the party systems in the new postcommunist democracies. Nevertheless, some common threads can already be picked out regarding the types of parties that have developed and the sorts of families they belong to (Berglund et al.; Lawson). Five are particularly important.

First, there are the new parties that emerged in opposition to the former regime and at the same time reflected broad-based alliances containing diverse strands of ideological and partisan opinion. Examples include the former Solidarity opposition in Poland, the Popular Front in Latvia, the Civic Forum in the Czech Republic, and People Against Violence in Slovakia. These alliances often broke up soon after the transition to democracy and split into various conservative, liberal, or even nationalist groupings. Second, there are the new parties that also emerged in opposition to the old regime but from the beginning were already characterized by a more distinctive political ideology, such as the Democratic Forum (HDF) or Alliance of Free Democrats (AFD) in Hungary, or the Confederation for an Independent Poland. With time, however, the distinction between this and the first category has become blurred as a result of the disintegration of the broad anticommunist fronts. Third, there are the successors of the former ruling communists themselves, which have since reformed and reconstituted themselves as parties that claim to support the new democratic systems but continue to favor state intervention and argue against the wholesale introduction of liberal market policies, such as the Polish Democratic Left Alliance (SLD), or the Hungarian Socialist Party (MSzP). Fourth, there are the old "satellite" parties that once formed part of the former communist political leadership, such as the Polish Peasant Party (PSL), which seek to restore an independent electoral credibility. Fifth, there are also the historic precommunist parties, such as the Latvian Social Democratic and Farmers' Parties, or the Hungarian Smallholders' Party, many of which reemerged after 1989 in the hope of capitalizing on their earlier legitimacy. To these might also be added some of the small Christian democratic parties that also trace their roots back to the interwar years.

Despite such common threads, however, there is clearly no uniform pattern, and the precise shape of each individual system has been at least partially determined by the specific legacy of the precommunist regime, on the one hand, as well as by the particular way in which the postcommunist transition proceeded, on the other. In Poland, as in the Czech and Slovak Republics, for example, the regime was attacked from the ground, and the transition involved the mobilization of a broadly based opposition movement that was later to fragment into a variety of different political parties in the wake of the first democratic elections. In Hungary, in contrast, where the regime had begun to reform itself in the mid-1980s, different parties began to emerge and to compete with one another well before the first elections, and an embryonic multiparty system was already in place before the communist regime actually collapsed. In Latvia and the other Baltic states, the struggle against communism was also a struggle for national independence, and the dominant forces in the new democracies were nationalist in character. In these states also there existed the specific problem of an ethnic Russian minority, and hence issues relating to ethnicity and citizenship rights figured high on the new political agenda.

All of these national experiences, as well as the more or less enormous burden of reconstruction shouldered by each of the polities, inevitably led to a set of political oppositions that was without real parallel in western Europe. This, at least, is one way of looking at the issue. Dealing with Russian, Roma, or irredentist minorities, for example, is not something that has figured very strongly in the recent experiences of western political leaders. Converting an outdated, bureaucratic, and state-controlled economy into a late-twentieth-century market economy is also not a problem that has been faced in the west—except in the eastern part of Germany, of course, where unification of west and east had not yet had the effect of pulling the east up to the living standards of the west. Nor have the present batch of western leaders ever been obliged to engineer a democratic constitution more or less from scratch or to build a competitive party system. In contemporary western Europe, democracy has been inherited. In postcommunist Europe, it has had to be constructed. As one central European political leader recently remarked, "It must be so boring being prime minister of a country like Denmark. We do more reform in a single session of parliament than they do in five years" (*The Economist,* November 6, 2004, p. 42). It is then hardly surprising that political alignments should look different once we go beyond the west, or that they should sometimes prove more challenging.

But there is also another side to the story (Lewis; Chan). Even when political institutions and party systems are constructed from scratch, it is often with one eye on the experiences of more seasoned models. Lessons have been learned from the west, and existing party models, and even current issue positions, have sometimes been absorbed by the new polities. In addition, regardless of the location of the polity or its level of institutional development, some key problems are of pan-European concern and hence prompt the emergence of similar political coalitions and alignments—issues relating to the reorganization of welfare states, for example (Kovács), or those relating to the positions to be adopted in the new international order. The development of comparable political profiles has also been fostered by the enlargement of the European Union, forcing adaptation to the common *aquis,* on the one hand, and bringing many of the new postcommunist parties into transnational and specifically European party federations, on the other. In other words, even when the postcommunist path to party politics has been forged by national and systemic peculiarities, it is often standardized by the need for the new actors to forge links with like-minded forces throughout the enlarged European Union (Zielonka and Pravda).

In sum, although substantial differences exist between the development of west European party systems and the development of postcommunist party systems, and although it is therefore not always easy to detect family resemblances between the two groups of countries, some links can nevertheless be established. Christian democratic parties can be found in each of the two groupings, for example, even though this family still has a more powerful hold among the west European polities. Conversely, conservative parties prove to be stronger in the postcommunist world, even though in this case they are concerned more with reforming than with conserving, as such. In many cases, these parties grew out of the popular coalitions and citizens' movements that initially challenged the communist regimes, and hence they reflect the sort of radical and protest-based traditions that, in the west at least, are normally associated with the left. In this sense it is the socialist, or ex-communist parties that might be seen as the real conservatives of postcommunist Europe—parties that once held a monopoly of political power and that now, as democrats, seek to slow down the speed of liberal reform. With the exception of the (East) German PDS, these parties have no equivalent in the west, of course. Their social democratic counterparts in the west come from a wholly different political tradition, and their fading ex-communist counterparts were never regime parties. In some cases, however, such as in the Czech Republic or Lithuania, there are now major social democratic parties that do share common roots with the social democratic parties in the west and trace their identity back to the precommunist interwar years. In this sense we can speak of two distinct socialist party families in postcommunist Europe—the ex-communists, who are strongest in Hungary and Poland and appear to have a growing appeal in the Czech Republic, and the more conventional Social Democrats.

The different levels of support for the various families in the different postcommunist countries are summarized in Table 8.10 and are based simply on the first elections of the twenty-first century rather than on any longer run of contests. Given the lack of continuity of many party organizations in postcommunist Europe, as well as the formation and collapse of so many short-term electoral alliances, it is as yet almost impossible to trace meaningful long-term patterns. For purposes of comparison, however, Table 8.10 also reports the breakdown by party family of the recent election results from the west European polities.

As can be seen from the table, a number of party families can be identified in reasonably familiar western terms. There is a small set of Green parties, for example, with a presence in both the Czech Republic and Latvia, although in the latter case the party forms part of an electoral alliance with the agrarian party. There are also the agrarian parties themselves, which are more pervasive than their western counterparts but now win relatively little support. Indeed, this is one of the surprises of postcommunist party development, for it had been widely anticipated that farmers' parties would do particularly well after the transition to democracy. However, as Mudde, ("In the Name," p. 229) notes, "Today, farmers in the region are 'rural workers' rather than 'peasants,' and they give their support to (former) Communist parties rather than populist peasant parties." Another group that is common to the west is that of the far-right populist parties, but here too levels of electoral support are proving less than anticipated. Indeed, across the eight postcommunist polities for which data are reported in Table 8.10, far-right populists poll on average less than in the western polities. Christian democrats also poll less than in the west, which is perhaps also surprising given that, especially in Poland, they formed a core part of the old opposition to the former communist regimes. However, the Christian element is often subsumed within ostensibly conservative parties, such as in the case of the Hungarian Democratic Forum (MDF).

So where does the postcommunist vote go? In the first place, and most obviously, it goes to the postcommunists themselves. In the first elections of the new century, former communist parties polled an average of more than 13 percent in the EU accession countries. This average figure is misleading, however, because the former communists have a presence only in east central Europe—the Czech Republic and Slovakia, Hungary and Poland, where they won an average of 27 percent of the vote—and win no support at all in the three Baltic states (on the different clusters of postcommunist states, see Berglund et al.). Second, and on a scale that is massively greater than in the west, the vote goes to liberal parties—center–right and reformist parties that are sometimes difficult to distinguish from the conservatives but have always been in the forefront of the struggle for democracy. These parties are particularly strong in Estonia and Lithuania and somewhat less so in Poland and Slovenia. Third, the vote sometimes goes to parties representing ethnic or regional minorities, such as the Russians in the Baltic states or the

TABLE 8.10

Electoral Support for Party Families in the New Europe

Country	Election Year	(Ex)Communist/ Socialist[a]	Social Democrat	New Left	Green	Liberal	Christian Democrat	Conservative	Agrarian	Populist/ Far Right	Ethnic/ Regional	Others/ Not Aligned
Postcommunist polities												
Czech Republic	2002	18.5	30.2	—	2.4	4.3	10.0	24.5	—	1.0	—	9.1
Estonia	2003	—	7.0	—	—	43.1	1.1	44.9	0.8	—	2.2	1.7
Hungary	2002	42.1	—	—	—	9.4	—	41.1	4.7	4.4	—	2.2
Latvia	2002	—	6.0	—	4.7	4.9	9.6	40.6	3.3	—	18.9	10.6
Lithuania	2004	—	20.7	—	—	40.8	3.4	14.6	9.0	—	3.8	13.4
Poland	2001	41.0	—	—	—	25.3	13.5	—	—	10.2	0.4	0.6
Slovakia	2002	6.3	16.7	—	—	8.0	23.4	35.9	—	7.0	11.2	27.4
Slovenia	2004	—	10.2	—	—	22.8	9.0	—	—	—	—	22.1
Mean (N = 8)		**13.5**	**11.4**	—	**0.9**	**19.8**	**8.8**	**25.2**	**2.2**	**2.8**	**4.6**	**10.9**
West European polities												
Austria	2002	0.6	36.5	0.1	9.5	1.0	42.3	—	—	10.0	—	0.1
Belgium	2003	—	27.9	—	5.5	26.8	19.1	—	—	13.7	3.5	1.9
Cyprus	2001	34.7	6.5	—	2.0	17.4	—	39.2	—	—	—	0.2
Denmark	2001	—	29.1	6.4	2.4	7.0	2.3	9.1	31.2	12.9	—	4.3
Finland	2003	9.9	22.9	—	8.0	—	5.3	18.5	26.3	—	4.8	4.0
France	2002	4.9	26.7	2.7	5.6	—	—	45.0[b]	—	11.1	—	0.8
Germany	2002	4.0	38.5	—	8.6	7.4	38.5	—	—	0.6	—	1.4
Greece	2000, 2004	5.7	42.2	5.5	—	—	—	44.1	—	1.1	—	1.4
Iceland	2003	—	31.0	—	8.8	7.4	—	33.7	17.7	—	—	—
Ireland	2002	—	10.8	0.8	3.9	4.0	22.5	41.5	—	—	6.5	0.7
Italy[c]	2001	6.7	17.6	1.9	2.2	23.0	3.2	29.4	—	16.3	0.9	10.0
Luxembourg	2004	0.9	23.4	1.9	11.6	16.1	36.1	—	—	—	—	10.0
Malta	2003	—	47.5	—	0.7	—	51.8	—	—	—	—	1.8
Netherlands	2002, 2003	—	21.2	6.1	6.1	21.3	32.2	—	—	11.4	—	4.7
Norway	2001	—	24.3	13.7	—	3.9	12.4	21.2	5.6	14.2	—	3.7
Portugal	2002	6.9	37.8	2.7	—	40.2	8.7	—	—	—	—	—
Spain	2000, 2004	5.5	38.4	—	—	—	—	41.1	—	—	10.5	4.5
Sweden	2002	8.4	39.9	—	4.6	13.4	9.1	15.3	6.2	1.4	—	1.7
Switzerland	2003	0.7	23.3	—	7.9	20.0	17.1	1.3	26.7	1.0	0.4	1.8
United Kingdom	2001	—	40.7	—	—	18.3	—	31.7	—	—	5.3	4.0
Mean (N = 20)		**4.4**	**29.3**	**2.0**	**4.4**	**11.4**	**14.0**	**18.5**	**5.7**	**4.7**	**1.6**	**2.9**
Overall mean (N = 28)		**7.0**	**24.2**	**1.4**	**3.4**	**13.8**	**12.5**	**20.5**	**4.7**	**4.1**	**2.5**	**5.2**

Party Family

[a] In postcommunist Europe, as well as in the case of the German PDS, this refers to the former regime parties.

[b] Conservative includes the UDF, a coalition of liberal, Christian, and conservative groupings.

[c] Proportional representation (PR) vote shares only.

Sources: Mackie and Rose, *European Journal of Political Research*; *West European Politics*; European Parliament, 2004; http://www.electionworld.org ("Elections Around the World"). Because these tables report results for party families, the average figures for each country sometimes refer to two or more parties within any one family.

Hungarians in Slovakia. Problems of this sort are much more pronounced than in the west and often reflect an incomplete or forced nation- and state-building process. Finally, of course, the vote also goes to parties that are impossible to classify in conventional terms, such as the various small and single-interest parties in Slovenia, or such as the Movement for a Democratic Slovakia–People's Party (HZDS), the idiosyncratic and somewhat authoritarian party that is led by Vladimir Meciar and has played a major role in Slovak politics since the fall of communism.

But even if this mode of classification allows most of the main parties to be grouped within one or another of the more or less conventional political families, any comparison of the postcommunist alignments with those of the west must be extremely tentative. Despite recent electoral flux, the main parties in western Europe are still organizationally stable and ideologically embedded. Social democratic parties are easily recognized as such and continue to have much in common with regard to their ideological profile and policy preferences. The same is true for most of the Catholic or Catholic-influenced Christian democratic parties and also even for many of the secular conservative parties. Moreover, these are often old parties, which contest election after election with the same organization and under the same label, and which manage to protect their identities even when entering coalitions or electoral alliances. In such a context, it is therefore still very meaningful to speak of party families. In postcommunist Europe, by contrast, the parties are fragmented and often short-lived. With each election we tend to see a host of new party labels of new electoral alliances. Between elections, we see constant splits and divisions within existing parties. The result is that while a crude profile of the distribution of support between party families can be established at any one point in time—in 2001–4 in Table 8.10—there is no guarantee that anything like this pattern will still be seen in five or ten years hence, particularly as far as the distribution of support on the center–right is concerned. Indeed, as Sitter (p. 447) has noted, it is the ongoing struggle to define the right that remains one of the most powerful forces driving multiparty competition in the new postcommunist systems.

In general, therefore, and despite exceptions on both sides, contemporary postcommunist party politics can be distinguished from western European party politics by virtue of its lack of institutionalization. As shall be seen in the next chapter, however, this distinction may yet fade away—not only because postcommunist systems will become more institutionalized but also because western systems themselves are likely to become less structured.

References

Arter, David: *From Farmyard to City Square? The Electoral Adaptation of the Nordic Agrarian Parties,* Ashgate, Adershot, 2001.

Bartolini, Stefano: *The Political Mobilization of the European Left, 1860–1980: The Class Cleavage,* Cambridge University Press, Cambridge, 2000.

Berglund, Sten, Joakim Ekman, and Frank H. Aarebrot (eds.): *The Handbook of Political Change in Eastern Europe,* 2nd ed., Edward Elgar, Cheltenham, 2004.

Betz, Hans-Georg: *Radical Right-Wing Populism in Western Europe,* St. Martin's Press, New York, 1994.

Betz, Hans-Georg, and Stefan Immerfall (eds.): *The New Politics of the Right: Neo-Populist Parties and Movements in Established Democracies,* St. Martin's Press, New York, 1998.

Bull, Martin J., and Paul Heywood (eds.): *West European Communist Parties After the Revolutions of 1989,* Macmillan, Basingstoke, 1994.

Burchell, Jon: *The Evolution of Green Politics: Development and Change Within European Green Parties,* Earthscan, London, 2002.

Chan, Kenneth Ka-Lok: "Political Ideologies in Post-Communist Europe: Consensus or Disunity?" *Central European Political Science Review,* vol. 4, no. 14, 2003, pp. 28–53.

Cuperus, René, and Johannes Kandel: *European Social Democracy: Transformation in Progress,* Friedrich Ebert Stiftung/Wiardi Beckman Stichting, Amsterdam, 1998.

Delwit, Pascale, and Jean-Michel de Waele (eds.): *Les Partis Verts en Europe.* Éditions Complese, Brussels, 1999.

De Winter, Lieven, and Huri Tursan (eds.): *Regionalist Parties in Western Europe,* Routledge, London, 1998.

Flora, Peter: "Introduction," in Peter Flora (ed.), *Growth to Limits: The West European Welfare States Since World War II,* vol. 1, *Sweden, Norway, Finland, Denmark,* de Gruyter, Berlin, 1986, pp. v–xxxvi.

Gehlen, Michael, and Wolfram Kaiser: *Christian Democracy in Europe Since 1945,* Cass, London, 2004.

Giddens, Anthony: *The Third Way: The Renewal of Social Democracy,* Polity Press, Cambridge, 1998.

Girvin, Brian (ed.): *The Transformation of Contemporary Conservatism,* Sage, Beverly Hills, 1988.

Hainsworth, Paul (ed.): *The Politics of the Extreme Right: From the Margins to the Mainstream,* Pinter, London, 2000.

Hecke, Steven van, and Emmanuel Gerard (eds.): *Christian Democratic Parties in Europe Since the End of the Cold War,* Leuven University Press, Leuven, 2004.

Heinisch, Reinhard: "Success in Opposition—Failure in Government: Explaining the Performance of Right-Wing Populist Parties in Public Office," *West European Politics,* vol. 26, no. 3, 2003, pp. 91–130.

Heywood, Paul: "Political Corruption: Problems and Perspectives," *Political Studies,* vol. 45, no. 3, 1997, pp. 417–35.

Hix, Simon, and Christopher Lord: *Political Parties in the European Union,* Macmillan, Basingstoke, 1997.

Ignazi, Piero: *Extreme Right Parties in Western Europe,* Oxford University Press, Oxford, 2004.

Kalyvas, Stathis N.: *The Rise of Christian Democracy in Europe,* Cornell University Press, Ithaca, 1996.

Keman, Hans: "The Search for the Centre: Pivot Parties in West European Party Systems," *West European Politics,* vol. 17, no. 4, 1994, pp. 124–148.

Kersbergen, Kees van: *Social Capitalism,* Routledge, London, 1995.

Kirchheimer, Otto: "The Transformation of the West European Party Systems," in Joseph LaPalombara and Myron Weiner (eds.), *Political Parties and Political Development,* Princeton University Press, Princeton, 1966, pp. 177–200.

Kirchner, Emil J. (ed.): *Liberal Parties in Western Europe,* Cambridge University Press, Cambridge, 1988.

Kitschelt, Herbert P.: "Left–Libertarian Parties: Explaining Innovation in Competitive Party Systems," *World Politics,* vol. 40, no. 2, 1988, pp. 194–234.

Kitschelt, Herbert P.: *The Transformation of European Social Democracy,* Cambridge University Press, Cambridge, 1994.

Kovács, János Mátyas: "Approaching the EU and Reaching the US? Rival Narratives on Transforming Welfare Regimes in East-Central Europe," *West European Politics,* vol. 25, no. 2, 2002, pp. 175–204.

Lawson, Kay: "Cleavages, Parties and Voters in Central Europe," *Central European Political Science Review,* vol. 4, no. 14, 2003, pp. 6–27.

Lewis, Paul G.: "Political Parties," in Stephen White, Judy Batt, and Paul G. Lewis (eds.), *Developments in Central and East European Politics 3,* Palgrave, London, 2003, pp. 153–72.

Lijphart, Arend: *Democracy in Plural Societies,* Yale University Press, New Haven, 1977.

Luther, Richard, and Kris Deschouwer (eds.): *Party Elites in Divided Societies: Political Parties in Consociational Democracy,* Routledge, London, 1999.

Mackie, Thomas T., and Richard Rose: *The International Almanac of Electoral History,* 3rd ed., Macmillan, Basingstoke, 1991.

Mair, Peter, and Cas Mudde: "The Party Family and Its Study," *Annual Review of Political Science,* vol. 1, 1998, pp. 211–29.

Michels, Robert: *Political Parties: A Sociological Study of the Oligarchical Tendencies of Modern Democracy,* Free Press, New York, 1962 [first published 1911].

Moschonas, Gerassimos: *In the Name of Social Democracy: The Great Transformation from 1945 to the Present,* Verso, London, 2002.

Mudde, Cas: *The Ideology of the Extreme Right,* Manchester University Press, Manchester, 2000.

Mudde, Cas: "In the Name of the Peasantry, the Proletariat, and the People: Populisms in Eastern Europe," in Yves Mény and Yves Surel (eds.), *Democracies and the Populist Challenge,* Palgrave, London, 2002, pp. 214–32.

Mudde, Cas: "The Populist Zeitgeist," *Government and Opposition,* vol. 39, no. 4, 2004, pp. 541–63.

Müller-Rommel, Ferdinand: "The New Challengers: Greens and Right-Wing Populist Parties in Western Europe," *European Review,* vol. 6, no. 2, 1998, pp. 191–202.

Müller-Rommel, Ferdinand, and Thomas Poguntke (eds.): *Green Parties in National Governments,* Cass, London, 2002.

Rokkan, Stein, and Derek W. Urwin (eds.): *The Politics of Territorial Identity,* Sage, Beverly Hills, 1983.

Scharpf, Fritz: *Governing in Europe: Effective and Democratic?* Oxford University Press, Oxford, 1999.

Sitter, Nick: "Cleavages, Party Strategy and Party System Change in Europe, East and West," *Perspectives in European Politics and Society,* vol. 3, no. 3, 2002, pp. 425–51.

Steed, Michael, and Peter Humphreys: "Identifying Liberal Parties," in Kirchner (ed.), pp. 396–435.

Taggart, Paul: "New Populist Parties in Western Europe," *West European Politics,* vol. 18, no. 1, 1995, pp. 34–51.

Urwin, Derek W.: *From Ploughshare to Ballotbox: The Politics of Agrarian Defense in Europe,* Universitetsforlaget, Oslo, 1980.

Zielonka, Jan, and Alex Pravda (eds.): *Democratic Consolidation in Eastern Europe,* vol. 2, *International and Transnational Factors,* Oxford University Press, Oxford, 2001.

CHAPTER 9

CLEAVAGE STRUCTURES AND ELECTORAL CHANGE

Enormous historical legacies underpin the appeals that political parties make to the citizens of the various European polities, and similar legacies help determine how citizens respond to those parties. Indeed, Seymour Martin Lipset and Stein Rokkan, in one of the most cogent and influential accounts of the development of modern western European politics, begin their analysis with events that took place more than four centuries ago, at a time when the very idea of mass political parties, let alone that of mass democracy, was unthinkable. Those events and subsequent developments over the succeeding centuries continue to provide the parameters of contemporary politics in western Europe.

To take a very clear-cut example, we saw in Chapter 8 that one of the most important distinctions between European party systems concerns whether the major party of the center–right is a Christian democratic or a conservative party. We also saw that when there is a major Christian party, it typically depends on a substantial Catholic vote. And the presence or absence of this Catholic vote derives, in turn, from a history of religious division that dates back to at least 1517, when Martin Luther pinned his ninety-five theses to the door of a church in Wittenberg, thus initiating the Protestant revolt against the church of Rome and marking the beginning of what we now know as the Reformation.

The ensuing clash between traditional Catholic Europe and reforming Protestant Europe constituted the first serious division in what had previously been a unifying Christian culture. The western area of Europe was effectively fractured in two, and the boundary between the two parts can be seen on a map of Europe by drawing a line between the Dutch city of Rotterdam in the northwest and the Italian city of Venice in the southeast. To the south and west of this line lie most of the countries that remained loyal to Rome and that remain predominantly Catholic today: France, Spain, Belgium, Luxembourg, Italy, and Austria, as well as the southern part of the Netherlands and southern Germany. To the north and east of this line but still within the area of western Europe, lies the Protestant domain: the Scandinavian countries in particular, as well as northern and eastern Germany and the northern part of the Netherlands. Britain was also to form part of the Protestant north, whereas Ireland remained mainly Catholic (see also Table 1.1).

In most but not all of the Catholic countries, as we have said, the major party of the center–right has been or still remains an essentially Catholic Christian democratic party. In all of the Protestant countries, the major party of the center–right is a conservative party. In the Netherlands, the continental fissure also split the polity, leading, as we have said, to the early mobilization of both Catholic and Protestant Christian parties.

What is clear beyond any shadow of a doubt is that the religious history of the previous four centuries still overhangs the development of party politics in contemporary Europe—as well as helping to set the long-standing division between west and east (Prodromou). Given this, it is hardly surprising that the broad outline of the party systems in the long-standing democracies of western Europe has proved so enduring.

In this chapter, therefore, we discuss the traditional cleavage structures that have underpinned European politics, and we explore how they might have changed in recent years. We also explore whether the changes that have occurred might be leading toward the realignment of party systems or toward dealignment. As in the previous chapter, we often make a distinction between the traditional west European democracies, on the one hand, and the new postcommunist democracies, on the other. Although both sets of polities often share similar cleavage structures (Berglund et al.; Whitefield), the questions that we address to long-standing party systems are necessarily different from those we address to newly formed party systems.

✦ THE MEANING OF CLEAVAGE

Before we consider the actual substance of the divisions that underpin contemporary European politics, whether in the east or in the west, it is important to be clear about precisely what we mean by the notion of a cleavage, which implies much more than a mere division, more even than an outright conflict, between two sets of people. In the 1980s, for example, before the end of the Cold War, there was a sharp division in a number of countries between those who favored the continued deployment of nuclear missiles and those who favored nuclear disarmament. This division cut deep and often led to violent conflict in the form of protests and street demonstrations. It was also pervasive, being an important item on the political agenda in countries as diverse as the United Kingdom, Italy, West Germany, and the Netherlands. But the nuclear missile issue, though acute, pervasive, divisive, and conflictual, did not constitute a fundamental cleavage in the sense identified by Lipset and Rokkan, for whom a cleavage has three quite specific connotations (Bartolini and Mair, pp. 212–49; Bartolini).

First, a cleavage involves a social division that separates people who can be distinguished from one another by key social-structural characteristics such as occupation, status, religion, or ethnicity. Thus, a cleavage may separate workers from employers, or Catholics from Protestants, or, as in Belgium, those who speak French from those who speak Dutch, or, as in Latvia, those who are ethnically Latvian from those who are ethnically Russian. A cleavage cannot be defined at the political level alone (as with the division over nuclear disarmament, for example).

Second, the groups involved in the division must be conscious of their collective identity—as workers or employers, or as Latvians or Russians, for example—and must be willing to act on this basis. This sense of collective identity is of crucial importance in the emergence and maintenance of cleavages. Without it, no "objective" social division will be transformed into a salient sociopolitical cleavage. For example, although the gender division between men and women remains one of the most significant social divisions in all western societies, it has never really generated the sense of collective gender identity that could turn gender into a salient basis for a major political division (Kaplan; Lovenduski). Despite widespread feminist mobilization, Iceland is still the only west European country to have produced a distinct and important women's party.

Third, a cleavage must be expressed in organizational terms. This is typically achieved as a result of the activities of a trade union, a church, a political party, or some other organization that gives formal institutional expression to the interests of people on one side of the division. In Britain, for example, although an objective social reality of distinctive national groups has always existed in Scotland and Wales, and although there has also been a clear collective sense of national identity within these groups, Welsh and Scottish nationalist politics have only sporadically achieved organizational expression. Hence, the nationalist cleavage in Britain has often been dormant. In Ireland, by contrast, and in Irish relations with Britain, it was one of the dominant elements in mass politics prior to Irish independence and continued to shape electoral alignments well into the twentieth century. In Northern Ireland, of course, it was, and still is, all-consuming.

It is important to maintain an emphasis on each of the three components of a cleavage, because they help us to understand how cleavages can persist or decay. A change in the cleavage structure of a society can occur as a result of changes in the social divisions that underpin cleavages, as a result of changes in the sense of collective identity that allows cleavages to be perceived by those involved, or as a result of changes in the organizational structure that gives political expression to cleavages. As we will see, recent experiences in Europe suggest evidence of change in all three components.

✦ TRADITIONAL CLEAVAGE STRUCTURES

In their seminal analysis of European political development, Lipset and Rokkan argued that the parameters that determined contemporary political alignments resulted from the interaction of four major historic cleavages. The first of these was the cleavage that divided the dominant culture (in the center of the state and nation) from subject cultures (in the periphery). The second was the cleavage that divided church from state. The third was the cleavage dividing those involved in the primary economy (typically in the countryside) from those in the secondary economy (typically in the town). The fourth was the cleavage that divided employers from workers (Lipset and Rokkan, pp. 13–26, reprinted in shorter form in Mair, *West,* pp. 99–111; see also Rokkan, ch. 3).

The Center–Periphery Cleavage

The first of the cleavages to which Lipset and Rokkan refer is that between the "subject culture" and the "dominant culture," now more commonly described as the cleavage between a country's sociopolitical "center" and its "periphery." This center–periphery cleavage derives from the era during which both the boundaries and the political authority of modern European states were being forged. When these modern states were being built, an inevitable clash emerged. On one side were those, typically at the center of the political system, who sought to standardize the laws, markets, and cultures that lay within state boundaries. On the other side were those, normally in the periphery of the new states, who sought to preserve their independence and autonomy.

The desire for autonomy was rooted in a variety of factors. In some cases linguistic or minority national groups resisted the encroachment of what they regarded as essentially foreign government. In other cases religious groups resisted the new codes, customs, and values imposed from the center. Either way, pockets of resistance to centralization persisted in many of the developing nation states. In some cases this resistance led eventually to secession, as when southern Ireland left the United Kingdom. In some cases it led to the granting of substantial local autonomy within the largest state, as with the separate Dutch-speaking (Flemish) and French-speaking (Walloon) communities in Belgium. In some cases it ended with effective absorption, as with the Breton minority in northwest France. The most common outcome, however, of this conflict between nation builders and subject populations was a diffuse but persistent tension between the two. This created a center–periphery cleavage in many European countries that remains visible to this day. It manifests itself in patterns of political attitude and voting behavior, as well as in the persistence of small ethnic, linguistic, or other cultural minorities. The center–periphery cleavage is salient even among some of the "smaller" democracies in which the geographic, as opposed to the sociopolitical, distance between the center and the periphery is not very large. It is also marked in a number of the postcommunist countries, not least as a result of boundary problems that were never solved, or were sometimes even created, during the communist period. The division between ethnic Latvians and Russian is one obvious case in point, as is that between the Slovak majority and Hungarian minority in Slovakia.

The Church–State Cleavage

The process of state building also created a second cleavage, at once more sharply defined and more critical. This involved the conflict between state-builders and the church, a conflict epitomized by the secular challenge posed by the French Revolution more than two hundred years ago. This was, and remains, a conflict about rights and privileges. It had to do with whether policies on crucial questions of public morality and, above all, education would be determined by the state or by the church.

The church–state cleavage developed in very different ways in Protestant and Catholic societies. The newly formed Protestant churches were essentially national churches that had largely become "agents of the state" (Lipset and Rokkan, p. 15). They thus had little incentive to challenge the policies of the state. Indeed, it was often only as a result of an alliance with the state that these churches had been able to establish themselves as legal entities. (This was not always the case. In the Netherlands, for example, the more fundamentalist Protestant adherents of the Dutch Reformed Church also opposed the secular ideas of the French Revolution in 1789, prompting the creation of the Anti-Revolutionary Party, a party that remained a significant independent electoral force until the end of the 1970s, when it merged with two other Christian parties into the CDA.)

In the case of the Catholic Church, the potential for conflict with the state was enormous. First, the Catholic Church saw itself as being "above" the state, owing its allegiance to a supranational religious organization based in the Vatican. Second, the Catholic Church persistently sought to insulate its adherents from secularizing tendencies, creating an autonomous cultural environment that proved resistant to state penetration. Thus,

Catholics sought to maintain their own independent schools and rejected state provision of secular education. They also sought to ensure that state laws on issues of public morality, such as divorce and censorship, would reflect Catholic values. Conflict between church and state was thus almost inevitable. This was obviously true in those countries where Catholics constituted a substantial religious minority, as in the Netherlands and Germany. It was also true, however, in countries such as France and Italy. In both countries, although the population was nominally all Catholic, the French Revolution prompted a major secular impetus that found expression in the anticlericalism of the early liberal and radical parties. In the exceptional case of Ireland, where the vast majority of the population remained practicing Catholics, secularism failed to take root, and, until relatively recently, state policy actually enshrined the Catholic belief system. Following the fall of communism, issues of religious freedom and control also reemerged in eastern Europe and proved especially pronounced in Catholic Poland.

Thus, the practical impact of the church–state cleavage was very unevenly distributed, proving a major source of political mobilization only in those countries with a substantial Catholic minority. In those countries, as we have said, Christian Democratic parties now constitute a powerful electoral force. In the Protestant north and east of Europe, in contrast, an accommodation between church and state was reached without too much difficulty. No substantial religious cleavage emerged, and so room was left for the mobilization of alternative cleavages (for a recent overview, see Madeley and Enyedi).

That said, there is now increasing evidence of a partial revival of the religious cleavage, albeit in a different form than used to be the case in Europe. In this new guise, a religious cleavage emerges between a largely immigrant, or immigrant-descended Muslim minority and the indigenous Christian or secular majority. This division has always been present, but it has only recently become politicized, not least as a result of reactions to 9/11. The issues involved are in some ways familiar: As in past conflicts between Catholics and the state, the question is whether and to what extent the Muslim minority can be expected to integrate, or whether separate schools and cultural practices can be tolerated. At the beginning of the twenty-first century these issues took on a particularly sharp and often polarized character particularly in Belgium, Denmark, France, and the Netherlands, fueling violence and protest actions, on the one hand, and encouraging support for far-right populist parties, on the other. But although the protagonists who are now involved may be new, the sense of cleavage, and the logic of the division itself, is familiar.

The Rural–Urban Cleavage

The third cleavage identified by Lipset and Rokkan concerns the conflict between the traditionally dominant rural interests and the new commercial and industrial classes of the cities. This conflict was already apparent in the medieval period but became particularly acute with the beginning of the industrial revolution. Although acute, however, the rural–urban cleavage was not always persistent. In Britain and Germany, in particular, but also in most of the rest of continental western Europe, divisions between the two groups did not form an enduring partisan conflict. But in Scandinavia, as well as in parts of eastern Europe, urban interests proved much more dominant, and sustained rural opposition to the urban elites resulted in the creation of powerful agrarian parties that have persisted—in a modified form—into the beginning of the twenty-first century.

But although the rural–urban cleavage may now be largely dormant in relation to conflicts between traditional landed and urban interests, there is also a sense in which the cleavage may now be acquiring a new, "postindustrial" relevance. Three factors are involved. First, like the United States, many European countries now face severe problems in balancing the interests of city and country, problems that often derive from the concentrations of urban poverty and racial tension in inner cities, the remedies for which are seen to demand increasing government intervention and expenditure. At the same time, many more wealthy citizens flee inner cities in search of suburban or rural comforts, eroding the tax base of cities while continuing to take advantage of their services and thus generating a new clash of interests between city and country. Second, at least within the countries of the European Union (see Chapter 5), a new and sometimes violent conflict has arisen as a result of the drive to free the movement of agricultural produce between countries while reducing subsidies to farmers. City folk clearly favor the cheaper food produced by both strategies, but farmers are increasingly discontented with the threatened slump in their standard of living. Third, urban–rural interests may also clash over values and over the manner in which the countryside is managed. In Britain in 2003 and 2004, for example, a very bitter and sometimes violent row broke out between supporters of the primarily urban Labour Party and members of the newly formed Countryside Alliance over the question of whether foxhunting should be banned. This long-favored preference of Labour was resisted very heavily by individuals involved in the sport. Relations between Labour and many country-dwellers had already been soured by opposition to the slaughter policy pursued by Labour during the outbreak of a hoof-and-mouth epidemic among cattle and sheep. In this case, the traditional cleavage, though marginal, was experienced with great intensity. Conflict over the superficially minor political issue of banning foxhunting therefore had a much more profound social resonance because, apart from its inevitable class connotations, it was inextricably linked to a deeper, and possibly deepening, cleavage between city and country in Britain.

Farmers now make up a very small proportion of the workforce in most western European countries, of course, and so it is unlikely that they could generate and sustain major new agrarian political movements. But (for example, in France) there are often enough of them to tip the balance between the existing parties, and they can therefore pose a threat to their traditional representatives on the center–right. They also form an important lobby group (see Chapter 14), and anyone who recalls the very bitter conflict between the United Kingdom and France over beef exports in the late 1990s will need no reminding of the political weight farmers can wield.

The Class Cleavage

By far the most important cleavage to emerge from the industrial revolution was the conflict between the owners of capital together with their allies among the established elites, on the one hand, and the newly emerging working class, on the other. The process of industrialization meant that, throughout nineteenth-century Europe, workers became increasingly concentrated in an essentially urban factory system. This provided a social environment in which they began to develop organizations, both trade unions and political parties, that sought to improve their conditions of work and to enhance their life chances. The increasing concentration of production enabled the organizations of the emerging working class to compensate for their lack of economic resources by mobilizing large groups of workers in collective action.

However, although the class cleavage is present in all western European countries, its organizational expression shows at least two contrasting patterns (Bartolini). In all countries during the industrial revolution, and in the majority of countries thereafter, the political demands of workers were expressed by a socialist party. In the wake of the Russian Revolution of 1917, more radical workers shifted toward a communist alternative, and in a small number of countries support for such parties equaled and even surpassed that of the socialist party. According to Lipset and Rokkan (pp. 21–23), much of the explanation for the relative success of communist parties lies in how bourgeois elites first responded to the workers' demands. Where they were more accommodating and pragmatic, as in Scandinavia and Britain, workers eschewed radical alternatives and became integrated into national politics. Where the bourgeois response was more repressive and the extension of political and social rights to the working class was resisted most adamantly—as in France, Germany, Italy, and Spain—workers adopted a more radical agenda, preparing the ground for the later acceptance of communist parties. Thus, even though class cleavage has been characteristic of all European democracies, the political expression of working-class interests has in some countries been divided between a socialist party and a communist party, though this political division between socialists and communists does not itself have the properties of a separate cleavage, as we have outlined them.

The Interaction of Different Cleavages

History has left a complex mosaic of social and political divisions in Europe (see Box 9.1). The cleavage between workers and employers has found expression in almost every European country, both east and west, but cleavages relating to center–periphery, rural–urban divisions, or to church–state relations emerged in ways that were specific to particular countries. Thus, although the major similarities between the western European political systems in particular derive from the class cleavage, the major differences between them can be explained to a large extent by the idiosyncratic development of other, often preindustrial, social cleavages.

One way to distinguish these western European countries is in terms of the interaction between the various cleavages that are present in the system. As the class cleavage emerged in Austria, for example, it overlapped the important church–state cleavage. This resulted in a Christian democratic party, which represents both "owners" and the church, and a socialist party, which represents both workers and anticlericals. The two key cleavages cut along the same lines.

In the United Kingdom, in contrast, a single social cleavage has come to dominate politics. Church–state tensions were largely resolved through the creation of a national church during the Reformation, and the rural–urban cleavage was resolved when the landed aristocracy and the emerging industrial capitalists made common cause during the nineteenth century. The most important center–periphery tensions largely evaporated in 1921, with the secession of southern Ireland from the United Kingdom, a radical break that also helped to solve lingering problems of church–state relations reflected in opposition between overwhelmingly Catholic Ireland and largely Protestant Britain. Until the partial reemergence of Scottish and Welsh nationalism in the 1970s, therefore, nothing

BOX 9.1   TRADITIONAL CLEAVAGE STRUCTURES

France

Three cross-cutting cleavages have been of major importance in postwar France: a class cleavage, separating right from left; a religious cleavage, separating the Gaullists, the National Front, and the Catholic groups within the UDF from the Socialists, the Communists, and the liberal and conservative elements within the UDF; and a center–periphery tension that pervades all parties and reflects the inevitable and persistent response to the domination of Paris. Whether new divisions concerning Europe, concerning immigrants, or even concerning religion have the capacity to become translated into real cleavages is still an open question. Although the broad left–right division has remained remarkably stable in France, the individual party and other organizations that mobilize on left and right have never been particularly strong.

Germany

For much of the postwar period, the class cleavage has been the dominant cleavage in Germany, cross-cut by a formerly much stronger church–state cleavage. Rural–urban tensions, which proved important in the nineteenth century, have now effectively disappeared. Since the reunification of east and west in 1990, Germany has experienced the reemergence of a version of the center–periphery cleavage, with the interests of the relatively poorer east conflicting with those of the richer west. Germany was also seen as one of the first countries to reflect an important divide between the old and the new politics on the left, although it now seems that the new politics challenge is being increasingly absorbed within conventional left–right competition.

Italy

Much like France, postwar Italy also experienced the three separate but cross-cutting cleavages of class, religion, and center–periphery. Growing secularization undermined the salience of the religious divide and led Italy to adopt legislation permitting both divorce and abortion. In the 1990s, the dominant Christian Democrat Party broke apart and was replaced in part by the secular Forza Italia. The class cleavage has also waned, particularly since the split in the Communist Party and the formation of the more moderate Democratic Left. Center–periphery tensions, however, are acquiring a new and more powerful resonance. This is not only reflected in the growth of the Northern League but is exacerbated by the persistent inequalities between the richer north and the poorer south.

Latvia

Among the key questions facing analysts of postcommunist politics is whether communist rule created distinctive cleavage structures in the region as a whole and whether the precommunist cleavages have survived into the new democratic period. Up to now, three divisions have tended to dominate Latvian politics, relating to culture (with education and class as the main determinants), ethnicity (the divide between Latvians and non-Latvians), and the economy, particularly with regard to the transformation to the market. Divisions over accession to the European Union have proved very marginal. Ethnicity is an especially important source of division in Latvia, where non-Latvians—mainly Russian-speakers—constitute about 35 percent of the total population. This is also probably the closest that Latvia gets to having a classical cleavage in Lipset–Rokkan sense. Instability in the party system and at the electoral level make it difficult to discern any real consolidation of electoral alignments.

The Netherlands

Cleavages of class and religion are also the dominant cleavages in Dutch politics, although increased secularization and a blurring of class boundaries have tended to erode the strongly "pillarized" subcultures on which the traditional cleavage structure in the Netherlands rested. There are few if any remaining

remained to interact with the class cleavage in Britain itself, and the result has been the emergence of two large political blocs that were distinguished from each other almost exclusively on the basis of their traditional class appeals. As Pulzer (p. 98) once famously noted: "Class is the basis of British politics; all else is mere embellishment and detail."

center–periphery tensions in the Netherlands—the country is simply too small for these—but local identities prove remarkably strong and continue to be sustained by the very uneven geographic distribution of the different religious groups. In recent years the rise of far right has pushed established social divisions between the indigenous and immigrant populations to the top of the political agenda.

Poland

As in Latvia, one of the key divisions within contemporary Polish politics concerns the scale and pace of the transition to a full market economy, and the enduring success of the SLD in the postcommunist elections offers a good indicator of the desire among many voters to maintain a reasonable level of welfarism and social protection. A second major division in Poland is reflected in the survival of the church–state cleavage. Poland is a predominantly Catholic country with some of the highest levels of religiosity and church attendance in modern Europe, and the postcommunist period has seen frequent clashes between advocates of Catholic values, on the one hand, and more liberal or secular forces, on the other. Inevitably, these disputes became particularly acute during the period in which the new institutions were being designed. A third divide opposes the urban, industrial, and service economy to the traditional rural economy, which remains very important in Poland. Finally, overlapping many of these conflicts, as well as building on them, there is a new divide between westernization and nationalism, a divide that also finds expression in the opposition between various pro- and anti-EU forces. On this last issue there is now probably more consensus among the political elites than among the general public.

Spain

Two cleavages clearly dominate Spanish politics—the class cleavage and the center–periphery cleavage. Although the strength of the Socialist Party might sug-

gest that class is substantially more important, no other western European country contains such a range or variety of regionalist and nationalist parties. At the same time, however, the class cleavage also operates within the regional party systems, with left–right divisions cutting across local solidarities. Despite a long tradition of church–state conflict, religion has had a surprisingly marginal impact on politics since the transition to democracy.

Sweden

The rural–urban cleavage has been particularly important in Swedish politics, as in Scandinavian politics more generally. Since the strongly rural Agrarian Party changed its name to the Center Party in 1957 and began to appeal to a wider section of the Swedish electorate, however, the relevance of this cleavage has clearly waned. A secondary religious cleavage is reflected in the small but growing electoral following of the Christian Democrats, a Protestant party that campaigns against permissiveness and alcohol consumption, but the dominant cleavage in Sweden is clearly the class cleavage.

United Kingdom

Britain has perhaps the simplest cleavage structure in Europe. Class was by far the dominant traditional cleavage, with the less significant religious and rural–urban divisions having waned in the nineteenth century. A small center–periphery cleavage does persist, however, reflecting the multinational character of the United Kingdom state and pitting Scottish, Welsh, and Irish nationalists against the English center. Most recently, hope finally began to emerge for a settlement of the bitter conflict resulting from the cleavage between nationalists and unionists in Northern Ireland. This has always been the most bitterly contested division in the politics of the United Kingdom, but since it is largely confined to Northern Ireland, it has had little effect on mass politics in mainland Britain.

In other cases, important cleavages cut across one another. In the Netherlands, the church–state cleavage first resulted in the creation of the three different forces, representing Catholics, Protestants, and anticlericals. When the class cleavage emerged, however, it cut across the church–state cleavage. This implied the formation of a new party, the Labour Party (PvdA), which opposed both the bourgeois religious parties and the bourgeois anticlerical Liberal Party. In France, too, the church–state cleavage cuts across the class cleavage. The Catholic Popular Republican Movement (MRP) opposed the secular socialists and the communists on the one hand and the secular bourgeois liberals and radicals on the other, finding reasonably common ground with the more religiously inclined conservative Gaullist movement. In social and economic policy, however, the MRP looked left and found itself making common cause with the workers' parties against the liberals, radicals, and Gaullists.

Overall, therefore, what we might think of as the "cleavage structure" of a particular society has two distinct features. The first has to do with the particular cleavages that have survived historically as important lines of social and political division. The second has to do with the extent to which these important lines of division cut across one another. Thus, a religious cleavage and a class cleavage may both run along the same lines (if all workers are Catholic, for example, and all owners are Protestant), or they may cut across one another (if whether or not someone is a Protestant or a Catholic has no bearing on whether he or she is a worker). It is this pattern of interaction between cleavages that has underpinned the traditional structure of party competition in most western European states and that also played a major role in shaping the interwar patterns of those states that were later to come under Soviet control.

✦ THE PERSISTENCE OF CLEAVAGES AND THE FREEZING OF PARTY SYSTEMS

After the pathbreaking work of Lipset and Rokkan, it became common to speak of the "freezing" of western European party systems at about the time of the 1920s as a result of the remarkable persistence of the cleavages that underpin party politics. Cleavages could persist for four main reasons. First, they could persist when the interests with which the cleavage was concerned remained relevant and the groups that were polarized retained a sense of collective identity. Second, major alternative political identities were likely to be mobilized only when substantial bodies of new votes were incorporated into mass politics, and no such large-scale incorporation has occurred since the granting of universal suffrage. Third, the rules of the game are such that they tended to favor the persistence of those parties that devised the rules in the first place. Fourth, parties could attempt to isolate their supporters from competitors and thereby "narrow" the electoral market. Let us look at these elements more closely.

Cleavages persist first because they concern people who are divided from one another on the basis of real and enduring issues. As long as workers continue to feel that they have a common interest that is distinct from the interest of employers, or farmers, for example, and as long as this remains relevant at the level of politics and government, the cleavage around which workers are aligned is likely to persist. Conversely, if the social distinctiveness of being a worker becomes blurred or if it is no longer seen to be relevant politically, the class cleavage might become dormant. (This is precisely the argument that is now cited to emphasize the changing character of contemporary European politics.)

Second, cleavages persist because European electorates are now fully mobilized (Lipset and Rokkan; Rokkan). This helps explain why the "freezing" of many European party systems is typically said to have occurred around the 1920s. Lipset and Rokkan argued that the political alignments forged when a group of voters is newly enfranchised prove strong and enduring. They thus emphasized the importance of the 1920s, the period when universal suffrage was generally introduced. This is not, of course, to suggest that the cleavages that were relevant in the 1920s will always remain salient. Rather, it implies that subsequent political realignments involve winning the support of voters who are already aligned in terms of a particular cleavage structure, a more difficult task than attracting new voters with no established alignments. Another way of thinking of this is to consider the period leading up to universal suffrage as having set the parties in motion. Thereafter, these selfsame parties will tend to hold on to their monopoly of representation.

The third explanation for the persistence of cleavages has to do with the laws that govern the conduct of elections. As you will see in Chapter 11, the first-past-the-post electoral system that operates in Britain (and the United States) is often said to favor the development of a two-party system. The proportional representation (PR) systems that operate in the majority of western European states are more conducive to multiparty politics. It might be argued that by not penalizing minority parties, PR electoral systems help maintain minor cleavages. Conversely, first-past-the-post systems, by squeezing out small parties, may eliminate minor cleavages and allow the most salient cleavage to dominate the system as a whole.

As Lipset and Rokkan forcefully remind us, however, the rules of the game do not emerge out of thin air; rather, they are legislated by political parties. They will therefore tend to protect established interests (Lipset and Rokkan, p. 30; see also Sartori, "Influence"). Similarly, in a separate analysis of electoral systems, Rokkan (pp. 147–68) argued that the adoption of PR *resulted from,* rather than *led to,* multiparty politics. Proportional representation electoral systems were adopted in countries where there were distinct cultural or linguistic minorities. When the mass working class was enfranchised in countries where other cleavages were already present, the rules of the game were often modified to ensure the continued representation of the existing smaller parties. This, of course, facilitated the persistence of the cleavages along which they aligned.

A fourth factor that encourages the persistence of cleavages has to do with party organization (see Chapter 10). In a desire to insulate party supporters from the competing appeals of their opponents, many European parties initially involved themselves in a host of social activities. They attempted to establish a presence in many different areas of their individual supporters' lives, organizing social clubs, welfare services, recreational facilities, and the like, thus offering adherents a range of services to sustain them "from the cradle to the grave." Although such behavior was mainly a characteristic of working-class socialist parties (the best account is in Roth), this process of "encapsulation" was also attempted by some of the Christian parties, notably the old Catholic People's Party in the Netherlands (Bakvis) and the People's Party in Austria (Diamant; see also Houska).

This process of integrating and encapsulating supporters thus characterized many of the new mass parties that challenged the most elitist traditional "cadre" parties in the era of popular enfranchisement (Duverger; Neumann; Katz and Mair). These mass parties helped to create and sustain specific political subcultures in which they hoped that party voters would express a more permanent sense of "belonging" rather than make a more instrumental, and changeable, policy-oriented voting decision. These mass parties attempted to corner the electoral market by building long-term voter attachments. To the extent that they succeeded, they stabilized cleavage structures and the party systems on which these were based.

The persistence of cleavages and party systems is underlined most clearly in Lipset and Rokkan's work, which has since become the benchmark for many subsequent analyses of western European party systems. Writing from the perspective of the late 1960s, and noting that the last new cleavage that had emerged had been the class cleavage, solidified some forty years before, Lipset and Rokkan (p. 50) rounded off their analysis with the conclusion that "the party systems of the late 1960s reflect, with few but significant exceptions, the cleavage structures of the 1920s. ... The party alternatives, and in remarkably many cases the party organizations, are older than the majorities of the national electorates." This was to become known as the "freezing hypothesis"—that party systems in western Europe had "frozen" into place in the 1920s, with any subsequent changes proving either marginal or temporary (Mair, "Freezing").

The freezing hypothesis offered an influential theoretical and historical explanation for the stability of European electoral behavior in the 1950s and 1960s. During this period the potentially vulnerable new West German party system had begun to be stabilized by the success of Konrad Adenauer's Christian Democrats and by the abandonment of radical policies by the Social Democrats in 1959. It was the period in which the policies of the Labour Party in Britain had become almost indistinguishable from those of the centrist Conservative government in a process of convergence that became popularly known as "Butskellism," a neologism derived from the names of R. A. Butler, then Conservative treasury minister, and Hugh Gaitskell, then leader of the Labour Party. It was the period in which the polarized party system of Italy seemed set to stabilize under the center–right control of the Christian Democrats and in which the unstable French Fourth Republic had been replaced by the potentially more stable presidential system of the Fifth Republic. It was the period of unchanging social democratic hegemony in Scandinavia. In more general terms, it was a period described by some observers as one in which there was a "waning of opposition" (Kirchheimer, "Waning"; Kirchheimer, "Transformation") and an "end of ideology" (Bell).

This seemingly pervasive political consensus, together with the marked increase in mass prosperity that characterized western Europe in the first postwar decades, clearly enhanced the prospects for democratic stability in the continent. It also seemed to be accounted for rather neatly by the processes of inertia suggested by Lipset and Rokkan. When Rose and Urwin set out to conduct the first real empirical test of the freezing hypothesis at the end of the 1960s, they found that

> whatever index of change is used . . . the picture is the same: the electoral strength of
> most parties in Western nations since the war has changed very little from election to
> election, from decade to decade, or within the lifespan of a generation . . . [T]he first
> priority of social scientists concerned with the development of parties and party
> systems since 1945 is to explain the absence of change in a far from static period in
> political history. (Rose and Urwin, p. 295)

✦ From Persistence to Change

Thus, political scientists became convinced during the late 1960s that western European party politics had settled into a very stable pattern. However, while Lipset, Rokkan, and others were putting the finishing touches to their various analyses of persistence, the image of tranquillity began to be rudely shattered. Signs of change had actually been apparent in 1968, when student protests and violent street demonstrations raged throughout western Europe and the United States. There were also signs of a challenge to the consensus within more mainstream politics, however.

The stability of Norwegian politics, for example, was fractured in the early 1970s as a referendum on Norway's entry into the then European Community reawakened the dormant center–periphery conflict and provoked major splits in the traditional parties. In the United Kingdom in 1974, nationalist parties from Scotland and Wales won a record share of the vote, while in Northern Ireland the political violence that had erupted in 1968 continued unabated, claiming almost five hundred lives in 1972 alone. In Belgium, the rise of Flemish and Walloon nationalist movements provoked major splits in all three traditional parties, and in the Netherlands, the major Catholic party and its two traditional Protestant opponents were forced into an electoral alliance in order to stave off their severe electoral losses. Meanwhile, in Italy in 1976, the Communist Party won its highest share ever of the vote and came within 5 percent of overtaking the ruling Christian Democrats. In France in 1974, a candidate supported by both the Socialists and the Communists came within 1 percent of finally snatching the presidency from the center–right. In short, it now seemed to be the case that "a week is a long time in politics," as former British Labour leader Harold Wilson once observed. "Stability" was the catchword of the 1950s and the 1960s; "change" was to become the catchword of the 1970s.

Nowhere were these watershed changes of the 1970s better illustrated than in Denmark in 1973. For many scholars, this was also seen at the time as a major turning point. For a long time Denmark had been regarded as "one of the most dull countries to deal with for a student of voting behavior" (Pedersen, "Danish"). This image was utterly transformed by the election of December 1973, however, when the number of parties winning representation in the Danish parliament (Folketing) suddenly doubled from five to ten. The combined vote share of the four parties that had traditionally dominated Danish politics—Social Democrats, Social Liberals, Liberals, and Conservatives—fell more or less overnight from 84 percent to 58 percent, and a new far-right antitax party, the Progress Party, suddenly emerged as the second largest party. These dramatic changes occurred during a period of only twenty-seven months after the previous Danish election and are summarized in Table 9.1.

Table 9.1 shows big changes in the vote shares of the parties, and on this basis we can calculate what is known as the index of aggregate electoral volatility, one of the standard measures of electoral change (Pedersen, "Dynamics"; Pedersen, "Changing"). The Progress Party gained almost 16 percent of the vote. Other gains were made by the Center Democrats (7.8), Communists (2.2), Christians (2.0), and Justice Party (1.2). The Social Democrats lost 11.7 percent of the vote. Other losses were suffered by the Conservatives (−7.5), Liberals (−3.3), Social Liberals (−3.2), and Socialist People's Party (−3.1). If we summarize these changes by reference to Pedersen's index, then we see that the level of aggregate (or total) electoral volatility in Denmark between 1971 and 1973 was 29.1 percent,

TABLE 9.1

Denmark's "Earthquake" Election of 1973

Party	1971 % of Votes	1971 Seats	1973 % of Votes	1973 Seats
Social Democrats	37.3	70	25.6	46
Conservatives	16.7	31	9.2	16
Liberals	15.6	30	12.3	22
Social Liberals	14.4	27	11.2	20
Socialist People's Party	9.1	17	6.0	11
Christian People's Party	2.0	—	4.0	7
Justice Party	1.7	—	2.9	5
Left Socialists	1.6	—	1.5	—
Communists	1.4	—	3.6	6
Progress Party	—	—	15.9	28
Center Democrats	—	—	7.8	14
Others	0.2	—	—	—
Total	**100.0**	**175**	**100.0**	**175**

Source: Unless otherwise stated, the sources for all tables in Chapter 9 are the same as those for Tables 7.1 and 8.10.

a very high figure indeed.[1] During the 1960s, for example, volatility in Denmark averaged 8.7 percent. In the 1950s, it averaged just 5.5 percent (see Table 9.10). This election, though old, is therefore a valuable illustration of how extensive electoral change can be.

The first comprehensive analysis of changing levels of electoral volatility in western Europe came, appropriately enough, from a Danish researcher, Mogens Pedersen ("Dynamics"; "Changing"), whose work had been partly stimulated by the extraordinary level of change in his own country. Pedersen documented the changes that were also evident in Norway and the Netherlands and, to a lesser extent, in Switzerland, the United Kingdom, Finland, and Sweden. He concluded that there was a significant "unfreezing" of European party systems. A similar conclusion was reached by Maguire, who replicated and updated Rose and Urwin's analysis at the end of the 1970s. Just one decade later, using identical statistical measures to Rose and Urwin, Maguire found evidence of much greater instability and argued that western European party systems "cannot now be regarded as inherently stable structures" (p. 92). Although the priority stated by Rose and Urwin at the end of the 1960s had been to explain stability, by the end of the 1970s, for Maguire, the priority had become to explain why many party systems seemed to be subject to sudden change (see also Crewe and Denver; Dalton et al., *Electoral*).

---

[1] Calculations of levels of aggregate volatility must be treated very carefully, however, for the figures may be artificially raised as a result of one-off party splits and mergers. In this Danish example, for instance, the Center Democrats were not a wholly new party but rather a split from the Social Democrats. A more realistic index of volatility would therefore measure change in 1973 by comparing the combined vote share of the divided parties (25.6% + 7.8% = 33.4%) with the previous vote share of the Social Democrats (37.3%) in order to produce a figure of 3.9 percent for the net party change and a figure of 21.2 percent for the election as a whole (see Bartolini and Mair, pp. 311–12). Subsequent calculations of levels of electoral volatility reported in this chapter follow the latter rule.

✦ CHANGE IN EUROPEAN CLEAVAGE STRUCTURES AND ELECTORAL BEHAVIOR

The argument that post-1970s party systems in western Europe entered a period of sudden and pervasive change is by now received wisdom, and much of this change is attributed to fallout from the decline of traditional cleavages (e.g., Inglehart, "Changing"; Franklin et al; Dalton and Wattenberg). Indeed, contrary to the conclusions reached by Lipset and Rokan, most observers now prefer to speak of the *de*freezing of traditional political alignments and party systems. Needless to say, these arguments apply only to the long-standing party systems of Europe. In the postcommunist systems in particular, there was no structure of mass democratic politics that could have become frozen through the century, and hence the notion of defreezing is hardly relevant. That said, students of contemporary postcommunist alignments do point to continuities with the alignments that once characterized the interwar democracies in eastern Europe, suggesting that even if the traditional cleavage structure was dormant under communism, it has now been at least partially revived (Berglund et al.; Kitschelt et al.; Wittenberg).

Among the long-standing democracies, and following our earlier definition, cleavages can be subject to erosion or change in three distinct ways. First, the strength of cleavages may be affected by changes in the social structure, such as through shifting or blurring class and occupational boundaries, or through changes in religious affiliation. Second, the strength of cleavages may be affected by changes in collective identities and behavior, such as when workers might no longer feel a sense of collective identity as workers, or when Catholics might no longer act in concert in support of particular political preferences. Third, the strength of cleavages may be affected by the organizational and ideological behavior of parties, such as when parties begin to downplay their appeals to specific social or cultural constituencies.

For the purposes of this chapter, we now want to look briefly at the evidence of change in cleavage strength in the first two of these three factors, focusing mainly on the period from the 1950s to the 1980s, when a lot of the social change in particular is believed to have taken place. In Chapters 10 and 13, we pay much closer attention to party organizational and programmatic change (see also Kirchheimer, "Transformation"; Katz and Mair).

Changing Social Structure

In western Europe in 1960, an average of some 34 percent of all employment in the three main sectors of the economy was within agriculture; some 40 percent was in manufacturing, some 26 percent in the service sector. Already by 1995, these relative proportions had changed to 12, 31, and 56 percent respectively (calculated from Crouch, pp. 433, 439), and by 2003 they had changed to 4, 28 and 69 percent within the then EU-15 area (OECD figures). We need hardly reminding that changes such as these will have had profound implications for politics and political representation. It is not only important here to recognize that the last half century has seen a major sea change in the way people earn their livings. This transformation is already be all too familiar to even the most cursory observer. What is at least as important is to recognize that within the different sectors, technological changes and economic modernization have led to the erosion of many traditional social boundaries. As the population has become more educated and more prosperous, lifestyles have begun to converge, and previous lines of divisions between different sectors of the population have tended to become blurred. In 1960, for example, women constituted an average of 31 percent of the west European labor force; by 1990, this figure had risen to over 40 percent. Yet another indicator of change can be seen in the decline in the numbers of people belonging to the traditional blue-collar working class through to the mid-1990s. According to one set of figures, the proportion of manual workers in the labor force fell from an average of close to 50 percent in western Europe in 1960 to 40 percent in 1995, including a decline from almost 54 to 36 percent in the Netherlands, from 54 to 35 percent in Sweden, and from 61 to 33 percent in the UK (Crouch, pp. 456–57). In other words, as Ambrosius and Hubbard (pp. 76, 78) put it, dating the change to the 1960s in particular, postwar western Europe had witnessed the crossing of a major "socio-historical watershed."

Nor was it only the economic categories that were changing in the 1960s and after. Religious identities and practice were also subject to erosion as western Europe in general drifted toward a more secular society. One of the first comprehensive studies to tap into this change, the World Values survey of 1981–82, revealed some striking contrasts (Inglehart, *Culture,* p. 191). Thus while some 83 percent of those surveyed in the oldest cohorts (aged 65 or more) in western Europe proved willing to describe themselves as "a religious person," only 53 percent of those who were then in the youngest cohorts (aged 15 to 24) did so. Already by then, of course, religious practice had also fallen off considerably. In Italy in the twenty years between 1956 and 1976, for example, regular church attendance among Catholics had fallen from 69 to 37 percent (Amyot, p. 44). In West Germany in the late 1980s only 25 percent of the electorate regularly attended church—as against 40 percent in the 1950s. Among Catholics alone, regular church attendance had fallen from over 50 to just 30 percent in the same period (Dalton, "German," p. 103). Even in Ireland, where Catholicism had long held particularly powerful sway, figures indicated that weekly church attendance had fallen from 81 in 1990 to 67 percent four years later (Hardiman and Whelan, p. 72).

It is perhaps in the Netherlands that this widespread process of secularization has proved the most striking—and it is also in the Netherlands that it has been most tellingly documented and can best be illustrated (see Irwin and van Holsteyn). Religious identity and practice have always constituted a key component in Dutch culture, where the long-standing tolerance of religious differences were fostered by the existence of a sharp—or "pillarized"—division between three main denominations: Catholic, Protestant, and Calvinist. In 1959 these three main denominations covered some 75 percent of the Dutch electorate (see Table 9.2). Moreover, these religious affiliations were more than simply nominal: In that same year, some 51 percent of the electorate regularly attended church services, including some 87 percent of Catholics and some 88 percent of Calvinists. The Netherlands in 1959 was clearly a religious country. Already by 1986, however, when the various denominations were starting to pool their political forces, this picture had changed dramatically. Although nominal religious adherents still constituted a small majority of the electorate (some 52 percent), religious practice had declined substantially; only 17 percent of the electorate still regularly attended church, among whom were just 26 percent of Catholics. By 1986, in other words, the Netherlands had been effectively secularized.

TABLE 9.2

Decline of Religiosity in the Netherlands

| | 1959 | | | 1986 | | |
| | % of Adherents in the Electorate | % of Regular Church Attenders Among Adherents | % of Regular Church Attenders in the Electorate[a] | % of Adherents in the Electorate | % of Regular Church Attenders Among Adherents | % of Regular Church Attenders in the Electorate[a] |
Religion						
Catholic	37	87	32	31	26	8
Dutch Reformed	28	36	10	15	33	5
Calvinist	10	88	9	6	65	4
Total	75	n.a.	51	52	n.a.	17

[a] Calculated on aggregate percentages.

Source: Irwin and van Holsteyn.

Changing Voting Behavior

In addition to these dramatic changes in the social structure of many European countries, most of which have accelerated during the 1990s, there is also evidence of a waning of the sense of identification between particular groups and political parties that formerly represented their interests. In other words, even among the diminished pool of workers or religious practitioners there is evidence to suggest that there was a major falling-off in collective partisan preferences through the 1970s and 1980s.

One of the clearest illustrations of this change comes from survey data reporting the broad ideological (left versus right) preferences of the traditional social classes. If traditional cleavages still held sway, then even though there might be fewer workers in contemporary societies, we might still expect that they would maintain a preference for left-wing parties. And even though there might be more middle-class voters in the electorate, they should nevertheless reflect a preference for parties of the center and right. A simple—if somewhat crude—method of detecting these differential class preferences is by means of the "Alford index," which measures the extent to which support for the left among the working class is greater than among the middle class (Alford). In Britain in 1951, for example (Heath et al., 1985, p. 30), the Alford index was a relatively high 41 percent, a figure that is calculated by subtracting the amount of Labour support among nonmanual classes (22 percent) from that among manual workers (63 percent). The higher the value of the index, therefore, the more pronounced is class voting, in the sense that workers are more likely to be voting left, with other classes voting center and right.

As Table 9.3 shows, levels of class voting as measured by the Alford index declined quite substantially between the 1950s and the 1980s. From an average of almost 37 percent prior to 1960, the index falls to just over 29 percent in the 1960s, to 24 percent in

TABLE 9.3

The Decline in Class Voting, 1950s–1980s

Country	1945–60	1961–70	1971–80	1981–90
Austria	—	27.4	28.9	18.3
Belgium	—	25.4	17.9	16.4
Britain	37.3	38.3	24.3	23.4
Denmark	39.8	52.0	28.1	20.9
Finland	48.4	50.2	36.9	35.7
France	24.4	18.3	17.0	11.7
Germany	36.0	24.8	14.9	13.4
Ireland	—	14.1	8.7	7.3
Italy	26.6	14.5	17.8	13.1
Netherlands	14.0	14.7	21.8	15.5
Norway	52.5	32.0	33.8	20.5
Sweden	51.0	40.7	37.3	32.7
Mean (N)	**36.7 (9)**	**29.4 (12)**	**24.0 (12)**	**19.1 (12)**

Note: Values are those of the Alford index, measuring the difference between the percentage of manual workers voting for left-wing political parties and the percentage of nonmanual workers voting for these same parties. The higher the index, the stronger is class voting.

Source: Nieuwbeerta, p. 53.

the 1970s, and to just 19 percent in the 1980s. In other words, levels of class voting as indicated by this simple measure were cut by half. To be sure, this index is particularly crude, and there are problems with its comparability across countries, given different ways of categorizing social classes. In Sweden, for example, the decline in class voting during this same period proved much less pronounced when lower-level nonmanual workers were classified as middle class rather than working class (Sainsbury). In Britain, the adoption of a seven-category classification ranging from the higher service class to the unskilled working class suggests that that the decline in class voting has actually been much more muted than might appear from a simple two-category classification. In 1964, for example, the Conservatives enjoyed a lead over Labour of 47 percent among the higher service class; in 1992, the last election before the Labour landslide, this lead was 50 percent. Among the unskilled working class, Labour's lead over the Conservatives in 1964 was 40 percent; in 1992, Labour's lead was 32 percent. But among the skilled working class, Labour's lead had fallen from 45 percent to just 13 percent, while among the lower service class the Conservative lead had fallen from 41 percent to 29 percent. Indeed, by 1997, Labour had the lead in this group (Evans et al., p. 90; see also Evans, *End of Class*). Thus even though the core middle class and core working class might still tend to reflect traditional voting preferences, the leakage between intermediary classes, and the declining cohesiveness even within the core itself, suggest that voting behavior in general is now less predictable in such social-structural terms.

A similar pattern is obvious in the relationship between religion and partisan preferences, although the implications of this pattern are less far-reaching because religious divisions have been part of the political arena only in certain countries. We should not underestimate the importance of religion to traditional voting behavior, however, for religious differences exert a much more pervasive impact than the presence of explicitly religious parties might indicate. Religious differences may have helped to determine party choice in situations where the parties concerned were all ostensibly secular.

In France, for example, the decline of the Catholic party (MRP) in the early 1960s did not imply the wholesale decline of religion as a force in voting behavior. According to a 1978 survey, more than 50 percent of regular churchgoers supported parties of the center–right, against just over 20 percent of those who never attended church. This contrast led to the conclusion that about 20 percent of the variation in partisan choice between supposedly "secular" parties was actually explained by patterns of church attendance (Lewis-Beck, pp. 438–39). Overall, survey results in the 1960s indicated that religious divisions, when they were salient, actually had a stronger impact on party choice than did social class (Lijphart).

As the evidence of growing secularization would suggest, however, this picture is now quite different—even among that minority who still practice. In the Dutch case, for example, not only was the Catholic Church larger and more actively involved in the daily lives of its adherents in the 1950s (see Bakvis), but the vast majority of practicing Catholics also supported the then Catholic People's Party (KVP). Indeed, according to a 1956 survey, the KVP, which was then the second largest party in the Netherlands, enjoyed the support of an astonishing 95 percent of practicing Catholics! By 1977, the last election that the KVP contested as an independent party, its support among practicing Catholics had fallen to 67 percent (Irwin and van Holsteyn, p. 39). Since then, of course, Dutch Catholics do not even have the option of voting for their own party, because the KVP merged with its two Protestant rivals in 1980 to form the pan-Christian CDA, itself a powerful indication of the changes that were then taking place within the wider society.

The contraction of both the traditional working class and the churchgoing public in contemporary western Europe, together with a declining political cohesion even among those who retain traditional social-structural identities, has inevitably undermined the potential role of traditional social cleavages. This has resulted in the erosion of two of the most important subcultures in modern Europe, creating conditions in which individual preferences may replace collective identification as a basis for party choice.

Other forces also appear to be pushing European electorates in this direction. Already in the late 1980s, for example, Dalton (*Citizen,* pp. 18–24) suggested that Europe was experiencing the emergence of a more politically sophisticated electorate. This new electorate was characterized by high levels of education and had access, particularly through television, to a huge amount of information about politics. Dalton argued that these voters related to politics on an individual rather than a subcultural basis. This trend was also compounded by a shift toward the privatization of consumption—of housing, health care, education, car ownership, and so on—promoting individualistic and fragmented political responses that some suggested were likely to push patterns of partisan preference in western Europe much closer to those in the United States. It was also later compounded by the decline of the more standardized and often partisan mass

TABLE 9.4

The Declining Impact of Social Structure on Left Voting, 1960s–1980s

Country	% of Variance Explained in Earlier Period (Year)	% of Variance Explained in Later Period (Year)	Difference (%)
Belgium	29.9 (1973)	13.1 (1984)	−16.8
Britain	20.6 (1964)	11.3 (1983)	−9.3
Denmark	23.0 (1971)	9.0 (1987)	−14.0
France	8.3 (1968)	7.7 (1981)	−0.6
Germany (West)	8.2 (1968)	7.8 (1986)	−0.4
Ireland	11.2 (1969)	1.6 (1987)	−9.6
Italy	24.4 (1968)	28.5 (1988)	+4.1
Netherlands	35.0 (1967)	20.0 (1986)	−15.0
Norway	42.0 (1969)	34.0 (1985)	−8.0
Sweden	29.0 (1964)	18.0 (1985)	−11.0
Mean	**23.2**	**15.1**	**−8.1**

Note: This table summarizes the amount of variance in electoral support for parties of the left that can be explained (at the individual level) by a combination of social-structural variables including class, religion, trade union membership, church attendance, and so on. The variables in the West German study include only trade union membership, occupation, and education.

Source: Adapted from Franklin et al., pp. 92, 109, 154, 189, 229, 245, 266, and 313.

media—when more or less the same message went to very large groups of readers and viewers—and their replacement by more narrowly based, fragmented, and entertainment-oriented channels.

More generally, after one of the most comprehensive attempts to address this problem from a comparative perspective, Mark Franklin and his colleagues concluded that the end of the 1980s had witnessed a fundamental weakening of the relationship between social structure, including both class and religion, and voting behavior. The main findings of these authors are summarized in Table 9.4 and show that whereas social-structural variables (including class, religion, gender, region, trade union membership, church attendance, and so on) were able to explain an average of some 23 percent of the variance in left voting when the first mass surveys were undertaken in these countries, this figure had fallen to just 15 percent by the mid-1980s. Only in Italy did social-structural factors explain a greater share of the variance in the more recent period. The decline was most pronounced in Denmark, where the figure fell from 23 to 9 percent, and in Ireland, where it fell from 11 to less than 2 percent. The argument advanced by this study did not suggest, however, that these changes had been brought about by the emergence of new cleavages or even by a change in the traditional cleavage structures themselves. Rather, in much the same way as Dalton had argued, the researchers suggested that the traditional cleavages had simply become less relevant to partisanship as a result of what they defined as the growing "particularization," or individualization, of voting choice (Eijk et al.).

Let us try to knit these various strands together. A cleavage, it will be recalled, is sustained by three separate elements: a distinct social base, a sense of collective identity, and a clearly defined organizational expression. In its most extreme form, a cleavage is therefore sustained through the creation of distinctive subcultures within which voting is an expression of social identity rather than a reflection of instrumental choice. In short, voters belong. As Richard Rose once put it, at a time when this sense of belonging was particularly pronounced, "to speak of the majority of voters at a given election as choosing a party is nearly as misleading as speaking of a worshipper on a Sunday 'choosing' to go to an Anglican rather than a Baptist or a Catholic church" (Rose, *Problem,* p. 100).

Already by the end of the 1980s, however, there was ample evidence to suggest that these traditional demarcation lines were becoming blurred. Class divisions were becoming less pronounced, and widespread secularization had reduced the impact of religious divisions. Even within what remained of the traditional social groups, behavior was tending to become less collective, and the traditional variations in political preference between groups were tending to wane. Finally, as shall be seen in later chapters, and in what seems to be a response to these changes, political parties had begun to loosen their bonds with specific groups of voters and had begun to appeal much more emphatically to the electorate at large. In short, the evidence suggested and still does suggest a consistent trend toward a much less structured electorate and toward the fragmentation and "particularization" of political preferences.

However, before going on to look at where these changes might be heading, we do need to introduce a couple of important caveats. First, although class and religion may now have less impact on voting behavior than was the case in the 1950s and 1960s, their impact has not disappeared entirely. In Britain, for example, as we have said, the higher service class still continues to register a preference for the Conservatives, and both the skilled and the unskilled working classes still tend to opt for Labour. In the increasingly secular Netherlands, a majority of the now diminished set of religious practitioners still votes for the CDA.

Second, while class and religion may now offer fewer voting cues, other identities retain a powerful impact. The large majority of Basque voters in Spain still vote for Basque parties. An even larger majority of Catholics in Northern Ireland still vote for Irish nationalist parties. Almost all Swedish-speaking Finns—they are not very numerous—still support the Swedish People's Party. In Belgium, nearly every Flemish voter supports a Flemish party, and nearly every French-speaking voter supports a Walloon party. Indeed, these sorts of identity might even be becoming more pronounced. In 1972—and again in 1994—the old center–periphery cleavage in Norway was suddenly reawakened by the prospect of Norwegian entry into the European Union. A similarly dormant north–south conflict was reawakened in Italy thanks to the mobilization efforts of the Northern League. And while class politics may be waning in Britain, there is ample evidence to suggest that Scottish, Welsh, and—through the Conservatives' new appeals—even English nationalism is growing in importance.

✦ CHANGE TOWARD WHAT?

In a wide-ranging early discussion of electoral change in advanced industrial democracies, Russell Dalton and his colleagues (Dalton et al., *Electoral;* Flanagan and Dalton) put forward two general models that seek both to explain the nature of the changes occurring in western European politics and to predict their potential consequences. Their first explanation is based on the role of cleavages. It suggests that as traditional cleavages wane in importance and new cleavages emerge, voters go through a process of "realignment." Their second explanation concentrates on the declining role of political parties. It suggests that almost regardless of the new issues and concerns arising in postindustrial societies, political parties as such will become less and less relevant to the representation of interests. Citizens will turn increasingly toward interest groups and other social movements in order to press their demands, producing a widespread process of "dealignment." Although both explanations emphasize the declining political relevance of factors such as class and religion, the realignment thesis stresses the growth of postmaterialist—quality of life—concerns (Inglehart, "Changing"), whereas the dealignment thesis suggests that electorates will become ever more unstructured. We now turn briefly to assessing each of these arguments.

Toward Realignment?

Despite Lipset and Rokkan's earlier emphasis on the "freezing" of party systems, it has been argued that the new issues that arise in postindustrial societies reflect the emergence of a wholly new cleavage, one that, like more traditional cleavages, is characterized by a social base, a collective identity, and an organizational expression. In the first place, this "new politics" is associated with a distinct social base within the new middle class, particularly among younger voters and those with a university education. Second, the values of the new politics are also distinctive, laying particular stress on environmental protection, feminism, and the extension of democratic and social rights—what Inglehart (*Culture; Modernization*) has referred to as "postmaterialism" or "postmodernism." Third, this new politics is increasingly and pervasively reflected in the emergence of a distinct organizational expression, most clearly represented in the rise of Green parties in most parts of western Europe, as well as in the earlier new left parties, that are increasingly seen as part of the wider new politics constituency. It is in this sense that what has become known as postmaterialism can be seen to constitute a new cleavage, the mobilization of which implies a potential realignment of party politics (see also Inglehart, "Changing").

There are two reasons to suggest that this scenario may be exaggerated, however. First, and most obvious, despite the evident resonance of some of the issues associated with the new politics, these parties remain an essentially marginal electoral force. As seen in Chapter 8, Green parties polled an average of some 5 percent of the vote in western Europe in the 1990s, and around 5.5 percent in the first elections of the new century; a further 2 percent went to the new left. These figures are not to be dismissed, and they also conceal quite a bit of variation across the different polities. Nonetheless, they fail to signify a dramatic sea change in aggregate voting alignments.

The second reason why it may be precipitate to speak of realignment is that despite their own initial claims, the appeals of parties associated with the new politics are not really so very different from more traditional parties. There is a sense in which they need not be seen to represent a new dimension in mass politics, cutting across the left and the right; rather, they can be regarded as a new variation within the left. During their initial formation, Green parties often deliberately avoided applying terms such as "left" or "right" to their own politics. As Jonathon Porritt, a leading member of the British Green Party, then put it: "We profoundly disagree with the politics of the right and its underlying ideology of capitalism; we profoundly disagree with the politics of the left and its adherence, in varying degrees, to the ideology of communism. That leaves us little choice but to disagree, perhaps less profoundly, with the politics of the center and its ideological potpourri of socialized capitalism" (Porritt, *Seeing,* p. 43). With time, however, the capacity to maintain this distinctive approach was undermined. As Green parties began to win seats in local assemblies and national parliaments, they found themselves obliged to come to terms with mainstream politics, and like their long-established competitors, they found it difficult— and undesirable—to stand aloof from day-to-day political bargaining. Even more important, in such situations the Green parties have become increasingly associated with other parties of the left (Mair, "Green"). Thus, in both Belgium and Germany, Green parties forged local alliances with established left-wing parties, and both later joined governments together with the social democrats. A similar process happened in France and Italy. In the Netherlands, the tiny Green Party actually joined with the Communist Party and two small new left parties to form an electoral cartel, the Green Left. Indeed, already by the end of the 1980s, Porritt's own emphasis had changed: No longer rejecting notions of left and right, he argued that a crucial issue was the extent to which "today's Green parties [should] identify themselves specifically as parties of the left" (Porritt, "Foreword," p. 8).

In sum, if postmaterialist concerns do signify a potential for change within western European party systems, it is likely to be a limited realignment that changes some of the terms of reference of the left-wing divide while leaving its essential basis intact. Thus, one of the few studies to address these questions to the politics of gender, which has long been a major concern of postmaterialism, found that attitudes toward gender inequalities did not actually constitute part of any new cleavage but, rather, were strongly associated with and absorbed within the older "left–right" divide (Evans, "Is Gender"). This sort of change and adaptation is by no means novel. As was seen in Chapters 7 and 8, the terms of reference of the left-right divide have often been in flux, and it can even be argued that it is primarily because of this flux that the distinction itself has remained so relevant for so long, in that the terms "left" and "right" are capable of taking on new meanings for successive generations of voters and parties in European politics. As Smith once put it, "it is precisely the 'plasticity' of left and right which enables [parties] to combine coherence and flexibility, to absorb new issues and ward off challenges" (Smith, p. 159). On the left adaptation could be seen when the initial monopoly of the social democratic parties was challenged fundamentally by the mobilization of communist parties in the wake of the Russian Revolution of 1917 and again by the new left parties of the late 1960s and 1970s. The Green challenge of the late 1980s and the 1990s, to the extent that this challenge is contained within the broad left, may simply be another step in a long and continuing process of adaptation.

On the right, despite overall long-term continuity, the political terms of reference have also changed continually, most recently through the dramatic decline of Christian democracy. New politics at this end of the spectrum has also enjoyed greater success, with the rise of far-right parties in such countries as Austria, Belgium, Denmark, France, Italy, the Netherlands, and Norway, and with their overall mean levels of support rising

TABLE 9.5

The Persistence of the Left, 1950–2004 (in 16 countries)

Party Family	1950s	1960s	1970s	1980s	1990s	2000–4
Social democrats	33.6	32.1	31.8	30.7	29.9	28.8
Communists	7.9	7.3	7.5	5.4	3.5	2.3
New left	—	1.1	1.6	2.6	1.8	2.0
Greens	—	—	—	2.3	4.8	5.4
All left	**41.5**	**40.5**	**40.9**	**41.0**	**40.0**	**38.5**

Note: Figures refer to mean aggregate electoral support per decade—see the tables in Chapter 8.

from less than 1 percent in the 1960s to more than 6 percent in older democracies in the 1990s. Moreover, albeit often with difficulty, they have also sometimes joined government—in Austria, Italy, and the Netherlands, for example—or supported minority governments as external partners (in Denmark). Although this might offer stronger evidence of realignment than the Green case on the left, here too we may simply be seeing another step in the extended process of adaptation. As far-right parties gain votes, their desire for influence becomes more apparent, and hence their program becomes somewhat more pragmatic.

Taking left and right as a whole, however, the most remarkable feature of all is the extraordinary persistence across the postwar decades. To be sure, the individual countries have varied in their own national records (see Chapter 8). In addition, as we have shown, there has also been some limited reshuffling at the European level both *within* the left and *within* the right. But for compelling evidence of overall persistence, we need look no further than the summaries in Tables 9.5 and 9.6, as derived from the various family tables in Chapter 8.

Table 9.5 summarizes changes in the mean levels of electoral support for the different families of the left across the past half century. For the left as a whole, this has been almost invariant: from 41.5 percent in the 1950s to 40 percent in the 1990s. What is even more striking is to see this continuing even into the first elections of the new century, where the left averaged 38.5 percent in the long-established democracies, and 40.1 percent across all twenty west European cases. And this continuity ensued despite what was almost a wholesale transformation in society, economy, and culture across the postwar period. Within the left, and among the individual families, variation can of course be seen. The social democrats fell by almost 4 percent across the last five decades, while the communists fell by more than 4 percent. This slack was taken up by both the new left and the Greens, and in this sense the left as a whole appears to have become more modern—or postmodern—than was the case in the earlier postwar years. In other respects, however, this reshuffling has made little practical difference. Despite greater fragmentation, alliances between the different left parties are just as feasible now as during the 1950s and 1960s—perhaps even more so since the more hard-line communists have been partially edged out by the more accommodating Greens and new left. The left may now be more varied than before. It is certainly not weaker.

TABLE 9.6

The Persistence of the Center and Right, 1950–2004 (in 16 countries)

Party Family	1950s	1960s	1970s	1980s	1990s	2000–4
Christian democrats	22.9	23.4	22.2	21.5	17.6	16.9
Conservatives	15.4	15.8	15.2	16.3	15.0	15.4
Liberals	8.7	9.8	9.6	10.3	10.1	10.7
Agrarian/center	6.6	6.9	6.7	5.4	6.4	7.1
Far right	1.0	0.5	1.6	2.2	6.3	5.8
All center and right	**54.6**	**56.4**	**55.3**	**55.7**	**55.4**	**55.9**

Note: Figures refer to mean aggregate electoral support per decade—see the tables in Chapter 8.

Table 9.6 summarizes the parallel changes in the mean levels of support for the different families of the center and right. Here too, what is most striking the sheer persistence over time. These families of the center and right together accounted for 54.6 percent of the European vote in the 1950s and stayed steady through to the 55.4 percent recorded in the 1990s. (Because of the presence of "other" parties—see Chapter 8—the two sets of families do not sum up to exactly 100 percent.) In the early elections of the new century, the figures remained highly comparable: 55.9 percent in the long-established democracies, 54.3 percent when taking all 20 democracies together. In this group of families, however, reshuffling was more pronounced. While the conservative and agrarian/center parties remained more or less unchanged at the European level, Christian democratic parties fell by a quarter. Particularly in the bigger countries, an increasingly secular society has been clearly less hospitable to these latter parties. Part of this loss has been made up by liberal gains, but the bulk of it has been compensated for by the rise of the far right. In the short run, at least, this may also work to undermine the overall position of the right, in that some of these new extreme parties are difficult coalition allies. One result of their success might therefore be to weaken the strategic position of the right by pushing the parties of the center into closer alignment with the left; if the far-right parties moderate, however, the right will be strengthened strategically (see Bale).

In short, if realignment is taken to mean the replacement by an alternative divide of the fundamental division between right and left, then the evidence in favor of realignment is far from convincing. But if it is taken to mean a significant shift in party fortunes *within* both left and right, then a limited realignment may well be taking place. Then again, this is not a particularly new phenomenon—we have seen reshuffling before.

If, on the other hand, as Ignazi has suggested, there is something qualitatively different about the "new politics" of the left and the Green parties, and if this is now being challenged by the mobilization of "new right" parties, then we could be witnessing the emergence of a new cleavage in European politics. It is clearly too soon to speak of such a radical departure, however, and it must be remembered that, despite their success, the parties of the new right, like those of the new left and the Greens, still account for only a very small share of the popular votes. Taken together, average electoral support for the far right, the Greens, and the new left totaled a little more than 13 percent of the vote among the long-established democracies in 2000–4; even when taken together, in other words, they were still being outpolled by the ailing Christian democrats.

Toward Dealignment?

The argument that there has been a dealignment of western European party systems rests on three types of evidence. The first concerns a decline in the extent to which voters identify with political parties and prove willing to turn out to vote for them. The second concerns the emergence of new political parties and the growth in electoral support for such parties. The third has to do with the general increase in levels of electoral volatility (for a more detailed discussion, see Mair, "In the Aggregate"). As we shall see, evidence regarding all three factors suggests that the hold of traditional parties in western Europe is indeed being undermined, but even this conclusion should not be overstated.

Party Identification and Voter Turnout

One of the clearest symptoms of dealignment in western Europe can be seen in the declining levels of party identification—the psychological attachment that is seen to tie individual voters to particular party alternatives. At first sight, the evidence of such decline seems quite convincing. In one recent assessment, for example, Dalton and his colleagues (*Parties,* pp. 24–29) collated various Eurobarometer surveys and national election studies covering some fourteen European polities over the period from the 1960s through to the end of the 1990s, and they found that the evidence of declining partisanship was unequivocal. In all but two of the polities (the exceptions were Belgium and Denmark), the trend in levels of popular identification with parties was clearly downward—sometimes markedly so. Moreover, in *all* fourteen polities, this time without exception, the trend in levels of strong party identification was also clearly down. In other words, substantially fewer voters now feel a strong sense of attachment to their party of choice than used to be the case in Europe. A similar pattern is evident in the comparable data that are summarized for a group of key European polities in Table 9.7, and that in some cases extend to 2001 and 2002. Here, a decline in the general level of party identification is evident in each of the countries, albeit more pronounced in some cases (e.g., Ireland) than in others (e.g., Denmark). Moreover, here also it is the decline in the numbers of voters with a strong sense of identification that is most evidently marked and that is also sometimes very sharp (Austria, the UK). Although the sense of attachment to party has not been completely obliterated in western Europe, these figures suggest that it is clearly waning.

In practice, however, we must be careful not to read too much into such figures. In the first place, information on party identification is based on survey data, and the cross-national use of survey data is notoriously fraught with problems. Questions must be translated into different languages, and anyway the same questions tend to mean rather different things in different countries, often leading to contradictory results (Sinnott). In addition to these methodological problems, there have been conceptual problems in applying what is essentially a U.S. notion of party identification in the European context (Thomassen). For a range of institutional reasons (the voter registration process, the holding of primaries, the holding of separate presidential and congressional elections), U.S. voters may be able to distinguish between identifying with a party, on the one hand, and voting for that party, on the other. European voters, in contrast, often change their

TABLE 9.7

The Decline of Party Identification

Country: dates	Party Identifiers (%)		Strong Party Identifiers (%)	
	Past	**Present**	**Past**	**Present**
Austria: 1954, 2001	73	55	71	25
Denmark: 1971, 1988	56	50	30	23
Germany: 1972, 2002	75	65	17	12
Ireland: 1978, 1994	29	18	14	6
Italy: 1978, 1996	77	56	46	30
United Kingdom: 1964, 2001	93	84	44	15

Note: Data refer to the proportion of survey respondents reporting an attachment or a close attachment to a party.

Source: Eurobarometer, as derived from data reported in Mair et al.

party identification at the same time that they change their vote. Thus, even though party identification can remain quite stable in the United States, notwithstanding some electoral volatility, it does not tend to have the same degree of independent stability in Europe.

A second reason to be cautious when interpreting data on the dealignment of party identification in Europe is that many European voters have tended to identify primarily with social groups and only indirectly with political parties. Sections of the Italian electorate, for example, may have identified with the Christian Democrats only to the extent that they also identified with the Catholic Church, which was associated with the DC. In the same way, sections of the British electorate may have identified with the Labour Party only to the extent that they had a working-class identification, which then translated into a sense of belonging to the Labour Party as the party of the working class. In other words, precisely because many European parties were traditionally cleavage-based, the primary loyalty of a voter may be to the class or social group that defines a cleavage rather than to the party that represents it.

Perhaps the most serious problem with applying the notion of party identification in the European context is that there is evidence that voters in more fragmented party systems can identify with more than one party at the same time (Eijk and Niemoeller). Voters on the left, for example, may identify with both a socialist party and a communist party, maintaining a stable sense of belonging to the left bloc as a whole while shifting their preferences from one party to another according to the particular circumstances of a given election. Given the evidence that we have seen of the aggregate persistence of left and right over time, as well as that of the reshuffling that has taken place within each of these blocs, this interpretation seems at least intuitively plausible (see also Bartolini and Mair).

Thus, despite the fact that the evidence of declining party identification in Europe seems quite powerful and consistent, interpreting this evidence is quite difficult. Rather than showing that European party systems are becoming "dealigned," patterns in these data may be a product of applying an inappropriate concept to European multiparty parliamentary democracies.

The evidence is somewhat clearer with regard to trends in voting turnout. Participation levels in national elections in western Europe have usually far exceeded the levels recorded in the United States; but ever since observers began debating the extent to which traditional parties and party systems were being transformed, there has been a general expectation that these high levels of electoral participation would begin to decline. As we shall see in Chapter 11, voting has actually been obligatory in a small number of European polities. Even beyond these polities, however, turnout has been very high. In Malta, for example, where turnout is not obligatory, nearly every able voter now turns out on election day. In Denmark, Germany, Iceland, Italy, Luxembourg, the Netherlands, Norway, and Sweden, turnout levels well in excess of 80 percent have not been uncommon. Only in Switzerland, and then only since the 1970s (when women were first given the vote) does the exceptionally low level of turnout in national elections approximate to that in the United States, although it should also be pointed out that even in other countries levels of turnout in elections to the European Parliament (see Table 5.3) now often fall below those recorded in the United States. Moreover, as we shall see, levels of participation are also markedly low in Poland.

Nor, perhaps surprisingly, was there much change in this pattern of high turnout at national elections—at least through to the 1980s and at least at the cross-national European level. In the 1950s, for example, turnout levels averaged 84 percent (see Table 9.8). In the 1960s, the average was 85 percent, falling to just below 85 percent in the 1970s and to just under 83 percent in the 1980s. There was not much variation here.

In the 1990s, however the picture began to look quite different. Among the sixteen long-established democracies, turnout averaged less than 79 percent in the 1990s, falling below the 80 percent mark for the first time in postwar history and dropping by a full 4 percent with respect to the 1980s. More strikingly, all but five of these countries (Belgium, Denmark, Malta, Sweden, and the UK) recorded their own lowest decade average in the 1990s, while, with the exception of the UK, all recorded a lower turnout in the 1990s than in the 1980s. This was a marked change, and it suggested that European voters might be becoming more disengaged from the conventional political process. Such evidence would clearly serve the dealignment thesis. The evidence of the first elections of the new century also confirm this pattern. In 2000–4 turnout fell even further, to below 77 percent among the sixteen long-established democracies, and to a similar level when all twenty democracies are measured. To be sure, the differences are small, but they are still moving in a consistent direction. These latest figures also include the most recent elections in Ireland and the UK, in both of which turnout fell to the lowest level since the introduction of universal suffrage.

Support for New Political Parties

The second obvious symptom of partisan dealignment is a trend toward increasing electoral support for new political parties. As political responses to the parties have become more individualized and as the links between parties and voters have become more attenuated, the space for the creation of new parties has increased. In some cases, as with the environmental or Green parties, new parties reflect the emergence of new issues. In other cases, however, new parties are simply the results of splits in old parties. In Britain, Denmark, and the Netherlands in the 1970s and 1980s, for example, key figures abandoned mainstream socialist parties and formed new parties of the center–left. In Belgium,

TABLE 9.8

Mean Levels of Electoral Participation, 1950–2004

Country	1950s	1960s	1970s	1980s	1990s	2000–4
Austria	95.3	93.8	92.3	91.6	83.8	84.3
Belgium	93.1	91.3	92.9	93.9	92.5	91.1
Denmark	81.8	87.3	87.5	85.6	84.4	87.1
Finland[a]	76.5	85.0	81.1	78.7	70.8	69.6
France	80.0	76.6	82.3	71.9	68.9	64.4
Germany	86.8	87.1	90.9	87.1	79.7	80.3
Iceland	90.8	91.3	90.4	89.4	86.4	87.5
Ireland	74.3	74.2	76.5	72.9	67.2	62.7
Italy	93.6	92.9	92.6	89.0	85.5	81.2
Luxembourg	91.9	89.6	89.5	88.1	87.1	86.0[b]
Malta	78.7	90.3	94.0	95.2	94.7	96.2
Netherlands[c]	95.4	95.0	83.5	83.5	76.0	79.5
Norway	78.8	82.8	81.6	83.1	77.1	75.5
Sweden	78.7	86.4	90.4	89.1	85.0	80.1
Switzerland[d]	69.0	64.2	52.3	48.2	43.8	45.2
United Kingdom	79.1	76.6	75.1	74.1	75.4	59.4
Mean (N = 16)	**84.0**	**85.3**	**84.6**	**82.6**	**78.6**	**76.9**
Cyprus				95.2	92.2	91.8
Greece				83.5	81.6	77.4
Portugal				78.0	64.3	61.5
Spain				73.5	77.6	77.2
Overall mean (N = 20)				**82.6**	**78.7**	**76.9**

Note: As in Chapter 8, for Cyprus, Greece, Portugal, and Spain, decade averages are reported only since the 1980s.

[a] From 1975 onward, Finnish citizens residing abroad were given the right to vote, but the figures reported here refer only the turnout among Finnish residents.

[b] Estimate.

[c] From 1971 onward (that is, including all 1970s elections), it was no longer obligatory for Dutch voters to attend at the ballot box.

[d] Women in Switzerland were given the vote in federal elections for the first time in 1971.

the politicization of the linguistic divide in the 1970s led not only to the creation of new parties but also to splits in each of the main traditional parties.

In fact, and as can be seen from Table 9.9, aggregate electoral support for new parties has risen steadily over the past forty years. The operational definition of new parties that we are using here is a very simple—and generous—one: Recalling that Lipset and Rokkan spoke in the late 1960s of the fact that many of the parties then contesting elections "were older than the national electorates," we can make a very simple distinction between "old" parties, those that first began contesting elections prior to the 1960s, and "new" parties, those that first began to contest elections from 1960 onward. Indeed, the latter parties have proved thick on the ground: Of the almost 300 separate parties that contested at least one

TABLE 9.9

Mean Aggregate Electoral Support for New Political Parties, 1960–2004

Country	1960s	1970s	1980s	1990s	2000–4
Austria	1.7	0.1	4.1	11.5	10.5
Belgium	2.8	11.4	12.9	23.7	19.2
Denmark	8.7	26.9	30.7	24.9	25.1
Finland	1.6	8.2	13.7	22.3	19.5
France	16.3	29.1	27.1	41.7	57.7
Germany	4.3	0.5	7.5	13.9	13.2
Iceland	2.4	4.7	19.3	21.6	40.8
Ireland	0.3	1.4	7.9	10.0	9.4
Italy[a]	9.5	3.3	7.1	66.8	100.0
Luxembourg	3.1	12.0	11.5	22.4	27.4
Malta	13.1	0.0	0.1	1.5	0.7
Netherlands	2.3	26.6	44.5	45.9	61.5
Norway	3.9	13.6	15.1	19.7	30.0
Sweden	1.1	1.6	4.5	14.5	13.7
Switzerland	0.4	5.3	12.2	14.9	8.5
United Kingdom	0.0	0.8	11.6	2.3	1.5
Mean (N = 16)	**4.4**	**9.1**	**14.4**	**22.4**	**27.4**

Note: "New parties" are here defined as those that first began to contest elections no earlier than 1960 and that poll at least 1 percent in one election.
[a] Calculated on basis of PR votes only since elections of 1994.

election in the long-established democracies since 1960, some 60 percent have been formed since that date. To put it another way, only some 40 percent of parties contesting elections during these past four decades were formed prior to 1960 (Mair, "New").

Given these large numbers, and given that the later the period the more likely it is that the numbers will have accumulated, it is not then very surprising to see these parties' aggregate support building up. During the 1960s, when only some thirty of these new parties had already been formed, their total vote averaged just over 4 percent (see Table 9.9). In the 1970s, this number grew to just over 9 percent, and then in the 1980s to more than 14 percent. In the 1990s, the new-party share totaled more than 22 percent, and in 2000–4 more than 27 percent. By the new century, therefore, more than one in four of votes being cast in national elections in Europe was going to a "new" party.

In some of the countries involved, this growth has clearly been substantially above this average. In the newly made Italian party system, where new parties accounted for the vast majority of votes cast in 1996, their average share across the three elections of the 1990s was a massive 67 percent, and by 2001 new parties enjoyed a monopoly of the vote. None of the older protagonists was left in the field. In the Netherlands, where the CDA also counts as a new party, their share averaged almost 46 percent in the 1990s and then rose to more than 60 percent in 2002 and 2003, helped along in part by the success of the Pim Fortuyn List. In France, where party longevity is the exception, they averaged more than 40 percent in the 1990s and almost 60 percent thereafter. Indeed, only Malta and the United Kingdom have proved inhospitable to new parties, notwithstanding the flurry of success enjoyed by the SPD in Westminster elections in the 1980s.

Taking these figures at face value, we might be inclined to read them as signifying a fundamental transformation in party alignments in western Europe. The fact that the old parties formed before the 1960s have accounted for fewer than half of the parties contesting elections over the past forty years, and the fact that the new parties formed since 1960 pulled in more than a quarter of the vote in western Europe in the new century elections, must surely signal a major change.

But what sort of change? As we have already said (see Tables 9.5 and 9.6), most of the traditional party families are managing to hold their own in aggregate electoral terms. We have also shown that the really new families—the new left and Greens, on the one hand, and the new far right, on the other—have not proved great vote winners to date, at least not across western Europe as a whole. Moreover, some of the most successful "new" politics parties of the far right—including the Freedom Party in Austria and the National Alliance (ex-MSI) in Italy—are themselves quite old parties, albeit now dressed in new ideological costumes.

What this therefore seems to suggest is that many of the votes going to new parties are actually going to new organizational alternatives that operate within recognizable—if not wholly traditional—parameters. This is not exactly the old politics: After all, newly formed organizations are unlikely to present themselves as wholly belonging to the past. But neither is it necessarily the new politics. At best, it may be old politics in a new form. Hence it is not too surprising to find that the most successful of these new formations over the past forty years include parties such as the Dutch CDA, Forza Italia, and the Democratic Left in Italy, the UDF and later the UMP in France, and the Left Wing Alliance in Finland (Mair, "New"). To be sure, these are all new parties. But their politics will be familiar to even the most old-fashioned observer of west European politics.

Here again, then, we seem to see evidence that speaks more of dealignment than of realignment. Loyalties to traditional parties are certainly ebbing. Otherwise, even these familiar-sounding new parties would never have enjoyed any real success. But while voters may be willing to consider new alternatives, especially since the 1990s, and in this sense may be regarded as increasingly dealigned, they seem unwilling to transfer across to a wholly new politics.

Electoral Volatility

The third collection of evidence in favor of the dealignment thesis involves increased aggregate electoral volatility (Pedersen, "Dynamics"; Pedersen, "Changing"), which, precisely because it measures levels of flux from one election to the next, offers a very useful summary indicator of short-term changes in party support.

When the trend toward increased electoral volatility was first noted in certain countries in the 1970s, it was not in fact then seen to apply to western Europe as a whole. Pedersen's own evidence from the 1970s, for example, pointed to an actual decline in volatility in France and West Germany and, albeit less marked, in Italy. In each of these countries, the party system was restructured in the early postwar years, following the reestablishment of the democratic process, and each party system was soon to be stabilized by a strong center–right party. In many other western European countries, however, the 1970s did witness an erosion of the steady-state politics of the 1950s and 1960s, and

TABLE 9.10

Mean Aggregate Electoral Volatility, 1950–2004

Country	1950s	1960s	1970s	1980s	1990s	2000–4
Austria	4.1	3.3	2.7	5.5	9.4	21.1
Belgium	7.6	10.2	5.3	10.0	10.8	12.8
Denmark	5.5	8.7	15.5	9.7	12.4	13.3
Finland	4.4	7.0	7.9	8.7	11.0	4.8
France	22.3	11.5	8.8	13.4	15.4	12.6
Germany	15.2	8.4	5.0	6.3	9.0	7.8
Iceland	9.2	4.3	12.2	11.6	13.7	8.0
Ireland	10.3	7.0	5.7	8.1	11.7	8.5
Italy[a]	9.7	8.2	9.9	8.6	22.9	22.0
Luxembourg	10.8	8.8	12.5	14.8	6.2	9.7
Malta	9.2	14.4	4.6	1.4	3.6	0.5
Netherlands	5.1	7.9	12.3	8.3	19.1	23.4
Norway	3.4	5.3	15.3	10.7	15.9	16.1
Sweden	4.8	4.0	6.3	7.6	13.8	13.9
Switzerland	2.5	3.5	6.0	6.4	8.0	8.7
United Kingdom	4.3	5.2	8.3	3.3	9.3	5.6
Mean (N = 16)	**8.0**	**7.4**	**8.6**	**8.4**	**12.0**	**11.8**
Cyprus				12.8	8.4	6.2
Greece				11.3	5.5	6.2
Portugal				15.0	11.9	8.3
Spain				14.2	8.8	9.6
Overall mean (N = 20)				**9.4**	**11.3**	**11.0**

Note: The values refer to levels of aggregate electoral volatility, measured as the sum of the percentage vote gains of all the winning parties (or the sum of the percentage vote losses of all the losing parties) from one election to the next. See Pedersen ("Dynamics"; "Changing"). As in Chapter 8, for Cyprus, Greece, Portugal, and Spain decade averages are reported only since the 1980s.

[a] Calculated on basis of PR votes since elections of 1994.

since then the expectation has been that this sense of flux would eventually pass on to even the more stable polities.

Even by the 1980s, however, these expectations had not been borne out. Indeed, in western Europe as a whole (see Table 9.10) the 1980s witnessed a marginal decline in volatility, a decline that was particularly marked in Denmark, the Netherlands, Norway, and the United Kingdom. Moreover, what could also be seen by the 1980s was that the level of aggregate vote shifts between the main class blocs on the left and right was much less than the volatility within these class blocs (Bartolini and Mair; Mair, *Party*, pp. 76–90). In other words, at least as far as the class cleavage is concerned, a much greater proportion of electoral instability proved to be the result of switching votes between friends rather than between enemies, a trend that is also compatible with the notion that European voters may identify with more than one party at the same time.

But although this bloc volatility continues to remain relatively low, it is striking to note that elections since the 1990s reveal that aggregate volatility as a whole has increased quite suddenly and quite markedly (see Table 9.10), averaging some 12 percent among the long-established European democracies. The 1990s marked the first postwar decade in which the mean level of volatility across western Europe as a whole pushed above 10 percent, marking an increase of almost half as much again relative to the 1980s. The growth in volatility in the 1990s has also proved remarkably consistent, with almost three-quarters of the individual countries registering their own peak postwar levels. The exceptions to this pattern include Denmark, where the really big electoral earthquakes hit in the 1970s, as well as France and Germany, which experienced considerable volatility in the wake of immediate postwar reconstruction. Luxembourg and Malta also peaked during earlier decades. Remarkably, however, only in Luxembourg did volatility in the 1990s prove lower than in the 1980s. Moreover, despite a slight average decline, the few elections that have so far taken place in the new century confirm this new trend. Italy still remains remarkably volatile, for example, despite the emergence of two broadly based electoral cartels, and both Austria and the Netherlands have gone on to new record highs. Indeed, in both cases, the sudden growth in support for the far right (in the Netherlands in 2002), or its sudden decline (in Austria in 2002) produced election outcomes that rank among the most volatile in western European history (see Table 9.11). But although these elections were exceptional, they can be related to a trend toward

TABLE 9.11

The Most Volatile Elections Since 1900 in Europe's Long-Established Democracies

Country	Year	Level of Volatility (%)
Italy	1994	36.7
Germany	1920	32.1
France	1906	31.1
Netherlands	2002	30.7
France	1910	30.5
Germany	1924	27.1
France	1958	26.7
Switzerland	1919	23.4
Italy	1948	23.0
Switzerland	1917	22.8
Italy	2001	22.0
Netherlands	1994	21.5
Denmark	1973	21.2
Germany	1953	21.2
Austria	2002	21.1
Ireland	1927	20.8

Note: All elections with a level of volatility greater than 20.0 percent.

greater electoral instability. Among the nine postwar elections included in Table 9.11, for example, five have occurred since 1990. Here again, then, as we have seen with regard to levels of turnout and support for new parties, we see evidence to suggest that the period around the turn of the new century is different from what has gone before. Here again, we may be witnessing real signs of dealignment.

✦ Evaluating Change and Stability in Western Europe

Studies of western European politics that set out to chart and explain change often conclude with the observation that change is neither so extensive nor so pervasive as was first imagined. "Even if change is widespread," concluded one early account, "it is important not to overstate its extent. Although few party systems have been as constant as they once appeared to be, all exhibit substantial elements of continuity" (Wolinetz, p. 296). Taking all the evidence presented in this chapter together, we can see that contemporary western European politics is characterized at least as much by continuity as it is by change. To be sure, the image of transformation is seductive; but the shock of the new can blind us to the persistence of the old.

The continuities can be easily summarized. The overall balance between the broad left bloc and the broad center–right bloc is remarkably constant. There is also a very low level of aggregate vote redistribution across the key left–right boundary. The principal political protagonists, most notably the social democrats and the conservatives, have proved very resilient. New parties, despite their pervasiveness and their electoral success, do not seem to have challenged the core of traditional alignments.

The changes are also evident, particularly since the 1990s. There is a growing individualization of political preferences and a weakening of collective identities. There is a decline in the distinctiveness of the social bases of party support. There have been changes in the terms of reference of the division between left and right. The balance of support for parties within each bloc has sometimes changed. And a "postmaterialist" or "new politics" dimension has emerged, albeit without substantial electoral weight, in many of the more established European democracies. Above all, one of the most important party families, the Christian democrats, has experienced a major decline in its aggregate electoral support. Perhaps most important of all, it seems that voters have become less willing to participate, while those who still do turn out to vote are now more willing to play around with their individual party preferences.

The overall picture, then, seems to be one of "peripheral" change, with the "core" of most of the party systems remaining intact (Smith) and with the voters who continue to opt for these parties proving increasingly disengaged. European voters are less tied to parties than before and have shown themselves more willing to shift their preferences from one party to another. But they do so cautiously. On the left, voters may shift from a communist party to a socialist party, or from a socialist party to a new left or Green party, but they tend to remain on the left. Voters on the right may shift from a Christian party to a secular party, or from a liberal party to a more conservative party, or from a conservative party to a far-right party, but they tend also to stay on the right. Ties to individual parties may have weakened, but ties to the broader identities of left and right appear to have been maintained. In this important sense, the notion that European party systems are "frozen" should not be dismissed too easily.

It must be emphasized, moreover, that the long-term stabilization of west European party systems is not simply a function of the ties that bind distinct social groups (Catholics, workers, farmers, and so on) to parties or to blocs of parties. To be sure, social structure has certainly proved to be an important stabilizing element, especially in systems with strong social cleavages or subcultures, such as Italy, the Netherlands, and Sweden. But if social structure were the only freezing agent, then we would already have witnessed much greater change in electoral alignments in the 1970s and 1980s than was actually the case. The fact is that many of the old traditional party families in Europe remain alive and kicking despite what we have seen to be the widespread weakening of religious and class identities, and the long-term process of individualization. More specifically, if social structure were all that mattered, then we would have witnessed much more continuous change in a party system such as that in Ireland, where partisanship has long been characterized by a remarkable absence of social roots yet, at least until recently, the party system proved to be one of the most stable in western Europe. In other words, to suggest that social structure alone is the freezing agent is to suggest that a frozen party system can exist only in a country in which there is also a frozen society, and this contention is patently implausible.

Party systems are in fact frozen by a variety of factors, of which social structure is just one of the more important (Bartolini and Mair, pp. 251–308; Sartori, "Sociology"; Mair, *Party,* pp. 199–223). They are also frozen by the constraints imposed by institutional structures such as the electoral system (see Chapter 11) and by the organizational efforts of the parties themselves (see Chapter 10). Most important, party systems are also frozen by the constraints imposed by the structure of party competition. In Italy, for example, the basis for a wholesale change in electoral preferences in the 1990s was laid partly by the "legitimation" of the DS, which undermined the terms of reference by which Italian party competition had been structured since the late 1940s. Italian voters, as well as the Italian parties themselves, had long been constrained by the belief that there was no alternative to Christian Democratic government. And once such an alternative finally did emerge through the transformation of the unacceptable PCI into the highly acceptable DS, this particular anchor was cut loose and voters began to shift in relatively great numbers.

Up to now, however, the sort of dramatic changes that have recently had an impact on the Italian party system remain exceptional, and whether similar ruptures will yet come to affect other long-standing European party systems is still to be seen. It still remains to be seen, for example, whether the innovative Red–Green coalition that took office in Germany in 1998 will lead to a sea change in how Germans understand the dynamics of their party system. It still remains to be seen whether the huge flux that characterized Dutch politics in 2002 and 2003 will signal a new and lasting change in patterns of government formation and party competition. It also still remains to be seen whether contemporary new divides will be strong enough and persistent enough to develop into new cleavages, or even into a recrudescence of old cleavages. The growing tension between indigenous and immigrant populations, for example, particularly relating to the position of Islamic communities and practices, might well lead to a revitalization of old-style church–state issues. The growth of Euroskepticism in both western and postcommunist Europe, and the growing opposition to the deepening and widening of European integration may also begin to force new electoral alignments (see Chapter 5). Eijk and Franklin (p. 47) speak of this latter issue as the equivalent of a "sleeping giant" and argue that it is now ripe for politicization: "it is only a matter of time before policy entrepreneurs ... seize the opportunity ... to differentiate themselves from other parties in EU terms." One direction in which such politicization might lead is toward a wholly new divide, with pro- and anti-EU parties lined up in a new set of alliances. Alternatively, as in the Norwegian case, it might simply play out within the older alignments defined by center and periphery. Europe may also have a depoliticizing effect, however, and hence one of the most important questions for the future is whether voters in the future might become even more disengaged, and whether aggregate voting outcomes will begin to reflect an ever more random distribution of preferences, leading to the possible erosion of long-familiar structures. New and potentially enduring divides might not actually emerge, or at least they might not translate so directly into the national electoral arena, and hence the result could be continuing dealignment and disaffection. It is this possibility, rather than the challenge of new issues as such, that still poses the greatest challenge to contemporary political leaders in Europe.

✦ PARTIES AND VOTERS IN POSTCOMMUNIST EUROPE

One of the most important lessons that we have learned from looking at the development of parties and party systems in western Europe is that the structure of mass politics takes time to stabilize. When mass politics begins, in other words, it is often unsettled. As was the case in Portugal and Spain in the late 1970s and 1980s, as well as in the rest of Europe in the wake of full democratization in the early part of the twentieth century, the formative years of mass politics are often characterized by significant volatility and change. New parties emerge and then disappear. Parties fuse with one another and then split away again. And the process by which voters learn about the limits and possibilities afforded by new electoral systems, on the one hand, and about the constraints and opportunities imposed by the new structures of party competition, on the other, can often take years to develop. In postcommunist Europe, then, as was noted in Chapter 7, as well as in most other new democracies, we cannot expect to witness the immediate settling down or institutionalization of stable party systems.

There are three principal factors involved here, each of which sets the postcommunist experience apart from that in western Europe, and each of which was also likely to have promoted high levels of electoral instability (see Mair, *Party*, pp. 175–98; see also Tóka; Kitschelt et al.). First and most obvious, the path toward democracy in postcommunist Europe has been radically different from that taken in most of western Europe. Not only are we talking here about a massive and quite overloaded process of transition—from communism to multiparty democracy, and from command economies to the free market—but we are also talking about a different mode of democratization. When most of the west European polities democratized at the beginning of the twentieth century, the process involved opening up to the mass of new voters a regime in which political competition was already an accepted principle. In other words, the regimes were competitive but exclusive—they denied the mass of ordinary citizens the right to participate. Democratization involved enfranchisement, the advent of mass suffrage. In postcommunist countries, by contrast, the process occurred the other way around. The principle of mass participation had been accepted under communism—indeed, if the mock elections that took place under communism recorded turnouts of less than 90 percent, the regime took umbrage—but not the right of competition. Elections were held, but they were not free elections. Given these different paths to democracy, then, we should not necessarily expect that the resultant parties and party systems will prove easily comparable (Biezen).

Second, the electorates in postcommunist Europe are different. One obvious difference is the absence of a long-standing cleavage structure (see Tóka), at least in the sense that has been discussed earlier—a structure that is characterized by distinct social divisions, a strong sense of collective identity within different groups in society, and strong organizations to which citizens might feel a sense of belonging. Social divisions in postcommunism are still essentially fluid, with the transition from a command to a market economy initially breaking down those few lines of social stratification that previously existed. And although this market economy is beginning to lead to new lines of stratification, these are emerging in the wake of societies that experienced through transition what Batt (p. 50) once tellingly described as "an unprecedented degree of social destructuring, volatility and fluidity." To be sure, identities other than those eroded by the communist economic system have survived—national or ethnic identities in a number of the postcommunist states, such as in Latvia, for example, and a religious, Catholic, identity in Poland in particular. Thus it is possible in some cases to link patterns of postcommunist partisanship to patterns of partisanship that existed over forty years earlier, before the era of communist rule, and to attribute at least some of this persistence to the enduring role of religious affiliations, as Wittenberg does for Hungary (Wittenberg). But such long-standing patterns of cleavage are the exceptions.

The emergence of new cleavages is also hampered by the fact that the parties in these new democracies have not yet invested a great effort to build a popular sense of identification and belonging among voters. There are exceptions, of course. The Czech and Slovak parties, for example, have grown to dominate their respective systems, and they also have been intent on building powerful organizational networks within their polities (Kopecký). In the main, however, postcommunist parties scarcely exist beyond parliament, with little continuity over time in terms of identity or organization, and with little evidence of any substantial organizational presence on the ground. As such, they do little to promote the structuring of electoral choice (see Chapter 10; see also Biezen; Lewis). In short, the electorates in postcommunist countries tend to be different in the sense that, as Rose ("Mobilizing") puts it, they are demobilized—lacking in any strong affective ties to the parties that compete for their votes and often skeptical about the idea of party itself. It is not so much that these voters are *de*aligned, as is perhaps increasingly the case in contemporary western Europe; rather, they are not *yet* aligned. And while the opposition between supporters and opponents of the former regime has had some structuring impact—most notably in Hungary and Poland—this is unlikely to persist into the future as a major alignment.

Third, the parties themselves are different. This is not so much a matter of differences in ideology or in programmatic identity—although these are also important—as it is of organizational behavior and practice. In brief, parties in new democracies in general, and parties in the postcommunist democracies in particular, are less frequently characterized by a sense of organizational loyalty and commitment. Where conflicts arise inside a party, then, the solution is often to split the party apart, with the dissenting factions establishing their own separate alternative organizations. At the same time, when common interests are perceived among different parties, even in the short term, the decision is often made to merge the parties into a broad electoral or even organizational coalition. The result is a constantly shifting array of actors, with parties entering elections in one guise and then adopting yet another guise in parliament itself, and with relatively little continuity in alternatives from one election to the next.

To be sure, there is substantial variation among across the postcommunist systems in this regard. At one extreme lies the Polish or Latvian cases, where the huge variety of party alternatives move in and out of diverse alliances from one election to the next and where, within parliament itself, there is such a constant shifting between parliamentary fractions and clubs that it becomes almost impossible even to identify some of the individual parties and to pin them down to particular positions. In the Czech Republic and Hungary, by contrast, the alignments at both the electoral and the parliamentary levels seem much more predictable, although in the Hungarian case electoral support still does shift considerably from one election to the next (see Table 9.12). Such complex processes of party fission and fusion are very uncommon in long-established party systems—almost by definition. Among the west European cases discussed here, for example, it is really only in France and, since 1994, in Italy that this sort of reshuffling is so pervasive. Indeed, were such organizational behavior to be a feature of these western systems, then it would be almost impossible to speak of them as party "systems." For a system of parties to emerge in the first place, and for it to persist, it must necessarily be characterized by regularity and predictability. This is what any system entails. And this is also why it still remains quite difficult to speak of real "party systems" in a number of the new postcommunist democracies. Neither the parties themselves, nor their modes of interaction, have yet been fully regularized.

TABLE 9.12

Aggregate Electoral Change in Postcommunist Europe

Country	1990s		2000–4	
	Turnout	Electoral Volatility[a]	Turnout	Electoral Volatility[a]
Czech Republic	77.8	19.3	57.9	11.5
Estonia	63.8	48.7	58.2	38.0
Hungary	63.8	26.9	70.5	22.5
Latvia	80.1	40.3	71.5	44.3
Lithuania	64.1	41.0	51.0	49.7
Poland	46.4	32.7	46.3	21.3
Slovakia	80.1	24.0	70.0	27.6
Slovenia	74.5	28.9	64.2	30.4
Mean ($N = 8$)	**68.8**	**32.7**	**61.2**	**30.6**

[a] Because precise information is often missing on the relationship between some of the parties that contest sequential elections, these provisional estimates of electoral volatility have a substantial margin of error. In general, they are likely to overestimate the real levels of aggregate volatility.

This sense of flux is also clearly compounded by unpredictability at the level of the voters themselves. Over and above the uncertainties that follow from the relative absence of affective loyalties to parties, as well as those that can be associated with the continuing institutional fluidity (see above), there are also uncertainties regarding how even short-term voter preferences will be reflected. Two factors are important here. First, turnout levels are still often relatively low by European standards (see Table 9.12), and hence a lot of voters may not yet have become socialized into the electoral process. In this sense, they remain demobilized and unpredictable. Second, because of the high thresholds imposed by the new electoral systems (see Chapter 11), and because both the voters and some of the parties have needed time to learn how to operate within the constraints imposed by these systems, a lot of votes in the formative elections were wasted by the failure of the parties concerned to win through to parliamentary representation. In the Czech Republic in 1992, for example, parties failing to reach the threshold accounted for almost 19 percent of the total vote. In Slovakia in 1992, the equivalent figure was almost 24 percent, and in Poland in 1993, following the imposition of the new thresholds, more than 34 percent of votes were cast for unsuccessful parties.

Putting all of these factors together, the picture that emerges is one of instability and flux among voters and their parties. This picture is summarized in Table 9.12, which reports levels of turnout and electoral volatility in elections in the eight postcommunist countries that concern us in this volume and offers a useful contrast with the patterns evident in the long-established west European democracies during the same period (see Tables 9.8 and 9.10). Through the 1990s, when these new party systems were first emerging, turnout averaged some 69 percent, almost 10 percent less than the "trough" recorded among the established European democracies during the same period. Of course, sharply contrasting patterns are also recorded here. Average turnout levels in Latvia, Slovenia, the Czech Republic, and Slovakia approximate the west European levels, and the level in Poland just manages to exceed that in Switzerland. This alone might suggest that it is also difficult to generalize even among this limited set of countries. On the other hand, by the beginning of the new century, turnout had actually fallen, to just over 60 percent, and this decline was marked in all of the countries with the exception of Hungary. This also serves to widen the gap with western Europe. To be sure, there are very few elections involved here, whether in the west or in the east, and a proper assessment should not be made until the full decade can be analyzed. Nevertheless, it is worth underlining here that the *average* turnout among the postcommunist countries in 2000–4 is lower than the turnout in *each* of the west European countries with the exceptions of Switzerland and the UK.

It is even more striking to observe the contrast in volatility levels. Across all the eight postcommunist countries in the 1990s, volatility averaged 32.7 percent, falling marginally to 30.6 percent in the first elections of the new century. This average is almost three times the equivalent figures in western Europe (see Table 9.10); indeed, this *average* figure of 32.7 percent is higher than all but one of the most volatile *single* elections ever recorded among the long-established democracies (see Table 9.11)—the only exception being the massive restructuring election in Italy in 1994, which produced a volatility level of almost 37 percent. What is also evident from the figures in Table 9.12 is that there is a reasonably marked difference between the small Baltic states, on the one hand, which remain extraordinarily volatile, and the slightly more stable east-central European states, on the other hand. In Estonia, Latvia, and Lithuania, volatility in the 1990s averaged some 43 percent, as against 26 percent in the other states. Moreover, while volatility actually increased in both Latvia and Lithuania in the first elections of the new century, it fell in the Czech Republic, Hungary, and Poland. The figure for the Czech Republic in this period is actually quite exceptional for the region, being lower than that recorded in many of the long-established polities during the same period. That said, we must treat all of these figures with caution. As noted above, these are nascent party systems, and they are often constituted by noninstitutionalized parties. Groups of leaders adopt particular labels in elections but then are quite prepared to reshuffle their alliances within parliament. Moreover, when labels change, or when parties split or merge, it is often difficult for the outside observer to trace the precise details of who has gone where, or with whom. The result is that new parties are deemed to have emerged and old parties are deemed to have failed, even though core elements of continuity might well be present. This also means that the real levels of aggregate volatility are probably lower than those that we indicate, and hence that the contrast with the stable and highly transparent party politics is probably exaggerated. To be sure, the electorates in postcommunist Europe are less stable than those in the west, but it is sometimes difficult to be precise when pinning this difference down.

When turnout levels began to dip in western Europe in the 1990s, and when levels of volatility began to climb, it suggested the onset of a new period of dealignment. Party systems and electoral support patterns had been frozen in the past, but they now appeared to be thawing out. With even lower turnout levels and even higher peaks in volatility becoming apparent in postcommunist Europe, the interpretation must necessarily be different. These systems are not emerging out of a frozen landscape—at least as far as democratic party systems are concerned. Rather, they are being formed for the first time. In other words, while the western systems may be becoming dealigned, these postcommunist systems might well be on the way to an initial alignment. In this sense, we may conceive of each set of systems as beginning from opposite ends of some notional continuum in which the western systems come from a point of stability and head toward a more uncertain and unpredictable future while the postcommunist systems emerge from a point of total uncertainty and unpredictability—an inevitable characteristic of newly created party systems—and perhaps head toward a more stable future (see also Ágh; Sitter). This would suggest that we might eventually see them meeting in the middle, converging on a point that is neither frozen not wholly fluid, and in which broad continuities combine with sometimes rapid and short-term change. What also follows from this, of course, and what may well be the most interesting aspect of this contrast between the two sets of systems, is not that the postcommunist countries are catching up with the already developed party politics of the west but rather that the patterns evident in the postcommunist countries may well represent one version of the possible future facing their western neighbors.

✦ EAST *VERSUS* WEST, OR EAST *AND* WEST?

Although parties and party systems in postcommunist democracies may not be stabilized by new cleavage structures—the consolidation of new cleavages will prove difficult in the increasingly individualized Europe of the twenty-first century—they may well be stabilized by persisting dimensions of competition. In other words, key issues and alternatives are likely to remain relevant for some years to come, even if the manner in which individual voters line up on these issues may reflect particularistic concerns. Tóka (p. 607), for example, convincingly argues that postcommunist alignments in the future will be likely to hinge firmly on value preferences and on what he calls "value voting," with the important dimensions being those constituted by religion versus secularism, left versus right, and nationalism versus antinationalism. In contemporary politics, he notes, such values are likely to remain relatively independent of circumstances related to status and demography, and, when it comes to generating partisan commitment, they "are at least as effective as is the political mobilization of organizational networks. ... Rather than stick with parties whose followers or leaders 'look like them,' voters are most likely to stick with the parties with whom they agree on major issue dimensions." Here too, then, we can see a possible convergence between the directions in which the eastern and western systems are heading, with the freeing of political preferences from long-term social determinants.

In this chapter we offered a very brief overview that sets the experience of postcommunist Europe against the more lengthy analysis that we devoted to the development of cleavages and mass politics in western Europe. As we noted earlier, these two separate worlds are not easily integrated with one another. The western polities have, in the main, more than a half century of peaceful democratic development already behind them. The postcommunist polities, in contrast, have experienced a long history of authoritarianism and only managed to effect a transition to democracy at the end of the twentieth century. What this brief overview indicates, however, is that the evident contrasts between these two parts of Europe may not last for long. It is not that the postcommunist polities are necessarily catching up with their longer-established western counterparts. That would leave a misleading impression. Instead, the politics of postindustrial society at the beginning of the new century, whether practiced in east or west, is sufficiently different from what went before that both sets of countries may well be converging on a new equilibrium. In the end, what matters may not be the former contrasts between the traditional capitalist democracies and the new postcommunist democracies but rather the difference between, on the one hand, both sets of polities and their contemporary functioning within a context of individualized preferences, communication, and behavior and, on the other hand, the patterns that used to prevail through most of the twentieth century. The relevance of this distinction for the way in which contemporary political parties are organized is one of the issues that we address in Chapter 10.

References

Ágh, Attila: *The Politics of Central Europe,* Sage, London, 1998.

Alford, Robert R.: *Party and Society: The Anglo-American Democracies,* Rand McNally, Chicago, 1963.

Ambrosius, Gerold, and William H. Hubbard: *A Social and Economic History of Twentieth-Century Europe,* Harvard University Press, Cambridge (MA), 1989.

Amyot, G. Grant: "Italy: The Long Twilight of the DC Regime," in Wolinetz (ed.), pp. 31–58.

Bakvis, Herman: *Catholic Power in the Netherlands,* McGill–Queens University Press, Kingston and Montreal, 1981.

Bale, Tim: "Cinderella and Her Ugly Sisters: The Mainstream and the Extreme Right in Europe's Bipolarising Party Systems," *West European Politics,* vol. 26, no. 3, 2003, pp. 67–90.

Bartolini, Stefano: *The Political Mobilization of the European Left, 1860–1980: The Class Cleavage,* Cambridge University Press, Cambridge, 2000.

Bartolini, Stefano, and Peter Mair: *Identity, Competition, and Electoral Availability: The Stabilization of European Electorates, 1885–1985,* Cambridge University Press, Cambridge, 1990.

Batt, Judy: *East Central Europe from Reform to Transformation,* Royal Institute of International Affairs/Pinter, London, 1991.

Bell, Daniel: *The End of Ideology,* Free Press, New York, 1960.

Berglund, Sten, Joakim Ekman, and Frank H. Aarebrot (eds.): *The Handbook of Political Change in Eastern Europe,* 2nd ed., Edward Elgar, Cheltenham, 2004.

Biezen, Ingrid van: *Political Parties in New Democracies: Party Organization in Southern and East-Central Europe,* Palgrave, London, 2003.

Crewe, Ivor, and David Denver (eds.): *Electoral Change in Western Democracies: Patterns and Sources of Electoral Volatility,* Croom Helm, London, 1985.

Crouch, Colin: *Social Change in Western Europe,* Oxford University Press, Oxford, 1999.

Daalder, Hans, and Peter Mair (eds.): *Western European Party Systems: Continuity and Change,* Sage, London, 1983.

Dalton, Russell J.: *Citizen Politics in Western Democracies: Public Opinion and Political Parties in the United States, Great Britain, West Germany, and France,* Chatham House, Chatham (NJ), 1988.

Dalton, Russell J.: "The German Voter," in Gordon Smith, William E. Paterson, and Peter H. Merkl (eds.), *Developments in West German Politics,* Macmillan, London, 1990, pp. 99–121.

Dalton, Russell J., Scott C. Flanagan, and Paul Allen Beck (eds.): *Electoral Change in Advanced Industrial Democracies: Realignment or Dealignment?* Princeton University Press, Princeton, 1984.

Dalton, Russell J., Ian McAllister, and Martin P. Wattenberg: "Parties and Their Publics," in Kurt Richard Luther and Ferdinand Müller-Rommel (eds.), *Political Parties in the New Europe,* Oxford University Press, Oxford, 2002, pp. 19–42.

Dalton, Russell J., and Martin P. Wattenberg (eds.): *Parties Without Partisans: Political Change in Advanced Industrial Democracies,* Oxford University Press, Oxford, 2000.

Diamant, Alfred: "The Group Basis of Austrian Politics," *Journal of Central European Affairs,* vol. 18, no. 2, 1958, pp. 134–55.

Duverger, Maurice: *Political Parties,* Methuen, London, 1954.

Eijk, Cees van der, and Mark Franklin: "Potential for Contestation on European Matters at National Elections in Europe," in Gary Marks and Marco R. Steenbergen (eds.), *European Integration and Political Conflict,* Cambridge University Press, Cambridge, 2004, pp. 32–50.

Eijk, Cees van der, and B. Niemoeller: *Electoral Change in the Netherlands,* C. T. Press, Amsterdam. 1983.

Eijk, Cees van der, et al.: "Cleavages, Conflict Resolution, and Democracy," in Franklin et al., pp. 406–31.

Evans, Geoffrey: "Is Gender on the 'New Agenda'?" *European Journal of Political Research,* vol. 24, no. 2, 1993, pp. 135–58.

Evans, Geoffrey (ed.): *The End of Class Politics? Class Voting in Comparative Context,* Oxford University Press, Oxford, 1999.

Evans, Geoffrey, Anthony Heath, and Clive Payne: "Class: Labour as a Catch-All Party?" in Geoffrey Evans and Pippa Norris (eds.), *Critical Elections: British Parties and Voters in Long-Term Perspective,* Sage, London, 1999, pp. 87–101.

Flanagan, Scott C., and Russell J. Dalton: "Parties Under Stress: Realignment and Dealignment in Advanced Industrial Societies," *West European Politics,* vol. 7, no. 1, 1984, pp. 7–23.

Franklin, Mark, Tom Mackie, Henry Valen, et al.: *Electoral Change: Responses to Evolving Social and Attitudinal Structures in Western Countries,* Cambridge University Press, Cambridge, 1992.

Hardiman, Niamh, and Christopher Whelan: "Changing Values," in William Crotty and David E. Schmitt (eds.), *Ireland and the Politics of Change,* Longman, New York, 1998, pp. 66–85.

Heath, Anthony, Roger Jowell, and John Curtice: *How Britain Votes,* Pergamon, Oxford, 1985.

Houska, Joseph J.: *Influencing Mass Political Behavior: Elites and Political Subcultures in the Netherlands and Austria,* University of California, Institute of International Affairs, Berkeley, 1985.

Ignazi, Piero: *Extreme Right Parties in Western Europe,* Oxford University Press, Oxford, 2004.

Inglehart, Ronald: "The Changing Structure of Political Cleavages in Western Society," in Dalton, Flanagan, and Beck (eds.), pp. 25–69.

Inglehart, Ronald: *Culture Shift in Advanced Industrial Society,* Princeton University Press, Princeton, 1990.

Inglehart, Ronald: *Modernization and Postmodernization: Cultural, Economic, and Political Change in 43 Societies,* Princeton University Press, Princeton, 1997.

Irwin, Galen A., and J. J. M. van Holsteyn: "Decline of the Structured Model of Electoral Competition, *West European Politics,* vol. 12, no. 1, 1989, pp. 21–41.

Kaplan, Gisela: *Contemporary West European Feminism,* Allen & Unwin/UCL Press, London, 1992.

Katz, Richard S., and Peter Mair: "Changing Models of Party Organization and Party Democracy: The Emergence of the Cartel Party," *Party Politics,* vol. 1, no. 1, 1995, pp. 5–28.

Kirchheimer, Otto: "The Transformation of Western European Party Systems," in Joseph LaPalombara and Myron Weiner (eds.), *Political Parties and Political Development,* Princeton University Press, Princeton, 1966, pp. 177–200.

Kirchheimer, Otto: "The Waning of Opposition in Parliamentary Regimes," *Social Research,* vol. 24, no. 2, 1957, pp. 127–56.

Kitschelt, Herbert, Zdenka Mansfeldova, Radoslaw Markowski, and Gabor Toka: *Post-Communist Party Systems: Competition, Representation and Intra-Party Cooperation,* Cambridge University Press, Cambridge, 1999.

Kopecký, Petr: "Building Party Government: Political Parties in the Czech and Slovak Republics," in David Stansfield, Paul Webb, and Stephen White (eds.), *Political Parties in Transitional Democracies,* Oxford University Press, Oxford, 2005.

Lewis, Paul (ed.): *Party Development and Democratic Change in Post-communist Europe,* Cass, London, 2001.

Lewis-Beck, Michael: "France: The Stalled Electorate," in Dalton, Flanagan, and Beck (eds.), pp. 425–48.

Lijphart, Arend: "Religious vs. Linguistic vs. Class Voting," *American Political Science Review,* vol. 73, no. 2, 1979, pp. 442–58.

Lipset, S. M., and Stein Rokkan: "Cleavage Structures, Party Systems and Voter Alignments: An Introduction," in S. M. Lipset and Stein Rokkan (eds.), *Party Systems and Voter Alignments,* Free Press, New York, 1967, pp. 1–64.

Lovenduski, Joni: *Women and European Politics: Contemporary Feminism and Public Policy,* Wheatsheaf, Brighton, 1986.

Madeley, John T. S., and Zsolt Enyedi (eds.): *Church and State in Contemporary Europe,* special issue of *West European Politics,* vol. 26, no. 1, 2003.

Maguire, Maria: "Is There Still Persistence? Electoral Change in Western Europe, 1948–1979," in Daalder and Mair (eds.), pp. 67–94.

Mair, Peter: "The Freezing Hypothesis: An Evaluation," in Lauri Karvonen and Stein Kuhnle (eds.), *Party Systems and Voter Alignments: Looking Back, Looking Forward,* Routledge, London, 2001, pp. 27–44.

Mair, Peter: "The Green Challenge and Political Competition: How Typical Is the German Experience?" in Stephen Padgett and Thomas Poguntke (eds.), *Continuity and Change in German Politics: Beyond the Politics of Centrality? A Festschrift for Gordon Smith,* Cass, London, 2002, pp. 99–116.

Mair, Peter: "In the Aggregate: Mass Electoral Behaviour in Western Europe, 1950–2000," in Hans Keman (ed.), *Comparative Democratic Politics,* Sage, London, 2000, pp. 122–42.

Mair, Peter: "New Political Parties in Long-Established Party Systems: How Successful Are They?" in Erik Beukel et al. (eds.), *Elites, Parties and Democracy: Festschrift for Mogens N. Pedersen,* Odense University Press, Odense, 1999, pp. 207–24.

Mair, Peter: *Party System Change: Approaches and Interpretations,* Clarendon Press, Oxford, 1997.

Mair, Peter (ed.): *The West European Party System,* Oxford University Press, Oxford, 1990.

Mair, Peter, Wolfgang C. Müller, and Fritz Plasser (eds.): *Political Parties and Electoral Change,* Sage, London, 2004.

Neumann, Sigmund: "Toward a Comparative Study of Political Parties," in Sigmund Neumann (ed.), *Modern Political Parties,* University of Chicago Press, Chicago, 1956, pp. 395–421.

Nieuwbeerta, Paul: *The Democratic Class Struggle in Twenty Countries, 1945/1990,* Thesis Publishers, Amsterdam, 1995.

Pedersen, Mogens N.: "Changing Patterns of Electoral Volatility: Explorations in Explanations," in Daalder and Mair (eds.), pp. 29–66.

Pedersen, Mogens N.: "The Danish 'Working Multiparty System': Breakdown or Adaptation?" in Hans Daalder (ed.), *Party Systems in Denmark, Austria,*

Switzerland, the Netherlands and Belgium, Pinter, London, 1987, pp. 1–60.

Pedersen, Mogens N.: "The Dynamics of European Party Systems: Changing Patterns of Electoral Volatility," *European Journal of Political Research,* vol. 7, no. 1, 1979, pp. 1–26.

Porritt, Jonathon: "Foreword," in Sara Parkin, *Green Parties: An International Guide,* Heretic Books, London, 1989, pp. 7–9.

Porritt, Jonathon: *Seeing Green: The Politics of Ecology Explained,* Blackwell, Oxford, 1984.

Prodromou, Elizabeth H.: "Paradigms, Power, and Identity: Rediscovering Orthodoxy and Regionalizing Europe," *European Journal of Political Research,* vol. 30, no. 2, 1996, pp. 125–54.

Pulzer, Peter: *Political Representation and Elections in Britain,* Allen and Unwin, London, 1967.

Rokkan, Stein: *Citizens, Elections, Parties,* Universitetsforlaget, Oslo, 1970.

Rose, Richard: "Mobilizing Demobilized Voters in Post-Communist Societies," *Party Politics,* vol. 1, no. 4, 1995, pp. 549–63.

Rose, Richard: *The Problem of Party Government,* Macmillan, London, 1974.

Rose, Richard, and Derek Urwin: "Persistence and Change in Western Party Systems Since 1945," *Political Studies,* vol. 18, no. 3, 1970, pp. 287–319.

Roth, Günther: *The Social Democrats in Imperial Germany: A Study in Working-Class Isolation and National Integration,* Bedminster Press, Totowa (NJ), 1963.

Sainsbury, Diane: "Class Voting and Left Voting in Scandinavia," *European Journal of Political Research,* vol. 15, no. 5, 1987, pp. 507–26.

Sartori, Giovanni: "The Influence of Electoral Laws: Faulty Laws or Faulty Method?" in Bernard Grofman and Arend Lijphart (eds.), *Electoral Laws and Their Political Consequences,* Agathon Press, New York, 1987, pp. 43–68.

Sartori, Giovanni: "The Sociology of Parties: A Critical Review," in Mair (ed.), pp. 150–82.

Sinnott, Richard: "Party Attachment in Europe: Methodological Critique and Substantive Implications," *British Journal of Political Science,* vol. 28, no. 4, 1998, pp. 627–50.

Sitter, Nick: "Cleavages, Party Strategy and Party System Change in Europe, East and West," *Perspectives in European Politics and Society,* vol. 3, no. 3, 2002, pp. 425–51.

Smith, Gordon: "Core Persistence: System Change and the 'People's Party,'" *West European Politics,* vol. 12, no. 4, 1989, pp. 157–68.

Thomassen, J. J. A.: "Party Identification as a Cross-Cultural Concept: Its Meaning in the Netherlands," in Ian Budge, Ivor Crewe, and Dennis Farlie (eds.), *Party Identification and Beyond,* Wiley, London, 1976, pp. 63–80.

Tóka, Gábor: "Party Appeals and Voter Loyalties in New Democracies," *Political Studies,* vol. 46, no. 3, 1998, pp. 589–610.

Whitefield, Stephen: "Political Cleavages and Post-Communist Politics," *Annual Review of Political Science,* vol. 5, 2002, pp. 181–200.

Wittenberg, Jason: *Sustaining Political Loyalties: Religion and Electoral Continuity in Hungary.* Cambridge University Press, Cambridge, 2005.

Wolinetz, Steven B. (ed.): *Parties and Party Systems in Liberal Democracies,* Routledge, London, 1988.

CHAPTER 10

INSIDE EUROPEAN POLITICAL PARTIES

As earlier chapters in this book make clear, political parties play a vital role in European politics. They control governments, dominate parliaments, and have a strong role in the appointment of members of constitutional courts. In many parts of the world, parties are inclined to be peripheral or transient bodies. They may be built around a single leader and cease to exist when this leader disappears from the scene, as has occurred in some third-world countries. They may play a secondary role in what are in many ways candidate-centered politics, as in the United States. In Europe, however, parties really matter, and many authors have quoted with approval Schattschneider's statement that "modern democracy is unthinkable save in terms of the parties" (Schattschneider, p. 1). Voters themselves agree with this, acknowledging that parties are necessary to make politics "work" even if they do not particularly love the parties they have (Holmberg, p. 291; Torcal et al., p. 266).

We have seen in earlier chapters that some European parties have a long history, surviving world wars and fundamental changes of regime. We saw in Chapter 3 that the institutions of European parliamentary democracy mean that it is party, rather than candidate, that Europeans vote for at election time. On the whole, government in Europe is party government, although other organizations, such as interest groups, sometimes appear to challenge this, as we shall see in Chapter 14. Consequently, the internal affairs of parties, although many Europeans regard them as mundane and uninteresting, may make a significant difference to the politics of a country by determining the nature of both the politicians and the policy packages among which voters choose at elections. In this chapter, therefore, we move inside parties and ask what sort of bodies they are. We consider how well they are organized; how they make decisions; where they get their resources; how they are adjusting to important social changes, such as the increasing role of the mass media in politics; and how political parties make their distinctive contribution to the politics of representation in Europe.

✦ WHAT DO PARTIES DO?

Political parties are present in, and indeed at the core of, politics in all European countries. Even though many Europeans are cynical about parties and their motives, European politics would scarcely operate without them. They perform a number of functions that are crucial to the operation of modern political systems. Among these functions, four are particularly important.

First, political parties structure the political world. As we have seen in earlier chapters and will also see in Chapter 12, parties are the key actors in the operation of governments and parliaments. If there were no parties—in other words, if every member of parliament was an independent with no institutionalized links with other members—the result would be something close to chaos. The only west European country that has come anywhere close to this situation in living memory was Fourth Republic France prior to 1958, when the parliamentary groups were numerous and internally incohesive, rendering stable government and cohesive policy making, except to the extent that the civil service filled the breach, impossible. Parties also structure the political world for many voters, who see politics in terms of the fortunes of parties as much as the fate of issues, especially at election times. Most individual voters don't have time to work out their view on every political issue, and many tend to follow their party's judgement on matters about which they have not thought deeply.

Second, parties recruit and socialize the political elite. To become a member of parliament in Europe it is almost essential first to be selected by a political party as an election candidate. Likewise, to become a government minister in most countries it is usually necessary to be a senior member of a political party. Thus gaining access to political power requires being accepted by a party, and usually being a leading figure in it. Parties also socialize the political elite; most government ministers have spent a number of years as party members, working with other party members and learning to see the political world from the party's perspective. In doing this, they become accustomed to working with others, learning about teamwork, about the need to coordinate their activities with other figures in the party and, most important, about the constraints that party discipline imposes on them. The control that European parties possess over elite recruitment and socialization marks one major difference between most of Europe on the one hand and the United States and certain other presidential systems on the other. In the latter, the country's political leader often does not emerge from within the party organization, and in some cases complete political outsiders, such as Alberto Fujimori in Peru, can come through and win political power. This means that the political direction of such systems is inclined to be inherently less stable, whereas in Europe, where political parties control the channels of elite recruitment and socialization, the behavior of political leaders is usually more predictable, for better or worse.

Third, parties provide linkage between rulers and ruled, between civil society and the state. They constitute one of the mechanisms by which voters are linked to the political world, providing a flow of information in both directions. As we shall see later, there are many doubts as to whether parties are still performing their linkage role effectively.

Fourth, parties aggregate interests. Unlike interest groups, which we look at in Chapter 14, they put forward and try to implement packages of proposals, not just policies in one area of government. Most parties at elections put forward manifestos containing policies on many different issues and thereby stand ready to give direction to government. By doing this, they offer meaningful choices to voters between alternative policy packages and thus play a crucial part in converting voters' preferences into government policy. Party control of government, whether by one party or by a coalition of parties, should mean some more or less coherent program that the government aims to follow, rather than a situation where disparate individual ministers each pursue their own ideas.

✦ BASIC PARTY ORGANIZATION

Party organizations differ in detail around Europe, but the basic organizational elements are similar. Members of parties belong to a local unit based on a geographic area, usually known as the *branch.* Ideally, the party will aim to establish branches all over the country in order to maintain a presence on the ground and to mobilize potential voters. The branches usually have a role in selecting election candidates, and they are entitled to send delegates to the party's *annual conference,* which in many parties is nominally the supreme decision-making body. Delegates at the annual conference usually elect most members of the party's *national executive,* which runs the party organization between conferences, adjudicating on internal disputes. This works in conjunction with the party's head office, staffed by the party's own employees, who constitute a permanent party bureaucracy. The other main element in the party is the *parliamentary party* or *caucus,* comprising the party's elected deputies.

In the case of some parties, this basic picture is complicated by the presence of other bodies. A few parties, such as the French Socialists, are highly factionalized. Such parties contain a number of clearly defined groups, often quite institutionalized, with a continuous existence over time; the various factions jostle for power and position within the party. Factionalization is generally something that parties aim to avoid: Factions were an important element in the death of the Italian Christian Democrats (DC) in the early 1990s. Other parties have in the past had interest groups affiliated to them; examples include the labor parties in Britain, Norway, and Sweden, though in each case the links have become much weaker in recent years. In federal countries, the party organizations in the various states may have considerable freedom of action. This is especially true of the German Christian Democrats and the Austrian People's Party (the latter also has interest groups, in the form of farmers', workers', and business leagues, attached to it).

Party constitutions usually give the impression that the party is a smoothly functioning organization in which important decisions are reached through a fully participatory process. The reality, as might be expected, is often rather different. Although some parties do operate reasonably peacefully (though not necessarily very democratically), others are wracked by constant internal tension. One very common source of conflict concerns the ideological "purity" of party policy. The battle lines are often drawn between party activists, for whom it may be of prime importance that the party adhere to the ideals that led them to join it in the first place, and party legislators, who may well wish to trim ideological sails in order to get into office. Internal conflict along these lines was very prominent, for example, in the British Labour Party during most of the 1980s. Overall, in any case, what is important to remember is that every European political party is a political system in its own right. In order to understand what parties do, therefore, it is important to understand what is happening inside them.

✦ PARTY MEMBERSHIP

Who Becomes a Party Member?

Belonging to a party in Europe is slightly more formal than in some other parts of the world, involving more than just expressing an inclination toward the party in question. Typically, to become a party member a person has to pay a small annual membership fee and indicate (by signing some kind of pledge) that he or she accepts the basic prin- ciples of the party. Members are also expected, at least in theory, to attend regular local branch meetings.

Not surprisingly, most people who vote for a party do not go to the trouble and expense of actually joining it. Party members make up only a minority of party sup- porters as a whole. Just how large or small this minority is varies a lot, both from country to country and from party to party within countries. Indeed, it can be difficult to pin down exactly how many people really do belong to parties. Some parties are simply not sufficiently centralized for anyone in a party to know how many members it has. In Switzerland, the most decentralized country in Europe, for example, party headquarters may have little knowledge of the party's position in the various cantons around the country. Similarly, most of the Green parties that began to emerge as a significant polit- ical force in the 1980s shunned the formal organizational structure of the established parties on principle, though in many cases they have had to think again about this position in order to compete effectively with other parties (Burchell). Other parties may have a good idea of their membership but may be reluctant to disclose the information publicly. In Poland, for example, one writer comments that all parties "maintain high levels of secrecy regarding data on membership" due to their "embarrassingly low memberships" (Jasiewicz).

Even when we do manage to get membership figures for a particular party, we sometimes need to treat them skeptically. Parties have an obvious incentive to claim more members than they really have, in the hope of increasing their legitimacy. In addition, the figures passed on to the head office by the local organizational units around the country may not be reliable; the number of delegates each branch can send to the annual conference may depend on how many members it has, for example, so the larger it claims to be, the more delegates it can send. Local members may even pay membership dues for "ghost" members, creating "paper" branches, either in order to boost local represen- tation in national bodies or to boost their own influence in local intraparty competition over, for example, candidate selection. Another problem is the relatively subjective def- inition of membership in some cases. There may be people in some parties who invari- ably help the party campaign during elections but never actually join and thus are not formally considered members. Other parties might still count as members people who, in fact, drifted away years ago but never explicitly resigned. There is also a degree of "noise" in the annual membership figures, which may fluctuate randomly or in a man- ner linked to the electoral cycle.

A good, through probably extreme, example of the difficulty of counting members comes from one of the countries that on paper appears to have an exceptionally high proportion of party members, namely Iceland. Perhaps appropriately, given the island's geographical location in mid-Atlantic, the concept of "party membership" bears as much resemblance to the U.S. model as to the standard European one. In the 1990s, the par- ties' records claimed that around 25 percent of the electorate belonged to a party (Kristjánsson, p. 165). Evidence from surveys found that around 17 percent of respon- dents reported that they were party members—a lower figure but still very impressive. However, Kristjánsson suggests that most of the people describing themselves as "party members" really meant only that they had a feeling of identity with a party, not an organizational connection. None of the parties collects annual dues from members, and neither do they purge their membership lists, so anyone who ever joined is counted as a member until death. In reality, Kristjánsson, suggests, all party work is carried out by about 0.5 to 1 percent of the electorate.

Still, when all the qualifications are made, we can come up with at least some reasonably hard facts about party membership in individual countries. The pattern for each country is summed up in Table 10.1. In most countries, only a small fraction of the people who vote for a party are sufficiently committed to join it, and, as we shall see, only a minority of this minority can be considered active in the party. There are only three countries, besides the dubious case of Iceland, where a tenth or more of electors join a party: Austria, Malta, and Finland. The way in which the parties in Austria saturate society is well documented; over one in six of all Austrians belong to a political party, and the parties permeate many aspects of ordinary life by providing social outlets together with a patronage system so extensive that even the most menial public sector job can be hard to obtain unless the job-seeker belongs to the party in whose domain it lies. An even higher proportion of Maltese electors are members of a party: In nearly every town of any size, the two main parties, the Maltese Labour Party (MLP) and the Partit Nazzjonalista or Nationalist Party (PN), have a social club that is the center of social life for many members, and the parties have a range of ancillary organizations. For example, the PN has separate associations for workers, the self-employed, pensioners, women, and young people; it runs its own travel agency; and it has a section called "Team Sports PN" that organizes tournaments for members and supporters in various sports, such as football, athletics, and snooker (information from the party's Web site at www.pn.org.mt).

It is generally accepted that membership figures are declining across western Europe. From a survey of membership data in twenty-one European countries between 1980 and the late 1990s, Mair and van Biezen found that the trend was downward everywhere except Greece and Spain (and, for a more recent period, Hungary and Slovakia), in each of which parties were growing after a long period of authoritarian rule. The mean percentage of the electorate that belonged to a party in the west European countries was 10 percent in 1980 but only 6 percent in the late 1990s (Mair and van Biezen, pp. 11–12). The figure is less than 5 percent now if we exclude the small countries of Malta and Iceland from the calculations. Moreover, even the 1980 figures represent a decline from earlier decades. We can illustrate the decline by considering a few specific examples. In Denmark, over a fifth of all registered voters were party members in the early 1960s, but by the late 1990s only a twentieth belonged to a party (Damgaard, p. 123). In Britain, individual membership of the Labour Party fell from a peak of just over a million in 1952 to fewer than 300,000 in the early 2000s, and the drop in Conservative membership has been even more precipitous (Kingdom, p. 314). In France membership, low to begin with, has been declining further (Knapp, pp. 122, 127).

We can explain the decline in membership rolls by considering the reasons why people might join a party in the first place. In the 1960s Clark and Wilson suggested three main motives that might lead someone to join a party (see Ware, *Political,* pp. 68–78; Clark and Wilson). One is *material,* the desire to gain some tangible reward, such as a public office or a public resource controlled by the party. The material motive has been important in a few European countries, such as Austria, Belgium, and Italy; in Spain, too, "holders and seekers of public office make up a large proportion" of party membership (Colomer, p. 181; Holliday). Even so, it is generally a minor factor and is

TABLE 10.1

Party Membership as a Percentage of the Electorate

Country	% of Electorate That Belongs to a Political Party	Membership Trends in Recent Decades
Austria	17.7	Decline from 28% in 1980
Belgium	6.6	Slight decline in past twenty years
Cyprus	—	No information
Czech Republic	3.9	Decline from 7% in 1993
Denmark	5.1	Decline from over 20% in 1960s
Estonia	2.0	No information
Finland	9.6	Decline from 16% in 1980
France	1.5	Decline from 5% in 1978
Germany	2.9	Little change since 1960s
Greece	6.8	Figure has doubled since late 1970s
Hungary	2.2	Little change
Iceland	16.9[a]	Decline since 1980s
Ireland	2.7	Slight decline in past twenty years
Italy	4.0	Decline from 10% in 1980
Latvia	0.9	Stability since mid-1990s
Lithuania	2.4	Slight increase since mid-1990s
Luxembourg	—	Figure stood at 10% in late 1980s
Malta	30.0	Dramatic increase in early 1980s, stability since then
Netherlands	2.5	Now around half of the 1980 figure
Norway	7.3	Now around half of the 1980 figure
Poland	1.5	No significant or sustained changes
Portugal	4.0	Modest increase since 1980
Slovenia	4.7	No information
Slovakia	4.1	Slight increase since the early 1990s
Spain	3.4	Modest increase since 1980
Sweden	5.5	Slight decline in past twenty years
Switzerland	6.4	No information
United Kingdom	1.9	Now about a third of 1950s figures
Average	6.0	
Average excluding Iceland and Malta	4.6	

Sources: For Estonia and Slovenia: Norris, *Democratic,* p. 115; France: Andolfatto, p. 109; Iceland: Kristjánsson, p. 165; Ireland: Marsh, "Parties," p. 169; Latvia and Lithuania: Smith-Sivertsen, p. 231; Poland: Szczerbiak, "New Polish," p. 62. For Malta, data are from party Web sites (www.mlp.org.mt/min-ahna/organizzazjoni.asp; sites.waldonet.net.mt/alternativa/frames.htm) and from information supplied by the Nationalist Party (PN). For other countries, data are from Mair and van Biezen, p. 9.

[a] See caveat in text.

under attack in countries where "the party card" is still an asset when it comes to being given a public sector job. The second motive is *solidary,* referring to the desire for social contact and a sense of comradeship. With the rise of a wide range of leisure opportunities and the decline in cohesiveness among subcultures and communities, the solidary motive is of diminishing importance. The third motive is *purposive*—in other words, directed toward a specific end—referring to a desire to advance certain policy goals. The purposive motive, too, is under challenge: The attraction of joining a party in order to promote a particular issue is weakened by the rise of social movements, single-issue pressure groups, and community action groups, which provide other, perhaps more satisfying, ways of participating. For such groups, a particular issue is the members' top priority, whereas for a party any issue is just one among many and may get lost from view if the party enters government.

Across western Europe, then, membership levels are declining. In the postcommunist countries these levels were low to start with (for parties in postcommunist countries generally, see Bugajski). Under the communist regimes, many people felt that it was unwise or pointless to become politically active, and this pattern has generally continued since the collapse of communism. In some, such as Poland, the very concept of party partisanship had negative connotations going back before the communist era. Polish parties score very low on trust and are regarded as "selfish, quarrelsome, divisive and possibly corrupt" (Sanford, p. 195; Kostelecky, p. 153). Thus membership is low for both supply-side and demand-side factors: The great majority of Poles see no point in joining a party, and existing party leaders feel no burning desire to try to recruit members (Szczerbiak, "New Polish"). This applies in nearly all postcommunist countries. Particularly low membership in Latvia has been attributed partly to the "open-list" electoral system (see Chapter 11). This means that building support among voters is more important for candidates than having a strong base within the party organization. In neighboring Lithuania, the closed-list system means that candidates need support from within the organization to make sure that they are selected in a high position, so they have an incentive to recruit members who will back them, which in turn results in higher membership levels (Smith-Sivertsen). Even when membership is apparently quite high, we need to treat the figures with some suspicion. When Estonian membership lists were made public in 2002, it turned out that some "members" were unaware of their supposed membership, while some parties' membership claims surpassed the number of votes the parties won in the following year's election (Sikk, p. 16).

One reason why membership was low from the start in postcommunist countries is that nearly all the parties were founded after 1989 from the top down by elites looking to build support organizations, rather than emerging, as many of their western counterparts did in the early twentieth century, from significant social forces in society (Mair, pp. 183–87). A related reason is that by the time these parties were formed, parties no longer needed a lot of members. Therefore, rather like countries that missed out on the industrial revolution, skipping straight from an agricultural economy to a high-tech one, postcommunist countries simply arrived at once at the low membership levels to which western parties are gradually dwindling. Postcommunist parties emerging in recent times could be deliberately designed by elites as low-membership organizations, whereas most western parties retain an organizational structure that evolved many decades ago to meet the needs of ordinary members. We return to this later in the chapter.

As a general rule, party members are not entirely socially representative of party voters. Anders Widfeldt analyzed surveys of the public across Europe in 1988–89; because these surveys inquired about party membership, Widfeldt was able to compare members of a party with other supporters of the party. He found that members were less likely than voters to be women: in thirty-four of the thirty-seven parties for which there were data, the proportion of men was higher among party members than among other party supporters. Likewise, young people were underrepresented among party members while the middle-aged were overrepresented, and working-class people were underrepresented in almost every party in comparison with their strength among other party supporters. Widfeldt concluded: "the members of political parties in western Europe are, on the whole, not socially representative of party supporters. Party members tend to be disproportionately male, middle-aged and middle-class" (Widfeldt, "Party," p. 165). There was no consistent pattern as to which parties had memberships that were closest to being a social cross-section of party supporters; in some countries, this might be true of right-wing parties while in other countries left-wing parties had this position.

These broad findings tally with information on some specific parties that have been studied in greater detail (Seyd and Whiteley, *Party*). The first academic study of British Conservative members discovered, to the horror of the Conservative head office, that the average Conservative member was aged 62 (Whiteley, Seyd, and Richardson, p. 50). As one writer colorfully put it: When voting slips were sent to members in a 1997 leadership vote, "sacks ... were returned marked 'Deceased'" (Kingdom, pp. 314–15). Many parties in the postcommunist countries, especially the former communist parties, suffer from the same problem. In the German PDS (the ex-communists of East Germany), for example, more than two-thirds of the eastern members were aged over 60 in 2001 (McKay, p. 54).

The decline in membership numbers means that parties have become less firmly implanted in civil society than they were in earlier decades, and it calls into question their ability to perform their linkage role. It is one reason why well-resourced parties nowadays spend their money on setting up focus groups; in an ideal world, parties would have their ears sufficiently close to the ground so as not to need focus groups to tell them what the public is thinking. At the same time, while it is easy to be cynical about parties that test out their policies on focus groups in the same way that a soft-drinks manufacturer would seek consumer feedback on a new product, we should not adopt too rosy a view of the past. Party members are not necessarily a reliable touchstone of what the voters are thinking, for their views may be out of line with those of voters, as we discuss later in this chapter. Moreover, although parties risk appearing unprincipled if they adapt their policies according to what focus groups tell them, few people would take such a purist view as to insist that parties are obliged to stick to a fixed set of "principled" policies regardless of what the voters think. Even so, falling membership numbers do pose problems for parties, as we explain later in the chapter.

The Activities of Party Members

What do party members do? In virtually all parties nowadays, members tend to be most active at election time, playing an important role in campaigning at the grassroots level. They may not be particularly successful when it comes to trying to persuade the floating

Box 10.1   Membership of Political Parties

France

Reliable figures on party membership in France are hard to come by, but all reliable estimates concur on figures that represent a low proportion of voters. Prior to the formation of the UMP in 2002, the 80,000 members of the Gaullist party (the RPR) in the late 1990s represented only 2 percent of those who voted for it at the 1997 parliamentary elections. The second mainstream right-wing party, the UDF, was a conglomeration of a number of smaller groups and parties, which together did not have as many members as the RPR. The FN, despite its electoral growth, had fewer members than the UDF. The Socialist Party, though it had slightly more members than the RPR, has never been a mass membership party. According to its own claims, the Communist Party has more members than the RPR and the Socialists combined, but given its record of electoral decline over the last two decades, analysts believe it has at most half of what it claims. Members in all parties, with the occasional exception of the Socialists, have a reputation for being deferential toward their leaders.

Germany

Party membership in postwar Germany has fluctuated somewhat but has been consistently low by general western European standards. The Social Democrats (SPD) had the largest number of members prior to the 1990s, but by the end of that decade they had been overtaken by the combined strength of the two parties in the main right-wing bloc, the CDU and CSU. The CDU in particular traditionally attached low priority to the recruitment of members but after losing office in 1969, it set about strengthening its organization so as to challenge the dominance of the SPD on the ground. Its membership more than doubled during its thirteen-year period in opposition; in government from 1982 to 1998, its membership fell slightly but not to the same extent as SPD membership. The FDP has far fewer members, and the Greens are smaller still. After the reunification of Germany in 1990, all the parties sought to extend their membership in the former East Germany, but only the Free Democrats had much success. Conversely, the East German PDS has made attempts to organize in the west, where its few members

are much younger than its predominantly pension-age eastern members. The Greens, like their counterparts elsewhere, and despite (or because of) their ethos of membership participation in internal party decision-making, have relatively few members.

Italy

The party with the most members in postwar Italy was the Communist Party (PCI), which in the early 1990s was reborn as the PDS and then the DS (Democratic Left), with far fewer members than the PCI. In the late 1980s two of the government parties, the Christian Democrats (DC) and the Socialists (PSI), had over 2 million members between them, but these parties both disintegrated as a result of the scandals that convulsed Italian politics in the early 1990s, and the evidence suggests that most of their members drifted away from politics. The only party to show membership (as well as electoral) growth in recent years has been the far-right Alleanza Nazionale (AN). Particularly notable has been the rise of Forza Italia, founded by the media tycoon Silvio Berlusconi, which has been described as a "virtual party," having no real organizational structure and a small membership base yet able to poll over 20 percent of the votes at elections and play a leading role in government from 1994 to 1995 and again from 2001.

Latvia

Latvia is the only European country where less than 1 percent of the electorate are members of political parties (0.9 percent, or approximately 15,000 people). There are two major reasons for the low level of party membership in Latvia. First, party elites see no real need for members, and joining is not made easy: Applicants usually need to provide references from two or three existing members. Second, as in other postcommunist countries most people have very little trust in political parties and thus do not feel motivated to join them. Two parties—the Latvian Popular Front and the Christian People's Party—each claimed over 100,000 members in the early 1990s, but by the mid-1990s both had disappeared from the scene, an indication of the loose commitment implied by "party membership."

Continued

BOX 10.1   MEMBERSHIP OF POLITICAL PARTIES *(Continued)*

Netherlands

Over the last forty years, the membership of the Dutch parties has declined from a level that was never particularly high by general European standards. The drop has been most pronounced among the religious parties (now combined in the CDA); membership fell from about half a million in 1950 to around 77,000 some fifty-five years later. The membership of the Socialist PvdA halved from the early 1980s to the midpoint of the new century's first decade. In most parties, the activity of sections such as youth movements and women's groups has declined.

Poland

In reaction to the pervasive control of the communist party from the late 1940s onward, the Law on Political Parties adopted in 1990 banned all party activity from the workplace and required only fifteen signatures (raised to one thousand in 1997) for a political party to be registered. In 2002 there were 106 officially registered active parties, but most had few members. Overall, party membership in Poland remains low. Parties were mostly founded by political entrepreneurs rather than emerging from significant social forces, and thus, by design, they do not give a strong role to members in internal decision making.

Spain

The Spanish parties had exceptionally small memberships in the years after the return to democracy in the late 1970s, but, unlike most European parties, they have been gaining rather than losing members since then. The right-wing PP more than doubled its membership during the 1990s, and the Socialists (PSOE) also showed a steady increase. Even so, overall membership levels remain low. The legacy of dictatorship is sometimes suggested as an explanation for the phenomenon, as it led to a political culture that did not encourage active participation in politics, just as in communist regimes.

Sweden

Sweden displays the familiar pattern of a decline in party membership in recent years, although the number of members has fallen less dramatically than in many countries. The largest party, the Social Democrats, used to have "indirect members" who were deemed to be party members because of their membership in trade unions affiliated with the party, but this practice was ended in 1990. Taking this into account, the largest decrease has been in membership of the liberal People's Party (FP); the number of individual members of the Social Democrats has held up relatively well by comparison. At the end of the 1990s, nearly half of Swedish party members belonged to the Social Democrats.

United Kingdom

Party membership in Britain has declined markedly since the 1950s, even allowing for the patchy data available on membership. Research in the early 1990s discovered that the average Conservative member was aged 62; these members have a reputation for being more right-wing than Conservative MPs and are noted for their strong Euroskepticism. The party had an estimated 2 to 3 million members in the 1950s and 1960s, but this number had declined to only a third of a million by the end of the 1990s. Labour's figures followed a bell curve during the twentieth century. Up to the mid-1940s the party had on average around a third of a million members each year, but then membership rose to a peak of over a million in the early 1950s. Since then the pattern has been one of steady decline, back again to fewer than a third of a million in the early years of the new century. The membership of all the other British parties is small.

voters to come off the fence, let along trying to convert the supporters of other parties. But in most countries they have a part to play in mobilizing the faithful, by putting up posters, looking after party booths and handing out leaflets in public places, and even, in a few countries such as Britain and Ireland, going from house to house and knocking on doors to rekindle dormant loyalties and to show that the party has a local presence.

Between elections, undoubtedly, many party branches are not especially active. The more committed members attend branch meetings regularly, to discuss ways of expanding the organization at the local level or to decide their stance on issues due to arise at the next annual conference.

In most parties, only a small proportion of members can really be considered activists, that is, regular attenders at local branch meetings and participants in the party's internal affairs. Surveys in Britain, Denmark, and Ireland have found a majority of members reporting that they do not spend any time at all on party activities in the average month (Seyd and Whiteley, "British," p. 359; Pedersen et al., p. 375; Gallagher and Marsh, "Party," p. 413). It is also true that branch meetings may not be needed to bring members together these days; communication is possible by means of telephone, email, or—especially in rural areas—face-to-face contact in the course of daily life (Heidar and Saglie, "Decline," pp. 771–76; Heidar and Saglie, "Predestined," pp. 231–32; Gallagher and Marsh, *Days,* p. 103). Even so, the general impression is that most party organizations are nearly dormant most of the time, springing to life during election campaigns.

One concern for parties is that the humdrum nature of internal party life may mean that party organizations now attract only people who are interested in precisely that: party organization. Ware ("Activist–Leader," p. 79) quotes from a study of British Conservative members that concluded that "what all activists were interested in was not politics but organization." A few years earlier, a Conservative minister had put the point more pungently in his private diary, noting that his local party organization members were "boring, petty, malign, clumsily conspiratorial and parochial" (quoted in Kingdom, p. 313). Other parties, too, have concluded that the frequency of meetings meant that the organization was becoming "introverted" or "inward-looking" and was "literally talking to itself" rather than engaging with the public (Gallagher and Marsh, *Days,* p. 81). Members, or potential members, with ideas and enthusiasm find little to attract them in such an environment.

It was not always like this. As mentioned in Chapter 9, belonging to a party in the early years of the twentieth century could mean living within what was nearly a separate subculture in society. This was especially true of left-wing parties with a mass membership, such as the German SPD. Belonging to the SPD was almost a way of life. The party had its own newspaper, which members bought, read, and discussed with one another, and its branch offices all over Germany were centers of social activity for members, running stamp-collecting clubs and sports teams, organizing outings, and so on. It ran its own health service, paid for by members through a health insurance scheme, and it sought to look after members and their families from the cradle to the grave. In 1906 it founded a training school in Berlin for the political education of members, grooming the most committed to take up places in the ranks of its full-time employees. Given that many members worked in factories alongside fellow party members and belonged to trade unions associated with the party, they were almost cocooned from contact with the rest of German society.

But even in the heyday of mass parties, in the first half of the twentieth century, few European parties managed to encapsulate their members to this extent. Not only has the number of party members generally diminished, as we have said, but the commitment of those members may well have waned—though we should not imagine that a few decades ago party members behaved very differently, for the available evidence suggests that levels of activism among members were low throughout the twentieth century

(Scarrow, *Parties*, pp. 181–94). Certainly, some of the reasons why people might once have joined parties now have much less force. The modern welfare state has taken over many of the functions that party insurance schemes once performed. A rise in living standards, a huge increase in leisure outlets, and the advent of television have all combined to reduce the appeal of spending evenings playing table tennis in the local party hall. Fewer people are living in a party-dominated subculture, and the Maltese parties are now practically unique in Europe in their capacity to structure their members' leisure activities to a significant extent. Television has undermined much of the rationale for party newspapers, so few European parties nowadays run their own papers, and when they do, the papers often produce a loss. The dedicated party activist, spending much of his or her free time debating and propagating the party's policy and ideology, is becoming a creature of the past, maybe indeed of a mythical and nonexistent past.

All of this does not mean that ordinary members no longer play a role within European parties. On the contrary, they are important in giving these parties a character quite distinct from that of their American counterparts. The role of European party members in certain key areas gives parties a reasonable degree of coherence, as we see when we look at power within parties.

✦ POWER WITHIN PARTIES

Who controls European parties? Who wields power within them? Who determines the packages they offer to the voters at elections and the policies they implement if they get into office? In reality, there is no single answer to this question. It is just not the case that all power lies in one place and every other part of the party is powerless. Usually, the internal affairs of parties are characterized by a continuous process of accommodation and mutual adjustment. When it comes to the crunch, most party members at every level would rather keep the party together as an effective body than precipitate a destructive split—although, of course, sometimes internal differences are so great that a split does take place and a new party is formed, a development that is more common in new party systems than in established ones. More commonly, there is a constant process of give-and-take, and the party remains together precisely because a balance of power is respected and no one element tries to achieve complete control. The various elements in the party organization—the leader, MPs, rank-and-file members, and so on—may jostle for position, but there is rarely open warfare of the sort that in the United States is prone to break out at primaries. After all, they all belong to the same party and can be assumed to have a broadly similar political outlook. They are bound to disagree on details, but the leader and parliamentarians usually have some freedom of maneuver, provided that they stay within the broad parameters of what is acceptable to the membership.

There are several important areas of activity where conflict can arise within a party, and where we might look in order to try to identify the most powerful actors within the party. Three, in particular, have the potential to be key battle sites. The first is the writing of the party's manifesto, the set of policies on which it fights elections. The second is the election of the party leader, and the third is the selection of the party's parliamentary candidates. We examine each of these in turn.

The Party Manifesto and Program

Two of the party's policy documents are especially significant: the party manifesto, the formal declaration in which a party tells the voters what it will aim to do if it gets into government, and the party program, the statement of the party's aims and aspirations, which is generally updated every few years. Party members often differ among themselves as to what should be put in these documents, partly because not all members have exactly the same policy preferences and partly because some members are more concerned than others with winning votes as opposed to maintaining ideological purity. Arguments about the party's policies often surface at annual conferences, where tension is sometimes apparent between parliamentarians and rank-and-file members. The rank and file, especially in radical parties, are inclined to suspect the deputies of being seduced by the clublike atmosphere of parliament, of forgetting their roots, and of being willing to betray the party's principles in order to get into the comfortable seats of power. The deputies, in turn, may view some members as being unworldly zealots who are unaware that compromises and bargaining are necessary in order to achieve at least part of what the party stands for and who are obsessed with policies that have no hope of ever being acceptable to the wider electorate.

Although some party activists may feel like fighting over every semicolon in the party's manifesto and program in the belief that they are taking part in a battle for the party's soul, others conclude, as indeed do most political scientists, that the manifesto is probably not the most important arena of intraparty conflict. Parties feel that they must have a manifesto to show that they are to be taken seriously—and they certainly would be criticized if they didn't have one. However, there is no real expectation that many people will read it; realistically, everyone, including the party, knows perfectly well that most voters don't bother to read manifestos. At most, the party hopes that some of the main, or at least most vote-catching, ideas will be highlighted by the media. And although a manifesto is in theory a commitment by the party to do certain things if it gets into government, in practice few voters are so naive as to believe that a party, once in government, feels bound to do everything mentioned in its manifesto and to do nothing not mentioned there. Parties always have good excuses for not fulfilling their manifesto pledges; they will be able to point to some unexpected development that threw their plans off course, such as a worldwide economic downturn. As we shall see in Chapter 13, even academics who have spent a lot of time on the question acknowledge that there is usually room for disagreement about the extent to which parties actually do what they promised to do.

Many election manifestos are drawn up by groups close to the party leadership, with little real membership involvement. If manifestos and policy programs are drawn up in such a way that the leadership is not keen on the result, then these documents are likely to gather dust from the moment they are published. If a particular party is in government, furthermore, its ministers, while always trying to keep the party supportive, are unlikely to feel bound by the details of a manifesto that they can dismiss as the dreams of some youthful enthusiasts who were hired by head office for their theoretical expertise but who lack any experience of the real world. Examples abound of parties, especially left-wing parties, where membership participation in drawing up supposedly key documents has meant very little. For example, the Spanish Socialists engaged in a massive exercise from 1987 to 1990 to draw up a new program, involving 950,000 people and 14,900 debates, but once it was adopted little more was heard of it (Gillespie, "'Programa 2000,'" pp. 93–94). In other words, the content of manifestos and programs can hardly be said to determine the behavior of the party's ministers if the party gets into office. Most members are well aware of this and do not believe that, even if they have a major input into the manifesto, they will really be determining the behavior of their party ministers in a future government. Thus, in many cases, they may not care deeply about the contents of the manifesto.

Election of the Party Leader

A second important area of potential conflict is the election of the party leader. The leader of any organization can be expected to be more powerful than other members, and leaders of political parties are especially important because, during election campaigns, the focus of the media is often on them. In the case of some parties it may be hard to say who exactly the leader is: There may be a party chairperson, a party president, and a parliamentary leader, with different people holding these positions and no clear designation of one as "the" leader. For some of these parties, such as the Norwegian center–right Høyre, it is conventional to see the real leader as the person who would become prime minister if the party came to hold that position in a future government (Heidar, p. 133). The same is true in Belgium and the Netherlands. Even this, though, is not an acid test: In both France and Italy individuals who have become prime ministers were not necessarily the most important politicians in their parties. In Denmark, there is considerable variation among the parties as to the official position that the "real" leader holds (Bille, "Power," p. 140).

Among the parties for which we can clearly identify the leader, there are several distinct methods of selection (Scarrow et al.; LeDuc). In some parties—examples can be found in Denmark, Ireland, and the Netherlands—the parliamentary group, comprising the party's elected deputies, plays a major or indeed exclusive role in choosing the leader. In many other parties—including a number in Austria, Finland, Germany, Norway, and Sweden—a party congress or convention picks the leader. A model that is becoming more common allows a direct vote for the party leader among the entire membership, a method used in some or all parties in Belgium, Britain, France, and Ireland (for Britain, see Quinn). The motive for this system may be to encourage new members by giving them a meaningful role within the party or, to take a more cynical view, to bypass the influence of supposedly more "extreme" party activists, something that we discuss more fully later.

In any case, and whatever the leadership selection method, the leader's job will be very difficult if he or she does not have the confidence of the party's parliamentarians. This was shown in October 2003 when Britain's Conservative MPs voted out Iain Duncan-Smith, who had been chosen as leader by the members just two years earlier in a decision that rapidly came to seem a mistake. Widely regarded as "not up to the job," Duncan-Smith became a figure of fun in the media. After his removal from office, MPs prevented members from having any say in choosing his successor by rallying behind a single candidate, Michael Howard. Under the party's rules, members choose the leader but MPs propose candidates, so the members' power of choice can be rendered worthless if the MPs collectively agree on just one name.

Selection of Parliamentary Candidates

A third area of prime importance for politics within parties is candidate selection (Pennings and Hazan; Gallagher and Marsh, *Candidate;* Narud et al.). The selection of the individuals who are entitled to use the party's label when they stand for election plays a crucial role in the political recruitment process. Only the people selected as candidates can become members of parliament, and in almost every country, most or all government ministers are present or former members of parliament. After the 2001 election in the United Kingdom, for example, 578 of the 659 MPs elected represented either the Conservative Party or the Labour Party. Each of these parties nominated 641 candidates, one in each mainland British constituency. The people who selected these 1,282 Conservative and Labour candidates, therefore, exercised an enormous power over who could and who could not get into the House of Commons and, beyond that, into government. Moreover, many seats in Britain (approximately 500 of them) are known to be "safe seats" for one or the other party, and in these cases selecting the candidate is tantamount to picking the MP. In some other countries, too, the candidate selectors can reasonably be seen as choosing members of parliament. For example, in a number of European countries, as we shall see in Chapter 11, the electoral system presents voters with a number of "closed" party lists, each list containing the names of candidates in a fixed order that the voters cannot alter. If a party wins, say, five seats in a particular district, these seats go to the top five names on the list, and it is the candidate selectors who determine which individuals are chosen to occupy these positions.

In 1997 Tony Blair became prime minister of Britain, swept into office with a huge majority on a powerful wave of personal popularity. However, in order to attain this position, Blair first had to become a Labour MP, and in order to do so, he had to be selected as a Labour candidate somewhere in a seat that his party had a chance of winning. By far the most difficult hurdle that he had to overcome was the last. In the early 1980s, he made unsuccessful attempts to be picked as the Labour candidate in a number of constituencies where Labour might win the seat. Finally, shortly before the 1983 election, he sought to be selected as the party's candidate in the safe Labour seat of Sedgefield in the northeast of England, a constituency with which he had no previous connection. He had first of all to persuade the skeptical members of a Labour branch in the constituency to nominate him for inclusion on the panel from which the short-list would be picked. The branch did this, but all seemed lost when he was omitted from the short-list of six that was drawn up by the handful of people who comprised the constituency executive committee. However, one of the members of the branch that had nominated him was so impressed by Blair that he persuaded the committee at a late stage to add Blair to the short-list. The 119 members entitled to make the decision then met all seven people seeking the nomination, and they picked Blair as the Labour candidate; he duly won the seat at the election and, given that it was a safe Labour seat, became in effect an MP for life (Rentoul, pp. 91–137). If he had not managed to secure selection as a Labour candidate by a small number of people in one of the proverbial smoke-filled rooms, either in Sedgefield or in another constituency that was winnable for Labour, he could never have become prime minister.

Aspiring politicians who do not meet with the approval of these powerful gate-keepers, the major parties' candidate selectors, can start their own party, with very limited chances of success, or find that their political careers are dead in the water. Candidate selection is thus a crucial step in the political recruitment process. For this reason, it is also a key area of internal party activity. If one section of a party, such as the party leader or the national executive, has control over the selection process, then this section can almost be said to control the party. Candidate selection is thus a vital matter in every individual European political party; it is also important—indeed, it is one of the key factors—in making European political parties very different from American parties.

European parties control their own candidate selection—albeit, as we shall see, with considerable variation as to who exactly within the party can be said to occupy this controlling position. The only European country with parties that use American-style open primaries, in which anyone who wishes to participate can do so, is Iceland, where primaries have been used since 1914 and have become common since the early 1970s. At the 1983 election, it was found that 29 percent of voters had taken part in a primary at that election, and 46 percent had participated in a primary at some time in their lives (Hardarson, pp. 156–65). In every other country in Europe, the power to choose candidates is kept within the party.

Perhaps surprisingly, given the importance of candidate selection in affecting the composition of parliament, the process is regulated by law in only a few countries. In Finland, parties are legally obliged to open up the process of candidate selection to a direct vote of all their members. In both Germany and Norway the law ensures that candidates are selected by local party organizations, and the parties' national executives have no power to overturn the decisions reached locally. Parties in every other country are in effect treated as private bodies and can make whatever arrangements they wish when they pick parliamentary candidates, reflecting a strong constitutional norm of freedom of political association.

The furthest that any party outside Iceland goes down the road toward opening up its selection process to all and sundry is to adopt "party primaries" (sometimes known as OMOV, standing for one member one vote), which allow each paid-up party member a direct say in the choice of parliamentary candidates. This method of choosing candidates, though still employed by only a minority of parties, is becoming more common (Bille, "Democratizing"; Scarrow et al.; Caul Kittilson and Scarrow). It is a method employed in Austria, Britain (by Labour and some of the smaller parties), Finland (where it is obligatory under law), Ireland (by the second and third largest parties, Fine Gael and Labour), and the Netherlands (by Democrats 66). In addition, in some other countries, such as Belgium, Denmark, and Germany, there is provision for party primaries, though in practice other methods of candidate selection are sometimes employed. More commonly, candidate selection involves interplay between the local and central party organizations, with the balance varying from case to case (Bille, "Democratizing"). Often, the key decisions are taken locally, with national actors sometimes attempting to influence the process. In other parties, the balance is different, in that the ultimate decisions are taken nationally, with local organizations trying to influence the outcome.

The nature of the candidate selection process is determined partly by the electoral system. If a country is divided into single-member constituencies, then, quite obviously, each party will select only one candidate in each constituency, whereas in proportional representation (PR) systems based on multimember constituencies, it is common for several candidates from the same party to be picked. The evidence from many countries, as we discuss in greater detail in Chapter 11, is that under PR the selectors aim to "balance the ticket," ensuring that both men and women are represented, along with individuals who will appeal to different sectoral or geographical interests within the constituency (Gallagher). However, the degree of centralization of the process is difficult to explain in terms of the political institutional features of a country, and one of the few identifiable patterns is that large parties tend to have a more centralized procedure than small ones (Lundell). In addition, there is often considerable variation between different parties in the same country—as, for example, in Poland—a sign that neither institutional nor cultural features of a country can entirely determine the nature of candidate selection (Szczerbiak, "Testing"; Szczerbiak, *Poles,* pp. 58–62).

Does it matter who selects the candidates? It could indeed matter if different actors within the party have different values and priorities. In that case whoever gains control of candidate selection could ensure that only those people holding certain political views are picked as candidates and, hence, have a chance of becoming parliamentarians. In addition, variations in this essentially private process might have a discernible impact upon the sociodemographic composition of parliament, if these variations lead to differences in the proportions of women, young people, and ethnic minorities in parliament.

When we try to identify the values that selectors impart to the candidate selection process, we find that selectors everywhere tend to appreciate certain characteristics in aspiring candidates: Having local roots is always welcomed (even in Britain, though it is by no means essential there), as is possessing a solid record as a party member. Sometimes, though, parties are willing to offer a candidacy to nonmembers who have proven appeal in the hope of thereby boosting the party's votes. Another universal pattern is that incumbent MPs are only rarely deselected—that is, they are nearly always picked to run again.

Most candidates in most parties are of higher socioeconomic status than the voters for the same parties, but this is not necessarily due to bias on the selectors' part. British candidate selectors are sometimes accused of favoring wealthy, upper-class men when making their choices, though an investigation of the selection process at the 1992 election concluded that the backgrounds of successful seekers after a nomination were not very different from the backgrounds of unsuccessful ones, and so, apart from some possible discrimination against women by Labour selectors, there was little evidence of bias on the part of selectors (Norris and Lovenduski). In the Netherlands, a feeling that ordinary members overvalued long and faithful party service led to changes in candidate selection in several parties in the 1990s; the national party organizations increased their power and declared their aim of ensuring the selection of more women and young people (Leijenaar and Niemöller, pp. 119–25). Beyond this, how far the selectors' own views impinge on the nature of the candidates they select is a rather underresearched question. In some cases, there are suspicions that the members deliberately pass over aspiring candidates whose views are not the same as their own. In Britain's Conservative Party in recent years, it has become difficult for anyone without Euroskeptic views to gain selection as a candidate, and as a result the parliamentary party has become overwhelmingly Euroskeptic (Webb, *Modern,* p. 185). In the 1980s, there was a widespread perception that members of the Labour Party were left-wing "extremists" and that they were picking candidates of a similar persuasion and thereby potentially making the party unelectable. However, a study of British Labour Party activists found that although they saw themselves as further to the left than Labour voters, they deliberately selected

Box 10.2   SELECTION OF PARLIAMENTARY CANDIDATES

France

Parties in France tend to be dominated by a small number of prominent individuals (notables), a fact that manifests itself in the candidate selection process. Before the formation of the UMP in 2002, the two main right-wing parties, the RPR and UDF, usually fought elections in tandem, so they made arrangements about which of them would contest each constituency. The central authorities of the parties, especially the national executives, played a decisive role in this negotiation and were also important in picking the candidates, though they were always sensitive to the views of local notables. Communist Party candidates are chosen by the national executive. Local members have rather more say in the Socialist Party, although here too some central involvement is necessitated by the factionalized nature of the party; the factions are required to reach some overall arrangement about sharing the candidacies in order to preserve party unity. As in most countries, local roots are very important; most parliamentary deputies are simultaneously councillors (usually mayors) of their town or village, and resentment is created when candidates are "parachuted" by the central party authorities into a constituency with which they have no links.

Germany

Candidate selection is regulated by law, which ensures that the central authorities of the parties have very little power. Selection is carried out by local conventions consisting of delegates from party branches within the constituency. Once these local bodies have made their choice, the central bodies cannot enforce changes. There is very little variation between the parties. Although the German electoral system provides two routes to parliament (see Chapter 11), the parties do not look for different qualities in the candidates they nominate for the list seats and for the constituency seats; indeed, there is considerable overlap between the two sets of candidates.

Italy

The electoral system adopted in the mid-1990s, which is based primarily on single-member constituencies,

has led to negotiations and deals among parties of the left and right as to which among a number of allied parties should present a candidate in each specific constituency. These deals are especially complicated on the left, because the center–left is more fragmented than the center–right. Once the allied parties have decided which one will contest which seat, candidate selection itself is a relatively oligarchic process. Candidate selection in the DS (the former communists) is similar to that in the old PCI. National leaders have the choice of the safest seats, and the provincial and regional organizations make selections that require approval at national level. In the main right-wing party, Forza Italia, the dominance of the leader Silvio Berlusconi is reflected in the way candidates are picked, and, similarly, within the Lega Nord the leader, Umberto Bossi, retains considerable power over candidate selection as over other matters of internal party life. In the Alleanza Nazionale, candidate selection is mainly under the control of the leadership group around the party leader, Gianfranco Fini.

Latvia

Party membership in Latvia is particularly low, and this, combined with the open-list electoral system (see Chapter 11), presents opportunities for would-be candidates who have a degree of personal support among party voters. Because candidate selection in Latvia has not been extensively researched, the extent of leadership control of the process remains difficult to determine. The high degree of turnover of candidates from one election to the next leads Pettai and Kreuzer to conclude that candidate recruitment remains weakly institutionalized and wide open to entrepreneurial newcomers.

Netherlands

There is some variation among the Dutch parties. The largest two, the CDA and the PvdA, took some power away from party members in the 1990s. The central party organization exercised greater influence with the aim of selecting more women and young candidates than had been picked by the members, who had tended to place a high value on service to the party organization.

In the liberal VVD, the national executive was already the most important actor; this party has been affected less than the CDA and PvdA by demands for democratization since the 1970s. A fourth party, Democrats 66, in contrast, places heavy stress on internal democracy and gives a mail-in ballot in the candidate selection process to every paid-up member.

Poland

In most of the Polish parties the first stage of the candidate selection procedure is almost completely decentralized; central involvement consists at most of issuing general guidelines about the type of qualities that local parties should look for. In most cases the initial local candidate lists are composed without any interference from the party leaders. However, under electoral law candidate lists can be submitted only by a nationally approved plenipotentiary, and in addition most parties' statutes give the leadership the right to make changes to the local selections. The extent to which the center actually does intervene varies from party to party. In the PSL (Peasant Party) and the successor to the former Solidarity movement, local selections are left more or less untouched. In some other parties the center might "parachute" in a candidate without local connections or veto someone whom it feels will damage the party's image, and sometimes it alters the order of names on the list. Even though Poland has an open-list electoral system, the top two positions on the list are regarded as most likely to attract preference votes. The most centralized party is the Labor Union (UP), where central interest in the process is great and intervention is frequent.

Spain

Because Spanish parties are leader dominated and have few members, it is not surprising to find that candidate selection is largely controlled by the leadership group. Although the leadership usually feels it wise to pay some regard to the feelings of the local party organization when settling on its lists around the country, it nonetheless retains a fairly free hand in deciding who should carry the party flag. Local activists occasionally show their displeasure with the centrally made selections by running dissident lists in the election, but these rarely achieve any success.

Sweden

As in the other Scandinavian countries, central government and the central party authorities are less powerful in Sweden than across most of Europe. Local government is important, and the local party branches do not welcome or indeed expect any attempt by party headquarters to dictate to them. In all the Swedish parties, candidate selection is carried out at the constituency level by conventions composed of delegates from the party branches in the constituency and is firmly under the control of the local party organization. Even the Left Party deviates from the usual communist pattern of central control—a strong testimony to the Swedish concern for local autonomy.

United Kingdom

Candidate selection in Britain used to be dominated by local party activists, but in recent years there has been a movement toward giving ordinary members a direct voice. In the 1990s Labour adopted a "one member one vote" system, known by the acronym OMOV, allowing each member a direct vote in the selection process. This method is also employed by Britain's third party, the Liberal Democrats. The Conservative Party combines centralization and membership involvement. It maintains a list of about eight hundred centrally approved aspirant candidates, who have to go through a rigorous screening procedure, and constituency organizations are expected to draw up a short-list from these names; ordinary members make the final choice from this short-list. Aspiring Conservative candidates who do not share the Euroskeptic attitudes of party members face an uphill struggle to win selection. Candidate selection in Britain is unusual in one respect. Most parliamentarians elsewhere have roots in the constituency they hope to represent, but in Britain selectors often pick someone with no previous connection with the constituency—though even in Britain local roots are becoming more important.

Labour candidates whose views were more moderate than their own so as not to damage the party's electoral chances (Bochel and Denver, p. 60).

It may, indeed, not matter greatly exactly *who* within the party chooses the candidates, but it does matter a lot that it is *someone* within the party, and not the voters at large, who chooses them. Even if different actors within the party have different priorities and views on some issues, they all belong to the same party and are thus likely to have a broadly similar political outlook. Epstein (pp. 219, 225) points out that it is not necessary for the leadership to pick all the candidates directly, because the results of locally controlled selection are usually perfectly acceptable to it. Local party activists, just like the national leadership, want deputies who are loyal to the party line as defined nationally. For political parties, keeping candidate selection firmly under their own control has two great advantages. First, it helps retain the loyalty of ordinary party members. Deciding who will be allowed to use the party's name and resources in the election campaign is often the only real power members have, so allowing them to do this increases the party leaders' ability to retain a substantial body of cooperative members. Second, it enables the parties to behave as cohesive and disciplined bodies in parliament and in political negotiations with other parties, and this in turn means that the party label conveys valuable information to voters at election time (Bowler). European party organizations control access to their label at elections and can withhold it from parliamentarians who are not sufficiently loyal to it in parliament. Their American counterparts, lacking this power, cannot do this. The threats and blandishments of interest groups, political action committees (PACs), and constituents at large may all have to be taken seriously by American Congress members, but in Europe individual MPs must put the party first, last, and always. Defying the party line in parliament may lead to deselection at the next election, and MPs will have little chance of reelection without the party label. Outside the party there is no salvation, or at least no long-term prospect of a political career.

For parliamentarians, this system has the advantage of protecting them from the risk of being picked off one at a time by outside interests who might put pressure on them to defect from the party line, and from the threat of being targeted at the next election by powerful and well-funded single-issue groups. Whatever an interest group might threaten to do to a deputy who doesn't vote as the group wants, it is nothing compared with what the party will do if the deputy doesn't vote as *it* wants. At the same time, the prospect of being deselected by the candidate selectors is a remote one for deputies who are loyal to the party. Most European parties have adopted a style of organization that keeps deputies on a fairly long leash held by the ordinary members but does not go so far as to make them mere poodles of unelected activists. Clearly, one could argue either in favor of the European model of strong and disciplined parliamentary parties or in favor of the U.S. pattern of greater independence of the individual Congress member. Regardless of which has more advantages, it is beyond dispute that disciplined and cohesive political parties are central to European parliamentary democracy and that party control of candidate selection is essential to this. U.S.-style direct primaries are incompatible with strong political parties (Ranney), and, in the last analysis, all of the differences that are to be found within Europe are probably less significant than the differences between European and U.S. candidate selection practices as a whole.

Sources of Party Finance

Because European parties do so much more as party organizations than U.S. parties, they need more resources. This is not to suggest that there is more money floating around in European politics than there is in the United States—almost certainly, the reverse is true. But in the United States a significant proportion of political funds is raised and spent by and on candidates rather than parties, whereas in Europe parties are much more central in raising and spending money, as in everything else.

European parties need money for two main reasons. First, they need it to run their organizations: to pay their head office staff and their telephone, postage, and other bills; to hold annual conferences and other meetings; and in some cases to support research institutions linked to the party. Second, they need cash to fight election campaigns, and this has become the main item of expenditure for nearly all parties. In the past, parties in most European countries were not allowed to buy television advertising space, though this is now possible in a growing number of countries (including Austria, Germany, Italy, the Netherlands, and Sweden). Even where television advertising by parties is still illegal, parties find plenty of other ways to spend money at election time: on newspaper and poster advertising; on the public relations firms that increasingly design election campaigns; on private focus group and survey research; perhaps on a helicopter to whisk the party leader around the country on the campaign trail; on fax machines and mobile phones to keep candidates in touch with party headquarters; and on balloons, buttons, and general razzmatazz.

Parties get their money from a variety of sources (general overviews are given in Fisher and Eisenstadt; Katz, pp. 124–32; Pinto-Duschinsky; Williams). Dues paid by members play a role but nowadays rarely produce more than a quarter of a party's income; the Netherlands, where membership dues comprise about half of party revenues, is a notable exception (Koole, "Party"). A second source of income is a party's request or insistence that its parliamentary deputies and government ministers pay a proportion, perhaps as much as 10 percent, of their official salary into party coffers. Third, parties may engage in fund-raising activities, such as the garden fetes and church hall bazaars for which the British Conservatives are famous. Some parties publish their own newspapers, but these days, as mentioned, they are more often a drain on a party's coffers than a contributor to them.

Besides these three sources arising "internally"—that is, from the party's own activities—there are also two important "external" sources of money. First, major interest groups back political parties whose policies they think will help them. In particular, business gives money to right-wing parties, and trade unions give money to left-wing parties. Second, in the great majority of European countries the state gives public money to political parties. Moreover, in almost every country there are benefits in kind, including free party broadcasts and mailings during election campaigns, as well as grants to the parliamentary groups to enable them to pay for secretarial and research assistance.

These two external sources of funding, contributions from interest groups and from the state, are related, because concern about the consequences of parties becoming financially dependent on interest groups is one of the factors that has brought about the rise of state financing. Obviously, neither business corporations nor trade unions give money to parties simply as a charitable exercise. At the very least, they hope to help their chosen party get into government and implement policies broadly sympathetic to their own needs. Some sponsors may have more tangible benefits in mind. A business or a wealthy individual may give money to a party in the hope (or even on condition) that once in government, it will give the donor special access to decision makers or even that the party's ministers will make a specific decision, perhaps on a tax liability or a request for land use planning permission, that will repay the investment several times over. This is particularly likely to happen when, as is the case in many countries, there are no laws, or at most ineffective laws, compelling parties to disclose their financial sources.

The first European country to introduce state funding of its parties was West Germany in 1959. The German scheme has subsequently been expanded and altered several times and now involves huge sums of money (Scarrow, "Explaining"; Saalfeld). Parties winning more than 0.5 percent of the vote in an election receive €1.3 for each of their first 4 million votes and €0.7 for each additional vote, which adds up to a lot of money given that around 50 million votes are cast at postunification German elections. The result is that the German parties are awash with funds, and even after covering the costs of exceptionally large party bureaucracies and research institutes, they have enough left over to help like-minded parties in the poorer postcommunist countries. In Germany's case, the past history of dictatorship may create a heightened willingness to spend a lot of money on preserving the institutions of liberal democracy.

Other countries have rather more modest schemes, although the principle is the same—parties receive money in approximate proportion to their electoral strength. In some countries all the money is paid by the national government to the parties' national headquarters, while in others, especially in Scandinavia, a significant part of the cash flows from local government to the parties' local organizations. With expenditure rising constantly and most other sources of revenue proving erratic or unreliable, state-supplied income now looms large in the finances of parties in countries that have public funding schemes. In many countries that have state funding, this source of party income exceeds all other sources combined (Mair, pp. 141–42). This applies to most parties in postcommunist countries as well, though these parties have two other potential sources of income. Some benefited from the less than transparent distribution of state assets at the end of the communist era, and some secured admission to one of the main European party groups (such as the socialist or the Christian democratic group), which had the potential to bring significant material benefit (Lewis, *Political Parties,* pp. 111–12, 122; Lewis, "Political Parties," pp. 171–72). For example, at Poland's 1997 election, different parties were in receipt of assistance from counterparts in Britain, France, Sweden, and the United States (Szczerbiak, "'Professionalization,'" p. 86). Although the financial resources of postcommunist parties are not great in absolute terms, the parties' low number of members means that their ratio of head office employees to members is much higher than in the west (van Biezen, p. 207).

The pros and cons of public funding of political parties have been debated in many European countries. One argument, as we have said, is that it frees parties from having to dance to the tune of wealthy financial backers and thus reduces corruption in politics generally. In practice it certainly does not eliminate the sleaze factor entirely, as periodic scandals demonstrate. In Italy, for example, an extensive scheme of state funding of parties did not prevent a number of parties from engaging in corruption on a massive scale, in the "Tangentopoli" or *mani pulite* affair of the 1990s, which we outlined in

Chapters 4 and 7. In Portugal, a degree of corruption coexists with state funding, aided by the indifference of citizens (de Sousa). In postcommunist countries, too, the laws on transparency read well on paper but are laxly enforced, leading to a general impression among many voters of ongoing corruption. Defenders of state financing maintain that there would be even more of this kind of thing if parties were entirely dependent on private sources. Critics suggest that it will lead to a decline in party membership and make leaders less accountable to members as parties realize they no longer need members' dues, but the evidence is that the introduction of state finance makes no difference to membership trends (Pierre et al.). Right-wing critics argue that party funding should be left to the market and is none of the state's business; left-wing critics claim that state funding turns parties into mere agents of the state or "public utilities" instead of the autonomous forces they should be (Lipow, pp. 49–65).

Supporters of state financing emphasize that not all parties can find wealthy interest groups willing to give them money. Parties whose policies appeal to no wealthy interest group—Green parties, for example, or center parties—may receive only small sums from members and sympathetic individuals. Private money may wield undue influence in intra-party battles. For example, in the days leading up to the ousting of Iain Duncan-Smith as British Conservative leader in 2003, several large donors had stated that they would stop giving money to the party unless he were replaced. Moreover, state financing, besides coming without strings attached, is awarded according to a predetermined formula and thus seems to make competition "fairer." Critics of state funding, though, observe that this line of argument can be used to rationalize a situation in which the parties already in parliament form a tacit "cartel," using their control of the state to vote themselves public money in a manner that reinforces their position by placing parties outside the cartel at a disadvantage (Katz and Mair, "Changing," pp. 15–16). The evidence is, though, that challenger parties fare no worse in countries that provide state funding than they fare elsewhere (Pierre et al.).

Although some people claim that political parties are private bodies and as such have no right to expect money from the public purse, others point out that they fulfill a public function: They are essential to the workings of a democracy and therefore need to be sustained. Furthermore, the role of government has expanded greatly since the nineteenth century, and government is controlled by a ruling party or parties. Unless parties have the money to explore and expand policy options and to conduct research into the feasibility of their ideas, the country as a whole could suffer from the inadequately thought-out policies they promote.

The flow of money into a party is likely both to reflect and to reinforce the balance of power within the party. For donors other than the state, there is little point in giving money to people or groups within a party who have no power. It makes sense, obviously, for them to give money to those who wield the power and can make the policy decisions that the donors wish to see. By doing this, of course, they further strengthen those to whom they give money. The pattern in Europe generally since the 1960s has been one of a dramatic increase in the amount of money going to central party bodies, both to the parliamentary party and to the head office (Katz and Mair, "Ascendancy"; Farrell and Webb).

Although every European party would no doubt like more money to finance its activities, most parties with reasonable levels of electoral support have sufficient resources to get their message across at elections. Individual party candidates fight elections on a national party platform and thus do not need much money to mount a personal campaign. The need for a personal campaign arises only when a preferential electoral system pits two or more candidates of the same party against each other (see Chapter 11). Even in those cases, the amounts of money involved are not huge. The elected candidates in a Finnish constituency in 1999 spent an average of just over €11,000 each, for example, a sum that would not get anyone far in a U.S. campaign (Ruostetsaari and Mattila, p. 100). Moreover, a European candidate who flaunts his or her wealth on a personal campaign rather than fighting as part of the party's team might well incur disapproval, perhaps from voters as well as from party members. Consequently, candidates do not need huge sources of private funding to bankroll their election campaigns and are less dependent than their U.S. counterparts on nonparty groups. Once again, we see in Europe the dominance of party over candidate, in marked contrast to the situation in the United States.

✦ THE CHANGING SHAPE OF EUROPEAN PARTIES

Political parties, like other organizations, change and adapt in response to changes in their environment. There have been many attempts to assess evolving patterns of European party organizations. In the 1950s the French writer Maurice Duverger argued that during the nineteenth century most parties had been what he termed "cadre parties," which were dominated by local notables who in most cases were the parties' MPs. At local level these notables had their own support groups, but the people in these groups were not really "party members," for they did not pay a membership fee and had no formal rights within the party. These parties, said Duverger, were swept aside later in the nineteenth century and in the first half of the twentieth century by the "mass party." He maintained that the mass party, with a large number of fee-paying members, a sizable permanent bureaucracy in the head office, and a clear policy program, was the "new" or "modern" form of party, and he foresaw a convergence toward this model (Duverger, p. 427).

In contrast, Leon D. Epstein, writing in the 1960s, believed that mass parties belonged only to particular places and periods. He identified a number of "counter-organizational tendencies"—such as the increasing use of the mass media, especially television, during election campaigns, which reduced the need for thousands of ordinary party members to go out spreading the word in order to get the message across—that, he argued, would increasingly undermine the rationale for the existence of large-scale mass political parties (Epstein, pp. 233–60). In a similar vein, Otto Kirchheimer argued that changes in European society were bringing about changes in the type of party likely to flourish. Class lines were becoming less sharp, and the growth of the welfare state and the mixed economy had cut the ground from under the feet of old-style antisystem socialist parties, which had been dedicated to a radical transformation of society, with members living within a virtual subculture. The type of party best suited to current conditions was what Kirchheimer called "the postwar catch-all party" that tried to win votes from nearly all sections of society and would concentrate on general, bland issues such as better health and education services. Panebianco (pp. 262–74) elaborated this idea with the "electoral–professional" model, emphasizing in particular the central role of professionals with the expertise to perform certain tasks, such as designing election campaigns.

From this point of view, a party does not really need a large number of committed members. In the 1980s, Gunnar Sjöblom took this line of thought one step further and argued that members might actually be a handicap to a party, or at least to its parliamentarians. He suggested that various changes in society, such as increased mobility and the growing role of the mass media in conveying political messages, were leading to greater volatility among voters. People were suffering from "information overload"; they were confused by a never-ending stream of reports about proposals, decisions, and speculation; and they were increasingly likely to vote on the basis of "political paraphernalia"—trivial factors such as the style or appearance of the party leader (Sjöblom, p. 385). In this situation, members with a strong commitment to certain principles were a definite liability to the vote-hungry parliamentarians, who wanted the party to be able to change tack rapidly to take advantage of the shifting winds of public opinion. Party members trying to drum up support by faithfully plugging a traditional message were likely to have a counterproductive effect. Consequently, argued Sjöblom (p. 395), "it may be to the advantage of a party to have few and/or passive members." Indeed, the deputy leader of the Spanish Socialist Party said in the 1980s that he would sooner have ten minutes of television broadcasting time than ten thousand members (Gillespie, *Spanish,* p. 366).

This argument seems to become even more persuasive when we think about the types of people who might make up the bulk of party members. We pointed out earlier that the factors that motivate people to join a party might be categorized as material, solidary, or purposive, and although each of these motives seems to be losing power, the first two may have lost more of their force than the last. If this is the case, people joining for the third reason will form an increasing proportion of members, their ideological commitment no longer diluted by the more pragmatic members who joined for less explicitly political purposes. There is a plausible argument, backed up with evidence, to the effect that party members tend to be more "extreme" in their views than party voters (May). (The evidence is less clear-cut on the question of whether members are also more extreme than MPs, as May also claimed.) For example, in Sweden members of the main left-wing party hold views farther to the left than that party's voters, and members of the main right-wing party hold views farther to the right than that party's voters (Widfeldt, *Linking,* p. 263). This line of argument was expressed colorfully in the 1930s by an observer of the British Labour Party who claimed that its local constituency organizations were "frequently unrepresentative groups of nonentities dominated by fanatics and cranks and extremists" (quoted in McKenzie, p. 194). In addition, even if researchers feel that the jury is still out on whether May's law is true, party leaders might well believe it to be true and thus want to reduce the power of activists. Certainly, it is quite plausible that members impose programmatic "costs" on the party leadership by demanding that the party adopt certain policy stances as the price of their continued loyalty, and it may be that the policies they demand are sometimes ones that the voters as a whole do not find attractive (Strøm, "Behavioral"). Members, then, might saddle the party with vote-losing policies, in which case parliamentarians might prefer to dispense with members and instead communicate with the public entirely through the mass media.

This possibility suggests that parties will be less keen than in the past to recruit members, and as we have seen in this chapter, party membership levels have indeed been falling across Europe in recent decades. This does not necessarily mean that parties are becoming "weaker," any more than, say, an automobile factory is weaker because it employs far fewer workers now than four decades ago yet still produces the same number of cars. Rather, it is partly a reflection of the fact that the kind of tasks for which parties once needed a mass membership, such as providing cheap labor and a source of finance, are now taken care of by other means, principally the mass media, computerized databases, and state funding. The automobile factory is now less rooted in the community than it was when it had a mass workforce on the production line, but if it is still delivering a product that consumers want, it could be judged as being as successful as ever. The same, clearly, could be said about parties. This is one reason why many postcommunist parties have very few members; they were founded in a technological era and in a funding environment where a mass membership would simply be seen as a "deadweight" (Kitschelt et al., pp. 395–97).

The organizational structure of parties, too, seems to be changing, in response to the same set of factors. The main trend is one that we have already mentioned in connection with candidate selection and the election of leaders: the use of direct rather than representative democracy within parties. Increasingly, members are being given a vote on subjects that were previously decided by members' delegates within the organization, such as branch officials or conference delegates. This move tends to give party leaders greater freedom of action, since members, deciding as individuals how to vote by postal ballot on some leadership proposal, are less likely to block initiatives from the top than were branch activists, who were better able to mobilize and to act collectively. The potentially "troublesome" activist layer, comprising people who according to May's law are the most likely to hold "extreme" views, thereby becomes marginalized (Hopkin; Katz and Mair, "Ascendancy," pp. 128–29).

Some analysts feel that this reduces intraparty democracy, because they regard atomized members as more docile, more passive, or more easily manipulable by the leadership than a membership acting collectively through the previously dominant branch structure. They speak of the arrival of the "plebiscitary party," in which all proposals come from the top and members' role is simply to ratify these ideas; this kind of party "is characterized by a veneer of democracy overlaid by centralization and control" (Whiteley and Seyd, pp. 213–17; Lipow, pp. 1–2). The role of members now is to "pay up and shut up." Others, though, note that the old structures were often far from a paradigm of democracy and that today's party members, being better educated and having access to many more independent sources of political information than previous generations, are perfectly capable of making "informed and rational" judgements and are not just putty in the hands of party leaders (Scarrow et al., p. 150).

As parties move away from the structure of the mass party, which was dominant in Europe from around 1900 to 1960, their organizational form defies easy labeling. The concept of the "cartel party" (Katz and Mair, "Changing"), which we have already mentioned, has been very influential. It emphasizes the reliance of parties on state funding rather than members' dues, and it sees parties as having moved from their original role of linking civil society with the state to a position where they are practically agents of the state. It suggests, further, that parties collude with each other rather than compete full-bloodedly as in the past. Internally, it envisages parties as "stratarchies," with each level being nearly autonomous rather than being answerable to actors at other levels within the party. Carty also accepts the notion of parties as stratarchies and suggests that parties can be seen as "franchise systems," which, like a hamburger chain, have a centrally designed product plus a local network to distribute it. According to Carty, there is an implicit "contract" between the head office and the local outlets, under which each has its rights and its responsibilities, and as long as everyone is keeping to their part of the bargain, each level leaves the other alone.

Koole, in contrast, disputes the existence of stratarchy, arguing that every level of the party has a strong stake in what actors at other levels are doing. As reasons why actors at one level have good reason to take a great deal of interest in trying to influence what is going on at other levels. Koole emphasizes the reliance of party leaders and national executives on endorsement or election by ordinary members, the potential of the behavior of a "rogue" candidate at local level to damage a party's national image, and the impact on local elections of what a party is doing at national level. He also disputes the idea that parties systematically collude with each other, arguing that electoral competition is fiercer than ever (Koole, "Cadre"; see also Kitschelt). Koole has put forward the model of the "modern cadre party," one in which the parliamentary group is dominant yet to some degree accountable to the members, so that there remains a degree of internal democracy (Koole, "Vulnerability"). However, given that the original cadre parties had no members in the conventional sense of the word, and that there was no pretense that MPs were accountable to an extra-parliamentary organization, the name chosen for this model is perhaps misleading. Consequently, Heidar and Saglie, identifying pretty much the same features as Koole, prefer the name "network party," emphasizing the way in which policies are devised in informal networks rather than through the formal processes implied by the party constitution. They characterize Norwegian parties as "mass parties without a mass membership" and suggest plausibly that the picture they find in Norway would apply to most of modern Europe (Heidar and Saglie, "Predestined"). Whatever name is chosen, there is agreement on the most important aspects of the substance: Parties are financed primarily by the state, dominated by the upper echelons (the leader and MPs), and have a membership base that almost always amounts to less than 10 percent of their voters yet preserves the formal mechanisms of internal party democracy that, however attenuated, act as a continuing constraint on the leaders' freedom to maneuver.

✦ THE FUTURE OF EUROPEAN PARTIES

Despite the plethora of writings that discuss the "crisis" of parties or the "decline in party," political parties in modern Europe seem very likely to survive the falling membership levels and other trends that we have discussed. Gloomy analysts have been talking about "party decline" for pretty much as long as parties have existed (Scarrow, "Parties Without," p. 80). To see why parties are likely to survive, we can usefully distinguish three levels of parties, an approach devised in the 1960s by the American political scientist V. O. Key. First, there is the "party in the electorate" or "party on the ground"—the party's implantation in civil society. As we have said, there is a lot of evidence that parties are indeed becoming weaker at this level. Second, there is the "party in public office"—its elected representatives and their direct organizational support. Third, there is the "party in central office"—the headquarters and central organs of the party. There are no signs of decline at the second and third levels (Webb, "Conclusion").

Most observers believe that power increasingly lies with the parliamentary group, whose members are becoming ever more autonomous (Katz and Mair, "Ascendency"). It has been argued that power in postcommunist parties, at least according to their rulebooks, lies with the party in central office and the national executive rather than with the parliamentary group, but it is difficult to be certain about this, given that MPs control many of the positions on national executives (van Biezen). In terms of their resources—grassroots membership being the obvious exception—parties are becoming steadily stronger, and they continue to dominate parliaments and governments (Mair, pp. 120–54; Strøm, "Parties").

Moreover, as we observed in the first paragraph of this chapter, it is not just academics but most Europeans themselves who accept that parties are essential for the functioning of representative government in modern Europe. The apparent indispensability of parties is demonstrated by their dominance of politics in postcommunist countries since 1989: Despite the widespread public antipathy to them, parties in these countries play pretty much the same role as their west European counterparts. In some ways, they are even more central to politics. Although in resource terms they may seem weaker than their western counterparts, civil society and interest groups are even weaker, leaving parties nearly unchallenged as key political actors (Evanson and Magstadt).

It seems likely that parties will not only continue to exist but they will continue to have members, albeit not as many as in the period from the 1950s to the 1980s. Even on the most self-interested calculus, parliamentarians are aware that members have their uses. No matter how hi-tech election campaigns become, members demonstrating an active local party presence are still of benefit to the candidates. The presence of active local members tends to result in more votes for the party at election time (Gallagher and Marsh, *Days,* pp. 135–39; Seyd and Whiteley, *New Labour's,* pp. 111–37). Even though television is the main political arena during election campaigns, it is an addition to rather than a replacement for the work done by the local party organization. And although this local organization may not do a great deal between elections, there is a need to keep some kind of network in place at all times so that there is something that can be activated at elections; if the local organization is allowed to atrophy, reviving the party's unpaid workforce will become very difficult (Ware, "Activist," p. 89). In addition, as we have mentioned, specific actors within the party may have incentives to recruit members, seeing them as a resource in intraparty battles such as candidate or leadership selection.

Susan Scarrow (*Parties,* pp. 42–45) points out that, in theory at least, there are a number of other benefits that having members brings to a party. They bring legitimacy benefits, by fostering the impression, accurate or otherwise, that party leaders are at the apex of a principled movement rather than being merely a self-interested clique answerable to no one. Voters still expect their parties to be visible locally as well in the mass media; media strategies designed to market party elites need "validation" on the local level (Boll and Poguntke, p. 140). Members may also act as "ambassadors to the community," perhaps influencing the views of their friends and neighbors. Studies in Britain and in Denmark have found that members are a visible and articulate local manifestation of the party, frequently discussing politics with nonmembers (Martin and Cowley; Pedersen, p. 297). In addition, members provide a source both of linkage with the wider electorate and of new ideas, as well as providing a recruitment pool from which party candidates and leaders can be drawn.

Thus to talk about the "decline of party" in Europe is simplistic and misleading. European parties are adapting rather than declining or disappearing. In terms of the functions of parties, which we outlined earlier in this chapter, parties may not play the linkage role that they once did, but in other respects they face no serious challengers—which is why, though unloved, they dominate postcommunist political life. Parties are still indispensable after all these years. As Webb ("Conclusion," p. 458) puts it:

> Parties continue to perform vital tasks with a relatively high degree of effectiveness and are central mechanisms of popular choice and control. If they did not exist in the advanced industrial democratic world, somebody would undoubtedly have to invent them.

Parties thus continue to be vital organs of representation in European politics. Despite suggestions that their members' views and backgrounds are likely to be unrepresentative of voters, we have seen that the political values and social profile of party members are not such as to distort in any major way the process of representative government and the packages of policies on offer to voters. European parties will continue to be fundamentally different from American ones for as long as they retain control over the selection of their candidates, and there is no prospect of their relinquishing that prerogative. Elections in Europe will continue to center on parties, and on the programs that they offer, rather than on candidates. Electors will continue to vote for parties; seats in parliaments will continue to be divided among parties. The link between votes and seats is forged by electoral systems, and it is to this subject that we next turn.

REFERENCES

Andolfatto, Dominique: "Les Adhérents: Une Ressource Réévaluée," in Dominique Andolfatto, Fabienne Greffet, and Laurent Olivier (eds.), *Les Partis Politiques: Quelles Perspectives?* L'Harmattan, Paris, 2001, pp. 99–114.

Biezen, Ingrid van: *Political Parties in New Democracies: Party Organization in Southern and East-Central Europe,* Palgrave Macmillan, Basingstoke, 2003.

Bille, Lars: "Democratizing a Democratic Procedure: Myth or Reality? Candidate Selection in Western European Parties, 1960–1990," *Party Politics,* vol. 7, no. 3, 2001, pp. 363–80.

Bille, Lars: "A Power Centre in Danish Politics," in Knut Heidar and Ruud Koole (eds.), *Parliamentary Party Groups in European Democracies: Political Parties Behind Closed Doors,* Routledge, London and New York, 2000, pp. 130–44.

Bochel, John, and David Denver: "Candidate Selection in the Labour Party: What the Selectors Seek," *British Journal of Political Science,* vol. 13, no. 1, 1983, pp. 45–69.

Boll, Bernhard, and Thomas Poguntke: "Germany: The 1990 All-German Election Campaign," in Shaun Bowler and David M. Farrell (eds.), *Electoral Strategies and Political Marketing,* Macmillan, Basingstoke, 1992, pp. 121–43.

Bowler, Shaun: "Parties in Legislatures: Two Competing Explanations," in Dalton and Wattenberg (eds.), pp. 157–79.

Bugajski, Janusz: *Political Parties of Eastern Europe: A Guide to Politics in the Post-Communist Era,* M. E. Sharpe, Armonk (NY), 2002.

Burchell, Jon: "Organisational Reform Within European Green Parties," *West European Politics,* vol. 24, no. 3, 2001, pp. 113–34.

Carty, R. Kenneth: "Parties as Franchise Systems: The Stratarchical Organizational Imperative," *Party Politics,* vol. 10, no. 1, 2004, pp. 5–24.

Caul Kittilson, Miki, and Susan E. Scarrow: "Political Parties and the Rhetoric and Realities of Democratization," in Bruce E. Cain, Russell J. Dalton, and Susan E. Scarrow (eds.), *Democracy*

Transformed? Expanding Political Opportunities in Advanced Industrial Democracies, Oxford University Press, Oxford and New York, 2003, pp. 59–80.

Clark, Peter B., and James Q. Wilson: "Incentive Systems: A Theory of Organizations," *Administrative Science Quarterly,* vol. 6, 1961, pp. 129–66.

Colomer, Josep M.: "Spain and Portugal: Rule by Party Leadership," in Josep M. Colomer (ed.), *Political Institutions in Europe,* 2nd ed., Routledge, London, 2002, pp. 171–205.

Dalton, Russell J., and Martin P. Wattenberg (eds.): *Parties Without Partisans: Political Change in Advanced Industrial Democracies,* Oxford University Press, Oxford and New York, 2000.

Damgaard, Erik: "Developments in Danish Parliamentary Democracy: Accountability, Parties and External Constraints," *Scandinavian Political Studies,* vol. 27, no. 2, 2004, pp. 115–31.

de Sousa, Luís: "The Regulation of Political Financing in Portugal," *West European Politics,* vol. 27, no. 1, 2004, pp. 124–45.

Duverger, Maurice: *Political Parties,* 3rd ed., Methuen, London, 1964.

Epstein, Leon D.: *Political Parties in Western Democracies,* rev. ed., Transaction Books, New Brunswick (NJ), 1980.

Evanson, Robert K., and Thomas M. Magstadt: "The Czech Republic: Dominance in a Transitional System," in Clive S. Thomas (ed.), *Political Parties and Interest Groups: Shaping Democratic Governance,* Lynne Rienner, Boulder (CO) and London, 2001, pp. 193–209.

Farrell, David M., and Paul Webb: "Political Parties as Campaign Organizations," in Dalton and Wattenberg (eds.), ch. 6.

Fisher, Justin, and Todd A. Eisenstadt (eds.): *Comparing Party Finance Across Democracies—Broadening the Debate,* special issue of *Party Politics,* vol. 10, no. 6, 2004.

Gallagher, Michael: "Conclusion," in Gallagher and Marsh (eds.), pp. 236–83.

Gallagher, Michael, and Michael Marsh: *Days of Blue Loyalty: The Politics of Membership of the Fine Gael Party,* PSAI Press, Dublin, 2002.

Gallagher, Michael, and Michael Marsh: "Party Membership in Ireland: The Members of Fine Gael," *Party Politics,* vol. 10, no. 4, 2004, pp. 407–25.

Gallagher, Michael, and Michael Marsh (eds.): *Candidate Selection in Comparative Perspective: The Secret Garden of Politics,* Sage, London and Newbury Park (CA), 1988.

Gillespie, Richard: "'Programa 2000': The Appearance and Reality of Socialist Renewal in Spain," *West European Politics,* vol. 16, no. 1, 1993, pp. 78–96.

Gillespie, Richard: *The Spanish Socialist Party: A History of Factionalism,* Clarendon, Oxford, 1989.

Gunther, Richard, José Ramón Montero, and Juan J. Linz (eds.): *Political Parties: Old Concepts and New Challenges,* Oxford University Press, Oxford and New York, 2002.

Hardarson, Ólafur Th.: *Parties and Voters in Iceland: A Study of the 1983 and 1987 Althingi Elections,* Social Science Research Institute, University of Iceland, Reykjavík, 1995.

Heidar, Knut: "A 'New' Party Leadership?" in Kaare Strøm and Lars Svåsand (eds.), *Challenges to Political Parties: The Case of Norway,* University of Michigan Press, Ann Arbor, 1997, pp. 125–47.

Heidar, Knut, and Jo Saglie: "A Decline of Linkage? Intra-Party Participation in Norway, 1991–2000," *European Journal of Political Science,* vol. 42, no. 6, 2003, pp. 761–86.

Heidar, Knut, and Jo Saglie: "Predestined Parties? Organizational Change in Norwegian Political Parties," *Party Politics,* vol. 9, no. 2, 2003, pp. 219–39.

Holliday, Ian: "Spain: Building a Parties State in a New Democracy," in Webb, Farrell, and Holliday (eds.), pp. 248–79.

Holmberg, Sören: "Are Political Parties Necessary?" *Electoral Studies,* vol. 22, no. 3, 2003, pp. 287–99.

Hopkin, Jonathan: "Bringing the Members Back In: Democratizing Candidate Selection in Britain and Spain," *Party Politics,* vol. 7, no. 3, 2001, pp. 343–61.

Jasiewicz, Krzysztof: "Poland: Party System by Default," in Paul Webb, David M. Farrell, and Stephen White (eds.), *Political Parties in Transitional Societies,* Oxford University Press, Oxford and New York, 2006.

Katz, Richard S.: "Party Organizations and Finance," in Lawrence LeDuc, Richard G. Niemi, and Pippa Norris (eds.), *Comparing Democracies: Elections and Voting in Global Perspective,* Sage, Thousand Oaks (CA), 1996, pp. 107–33.

Katz, Richard S., and Peter Mair: "The Ascendancy of the Party in Public Office: Party Organizational Change in Twentieth-Century Democracies," in Gunther, Montero, and Linz (eds.), pp. 113–35.

Katz, Richard S., and Peter Mair: "Changing Models of Party Organization and Party Democracy: The Emergence of the Cartel Party," *Party Politics,* vol. 1, no. 1, 1995, pp. 5–28.

Katz, Richard S., and Peter Mair (eds.): *Party Organizations: A Data Handbook,* Sage, London and Newbury Park (CA), 1992.

Kingdom, John: *Government and Politics in Britain: An Introduction,* 3rd ed., Polity, Cambridge, 2003.

Kirchheimer, Otto: "The Transformation of the Western European Party System," in Joseph La Palombara and Myron Weiner (eds.), *Political Parties and Political Development,* Princeton University Press, Princeton, 1966, pp. 177–200.

Kitschelt, Herbert: "Citizens, Politicians and Party Cartellization: Political Representation and State Failure in Post-Industrial Democracies," *European Journal of Political Research,* vol. 37, no. 2, 2000, pp. 149–79.

Kitschelt, Herbert, Zdenka Mansfeldova, Radoslaw Markowski, and Gábor Tóka: *Post-Communist Party Systems: Competition, Representation and Inter-Party Competition,* Cambridge University Press, Cambridge and New York, 1999.

Knapp, Andrew: "From the Gaullist Movement to the President's Party," in Jocelyn A. J. Evans (ed.), *The French Party System,* Manchester University Press, Manchester and New York, 2003, pp. 121–36.

Koole, Ruud: "Cadre, Catch-all or Cartel? A Comment on the Notion of the Cartel Party," *Party Politics,* vol. 2, no. 4, 1996, pp. 507–23.

Koole, Ruud: "Party Finance Between Members and the State: The Dutch Case in Comparative and Historical Perspective," paper presented at the 17th World Congress of the International Political Science Association, Seoul, August 17–21, 1997.

Koole, Ruud: "The Vulnerability of the Modern Cadre Party in the Netherlands," in Peter Mair and Richard S. Katz (eds.), *How Parties Organize: Change and Adaptation in Party Organizations in Western Democracies,* Sage, London, 1994, pp. 278–303.

Kostelecky, Tomás: *Political Parties After Communism: Developments in East–Central Europe,* Woodrow Wilson Center Press, Washington (DC), 2002.

Kristjánsson, Svanur: "Iceland: Searching for Democracy along Three Dimensions of Citizen Control," *Scandinavian Political Studies,* vol. 27, no. 2, 2004, pp. 153–74.

LeDuc, Lawrence: "Democratizing Party Leadership Selection," *Party Politics,* vol. 7, no. 3, 2001, pp. 323–41.

Leijenaar, Monique, and Kees Niemöller: "The Netherlands," in Norris (ed.), pp. 114–36.

Lewis, Paul G.: "Political Parties," in Stephen White, Judy Batt, and Paul G. Lewis (eds.), *Developments in Central and East European Politics 3,* Palgrave Macmillan, Basingstoke, 2003, pp. 153–72.

Lewis, Paul G.: *Political Parties in Post-Communist Eastern Europe,* Routledge, London and New York, 2000.

Lipow, Arthur: *Political Parties and Democracy: Explorations in History and Theory,* Pluto Press, London and Chicago, 1996.

Lundell, Krister: "Determinants of Candidate Selection: The Degree of Centralization in Comparative Perspective," *Party Politics,* vol. 10, no. 1, 2004, pp. 25–47.

Mair, Peter: *Party System Change: Approaches and Interpretations,* Clarendon Press, Oxford, 1997.

Mair, Peter, and Ingrid van Biezen: "Party Membership in Twenty European Democracies, 1980–2000," *Party Politics,* vol. 7, no. 1, 2001, pp. 5–21.

Marsh, Michael: "Introduction: Selecting the Party Leader," *European Journal of Political Research,* vol. 24, no. 3, 1993, pp. 229–31.

Marsh, Michael: "Parties and Society," in John Coakley and Michael Gallagher (eds.), *Politics in the Republic of Ireland,* 4th ed, Routledge and PSAI Press, Abingdon and New York, 2005, pp. 160–82.

Martin, Alan, and Philip Cowley: "Ambassadors in the Community? Labour Party Members in Society," *Politics,* vol. 19, no. 2, 1999, pp. 89–96.

May, John D.: "Opinion Structure of Political Parties: The Special Law of Curvilinear Disparity," *Political Studies,* vol. 21, no. 2, 1973, pp. 135–51.

McKay, Joanna: "The PDS Tests the West: The Party of Democratic Socialism's Campaign to Become a Pan-German Socialist Party," *Journal of Communist Studies and Transition Politics,* vol. 20, no. 2, 2004, pp. 50–72.

McKenzie, Robert: "Power in the Labour Party: The Issue of 'Intra-Party Democracy,'" in Dennis Kavanagh (ed.), *The Politics of the Labour Party,* Allen and Unwin, London, 1982, pp. 191–201.

Narud, Hanne Marthe, Mogens N. Pedersen, and Henry Valen (eds.): *Party Sovereignty and Citizen Control: Selecting Candidates for Parliamentary Elections in Denmark, Finland, Iceland and Norway,* University Press of Southern Denmark, Odense, 2002.

Norris, Pippa: *Democratic Phoenix: Reinventing Political Activism,* Cambridge University Press, Cambridge and New York, 2002.

Norris, Pippa (ed.): *Passages to Power: Legislative Recruitment in Advanced Democracies,* Cambridge University Press, Cambridge, 1997.

Norris, Pippa, and Joni Lovenduski: "United Kingdom," in Norris (ed.), pp. 158–86.

Panebianco, Angelo: *Political Parties: Organization and Power,* Cambridge University Press, Cambridge and New York, 1988.

Pedersen, Karina: *Party Membership Linkage: The Danish Case,* PhD thesis, Department of Political Science, University of Copenhagen, 2003.

Pedersen, Karina, Lars Bille, Roger Buch, Jørgen Elklit, Bernhard Hansen, and Hans Jørgen Nielsen: "Sleeping or Active Partners? Danish Party Members at the Turn of the Millennium," *Party Politics,* vol. 10, no. 4, 2004, pp. 367–83.

Pennings, Paul, and Reuven Y. Hazan (eds.): *Democratizing Candidate Selection: Causes and Consequences,* special issue of *Party Politics,* vol. 7, no. 1, 2001.

Pettai, Vello, and Marcus Kreuzer: "Institutions and Party Development in the Baltic States" in Paul G. Lewis (ed.), *Party Development and Democratic Change in Post-Communist Europe: The First Decade,* Frank Cass, London, 2001, pp. 107–25.

Pierre, Jon, Lars Svåsand, and Anders Widfeldt: "State Subsidies to Political Parties: Confronting Rhetoric with Reality," *West European Politics,* vol. 23, no. 3, 2000, pp. 1–24.

Pinto-Duschinsky, Michael: "Financing Politics: A Global View," *Journal of Democracy,* vol. 13, no. 4, 2002, pp. 69–86.

Quinn, Thomas: "Electing the Leader: The British Labour Party's Electoral College," *British Journal of Politics and International Relations,* vol. 6, no. 3, 2004, pp. 333–52.

Ranney, Austin: *Curing the Mischiefs of Faction: Party Reform in America,* University of California Press, Berkeley and London, 1975.

Rentoul, John: *Tony Blair,* Little, Brown, London, 1995.

Ruostetsaari, Ilkka, and Mikko Mattila: "Candidate-Centered Campaigns and Their Effects in an Open List System," in David M. Farrell and Rüdiger Schmitt-Beck (eds.), *Do Political Campaigns Matter? Campaign Effects in Elections and Referendums,* Routledge, London and New York, 2002, pp. 92–107.

Saalfeld, Thomas: "Court and Parties: Evolution and Problems of Political Funding in Germany," in Williams (ed.), pp. 89–121.

Sanford, George: *Democratic Government in Poland: Constitutional Politics Since 1989,* Palgrave Macmillan, Basingstoke, 2002.

Scarrow, Susan E.: "Explaining Political Finance Reforms: Competition and Context," *Party Politics,* vol. 10, no. 6, 2004, pp. 653–75.

Scarrow, Susan: *Parties and Their Members: Organizing for Victory in Britain and Germany,* Oxford University Press, Oxford, 1996.

Scarrow, Susan E.: "Parties Without Members? Party Organization in a Changing Electoral Environment," in Dalton and Wattenberg (eds.), pp. 79–101.

Scarrow, Susan, Paul Webb, and David M. Farrell: "From Social Integration to Electoral Contestation: The Changing Distribution of Political Power Within Political Parties," in Dalton and Wattenberg (eds.), pp. 129–53.

Schattschneider, E. E.: *Party Government,* Greenwood Press, Westport (CT), 1977 [originally published 1942].

Seyd, Patrick, and Paul Whiteley: "British Party Members: An Overview," *Party Politics,* vol. 10, no. 4, 2004, pp. 355–66.

Seyd, Patrick, and Paul Whiteley: *New Labour's Grassroots: The Transformation of the Labour Party Membership,* Palgrave Macmillan, Basingstoke, 2002.

Seyd, Patrick, and Paul Whiteley (eds.): *Party Members and Activists,* special issue of *Party Politics,* vol. 10, no. 4, 2004.

Sikk, Allan: "A Cartel Party System in a Post-Communist Country? The Case of Estonia," paper prepared for the ECPR general conference, Marburg, September 18–21, 2003.

Sjöblom, Gunnar: "Political Change and Political Accountability: A Propositional Inventory of Causes and Effects," in Hans Daalder and Peter Mair (eds.), *Western Europe Party Systems,* Sage, London, 1983, pp. 369–403.

Smith-Sivertsen, Hermann: "Why Bigger Party Membership Organisations in Lithuania than in Latvia 1995–2000?" *East European Quarterly,* vol. 38, no. 2, 2004, pp. 215–59.

Strøm, Kaare: "A Behavioral Theory of Competitive Political Parties," *American Journal of Political Science,* vol. 34, no. 2, 1990, pp. 565–98.

Strøm, Kaare: "Parties at the Core of Government," in Dalton and Wattenberg (eds.), pp. 180–207.

Szczerbiak, Aleks: "The New Polish Political Parties as Membership Organizations," *Contemporary Politics,* vol.7, no. 1, 2001, pp. 57–69.

Szczerbiak, Aleks: *Poles Together? The Emergence and Development of Political Parties in Post-Communist Poland,* Central European University Press, Budapest, 2001.

Szczerbiak, Aleks: "The 'Professionalization' of Party Campaigning in Post-Communist Poland," in Lewis (ed.), *Party Development and Democratic Change in Post-Communist Europe,* FrankCass, London, 2001, pp. 78–92.

Szczerbiak, Aleks: "Testing Party Models in East–Central Europe: Local Party Organization in Postcommunist Poland," *Party Politics,* vol. 5, no. 4, 1999, pp. 525–37.

Torcal, Mariano, Richard Gunther, and José Ramón Montero: "Anti-Party Sentiments in Southern Europe," in Gunther, Montero, and Linz (eds.), pp. 257–90.

Ware, Alan: "Activist–Leader Relations and the Structure of Political Parties: 'Exchange Models' and Vote-Seeking Behaviour in Parties," *British Journal of Political Science,* vol. 22, no. 1, 1992, pp. 71–92.

Ware, Alan: *Political Parties and Party Systems,* Oxford University Press, Oxford, 1996.

Webb, Paul: "Conclusion: Political Parties and Democratic Control in Advanced Industrial Societies," in Webb, Farrell, and Holliday (eds.), pp. 438–60.

Webb, Paul: *The Modern British Party System,* Sage, London and Thousand Oaks (CA), 2000.

Webb, Paul, David M. Farrell, and Ian Holliday (eds.): *Political Parties in Advanced Industrial Democracy,* Oxford University Press, Oxford and New York, 2002.

Whiteley, Paul F., and Patrick Seyd: *High-Intensity Participation: The Dynamics of Party Activism in Britain,* University of Michigan Press, Ann Arbor, 2002.

Whiteley, Paul, Patrick Seyd, and Jeremy Richardson: *True Blues: The Politics of Conservative Party Membership,* Oxford University Press, Oxford, 1994.

Widfeldt, Anders: *Linking Parties with People? Party Membership in Sweden 1960–1997,* Ashgate, Aldershot, 1999.

Widfeldt, Anders: "Party Membership and Party Representativeness," in Hans-Dieter Klingemann and Dieter Fuchs (eds.), *Citizens and the State,* Oxford University Press, Oxford, 1995, pp. 134–82.

Williams, Robert (ed.): *Party Finance and Political Corruption,* Macmillan, Basingstoke, 2000.

CHAPTER 11

ELECTIONS, ELECTORAL SYSTEMS, AND REFERENDUMS

Elections are central to representative government in Europe. Their significance is both practical and symbolic. In practical terms, they play a large role in determining who becomes part of the political elite. In addition, they have a major bearing on the formation of governments, although, given the frequent complexity of government formation in modern Europe, their impact in this respect may be only indirect (see Chapter 12). As we saw in the previous chapter, elections have become the focal point of activity for most European parties.

Elections are also important symbolically in most competitive party systems, legitimizing a country's political system in the eyes of its citizens. They offer a means of participating in politics at relatively low cost to the individual in time, money, and mental effort. For most people, indeed, voting in elections is their only active participation in the political process. Elections also give citizens the feeling that they are exercising choices about who should represent them in the national parliament and about who should form the next government, even though the vote of any individual elector is highly unlikely to have much impact on either matter.

Elections themselves consist everywhere of citizens casting votes for candidates and/or political parties, but there is considerable variation across Europe in the precise set of electoral laws that determines how the votes that are cast are transformed into seats in the legislature in each country. In this chapter, we consider the variations in electoral systems in some detail, because these variations can have a significant bearing on some of the major differences between party politics across Europe. A country's electoral system can affect the nature of its party system, the sociodemographic composition of its parliament, the accuracy with which voters' preferences are reflected in the composition of the legislature, and the likelihood that governments will be formed by a coalition of parties rather than by just a single party.

Elections decide which parties and which candidates hold seats in parliaments, but they do not necessarily reflect a judgment on issues. At general elections, it is usually the case that many different issues are discussed during the course of the campaign, and even if a particular party pays particular attention to one particular issue, the degree of popular support for that party cannot necessarily be interpreted as the voters' verdict on the issue in question. In a number of European countries, therefore, referendums are used precisely to obtain the voters' decision on a specific issue. To some, the use of referendums is a good thing because it provides for greater popular participation in the decision-making process; to others, it raises the fear that existing political institutions such as parliaments, governments, and political parties will be weakened. Therefore we end this chapter by assessing the role of referendums in modern European politics and asking whether use of the referendum amounts to "direct democracy" and in this sense constitutes a challenge to representative government.

Before looking in detail at the nature and impact of electoral systems and the effects of referendums, we briefly outline some central aspects of the legal framework regulating elections in Europe, specifically the nature of the electorate and the timing of elections.

✧ WHO VOTES?

Elections in all European states are now held under a universal adult franchise. In most countries, universal male suffrage had been won by the time of World War I and female suffrage by World War II, although women did not receive the vote until immediately after World War II in Belgium, France, Greece, Italy, and Malta and until the 1970s in Switzerland. Evolving legal definitions of adulthood have lowered the voting age in many countries, characteristically to 18, although in a few countries it remains at 19 or 20. Certain categories of citizens are disfranchised in many countries, including people serving prison sentences and those confined to mental institutions. Generally speaking, the qualifications needed to be an election candidate are the same as those for being a voter (for details, see Katz, *Democracy,* pp. 246–61; Bowler et al., pp. 97–100).

In European countries it is the responsibility of the state to ensure that the electoral register—the list of eligible voters—contains the names of all who are entitled to vote. This means that European electoral registers tend to be far more accurate than those in the United States, for example, where the onus is on individuals to register themselves as voters. The proportion of the voting-age population that turns out to vote is higher in Europe than in the United States, in most countries reaching between 70 and 85 percent. It is particularly low in Poland and Switzerland (usually below 50 percent in both cases), and especially high in Italy and Malta along with some countries where voting is or has been compulsory (Belgium, the Netherlands, Luxembourg, and Austria), in all of which turnout at many elections since the war has approached or even exceeded 90 percent. Since the late 1970s, however, turnout has been decreasing at elections all across Europe (see Table 9.8).

✧ WHEN DO PEOPLE VOTE?

In most countries, the law or constitution prescribes a maximum period between elections but not a minimum; the maximum is four years in most European countries and five years in the rest (see Table 2.2). Within the prescribed limits, the timing of parliamentary elections is usually, on paper at least, at the discretion of the government of the day. To be precise, governments, or sometimes specifically the prime minister, typically have the power to recommend the dissolution of parliament to a head of state, who almost invariably takes this advice. In France, it is the president who has the right to call parliamentary elections at any time—even against the wishes of the government, which may be of a different political complexion—though not more than once a year. (We discussed this power of the French president in detail in Chapter 2.) French presidential elections are held at fixed five-year intervals (the term was seven years prior to 2002), and in a few European countries parliamentary elections too take place at set intervals: In Norway, Sweden, and Switzerland, parliaments have a fixed life span of four years.

Most European governments have complete legal freedom of action as to exactly when they call an election, subject to specified maximum terms. We might thus expect that governments tend to dissolve legislatures at times when they expect to do well in the subsequent election. This can undoubtedly make the timing of elections an important strategic variable. In a few European countries, Norway and Sweden, for example, the timing of elections is fixed by law, as it is in the United States; in others it is more or less determined by practice and convention, so all political actors have a pretty good idea several years in advance as to when the next election will be held. For example, in Luxembourg it has become accepted that elections take place every five years, on the same day as elections to the European Parliament. In other countries, however, election dates are decided either by the government of the day or by events outside its control, such as a collapse in the government's parliamentary support, matters that we turn to in greater detail in Chapter 12. (For a comprehensive theoretical and empirical analysis of strategic election timing in Britain, see Smith; see also Strøm and Swindle.)

Parliamentary elections, of course, are not the only opportunity that people have to vote in modern Europe. In all countries there are also elections for local councils (these are quite important in Scandinavia), and in several there are regional or provincial elections (for example, in Austria, France, Germany, Italy, Spain, and the United Kingdom), as we saw in Chapter 6. The twenty-five member states of the European Union (EU) hold elections to choose members of the European Parliament; these elections, which we discussed in detail in Chapter 5, take place every five years. In a number of countries, as we noted in Chapter 2, the president is directly elected by the people: besides France, this occurs in Austria, Cyprus, Finland, Iceland, Ireland, Lithuania, Poland, Portugal, Slovakia, and Slovenia. In addition, as we shall see in the last section of this chapter, the referendum is employed in a number of European countries.

✦ TYPES OF ELECTORAL SYSTEM

In this chapter we concentrate mainly on parliamentary elections, the most important political contests in every European country with the possible exception of France. In particular, we concentrate on electoral systems, the mechanisms that turn the votes cast by people on election day into seats to be occupied by deputies in the parliament. The electoral system structures the choices that the voters can make and then converts these choices into a legislature.

A wide variety of electoral systems are in use across Europe, and there is an equally wide selection of literature describing and tracing the history of these systems (see Carstairs; Delwit and De Waele; Farrell; Gallagher and Mitchell). This variety reflects in part the different weights attached to different criteria in different countries. It also reflects the fact that the electoral law a country adopts is usually determined by the political elite of the day, some of whose motivations may be partisan. In addition, electoral reformers have devised a plethora of systems and formulas, some of which have captured the imagination of politicians in various countries at various times.

Electoral systems in western Europe have been fairly stable since 1945; only in France and Greece could the electoral system be said to have been used as a political football (Cole and Campbell). Even in Greece, the electoral system has to some extent been depoliticized as an issue by a constitutional amendment in 2001 stipulating that any future change would come into effect not at the next election but at the one after that (Alivizatos and

Eleftheriadis, p. 70). In postcommunist Europe the picture varies: In some countries there has been stability and continuity (Slovenia, Hungary, and the Baltic states); in others (such as Poland and the Czech Republic) the electoral system has been the topic of constant political battles, with many attempts to make changes, some of them successful (Birch et al.).

For all this diversity, there are several systematic patterns in the profusion of electoral systems to be found across the continent. One vital distinction is between proportional representation (PR) systems on the one hand and plurality or majority systems on the other. The former put more stress on the concept of proportionality, the numerical accuracy with which the votes cast for parties are translated into seats won in parliament. Under a PR system, if a party receives, say, 25 percent of the votes, it can expect to win close to 25 percent of the seats. If every party participating in an election was guaranteed exactly the same share of seats as it won of the votes, we would describe that system as perfectly proportional, although this would not necessarily mean that the system was "perfect" in a normative sense. In practice, no electoral system can guarantee perfect proportionality, but PR systems attach greater priority to getting somewhere close to this goal. Plurality systems do not, of course, set out deliberately *not* to achieve high proportionality, but by prioritizing other criteria they accept a certain level of disproportionality as inevitable. For an overview of European electoral systems in these terms see Table 11.1.

✦ PLURALITY AND MAJORITY SYSTEMS

Throughout the nineteenth century, elections in most countries were held under plurality systems, but a combination of factors led almost all countries to adopt some form of PR in the twentieth century. At the moment, only two European countries do not use an electoral system that has at least an element of PR: the United Kingdom and France.

The electoral system used in the United Kingdom is the least complicated of all systems. It is the same as that employed for most elections in the United States, Canada, and India, for example. The country is divided into 659 areas known as constituencies or districts, each of which returns one member of parliament (MP) to the House of Commons. Within each constituency, the candidate with the most votes, whether or not this number is a majority over all others combined, wins the seat. The system is best named the single-member plurality (SMP) system, though it is often called "first past the post," in a rather dubious analogy with horse racing, or simply "the British system." Voters, on entering the polling station, are given a ballot paper listing all the candidates, and they write an X next to the name of the candidate they wish to vote for. An example of the operation of the system in the Taunton constituency in Somerset, in the west of England, in the 2001 general election is shown in Table 11.2.

This system has the merit of simplicity for voters. It is also defended on the ground that as the MP, in this case Adrian Flook, is the only representative for the constituency, responsibility for its interests lies unequivocally with him. This, it is claimed, helps forge a bond between an MP and his or her constituents that would be lost if several MPs were responsible for the same constituency. In terms of the national impact, as we discuss later, the system is praised for its tendency to produce single-party majority governments.

But the plurality system has many critics. Three of the main points made against it are illustrated by the Taunton result. First, Flook was elected despite winning little more than 40 percent of the total votes; in fact, 58 percent of the voters were not represented by a candidate of their favored party. It is probable that most Labour voters

TABLE 11.1

Electoral Systems in Europe, 2005

Country	Basic Category	Members of Lower House	Number of Constituencies (districts)	Significant Changes Since 1945/1990[a]
Austria	PR list	183	43[b]	Introduction in 1992 of a third tier, increase from 9 to 43 districts, and minor expansion of effectiveness of preferential voting
Belgium	PR list	150	11	Abolition of higher tier, and significant expansion of effectiveness of preference voting, prior to 2003 election
Cyprus	PR list	56	6[b]	This replaced "reinforced PR" in 1995
Czech Republic	PR list	200	14	Abolition of higher tier before 2002 election
Denmark	PR list	175	18[b]	Change of formula from DH to MSL in 1953[c]
Estonia	PR list	101	12[b]	Abandonment of STV after 1990 election[c]
Finland	PR list	200	15	None
France	Non-PR (2-round)	577	577	Many (see text account)
Germany	Mixed compensatory	598	300[b]	Minor changes in 1953, 1956, 1984 and 1990
Greece	PR list	300	56[b]	Many changes, usually designed to benefit the government of the day
Hungary	Mixed partially compensatory	386	197[b]	None
Iceland	PR list	63	7[b]	Changes in 1987 and 2000
Ireland	PR-STV	166	42	None
Italy	Mixed partially compensatory	630	476[b]	Abandonment in 1993 of previous highly proportional list system
Latvia	PR list	100	5	Threshold raised from 4% 1995
Lithuania	Mixed parallel	141	72[b]	Threshold raised from 4% 1996; in single-member constituencies, two-round system replaced by single-member plurality for 2000 election

Continued

Electoral Systems in Europe, 2005

Country	Basic Category	Members of Lower House	Number of Constituencies (districts)	Significant Changes Since 1945/1990[a]
Luxembourg	PR list	60	4	None
Malta	PR-STV	65	13	Winner in votes guaranteed majority of seats since 1987
Netherlands	PR list	150	1	Minor increase in effectiveness of preferential voting in 1998
Norway	PR list	169	20[b]	Change of formula from DH to MSL in 1953; addition of 8 national seats before 1989 election (increased to 19 before 2005 election)
Poland	PR list	460	41	Changes prior to three of first four postcommunist elections
Portugal	PR list	230	20	First democratic election in 1975
Slovakia	PR list	150	1	Replacement of 4 subnational constituencies by 1 national constituency prior to 1998 election
Slovenia	PR list	90	9[b]	Introduction of 4% threshold prior to 2000 election
Spain	PR list	350	52	First democratic postwar election in 1977
Sweden	PR list	349	29[b]	Change of formula from DH to MSL in 1952; introduction of higher-tier seats in 1970; introduction of meaningful preference voting in 1998
Switzerland	PR list	200	26	None
United Kingdom	Non-PR (plurality)	659	659	None at national level

[a] In the case of postcommunist countries, only changes since 1990 are noted.

[b] The country has "complex districting"—that is, higher-tier constituencies to iron out discrepancies arising from lower-level constituencies.

[c] Electoral formulas: DH—D'Hondt; MSL—modified Sainte-Laguë; STV—single transferable vote.

Source: Mackie and Rose; Rose and Munro; annual updates in the *Political Data Yearbook* of the *European Journal of Political Research;* Birch.

would have preferred the election of the Liberal Democrat candidate to the actual outcome, and so in a straight fight between the Conservative and the Liberal Democrat, the latter would have won. Therefore, the British system is criticized for not necessarily producing the MP who would be most representative of the voters' wishes and, worse, for producing results that are in some sense arbitrarily determined by the nomination of "vote-splitting" losing candidates.

TABLE 11.2

The British Electoral System in Operation, Taunton Constituency, 2001 Election

Candidate	Votes	% of Votes
Adrian Flook (Conservative)	23,033	41.7
Jackie Ballard (Liberal Democrat)	22,798	41.3
A. Govier (Labour)	8,254	14.9
M. Canton (UK Independence Party)	1,140	2.1
Total	55,225	100.0

Second, the Taunton contest presented Labour supporters in particular with a tactical choice: Should they vote for the Labour candidate, or should they vote for the Liberal Democrat in order to keep the Conservative out? If they vote sincerely, in accordance with their true preferences, then this might have the effect of helping to bring about the election of the candidate they like least. Although no electoral system is completely "strategy-proof," the plurality system is almost guaranteed to force at least some voters to think strategically if there are more than two serious candidates.

Third, if the pattern of the Taunton result, with nearly 60 percent of the votes wasted on losing candidates, were repeated over the entire country, the House of Commons could be very unrepresentative of public opinion. In practice, the lack of "fairness" in individual constituencies evens itself out to some extent across the country; an overall election is never as "unfair" as a sample constituency outcome repeated 659 times over (Gallagher and Mitchell, app. C). Consequently, between 1945 and the 1970s, when nearly all the votes were won by the two main parties, Labour and the Conservatives, the national outcome in terms of seats was not grossly unrepresentative. But when a third party (the Liberals in 1974 and 1979, the alliance between the Liberal and the Social Democratic Parties in 1983 and 1987, the Liberal Democrats from 1992 onward) began winning significant support, the national outcome fell much farther short of perfect proportionality, and the third party was the main victim. This outcome is illustrated by the result of the 2001 election (see Table 11.3). In this election, just as in 1997, what appeared to be an overwhelming Labour win in parliament was in fact "manufactured" by the electoral system, as nearly three out of every five voters voted against Labour. The capriciousness of this electoral system was perhaps best illustrated by an election held outside Europe: The Progressive Conservatives in Canada, who had won a large majority of the seats on 43 percent of the votes in the 1988 election, found themselves reduced to just two seats in parliament after winning 16 percent of the votes in the October 1993 election.

Although the plurality electoral system may seem very firmly entrenched in the United Kingdom, it has come under increasing challenge in recent years. Indeed, the country now employs a variety of different electoral systems in different settings (Mitchell; Independent Commission on PR). Elections to the Scottish parliament and the Welsh assembly are held under a mixed member system (we discuss this and other systems later in the chapter) comparable to that used in Germany. Elections to the Northern Ireland

TABLE 11.3

Votes and Seats in the United Kingdom General Election of 2001

Party	% of Votes	% of Seats
Labour	40.7	62.5
Conservatives	31.7	25.2
Liberal Democrats	18.3	7.9
Others	9.3	4.4
Total	100.0	100.0

Source: See source note of Table 7.1.

assembly, like all other elections in the province (other than those to the Westminster parliament), are held under the single transferable vote, which is used in the Republic of Ireland. The elections to elect Britain's MEPs take place using a closed-list system like the one used for parliamentary elections in Spain. The country is divided into eleven constituencies; the other three MEPs from the United Kingdom, those representing Northern Ireland, are elected under the single transferable vote. After its 1997 election victory, the incoming Labour government set up a commission, headed by the former minister Roy Jenkins, to examine the case for a new electoral system, with the idea of putting its recommendation to a referendum. The Jenkins commission reported in favor of a mixed system, but plans for a referendum were put firmly on the back burner by the government.

One relatively modest modification that has been suggested by some British electoral reformers is the introduction of ordinal voting rather than "X" or "nominal" voting. Voters would rank the candidates in order of preference by placing a number (1, 2, etc.) next to each name. The counting process would no longer finish with the counting of the first preferences. Instead, if no candidate had a majority, the lowest-placed candidate would be eliminated, and his or her votes would be transferred to the other candidates in accordance with the second preferences marked on the ballots. So, in Taunton (see Table 11.2), first the UKIP candidate and then the Labour candidate would be eliminated. Assuming that a majority of Labour voters gave their second preference to the Liberal Democrat candidate rather than to the Conservative, the Liberal Democrat would almost certainly be carried above the Conservative and would therefore win the seat. This electoral system is known as the *alternative vote,* or the single transferable vote in single-member constituencies (in the United States it is known as "instant runoff"). It is a majority system, as opposed to the British plurality systems, because the counting process continues until one candidate has a majority (50 percent plus 1) over all other remaining candidates.

No European country uses the alternative vote to elect its parliament (though it is employed in Australia), but a system that has some of the same properties is used in France. There, as in Britain, deputies are returned from single-member constituencies, but there is provision for two rounds of voting, on successive Sundays. If a candidate wins a majority of votes in the first round, he or she is elected, but that occurs in only a small minority of constituencies. Otherwise, the first round of voting is followed by a second round, which only the top candidates are allowed to enter (see Box 11.1). The

Box 11.1   ELECTORAL SYSTEMS

France

France does not use proportional representation to elect deputies to the National Assembly. Instead, it employs a two-round or "double-ballot" system. Metropolitan France is divided into 555 single-member constituencies (the overseas territories and departments return an additional 22 deputies). Within each constituency there can be two rounds of voting on successive Sundays. If a candidate wins an overall majority in the first round, he or she is elected as the deputy for the constituency, but in the great majority of constituencies, no candidate achieves an overall majority, and the second round takes place a week later. Only candidates whose first-round votes exceeded 12.5 percent of the electorate (which on the basis of turnout at the 2002 election equates to about 20 percent of the votes cast) are permitted to participate in the second round, unless the operation of this rule would leave fewer than two candidates entitled to take part, in which case the top two are both allowed through. In the second round the candidate with the most votes, whether or not the tally amounts to a majority, wins the seat. Hence the system is sometimes described as "majority–plurality," in that a majority in the first round, or a plurality in the second, suffices for election.

Germany

The German electoral system provides two routes to the lower house of parliament, the Bundestag. When voters enter the polling booth, they are faced with a ballot paper with two columns. One gives them a vote in the election of a member of parliament (MdB) for the local single-member constituency; half of the 598 members of parliament are elected from single-member constituencies in exactly the same way as in the United Kingdom. The second column enables them to cast a list vote; the other half of the parliament is elected from party lists. The overall allocation of seats in the Bundestag is decided by these list votes. Each party is awarded as many list seats as it needs to ensure that its total number of seats (constituency seats and list seats combined) is proportional to the share of list votes it received. However, parties do not receive any list seats unless they have either won at

least 5 percent of the list votes or won three constituency seats. If a party wins more constituency seats within any Land (province) than it is entitled to on the basis of its list votes, it is allowed to keep these extra seats (which are termed *Überhangmandate*), and the size of the Bundestag is expanded accordingly. At recent elections these *Überhangmandate,* which represent a distortion of proportionality, have significantly increased the size of the government's majority: from 2 to 10 in 1994, from 8 to 21 in 1998, and from 6 to 9 in 2002.

Italy

From the end of World War II until 1993, Italy had a very proportional type of PR system. Seats were awarded within large constituencies (average district magnitude was around thirty), with a higher tier to balance up the number of seats awarded to parties that had received less than their "fair share" in the constituencies. The system was a preferential form of PR—that is, voters for a party could indicate preferences for specific candidates on that party's list, thus generating competition for preference votes between candidates of the same party. Within the Christian Democrats (DC) in particular, various factions and affiliated interest groups all tried to motivate voters to cast preference votes for their particular candidates. Politicians found guilty of corruption were inclined to blame the electoral system for forcing them into clientelistic vote-buying exercises of one sort or another, so the electoral system moved to the top of the hit list of Italy's political reformers and was fundamentally altered in 1993. The new system was a compromise between those who wanted to adopt the British single-member plurality system and those who wanted to retain PR. It is a mixed system that is partially compensatory, in that the share-out of list seats takes some but not full account of the seats that parties win in the single-member constituencies. Just over three-quarters of the deputies (475 out of 630) are elected from single-member constituencies, and the rest are elected from national lists and shared out among parties that pass the qualifying threshold of 4 percent of the national vote.

Latvia

Latvia's 100 members of the Saeima are elected from five multimember constituencies whose size ranges from 14 to 28 seats. Seats are awarded to parties by the Sainte-Laguë highest average method, which is completely fair as between large and small parties (and, perhaps not surprisingly, is used in very few countries). However, no party receives any seats unless it has won at least 5 percent of the votes nationally. Voters can cast not only a positive preference vote for individual candidates; they can even award a negative preference by crossing out the candidate's name (a hangover from the old Soviet system), which counts against the candidate. These preference votes are decisive in determining which candidates take the seats, though the Latvian parties have a habit of running candidates in more than one constituency. This means that the candidates who receive the most preference votes in a given constituency do not necessarily take their seat there, reducing the voters' power to choose their representatives.

Netherlands

The Tweede Kamer (Second Chamber) contains 150 deputies, and when it comes to awarding seats to parties, the whole country is treated as one 150-member constituency. Each party presents a list of candidates, and the parties receive seats in proportion to their votes. The seat allocation formula used is the D'Hondt highest averages method. Parties receiving fewer than two-thirds of 1 percent of the total votes cast do not qualify for any seats; this is the lowest threshold, as a share of the national vote, employed by any country in Europe. It rarely happens that the threshold debars a Dutch party from receiving seats. Voters can cast a preference vote for a candidate on a party list, but in practice the casting of preference votes in the Netherlands has had very little impact on the composition of the parliament. Because there are no subnational constituencies, the system is sometimes criticized for being impersonal. In response, the government that took office in 2003 outlined plans for a mixed system that would see half of the deputies elected from small multimember constituencies and the other half from a national list.

Poland

The 460 members of the Sejm are elected from forty-one constituencies, in which seats are awarded to parties by the modified Sainte-Laguë method. Parties require 5 percent of the votes nationally to qualify for any seats (coalitions need 8 percent). Voters can cast preference votes for individual candidates on a party's list, and these preferences determine which candidates are elected. Poland's electoral system was changed before the elections of 1991, 1993, and 2001; since the end of communism, only the elections of 1993 and 1997 have taken place under a common electoral system, and the 2001 system is not regarded by many political actors as final.

Spain

The Congress of Deputies is elected from fifty-two constituencies, each of which is based on a province and returns on average only seven deputies, a relatively small figure for a PR electoral system. Within each constituency, the D'Hondt highest averages formula is employed; this tends to favor the large parties rather than the small ones. There is no higher-tier allocation to compensate parties for any underrepresentation in the constituencies. Voters have no choice of candidate; they simply cast a vote for one of the party lists that are offered.

Sweden

The Riksdag has 349 members and is elected by proportional representation based on two tiers. The lower tier consists of twenty-eight constituencies covering the country, which between them return 310 deputies. The remaining 39 seats are held back for allocation at the second tier. They are distributed among the parties in such a way as to ensure that the total number of seats received by each party comes as close to its proportional share as possible. However, a threshold discriminates against small parties: Those receiving fewer than 4 percent of the national votes are not awarded any of the 39 higher-tier seats. There is provision for voters to indicate a preference for an individual candidate on a party list. Until 1998, the initial ranking order of the candidates on each party's

Continued

Box 11.1   ELECTORAL SYSTEMS *(Continued)*

list was in practice almost immune to alteration by the voters, but since then a rule change has meant that the preference votes that are cast can have a real impact on the outcome. Candidates who receive preference votes from at least 8 percent of their party's voters now leapfrog candidates who were placed above them on the list but receive fewer preference votes. In characteristic Swedish style, this reform was made not by a transient parliamentary majority in order to secure partisan advantage but on the basis of careful study of the subject. In the 2002 election, about 26 percent of voters availed themselves of the option to cast a personal vote, and an estimated 10 of the 349 MPs owed their election to the personal votes they received.

United Kingdom

The UK employs the single-member plurality system. The country is divided into 659 constituencies, each returning one member of parliament (MP) to the House of Commons. Within each constituency, the candidate winning the most votes, whether or not the tally amounts to a majority, becomes the MP. Other bodies within the UK are most commonly elected by forms of PR: either mixed compensatory systems (the institutions of devolution in Scotland and Wales), the single transferable vote (the Northern Ireland assembly), or a closed PR list system (the 75 members of the European Parliament elected from England, Scotland, and Wales).

candidate with the most votes (a simple plurality) in the second round wins the seat, even if he or she fails to achieve an overall majority. (French presidential elections are held under the same system, except that only the top two candidates from the first round are allowed to proceed to the second, thus guaranteeing that the eventual winner will emerge with an absolute majority.) This system is also used in Lithuania to elect 71 of the 141 MPs, as we discuss later; as in French presidential elections, only the top two candidates are allowed to proceed to the second round.

This two-round double ballot system has some advantages over the British system, for it gives supporters of losing first-round candidates a chance to switch their second-round votes to one of the serious contenders. The first of the two rounds could also be used by the two main blocs as quasi-primaries, but the established right-wing parties, the Gaullists and the UDF, generally agreed on a single right-wing candidate in each constituency before the first round, sharing the constituencies out between them. The 2002 merger between the Gaullists and most of the UDF into the UMP has simplified matters on the right-hand side of the political spectrum. On the left, in contrast, the two main parties, the Socialists and the Communists, usually nominate a candidate each in every constituency for the first ballot, and the one with fewer votes then stands aside for the stronger on the second ballot. Over the years this has increasingly benefited the Socialists more than the Communists; the latter's first-ballot votes have steadily fallen, to the extent that many more Communist candidates stand aside for Socialists than vice versa, and, in addition, Communist voters switch to Socialist candidates on the second ballot more solidly than Socialist voters switch to Communist candidates.

But even if the French system does have the potential to give a slightly greater choice to the voters, like the British system it does not overcome the problem of disproportional overall results. In 2002, for example, the UMP won only 33 percent of the votes but 63 percent of the seats. Like the British system, the French two-ballot system assists the largest parties and penalizes smaller ones. In addition, it benefits parties close to the center, such as the UMP and the Socialists, and works against more extreme parties, such as the Communists (PCF) or the far-right Front National (FN). Such parties, even if their candidates make it into the second round, are very unlikely to win the runoff against a more centrist candidate, and so they win a smaller share of the seats than of the votes. The PCF has some scope for deal making with the Socialists, albeit on the Socialists' terms, and thus wins some seats, but the FN is generally treated as a pariah by the other parties and usually ends up with few or no seats; in 2002, for example, it received 11 percent of the votes but won none of the 577 seats. For supporters of the double-ballot system, this pronounced penalization of "antisystem" parties is a definite merit (Sartori, p. 67).

One disadvantage of the two-round system when compared to the alternative vote is that the candidates whom it allows through to the second round may not be the most popular. This was dramatically illustrated at the French presidential election of 2002, when almost everyone expected that the second round would be fought between the main right-wing candidate, the incumbent Jacques Chirac, and the Socialist leader Lionel Jospin. Instead, due to fragmentation of the left-wing vote, Jospin was pushed narrowly into third position by the far-right candidate Jean-Marie Le Pen, whom Chirac defeated by 82 percent to 18 percent in the second round. Under the alternative vote, vote transfers from the lower-placed candidates of the broad left would have taken Jospin into second or perhaps even first place by the end of the count; under the two-round system this counted for nothing because his first-round votes were slightly fewer than Le Pen's.

In France, more than in any other country, the electoral system has been manipulated by ruling parties for their own benefit (for details, see Cole and Campbell; Elgie). The two-round system was used for most of the period between 1831 and 1939, though other systems were often tried for short periods. After World War II, a PR system was briefly used, but in the early 1950s a new system was introduced, with the clear aim of discriminating against the Communist Party. The double ballot was brought back under de Gaulle in the late 1950s. The Socialists replaced it with PR for the 1986 election, partly to minimize their electoral losses, but the incoming right-wing administration promptly reintroduced the double-ballot system, under which subsequent parliamentary elections have been held.

✦ PROPORTIONAL REPRESENTATION

Discontent with the anomalies produced by plurality or majority systems, combined inevitably with self-interested calculations by those parties that were faring, or seemed likely to fare, badly under such systems, led to discussion of electoral reform throughout Europe in the second half of the nineteenth century. As the franchise expanded to include the working class, the prospect of seeing left-wing parties sweep the board under the existing system brought about a sudden appreciation of the principle of PR among the existing conservative and liberal parties in most countries. By the end of World War II, nearly all countries had electoral systems based on PR. The key element in any PR electoral system is the multimember constituency. Seats are allocated to

TABLE 11.4

Features of European Electoral Systems, 2005

Electoral System	Constituency-Level Seat Allocation Formula[a]	Higher-Tier Seat Allocation? (formula)	Threshold (for participation in higher-tier seat share-out unless otherwise specified)[b]	Choice of Candidate Within Party?
PR List Systems				
Austria	Hare	Yes (DH)	1 constituency seat or 4% of votes nationally	Yes, but largely ineffective
Belgium	DH	No	5% needed within a constituency for any seats there	Yes
Cyprus	Hare	LR–Hare	1.8% national vote	Yes
Czech Republic	DH	No	5% of votes nationally for any seats	Yes
Denmark	MSL	Yes (LR–Hare)	2% of votes nationally needed for parliamentary representation	Yes
Estonia	Hare	Yes (DH)	5% of votes	Yes
Finland	DH	No	—	Yes
Greece	DH	Yes (LR)	3% of votes nationally needed for parliamentary representation	Yes
Iceland	DH	Yes (DH)	5% of votes nationally	Yes, but largely ineffective
Latvia	SL	No	5% of votes nationally for any seats	Yes
Luxembourg	DH	No	—	Yes
Netherlands	DH	No[c]	0.67% of votes nationally needed to qualify for seats	Yes, but largely ineffective
Norway	MSL	Yes (MSL)	4% of votes nationally	Yes, but largely ineffective
Poland	MSL	No	5% needed for any seats	Yes
Portugal	DH	No	—	No
Slovakia	LR–Droop	No[c]	5% needed for any seats	Yes, but largely ineffective
Slovenia	Droop	Yes (DH)	4% of votes	Yes, but largely ineffective
Spain	DH	No	—	No
Sweden	MSL	Yes (MSL)	4% of votes nationally or 12% in one constituency needed for parliamentary representation	Yes
Switzerland	DH	No	—	Yes

Continued

Features of European Electoral Systems, 2005

Electoral System	Constituency-Level Seat Allocation Formula[a]	Higher-Tier Seat Allocation? (formula)	Threshold (for participation in higher-tier seat share-out unless otherwise specified)[b]	Choice of Candidate Within Party?
Mixed Systems				
Germany	Plurality	Yes (LR–Hare)	5% of votes or 3 constituency seats	No
Hungary	2-round	Yes (DH)	5% of votes nationally	No
Italy	Plurality	Yes (LR–Hare)	4% of votes nationally	No
Lithuania	2-round	Yes (LR–Hare)	5% of list votes	No
Other PR Systems				
Ireland	STV	No	—	Yes
Malta	STV	Yes[d]	See note[d]	Yes
Non-PR Systems				
France	2-round	No	—	No
United Kingdom	Plurality	No	—	No

Source: See source note of Table 11.1.

[a] Electoral formulas: DH—D'Hondt; LR—largest remainders; MSL—modified Sainte-Laguë; SL—Sainte-Laguë; STV—single transferable vote.

[b] In some countries, especially postcommunist ones, there are higher thresholds for coalitions.

[c] There is only one (national) constituency.

[d] In Malta, whichever of the two main parties wins a plurality of first-preference votes is awarded extra seats to give it a bare overall majority of seats, if it has not won an overall majority from the constituencies. This is the only situation in which there is any higher-tier allocation.

parties within each constituency in broad proportion to the votes each party receives. Proportional representation systems cannot be based on single-member constituencies, because a single seat cannot be divided up proportionately, no matter what method is used to allocate it. As a general rule, indeed, the larger the district magnitude (i.e., the number of members returned from each constituency), the more proportional the national election result is likely to be. This, it should be stressed, applies only when a PR formula is used. If a plurality or majority formula is employed in multimember constituencies, as when American public representatives are elected from "at-large" districts, the result is highly disproportional, being even more crushing to minorities than a series of single-seat constituencies.

There are important variations between PR systems, but basically they can be grouped into three categories: list systems, mixed systems, and the single transferable vote.

List Systems

The basic principle of a list system is that each party presents a list of candidates in each constituency. Each list usually contains as many candidates as there are seats to be filled in the constituency. The seats are then shared out among the parties in proportion to the votes they win, in accordance with a predetermined formula. Although PR is scarcely used at any level of elections in the United States, Americans were the first to think about ways of achieving proportional representation. They were interested not in the proportional allocation of seats to parties in accordance with the votes that each party receives but in the proportional allocation to states of seats in the House of Representatives in accordance with the population of each state. Most of the PR methods used in Europe today were either used or discussed in the United States long before Europeans thought of them (Balinski and Young).

List systems differ from one another in a number of respects, and we discuss them in sequence. They include

1. the formulas used to award seats to parties within each constituency
2. the matter of whether or not there is a second, higher, tier at which seats are awarded to override any imbalances that may arise at the constituency level
3. the existence of thresholds
4. the degree of choice, if any, given to voters to express a preference for one or more specific candidates on the party list

The picture is summarized in Table 11.4.

Electoral Formulas

A number of different methods are used to decide how seats are shared out among parties. The most common are largest remainders (using the Hare or Droop quota), highest averages using the D'Hondt method, and highest averages using the modified or pure Sainte-Laguë method. In the United States, largest remainders with the Hare quota is known as the Hamilton method and D'Hondt as the Jefferson method, used for apportioning seats in the House of Representatives from 1790 to 1830. The "pure" Sainte-Laguë method is known in the United States as the Webster method; the modified version used in some Scandinavian countries and in Poland has the effect of making it more difficult than under the pure version for small parties to win seats.

We do not elaborate the differences between these formulas in any detail here (the mechanics are explained in Farrell, ch. 4; Gallagher and Mitchell, app. A), because these differences are less important than the similarities. However, it should be noted that of these five methods, both pure Sainte-Laguë and largest remainders with the Hare quota are completely even-handed between large and small parties; modified Sainte-Laguë and largest remainders with the Droop quota tilt the balance slightly toward larger parties; and the D'Hondt method favors large parties even more (Lijphart, *Electoral*, pp. 96–97). All variants of PR are essentially similar in that they set out to award seats as "fairly" as possible to each party according to how many votes it won, although they are based on slightly different ideas as to exactly what is meant by the concept of "fairness" (Gallagher, "Proportionality"). They share a common attachment to the idea of proportionality, and in this they differ fundamentally from the plurality method, where other criteria take priority.

District Magnitude and Higher Tiers

The seat allocation method is just one factor determining how proportional the distribution of seats will be in relation to the way votes were cast. A second and often more important factor is district magnitude. If the average district magnitude is small, an election outcome is unlikely to be highly proportional, no matter what allocation formula is used. When France introduced PR for the 1986 election, the D'Hondt formula was used in constituencies that returned only six deputies on average, so although the outcome was much more proportional than the outcomes of elections held under France's usual single-member constituency system, it was less proportional than under most PR systems. In Spain, too, this has an impact: Spain employs relatively small constituencies (district magnitude averages seven seats), and in addition its rural areas are significantly overrepresented in parliament (Hopkin). Consequently, the major parties derive a sizable bonus, and there is usually significant deviation from perfect proportionality, albeit not on the same scale as in countries using the British plurality system.

One way of overcoming the problem is to use larger constituencies, averaging around twelve seats or more, as in Cyprus, Finland, and Latvia. This is taken to the extreme in the Netherlands and Slovakia; in each case, the whole country forms one giant constituency. Employing large constituencies is sometimes criticized on the grounds that voters are likely to feel remote from their deputies. Another method is to have a second level of allocation at which disproportionalities arising at the constituency level can be ironed out (Taagepera and Shugart, pp. 126–33). In some countries, a certain proportion of seats is set aside at the start for this purpose: about 20 percent in Denmark and Iceland, and 11 percent in Norway and Sweden. These "higher-tier" seats are then awarded to the parties in the appropriate numbers to compensate them for any shortfall in the seats they won in the constituencies and thereby bring the overall distribution of seats as close to perfect proportionality as possible. In other countries, such as Austria, the number of higher-tier seats is not fixed in advance, but the effect is the same. What happens is that each party's "wasted" votes from the constituencies—that is, the votes it has not used to earn seats—are pooled on a national or regional basis, and a distribution of the unallocated seats takes place in accordance with each party's unused vote totals. This ensures that very few of a party's votes are wasted.

Mixed Systems

The wisest investment in electoral systems futures markets in the late 1980s would have been in mixed systems, because these have been the real growth area in recent years (for mixed systems see Shugart and Wattenberg; Farrell, ch. 5; Gallagher and Mitchell, chs. 10–15; Massicotte and Blais). Much of the growth has been outside the region we are covering (Japan, Mexico, New Zealand, and Russia are the most prominent examples), but four of the twenty-eight countries covered by this book now employ a mixed system. The essence of these systems is that MPs can be elected by two different routes. There is a wide range of possible (and even actual) variants, but the most widely employed is the one where the voter has two votes: one to choose a local constituency MP, the other to choose a party list. There is terminological profusion when it comes to naming this kind of system: It is known not only as "mixed" but also as "mixed member," "additional member" (particularly in Britain), or "personalized PR" (particularly in Germany).

The link between the two types of seat—constituency and list—is made in two different ways in different types of mixed electoral system. In some, termed "compensatory" mixed systems, the list seats are awarded to parties to ensure that their overall seat total (list seats plus constituency seats) is proportional to their list votes. Thus, if a party has been underrepresented at the constituency level, which is usually the case for small parties, it is allocated relatively more list seats to "compensate" it and bring it up to its overall "fair" share. The other type of mixed system is "parallel," where the list seats are shared out purely on the basis of list votes, without taking any account of what has happened in the constituency component. Parallel mixed systems produce a less "fair" overall outcome than compensatory ones, because the list seats are not used to counterbalance the disproportionalities produced in the constituency component.

Germany's is the archetypal mixed system (Saalfeld). The country is divided into 299 single-member constituencies, in each of which the seat goes to the candidate with the most votes, just as in Britain. The sharing out of the national seats is then carried out in such a way as to ensure that each party's total number of seats (constituency seats plus national seats) is proportional to its share of the list votes—in other words, it is a compensatory system (see Box 11.1). Usually, the two main parties, the SPD and the CDU–CSU, win over 99 percent of the constituency seats, the PDS wins the others, and the Greens and FDP win none at all. Consequently, the last two parties are reliant on the list seats to achieve their overall fair share.

In contrast, Lithuania employs the other type of mixed system, the parallel version. There are 71 single-member constituencies, in which the French two-round system is used, and a list component with 70 seats. Once again, each voter has two votes, one in the constituency and one for a list. Because it is a parallel system, the list seats are awarded entirely on the basis of the list votes won by each party, without regard to what happened in the single-member constituency component. This is better for the large parties, which, given the 5 percent threshold for qualification for list seats, get a bonus from the list section to add to the one they already got from the single-member constituency component. In 2000, for example, the social democratic coalition in Lithuania took 40 percent of the list seats with just 31 percent of the list votes—having already won 32 percent of the single-member constituencies with just 20 percent of the votes.

Mixed systems have grown in popularity in recent years because they can be perceived as offering "the best of both worlds" (Shugart and Wattenberg). Citizens have an individual MP to represent them, as they would under a non-PR system, but the provision of a list component means that, overall, the relationship between seats and votes is much closer than it would be under a non-PR system. This combination of proportionality and local representation is what has made mixed systems the alternative of choice for electoral system reformers and designers in a number of countries. At the same time, while no one would describe them as "the worst of all worlds," some of the claims made for them can be criticized. In particular, the impression that voters have a local MP who is in some way accountable to them can be misleading. In most countries that employ mixed systems, constituency candidates also stand on party lists, and if they are defeated in the constituency this makes no difference to their fate provided they have been placed in a high position on the list, as they will be elected anyway. Thus, even for a constituency MP, it can make more sense to concentrate on being given a high place on the party list at the next election than on serving his or her constituents.

Thresholds

Even PR electoral systems, despite their name, sometimes have features that give a built-in advantage to larger parties. This is due either to self-interest on the part of the larger parties (who usually make the rules), or to a disinterested concern that perfect proportionality could lead to a proliferation of small parties in parliament and thus to difficulty in forming a stable government—or to a combination of both factors. It is common, therefore, for electoral systems to employ a threshold that a party must overcome before it qualifies for seats. The best known example is the German system, which allows only those parties that have either won at least 5 percent of the second votes, or won at least three constituency seats, to share in the national list allocation. Only once has a party qualified for list seats without winning 5 percent of the list votes. This occurred in 1994 when the former communists, the PDS, qualified via the three-constituencies route due to their strength in east Berlin. In order to prevent fragmentation and to encourage the consolidation of a coherent party system, postcommunist countries generally impose higher thresholds than their west European counterparts: Often parties must reach 4 or even 5 percent of the vote in order to qualify for *any* seats (see Table 11.4). The impact has generally been to create somewhat more disproportionality than is found in most PR systems, exaggerating the impact of vote changes (Moraski and Loewenberg, p. 168). Some countries apply a threshold at the level of individual constituencies. For example, in Belgium no party can receive any seats within one of the multimember constituencies unless it has won at least 5 percent of the votes there.

Thresholds are usually employed to limit the degree of proportionality achieved and if set too high could significantly distort the election outcome. For example, in the 1980s the Greek electoral system imposed a threshold of 17 percent for qualification for higher-tier seats, which gave a sizable bonus to the large parties. This was termed "reinforced PR"—it was also used in Cyprus—but in fact it was not proportionality but the parliamentary strength of the largest parties that was reinforced (Dimitras, p. 160).

The effect of thresholds can be seen most starkly in Poland. At its first postcommunist election, in 1991, there were no thresholds and an amazing twenty-nine different parties won seats. For the next election, in 1993, thresholds were introduced (5 percent within constituencies and 7 percent to qualify for national list seats). This time, only seven parties won any seats, and 40 percent of the votes were cast for parties that won no seats. By the time of the following election in 1997, parties and voters showed that they had learned the lesson of the threshold: The fragmentation of the vote and overall disproportionality both plummeted, and only 12 percent of votes were wasted on parties that failed to reach the threshold. Like several other postcommunist countries, Poland imposes two thresholds: one for single parties and a slightly higher one (8 percent in this case) for coalitions.

Which Candidates Get the List Seats?

So far, we have been discussing the ways in which the seats are divided up among the parties under list and mixed systems. Once this has been decided, a second question arises: Which candidates on the party's list are awarded the seats that the party has won? This is dealt with in different ways. In some countries, the order of candidates drawn up by the party organization is a fixed ranking that the voters cannot alter. These systems are termed *nonpreferential,* with *closed* or *blocked* lists. In a second group of countries, in contrast, there is no default order—the voters alone decide which candidates are elected. These systems are termed *preferential,* with *open* or *unblocked* lists. Under such systems there is intraparty electoral competition, because candidates of the same party are competing against each other for personal votes. In between these two are cases where the party's ranking may stand as a default ordering but can be overturned if enough voters combine against it. These cases may in practice be either essentially preferential or essentially nonpreferential, depending on what degree of coordination is needed among voters to overturn the ordering decided on by the party organization. In some countries it is very easy for voters to do this, and in others it is nearly impossible. The systems in operation are listed in Table 11.4 (for a more detailed analysis, see Marsh; Katz, "Intraparty"; Shugart).

There are relatively few examples of PR list systems where the lists are completely closed. Countries in this category include Portugal and Spain; the lists used on the one recent occasion when France used PR, in 1986, were also closed. In all of these cases, the order of candidates' names on the list is decided by the parties, and voters cannot alter it. Moreover, where mixed systems are used, the lists are usually in practice closed (as in Germany, Hungary, and Italy). In these countries, then, candidate selection plays an especially important role in the political recruitment process, as we saw in Chapter 10, because the selectors are in effect choosing the MPs.

Countries in the second category, employing genuinely open lists where the voters determine which of a party's candidates are elected, include Finland, Latvia, Luxembourg, Poland, and Switzerland. In Finland the voters are all-powerful; they are obliged to express a preference for one specific candidate, and, within each party, those candidates receiving the most preferences win the seats. In Switzerland and Luxembourg, voters express as many preferences as there are seats in the constituency. They can cast a "list vote" for a party, which has the effect of giving one preference vote to each of the party's candidates, or they can cumulate two preference votes on one candidate. They can give their preferences to candidates on more than one party's list, an option known as *panachage,* which is confined to these two countries. Candidates near the top of the lists tend to receive the most preference votes. This could be either because the candidate selectors place the most attractive candidates in the most prominent positions, or because being near the top of the list attracts votes from party supporters who do not know much about individual candidates. Most likely, both factors operate. Thus, in Poland, about a third of all preference votes go to the candidate placed at the top of the list, and around 40 percent of these list-heading candidates are elected—though in 2001 one candidate placed as low as thirty-eighth on a list also won enough preference votes to be elected (Millard, pp. 93–94).

Turning to the third category, we find that in most cases the party candidate selectors draw up a list on which the candidates appear in a particular order, and the voters have a greater or lesser degree of power to overturn this order. Sometimes, the voters can cast either a "list vote" endorsing the order drawn up by the party or a "personal vote" for an individual candidate on the list; what varies is how likely these personal votes are to make any difference to the outcome. A number of postcommunist countries chose such systems, under which a degree of coordination by voters is needed to disturb the order drawn up by the party. As a result, whereas in open-list countries all MPs owe their election to preference votes, and in closed-list countries no MP does, in this third category of countries a proportion of MPs are elected because of the impact of preference votes. In Estonia around 15 percent of MPs are elected thanks to preference votes, while in the Czech Republic the proportion is smaller—5 percent in 2002 (Millard, pp. 92–95). The Estonian electoral system is particularly complex, being based on three tiers of voting, and because the highest tier is based on closed lists, voters can end up frustrated with the outcome. Quite frequently, "a popular candidate will receive thousands of votes, but will not be elected due to low placement on the national list, while unheard-of candidates get into parliament thanks to their prominent list position" (Pettai and Kreuzer, p. 111). However, a change made prior to the 2003 election reduced the number of MPs elected via the national list and thus increased the weight of preference votes (Sikk, pp. 5–6). In Sweden preference votes had little impact prior to 1998, but then the rules were changed (see Box 11.1); even so, only around 3 percent of MPs in 2002 were elected due to preference votes (Widfeldt, p. 784). Under the Danish system, the parties can choose how to present their lists; some forms give considerable choice to the voters, whereas others restrict it, and the degree of voter choice can vary from party to party as well as between and even within constituencies. In practice, it is the voters who wield the decisive voice (Elklit). The list component of Lithuania's mixed system used to employ lists that were in effect closed, but the rules were changed before the 2000 election to give preference votes more weight, and 15 of the 70 list candidates elected then owed their success to preference votes (Millard, p. 96).

In certain other countries, though, there are systems that in theory offer the opportunity for preferential voting for candidates but in practice are such that voters' preferences rarely overturn the ordering set by the parties. In Norway, personal votes have never made any difference to the personnel elected because they have been unable to have an effect unless at least half of a party's voters made exactly the same change to the list, and in Iceland no candidate has been elected due to preference votes since the mayor of Reykjavik managed this in 1946 (Aardal, p. 189; Kristjánsson, p. 403). Although the Norwegian rules were changed slightly in 2003, the impact is expected to be minimal (Aalberg, p. 1102). In Austria, similarly, even though a change to the electoral law in 1992 was supposed to make preferential voting more effective, only two candidates were elected out of list order in the four elections since then (Müller, p. 409). The system in the Netherlands differs in some of the details, but the essential feature is the same: The party supplies a default order of candidates, and such a high degree of concerted action by voters has been needed to overturn it that the party's rank ordering has almost always stood. Only three candidates were elected because of preference votes between 1945 and 1994. A recent change liberalized the position slightly, but at the three elections since then only five candidates were elected out of list order (Andeweg, p. 494). Even this limited opportunity has been resented by the Dutch parties, which sometimes demand pledges from their candidates that if they are elected "out of order," owing to preference votes, at the expense of a candidate higher on the list, they will resign their seat in favor of the candidate whom the party organization had placed higher on the list.

The Single Transferable Vote

The STV electoral system was devised in Britain in the middle of the nineteenth century, and enthusiasm for it has been largely confined to English-speaking countries. It is used to elect the parliaments of Ireland and Malta, and it was employed to elect Estonia's parliament at the 1990 election (for assessments of STV see Bowler and Grofman). In Ireland, the largest party, Fianna Fáil, has twice (in 1959 and 1968) attempted to have the system replaced by the British plurality system, mainly because it believed it would fare better under the latter, but on each occasion the electorate rejected the proposed change in a referendum. Like list systems, STV aims to give proportional representation to the shades of opinion within the constituency. Unlike them, it does not presuppose that those opinions are organized in terms of parties.

Voters cast a vote by ranking as many as they wish of the candidates, regardless of party, in order of their preference; they place a "1" next to the name of their favored candidate, a "2" next to the name of their second favorite, and so on (for detailed explanations of how STV works see Farrell, ch. 6; Sinnott, pp. 112–16). The counting of votes revolves around the Droop quota. This is calculated as the smallest whole number greater than $[v/(s + 1)]$, where v is the number of valid votes and s the number of seats in the constituency. The Droop quota is therefore one more than a quarter of the votes in a three-seat constituency, one more than a fifth in a four-seater, and so on. Any candidate who achieves the Droop quota is certain of election and does not need votes over and above this number, which are surplus to requirements.

Any candidate whose total of first-preference votes equals or exceeds the Droop quota is declared elected. Unless it should happen that sufficient candidates are elected at this stage, the count then proceeds by distributing the surplus votes of the elected candidate(s)—that is, the votes they possess over and above the quota. These votes are transferred to the other candidates, in proportion to the next preferences marked for them. If this were not done, some votes would be "wasted" by remaining in the possession of a candidate who did not need them. If no candidate has a surplus, the candidate with the fewest votes is eliminated, and his or her votes are transferred to the other candidates, again in accordance with the next preferences marked. This process continues until all the seats have been filled.

What are the pros and cons of STV when compared with other proportional representation systems? Its advocates emphasize several points. First, PR-STV gives voters the opportunity to convey a lot of information about their preferences; they may rank all the candidates in order of choice, whereas under almost every other system they are limited to expressing a "Yes" verdict on one (or a few) and "No" on the rest. Second, when ranking candidates, voters are not constrained by party lines. They vote for candidates, not for parties, and STV works perfectly well—some say better—in nonpartisan elections. Some voters' preferences are not determined primarily by the candidates' party affiliations. These might be voters whose main concern is with an issue that cuts across party lines (such as abortion, European integration, or nuclear power); or voters who want to affect the social composition of parliament and thus wish to vote, say, for women or young candidates across party lines; or voters who want to elect a representative whose home base is in their own area of the constituency. Such voters can give their first preference vote to, say, a pro-EU candidate from one party and their second preference to a pro-EU candidate from a different party. List systems do not offer this opportunity, and the apparent exceptions—those of Switzerland and Luxembourg, which offer *panachage*—are not really comparable.

This is because of the third argument in favor of STV—namely, that voters control the way their votes will be used. No vote can help a candidate unless it expresses a preference for him or her. This sets STV apart from all list systems, where a preference given to one candidate of a party might end up helping another candidate of the same party—a candidate whom, perhaps, the voter does not like. Under STV, voters can continue to give preferences after their first, knowing that a preference given to a candidate can never help that person against a candidate to whom the voter gave a higher preference. This is not the case under *panachage;* the voter giving a preference to a candidate of one party does not know which candidate of that party it will ultimately help, as it is added to the party's pool and could benefit any of its candidates.

Fourth, STV gives voters the opportunity to express an opinion as to the direction their party should take. If there is more than one tendency or faction within a party, voters can express higher preferences for candidates from the one they favor and affect the composition of the parliamentary group accordingly. STV shares this quality with preferential list systems and American primaries. In addition, voters can, by the way they order candidates of other parties, send signals about the coalition partner(s) they would like their own party to take, and indeed help designated partners to benefit from their vote if their own party cannot make use of it.

Fifth, STV ensures that voters can vote sincerely, knowing that even if their first-choice candidate is unpopular, the vote will not be wasted, as it can be transferred to another candidate in accordance with the second preference the voter has marked on the ballot paper.

But STV also has its critics, which explains why it has inspired so little enthusiasm on the European mainland, although it has been seriously considered in Sweden (Petersson et al., p. 114). They make three points in particular.

First, they are not impressed with the opportunity it gives voters to cross party lines. On the contrary, they feel that this might weaken the internal unity of parties and make them less cohesive. In elections, candidates of one party, rather than being able to concentrate on propagating party policies, must be alive to the possibility of attracting lower preferences from other parties' supporters. This might make the parties "fuzzy at the edges" as candidates adopt bland positions for fear of alienating any voter who might possibly give them a lower preference. Critics of STV argue that modern democratic politics, certainly in parliamentary systems, needs strong, cohesive parties to work properly, a subject that we discussed in Chapters 3 and 10, and that the idea of voting for candidates rather than parties, though all very well for other kinds of elections, is inappropriate for parliamentary elections. This argument is difficult to evaluate, because STV is used in too few countries for us to be able to tell whether it will tend to weaken parties. But it must be said that there is no evidence at all that parties in either Ireland or Malta are any less cohesive and disciplined than parties anywhere else (Gallagher, "Ireland," pp. 524–5). And even though Irish politics do tend to be relatively consensual, with few clear policy differences between the two main parties, Fianna Fáil and Fine Gael, the opposite is true in Malta, where the bitter rivalry between Labour and the Nationalists sometimes spills over into low-level violence.

The second criticism is that STV can realistically be used only in relatively small constituencies, thus raising the prospect of disproportionality (lack of complete correspondence between parties' shares of the votes and the seats). For example, STV is difficult to operate in constituencies larger than about ten seats, because the ballot paper could then contain thirty to forty names and most voters' preferences will become meaningless after the first half dozen or so. In both Ireland and Malta, the largest constituency size now used is five seats. Because votes are assumed to be cast

Under the STV electoral system, candidates have to appeal for personal support from the voters. The picture shows election banners for four candidates of the Nationalist Party in the Valletta constituency (district 1) in the Maltese election of 1996. In effect, these candidates were competing against each other as well as against candidates from the rival Maltese Labour Party. Guido de Marco and Austin Gatt were both elected, but Louis Cuschieri and Paul Borg Olivier were defeated. Courtesy of John C. Lane/State University of New York at Buffalo

for candidates rather than for parties, it is impossible, without contradicting the principles on which STV is based, to have higher-tier seat allocation (without the use of a second vote as in Germany), although, as Table 11.4 explains, Malta does have such an allocation in reserve. In practice, though, the possibility of disproportionality does not seem to be a major problem, as election results in Ireland and Malta have been as proportional as those of other PR systems.

Third, it has been argued that STV facilitates the election of independent candidates, who may be able to wield undue power over a government that lacks a secure majority. Independents, like center party candidates, stand to benefit from an electoral system in which voters can rank order the options as, precisely because they do not have a party label and thus do not alienate anyone, they may well be the second choice of many voters. Empirically, it is true that the election of independents is quite common in Ireland (thirteen were elected in 2002 and six in 1997), whereas elsewhere in western Europe independent members of parliament are virtually unknown. In times of minority government in Ireland, some independent deputies have been able to extract concessions from the government on local matters. Sinnott argues that STV thus makes possible circumstances in which independents wield disproportionate power and create a potentially serious underlying threat to the stability of government (Sinnott, p. 120). However, no independent has been elected to the parliament of Malta since independence in 1964.

→ WHY ELECTORAL SYSTEMS MATTER

The plethora of electoral systems used across Europe suggests that there is no simple answer to the question "Which is the best electoral system?" But although there has been no trend toward a uniform electoral system, the great majority of countries have systems based on PR. Only Britain and France use systems that do not embody the principle of PR. All the remaining countries that we are looking at employ some type of PR: In twenty countries a list system is used, four employ a mixed system, and Ireland and Malta have the single transferable vote. We have already reviewed the arguments about the relative merits of list systems and STV; we must now look at the wider question of the advantages and disadvantages of PR systems generally in comparison with plurality systems (for general discussions of the consequences and merits of different electoral systems, see Cox; Gallagher and Mitchell; Katz, *Democracy;* Lijphart, *Electoral*).

One obvious criterion for judging electoral systems is proportionality: How closely does the distribution of seats in parliament reflect the preferences of the voters as expressed in an election, and are some electoral systems better than others on this dimension? Another criterion is stable effective government. This is sometimes argued to be in conflict with the first, in that a very proportional electoral system might lead to a highly fragmented parliament from which it is difficult to put together a majority government, while a system that gives the largest parties a sizable seat bonus is less proportional but more likely to produce stable government. Others, though, are not convinced that government stability is any lower under PR systems. Other criteria, too, could be taken into account in an assessment of the merits of electoral systems. Do some systems give a better chance than others to women and minorities to win election to parliament? The overall picture, based on the most recent election in each of our twenty-eight countries, is summarized in Table 11.5.

Proportionality

The proportionality of election results—the degree to which parties' shares of the seats correspond to their shares of the votes—does indeed tend to be significantly greater under PR than under plurality systems. Table 11.5 shows clearly that there was a large difference between the plurality systems of Britain and France, on the one hand, and all PR systems, on the other hand, at the most recent elections. Among PR systems, there is some variation. The most proportional outcomes occur in countries that use large district magnitudes (Austria, Denmark, the Netherlands, Slovenia, and Sweden), and also in Malta, despite its small district magnitude of just five seats per constituency. Although Germany, Latvia, Poland, and Slovakia also award seats in large districts, their employment of a 5 percent national threshold creates disproportionality because a significant number of people vote for parties that fail to reach the threshold. Disproportionality is also likely to be high when thresholds or small district magnitude assist the large parties and penalize small ones, as in Greece and, usually, Spain (Anckar). The pattern in Table 11.5 matches that found by Lijphart (*Electoral*, pp. 96–97) for the period 1945–90.

The Number of Parties

The formulation of the best-known causal relationship in the study of the effects of electoral systems is attributed to Maurice Duverger. It holds that the single-member plurality

TABLE 11.5

Aspects of Electoral Outcomes in Europe

Country	Most Recent Election	Dispropor-tionality	Effective Number of Parties (elective level)	Effective Number of Parties (legislative level)	% of Parliament Seats Held by Women
Austria	2002	1.3	3.0	2.9	34
Belgium	2003	5.2	8.8	7.0	35
Cyprus	2001	3.8	3.6	1.6	16
Czech Republic	2002	6.3	4.8	3.7	17
Denmark	2005	1.8	5.2	4.9	37
Estonia	2003	3.5	5.4	4.7	19
Finland	2003	3.2	5.7	4.9	38
France	2002	21.9	5.2	2.3	12
Germany	2002	4.6	4.1	3.4	33
Greece	2004	7.4	2.7	2.2	14
Hungary	2002	7.6	2.8	2.2	9
Iceland	2003	1.9	3.9	3.7	30
Ireland	2002	6.6	4.1	3.4	14
Italy	2001	—	6.3[a]	5.3	12
Latvia	2002	7.4	6.8	5.0	21
Lithuania	2004	—	5.8[a]	6.2	22
Luxembourg	2004	3.4	4.3	3.8	23
Malta	2003	1.8	2.0	2.0	9
Netherlands	2003	1.1	5.0	4.7	37
Norway	2001	3.4	6.2	5.4	38
Poland	2001	6.3	4.5	3.6	20
Portugal	2005	5.7	3.1	2.6	20
Slovakia	2002	7.0	8.9	6.1	17
Slovenia	2004	5.1	6.0	4.7	12
Spain	2004	4.3	3.0	2.5	36
Sweden	2002	1.8	4.5	4.2	45
Switzerland	2003	2.5	5.4	5.0	25
United Kingdom	2001	17.7	3.3	2.2	18
Mean		**5.5**	**4.8**	**3.9**	**24**

Note: "Disproportionality" refers to vote–seat disproportionality as measured by the least squares index (Gallagher and Mitchell, app. B). The scale runs from 0 to 100, 0 representing full proportionality and 100 representing total disproportionality. "Effective number of parties" at the elective level and at the legislative level refers to the level of fragmentation of votes and seats respectively (Laakso and Taagepera). The "actual number of parties in parliament" excludes independent deputies.

[a] List votes only.

Sources: For election results, see the source note of Table 7.1. For women in parliaments, see the Web site of the Inter-Parliamentary Union (www.ipu.org). All other figures are authors' calculations.

system favors a two-party system, the double-ballot majority system tends to produce multipartism tempered by alliances, and PR tends to lead to the formation of many independent parties (Duverger, p. 70). PR might be associated with a multiparty system either because it allows parties representing existing minorities to be viable or, as Duverger sees it, because it artificially "multiplies parties in an otherwise dualistic world, while plurality ... conforms to that natural dualism" (Taagepera and Shugart, p. 53). Under the French double-ballot system, many parties may contest the first round of voting, but there are strong incentives for parties to form alliances for the second-round contests. The British-style SMP system is associated with a two-party system because of both mechanical and psychological effects, as Duverger terms them. The mechanical effect is simply that smaller parties with support spread across the country do not reap a proportional reward in seats for their share of the votes. Whereas under a PR system a party winning, say, 10 percent of the votes in every part of the country would end up with about 10 percent of the seats, under an SMP system such a party would probably win no seats because it would not be the strongest party anywhere. The psychological effect comes about precisely because voters are aware of the mechanical effect. They know that if they cast their vote for a small party, this vote is likely to be wasted, and therefore the votes for such parties do not reflect their true level of underlying support. We saw in the earlier discussion of the Taunton result in Britain in 2001 (see Table 11.2) that the electoral system compelled supporters there of Labour and the UK Independence Party to decide whether to waste their vote on a candidate who was almost certain to lose or to vote instead for one of the two candidates who had a real chance. In this example, Labour was the main party affected, but in most constituencies the Liberal Democrats are the third party and hence the main losers.

The precise meaning, status, and accuracy of Duverger's predictions have been the subject of an extensive literature (see, for example, Sartori, pp. 27–52; Taagepera and Shugart, pp. 142–55; Cox, pp. 13–33), and this is not the place to explore these issues fully. However, we can examine the evidence to see whether there are indeed fewer parties under non-PR than PR systems. In order to do this, we need some satisfactory measure of the number of parties. Simply counting the number of parties is not sufficient; for example, in the British House of Commons around eight or ten different parties are usually represented (there were nine in 2001), but Britain has never had anything like a genuine nine-party system. To deal with this, Laakso and Taagepera devised a measure that takes into account not only the number of different parties but also the relative size of each, which they call the "effective number" of parties. It is essentially a measure of fragmentation, registering the extent to which strength is concentrated or dispersed. The intuitive meaning to be put on an effective number of, say, 3.6 parties, is that there is the same degree of fragmentation as if there were 3.6 equal-sized parties (Laakso and Taagepera). This number can be calculated both at the elective level, by measuring the degree to which votes are dispersed among the parties, and at the legislative level, by measuring the degree to which seats are dispersed among the parties.

Table 11.5 shows that the pattern of party competition in Europe in the period 2001–4 corresponded well to Duverger's predictions. In the two plurality countries, Britain and France, the reduction from the elective to the legislative level, brought about by the "mechanical" effect of the electoral system, is very marked. In Britain, something like a three-party system at the elective level is reduced to a two-party system in parliament. In

France, the votes at elections are spread among many more parties than in Britain, but, partly because of the alliances and deals that Duverger predicts, parliamentary strength is far less fragmented than this. In PR systems, the fragmentation in parliament is only marginally less than that seen at the electoral level, as we would expect.

However, it is not invariably the case that PR is associated with multipartism. Certainly, this is true in some countries, most notably Belgium, where fragmentation has reached remarkable levels; at the 2003 election, the strongest two parties received only 28 percent of the votes between them. In Italy, Latvia, Norway, Slovakia, and Switzerland, too, the effective number of parties in parliament exceeds five. Yet in some other PR countries (Greece, Hungary, Malta, Portugal, and Spain) parliamentary strength is little if at all more fragmented than in France or the UK, with their plurality systems.

Two cases in particular show that the relationship between electoral systems and party systems is not a deterministic one. In Malta, the party system since independence has been the purest two-party system in Europe; since the start of the 1970s, the combined vote share of Labour and the Nationalists has averaged over 99 percent, neither party has fallen below 46 percent of the votes, and no other party has won a seat. This shows that while PR systems may well give parliamentary expression to a multiparty system if other factors, such as the number of political or social cleavages, cause voters to create one in the first place, PR does not by itself bring a multiparty system into being. Another interesting counterexample is Italy, where the change in the electoral system that was made in the mid-1990s, from a highly proportional version of PR to one in which three-quarters of the seats are filled by plurality contests in single-member constituencies, was expected to reduce the number of parties and present the voters with a clear choice between alternative governments. The second of these aims was met, in that since the change voters have been able to identify a right-wing and a left-wing option for government. But the effective number of parties in parliament actually rose, because the parties chose to "proportionalize" the plurality element of the new system, doing deals that mean that small parties that are part of an alliance get a clear run in a few constituencies (D'Alimonte). This shows that a preexisting party system can adapt to a new electoral system and will not necessarily be reshaped by it.

Electoral systems, then, do play a major part, albeit not a deterministic one, in influencing the shape of party systems. If Britain and France adopted PR systems, seats in their parliaments would be much less concentrated in the hands of the two main parties. In France, if we assume that French voters would behave in more or less the same way after the electoral system had been changed, the far-right FN would be a much more powerful presence in the National Assembly, and government formation might require alliances between the left and the mainstream right. In Britain, again assuming that voters would behave in the same way if the electoral system were changed, smaller parties such as the Liberal Democrats and perhaps the Greens and the anti-EU UKIP (United Kingdom Independence Party) would win both more votes and more seats, and single-party government might well become a thing of the past. The plurality electoral system may be all that has kept Britain (and, indeed, the United States) looking like a two-party system since the 1970s, and it has certainly been the key to two-party domination of the legislature.

A plurality electoral system, with its tendency to produce competition between just two large parties, reflects the view that a majority should prevail over a minority. This in itself is an impeccable democratic principle. But it encounters problems in societies that are divided into a number of segments or interests, and on issues where there are more than two positions. When there is no majority to represent, plurality systems tend to produce outcomes that favor inordinately the larger minorities and discriminate against the smaller ones. PR systems, in contrast, seek to reflect in parliaments the divergences that exist in society.

Coalition or Single-Party Government?

One common argument against PR systems is that the very accuracy with which they reflect parties' electoral strengths in parliament creates problems when it comes to forming a government. It is extremely rare, under any type of electoral system, for one party to win a majority of the votes cast, so a single-party majority government is likely only if the largest party receives a bonus of seats that takes it over the magic 50 percent mark. Obviously, this is most likely to happen under a plurality system, where proportionality is lower and the largest party often wins a substantial bonus. For example, in Britain's 2001 election, Labour received only 41 percent of the votes but won 63 percent of the seats, a bonus of 22 percent (see Table 11.3). Under a PR system, assuming that disproportionality is not introduced as a result of small district magnitudes, no party's seat bonus is very large. Consequently, a single-party majority government is possible only if one party actually wins a majority of votes or comes very close to it so that it needs only a small bonus to achieve a parliamentary majority. A survey of the record in twenty countries found that although single-party majority governments were formed after only 10 percent of elections held under PR, such governments emerged after 60 percent of elections held under plurality or majority electoral systems (Blais and Carty, p. 214).

Having said this, we should be clear that the relationship between electoral systems and government types is not entirely straightforward. It is true that in countries with the most fragmented party systems, such as Belgium, Finland, Iceland, Italy, Latvia, Luxembourg, the Netherlands, Slovakia, and Switzerland, all or nearly all governments are coalitions. It is also true that Britain, owing to its non-PR electoral system, has not had a coalition government since 1945. However, the British electoral system has not always produced a stable majority government. Some British elections—the most recent being that of February 1974—produced no overall parliamentary majority for any party, and between 1976 and 1979 the minority Labour government was able to survive in office only because of the support of the Liberals, under the terms of an arrangement known as the "Lib–Lab pact." In France, too, the plurality system did not produce a majority government in either the 1988 or the 1997 elections, and indeed, bearing in mind that the RPR and UDF were separate (albeit allied) parties, the Fifth Republic has had very few single-party governments (see Box 11.2). Likewise, in countries using PR systems, even though coalitions are far more common, there are still many cases of single-party government. The Austrian Socialist Party, Ireland's Fianna Fáil, the Norwegian Labor Party, the Swedish Social Democrats, and both Labour and the Nationalists in Malta have all had long spells in office alone, and other countries with PR have experienced single-party government for periods.

Some defenders of non-PR systems have argued that even if these systems do not produce proportional representation in any given parliament, they are likely to produce proportional tenure in government over a series of parliaments. The rationale for this is

BOX 11.2   THE IMPACT OF ELECTORAL SYSTEMS

France

As in Britain, the electoral system, being based on single-member constituencies, greatly favors the large parties. Single-party majority government, though, is uncommon; only three times in the post-1958 Fifth Republic has one party won a majority of seats (the Gaullists in 1968, the Socialists in 1981, and the UMP in 2002). The potential of single-member constituency systems to produce startling results was demonstrated by the March 1993 election, one of the most disproportional ever to have taken place in any country. The right-wing parties won 460 of the 577 seats in parliament despite having attracted only 38 percent of votes in the first round of voting (which under a "pure" PR system would have earned them just 221 seats). The main beneficiaries of the high disproportionality that is characteristically produced by the French system are the mainstream right-wing parties and, to a lesser extent, the Socialists. The main losers are small parties, together with the "extreme" parties: the Communists on the left and the FN on the right.

Germany

Under the Weimar Republic established after World War I, Germany had highly proportional election results and very unstable governments. The electoral system adopted after World War II is often seen as having produced the best of both worlds: Election results are still highly proportional, but there is no problem of government instability. The threshold that parties need to reach before qualifying for list seats has prevented the development of a situation where a multitude of small parties hold the balance of power. During the 1960s and 1970s only three parties (the SPD, the CDU/CSU, and the FDP) were represented in the West German Bundestag, before they were joined by the Greens in the 1980s and the PDS in the 1990s.

Italy

Italy's pre-1993 electoral system guaranteed a high degree of proportionality, and a large number of minor parties usually gained representation. Voters' ability to indicate a preference for individual candidates on their chosen party's list generated considerable intraparty competition in and between elections; this was especially pronounced within the Christian Democrats and reinforced the highly factionalized nature of that party. The new system adopted in 1993 was designed to have a very different impact. It is inherently less proportional than the previous system, and the element of intraparty competition for preference votes from the electorate has been eliminated. The first three elections held under this system have all been less proportional than previous Italian elections had been. For example, in Italy's 2001 election, Silvio Berlusconi's right-wing coalition won 45 percent of the constituency votes and 50 percent of the list votes yet received 58 percent of the seats. Although the new electoral system had been expected—and, by many, hoped—to reduce the number of different parties in parliament, this number actually rose, because the major parties prefer to make deals with the smaller parties that are close to them on the political spectrum rather than try to use the majoritarian tendency of the plurality seats to crush them. Nonetheless, the electoral system has encouraged the formation of two large preelection alliances between parties, giving Italians for the first time a clear choice between a center–right or a center–left government.

Latvia

The high degree of proportionality that could be generated by Latvia's large district magnitudes (an average of 20 seats per constituency) is not realized because of the 5 percent national threshold that a party must reach in order to receive any seats. Quite a number of votes (16 percent in 2002) are cast for parties that do not reach the threshold. Latvia's party system was highly fragmented in the 1930s, with as many as twenty-seven parties represented in parliament at one stage. The postcommunist party system was also very fragmented initially—its 1995 election was remarkable for the fact that even the strongest party won only 15 percent of the votes—but the fragmentation within parliament is much lower because of the threshold. Turnout has consistently exceeded 70 percent at postcommunist elections.

Netherlands

Because the Netherlands returns all its members of parliament in one nationwide constituency, proportionality is high, with the largest parties receiving a negligible bonus of seats over and above their share of the votes. The absence of any subnational constituencies has led to some complaints that citizens do not have any local constituency representatives with whom they can identify and to whom they can take casework problems. Over the years there have been attempts to counteract this by introducing provisions under which "personal votes"—that is, preference votes cast for individual candidates—would be more effective in determining which individual candidates are elected, and a change made before the 1998 election made it slightly easier for these personal votes to have an impact. Under the existing system, though, connections between citizens and MPs are weak, leading to pressure for electoral reform.

Poland

The first free election, that of 1991, was remarkable for the numbers of parties that competed (111) and won seats (29). The success of the Polish Friends of Beer Party (Polska Partia Przyjaciol Piwa), which won 16 seats, gained news coverage around the world (though it was claimed that the party had a serious anti-alcoholism message and was aiming to wean drinkers away from the harder stuff). Thresholds introduced for subsequent elections have drastically reduced the number of parties securing representation in the Sejm and have consequently increased government stability. Parliamentary strength now shows only moderate fragmentation. Despite the degree of activism and protest under the communist regime (higher than in other communist countries), turnout levels are low; only one postcommunist election brought more than 50 percent of the electorate out to vote.

Spain

Spain's electoral system is a version of PR, but it does not produce highly proportional outcomes, mainly because of the low number of members returned from the average constituency, together with malapportionment (the deliberate overrepresentation of rural areas). In consequence, the largest parties receive a significant bonus from the electoral system and are able to govern without the need for coalition partners. In 2000, for example, the right-wing Popular Party received 52 percent of the seats for 45 percent of the votes, and in 2004 the Socialists won 47 percent of the seats with 43 percent of the votes. Small parties with a strong regional base also fare well, but small parties whose support is spread thinly across the country are invariably underrepresented.

Sweden

The Swedish electoral system gives highly proportional results. Consequently, the largest party, the Social Democrats, rarely wins an overall majority of seats even though its average share of the votes makes it one of Europe's strongest parties. By international standards, women are strongly represented in the Riksdag. Following the election of September 2002, Sweden had the highest proportion of women in parliament of any country in the world, 146 women out of 349 MPs.

United Kingdom

The single-member constituency electoral system gives a large bonus of seats to the two largest parties, Labour and the Conservatives, which regularly win nearly all the seats in parliament even though smaller parties may take up to a third of the votes. An observer sitting in the gallery of the House of Commons would infer from the distribution of seats among the parties that Britain has something close to a two-party system, but this impression is largely created by the electoral system. If Britain adopted a proportional electoral system, small parties, especially the Liberal Democrats and the UK Independence Party, would win many more seats in the Commons, and the likelihood of single-party majority government, currently the norm, would be greatly reduced. Electoral reform is often discussed, but neither of the major parties, especially when it is in power, is keen on a move to proportional representation.

that a large party winning, say, between 40 and 50 percent of the votes, will have all the government power for about half the time, whereas under PR, it is argued, small centrist parties may be almost permanent fixtures in government, thus earning tenure in government way above their electoral support. However, empirical analysis does not support the claim that non-PR systems perform better on this criterion than do PR ones (Vowles). Under both kinds of electoral system, large parties' share of time in office tends to be greater than their share of electoral support, while "extreme" parties fare badly. The supposed bias toward centrist parties under PR largely disappears when account is taken of the (usually small) share of cabinet seats they occupy while in office.

Defenders of majoritarian systems also claim that the identifiability of government options is lower under PR systems, where voters may not know in advance of the election what government possibilities are on offer given that the government will be put together by interparty deals after the election (we discuss this in detail in Chapter 12). Empirical research shows that this is, indeed, the case. However, while majoritarian visions of democracy score well on identifiability, proportional ones score better when it comes to the representation of voters (Powell, pp. 87, 112–13). In other words, while single-party government gives some voters pretty much all of what they want and takes no account of the views of the others, coalitions give many voters at least some of what they want.

The Backgrounds of Parliamentarians

Proportional representation elections produce parliaments that differ from those produced by plurality elections. This is true not just as far as the representation of parties is concerned; it also applies to the profile of the individuals who sit on the parliamentary benches.

This is especially obvious when we look at the proportion of women in legislatures around the world. Table 11.5 shows that the average for Britain and France, the two countries that do not use PR, is a mere 15 percent, compared with 24 percent for the other twenty-six countries. In ten countries, 30 percent or more of parliamentarians are women; the Scandinavian countries and the Netherlands lead the way. Of course, these countries have a progressive attitude toward female participation in politics and in society generally (see the Gender Empowerment Index in Table 1.1), but the broad tendency remains true even when we look at less progressive countries. Thus, Ireland, Italy, Poland, and Portugal, where the relatively traditional nature of society and the strength of Catholicism might suggest that women would find it hard to gain entry to the political elite, and Switzerland, where women were denied the vote until the 1970s, all had more women in their national parliaments than Britain until 1997, when positive action by the Labour Party, which deliberately chose women candidates in a number of safe and marginal seats, led to a great increase in the number of female British MPs.

While the variation among the PR countries shows that many factors beside the electoral system affect the strength of women in the legislature, it is well established that, other things being equal, PR facilitates the election of women to parliament (Norris, pp. 179–208). The explanation is to be found primarily in the multimember constituencies necessitated by PR. Under a single-member constituency system, the candidate selectors might be reluctant to pick a woman as the party's sole candidate, using the excuse, genuine or otherwise, that they believe some voters will be less likely to vote for a woman than for a man. But when several candidates are to be chosen, it is positively advantageous for a ticket to include both men and women, for an all-male list of three or more candidates is likely to alienate some voters.

The evidence as to whether, within the PR group, either STV, open-list systems, or closed-list systems give any special advantage to women is inconclusive. In closed-list systems, where the voters cannot alter the candidate selectors' rankings, the selectors could, if they wished, bring about gender equality in parliament by employing the "zipper" system of alternating women and men on the list—placing a woman first, a man second, a woman third, and so on. But in countries where the selectors might wish to do this, it is quite likely that the voters too will believe in gender equality and will not use their preference votes specifically against women candidates. If this is the case, an open-list system and PR-STV will neither assist nor damage women's electoral chances. The empirical evidence is inconclusive. Table 11.5 shows that the three countries with most women (Sweden, Denmark, and Finland) all employ open-list systems, while in the next three (Netherlands, Norway, and Spain) the voters have little or no opportunity to alter the rankings of the candidate selectors. The number of women elected in the two PR-STV countries is even lower than in the plurality countries (the averages are 11 percent and 15 percent respectively), but this may be due less to their use of STV and more to the fact that both countries, Ireland and Malta, are very Catholic; it is clear that, other things being equal, attitudes toward a political role for women are more favorable in Protestant countries.

There is less research on other underrepresented groups, but the same argument applies. Those who pick the party's candidate in a single-member constituency may be reluctant to take the risk of selecting a representative of an ethnic, religious, or linguistic minority, but candidate selectors in a multimember constituency will usually feel it wise to ensure that the ticket includes a cross section of the groups to which the party is hoping to appeal. Legislatures produced by PR elections thus tend to be more representative of the population that elects them, both in the backgrounds of the parliamentarians and in the relationship between votes won and seats received by political parties.

✦ REFERENDUMS

Elections are archetypal institutions of representative democracy, but in a number of countries the people make certain decisions themselves, by means of the referendum. In a referendum the people decide directly on some issue, rather than electing representatives to make decisions on their behalf. In the great majority of European countries, a referendum can be triggered only by one of the institutions of representative government, such as the government, a parliamentary majority, a specified minority in parliament, or the president. In just five countries—Italy, Latvia, Lithuania, Slovakia, and Switzerland—the people themselves can bring about a popular vote by means of provisions for the initiative (Uleri, "Introduction," p. 12), without needing the endorsement of any other political actor.

The use of the referendum varies hugely across Europe. Between 1945 and 1995, around 400 referendums took place in western Europe—and one country, Switzerland, was responsible for 300 of these (Gallagher, "Conclusion," p. 231). Referendums are relatively common in Italy (40 cases during the same period), Ireland (17), and Denmark (14). In contrast, Germany and the Netherlands held no national referendums, Belgium, Finland, and the UK held one each, and Austria and Norway had two. The use of referendums worldwide increased steadily during the course of the twentieth century (LeDuc, p. 21).

Most commonly, referendum issues are ones that cut across party lines, and given that party systems are usually based on the left–right spectrum, as we saw in Chapter 8, socioeconomic issues are not usually the subject of referendums (Bogdanor, pp. 91–95). Instead, questions that concern national sovereignty or moral issues are often seen as particularly suitable for a direct vote by the people. In relation to sovereignty, sixteen countries have held referendums on membership of the European Union. Of the first fifteen members, Austria, Denmark, Finland, Ireland, and Sweden held a referendum before joining, and nine of the ten 2004 entrants (Cyprus was the exception) did the same (Szczerbiak and Taggart). Several other countries have held referendums on aspects of European integration, as we saw in Chapter 5.

Iceland and Norway held referendums on independence—in each case there was near unanimity in favor—as did the three Baltic states in the early 1990s (the votes were heavily in favor, but there was strong opposition from Russians living in these countries).

The people of Cyprus, too, voted on a sovereignty issue in April 2004, when a simultaneous vote was held in both parts of the divided island on a EU plan to reunify the island. If both sections had voted in favor, the island would have been reunited and would have joined the EU a week later as one political entity. Turkish Cyprus supported the proposals (65 percent were in favor), but Greek Cyprus voted three to one against. The outcome was that only the Greek part of Cyprus joined the EU—leading to some unhappiness among other EU member states, who felt that the Greek Cypriots had in effect prevented Turkish Cyprus from gaining EU entry.

Moral issues occasionally feature as referendum topics. In Italy, after parliament had legalized divorce in 1970, opponents of this measure brought about a popular vote in 1974 to try to strike it down, and the people's decision to retain the divorce laws confirmed the liberalizing trend in Italian society. In Ireland, too, the legalization of divorce required the approval of the people in a referendum; in 1986 the vote was against change, but when a further referendum was held in 1995, there was a slim majority in favor, thus opening the door to the provision of divorce. Both Italy and Ireland have also held referendums on abortion.

Several postcommunist regimes made provision for the referendum and also for the initiative, allowing a number of citizens to promote laws or to challenge existing ones. This was taken furthest in Lithuania, whose number of referendums soon reached double figures (Møller; Krupavicius and Zvaliauskas). One of the proposals in 1996, very unusual for a referendum topic, was to amend the constitution to specify that at least half of the annual budget should be spent on social welfare, health care, education, and science. However, very high thresholds—proposals must be supported by at least half of the electorate, which is much more difficult to achieve than the support of half of those actually voting—have led to a low acceptance rate. It is clear that some proposals have been promoted by parties more in order to impress or mobilize a group of voters than in any serious expectation of seeing their proposals passed.

The impact of the referendum, not surprisingly, has been greatest in Switzerland, where, by signing a petition, fifty thousand people can launch an initiative and bring about a popular vote on any bill recently passed by parliament. Over the years only about 7 percent of bills have been challenged in this way; about half of these bills have been endorsed by the people and the other half have been rejected (Trechsel and Kriesi, p. 191). The impact on policy making is to incline the individuals drawing up legislation to consult widely in order to bring aboard any group that might otherwise launch an initiative against the bill.

In Italy, too, the use of the referendum has been very significant. Here, most popular votes have been "abrogative initiatives"—that is, they are launched by a petition signed by a prescribed number of voters, and they have the aim of repealing an existing law (Uleri, "Italy"). In the early 1990s, two popular votes on aspects of the electoral system dealt hammer blows to the corrupt political establishment dominated by the Christian Democrats (DC) and the Socialists (PSI). The overwhelming support for both reforming measures was interpreted as an expression of popular disgust at the behavior of the ruling elite, which bowed to public pressure and left power, leading to a change in the electoral system used for elections to the lower house and to elections held three years ahead of schedule in March 1994. The Constitutional Court, which we discussed in Chapter 4, plays an important gatekeeper role by deciding whether questions may be put to a vote of the people. In the past it disallowed a high proportion of proposals, though by the mid-1990s it was more often criticized for allowing too many, and too trivial, questions through (Volcansek, pp. 91–115).

The rules in Italy require that for a law to be struck down by a referendum, there must be not only a majority of votes in favor of such a proposal but also a turnout of at least 50 percent. Consequently, if public opinion is known to be strongly supportive of some proposal, opponents are best advised not to vote at all in the hope of thereby invalidating the result by preventing turnout reaching the 50 percent threshold. In 1991 the Italian prime minister Bettino Craxi (later disgraced and indicted for corruption) advised Italians to "go to the beach" rather than vote on a change to the electoral system (most of them defied him and voted). However, no referendum since 1995 has generated a turnout as high as 50 percent (Uleri, *Referendum,* p. 323).

The disadvantages of imposing thresholds in referendums are manifold (Kobach, pp. 303–06), yet several postcommunist countries adopted very similar rules (Albi, pp. 65–69; Brunner, pp. 222–23). The most common requirement is a turnout of at least 50 percent, a hangover from the days of communism when this threshold was nominally in place for all elections. Some countries complicate matters more by having different thresholds for different kinds of referendum (for example, "ordinary" referendums or constitutional amendment referendums). Only a few postcommunist countries have no such high hurdles: Estonia and the Czech Republic, where a simple majority suffices, and Hungary, where the majority supporting a proposal must amount to at least a quarter of the electorate. The result of these requirements, coupled with declining turnout in most postcommunist countries, is that "more than half of referendums within recent years have failed to meet these high quorums" (Albi, p. 66).

The referendum is an institution that might seem to be inherently in conflict with the system of "representative government" that this book is about. Indeed, some critics of the referendum argue against it precisely on the grounds that it will weaken or

Box 11.3   The Referendum

France

France has a long history of referendums, going back to 1793. Most of its pre-1945 referendums were widely seen as dubiously democratic, being used by authoritarian rulers to legitimize their positions. More recently, the transition from the Third to the Fourth Republic was achieved by referendums in the mid-1940s, and in 1958 voters approved the inauguration of the Fifth Republic. The character of the Fifth Republic was transformed by the referendum called by Charles de Gaulle in October 1962 on direct election of the president. De Gaulle had been made president in 1958 by the established parties, and by 1962 he had fulfilled the tasks they had hoped he would undertake. They may have planned to dispense with his services once his term ended, but de Gaulle outflanked them by his decision to call a referendum. The people voted in favor of the change, and this outcome considerably enhanced the power and prestige of the president, at least when the president's party holds a parliamentary majority, as we saw in Chapter 2. In 1969, though, a referendum brought about de Gaulle's downfall. He had tied his continuation in office to the success of an administrative reform proposal, and when the people rejected this measure, he resigned from office. From then to the end of the century there were only three more referendums. The September 2000 referendum on reducing the term of the president produced a turnout (valid votes) of only 25 percent—the lowest for any national vote since records began.

Germany

Two referendums were held under the Weimar Republic in the 1920s, and another four took place under the Nazis in the 1930s. Needless to say, the last four were not in any way democratic exercises, and Hitler's use of the referendum brought the institution into lasting disrepute in Germany. The postwar German constitution makes no mention of national referendums, and none has been held since 1938, although referendums occur at state level. Despite exaggerated fears, dating from the Nazi era, about the possible undemocratic overtones of referendums, there was even some dis-

cussion for awhile about the possibility of putting the draft European constitution agreed to in June 2004 to a national referendum.

Italy

Italy is second only to Switzerland in the number of popular votes that take place. It is one of the few European countries where the voters themselves can bring about a popular vote by means of the initiative, without needing the agreement of the government, parliament, or political parties. Some Italian referendums have been particularly important. In 1974 Italians voted to retain the laws permitting divorce, which the Catholic Church and conservative groups had hoped would be struck down by the referendum, and in the early 1990s the votes to reform the electoral system constituted decisive blows against the corrupt and tottering political establishment. The rule that a referendum result is not valid unless turnout reaches 50 percent allows opponents of popular proposals to thwart them by not turning out.

Latvia

The Latvian constitution provides numerous possibilities for referendums—they are obligatory in some areas and can also be initiated by citizens—but only four have been held so far. One was on independence, one concerned citizenship, one was about pensions, and the fourth, in 2003, was on EU membership. The citizenship referendum (in 1998) liberalized citizenship laws dating from 1994 that were seen by the EU as discriminatory against Latvia's substantial ethnic Russian population. As in most other postcommunist countries, in Latvia there is a turnout requirement to make the result valid: Turnout must reach half the number of electors who voted in the previous general election—an unusual requirement.

Netherlands

Prior to 2005, the Netherlands was unique in western Europe in never having held a national referendum. Despite this, or possibly because of it, the question of whether referendums support or damage democracy is debated more intensively in the Netherlands than nearly anywhere else. A number of referendums have been held at the local level on an experimental basis, and in the late 1990s there were moves to introduce legislation that would allow national referendums for the first time. The first national referendum was scheduled to take place in June 2005 on the subject of the proposed EU constitution.

Poland

The political space (unique in the communist world) that was won in Poland during the 1980s by the Solidarity movement saw the holding of two referendums in November 1987 on political and economic reforms proposed by the regime. That they were not mere formalities was shown by the fact that neither set of proposals won the support of as many as 70 percent of those voting and, moreover, a further 30 percent heeded Solidarity's call to boycott the referendums. Only three referendums have been held in postcommunist Poland. In 1996, only 32 percent bothered to vote in a referendum on privatization. Second, in 1997 the people voted narrowly (53–47) to adopt a new constitution, and in 2003 they voted by nearly four to one in favor of joining the EU. Referendum results are not binding unless turnout reaches 50 percent (if it does not, the referendums are deemed merely "consultative"). Given that Poland's citizens have proved difficult to mobilize politically—the country has consistently low turnout—opponents of change have the same opportunity as that provided by a similar rule in Italy—that is, the chance to block a popular proposal by simply not voting.

Spain

Spain has used the referendum institution sparingly. Two nondemocratic referendums took place under the authoritarian Franco regime. After Franco's death in 1975, two more referendums authorized the transition to democratic politics, with a vote in favor of the political reform program in 1976 and approval of a new constitution in 1978. The only national referendums since then came in 1986, when the people voted narrowly in favor of Spain's remaining within NATO, and in 2005, when on a low turnout there was a strong vote in favor of the proposed EU constitution. In addition, a number of referendums have taken place at the regional level.

Sweden

Sweden held only five referendums during the twentieth century, on a rather eclectic range of subjects including the prohibition of alcohol and even the side of the road on which motorists should drive. The most important referendum took place in 1994, when Swedes voted by a narrow margin in favor of their country joining the European Union. In September 2003 the country voted against joining the European monetary union, a vote overshadowed by the murder a few days earlier of the popular foreign minister Anna Lindh.

United Kingdom

Only one national referendum has taken place in the United Kingdom; that was in 1975, when by a two-to-one majority the people voted to remain within the European Community, which the UK had joined in 1973. However, the referendum has been used rather more within the component parts of the United Kingdom. In 1979 and 1997 there were referendums in Scotland and Wales on the devolution of powers. In each nation, the 1979 proposals did not receive enough support, but the 1997 proposals did, and they led to the creation of the Scottish parliament and the Welsh assembly that we discussed in Chapter 6. In addition, the package of proposals agreed to by political leaders in Northern Ireland in April 1998 (the "Good Friday Agreement") was put to the people of the province a month later and received endorsement by a margin of 71 to 29 percent. Whether a referendum is held on a given issue is decided by the government of the day, and the Labour government of 2001–5 declared that both the new EU constitution and any government decision that the UK should join the European monetary union would be put to referendums.

undermine representative institutions. Perhaps, whenever a difficult issue arises, governments and parliaments will pass the buck to the people and propose holding a referendum rather than take the responsibility themselves. Or, in countries where the people can launch an initiative against a law passed by parliament, governments and parliaments may avoid taking tough but necessary decisions for fear of a popular vote overturning them. Another risk is that people might vote for attractive ideas that can't really be implemented, or for expensive plans for which they are unwilling to pay (by, for example, increasing taxes), or for ideas that are so at odds with the overall program of the government that the government is prevented from following any coherent policy. There are also elitist concerns that the mass public, being ill-informed and easily manipulable, will thus be likely to endorse whatever proposals government leaders place before them without thinking deeply about the issues. In this rather far-fetched line of thought, the use of referendums could transform a representative democracy into a "plebiscitarian democracy."

Despite these fears, representative institutions have not been seriously challenged by the referendum. For one thing, in most countries that hold referendums elected representatives control access to them. Indeed, in most cases the government, acting by virtue of its support in parliament, determines the wording and timing of proposals to be voted on. Consequently, it is, as Butler and Ranney (p. 21) observe, "hard to believe that ... the referendum seriously subverts representative democracy." Qvortrup (pp. 152–61) argues that it is likely to strengthen rather than weaken representative government. In Switzerland representative institutions are by now well accustomed to operating in conjunction with the referendum. Only in Italy can the referendum be said to have had a destabilizing effect. Initiatives played a major role in bringing down the corrupt *partitocrazia* in the early 1990s and could in theory make life difficult for more creditable political actors in future. Political parties may also be seen as under threat from the referendum, because during referendum campaigns the debate is often dominated by single-issue groups (or umbrella organizations covering a number of such groups), and parties, which may be internally divided on a referendum issue, become sidelined. Nevertheless, referendums can in fact be useful devices for parties, acting as a "lightning rod" by removing awkward issues from the party political agenda (Bjørklund, pp. 248–49).

The idea of replacing representative government by some kind of "direct democracy" in which citizens would vote on almost every issue is clearly completely unrealistic in a modern complex society. The sensible question to ask is thus not whether "direct democracy," which in any case is an ill-defined concept, is better than representative democracy. It is, rather, whether representative government and the referendum are inherently in conflict, or whether they can usefully complement each other. For the most part, the record in modern Europe suggests that the latter is the case.

✦ CONCLUSION

Studies of electoral systems have come a long way in recent decades (Shugart). During the first half of the last century, some writers used to argue seriously that the adoption of PR in any country was virtually bound to lead to the collapse of democracy and the establishment of a dictatorship. Others claimed that PR was almost a guaranteed recipe for harmony, enlightened government, and a contented citizenry. Expectations of the difference that electoral systems can make are now more realistic.

Even so, there is no doubt that electoral systems do matter. Proportional representation systems lead to parliaments that more closely reflect the distribution of votes than do plurality systems, are more likely to be associated with a multiparty system, and facilitate the entry of women and ethnic minorities into parliament. From a study of government performance in thirty-six countries, Arend Lijphart concludes that PR systems can make a bigger difference than this; they can have an impact on many aspects of public policy. In countries that are close to the model of "consensus democracy," of which a PR electoral system is a key component, the record of government tends to be "kinder and gentler" when it comes to welfare spending, protection of the environment, use of harsh penal measures, and aid to developing countries, than it is in "majoritarian democracies," which use plurality or majority electoral systems. When it comes to macroeconomic performance and control of violence, too, consensus democracies have a slightly better record (Lijphart, *Patterns,* pp. 258–300). Similarly, Powell shows that the policy positions of governments in countries employing the "proportional vision" of democracy are closer to the position of the median voter than are governments in countries using the "majoritarian vision." He concludes that in the twenty democracies he analyzed, "the proportional vision and its designs enjoyed a clear advantage over their majoritarian counterparts in using elections as instruments of democracy" (Powell, p. 254).

One of the areas in which electoral systems have their most visible consequences is government formation. PR formulas are much less likely than a plurality or majority system to manufacture single-party governments. Because it is very uncommon for a single party to win a majority of the votes cast, PR systems tend to be characterized by coalition government, the subject to which we turn in Chapter 12.

References

Aalberg, Toril: "Norway," *European Journal of Political Research,* vol. 43, no. 3–4, 2004, pp. 1098–1104.

Aardal, Bernt: "Electoral Systems in Norway," in Bernard Grofman and Arend Lijphart (eds.), *The Evolution of Electoral and Party Systems in the Nordic Countries,* Agathon Press, New York, 2002, pp. 167–224.

Albi, Anneli: "Referendums in the CEE Candidate Countries: Implications for the EU Treaty Amendment Procedure," in Christophe Hillion (ed.), *EU Enlargement: A Legal Approach,* Hart, Oxford, 2004, pp. 57–76.

Alivizatos, Nicos, and Pavlos Eleftheriadis: "The Greek Constitutional Amendments of 2001," *South European Society and Politics,* vol. 7, no. 1, 2002, pp. 63–71.

Anckar, Carsten: "Determinants of Disproportionality and Wasted Votes," *Electoral Studies,* vol. 16, no. 4, 1997, pp. 501–515.

Andeweg, Rudy B.: "The Netherlands: The Sanctity of Proportionality," in Gallagher and Mitchell (eds.), pp. 491–509.

Auer, Andreas, and Michael Bützer (eds.): *Direct Democracy: The Eastern and Central European Experience,* Ashgate, Aldershot, 2001.

Balinski, Michel L., and H. Peyton Young: *Fair Representation: Meeting the Ideal of One Man, One Vote,* Yale University Press, New Haven and London, 1982.

Benoit, Kenneth: "Hungary: Holding Back the Tiers," in Gallagher and Mitchell (eds.), pp. 231–252.

Birch, Sarah, Frances Millard, Marina Popescu, and Kieran Williams: *Embodying Democracy: Electoral*

System Design in Post-Communist Europe, Palgrave Macmillan, Basingstoke and New York, 2002.

Birch, Sarah: *Electoral Systems and Political Transformation in Post-Communist Europe,* Palgrave Macmillan, Basingstoke and New York, 2003.

Bjørklund, Tor: "The Demand for Referendum: When Does it Arise and When Does It Succeed?" *Scandinavian Political Studies,* new series, vol. 5, no. 3, 1982, pp. 237–59.

Blais, A., and R. K. Carty: "The Impact of Electoral Formulae on the Creation of Majority Governments," *Electoral Studies,* vol. 6, no. 3, 1987, pp. 209–18.

Bogdanor, Vernon: "Western Europe," in Butler and Ranney (eds.), pp. 24–97.

Bowler, Shaun, Elisabeth Carter, and David M. Farrell: "Changing Party Access to Elections'" in Bruce E. Cain, Russell J. Dalton, and Susan E. Scarrow (eds.), *Democracy Transformed? Expanding Political Opportunities in Advanced Industrial Democracies,* Oxford University Press, Oxford and New York, 2003, pp. 81–111.

Bowler, Shaun, and Bernard Grofman (eds.): *Elections in Australia, Ireland, and Malta Under the Single Transferable Vote: Reflections on an Embedded Institution,* University of Michigan Press, Ann Arbor, 2000.

Brunner, Georg: "Direct vs. Representative Democracy," in Auer and Bützer (eds.), pp. 215–27.

Butler, David, and Austin Ranney: "Theory," in Butler and Ranney (eds.), pp. 11–23.

Butler, David, and Austin Ranney (eds.): *Referendums Around the World: The Growing Use of Direct Democracy,* Macmillan and St. Martin's Press, Basingstoke and New York, 1994.

Carstairs, Andrew McLaren: *A Short History of Electoral Systems,* Allen and Unwin, London, 1980.

Cole, Alistair, and Peter Campbell: *French Electoral Systems and Elections Since 1789,* Gower, Aldershot, 1989.

Cox, Gary W.: *Making Votes Count: Strategic Coordination in the World's Electoral Systems,* Cambridge University Press, Cambridge, 1997.

D'Alimonte, Roberto: "Italy: A Case of Fragmented Bipolarism," in Gallagher and Mitchell (eds.), pp. 253–276.

Delwit, Pascal, and Jean-Michel De Waele (eds.): *Le Mode du Scrutin Fait-il L'Election?* Editions de l'Université de Bruxelles, Brussels, 2000.

Dimitras, Panayote Elias: "Electoral Systems in Greece," in Stuart Nagel (ed.), *Eastern Europe Development and Public Policy,* Macmillan, Basingstoke, 1994, pp. 143–75.

Duverger, Maurice: "Duverger's Law: Forty Years Later," in Grofman and Lijphart (eds.), pp. 69–84.

Elgie, Robert: "France: Stacking the Deck," in Gallagher and Mitchell (eds.), pp. 119–136.

Elklit, Jørgen: "Denmark: Simplicity Embedded in Complexity (or Is It the Other Way Round?)," in Gallagher and Mitchell (eds.), pp. 453–471.

Farrell, David M.: *Electoral Systems: A Comparative Introduction,* Palgrave, Basingstoke and New York, 2001.

Gallagher, Michael: "Conclusion," in Gallagher and Uleri (eds.), pp. 226–52.

Gallagher, Michael: "Ireland: The Discreet Charm of PR-STV," in Gallagher and Mitchell (eds.), pp. 511–532.

Gallagher, Michael: "Proportionality, Disproportionality and Electoral Systems," *Electoral Studies,* vol. 10, no. 1, 1991, pp. 33–51.

Gallagher, Michael, and Paul Mitchell (eds.): *The Politics of Electoral Systems,* Oxford University Press, Oxford and New York, 2005.

Gallagher, Michael, and Pier Vincenzo Uleri (eds.): *The Referendum Experience in Europe,* Macmillan and St. Martin's Press, Basingstoke and New York, 1996.

Grofman, Bernard, and Arend Lijphart (eds.): *Electoral Laws and Their Political Consequences,* Agathon Press, New York, 1986.

Hopkin, Jonathan: "Spain: Proportional Representation with Majoritarian Outcomes," in Gallagher and Mitchell (eds.), pp. 375–394.

Independent Commission on PR: *Changed Voting, Changed Politics: Lessons of Britain's Experience of PR with PR Since 1977,* Constitution Unit UCL, London, 2004.

Katz, Richard S.: *Democracy and Elections,* Oxford University Press, New York and Oxford, 1997.

Katz, Richard: "Intraparty Preference Voting," in Grofman and Lijphart (eds.), pp. 85–103.

Kobach, Kris: "Lessons Learned in the Participation Game," in Auer and Bützer (eds.), pp. 292–309.

Kristjánsson, Svanur: "Iceland: A Parliamentary Democracy with a Semi-Presidential Constitution," in Kaare Strøm, Wolfgang C. Müller, and Torbjörn Bergman (eds.), *Delegation and Accountability in Parliamentary Democracies,* Oxford University Press, Oxford and New York, 2003, pp. 399–417.

Krupavicius, Algis, and Giedrius Zvaliauskas: "Lithuania," in Auer and Bützer (eds.), pp. 109–28.

Laakso, Markku, and Rein Taagepera: "'Effective' Number of Parties: A Measure with Application to West Europe," *Comparative Political Studies,* vol. 12, no. 1, 1979, pp. 3–27.

LeDuc, Lawrence: *The Politics of Direct Democracy: Referendums in Global Perspective,* Broadview Press, Peterborough (Ont.), 2003.

Lijphart, Arend: *Electoral Systems and Party Systems: A Study of Twenty-Seven Democracies, 1945–1990,* Oxford University Press, Oxford and New York, 1994.

Lijphart, Arend: *Patterns of Democracy: Government Forms and Performance in Thirty-Six Countries,* Yale University Press, New Haven and London, 1999.

Mackie, Thomas T., and Richard Rose: *The International Almanac of Electoral History,* 3rd ed., Macmillan, London, 1991.

Marsh, Michael: "The Voters Decide? Preferential Voting in European List Systems," *European Journal of Political Research,* vol. 13, no. 4, 1985, pp. 365–78.

Massicotte, Louis, and André Blais: "Mixed Electoral Systems: A Conceptual and Empirical Survey," *Electoral Studies,* vol. 18, no. 3, 1999, pp. 341–66.

Millard, Frances: *Elections, Parties, and Representation in Post-Communist Europe,* Palgrave Macmillan, Basingstoke, 2004.

Mitchell, Paul: "United Kingdom: Plurality Rule Under Siege," in Gallagher and Mitchell (eds.), pp. 157–183.

Møller, Luise Pape: "Moving Away from the Ideal: The Rational Use of Referendums in the Baltic States," *Scandinavian Political Studies,* vol. 25, no. 3, 2002, pp. 281–93.

Moraski, Bryon, and Gerhard Loewenberg: "The Effect of Legal Thresholds on the Revival of Former Communist Parties in East-Central Europe," *Journal of Politics,* vol. 61, no. 1, 1999, pp. 151–70.

Morel, Laurence: "France: Towards a Less Controversial Use of the Referendum?" in Gallagher and Uleri (eds.), pp. 66–85.

Müller, Wolfgang C.: "Austria: A Complex Electoral System with Subtle Effects," in Gallagher and Mitchell (eds.), pp. 397–416.

Norris, Pippa: *Electoral Engineering: Voting Rules and Political Behavior,* Cambridge University Press, Cambridge and New York, 2004.

Petersson, Olof, Klaus von Beyme, Lauri Karvonen, Birgitta Nedelmann, and Eivind Smith: *Democracy the Swedish Way: Report from the Democratic Audit of Sweden 1999,* Center for Business and Policy Studies, Stockholm, 1999.

Pettai, Vello, and Marcus Kreuzer: "Institutions and Party Development in the Baltic States," in Paul G. Lewis (ed.), *Party Development and Democratic Change in Post-Communist Europe: The First Decade,* Frank Cass, London, 2001, pp. 107–25.

Powell, G. Bingham, Jr.: *Elections as Instruments of Democracy: Majoritarian and Proportional Visions.* Yale University Press, New Haven and London, 2000.

Qvortrup, Mads: *A Comparative Study of Referendums: Government by the People,* Manchester University Press, Manchester and New York, 2002.

Rose, Richard, and Neil Munro: *Elections and Parties in New European Democracies,* CQ Press, Washington (DC), 2003.

Saalfeld, Thomas: "Germany: Stability and Strategy in a Mixed-Member Proportional System," in Gallagher and Mitchell (eds.), pp. 209–229.

Sartori, Giovanni: *Comparative Constitutional Engineering: An Inquiry into Structures, Incentives and Outcomes,* 2nd ed., Basingstoke, Macmillan, 1997.

Shugart, Matthew Søberg: "Comparative Electoral Systems Research," in Gallagher and Mitchell (eds.), pp. 25–55.

Shugart, Matthew Søberg, and Martin P. Wattenberg (eds.): *Mixed-Member Electoral Systems: The Best of Both Worlds?* Oxford University Press, Oxford and New York, 2003.

Sikk, Allan: "A Cartel Party System in a Post-Communist Country? The Case of Estonia," paper prepared for the ECPR general conference, Marburg, September 18–21, 2003.

Sinnott, Richard: "The Rules of the Electoral Game," in John Coakley and Michael Gallagher (eds.), *Politics in the Republic of Ireland,* 4th ed., Routledge and PSAI Press, Abingdon and New York, 2005, pp. 105–34.

Smith, Alastair: *Election Timing,* Cambridge University Press, Cambridge, 2004.

Strøm, Kaare, and Stephen M. Swindle: "Strategic Parliamentary Dissolution," *American Political Science Review,* vol. 96, no. 3, 2002, pp. 575–91.

Szczerbiak, Aleks, and Paul Taggart (eds.): *Choosing Union: The 2003 EU Accession Referendums,* special issue of *West European Politics,* vol. 27, no. 4, 2004.

Taagepera, Rein, and Matthew Søberg Shugart: *Seats and Votes: The Effects and Determinants of Electoral Systems,* Yale University Press, New Haven and London, 1989.

Trechsel, Alexander H., and Hanspeter Kriesi: "Switzerland: The Referendum and Initiative as a Centrepiece of the Political System," in Gallagher and Uleri (eds.), pp. 185–209.

Uleri, Pier Vincenzo: "Introduction," in Gallagher and Uleri (eds.), pp. 1–19.

Uleri, Pier Vincenzo: "Italy: Referendums and Initiatives from the Origins to the Crisis of a Democratic Regime," in Gallagher and Uleri (eds.), pp. 106–25.

Uleri, Pier Vincenzo: *Referendum e Democrazia: Una Prospettiva Comparata,* Il Mulino, Bologna, 2003.

Volcansek, Mary L.: *Constitutional Politics in Italy: The Constitutional Court,* Macmillan, Basingstoke, 2000.

Vowles, Jack: "Electoral Systems and Proportional Tenure of Government: Renewing the Debate," *British Journal of Political Science,* vol. 34, no. 1, 2004, pp. 166–79.

Widfeldt, Anders: "The Parliamentary Election in Sweden, 2002," *Electoral Studies,* vol. 22, no. 4, 2003, pp. 778–84.

CHAPTER 12

Building and Maintaining a Government

Almost all European countries, including most of the newly democratized countries of eastern Europe, operate under a constitutional system of "parliamentary government" (see Chapter 2). Governments are not chosen directly by the people. Rather, the people vote to choose a parliament, and this elected parliament has the power both to choose a government and to dismiss it from office. The system of parliamentary government means that, whatever the fine constitutional theory, the raw political reality is that parliamentary elections are much more about choosing governments than they are about choosing a set of people to legislate, to pass laws. Bagehot's memorable description of the British system of government, which applies more generally to parliamentary government, is that "[t]he legislature chosen, in name, to make laws, in fact finds its principal business in making and in keeping an executive" (Bagehot, p. 48). The real prize that is won or lost at parliamentary elections, for most politicians at least, is a place in the government.

Very few European political parties ever win an overall majority of parliamentary seats, because in practice it is very unusual for a political party to win a majority of all votes cast in any country. As we explained in Chapter 11, the proportional representation (PR) electoral systems used in almost all European counties create legislatures that reflect this pattern of electoral preference. Almost all parliaments in which a single party has a majority of seats are actually creations of nonproportional electoral systems, such as those used in Britain or France, that award majorities of seats to parties that win less than 50 percent of the votes. Thus, governments formed by a single majority party are rare exceptions on the European scene, found in only a small number of countries. It is much more common for the result of an election to be that no single party has won a parliamentary majority. This means that no unambiguous choice of government has been indicated by those voting in the election. When no single party wins a parliamentary majority, a *coalition* of different parties is needed to provide parliamentary support for any government—even if this government is made up of politicians from only a single party. And it is a matter of simple arithmetic that there are always several different ways to put together a majority coalition when there is no single majority party; there are thus several different possible governments. The voters have not definitively "chosen" a government, and in most European countries, the precise membership of the government is decided, sometime after the parliamentary election is over, on the basis of bargaining between senior politicians.

Actually, even single-party majority governments are more accurately seen as being supported by parliamentary coalitions formed on the basis of bargaining between senior politicians—except in this case the bargaining takes place *within* rather than *between* parties. These intraparty coalitions may be kept together not as a result of any great affinity between those involved but by little more than the mutual fear of electoral disaster. The best-known example of a single-party "coalition" of factions has been outside Europe, in Japan's Liberal Democratic Party (LDP). The LDP is split into well-defined factions but has governed Japan as a single-party administration for much of the postwar era. Japanese politics during this period has been as much about shifting coalitions within the LDP as about competition between different parties. Within Europe, the Italian Christian Democratic Party (DCI) was also divided into clearly defined factions before it broke up in the early 1990s after a series of corruption scandals. Each DCI faction within the government was typically rewarded with a very precise share of the cabinet portfolios, almost as if it had been a distinct party in its own right (Mershon, "Party"). Both of the main British parties, Labour and the Conservatives, have formed single-party governments marked by deep internal divisions. As in Japan, the factions have stayed together within the same party largely because of the way in which the electoral system would penalize them if they split. Because the first-past-the-post electoral system used in Britain typically punishes smaller parties and splinter groups so viciously, explicit party splits can be very damaging; the fate of those who broke away from the British Labour Party to form the Social Democratic Party is a notorious example. One interpretation of the real political impact of the British electoral system, therefore, is that it forces big parties to stay together in one piece, however hair-raising the intraparty politics might be.

In a very real sense, therefore, the notion of any government as a coalition of diverse interests is fundamental to all political systems. In Britain (and in the United States), such coalitions of interests are found for the most part inside political parties as a result of the distorting effects of the plurality electoral system. In most continental European countries, election results are translated more or less proportionally into parliamentary seat distributions, and so bargaining to form a government takes place both within and between political parties. Election results mean that most European governments are *executive* coalitions, in which more than one party is represented at the cabinet table. Most European single-party cabinets, furthermore, are not made up of parties that control parliamentary majorities on their own. These "single-party" cabinets must thus rely for their continued existence on parliamentary support coalitions comprising more than one party; thus a group of parties supports the government in parliament, even if only one party controls seats in the cabinet.

The system of parliamentary government fundamentally implies that even after a government has been installed by parliament, this is by no means the end of the story. The ability of the government to keep hold of the reins of power crucially depends on the continuing support of parliament—implying a continuing process of bargaining and negotiation between senior politicians to deal with the shocks and surprises that any political system is always throwing up. The deals made to put the government together in the first place can just as easily fall apart, bringing the government tumbling down. At a certain point in time, a wide range of political factors combine to encourage politicians to create a particular government. If these factors change in unforeseen ways, then the same politicians face different incentives and may choose to destroy the same government they earlier created. A key implication of parliamentary government is thus that the government can be brought down at any moment, at least when parliament is in session, by the defection of key elements of its parliamentary support coalition. In reality, as we shall see, things are very much less chaotic than this description might imply. Members of parliament have an incentive to bring down any government only when a majority of them can agree on some precise alternative they all would prefer to the incumbent regime—which is very often much easier said than done.

In the rest of this chapter, therefore, when we explore the making and breaking of governments in modern Europe, we for the most part are considering the politics of executive and legislative coalitions. We examine factors affecting the formation of European cabinets and the allocation of cabinet portfolios among parties, before moving on to explore why some European governments last as long as is constitutionally possible while others form, collapse, and re-form at a very much faster pace.

✛ GOVERNMENT FORMATION

The typical European election does not in any final sense settle the matter of who gets into government, although elections are often more decisive, even in a coalition system, than many people realize. Thus, if members of the incumbent government are reasonably happy with one another, if the election results are not too unfavorable for them, and especially if the government parties between them control a legislative majority, then the incumbent government may well decide to continue in office. No serious consideration may be given to a change of administration. The situation after the 2002 election in the Ireland was a case in point. When the election was held, the incumbent government—formed in 1997—was a coalition comprising the large center–right Fianna Fáil Party and a small party, the Progressive Democrats (PDs), widely seen as having a more right-wing economic program. This government did not in itself command a majority of the Irish parliament, the Dáil, but was kept in power by a small group of independent deputies in exchange for having the ear of government in relation to the problems of their local constituencies. The Fianna Fáil–PD coalition had presided over the "Celtic Tiger" boom that resulted in sustained growth of the Irish economy, and the two government parties fought the 2002 Dáil election on the basis that they would continue in government together if they were able to do so. When the votes were counted, they had increased their combined share of seats, now commanding a parliamentary majority between them. Although some members of Fianna Fáil, now close to a parliamentary majority in its own right, might have flirted with the idea of going it alone as a one-party "minority" government, the outcome of the government formation process, to nobody's surprise, was that the incumbent Fianna Fáil–PD coalition government continued in office. In this particular case, Irish voters can be seen to have "chosen" their coalition government at the parliamentary election. They had a clear opportunity to punish the incumbent coalition, and they chose not to do so.

Election results may also lead to predictable *changes* of coalition government. The Italian general election of 2001, for example, was fought between two rival electoral coalitions. The need to form coalitions of parties that fight elections as a cartel was brought about by a change in Italian electoral law, which, as we said in Chapter 11, set out to reduce the number of parties in Italy by introducing a system of single-seat first-past-the-post elections for 75 percent of seats in the Italian legislature. The 2001 elections were fought out between a cartel, or electoral coalition, of parties on the center–right, and an opposing cartel of parties on the center–left. The center–left coalition of parties had won the previous election, in 1996, and had gone on to form the government. They thus fought the 2001 election as the incumbent coalition with an agreed candidate for prime minister, on the basis that they would continue in government if able to do so. The center–right cartel of parties fought the 2001 election as an alternative government, also led by an agreed candidate for prime minister in Silvio Berlusconi—leader of the largest of the coalition's component parties, Forza Italia. In this case, therefore, Italian voters had a clear choice between two possible government coalitions when they went to the polls and chose Berlusconi's center–right government. Italian voters had spoken and had played a big part in changing their government even in a political system with a large number of parties.

Thus, no one should get bewitched by an image of the political future of most European countries being settled not by voters but by the wheeling and dealing of party leaders in smoke-filled rooms. Even in countries where coalition governments are part of the political landscape, election results in practice may be politically decisive and voters may have a direct say in government formation. They may confirm an incumbent coalition in office, as in Ireland in 2002, or they may make it possible for a prearranged coalition in opposition to take over the reins of power, as in Italy in 2001. Notwithstanding this, and going to the constitutional heart of the matter in European parliamentary democracies, the final say in government formation always lies with elected politicians, not voters. Whatever the election result, no government can form without an agreement between senior politicians. Once formed, any government can fall if this agreement collapses. The constitutional and political bedrock is that the government remains in office as long as, but no longer than, a majority of parliamentarians prefer it to any realistic alternative. This means that the way politicians feel about the precise composition of any government is an absolutely vital matter. Before we can tell a sensible story about how European politicians set out to bargain their way into government, and before we can discuss the factors that Europe's parliamentarians take into account when trying to decide which government to support, we must consider what it is that motivates these people.

Office-Seeking Politicians?

Each European government comprises a cabinet led by a prime minister. The prime minister is typically, though not invariably, leader of one of the main political parties. Thus, in order to become a prime minister, it is almost always necessary to become a party leader first, a fact that adds much of the fire and brimstone to the business of leadership selection in major European political parties (see Chapter 10). After the prime ministership, cabinet ministries are the most powerful political offices in the land. A seat at the cabinet table represents the pinnacle of a politician's career. Cabinet ministers are typically, but not invariably, senior party legislators, though who is or is not "senior" in a political party is a far less clear-cut matter than who is the party leader. Indeed, a party leader can turn colleagues into senior politicians at the stroke of a pen by nominating them to the cabinet.

The fact that the positions of prime minister and cabinet minister are such glittering political prizes provides one distinctive perspective on the making and breaking of governments in modern Europe. This perspective sees politicians as being mainly interested in the "intrinsic" rewards of office. To be a cabinet minister, after all, is to be a famous and powerful person. The desire for such fame and power—for the "smell of the leather" in the ministerial car—may be the most important motivation for many politicians even if few would ever admit this openly or perhaps even to themselves. In many ways, achieving high office is in itself the mark of "success" in any political career.

Policy-Oriented Politicians?

Another important set of reasons for trying to get into government has to do with influencing public policy. If politicians want to make a difference to the way their country is run, one of the most effective ways they can do so is to get into the cabinet. This motivation, of course, is far more acceptable to the wider political world than naked political ambition and is one that politicians are much more inclined to promote in public. Very few politicians, whatever their real hopes and fears, look for votes on the grounds that what they want to do if elected is make lots of money, get their picture in the newspaper every day, ride around in the back seat of a chauffeur-driven limousine, and have a large staff to boss around. Most European politicians, like their U.S. counterparts, campaign on the basis of promises about all the good that they can do for their country if voters put them in a position of power. They usually claim that they want all of this power not for its own sake but rather in order to implement cherished and lofty policy objectives for the benefit of everyone.

The desire to consume the intrinsic rewards of office and the desire to have an impact on public policy, therefore, are different plausible motivations for the politicians involved in the making and breaking of governments. (For an extended discussion of this theme, see Müller and Strøm.) Different interpretations of government formation in modern Europe flow from these alternative assumptions about what drives politicians.

Office-Seeking Politicians and "Minimal Winning" Governments

Perhaps the best-known approach to the analysis of government formation in modern Europe is based on the assumption that politicians are driven above all else by the desire to enjoy the rewards of office for their own sake. This approach leads to predictions that the governments that form will be just enough to take the prize and no bigger—that "minimal winning" cabinets are the most likely to be the European norm. Minimal winning cabinets carry no passengers; they include only parties whose seats are essential to maintain the government's parliamentary majority.

The logic of this argument is straightforward. If being in government is valued in and of itself, then the set of cabinet positions is like a fixed set of trophies to be shared out by the winners of the government formation game. Any cabinet party whose votes are not essential to the government's parliamentary majority will be enjoying some of these scarce trophies without contributing any of the political resources needed both to capture them and to hold on to them. Office-seeking politicians are likely to exclude such "passenger" parties from the cabinet. This logic implies that government coalitions should comprise as few parties as possible, consistent with the need to win confidence votes in the legislature (Riker). The result is a minimal winning government. If a government does indeed include parties whose seats are not needed for its legislative majority, then it is called an "oversized" or "surplus majority" government. Both names, of course, suggest the rather curious—and, as you will see, unwarranted—implication that some governments can in some sense have "too much" support. Nonetheless, if a cabinet includes a party whose votes are not essential to keeping the government in office, then we do have to ask what else this party might be contributing. In this way, the notion of the minimal winning cabinet provides a useful basis from which to start thinking about the making and breaking of European governments. (For reviews of "office-driven" models of government formation, see Laver, "Models"; Laver and Schofield.) In a careful and widely cited empirical review by Martin and Stevenson (p. 41) of the formation of various types of government in parliamentary democracies, furthermore, one of the headline conclusions is that "[i]t is immediately clear … that minimal winning theory is a significant improvement on the intuitive idea that majority cabinets are more likely to form than cabinets that control only a minority of legislative seats." In short, there is a systematic real-world tendency for the governments that form to contain sufficient parties to allow them to control a legislative party but no more than this. This effect remains even after controlling for policy differences between the partners in government (see below), and does indeed suggest that politicians have office payoffs on their minds when they bargain over government formation.

The "office-seeking" assumption about the motivations of politicians also provides the basis for a number of "power indexes," which measure the extent to which parties can exploit their bargaining positions in the legislature. Two well-known power indexes are the Shapley-Shubik and Banzhaf indexes, named after their inventors. Such power indexes have been the subject of intense and ongoing intellectual controversy based on arguments about whether they reflect the ways in which real people vote (Gelman, Katz, and Bafumi) or whether they should take account of the substantive preferences of the actors concerned (Garrett and Tsebelis, 1999a, 1999b, 2001; Napel and Widgren). Nonetheless, the intuition behind them all is that they help highlight ways in which the distribution of bargaining power can sometimes differ quite starkly from the distribution of seats in the legislature. One classic example occurs when there are two large parties, each falling somewhat short of a parliamentary majority, with the "balance of power" held by a much smaller party. Imagine a legislature in which two parties win about 45 percent of the seats and a smaller party wins about 10 percent. In this situation, and if politicians are concerned above all else to get into office, the political facts of life are that neither of the two large parties can take power on its own but any two parties can take power as a coalition. All three parties have equal bargaining power despite their unequal size, giving the smaller party a level of power quite disproportionate to its size. This is actually quite similar to a situation that often arose in preunification Germany. The small Free Democrat Party held the balance of power and was able to be a maker and breaker of German governments despite its small size and indeed was in most postwar German coalition cabinets, often with the most coveted cabinet portfolios.

Policy-Oriented Politicians and Ideologically Compact Governments

If the politicians who make and break governments want to leave their mark on public policy rather than merely to consume the fruits of office, then a different interpretation of government formation is called for. Public policy, after all, applies to everybody. It applies to people who are in government and those who are not, to voters and nonvoters alike. Above all, public policy cannot in any sense be "used up" at a faster rate if there are more parties in the government. Thus, abolishing the death sentence for convicted murderers is a policy that applies to all, whether they are in the government or outside it, murderers or not. If more people join the government, the policy is in no sense "diluted"; it is no better and no worse than it was before. Those who want no more than to see the death penalty abolished will be delighted when it goes, whether they are in or out of office at the time.

If politicians are driven by nothing but the desire to affect public policy when they set out to bargain their way into government, then the logic of the minimal winning cabinet is eroded. If some other politician shares your policies, then there is no reason in the world, if all you are concerned with is policy, to keep this person out of office. In its pure form, this approach suggests that the only criterion that will be used in government formation is the ideological closeness of the cabinet partners. The cabinets that take office should contain parties whose policies are as compatible as possible. They will thus be ideologically "compact" in the sense that cabinet parties will tend to be closer together, rather than farther apart, in their ideological positions. In the extreme, if parties are concerned only with policy, then this focus should lead to cabinets that are so compact that they comprise only a single party—even a very small one—with a very central policy position. If the other parties do not care at all about getting into office, then they may regard the policies of this very central government as being better than those of any other government that is likely to form. They may thus allow the central party to take power on its own and implement its policy program. As we will see, this logic underpins the formation of the so-called minority governments that have been quite common in postwar Europe.

Obviously, however, it is rather extreme to assume either that politicians are concerned only with feathering their own nests or that they are concerned, whatever personal sacrifice is required, only with the good of the country. The truth is most probably somewhere in between, and some accounts of the politics of government formation in modern Europe are based on the assumption that politicians are concerned both with getting into office for its own sake and with having an impact on public policy. This leads to predictions that "minimal winning" governments will tend to form, because office motivations are important, but that these governments will be ideologically compact, because policy is also important. This leads in turn to the prediction that "minimal connected winning" cabinets will form; these are cabinets comprising parties that are adjacent to each other in policy terms, and that cannot lose a party off either "end" without losing their majority. Figures 12.1, 12.2, and 12.3, later in this chapter, give examples of these.

Many authors have constructed "policy-driven" models of government formation in modern Europe. The models differ in a number of important respects, although most assume that there is more to policy-driven government formation than a single left–right dimension of public policy. For example, other policy dimensions that might have a bearing on government formation in particular countries include foreign policy, environmental policy, and the "liberal–conservative" dimension of social and moral policy on matters such as abortion or capital punishment. Some of these authors have constructed models that concentrate more or less exclusively on the policy positions of the political parties and their relative strengths in the electorate or legislature (Schofield, "Coalition"; Schofield, "Equilibrium"; Grofman). Others have focused more on institutional features of the government formation process. These features include the order in which parties are chosen to be *formateurs* (Baron; for a discussion of the role of *formateurs* see Chapter 2). The vote of confidence procedure, also discussed in Chapter 2, is seen as being very important in a widely cited book by John Huber, as is the need to allocate control of particular policy areas to particular cabinet ministers (Laver and Shepsle, *Making*). Michael Thies has drawn attention to the need to balance the allocation of cabinet portfolios with the allocation of junior ministers. Carruba and Volden have focused on the need for coalition partners to put together "logrolls," whereby one partner makes concessions in policy areas that are lower on its list of priorities, in exchange for concessions from a coalition partner on policy areas much closer to its heart (Carruba and Volden; Volden and Carruba). A common feature of most of such models is that they highlight a tendency for the governments that form to adopt positions relatively close to the center of whatever policy dimensions are important. And a strong empirical result found by Martin and Stevenson is that policy divisions between the members of all types of potential government do indeed reduce the probability that such divided governments will form. The net result from all of this is that the government formation process in a coalition system is likely to produce government policies that are less extreme than the policies of many parties winning seats in the legislature. In this important sense, the politics of coalition appear to have a moderating effect on public policy outputs.

Minority Governments

So far, we have been implicitly assuming that the cabinets that take office in modern European countries are made up of parties that between them control a majority of seats in parliament. This need by no means be the case, however. At first glance, the idea of a minority government—one whose members do not control a majority of seats in parliament—might seem at best a paradox and at worst downright undemocratic. When there is a minority government, after all, there must be a majority opposition in parliament. In the typical European country with a PR electoral system, furthermore, the majority opposition will have been supported in the most recent election by a majority of voters. This opposition controls enough seats in parliament to throw the government out on its ear but, for some reason, chooses not to do so. When there is a minority government, furthermore, a cabinet has taken office with no parliamentary guarantee that it can stay there for any length of time, because it can be defeated at any moment at the pleasure of the opposition. Yet Kaare Strøm has argued convincingly that minority government should be seen as a normal and "democratic" outcome of the process of party competition in modern Europe, rather than as a sign of its failure (Strøm).

The main reason why minority governments are such a common outcome of party competition in modern Europe has to do with the role of party policy. After all, if politicians are motivated solely by the desire to get into power, then it is hard to see why they would languish in opposition when they have the legislative muscle to force their way into government and take control of the spoils of office. If politicians are concerned about policy, however, then there may well be circumstances in which policy objectives are better served from a place on the opposition benches than from a seat at the cabinet table. Parties may choose to stay in opposition, the better to fulfill their policy objectives. Strøm therefore looked at the influence over policy that can be wielded by the opposition, concentrating mainly on formal influence exercised through the legislative committee system (Strøm). The influence of the opposition arises because it is actually rather rare for bottom-line decisions on important policy matters to be slugged out on the floor of the legislature. Many more political wars are waged in committees. As we saw in Chapter 3, different European countries differ considerably, furthermore, in the effectiveness of their committee systems and the policy influence that committees give the opposition. The more powerful the committee system and the greater the influence of the opposition, so the story goes, the lower is the incentive for opposition parties to get into the government, because they can be almost as effective outside it. And the lower the incentive to get into government, obviously, the greater is the likelihood of minority governments. Strøm tested this argument by looking at the size, scope, specialization, and power of the committee system in a number of European democracies. He found that the Norwegian committee system is the one that gives the opposition the most influence over policy. This is followed, according to Strøm, by the committee systems of Iceland, Italy, Portugal, Sweden, and France. Strøm suggested that the committee systems that give the opposition least influence over policy are in Britain and Ireland, followed by the Netherlands. The general pattern is clear; the relatively high frequency of minority government in Scandinavia and Italy is consistent in these terms with the relatively high formal policy influence of the opposition, exercised through the committee system.

Laver and Hunt collected data that shed more light on the relationship between minority government and the political role of the opposition. A group of experts in the politics of each country was asked to rate that country in terms of the potential impact of the opposition on government policy. The scores are shown in Table 12.1, and the pattern is striking. The five countries scoring highest on opposition impact are the Scandinavian countries and Italy: the precise group with the highest frequency of minority governments. Although we can never be quite sure which is the chicken and which the egg, the accumulation of evidence lends strong support to the argument that, if the opposition parties have a greater chance of having an impact on government policy, opposition will be more attractive than would otherwise be the case and the frequency of minority governments will increase.

A second interpretation of the ability of minority governments to stay in power—one that may be more appropriate outside Scandinavia—is based on policy divisions within the opposition (see, for example, Laver and Shepsle, *Making*). On this account, a minority government can survive and can even be quite stable simply because the opposition parties cannot agree on a replacement. Thus, governments can be politically "viable" with far less than a parliamentary majority. Although control over a parliamentary majority guarantees victory, failure to control a majority does not inevitably spell

TABLE 12.1

Impact of Opposition Parties on Government Policy

Country	Score
Italy	7.1
Norway	6.8
Denmark	6.5
Sweden	5.2
Finland	4.9
Iceland	4.8
Portugal	4.3
Austria	4.1
Ireland	4.1
Luxembourg	4.0
Netherlands	3.6
Germany	3.5
France	3.4
Malta	3.3
Belgium	2.6
Greece	2.2
Spain	2.0
Britain	2.0

Note: Mean scores on a scale ranging from 1 (low) to 9 (high).

Source: Laver and Hunt, app. B.

defeat. In particular, a party whose policies place it at the center of the political system may often find itself a member of every viable government. Laver and Shepsle call such a party a "very strong" party; its strength derives from the fact that any government that excludes it is likely to be defeated on policy grounds in favor of a minority government comprising only the very strong party. In such a situation, a very strong party obviously can credibly demand to be allowed to govern alone, even in a minority position. Thus, if some party is sufficiently central that it can split its political opponents in this way, it can form a viable minority government, a conclusion for which Martin and Stevenson (p. 48) found systematic empirical support.

This logic may well underwrite a number of the minority governments formed in the past by the Christian Democrats in Italy and by the Social Democrats in Denmark. In each case, a substantial party with an ideological position toward the center of the ideological spectrum won less than a majority of seats but faced a divided opposition. Some of the opposing parties were to the left, some to the right. As a result of this ideological positioning of the parties, it was difficult to envisage a coalition of ideologically diverse opponents that could somehow combine to evict the center party in favor of an alternative they could all agree on. Because it was very difficult for this reason to evict the "strong" center party from office, this party was in a very powerful bargaining position and could have decided to go it alone. Even without a majority it could not be beaten. Indeed, the ability of a particular party to go it alone as a minority government, in the face of a divided opposition, is one of the acid tests of real bargaining power in the making and breaking of governments.

An additional factor that might plausibly affect the formation of minority governments is the existence of a constitutional requirement that any new government must win a formal vote of investiture before it can take office (Strøm). Such investiture requirements force the incoming government to demonstrate majority legislative support quite explicitly, and thus they impose a sterner test on potential minority governments than can be found in countries where there is no need for the government to win a legislative vote before it forms, so that legislative majorities on individual matters to be decided can if necessary be put together on an ad hoc basis. And indeed we do find a systematic empirical pattern that, holding many other factors constant, minority governments are less likely when a formal investiture vote is required (Martin and Stevenson, p. 44).

It should be quite clear from the foregoing discussion that minority government is very much a part of the political scenery in modern Europe, for quite understandable reasons. Any model of European politics that cannot give a convincing account of minority government, therefore, is seriously deficient. We should also note that each of the more plausible interpretations of minority government depends on taking policy seriously. One possibility is that the opposition to a minority government is so divided over policy that it can provide no alternative. Another possibility is that the other parties accept a minority government because they expect to be able to fulfill policy objectives from a position on the opposition benches—by exploiting the committee system, for example. If voters are motivated by policy considerations, then a party may even *prefer* to stay on the opposition benches so that it can pick and choose the issues on which it makes a policy intervention. If the same party were in government, in contrast, it would be forced to make heavily constrained policy decisions on many issues that were not of its own choosing, in this way alienating at least some of its supporters. However we look at it, policy figures prominently in accounts of minority government. We might conclude, then, that in those countries where minority government is common, policy must be an important factor in political competition. Policy also figures prominently in accounts of "surplus majority" government, the matter to which we now turn.

Surplus Majority Governments

Just as some cabinets may be able to survive with less than a parliamentary majority, others may include parties whose seats are not crucial to the government's majority in the legislature. There may be several reasons for the formation of such "surplus majority" or "oversized" governments.

Immediately after World War II, for example, governments of "national unity" were formed in many western European countries, with the intention of involving all sections of society in the job of postwar reconstruction. These were typically surplus majority coalitions comprising all, or nearly all, major parties. Examples can be found in Austria, Belgium, Finland, France, Germany, Italy, Luxembourg, and the Netherlands. In most cases, and perhaps somewhat surprisingly in the circumstances, these arrangements tended to be short-lived. "Normal" party competition soon reestablished itself. Government formation quickly came to involve some parties going into power and consigning others to the opposition. A similar pattern can be seen in the "founding" governments formed at the beginning of the transitions to democracy in eastern Europe, where there was a strong tendency not for grand coalitions of all parties but certainly for "oversized" coalitions involving more parties than needed to control a parliamentary majority. Although trends are difficult to establish over the short period since the beginning of the postcommunist transition in the early 1990s, there also seems to be a trend away from surplus majority governments as the new system of eastern European party competition becomes consolidated.

There are still occasional forlorn popular appeals, at times of major political or economic crisis, for governments of national unity. Although there may be public support for the idea that everyone should get together and pull the country out of trouble, politicians almost never respond to these appeals. Grand coalitions are rare in modern Europe, and government formation is typically as much about who is left out of office as about who gets in.

Another reason we may find surplus majority governments has to do with the constitution. Countries have different requirements for constitutional amendments but, as we saw in Chapter 4, one requirement used by some countries involves winning a "qualified" majority vote in the legislature, a majority of more than 50 percent of legislators—two-thirds or three-quarters, for example. In such circumstances, if constitutional reform is on the political agenda, a cabinet may need a legislative majority of more than 50 percent to implement its policies. Additional parties may then be included in the cabinet, whose seats are needed to achieve a 50 percent majority, so as to achieve this higher threshold. In Belgium, for example, divisions between language communities have resulted in constitutional provisions that laws affecting relations between the communities require the assent of a majority in each language group and two-thirds of legislators overall. This requirement in effect has meant that Belgian cabinets may sometimes need a two-thirds legislative majority in order to govern effectively. Such cabinets may superficially look "oversized," but they are in practice no larger than legally necessary in the circumstances.

There is another reason why a party whose votes are not essential for a government's parliamentary majority may still be a vital member of the cabinet. Laver and Shepsle (*Making*) argue that a party may be essential for a stable government because its presence is required to send out certain signals about some aspect of government policy. For example, the seats of a party with a tough policy of cutting public spending may not be needed for a cabinet's majority. If this party is nonetheless in the cabinet, then public perceptions of the government as a whole may be that it is tough on public spending. If the party is excluded, then public perceptions may be that the government is softer on public spending. The party thereby contributes to the perceived policy profile of the government, rather than to the government's parliamentary majority, and in this sense is not at all "surplus" to political requirements viewed broadly.

Finally, Luebbert argued that a very clear strategic benefit can arise from carrying "passengers" in cabinet coalitions, especially for a large government party. Once a government takes office, any party that is crucial to the government's majority can bring the entire executive tumbling down by withdrawing its support. Even very small parties have a potent threat with which to attempt to extract concessions from their cabinet colleagues, provided, that is, that their votes are critical to the government majority. In anticipation of this, a large party may choose to surround itself with a protective screen of weaker passengers so that no single other party is critical to the cabinet's parliamentary majority. In this event, none of the weaker passengers can make serious demands once the government has formed, because every one of them is expendable (Luebbert, p. 79). To put it rather crudely, powerful parties might actually choose to carry passengers so that one or two can be tossed overboard without too much fuss if they start to get greedy.

This argument was recently expressed in a more systematic way by Carruba and Volden and tested empirically by the same authors (Volden and Carruba). Carruba and Volden focus explicitly on the need of governments to get a diverse package of policy proposals through the legislature. In putting together a potential government, different parties will have to do "logrolling" deals with each other: Party A will concede to Party B on some issue that Party A opposes but cares rather little about, in exchange for a concession from Party B to Party A on a matter that Party B opposes but is close to Party A's heart. Each party benefits by getting its way on what it cares more about, in exchange for giving way on what it cares less about. Any policy agreement between prospective partners in government can be seen as a complex deal of this type. But in the real world such agreements are put into practice not in a single giant piece of "omnibus" legislation that deals with absolutely everything but in a particular sequence of legislative proposals. The danger for members of a coalition cabinet is that after members of some cabinet party have achieved the passage of the measures they are most concerned about, they will defect from the government rather than stay in office and honor their end of the deal—supporting policies they oppose but care less about than cabinet colleagues. Because policy proposals must inevitably be dealt with in sequence rather than all at once, any logroll that puts together a coalition cabinet is vulnerable to such defections by individuals who achieve their main objectives early in the sequence. One way to minimize the risk of this happening is to put together an oversized government. This reduces the incentive of any single member to defect because the government can remain in office, and can continue to implement its policy program, even after such a defection.

Overall, therefore, surplus majority governments are easier to understand than they might seem to be at first glance. This is just as well, because they are in practice quite common, particularly in the former communist states of eastern Europe. Drawing together the various possible explanations set out above, we can come to a conclusion quite similar to the one we came to for minority governments: Policy is important in government formation. Almost all of the theoretical ways in which we can make sense of surplus majority governments have to do, in some way or another, with the desire of potential members of the government to fulfill their policy objectives. This holds whether the objectives reflect what politicians deeply feel about policy in their hearts or instead indicate a more pragmatic desire to redeem policy pledges made to voters at the previous election.

A Minimal Winning Cabinet in Germany

Later in this chapter we take a comprehensive look at the types of government that form right across modern Europe. The best way to get a feel for these types of government, however, is to consider some specific examples. We begin with a straightforward and instructive example of a minimal winning cabinet.

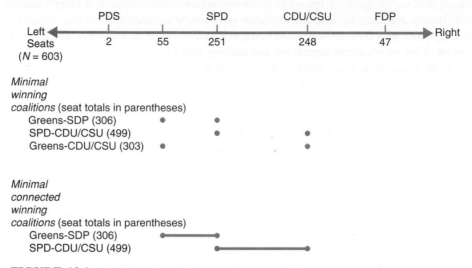

FIGURE 12.1   *Coalition Possibilities in Germany, 2002*

The top part of Figure 12.1 provides some information about the situation in Germany after the general election of 2002. Five parties were represented in the parliament that was given the job of choosing a government. The policy positions of these parties are placed on a left–right dimension of economic policy, and the number of seats won by each party, out of a total of 603, is also given. (Policy positions are taken from a collection of expert surveys of party positions in a wide range of countries, reported by Benoit and Laver.) From left to right, the parties involved were the former East German Communists (PDS), the Greens, the Social Democrats (SPD), the Christian Democrats (CDU/CSU), and the Free Democrats (FDP). The incumbent government at the time of the election was a coalition between SPD and the Greens.

The essential parliamentary arithmetic of government formation in Germany after the 2002 election, which determined the different ways to put together a parliamentary majority of 302 seats, is shown in the bottom part of Figure 12.1. First, the three minimal winning coalitions are listed. These are coalitions between Greens and SPD, between SPD and CDU/CSU, and between Greens and CDU/CSU. Obviously, any other party or parties could be added to each of these coalitions to create surplus majority coalitions. Minority governments would comprise less than the minimal winning coalitions; but minority governments still need to win votes of confidence, so they need the explicit or implicit support of a majority coalition in the legislature, even if the cabinet partners themselves do not constitute a majority. Thus one thing is very striking about German government formation in 2002: Neither PDS nor FDP was a member of any minimal winning parliamentary coalition. The 2002 German parliamentary arithmetic put the FDP, with 47 seats, in a very different bargaining position from that of the Greens, only slightly larger at 55 seats. Any two of the three largest parties, including the SPD, could form a minimal winning coalition without the FDP, but not one of them could form a majority with it. Quite simply, neither PDS nor FDP was an *essential* party of *any* parliamentary majority. In the indelicate language of government formation studies, they were "dummy" parties—by implication, destined to watch government formation from the sidelines. A dummy party in a multiparty system is the equivalent of the losing party in a two-party system, with no clear-cut impact on the making and breaking of governments. In this particular case, we also see quite clearly how bargaining power in government formation can be quite disproportional. The Greens in 2002 were much more powerful than the only slightly smaller FDP—and indeed the Greens went on to play a prominent role in the ensuing German government.

If party policy is important in government formation, as it usually is, then we need to consider the policy differences within various potential governments. Looking at the bottom part of Figure 12.1 again, we see that there were two minimal connected winning coalition cabinets after the 2002 German election, comprising only parties that were adjacent to each other on the left–right spectrum. These were coalitions between the Greens and SPD, and between SPD and CDU/CSU. The minimal winning cabinet involving both Greens and CDU/CSU did not comprise ideologically adjacent parties—and such cabinets may be considered less likely to form than those comprising parties whose policy positions are closer together. We already noted that "grand" coalitions are rather rare in modern European politics, and the coalition between what are by far the two largest parties in Germany, although it formed in the past, could in many ways be considered a grand coalition. Most recent German elections, indeed, are to a large extent head-to-head contests between two potential chancellors who are leaders, respectively, of the SPD and CDU/CSU. This makes it somewhat unlikely, if the possibility can be avoided, that the two will agree to go into government together immediately after having locked horns during the election. This left the minimal connected winning coalition between SPD and Greens, which had the added advantage of being the incumbent government and was in fact the government that formed very soon after the election results were declared, headed by SPD leader Gerhard Schröder. More generally in recent times, most German governments have been minimal winning cabinets.

Minority Cabinets in Norway

Although any government does need to win majority votes in parliament if it is to be able to govern effectively, the parties in the cabinet do not themselves need to command a majority and may instead form a minority administration. This is what happened after the September 1997 general election in Norway. Some information on the Norwegian party system after this election is given in the top part of Figure 12.2. Once more, party positions on a left–right dimension are given, together with legislative seat totals. Ranging from left to right, the parties are the Socialist Left (SL), Labor, the Liberals (Lib), the Christian Peoples' Party (CPP), the Center Party, the Conservatives (Con), and the Progress Party (Prog).

The traditional pattern of government formation in Norway over most of the postwar era was an alternation in power between two "blocs" of the center–right and the center–left. Center–right governments have comprised a coalition of medium-sized and small parties, based around the Conservatives. Center–left Norwegian governments have

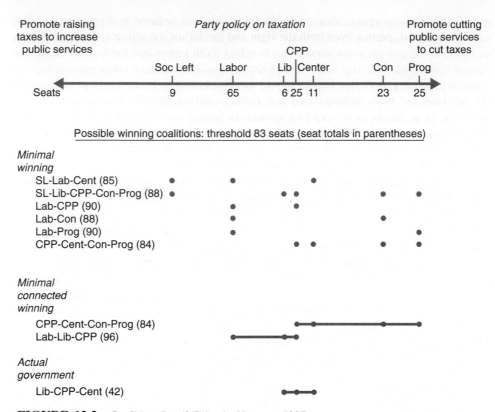

FIGURE 12.2 *Coalition Possibilities in Norway, 1997*

SOURCE: Policy positions taken from Laver and Hunt.

typically been single-party Labor administrations, often kept in office on the basis of "outside" support from other left-wing parties. The outgoing government in 1997 was a single-party minority administration controlled by the Labor Party. Although the Norwegian economy was in good shape, it quickly became clear that the incumbent Labor Party was not doing well in the opinion polls. While the right as a whole remained divided over the controversial issue of EU membership, an issue that had dominated Norwegian politics in the 1990s, the three parties of the center—the Liberals, the Christian Peoples' Party, and the Center Party—announced their intention to form a government if Labor was defeated.

As it turned out, all left-wing parties lost votes and seats in the election, dropping to their lowest combined level of support since 1936 (Narud). The Labor government was thus forced to resign. It was replaced by the small center coalition proposed during the election campaign, a coalition that fell far short of a parliamentary majority and excluded the traditional anchor of right-wing governments in Norway, the Conservative Party. Indeed, the administration that took over the government in October 1997 controlled only 42 of the 165 seats in the Norwegian legislature. Divisions within the right over the EU had thus broken the typical pattern of two-bloc politics in Norway. This minority government conformed very closely to the pattern of a small government at the center of the party system that could continue in office because it divided the opposition. To defeat it, parties from both the right and the left of the minority government had to be able to agree on some alternative. In effect, both Labor and the Conservatives had to find something that they both liked better than the incumbent minority government— a rather unlikely possibility. Since Norway has fixed-term parliaments, furthermore, with no provision for early dissolution, the opposition parties lacked any incentive to bring down the government in the hope of cashing in on election gains. They really did need to agree on some alternative if they were to have an incentive to bring down the government. (For more on the formation of this government, see Narud.)

Led by Kjell Magne Bondevik of the Christian Peoples' Party, this government lasted three years, despite the fact that it controlled far less than a majority of parliamentary seats, before being forced to resign in March 2000 after losing a vote of confidence in the Norwegian parliament. It was replaced in March by another minority government, this time led by Jens Stoltenberg of the Labor Party, which stayed in office until the next scheduled elections in September 2001. These elections resulted in heavy losses for Labor and significant gains for the Conservatives, opening the way for Bondevik to form his second center–right minority administration, this time including the Conservatives, a government that was well placed to complete a full term until the scheduled parliamentary elections of 2005. One of the main reasons why it is so hard to find a majority cabinet is that right and left tend to be evenly balanced and in each of the last two elections the radical right-wing Progress Party won 25 of the 165 seats with policies that mean it is not considered a suitable partner in government by either the center–left or the center–right. This makes the parliamentary arithmetic very tight. With the Progress Party's 25 seats out of the equation and only 140 seats in play, either right or left still needs to find the 83 seats needed for a parliamentary majority—an effectively impossible task. The result is that a pattern of alternating left- and right-leaning minority cabinets has been established in Norway.*

Surplus Majority Cabinets in Italy

Just as cabinets can sometimes be stable while controlling less than a majority of legislative seats, they may sometimes include more members than are strictly needed in order to control the legislature. This may be the case because the government needs a qualified majority of more than 50 percent for certain vital votes, as in Belgium, or there may be less tangible political considerations. Italy, for example, has a long tradition of "surplus majority" coalitions, one of which formed in May 1994. A simplified version of the Italian party system at this time is described in the top part of Figure 12.3. Party positions on a general left–right scale are listed at the top of the figure. From left to right, the main parties were the Reformed Communists (RC), the Democratic Left (PDS), the Greens, the Democratic Alliance (AD), the Popular Party (PPI), Italian Renewal (RI), the Christian Democratic Center (CCD), the Democratic Union of the Center (UDC), the Northern League (LN), the National Alliance (AN), and Forza Italia (FI). A number of smaller parties have been omitted for the sake of clarity.

---

*In addition to the 164 seats won by parties shown in Fig 12.2, one of the 165 seats was won by a minor party.

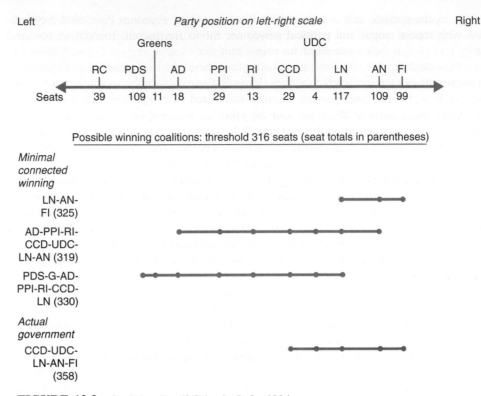

FIGURE 12.3 *Coalition Possibilities in Italy, 1994*

SOURCE: De Vries et al., supplemented by Ignazi.

The Italian political system in the period leading up to the 1994 election had been thrown into convulsions by a range of corruption scandals that had undermined the traditional parties (see Chapter 7). Many formerly strong parties had declined dramatically or disappeared altogether, while many new parties had formed. In an attempt to produce a more stable party system, the electoral system had been reformed to one in which 75 percent of all seats were allocated in single-seat constituencies on a first-past-the-post basis, while the remaining 25 percent of seats were allocated in regional constituencies using list-PR. The new system created very strong incentives for the formation of preelectoral coalitions of parties. This was the case because in order to avoid electoral disaster, "cartels" of parties needed to get together to decide which of them would fight which single-seat constituency. The PR element of the electoral system, however, which allocated seats to parties in a way that provided no incentive to form cartels, acted to preserve the identity of individual parties and held in check any pressure for wholesale mergers, resulting in a small number of large parties.

The result, for the 1994 election, was the formation of three "party cartels" to contest the single-seat constituencies. There was the "Freedom Pole" on the right, comprising the CCD and parties to the right in Figure 12.3. There was the centrist "Pact for Italy," comprising the PPI and RI, and there was the "Progressive Alliance," comprising

AD and parties to the left in Figure 12.3. The right-wing Freedom Pole, won the election with media mogul and political newcomer Silvio Berlusconi, founder of the new party Forza Italia, as its candidate for prime minister.

The list of possible minimal winning coalitions in this eleven-party system is immense; its calculation is left to any reader with a spare afternoon to while away. However, there were only three possible minimal connected winning coalitions. Two of these involved a large number of parties, and the third involved the three large parties of the right. A government based on the Freedom Pole did in fact take office after twelve days of hard bargaining, with Berlusconi at its head. The government was remarkable in a number of ways. None of the main parties had been in government before, and the National Alliance was a party that could trace its traditions back to Italy's wartime fascists. Forza Italia was a brand-new, media-driven, party, and the Northern League was strongly driven by regionalist concerns. These three parties between them controlled a legislative majority, but despite this, the two smaller parties that had been part of the electoral cartel were also brought into government and awarded cabinet seats. Neither of these parties was needed to keep the government in office in terms of legislative seats, but both nonetheless formed part of this "surplus majority" administration.

There is a long tradition of surplus majority governments in Italy (see Table 12.2), so there is no reason to suppose that this one was a product of the new electoral system, although it does give added impetus toward surplus governments by encouraging the formation of large electoral cartels. Traditionally, the level of party discipline has been low, and senior politicians may have felt the need for some additional legislative cushion, over and above a bare majority, before agreeing to form a government. As we shall see when discussing Table 12.5, surplus majority governments, despite having additional legislative support, tend on average to last less long than governments with bare majorities—perhaps because the political circumstances that encourage a prospective government to take on surplus partners may be more troubled and thus unstable than the norm.

As it happens, this particular surplus majority government did not last long. A number of serious divisions quickly opened up between the Northern League and Forza Italia, concerning among other things the issue of federalism (a fundamental matter for the Northern League) as well as the fight against corruption and antitrust legislation (the latter very sensitive given Berlusconi's dominant position in the Italian media). The government ceased to be viable after the withdrawal of the Northern League, a pivotal rather than a "surplus" member of the coalition whose votes were essential to its survival. Facing a motion of no confidence that he would surely have lost, Silvio Berlusconi resigned in late December 1994. (For more information on the rise and fall of this government, see Ignazi.)

The pattern of center–right surplus majority government in Italy was repeated in June 2001. The 2001 election was essentially contested by two cartels of parties, one from the center–left and one from the center–right, and resulted in significant losses for the incumbent "Olive Tree" (Ulivo) coalition of the center–left. Given these results, a new center–right government formed, once again under the prime ministership of Silvio Berlusconi. The cabinet included members from Berlusconi's party, Forza Italia, as well as the Northern League, the National Alliance, and the Christian Democrats. Both Forza Italia and the National Alliance were "pivotal" to this coalition cabinet; their withdrawal would have taken away the government's majority. This was not true of either the Northern League or the Christian Democrats; one of these parties was needed for a parliamentary majority, but not both. Two factors are probably at work here. The first is the fact that these four right-wing parties contested the election as a cartel—presenting themselves as an alternative government. Given the Italian electoral system, there is a strong incentive to form putative government coalitions *before rather than after* the election has been held. In going into government together despite the fact the one or other of the two smaller parties was "surplus" to requirements, the parties were honoring a deal that had already been made. This may be because of a genuine sense of honor among Italian politicians, or it may be for fear of an electoral backlash if voters are not given what they were promised in the election. The second thing to note is that a canny politician such as Berlusconi might well have seen the strategic advantage of carrying a "passenger" party in his cabinet. Mindful of the fact that the withdrawal of the Northern League had brought down his last government, Berlusconi might have taken some satisfaction from the fact they could not bring down this one—and as a consequence were likely to be more modest in their ongoing demands on him. In this context it is striking that Berlusconi then went on to lead the longest-surviving government in postwar Italy.

✦ TYPES OF GOVERNMENT IN MODERN EUROPE

Although the preceding case studies can give us a feel for the government formation process in modern Europe, they cannot give us a systematic picture of the types of government that form. This picture is provided in Table 12.2, which summarizes the types of government that have formed since World War II in a wide range of European countries.

The bottom line of the table indicates a wide diversity of government types. Only about 13 percent of governments are single-party majority administrations. This type of government is typical in Britain, Greece, and Malta—the first two of which in particular have electoral systems highly likely to produce single-party parliamentary majorities even when no single party wins a majority of the popular vote. This is the sense in which single-party majority governments in modern Europe tend to be artifacts of particular electoral systems. About one-third of the large number of governments categorized were minimal winning coalitions, and this type of government can be found in nearly every European country (with obvious exceptions such as Britain and Greece, for the reasons we just discussed). Taking these two government types together, we see that well under half of European administrations are "conventional" majority cabinets, in the sense that the government controls a parliamentary majority but includes no "surplus" members. Conversely, well over half of the governments analyzed either had too few parties to control a majority or had more parties than they needed to do so.

About 30 percent of postwar European cabinets were minority administrations. The body of the table shows that minority governments tend to be especially common in certain countries, in particular in Scandinavia and Italy. We already explored the reasons for this, which may have to do with the impact that opposition parties can have on

TABLE 12.2

Types of Government in Modern Europe, 1945–2003

Country	Single-Party Majority	Minimal Winning Coalition	Surplus Majority Coalition	Single-Party Minority	Minority Coalition	Total
Western Europe						
Austria	4	17	1	1		23
Belgium	3	24	7	1	2	37
Denmark		4		14	13	31
Finland		6	23	4	7	40
France		7	41	4	5	57
Germany		17	5	1		23
Greece	8		1			9
Iceland		21	1	2		24
Ireland	7	8		4	3	22
Italy		2	31	11	9	53
Luxembourg		17	1			18
Malta	9					9
Netherlands		10	9			19
Norway	6	3		13	6	28
Portugal	2	4	1	4		11
Spain	4			4		8
Sweden	3	5		16	2	26
United Kingdom	20			1		21
Total	**66**	**145**	**121**	**80**	**47**	**459**
Percentage	**14.4**	**31.6**	**26.4**	**17.4**	**10.2**	**100.0**
Eastern Europe						
Czech Republic		2		1	1	4
Estonia		6		2	1	9
Hungary		1	4			5
Latvia		4	3		4	11
Lithuania	2	1	3		1	7
Poland		5		2	2	9
Slovakia		4	1	1	1	7
Slovenia		2	3		2	7
Total	**2**	**25**	**14**	**6**	**12**	**59**
Percent	**3.4**	**42.4**	**23.7**	**10.2**	**20.3**	**100.0**
Europe total	**68**	**170**	**135**	**86**	**59**	**518**
Europe percentage	**13.1**	**32.8**	**26.1**	**16.6**	**11.4**	**100.0**

Source: Western Europe: Woldendorp et al. "Party"; annual *Data Yearbooks* of the *European Journal of Political Research;* authors' calculations. Eastern Europe: Müller-Rommel, Fettelschoss, and Harfst, "Party"; authors' calculations.

government policy. Another pattern that emerges is that single-party minority governments are far more common than minority coalitions in western though not in eastern Europe. This finding gives some support to the view that many minority governments may be formed around particular "strong" parties, whose position in the party system means that even though they do not command a majority on their own, they do not need coalition partners in order to be able to form a government.

Table 12.2 also shows that surplus majority governments are very common in modern Europe, east and west, although such governments tend to be concentrated in a small number of countries, notably Finland, France, and Italy. Just under 30 percent of cabinets are oversized, containing more members than they need for a majority. Many of the French oversized governments occurred during the French Fourth Republic, when party discipline was notoriously poor and governments needed a wide margin of legislative safety to be able to govern. Low party discipline may also account for many of the earlier Italian oversized governments, although a more recent explanation could have to do with the incentive under Italy's new electoral system to form pre-electoral cartels of parties that then go into government together as a group.

Also apparent from Table 12.2 is the fact that the types of government formed in the eastern European EU accession states after their first open elections conform to broadly the same pattern as government types of their western European neighbors, although "conventional" single-party or minimal winning cabinets tend to be rarer in eastern (about 39 percent) than in western (about 46 percent) Europe. In general, there are notably fewer single-party governments, and more minority coalitions, in eastern Europe. One explanation for this difference may be that the new eastern European party systems are still in a state of flux—often having a large number of parties with many party splits, fusions, and reincarnations, as well as considerable movement of politicians between parties (Shabad and Slomczynski). Perhaps the best-known example of this phenomenon can be seen in the aftermath of the 1991 election in Poland, in which twenty-nine different parties won seats in the 460-seat parliament, and the biggest single party won no more than 13 percent of the seats. Table 12.3 shows the distribution of seats between parties in the Polish parliament after this election, creating what amounted to an almost insoluble puzzle in the parliamentary arithmetic of how to put together a stable government majority. In the event, the government that formed was a minority coalition involving PC, PSL, PL, and ZChN—four medium-sized parties from the right of center—under the premiership of Jan Olszewski from the PC. This coalition survived about six months before being defeated in the legislature. Largely as a result of the government instability engendered by this type of election result, what was then the very open Polish electoral system was, as we reported in Chapter 11, reformed with the explicit intention of reducing the number of parties winning seats. Following this, as Table 12.2 indicates, Polish governments tended to be rather stable minimal winning coalitions. (For a series of country reports on government formation in eastern Europe, see Blondel and Müller-Rommel).

Overall, Table 12.2 sends a very clear message that although cabinets do need to be able to win the support of legislative majorities if they are to be able to govern in a parliamentary democracy, the government parties by themselves do not need to control a majority of seats. Both oversized and minority cabinets are clearly quite normal results of government formation in modern Europe.

TABLE 12.3

Parliamentary Parties in Poland, 1991

Party	Seats
Democratic Union (UD)	62
Democratic Left Alliance (SLD) (former Communists)	60
Catholic Electoral Action (ZChN)	49
Polish Peasant Party (PSL)	48
Confederation for an Independent Poland (KPN)	46
Center Alliance (PC)	44
Liberal–Democratic Congress (KLD)	37
Agrarian Alliance (PL)	28
Independent trade union "Solidarity" (S)	27
Polish Beer-Lovers' Party	16
German Minority (MN)	7
Christian Democracy (ChD)	5
Solidarity of Labor (SP)	4
Party of Christian Democrats (PChD)	4
Union of Real Politics/Republic's Rightists (UPR)	3
Social-Democratic Movement (RDS)	1
For Wielkopolska and Poland (W)	1
Others	18
Total	460

✧ THE ALLOCATION OF CABINET PORTFOLIOS

The cabinet is the key organ of government in most European countries, acting both as a committee for making decisions in the name of the entire government and as a collection of individuals with responsibility for making and implementing policy in particular areas (see Chapter 2). It may come as something of a surprise to people who think of elections and parliaments as being at the heart of representative democracy to realize that most important policy decisions do not require the direct assent of the legislature. Rather, it is the legislative vote of confidence or no confidence in the executive that gives parliament technical control over the government in all matters: Legislators can instruct the government to act in a particular way, on pain of defeat in a confidence motion. In practice, however, the threat of such a dire sanction is a constraint on executive action only if the issue is one that a majority of legislators feel very strongly about, strongly enough that they actually would bring down the government. When legislators do not feel this strongly, then having at their disposal a threat to bring down the government gives them a sledgehammer with which to crack a nut. As a result, cabinet ministers in practice have considerable autonomy vis-à-vis most aspects of public policy that fall within the jurisdiction of their portfolios.

We said earlier in this chapter that the motivations of the politicians who bargain over coalition formation are the key to understanding the party composition of governments in most European states. Some may be most interested in changing public policy;

others may be most interested in consuming the spoils of office. Whatever their motivations may be, however, the politicians who do the bargaining are the very same people who actually get to consume the spoils of office if they are successful. If they manage to negotiate their party into government, then most of them will also get their feet under the cabinet table, enjoying considerable control over government policy as well as the lifestyles of important public figures. Therefore, notwithstanding the control over public policy that can be wielded by cabinet ministers and the evidence that policy is important in government formation, we should not be too quick to ignore the perks of office. To win a seat at the cabinet table is, after all, the pinnacle of a career in politics for most European politicians. The job brings public recognition, power, patronage, and many other pleasant trappings of success. We should not be surprised to find that many politicians dedicate their political lives single-mindedly to the pursuit of these coveted positions. Given the two basic drives that we might assume motivate politicians—the desire to consume the benefits of office and the desire to influence public policy—we can interpret the political value of getting into the cabinet in two basic ways. On the one hand, cabinet seats may be seen as political trophies to be distributed among members of the winning side. On the other hand, they may be seen as the vital levers of power with which to control the direction of government policy.

Proportional Cabinet Payoffs in France

If cabinet portfolios are seen as political trophies, then we can easily observe how they are divided up in different European countries. The patterns that we see are quite striking. Cabinet portfolios tend to be distributed among government parties in strict proportion to the number of seats that each party contributes to the government's legislative majority. As an example, consider the coalition cabinet that formed in France in June 1997, details of which are given in Table 12.4. This cabinet was formed after an early election called by President Jacques Chirac in what some saw as an attempt to preempt the possibility of a left-wing victory if the parliament ran its full term. If this was the intention, it failed, however.

TABLE 12.4

Allocation of Cabinet Seats in France, June 1997

Party	Number of Parliamentary Seats[a]	Proportionate Contribution to Cabinet's Legislative Majority (%)	Number of Cabinet Portfolios	Share of Cabinet Portfolios (%)
Communist Party	37	12	2	12
Socialist Party	246	79	12	71
Movement for Citizens	7	2	1	6
Left Radicals	13	4	1	6
Greens	8	3	1	6

[a] Winning threshold: 289 seats.

The incumbent right-wing government was defeated at the polls. The Socialist Party and leftist allies made strong gains but did not win quite enough seats to govern alone. Accordingly, when President Chirac asked Socialist leader Lionel Jospin to form a government, Jospin invited both the Communists and the Greens to join him.

As Table 12.4 shows, Jospin formed a surplus majority coalition; only one of the three smaller parties was strictly needed for the government to control a parliamentary majority. (For more information on the formation of this government, see Ysmal.) Nonetheless, what is striking about the figures in Table 12.4 is the close way in which the sharing of cabinet portfolios matched the proportion of seats that each party contributed toward the government's majority in the legislature. Clearly this situation did not arise by accident. When the government was being formed, it was taken more or less as a given that each party was due a certain number of cabinet portfolios by virtue of the number of seats that it had won in the election. This was despite the fact that some of the parties might well have been able to use their bargaining power to win more portfolios than their "fair" share.

Bringing any party into the cabinet involves giving it at least one cabinet portfolio; in this case, one cabinet portfolio was 6 percent of the total. Without sawing politicians in half and appointing a half politician from each of two parties to the same portfolio, this was the smallest payoff that could be given to any government member, despite the fact that each of the three smallest parties contributed only between 2 and 4 percent of the government's total legislative representation. The largest party underwrote this inevitable "overpayment" to the small parties, and the medium-sized Communist Party got a precisely proportional payoff.

This example is very typical of the pattern to be found elsewhere; Browne and Franklin demonstrated that a "proportionality norm" such as this is a very good predictor of the allocation of cabinet portfolios. This research also found a tendency for very small parties to be "overpaid" and for larger parties to underwrite this—almost certainly because of the "lumpy" nature of cabinet payoffs, which means that even the smallest cabinet party cannot be given less than one portfolio. Browne and Franklin's findings, which have been confirmed by a number of more recent studies, are based on empirical analyses that explain about 90 percent of the variation in the allocation of cabinet seats in the real world, and as such they have gone down in the annals of political science as some of the most dramatic nontrivial empirical relationships thus far encountered. The facts suggest strongly that European politicians treat the allocation of cabinet portfolios very seriously indeed. This is hardly surprising, because, as we have argued, a cabinet portfolio represents the ultimate ambition for most of them.

Qualitative Portfolio Payoffs in Germany

Although the quantitative proportionality of portfolio payoffs is quite striking, these findings do not undermine the assumption that many European politicians participate in politics to have an impact on public policy—the interpretation that fits squarely with the facts on the frequency of minority and surplus majority governments. Being in command of a cabinet portfolio, after all, is the best means for a European politician to have an impact on public policy. This means that we must do much more than count portfolios when we analyze coalition outcomes. The allocation of particular portfolios to particular parties is a vitally important matter.

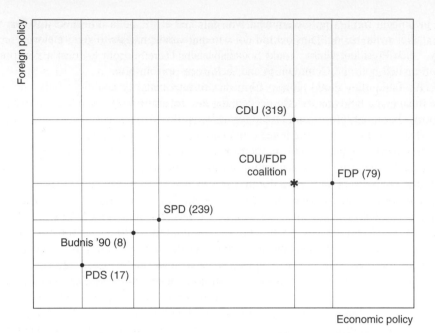

FIGURE 12.4 *The Allocation of Cabinet Portfolios in Germany*

SOURCE: PDS position: authors' estimate. Other positions: Laver and Hunt.

Consider the German example set out in Figure 12.4. The figure describes the key players in the government formation process in early 1991, after the first all-German elections of December 2, 1990. It shows the five German parties that won seats in the 1990 election, describing them in terms of their positions on two key dimensions of politics. The first is economic policy, seen in terms of the conflict between taxation and public spending. The second is foreign policy, which at that time could still be seen in terms of attitudes toward the then-disintegrating Soviet Union. From left to right on economic policy—see the horizontal axis in Figure 12.4—are the former East German Communists (PDS), the East German Greens (Bundnis '90), the Social Democrats (SPD), the Christian Democrats (CDU), and the Free Democrats (FDP). From left to right on foreign policy—the vertical axis in Figure 12.4—are the PDS, the Greens, SPD, FDP, and CDU. The number of legislative seats won by each party, out of a total of 662, is shown in parentheses. From this it can be seen that the party at the median position on economic policy was the CDU. Counting from either left or right on economic policy, we find that the CDU's votes turn a minority into a majority. Similarly, the party with the median position on foreign policy was the FDP.

The horizontal and vertical lines that form a sort of lattice in Figure 12.4 show what each party might be expected to do if put in charge of the policy area in question. Thus, the vertical line through the CDU position shows what would happen if the CDU were put in charge of economic policy. We would now know what economic policy was likely to be, although, without knowing who was in charge of the foreign affairs portfolio, we could place foreign policy anywhere on this vertical line. In the same way, the horizontal line through the FDP position shows what would happen if the FDP were put in charge of foreign policy. We would now know what foreign policy would be, although, without knowing who was in charge of the finance portfolio, we would have to concede that economic policy could be anywhere on this horizontal line.

If we knew who controlled both of these key cabinet portfolios, of course, we could forecast government policy on both policy dimensions. Thus, if the CDU were in charge of economic policy and the FDP were in charge of foreign policy, then we would know that what would happen would be on both the vertical line through the CDU position and the horizontal line through the FDP position. The policy that is on both lines is situated at their intersection, marked with a star in Figure 12.4. This is in fact the government that formed on January 18, 1991. Theodor Waigel of the Christian Democrats became minister for finance, and Free Democrat leader Hans-Dietrich Genscher became minister of foreign affairs. Note that the government that formed was forecast to implement median policies on both the economic and the foreign policy dimension; this is quite often the most likely type of government to form in European coalition systems (Laver and Shepsle, *Making*). This policy coalition, indeed, with the Christian Democrats in charge of economic policy and the Free Democrats in charge of foreign policy, was one of the more enduring governments in postwar Europe. Under the leadership of Helmut Kohl, it governed Germany from 1982 until 1998, winning five general elections in the process.

Cabinet Portfolios and Government Policy

Looking in more general empirical terms at the qualitative allocation of cabinet portfolios, we note a general tendency for parties to be rewarded with the ministries that are crucial in the policy areas of special interest to them. There is a very strong tendency for agrarian parties to get the agriculture portfolio, for example, and there are weaker but still distinct trends in relation to other portfolios (Budge and Keman). This means, as we saw in the German case, that the allocation of cabinet portfolios is not just the handing out of a set of spoils to senior politicians who have managed to take control of the government. It is also a very important way in which the policy profile of any new government is defined, because allocating a cabinet portfolio to one senior politician rather than to another makes a big difference to the expected policy output of the government in question. It also means that cabinet "reshuffles"—changes in the precise allocation of cabinet portfolios—are more significant than many commentators have realized.

Indeed, one account of government formation sees the allocation of cabinet portfolios as a fundamental defining characteristic of any government, since a cabinet minister is not just a member of the government but has considerable discretion over government policy in particular areas (Laver and Shepsle, *Making*). Thus, a minister of health, for example, has huge influence over public policy in the area of health; a minister of education has tremendous power over education policy; and so on. This implies that if you want to know a government's policy position on any issue, you do not necessarily take official policy statements at face value: They may well be unreliable "cheap talk." Rather, you might do better to look at the policy preferences of the politicians who have been given the relevant portfolios, as well at what these people actually do when in office.

When all is said and done, these constitute the most credible signals about the effective policy positions of a government.

This approach also allows us to look inside parties at the role played by senior politicians in government formation. A particular government may be made possible by a particular cabinet appointment. The appointment of a hard-line defense minister or a liberal minister for justice, for example, may make all the difference to the political viability of a given administration. This phenomenon can even be found inside single-party majority governments with huge majorities, because the position of a single-party majority government depends crucially on its ability to hold together and maintain party discipline. In one sense, for example, the British Conservatives under Margaret Thatcher enjoyed some of the most secure government majorities in postwar Europe. Yet the unity of the Conservative Party during this era had to be maintained in the face of deep internal divisions, especially over policy toward the European Union. Euroskeptic Conservatives were deeply suspicious of any move toward closer integration with Europe, and pro-European Conservatives were just as deeply committed to forging closer links. Feelings ran so deep that the party always had the potential to split on this issue, losing its huge majority. This meant that Conservative leaders making cabinet appointments to cabinet portfolios with an important role in European policy had to take care that these appointments did not aggravate the potential for party splits. Even single-party governments can sometimes usefully be seen as coalitions of factions, and this is why the allocation of cabinet portfolios between party factions is always a politically important matter.

Demonstrating the policy impact of individual ministers within the cabinet, and thus showing that the precise pattern of portfolio allocation between government ministers really does make a difference, is easier said than done. Nonetheless a recent study by Giannetti and Laver looked at the impact of ministers in one Italian cabinet on what happened in the departments under their jurisdiction. Giannetti and Laver estimated the left–right economic policy positions of individual ministers in the center–left Ulivo cabinet that held office in Italy between 1996 and 1998. They did this by conducting computerized analysis of the content of all parliamentary speeches made by each minister during 1996. When they plotted the policy positions of individual cabinet ministers against the change in the share of total government spending observed in the government departments under the ministers' jurisdiction between 1996 and 1998, they uncovered the pattern shown in Figure 12.5. Looking at the bottom right side of the plot, we can see that more right-wing ministers tended strongly to preside over departments for which the share of government spending declined, and (looking at the top left side of the plot) that more left-wing ministers tended to preside over departments whose share of total government spending increased. In this case, therefore, there is a strong association between the policy positions of individual cabinet ministers and at least one measure of the policy profile of their department, and the allocation of cabinet portfolios does seem to make a difference.

Overall, there can be no doubt that the cabinet is a vital institution in European parliamentary democracy. In theory it is permanently beholden to the legislature, which can evict it at any stage by a vote of no confidence in the executive. In practice, however, the considerable autonomy of cabinet ministers to set public policy in their respective areas of jurisdiction means that the cabinet is much more independent than formal

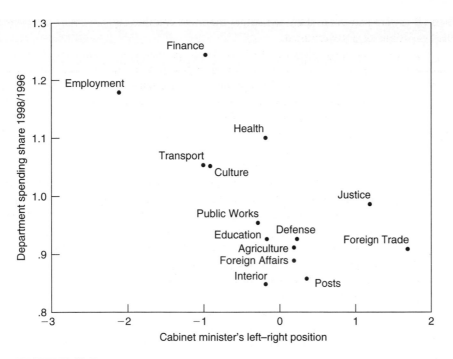

FIGURE 12.5   *The Impact of Cabinet Ministers in Italy, 1996–1998*

SOURCE: Giannetti and Laver.

constitutional theory might suggest. This means that the question of who gets into the cabinet, whether he or she is motivated by the desire to change the course of public policy or by nothing more elevated than the desire to be a big shot, should be seen as one of the fundamental political questions with which party competition in each European system is concerned. In the last analysis, voters choose between alternative sets of politicians; these politicians bargain over who gets what in the cabinet. The ideological complexion of the cabinet that they form represents the most important single way in which party politics in general and the voters in particular can be said to have an impact on what European governments actually set out to do.

✦ THE STABILITY OF EUROPEAN GOVERNMENTS

In some European countries governments tend to last significantly longer than they do in others. Toward the "stable" end of the stability spectrum in western Europe we find Luxembourg, Britain, Austria, and Ireland—all with governments that tend to last a full parliamentary term. We can be less confident about long-term trends in government stability within eastern Europe, since we have information only from the early 1990s, but thus far governments in the Czech Republic and Hungary have lasted as long on average as governments anywhere else in Europe (Müller-Rommel and Fettelschoss). Toward the "unstable" end of the spectrum in western Europe, with by far the shortest average

TABLE 12.5

Average Durations, in Days, of Different Government Types in Modern Europe

Country	Single-Party Majority	Minimal Winning Coalition	Surplus Majority Coalition	Single-Party Minority	Minority Coalition	Mean Duration
Western Europe, 1945–98						
Luxembourg		1,180	466			1,136
United Kingdom	1,038			227		995
Austria	1,424	763	1,420	548		933
Ireland	861	1,006		872	732	901
Netherlands		1,200	942			879
Iceland		876	1,202	224		830
Norway	965	960		777	235	757
Sweden	493	708		816	802	752
Germany		815	703	501		660
Denmark		807		567	674	641
Belgium	464	644	316	134	35	511
Finland		507	548	494	140	404
France		363	323	585	303	334
Italy		347	360	285	351	331
Mean duration	**953**	**814**	**462**	**601**	**410**	
Eastern Europe, 1990–2003						
Hungary			1096			1,096
Czech Republic		1,280		1,458	545	870
Slovenia		679	794		280	604
Slovakia		533	1,446	242	271	593
Estonia		507		423	436	477
Poland		582		498	228	449
Lithuania	682		471		249	447
Latvia		232	503		299	340
Mean duration	**682**	**636**	**862**	**655**	**330**	

Note: Table excludes caretaker and nonpartisan cabinets.

Sources: Woldendorp et al., "Party"; Müller-Rommel and Fettelschoss; *Data Yearbooks* of the *European Journal of Political Research;* authors' calculations.

cabinet durations, we find Italy, France, and Finland, although cabinets in each of these countries have been more stable in recent times, and the short average cabinet durations in Table 12.5 reflect patterns prevalent early in the postwar era. Latvia has the least durable governments of the eastern European countries with which we are concerned. To give a sense of the types of duration we are talking about, countries with more stable cabinets have governments that last, on average, about three years. Those with unstable cabinets have governments that tend to last about a year or even less.

The stability of governments is obviously an important matter for all who are interested in politics, and considerable intellectual energy has been devoted to exploring it. Before we move on to look at these patterns, we need to comment on one unexpectedly tricky matter: deciding when a government has actually come to an end. Unfortunately, different researchers have looked at this in different ways. To begin with the easy part, all researchers agree that one government ends and a new one takes office when the party membership of the cabinet changes. If an incumbent party leaves, or if new parties join, then there is effectively a new government. Some commentators take this as being the only definitive sign that a government has changed. Others regard a new government as having formed after every new election, even if exactly the same parties and the same prime minister resume control. They do this on the grounds that every new parliament represents a new political environment, typically with a host of new faces and a new legislative arithmetic, so that explaining what might appear to some people to be effectively the "same" government does present a new problem for political analysts.

A further important matter concerns the overall "turnover" of cabinet ministers from one government to the next. After all, if a government changes its prime minister and even its party composition, but most of the cabinet ministers remain the same, then it could be argued that it has not really changed very much. This argument is particularly important when we evaluate the apparent instability of governments in, for example, Italy. According to most definitions, postwar Italian governments have on average been very short-lived, but it is also the case that the turnover of Italian cabinet ministers from one government to the other is often very limited. Some considerable stability in the ranks of senior personnel underlies the apparent instability of Italian cabinets (Mershon, "Costs"; Mershon, "Party"). In a comprehensive comparative analysis, Huber and Martinez-Gallardo show that cabinet stability and cabinet turnover are indeed quite distinct from each other. They confirm the finding that Italy over the postwar period has tended to have short-lived cabinets but also to have relatively low turnover of cabinet ministers by international standards. Austria, Sweden, and Iceland are other countries in which cabinet ministers tend to stay in office for much longer than the average duration of cabinets—implying far less instability of cabinet personnel than might be inferred from simply looking at cabinet durations.

All of this shows that the question "How long did this government last?" is easier asked than answered. The classification of governments reported in Table 12.2 is based on data from Woldendorp et al. ("Party"), who have a "permissive" definition of the end of a government. They see a wide range of factors (elections, new party composition, new prime minister, resignation of incumbent prime minister even if she or he resumes office) as marking the end of a government's life. Obviously, this approach is likely to show cabinet durations as being shorter than if the sole indicator of the end of a government were a change in its party composition. Lijphart, however, has shown that different definitions do not make too much difference to the *relative* durations of different types of cabinet in different countries.

Most studies of the duration of European cabinets concentrate on two things. First, cabinets themselves may possess certain *attributes* that lead some to be more durable than others. It is widely believed, for example, that coalition governments are less stable than single-party governments, and that majority governments are more stable than minority governments. Second, there are features of the *political environment* in which a government must survive. This, if party competition is fragmented between many parties, for example, or if there is a powerful antiregime party that refuses to take party in any government, then these features of the political system may lead to greater cabinet instability.

Cabinet Attributes and Cabinet Stability

Several researchers have confirmed the expectation that single-party governments last longer than coalitions and the expectation that majority governments last longer than minority governments. These patterns can be seen by looking at the top part of Table 12.5. On average across the whole of western Europe, single-party majority governments last noticeably longer than minimal winning coalitions; they last about a year longer than single-party minority governments and more than twice as long as minority coalitions. Minimal winning governments, in turn, last much longer than minority or surplus majority governments. Overall, minority coalitions are notably the least stable type of government in western Europe.

There is only a very short history of parliamentary government in eastern Europe from which to draw conclusions about government stability. Nonetheless, the bottom part of Table 12.5 indicates some emerging trends and what look like some interesting differences from the pattern in western Europe. We can draw no conclusion at all about the longevity of single-party majority cabinets in eastern Europe because they hardly exist at all. What is quite striking, however, is that the most stable type of cabinet in eastern Europe is the surplus majority cabinet—comprising more parties than are needed to control a parliamentary majority. This sharp contrast with the situation in western Europe, where surplus majority cabinets are among the *least* durable, certainly suggests that in the more volatile party systems of eastern Europe during the transition era—with parties forming, splitting, fusing, and disappearing in between as well as during election campaigns—politicians have found that they may be able to bolster cabinet stability by including more parties than the bare minimum needed to control parliament at the time the government forms. This contrast also lends credibility to the interpretation of surplus majority cabinets as responses to uncertainty and flux in the political environment. Nevertheless, the pattern of government durations in eastern Europe resembles the western Europe pattern in one important respect: The least durable cabinet type is the minority coalition. As in western Europe, single-party minority cabinets are much more durable than minority coalitions. This similarity lends further support to the idea that single-party minority governments, as opposed to minority coalitions, tend to be based on parties that find themselves in a strong bargaining positions in the legislature, albeit short of a full parliamentary majority.

Broad European averages are a crude measure of the durability of different types of government, however, and the body of Table 12.5 shows that the pattern is more complex than it seems at first glance. Some general patterns hold when we compare different types of government within individual countries, but others do not. For example, minority coalitions are almost invariably less stable than majority coalitions, regardless of country. In most countries, single-party minority governments are also less stable than single-party majority governments. Majority status does tend to extend government stability in all political systems. Comparing the stability of minimal winning coalitions with that of single-party majority governments is instructive, however. With the exception of Austria, there is no evidence that minimal winning coalitions are less stable; indeed, in those countries that experience both types of government, minimal winning coalitions are likely to be just as stable as single-party majority governments. The reason Europe-wide averages make single-party majority governments look more stable is that this type of government tends to be found more often in countries where the stability of *all* types of government is higher. In other words, as long as the government has majority status, there is no strong evidence that coalitions per se are less stable than single-party governments.

Policy differences between members of a coalition cabinet can also have a big impact on government stability. This has been shown most clearly by Warwick, who measures the ideological diversity of coalition cabinets along three important policy dimensions: the traditional left–right dimension; a dimension contrasting proclerical and secular ideologies; and a dimension that captures the extent to which party policy is "anti-system." Warwick shows that increasing cabinet diversity on any one of these three dimensions reduces the life expectancy of the cabinet, presumably because of the greater possibility for policy disputes.

Not all sources of government instability come from within the cabinet, however. There are large differences between countries in government durability, in both eastern and western Europe, even when we take account of the different types of cabinet that form. Single-party minority governments are much more stable in Ireland, Sweden, and Norway, for example, than in Italy and Belgium. Surplus majority cabinets are much more stable in Hungary than in Latvia. Thus, the political system within which a government must survive, as well as the type of government itself, must have a major impact on government stability.

System Attributes and Cabinet Duration

One of the patterns to emerge quite clearly from comparing government stability in different European countries is that countries in which governments are more short-lived tend to be those with relatively large numbers of relatively small parties generating a more complex and unstable parliamentary arithmetic. In Latvia, for example, where average government duration since independence from the former Soviet Union has been less than one year, the 1995 election to the 100-seat parliament generated the parliament described in Table 12.6. There were nine parties, none of which controlled more than 18 percent of the seats, generating a simply enormous range of coalition possibilities. No "obvious" government emerged from this election result. Furthermore, the Latvian parties were still merging and splitting, and individual legislators were also on occasion switching parties. Any change in the party system, however tiny, could change the legislative arithmetic and hence the parliamentary support base of the incumbent government. Clearly this does not seem to be a political environment conducive, under the rules of parliamentary government, to sustaining stable administrations. Perhaps not surprisingly, four different coalition cabinets, each comprising six or seven parties, formed and fell in Latvia during the three-year period between the elections of October 1995 and those of October 1998.

In Luxembourg, in contrast, almost no election result that can realistically be forecast is likely to change the power structure in the legislature. After any election, the parliamentary arithmetic almost inevitably reveals that any two of the three largest parties are needed to form a majority administration and that the large, centrist Christian Social

TABLE 12.6

Parliamentary Parties in Latvia, 1995

Party[a]	Seats
DPS	18
LC	17
TKL	16
TB	14
LPP/LZS	8
LVP	8
LNNK	8
TSP	6
LSP	5
Total	100

[a] DPS—Democratic Party-Saimnieks; LC—Latvia's Way; TKL—People's Movement; TB—Fatherland and Freedom; LPP—Latvia's First Party; LZS—Latvian Peasants Union; LVP—Latvian Unity Party; LNNK—Latvian National Independence Movement; TSP—People's Harmony Party; LSP—Latvian Socialist Party.

Party is going to be very difficult to keep out of office. Because the party system in Luxembourg is so stable, there are almost no shocks, surprises, or likely changes in the legislative arithmetic that could change the support base of an incumbent government that demonstrated the support of a parliamentary majority when it took office.

Differences between countries in the complexity of their parliamentary arithmetic, in short, can have a major bearing on government stability. Countries with a record of short-lived cabinets (Italy, Belgium, Finland, and Latvia, for example) all tend to have fragmented party systems in which election results generate a rather large number of rather small parties (see Table 11.5). These systems yield a large number of coalition possibilities—as in the Latvian case—and a consequently high probability that small changes in the political environment are likely to destabilize an incumbent administration. Countries with a record of longer-lasting cabinets (Austria, Britain, Hungary, and Luxembourg, for example) all tend to have less fragmented party systems in which elections generate a much simpler parliamentary arithmetic. This outcome may occur because one party typically wins a majority, as in Britain. Or it may occur because there are only two or three large parties from which a majority coalition in parliament can be formed, as is typically the case in Austria and Luxembourg and after recent elections in Hungary. Extensive cross-national empirical analyses of factors affecting the stability of cabinets reinforce these conclusions (King et al.; Warwick; Diermeier and Stevenson, "Cabinet Survival"; Diermeier and Stevenson, "Cabinet Terminations"). They show that government duration is significantly affected by two factors that contribute directly to the complexity of the political environment within which the government must survive: the fragmentation and the ideological polarization of the party system. The more fragmented the party system is, and the greater the ideological polarization of the parties, the less conducive is the political environment to durable cabinets.

Government Stability and Political Events

The "political science" account of the stability of European governments that we have just discussed stands in stark contrast to the way that political journalists and practicing politicians tend to think about this subject. Those who are deeply involved in the rough-and-tumble of day-to-day politics are likely to see the defeat or resignation of any government as the direct product of a particular sequence of events, not of some abstract configuration of the party system. When a government falls, political journalists typically regale their audiences with their versions of the sequence of events that led to its demise. And even a government that seemed solid as a rock can sometimes be "ambushed" by events that are largely beyond its control. Although we have seen strong general patterns in the stability of European governments, we must not forget that these patterns are no more than trends. In the case of any *particular* government, such trends may inform our views on how stable it is *likely to be;* but how stable it *actually turns out to be* depends to a large extent on the slings and arrow of outrageous fortune.

This caveat alerts us to an important and often neglected distinction between the duration and the durability of governments. The *duration* of any government is a simple observable quantity—the elapsed time between the birth of the government and its replacement by parliament with an alternative. Political scientists can collect large numbers of observations of government durations and infer trends from them. The *durability* of any government is an abstract and unobservable quality. It refers to how long a government is *likely to last* in a specified range of circumstances, or to how long a past government *might have lasted* if only things had been different. There is a big difference between the durability of any particular government and its actual duration. A government that seems on the face of it to be rather durable—perhaps a single-party cabinet with a huge parliamentary majority—can still collapse when people least expect it to. There might be a huge scandal involving the financial affairs of the prime minister, or some pivotal political figure may have a heart attack. Such events can destroy even a "durable" government like a bolt out of the blue—just days after it looked as though it would govern for several more years. (For a discussion of the distinction between the duration and durability of governments, and a more general review of government stability, see Laver, "Government".)

Every government must live its life in a world of "critical events"—of shocks, scandals, and other disasters that put its ability to survive to the test. Any one of these events may be a bullet with the government's name on it. By definition, all of these events are things that could not have been foreseen when the government formed. Indeed they are precisely the things that could not possibly have been foreseen and thus could not have been taken into account by the individuals who negotiated about the size and shape of the government. The durability of a government, in these terms, can be seen as its ability to withstand critical events. Rather like boxers, durable governments can take a lot of punches and come back fighting. Less durable governments, in contrast, tend not to survive the first really nasty surprise.

Critical events can take many, many forms. It is always easy to be wise after the event. It is much harder for political scientists to identify in advance the type of critical event that will bring down a given government. For example, an unexpected turnaround in opinion poll ratings may modify the expectations of politicians about the outcome of

The 1985 soccer riot at Heisel Stadium: this completely unexpected event brought down a Belgian government.
© Photo News/Liaison Agency

an upcoming election. Their changed expectations may provoke a reallocation of power within the incumbent government or may even destabilize a sensitive deal already made and bring the government down (Lupia and Strøm). More generally, a wide range of different types of political shock may put pressure on the government. As well as "public opinion shocks," there may be shocks to the political agenda, arising when unexpected and quite possibly unwelcome issues simply must be decided. Perhaps an oil tanker goes aground on the coast—forcing hard decisions on environmental policy. Perhaps a major company goes bankrupt—forcing unwelcome decisions on industrial policy. To such scenarios can be added unexpected ministerial departures, as a result of death, ill-health, or scandal. Laver and Shepsle ("Events") set out to classify different types of political shock and explore the types of effect that they might have on government stability.

When we set out to predict the durability of any particular government, therefore, we are talking only about the *probability* that it will last for a specified time. A fuller account of the life cycle of governments must take account not only of the key "stability-inducing" attributes of cabinet but also of the possibility that even an apparently stable government can be shot down out of a clear blue sky by an unexpected event. Using appropriate statistical assumptions to model the impact of random events makes it possible to combine both approaches into a single account of government duration in western Europe. Quite a number of political scientists have now done this, using a statistical technique known as "event history" modeling (King et al.; Warwick; Diermeier and Stevenson, "Cabinet Survival"; Diermeier and Stevenson, "Cabinet Terminations"; Diermeier and Merlo; for a review of these see Laver, "Government"). These systematic statistical analyses have tended to confirm the more informal judgments we made above about trends in government duration. Longer-lasting governments tend to have majority status; they tend to arise in less fragmented party systems; they tend to arise when there is not a substantial antisystem opposition; they tend to arise when there is a formal parliamentary investiture requirement that tests the government strength before it takes office; and they tend to be less internally divided over policy. Thus we can use this work to write down the recipe for an unstable government: It would exist in a party system with a large number of small parties, including at least one antisystem party; it would be a minority coalition of ideologically diverse partners; and it would take office without having to pass an investiture requirement. Given a government with all of these attributes, we would not expect the cabinet to be able to survive many unwelcome political shocks.

The statistical techniques of event history analysis that were used in these studies also allow us, almost miraculously, to "remove" the effect of holding scheduled elections on the life span of governments. Although many governments never make it to the end of a full parliamentary term, many more durable governments might have been able to survive much longer had it not been for the constitutional need to hold a scheduled election. Thus King et al. found that scheduled elections have little effect on the duration of governments in high-turnover systems such as Finland and Italy. In contrast, if it were not for scheduled elections, governments in Britain would last even longer, on the average, than they do at present. In other words, for the more stable systems, turnover in governments is more a product of the constitutional requirement that elections be held at regular intervals, generating a new parliament, than it is of political forces at work within a particular parliament. In less stable systems, the high turnover of governments seems to arise because governments collapse, even without a constitutional limitation on their tenure, as a result of the forces at work in the very same parliaments that put them in office in the first place.

The same statistical techniques also allow us to estimate whether or not a government faces increasing risks of failure as it goes farther into its term of office. Intuitively, this seems plausible. As a new government takes office, it might seem strong and better able to withstand large shocks than it would be after it has been bombarded for a year or two by an endless stream of nasty shocks. The model of cabinet termination put forward by Lupia and Strøm, furthermore, predicted that the risk of termination—or "hazard rate" as it is usually referred to—should rise during the lifetime of a government. For them, this is reasonable because, with less time to go before the next constitutionally mandated election, the incentives for coalition partners to renegotiate their deal in the face of unanticipated political shocks will be less. Indeed, if some surprise event were to ambush a government shortly before an election was due to be held anyway, there might be no point in trying to renegotiate the deal. Diermeier and Stevenson ("Cabinet Survival") addressed this problem, distinguishing between cabinet terminations brought about by early dissolutions and those brought about by the fall of a government between elections. They found that the risk of a government being replaced *between elections* tended to be constant throughout its life—not to increase as we might have imagined. However, they also found that the risk of a government falling *as the result of an early election* did tend to rise significantly during a government's life.

This interesting finding returns our attention to the fact that many European prime ministers have strategic control over the calling of elections. What seems to be going on

is that the typical prime minister becomes increasingly likely to exercise his or her crucial power to cut and run for an election as the life of the government progresses. This
preference is quite understandable, for letting the government run its full constitutional
term would leave the prime minister without the option to pick an election time favorable to the government. Once the government is at least a couple of years into its term,
any prime minister worth his or her salt will be keeping an eye on the opinion polls and
trying to figure out the best time to call the next election. A good recent example can
be found in the continued speculation about an early election in Britain from about 2003,
despite the fact that the incumbent Labour government under Tony Blair had secured a
new five-year term in 2001, having won 413 of the 659 seats in the House of Commons.
Throughout the life of this government, there never seemed any question of it running
its full term, despite having a crushing parliamentary majority. All of the talk was of
the best time for Blair to cut and run for a third term—and of the need not to wait too
late to do so. (For an excellent recent analysis of strategic election timing in Britain, see
Smith.)

The destabilizing effect of anticipated elections is compounded by a crucial feature of *coalition* cabinets; as the next election appears on the horizon, junior coalition
partners begin to calculate ways in which they might leave the cabinet and force an election on terms that will put them in the best light possible. Thus coalition partners may
begin actually looking for "deal-breakers" that can form the basis of their next election
campaign, with obviously destabilizing effects on the government. All in all, as soon as
the next scheduled election pops up on the far horizon, the chances increase that some
key player is going to cut and run, precipitating an early election. This possibility is why
rather few national parliaments in modern Europe run to the very end of their legally
mandated terms.

❖ CONCLUSION

The making and breaking of European governments has been more extensively studied
than many other aspects of the political process. Although there is always more work to
be done, our conclusions on this important subject can nonetheless be rather firmer than
those we have drawn on some of the other subjects we deal with in this book.

First and foremost, we reemphasize that the normal situation in modern Europe,
given the system of parliamentary government used in nearly every country, is for no
party to have a parliamentary majority. *Parliamentary* coalitions will always be needed
in such cases if the government is to gain and retain office. But it is by no means always
necessary that there be an *executive* coalition of parties. If a single-party "minority" cabinet can find favor with a majority of legislators, it can build and maintain a viable government. Such minority cabinets are very much part of the mainstream experience in
Europe. Minimal winning coalitions, albeit common, do not account for the majority of
governments that form, notwithstanding the preconceptions of many of the people who
write about the government formation process.

Second, the details of the composition of the cabinet are a matter of vital political
interest. The proportional allocation of cabinet portfolios among parties is a firmly established norm in most European systems. This does not mean, however, that the allocation
takes place according to a sterile political formula. What it means is that the real political

action is concerned with which particular politician gets which particular portfolio; the end product of this process determines the fundamental character, and the likely policy outputs, of the government.

Third, certain types of political system in which coalition government is the norm do generate more unstable cabinets than others. In countries with stable *coalition* governments, furthermore, these are effectively as stable as one-party governments in Britain, where the stability of one-party majority governments is often put forward as the main advantage of maintaining a non-PR electoral system. Many of these stable coalition cabinets, indeed, have provided some of postwar Europe's most successful governments.

Putting all of this together, we find that the making and breaking of governments in the parliamentary democracies of modern in Europe provides the vital link between legislative politics, on which citizens have at least some small impact when they vote for their members of parliament, and what the political executive actually does to run the country, over which voters have no direct control. The patterns we describe in this chapter show that the politics of representative government does not stop when an election result has been declared, but continue into the making and breaking of governments. The policy outputs of coalition cabinets are affected by politicians who do their deals while thinking about the possible results of the *next* election. The substantive effects of this can be seen in the way in which the policies of ideologically compact coalition cabinets tend to converge on the center ground—and in this way to please the maximum number of voters.

REFERENCES

Bagehot, Walter: *The English Constitution,* Fontana, London, 1993 [first published 1867].

Baron, David: "A Spatial Bargaining Theory of Government Formation in Parliamentary Systems," *American Political Science Review,* vol. 85, no. 1, 1991, pp. 137–65.

Benoit, Kenneth, and Michael Laver: *Party Policy in Modern Democracies,* Routledge, London, 2005.

Blondel, Jean, and Ferdinand Müller-Rommel (eds.): *Cabinets in Eastern Europe,* Palgrave, London, 2001.

Browne, E., and M. Franklin: "Aspects of Coalition Payoffs in European Parliamentary Democracies," *American Political Science Review,* vol. 67, no. 2, 1973, pp. 453–69.

Budge, I., and H. Keman: *How Party Government Works: Testing a Theory of Formation, Functioning and Termination in 20 Democracies,* Oxford University Press, Oxford, 1990.

Carruba, Clifford J., and Craig Volden: "Coalitional Politics and Logrolling in Legislative Institutions," *American Journal of Political Science,* vol. 44, no. 2, 2000, pp. 521–37.

De Vries, Miranda, Daniela Giannetti, and Lucy Mansergh: "Estimating the Positions of Political Actors in the Netherlands, Italy and Ireland," in Michael Laver (ed.), *Estimating the Policy Positions of Political Actors,* Routledge, London, 2001, pp. 193–216.

Diermeier, Daniel, and Antonio Merlo: "Government Turnover in Parliamentary Democracies," *Journal of Economic Theory,* vol. 94, no. 4, 2000, pp. 46–79.

Diermeier, Daniel, and Randy Stevenson: "Cabinet Survival and Competing Risks," *American Journal of Political Science,* vol. 43, no. 5, 1999, pp. 1051–69.

Diermeier, Daniel, and Randy Stevenson: Cabinet Terminations and Critical Events," *American Political Science Review,* vol. 94, no. 3, 2000, pp. 627–40.

Farrell, Brian: "The Formation of the Partnership Government," in Michael Gallagher and Michael Laver (eds.), *How Ireland Voted 1992,* Folens and PSAI Press, Dublin and Limerick, 1993, pp. 146–61.

Garrett, Geoffrey, and George Tsebelis: "Even More Reasons to Resist the Temptation to Apply Power Indices to the European Union," *Journal of Theoretical Politics,* vol. 13, no. 1, 2001, pp. 99–105.

Garrett, Geoffrey, and George Tsebelis: "More Reasons to Resist the Temptation to Apply Power Indices to the European Union," *Journal of Theoretical Politics,* vol. 11, no. 3, 1999a, pp. 331–38.

Garrett, Geoffrey, and George Tsebelis: "Why Resist the Temptation to Apply Power Indices to the European Union?" *Journal of Theoretical Politics,* vol. 11, no. 3, 1999b, pp. 291–308.

Gelman, Andrew, Jonathan N. Katz, and Joseph Bafumi: "Standard Power Indices Do Not Work: An Empirical Analysis," *British Journal of Political Science,* vol. 34, pt. 4, 2004, pp. 657–74.

Giannetti, Daniela, and Michael Laver: "Policy Positions and Jobs in the Government," *European Journal of Political Research,* vol. 44, no. 1, 2004, pp. 1–30.

Grofman, Bernard: "Extending a Dynamic Model of Protocoalition Formation," in Norman Schofield (ed.), *Collective Decision-Making: Social Choice and Political Economy,* Kluwer, Dordrech, 1996, pp. 265–80.

Holler, Manfred, and M. Widgren: "Why Power Indices for Assessing European Union Decision-Making?" *Journal of Theoretical Politics,* vol. 11, 1999, pp. 321–30.

Huber, John: *Rationalizing Parliament: Legislative Institutions and Party Politics in France,* Cambridge University Press, Cambridge, 1996.

Huber, John, and Cecilia Martinez-Gallardo: "Cabinet Instability and the Accumulation of Experience: The French Fourth and Fifth Republics in Comparative Perspective," *British Journal of Political Science,* vol. 34, pt. 1, 2004, pp. 27–48.

Ignazi, Piero: "Italy," *European Journal of Political Research,* vol. 28, 1995, pp. 393–405.

King, G., J. Alt, N. Burns, and M. Laver: "A Unified Model of Cabinet Dissolution in Parliamentary Democracies," *American Journal of Political Science,* vol. 34, no. 3, 1990, pp. 846–71.

Laver, Michael: "Government Termination," *Annual Review of Political Science,* vol. 6, 2003, pp. 23–40.

Laver, Michael: "Models of Government Formation," *Annual Review of Political Science,* vol. 1, 1998, pp. 1–25.

Laver, Michael: "Party Policy and Cabinet Portfolios in Ireland, 1992–93: Results from an Expert Survey," *Irish Political Studies,* vol. 9, 1994, pp. 157–64.

Laver, Michael, and W. B. Hunt: *Policy and Party Competition,* Routledge, New York, 1992.

Laver, Michael, and N. Schofield: *Multiparty Government: The Politics of Coalition in Western Europe,* University of Michigan Press, Ann Arbor, 1998.

Laver, Michael, and Kenneth A. Shepsle, "Events, Equilibria and Government Survival," *American Journal of Political Science,* vol. 42, 1998, 28–54.

Laver, Michael, and Kenneth A. Shepsle, *Making and Breaking Governments,* Cambridge University Press, New York, 1996.

Lijphart, Arend: *Patterns of Democracy: Government Forms and Performance in Thirty-Six Countries,* Yale University Press, New Haven, 1999.

Luebbert, G.: *Comparative Democracy: Policy Making and Governing Coalitions in Europe and Israel,* Columbia University Press, New York, 1986.

Lupia, Arthur, and Kaare Strøm: "Coalition Termination and the Strategic Timing of Elections," *American Political Science Review,* vol. 89, no. 3, 1995, pp. 648–65.

Martin, Lanny W., and Randolph T. Stevenson: "Government Formation in Parliamentary Democracies," *American Journal of Political Science,* vol. 45, no. 1, 2001, 33–50.

Mershon, Carol: "The Costs of Coalition: Coalition Theories and Italian Governments," *American Political Science Review,* vol. 90, no. 2, 1996, pp. 534–54.

Mershon Carol: "Party Factions and Coalition Government: Portfolio Allocation in Italian Christian Democracy," *Electoral Studies,* vol. 20, no. 4, 2001, pp. 509–27.

Müller-Rommel, Ferdinand, and Katja Fettelschoss: "Cabinet Government and Cabinet Ministers in Central Eastern European Democracies: A Descriptive Cross National Evaluation," Paper presented at ECPR Joint Sessions of Workshops, Uppsala, April 13–18, 2004.

Müller-Rommel, Ferdinand, Katja Fettelschoss, and Philipp Harfst: "Party Government in Central Eastern European Democracies: A Data Collection," *European Journal of Political Research* 43, 2004, pp. 869–93.

Müller, Wolfgang, and Kaare Strøm (eds.): *Policy, Office or Votes? How Political Parties Make Hard Choices,* Cambridge University Press, New York, 1999.

Napel, Stefan, and Mika Widgren: "Power Measurement as Sensitivity Analysis: A Unified Approach,"

Journal of Theoretical Politics, vol. 16, no. 4, 2004, pp. 517–38.

Narud, Hanne-Marthe: "Norway," *European Journal of Political Research,* vol. 34, 1998, pp. 485–92.

Nurmi, Hannu, and Tommy Meskanen: "A Priori Power Measures and the Institutions of the European Union," *European Journal of Political Research,* vol. 35, 1999, pp. 161–79.

Riker, W.: *The Theory of Political Coalitions,* Yale University Press, New Haven, 1962.

Schofield, Norman: "Coalition Politics: A Model and Analysis," *Journal of Theoretical Politics,* vol. 7, 1995, pp. 245–81.

Schofield, Norman: "Equilibrium in the Spatial 'Valence' Model of Politics," *Journal of Theoretical Politics,* vol. 16, no. 4, 2004, pp. 447–481.

Schofield, Norman: "Political Competition and Multiparty Coalition Governments," *European Journal of Political Research,* vol. 23, 1993, pp. 1–33.

Shabad, Goldie, and Kazimierz Slomczynski: "Inter-Party Mobility and Parliamentary Candidates in Post-Communist East Central Europe," *Party Politics,* vol. 10, no. 2, 2004, pp. 151–76.

Smith, Alastair: *Election Timing,* Cambridge University Press, Cambridge, 2004.

Strøm, Kaare: *Minority Government and Majority Rule,* Cambridge University Press, Cambridge, 1990.

Thies, Michael, "Keeping Tabs on Partners: The Logic of Delegation in Coalition Governments," *American Journal of Political Science,* vol. 45, no. 3, 2001, pp. 580–98.

Volden, Craig, and Clifford J. Carruba: "The Formation of Oversized Coalitions in Parliamentary Democracies," *American Journal of Political Science,* vol. 48, no. 3, 2004, pp. 261–77.

Warwick, Paul: *Government Survival in Parliamentary Democracies,* Cambridge University Press, Cambridge, 1994.

Woldendorp, Jaap, Hans Keman, and Ian Budge: "Party Government in 20 Democracies: An Update (1990–1995)," *European Journal of Political Research,* vol. 33, 1998, pp. 125–64.

Woldendorp, Jaap, et al.: *Party Government in 48 Democracies (1945–1998).* Kluwer, Dordrecht, 2000.

Ysmal, Colette: "France," *European Journal of Political Research,* vol. 34, 1998, pp. 393–403.

CHAPTER 13

Does Representative Government Make a Difference?

One of the main reasons why people are interested in politics at all is that they have a general sense that politics should, and indeed does, make a difference. In the context of European parliamentary democracy, this belief can be translated into a feeling that election results and government formation should, and indeed do, have an impact on how a country is run. Different election results and the formation of different governments should cause things to be done differently; otherwise, the whole edifice of representative government would be little more than a facade.

Some, however, argue that politics, at least national politics, is making less and less of a difference in an era when "globalization" increasingly constrains the freedom of governments to act independently and implement distinctive policy positions. Thus, as we said when discussing the role of the European Union, many aspects of economic policy that would once have been the exclusive preserve of national governments are now decided at the European level. A major example is evident in the creation of a common European currency, the euro (see Chapter 5). In exchange for the perceived benefits of a common currency, European governments within the eurozone have given up their traditional control over many of the traditional levers of macroeconomic policy making, forsaking many policy instruments that previously were central to how they ran their economies. Sharing a common currency removes all local freedom to set interest rates and print money. National governments in the eurozone can no longer try to cool down potentially inflationary booms by raising interest rates or choking off the money supply; they can no longer stimulate their local economies out of recessions by lowering interest rates. EU competition policy has also increasingly constrained governments in their ability to pump money into loss-making public enterprises if they choose to do so—a limitation that had a big impact on how governments could deal with ailing national airlines, for example, during the global turndown in the industry after the 9/11 terrorist attacks on the United States. This constraint accompanies the general development of a world economy characterized by increasingly free and rapid movements of capital that make it ever harder for any national government to buck world trends. In the face of all this, it might seem that most European governments are far less free these days to do what they want to do. As a consequence, it might also seem that the scope for *national* politics to make a difference is far narrower than it used to be.

These developments must be set in a social context in which, even in an era of rapidly expanding international travel, most people in most countries are not very mobile. The vast majority of European populations are born, live, love, work, and die in a single country, speak a native language that differs from that of people in other countries, define themselves in large part as "German," "French," "Hungarian," "Italian," "Greek," and so on, and do not expect things to be any different. Land is not mobile. Housing is not mobile. Hospitals, schools, roads, railway lines, airports, police, and fire stations are not mobile. For the most part, labor is not very mobile. Social values may be changing, but there are still very wide variations across countries in attitudes toward abortion, euthanasia, single-parent families, the role of women in the workplace, and many other matters besides. Even in the area of socioeconomic policy, different core values translate into the very different welfare systems found in different European countries. The net result is that even if some of the key levers of macroeconomic policy have indeed been pried from the hands of European governments, the big public policy differences that still exist between states, and the big public policy shifts sometimes observed within states, imply that representative government still does make a difference. (Schmidt and Garrett both provide excellent discussions of this debate.)

Nowhere can the relevance of representative government be seen more clearly than in the transitions from communism experienced by central and eastern European states. Indeed, before this process took hold, a truly striking manifestation of how politics makes a difference could be seen by everyone crossing "Checkpoint Charlie" between what used to be West and East Berlin, the two parts of the same city operating under quite different political systems. Money had to be changed, passports had to be stamped, and the very look of the two places—one with a huge amount of brash advertising, one with none—was quite different. In a very short period of time at the end of the 1980s, as a result of radical political developments in all central and eastern European countries formerly under Soviet influence, everything changed very quickly. Berlin was reunited and what had been East Germany joined the Federal Republic of Germany. Estonia, Latvia, and Lithuania broke away from the Soviet Union, which itself imploded. The former Yugoslav federation disintegrated and its constituent parts descended into bitter civil war. Throughout eastern Europe, a massive program to privatize state assets was set in motion and the economic environment was radically transformed. Later in this chapter, we return in more detail to some of these developments, but the main point to be made here is that events in eastern Europe have reminded us in no uncertain terms that politics really can make a huge difference when it comes to the big things. (For a review of postcommunist transitions in politics and property ownership, see Stark and Bruszt.) It is difficult now to think ourselves back into the Cold War mind-set in which the radically different political environments of different parts of Europe appeared to be stable and unchanging facts of life. When we might be tempted to think that politics these days does not make much of a difference, it is salutary to recall that the map of Europe could be so dramatically redrawn—as a result of political developments, not military conquest—in the space of just five years.

The short answer to the question "Does politics make a difference?" is self-evidently "Yes, it does!" We need look no further than the transformation of central and eastern Europe and the creation of the euro to see this difference very clearly. The story does not end here, however. Turning to what happens inside individual countries with more or less stable political systems, we are also interested in whether the ebb and flow of representative government make a difference to the formation and implementation of public policy—with whether the wishes of voters are ultimately transformed into something that actually happens. This question, difficult to answer systematically, presents us with an almost impossible intellectual task. To assess the impact of any given government, we need to know *what would have happened if a different government had been running the country in its place.*

The need to face up to that task is common to all policy evaluations in both the public and the private sectors. Thus, to come to a view on whether the effective decriminalization of soft drugs in Amsterdam has increased or reduced the use of hard drugs in the city, we need to know how many people in Amsterdam would have been using heroin if the Dutch police had adopted a much tougher policy on marijuana. We will never really know what would have happened in this "counterfactual" situation, but we can make educated guesses on the basis of careful research. The fact that it is in theory impossible to get a perfect answer to such a question does not mean that in practice we cannot get any answer at all—indeed it would be simply negligent to throw up our hands and abandon the effort. Furthermore, although it can be difficult to decide whether a particular government did make a difference to a particular policy area on a particular occasion, an accumulating collection of comparative studies does throw considerable light on whether representative government, in general, does make a broad difference to the real world of public policy.

Researchers who have tackled this problem have approached it from several different directions. Perhaps the most traditional approach has been to develop case studies of major government policy interventions, such as the comprehensive program of privatizing state assets pioneered by British Conservative governments during the 1980s and taken up with gusto in eastern Europe over the following decade. The logic of such studies is quite straightforward. A government launches a dramatic policy initiative with the intention of bringing about a major change. If the intended change does in fact occur, we conclude that the policy initiative was the cause of it. In effect, we assume that the world would not have changed in the same way without the policy initiative. When changes of direction are really dramatic, as with the privatization programs that we consider later in this chapter, then this logic seems plausible.

Such dramatic changes, of course, are rather rare in European politics. We must look elsewhere if we wish to find systematic evidence that the normal processes of representative government do in general make a difference. A second approach has been to compare what government parties promised voters during the previous election campaign with what they set out to do once installed in office. During election campaigns, of course, parties are trying to get as many votes as possible and may pitch their policy promises to maximize their electoral advantage. If politics makes a difference, however, policy promises made during election campaigns should have an impact on the policies of the governments that follow. We can see whether they do by comparing pledges made by the winning party or parties when trying to woo voters during the election campaign with what policies the same, victorious parties say they will implement.

A third strategy for determining whether representative government makes a difference is to look at the actual fulfillment by governments of campaign pledges and party programs. The theory of representative government, after all, is based on the premise that at least some of the pledges made to voters at election time are actually redeemed. Evidence about pledge fulfillment, however, is especially skimpy, for a number of reasons. Often a campaign pledge is so vague that it can be almost impossible to decide whether it has been fulfilled. Some pledges, furthermore, are not fulfilled for reasons that are quite beyond the control of the government. A flood or an earthquake may strike without warning, destroying a communications infrastructure that the government had promised to improve. A stock market crash in Hong Kong, Tokyo, or New York may leave a government's economic policy promises in tatters. Some other critical event completely outside the control of politicians may fundamentally change the political universe. Nevertheless, although it is no easy task to define the set of campaign pledges that in practice could have been redeemed but were not, some progress has been made on this in recent years.

A fourth strategy for investigating the impact of politics on public policy is to look at patterns of public spending. Of course, some of the most important policy decisions to face postwar Europe have been only vaguely related to public spending. These decisions have pertained to matters of social policy, such as dealing with the AIDS pandemic, capital punishment, and race relations; matters of economic management, such as deregulation and free trade; and matters of foreign policy, including wars in Bosnia, Kosovo, Afghanistan, and Iraq, and the enlargement and future constitution of the European Union (EU). On top of this, patterns of public spending are very "sticky" in the sense that much of the public money that is spent—on education, pensions, and welfare, for example—is committed over a very long term. Such patterns can be changed only very slowly.

Furthermore, many of the changes in spending patterns that we do observe are the result of changes in the size of various "client" groups—such as the young, the old, and the unemployed—and are certainly not the result of conscious spending decisions by the government. There is considerable variation in the proportion of the population in each country that is of school or retirement age, for example, and public spending on schools and pensions is likely to vary between countries for this reason alone. The age structure of the population, rather than anything to do with public policy, may explain this difference. A more striking example concerns public spending on unemployment assistance. Governments that set out to cut public spending and privatize state assets, as many eastern European governments did during the 1990s, often increase unemployment in the process, at least in the short run. They certainly do not set out to increase public spending on unemployment assistance; such an increase is the unsought consequence of policy changes in other areas.

Notwithstanding these important complications, parties often promise voters that, if elected, they will make dramatic policy changes with a significant impact on the direction and flow of public spending. Furthermore, the allocation of public spending between different policy areas is a very visible indicator of government policy, one that can reflect an explicit set of priorities that has been vigorously argued over and eventually decided at the cabinet table. This allows us to infer that, if representative government does indeed make a difference, then different types of government should be associated with different patterns of public spending. In particular, we might expect changes in government to be associated with changes in public spending flows.

A fifth strategy for determining whether politics makes a difference involves looking over a long time period at large-scale macroeconomic variables such as the overall size of the public sector and the extent of the welfare system. If representative government does make a difference, then different types of party systems should be associated with major differences in key macroeconomic variables.

In the rest of this chapter we examine these five general ways of looking at how representative government might make a difference. At the end of it all we still cannot get around the fact that we have no way of knowing what would have happened in a particular country if the particular government for a particular period had been different. But the accumulated weight of evidence we assemble by the end of this chapter, on the basis of the five different approaches we explore, leaves us in little doubt that representative government in modern Europe does make at least some difference in what goes on in the real world.

✦ CLEAR-CUT CASES OF POLICY IMPACT

The Privatization of State Assets in Britain and Eastern Europe

Large-scale privatization reached a spectacular climax with the massive privatizations of state assets in eastern European countries as part of their transitions from communist government, but the onset of such policies in Europe can be seen in the policies and subsequent actions of the British Conservative Party under Margaret Thatcher. The British privatization program of the 1980s, "rightly seen as one of the most extensive anywhere in the world" (Feigenbaum, Henig, and Hamnett, p. 60), gives us a neat example of a clear-cut discontinuity between the actions of an incoming government and the actions of its predecessor, even though the Conservative government that took office following the 1979 election had not fought this election on the basis of a comprehensive set of manifesto commitments on privatization, which had been only a "minor theme" in the campaign (Heald, p. 32). Indeed a number of the privatizations that followed this election—including those of both Cable and Wireless, and Britoil—had not been mentioned at all in the Conservative manifesto. The process of privatizing state assets in Britain started slowly, with the denationalization of a series of profitable companies, such as British Aerospace and Britoil, that were easy to sell at discounted flotation prices in a robust bull market. At the same time the Conservative government introduced an ambitious program of selling a large proportion of the existing stock of rented public housing to its occupants.

Once the program of privatization began, however, it rapidly acquired momentum and probably went farther than the Conservatives themselves had initially envisaged (Kavanagh, p. 221). The success of early privatizations fed back into Conservative policy and encouraged the party to boost the role given to privatization in the party manifesto. Thus, the 1983 election was fought and won by the Conservatives on the basis of a much more ambitious privatization program. Soon afterward, the Conservative government privatized a series of massive public companies such as British Telecom, British Steel, the British Airports Authority, British Airways, Rolls-Royce, and the Rover group. The government also sold off enterprises that had previously been thought of as "untouchable"—basic services and natural monopolies such as electricity, gas, and water services. Within seven years, about fifty state corporations—about half of the total state sector—was sold to private investors. The shareholding population in Britain increased threefold to almost 10 million people, and many billions of pounds sterling were raised for the government by asset sales. It is estimated that by 1992 total privatization proceeds in Britain totaled 12 percent of British GDP (Boix, p. 86). (Boix provides a wide-ranging review of the economic policies associated with this era of Conservative government in Britain. Feigenbaum, Henig, and Hamnet [pp. 59–86] provide an extensive discussion of the Conservatives' privatization programs.) By any account, the privatization program of successive Conservative governments in Britain involved a massive partisan redirection of public policy that would not have taken place under most conceivable alternative administrations. Representative government, without any doubt at all, made a big difference in this case. (For a general comparative discussion of major shifts in policy regimes, see Notermans.)

If what happened in Britain during the 1980s was big, what happened in eastern Europe during the 1990s was an order of magnitude bigger. We obviously do not have space here to do justice to the huge subject of the privatization of state assets in eastern Europe during the transition from communism, but the general patterns that we can observe to some extent speak for themselves. (For an extended discussion of privatization programs in four postcommunist countries—the Czech Republic, Hungary, Poland, and the former East Germany—see Stark and Bruzst.) What is striking about these huge eastern European privatization programs is that although they present intellectual challenges of almost mind-boggling complexity, they were all achieved very quickly by the political system. In each case, the main political challenges in these countries were to establish stable political institutions. Discussions of the specifics of privatization policy, though obviously central to these transitions from communism, played second fiddle to the main political imperative.

As Stark and Bruszt (p. 84) point out, postcommunist privatization policy had to confront three big issues. The first issue concerned the selection and valuation of the state assets to be disposed of. In setting a value on the assets selected for privatization, the main choice was between having the assets valued by bureaucrats or letting the market decide. The second issue concerned who would be entitled to acquire these assets. Here, the big decision was between giving individual citizens or private corporations, first call on the assets being disposed of. The third issue concerned the resources that could be used to acquire the assets. The obvious resource is money, but citizens of the transition states tended to have very little money and would have been unable to compete against the resources available in international capital markets. The alternative was to give priority to people in particular *positions*—such workers and managers in the enterprises concerned.

Politicians of different political stripes, in different eastern European countries, came to different conclusions about these important policy dilemmas. In the Czech Republic, a primary objective was to get shares in state enterprises into the hands of private citizens as fast as possible, after which the shares could be traded and market forces would determine at least their "price," if not their "value." All adult citizens were given a fixed set of "investment vouchers," for which they had to pay a registration fee; the vouchers could be exchanged for shares in companies being privatized. Risk-averse citizens could put all their vouchers into safe and stable companies, which would command a high price in vouchers; others might prefer to "invest" their limited stock of vouchers in more risky companies offering lower "priced" shares with potentially greater returns but a higher risk of failure. Poland also adopted a version of the voucher system. Hungary took a different route, in general giving much more of a role in the privatization process to the managers and employees of the enterprises concerned (see Stark and Bruszt for more details). The different trajectories of privatization programs in the eastern European countries show us that although the privatization of state assets was an obvious common priority for many postcommunist regimes, and while there were significant differences in how this was achieved, we observe huge changes in privatization policy that would have been inconceivable under previous political arrangements. Politics made a very big difference in these cases.

The Withdrawal of Spanish Troops from Iraq

Despite the desire of many senior European politicians for a common European foreign policy, foreign policy remains one area in which individual European governments can make a big difference. This was clearly illustrated in the variegated responses of different European governments in 2003 to the U.S.-led military intervention in Iraq. Some major western European governments—Britain, Spain, and Italy, for example—were staunch allies of the United States. Others—notably France and Germany—were far more skeptical. There was no common European position on this vital foreign policy issue. But events that unfolded in Spain after March 11, 2004, show that the process of representative government can make a big difference to the foreign policy positions of a single state.

March 11 was a Thursday, and Spain was in the final stages of an election campaign with voting due at the weekend. That morning, commuter trains pulled into the main Madrid rail station loaded with passengers and carrying bombs hidden by terrorists that were primed to go off causing maximum damage when the trains arrived at their platforms. There was a shocking toll of death and serious injury. José Aznar's conservative government, one of U.S. president George W. Bush's strongest European supporters on Iraq, implausibly blamed Basque separatists for the atrocity. This accusation was widely perceived as an attempt to sway the election in the government's favor, since any implication that the bombing was the act of Islamic terrorists (evidence for which was already in the hands of Spain's security services) could have resulted in voters punishing Aznar for sending a sizable contingent of Spanish troops to Iraq. The elections were not postponed, and voting went ahead in a hothouse atmosphere. The result was the defeat of the Aznar government and a surprise victory for the Socialist opposition, led by José Zapatero. The Socialists had campaigned against Spanish intervention in Iraq, and immediately after taking office, Zapatero announced that all Spanish troops would be withdrawn as soon as possible from Iraqi soil. They were home in Spain within weeks.

We will never know for certain whether the Madrid bombing or Aznar's fumbled attempt to shift the blame for it to the Basques changed the way people voted in the 2004 election in Spain. What is certain, however, is that Spanish voters voted to change their government; that they elected a party hostile to the outgoing government's policy of Spanish involvement in Iraq; that Spanish withdrawal from Iraq was announced immediately after the election; and that this withdrawal actually did take place shortly afterward. In this case, therefore, we see a textbook example of representative government in action.

In general, however, things are rarely so clear-cut when it comes to foreign policy, mainly because foreign policy is rarely at the top of the campaign agenda in general elections in modern Europe. Thus Tony Blair, as Bush's most steadfast ally, in 2003 committed Britain to a war and ongoing military engagement in Iraq in which British troops died, despite the fact that this was in no sense an issue considered by voters during the preceding election, held in 2001, and despite the very vocal opposition of many Labour supporters. Of course we do not know what British voters would have decided if they had been asked about Iraq. What we do know is that they were not asked. More generally we also know that, in anything other than exceptional times, it is rare to observe what governments do in the realm of foreign policy being influenced by the processes of representative government. The reason for this lack of influence has more to do with the fact that foreign policy dilemmas rarely become campaign issues than it does with governments' ignoring the wishes of the electorate on these matters.

→ PARTY MANIFESTOS AND GOVERNMENT POLICY PROGRAMS

The idea that what governments do is affected by which parties get into office is what makes sense of the notion of representative democracy. If government policy does not respond to the intentions of elected government members, then why have elections in the first place? We just provided some dramatic examples of cases in which almost everyone would agree that representative government made a big difference. In the contrast of the day-to-day ebb and flow of public decision making, however, what is much more difficult to establish is how far we can generalize from this experience.

The first step along the rocky road from what is promised at election time to what is actually done by governments in office is to compare parties' election manifestos with the policy positions of the governments they join. Policy positions are recorded in the official policy programs typically published by newly formed governments as part of the investiture process, and in the formal statements of official government policy typically issued at the beginning of each new session of parliament. A key area of party policy in modern Europe, for example, is the running of the economy. This topic, of course, generates many policy problems related to unemployment, inflation, exchange rates, investment, government spending, and so on. One general set of policy prescriptions for these matters can be characterized as the promotion of "free-market economics" through the encouragement of private enterprise, private incentive structures, free trade, balanced budgets, and general economic orthodoxy, together with opposition to the expansion of the welfare state.

A group of researchers in the Comparative Manifestos Project (CMP) systematically analyzed party manifestos and government declarations in many countries over the entire postwar period, assessing the relative emphasis that each policy document gives to free-market economics, for example, as well as to many other themes. (For a description of the work of the CMP, and a huge amount of data on party policy positions in many European countries, see Budge et al., *Ideology;* Budge et al., *Mapping.*) To compare what *parties* promise voters they will do with what *governments* containing those same parties promise to do having taken power, we can conduct a content analysis of party manifestos and compare the results with a content analysis of government policy declarations. A collection of analyses making precisely these comparisons can be found in Laver and Budge.

The general pattern of these analyses is reasonably clear. There is a group of countries—for example, Norway and Denmark—in which there has typically been a clear-cut alternation of power between coalitions or single-party governments of the center–left and coalitions of the center–right. In such countries, there is little overlap between the parties in cabinets of the center–left and those in cabinets of the center–right. And in such countries, we do tend to see significant shifts in the ideological complexion of government policy declarations, depending on which parties are in power. In these cases, it is relatively easy to infer the party composition of a government just by looking at the government's published policies, and we may say that the partisan composition of the cabinet clearly does make a difference to government policy.

There are other countries—Italy before 1994 or Germany before 1998, for example— in which a single party with a changing set of coalition partners was a more or less permanent fixture of government. The alternation of government parties between elections has typically also only been partial in a number of other European countries—such as the Netherlands, Luxembourg, and Austria. When comparing party manifestos with government policy declarations in these cases, we should not be surprised to find that the more limited the turnover in the partisan composition of the government is, the more difficult it is to track the changing substance of government policy declarations. And that is exactly what the CMP researchers found: Adding and subtracting parties from the cabinet makes less of a difference to government policy when a single party remains in office for a long period, than it does when all government parties tend to change from election to election.

Overall, therefore, the rather limited evidence available—systematic patterns have yet to be established for eastern Europe—suggests that parties do make a difference to the published policy programs of European governments. Not surprisingly, this pattern is far more clear-cut when the entire party membership of the cabinet is likely to change from one government to the next.

✦ REDEEMING CAMPAIGN PLEDGES

It is one thing for a party that has just formed a government to announce that it is going to redeem a particular election pledge. It is quite another thing actually to do so. The next major step on the path that takes us from the promises made by politicians in the excitement of an election campaign to what actually happens in the real world is the redeeming of campaign pledges. Before we can get down to the systematic analysis of this matter, however, we must deal with a number of tricky methodological problems.

First, we must decide in a systematic way what is a genuine pledge to voters and what is a piece of typical campaign rhetoric and hyperbole that no sensible person would take seriously. This distinction, of course, is highly subjective. It has to do with how specific the promise is, with how literally it is intended to be taken by those who hear it, and with whether a campaign pledge proposes real actions or merely expresses pious hopes. Thus, promises to "make this great country of ours a better place to live in" or to "banish hunger and poverty from the face of the earth" ought not to be seen as campaign "pledges" in any real sense of the word. They are either too vague to be taken seriously or no more than general aspirations. In contrast, a promise to "increase old age pensions by ten percent over the next two years" is an explicit statement about something within the competence of any government, for which the person making the pledge can be held to account.

Second, we must decide who is to blame when campaign pledges are not redeemed. Has the politician who promised to double the rate of economic growth broken that pledge to voters if he or she tries as hard as possible but fails? Has that politician broken the pledge if he or she doesn't try at all? Has the pledge been broken if the politician doesn't try very hard? If we are going to excuse pledges that are thwarted for reasons beyond the control of the person who makes them, someone will have to keep score, pledge by pledge, on who was to blame for the breaking of each.

A third problem relates to the business of giving credit for pledges that do indeed appear to have been redeemed. After all, if a politician promises that the sun will rise tomorrow and it does, is it sensible to give any credit for having redeemed this promise? Finally, there is the problem that many campaign pledges tend to be carried out a little bit; few are enacted in their full splendor. A little progress may be made on cutting public spending or reforming the tax system, for example. Unemployment may be reduced somewhat, quite possibly not thanks to the government of the day. Once more, to classify these as pledges broken or as pledges fulfilled is a matter of highly subjective judgment.

There are no easy answers to these problems. The solution adopted by most of the people doing empirical research on the redemption of campaign pledges in Europe is to agonize a little about the types of problems outlined above and then just get down to work and do the best they can. It is difficult to see what else can be done.

Much of the early work on the fulfillment of campaign pledges in Europe related to Britain. The first detailed study was conducted by Richard Rose, who compared the record of redeemed pledges for the 1970–74 Conservative government with the record for the 1974–79 Labour government (Rose, pp. 55–73). His conclusion, confounding the skeptics, was that manifesto pledges do make a difference, that "Conservative and Labour governments act consistently with the Manifesto model of governing; in office they do the majority of things to which they pledge themselves" (Rose, p. 64). The skeptics might retort that this conclusion is a product of an exclusive concentration on manifesto pledges that Rose deems "doable." This problem is compounded by the fact that one of the reasons why the record of these parties seems so good is that they promise many things that are straightforward and uncontroversial. Rose finds that about half of all pledges are nonpartisan, representing a consensus between the parties (Rose, p. 69). Such pledges are easy to make and are much easier to carry out than others. Whether we should set much store by them when trying to decide whether politicians keep their promises is another matter.

Rallings applied the general features of Rose's analysis to the period from 1945 to 1979 in Britain and came up with similar conclusions. He found that about 70 percent of all manifesto pledges were implemented, though some types were much more likely to be implemented than others: "Clear promises to increase pensions and other benefits (often by a named amount) and to repeal ideologically unacceptable legislation passed by the previous administration, are almost invariably kept. … The pledges least likely to be fulfilled are the small minority where the government cannot ensure their passage or which involve the expenditure of large amounts of public money on electorally unappealing and/or low priority projects" (Rallings, p. 13). This approach has also been applied to analyze the record of the PASOK (Socialist) government in Greece from 1981 to 1985, and once more a pledge fulfillment rate of about 70 percent was found (Kalogeropoulou, p. 293).

Terry Royed extended this work to a comprehensive comparative evaluation of the role of campaign pledges in Britain and the United States, looking at the relative rates of fulfillment of pledges made by government and opposition parties. Using a more precise definition of "campaign pledge" than earlier authors, she found that over 80 percent of pledges made in Conservative election manifestos were enacted by the Conservative governments of 1979–83 and 1983–87—a significantly higher rate than was found in the United States. The high rate of pledge fulfillment by the government party in Britain compares with a much lower rate for the opposition party. (Opposition party pledges may be enacted if the opposition made the same promises as those made by the parties that go into government.) In fact, when government and opposition disagreed in Britain, Royed found that the opposition had almost zero chance of seeing its pledges enacted (Royed).

Most of the research on the fulfillment of campaign pledges has been conducted in countries where one-party government is the norm, but Thomson investigated the fulfillment of campaign pledges in the Dutch coalition system during the 1980s and 1990s. The expectation in a coalition system is that fewer pledges will be fulfilled because of the policy compromises between parties that must be made in order to form a government. Not only must some pledges be dropped to achieve a compromise, but the subsequent need to do deals with other parties also provides a ready-made excuse for the nonfulfillment of campaign pledges. Using comparable definitions of "pledge" in the Netherlands and Britain, Thomson found pledge fulfillment rates of close to 80 percent in Britain and of about 50 percent, or even less, in the Netherlands. He quite firmly concluded that "[p]ledges made by parties that go on to form Dutch governments are significantly less likely to be acted upon than those made by parties that form single-party governments in the United Kingdom" (Thomson, p. 202).

Coalition systems create a more complex environment for the fulfillment of campaign pledges than the environment created by single-party governments, and Thomson's work throws some useful light on this. He found, for example, that campaign pledges are significantly more likely to be enacted if the party that made them controls the cabinet ministry with jurisdiction over the policy area in question. He found that pledges are significantly more likely to be enacted once they have found their way into the formal agreement signed between the government parties. And he found that pledges are significantly more likely to be enacted if they represent a consensus between the government parties. When a single party controls all cabinet seats, these issues do not arise. When power is shared between parties, Thomson's work on the Netherlands suggests, the level of consensus between cabinet partners, the specific policy agreement between them, and the allocation of cabinet portfolios to different parties, all have an important bearing on the redemption by parties of pledges made during election campaigns.

Taken overall, the research that has been conducted to date—and again there is as yet no systematic body of evidence on pledge fulfillment in eastern Europe—does suggest that parties honor more of their campaign pledges than skeptics, rivals, and journalists typically give them credit for. This finding may, in part, be an artifact of the data, arising because researchers regard as firm pledges only proposals that can be carried out. It may also be a product of real-world party competition, if parties tend to promise a lot of easy and uncontroversial things so that they can go back to the voters and boast about how they fulfilled most of their promises. Parties may anticipate all the easy things that they can actually deliver and make a great song and dance at election time about promising to deliver them. Notwithstanding these reservations, however, the growing body of work on this topic suggests that parties do redeem campaign pledges to a greater degree than many cynics previously thought, and that representative government does make a difference in this particular sense.

✦ Party Government and Public Spending

When public policy has a bearing on patterns of public spending, we can find at least one concrete indicator of what the government is actually doing. If a promise is made to do something that involves public spending—to build more schools, for example— then we can see whether or not spending on school construction does in fact increase.

Patterns in the flow of public expenditure, and the links between these patterns and the partisan composition of the government, have been the subject of an increasing body of academic research. The problem has been approached from two basic perspectives. The first is to look at different countries in the same time period in order to establish whether countries with particular types of government have particular types of public spending patterns. The second is to look at the same country in different time periods in order to establish whether changes in spending patterns can be traced to changes in government.

Differences Between Countries

The basic patterns of public spending in modern western European states can be seen in Table 13.1. The first two columns of data give alternative indicators of the average ideological complexion of each European country's governments over the fifty-year era following the Second World War. The first column gives the average share of cabinet seats controlled by social democratic and other left-wing parties over the period. The second column reports an index of the average ideological complexion of the government. This index would score 1.0 if a country was governed by a right-dominated government for the entire period, 5.0 if it was governed by a left-dominated government for the entire period. Countries are ranked in the table according to the average ideological complexion of their governments. Ireland experienced the lowest incidence of left-wing parties in government over this postwar era, Norway and Sweden the highest.

The third column of data in Table 13.1 shows total public spending in each country, expressed as a percentage of the overall gross domestic product (GDP), averaged over the decade 1996–2005 (that is, over the decade immediately following the era for which we have established the "left-wingness" or "right-wingness" of governments in

TABLE 13.1

Relationship Between the Long-Term Ideological Complexion of Government and Government Spending

Country	% of Cabinet Seats Controlled by Social Democrats and Other Left-Wing Parties, 1950–94	Mean Left Score of Government, 1945–95	Total Government Outlays as Percentage of GDP, 1996–2005	Public Social Expenditure as Percentage of GDP, 1995–98
Western Europe				
Portugal	5.7	n.a.	45.9	17.9
Ireland	9.7	1.5	35.2	17.8
Italy	12.4	1.6	49.3	24.5
Netherlands	18.6	2.0	47.5	25.0
Greece	19.7	n.a.	47.8	21.9
Switzerland	23.8	1.9	n.a.	27.6
France	24.5	2.0	53.8	29.1
Germany	24.8	2.0	48.4	27.4
Spain	26.0	n.a.	40.5	20.4
Belgium	27.6	2.3	50.6	24.8
United Kingdom	28.1	2.3	41.0	25.4
Luxembourg	28.4	2.1	43.5	22.8
Iceland	31.7	2.3	44.4	18.4
Finland	33.6	2.8	52.1	29.4
Denmark	50.7	3.0	56.4	31.1
Austria	60.7	3.4	52.6	27.4
Norway	73.1	4.0	47.4	26.8
Sweden	76.3	4.1	59.6	32.3
Correlation with left cabinet seats			.56	.63
Eastern Europe				
Czech Republic			47.7	19.0
Hungary			50.9	n.a.
Poland			46.4	24.2
Slovakia			55.0	13.4

Sources: Cabinet seat share for left: Schmidt, p. 160. Scores for Greece, Portugal, and Spain recalculated to cover the entire postwar period. Left scores: Woldendorp, Keman, and Budge. Public spending data: OECD.

the countries concerned). The data indicate that government spending, as a percentage of GDP, does tend to be higher in those countries—such as Finland, Denmark, Austria, and Sweden—that have a long history of left-wing participation in government. Conversely, where there was extensive right-wing participation in government, as in Ireland, the proportion of GDP devoted to public spending tends to be low. There are, however, some striking exceptions. France, for example, and to a lesser extent Italy, experienced considerable right-wing participation in government during the postwar period yet had relatively high levels of public spending.

Overall public expenditure, of course, covers a multitude of sins, from welfare schemes to weapons of mass destruction, from schools to pensions to prisons. It might well be argued that the general level of public spending in a given country conceals as much as it throws light on. For this reason, the final column of data in Table 13.1 shows the level of government social expenditure on matters such as social welfare, pensions, education, and housing. The figures do show more or less the same pattern as the figures for overall government spending. Countries—such as Ireland, Portugal, and Greece—that tended to have right-wing governments also had distinctly lower levels of public expenditure. Austria and the Scandinavian countries, which tended to have more left-wing participation in government, are at the other end of the social expenditure scale. The correlations between the rate of left-wing participation in government, and the two measures of the level of public spending are also given in Table 13.1. These correlations show that there is indeed a systematic pattern to be observed: higher levels of public spending arising in countries with a tradition of left-wing government.

The bottom rows of Table 13.1 give the limited information that is available for a number of eastern European countries. It is not yet possible to provide equivalent systematic estimates of long-term trends in the ideological composition of eastern European governments coming out of the long postwar period of communist government. What we can say is that these countries are very much on a par with western European fellow members of the EU in overall government spending as a proportion of GDP and, perhaps surprisingly, at the low end of the spectrum when it comes to public social expenditure. It is dangerous to draw firm conclusions from these early data on eastern Europe. What Table 13.1 does tell us, however, is that, taking the broad view, variations between countries in levels of public spending are indeed related to variations in the long-term ideological complexion of those same countries' governments. In this particular sense, therefore, representative government does seem to make a difference. (For an extended discussion and empirical analysis of this argument, see Garrett.)

Differences Within Countries

One way to look for evidence of whether governments make a difference is to look at whether changes in the parties of government in a given country tend to be associated with changing patterns of public spending. Research on this matter must take into account the fact that patterns of public spending can be shifted only a little bit from one year to the next. Governments can in practice have an impact on spending patterns only at the margin, controlling year-to-year changes in spending flows much more than they control the overall scale of spending. The actual level of welfare or defense spending, for example, might be much higher in one country than in another not because of the current political situation but as a result of the interplay of a complex set of historical and structural factors. What an incoming government can do in the short and medium run is to cut or boost welfare or defense spending. But even savage cuts and generous boosts do not, unless they are repeated year after year, have a huge impact on the overall level of spending in these areas.

Manfred Schmidt tackled this problem by analyzing the year-by-year changes in government spending in a wide range of countries and relating these data to the partisan composition of the cabinet, controlling for important economic variables such as the growth rate and changes in the level of unemployment. He found quite clear evidence that having left or center–right parties in office contributed to annual increases in the level of government spending, and having a right-wing party in government contributed to decreases. His conclusion was that "social democracy and Christian democracy have been major political 'engines' in the growth of government. … [I]n contrast to this, conservative parties have been major inhibitors of the growth of government in modern democracies" (Schmidt, p. 177).

Looking further into the relationship between partisan control of the government and public spending, Andre Blais and his colleagues found that the majority status of the government was an important factor. First, they found that "parties do not make a difference when the government is a minority one" (Blais et al., p. 55). This is not surprising, given our discussion of minority governments in Chapter 12. Minority governments typically can remain in place because they are at the center of the political spectrum and opposition to them is divided. In a sense, they can govern precisely because they do not make a difference in the sense of imposing their will over the will of a majority of the legislature. As soon as a minority government begins to implement distinctive policies, it is liable to be defeated. In contrast, Blais et al. found, majority governments controlled exclusively by the left did increase overall public spending by a small but significant amount, relative to majority governments controlled exclusively by the right. As might be expected, the difference between left- and right-wing governments is greater for governments that have held office for five years or more. Thus, considering the overall size of the public sector, Blais and his colleagues concluded that "governments of the left spend a little more than governments of the right. Parties do make a difference, but a small one. That difference, moreover, is confined to majority governments and takes time to set in" (Blais et al., p. 57).

Hicks and Swank found that the partisan composition of the *opposition* can make a difference to public policy. Thus, a left-wing government facing a numerically strong right-wing opposition tends to spend less on welfare than one facing a weaker right-wing opposition. Hicks and Swank called this phenomenon an "embourgeoisement" of the left party. Conversely, a right-wing government facing a numerically strong left-wing opposition tends to spend more on welfare than one that does not. They called this phenomenon "contagion from the left," and Petry provided further evidence of it for a number of different spending areas in the specific case of the French Fifth Republic.

As Margaret Thatcher found in Britain, massive efforts of political will are needed to produce modest effects on public spending. It is not surprising, therefore, that we do not find public spending patterns changing dramatically with every change in government. In general, however, the accumulating evidence does suggest that parties do make a difference to patterns of public spending. The overall effects that we can observe on public spending are small, but if we focus on particular spending areas or on the impact of long-serving single-party governments, the impact of parties on public spending becomes easier to see. If we look carefully and know what we are looking for, we should indeed be able to detect a change in the party composition of governments by examining patterns of public spending—our acid test of whether representative government does make a difference.

→ BEYOND PUBLIC SPENDING

There is, of course, much more to public policy than government spending patterns. Even in the realm of economic management, governments must have policies on matters such as industrial relations and income inequality, for example.

The extent of political control over national European labor markets is elaborated by Armingeon, who argued that the key precondition for political control of labor markets is the combination of a strong labor movement and a powerful social democratic party. One or the other acting alone does not seem to be enough to make a real difference (Armingeon, p. 234). But a strong social democratic party together with a strong union movement fosters the development of policies on wage restraint, employment, the "social wage," and the role of trade unions. In countries such as Austria, Belgium, Denmark, Finland, Germany, and Sweden, where the connection between the social democratic party and trade unions is strong, changes in the government are associated with changes in the effective political control of wages. In Sweden, for example, the social democratic–trade union nexus was strong for much of the postwar era, though it weakened significantly in the 1990s. Political control of wages in Sweden has tended to be high relative to that in other countries, although there has not been enough alternation in government to allow the impact of changes in party control of government to be estimated. In Britain, France, and Italy, the social democratic–trade union nexus is much weaker, and political control of wages is much less obvious.

Given that, if they choose to do so, governments can attempt to modify the distribution of both wealth and income by means of the welfare and tax systems, it is interesting to explore the impact of parties on income redistribution. Trade unions can have the greatest impact on gross income. Governments can have the greatest impact on net income, which reflects how actual take-home pay is affected by taxes and by transfer payments in the social welfare system. The bigger the change in inequality between gross and net income, the greater is the impact of public policy.

E. N. Muller conducted an extensive comparative analysis of the impact of politics on income distribution. Controlling for a wide range of factors and analyzing data from a long list of countries, he concluded confidently that politics makes a considerable difference to income redistribution. According to Muller's empirical findings, socialist governmental strength depresses the income share going to the richest 20 percent of the population and narrows the income gap between the richest and the poorest 20 percent, and conservative governmental strength increases the income share going to the richest 20 percent and widens the income gap between the richest and the middle income groups (Muller, p. 394). Muller reported that the negative impact of conservative parties on income equality is greater than the positive impact of socialist parties, and he concluded, quite unequivocally, that "most of the cross-national variation [in income inequality] is explained by the inegalitarian influence of strong conservative parties" (p. 396).

Turning to inflation and unemployment, we find further evidence of the policy impact of government composition. Warwick found that the average monthly increase in unemployment was noticeably smaller under left-wing governments than under bourgeois governments or those that "mixed" right and left. Conversely, he found that the average monthly level of inflation was higher under left-wing governments and lower under bourgeois or mixed governments. This pattern of party effects on inflation was strongly confirmed by Suzuki: Left-wing governments tend to deliver lower unemployment and higher inflation, and right-wing governments tend to deliver lower inflation and higher unemployment. According to these findings at least, governments that mix right and left tend to deliver the worst of both worlds: higher unemployment as well as higher inflation. Thus we can extend our conclusions based on patterns of public spending to economic policy more generally. Most of the research that has been done to date does imply that politics makes a difference.

Allan and Scruggs recently analyzed the relationship between the partisan composition of the government and two significant manifestations of the modern welfare state: the proportions of full-time income replaced by unemployment assistance and by sick pay. They found clear-cut though time-specific partisan effects on public policy. Up until the 1980s, during the era of welfare state expansion, they detected a clear tendency for left-wing governments to increase both unemployment benefits and sick pay in real terms, and they found no opposing tendency for right-wing governments to reduce either one. After the 1980s, during the era of welfare state contraction, they saw the opposite pattern: right-wing governments tending to reduce the real value of these welfare benefits and left-wing governments having no significant effect on them.

Moving beyond economic policy—for example, to environmental or foreign policy, or to policy on social and moral issues—we might expect policy to be more responsive to politics because there is no need to shift the deadweight of public finances. Furthermore, for a number of aspects of social policy, particularly those involving the reform of existing social legislation, action is either taken or not taken. For example, the law on abortion, on divorce, on the status of women, or on capital punishment is either reformed or not reformed. Public policy is easy to see in these areas for particular cases—laws on such matters do change after changes in the partisan control of governments—but unfortunately there is little comparative research assessing the impact of parties on social policy.

✦ So, *Does* Politics Make a Difference?

It used to be fashionable to denigrate the impact of politicians on public policy, to argue that the political world has reached the "end of ideology" and that politics no longer makes much of a difference. More recently, the steady globalization of economic policy has appeared to remove from politicians many of the levers of public policy that were formerly in their hands. Nonetheless, we have seen the impact of particular parties on the ambitious privatization programs of the 1980s and 1990s, in both Britain and eastern Europe, as well as the dramatic effect on Spanish foreign policy of the 2004 general election in Spain. It is hard to deny that representative government made a big difference in these cases. If we look at the problem more generally, furthermore, we see that almost all recently published studies conclude that party politics has a major impact on policy outputs in the real world, although more years will need to pass before systematic patterns can be seen for eastern Europe.

It seems to be the case that government programs tend to reflect the published policies of government members. At least in the countries in which there is a clear-cut alternation in the party composition of governments, promises made to the voters in the heat of an election campaign do seem to filter through to government policy. It seems to be the case that parties enact their promises more often than the cynics would have us believe. In part they may do so because many of the promises that politicians make are not controversial; nevertheless for one-party governments, pledge fulfillment rates of 70 percent or more have consistently been found.

It seems that changes in government spending flows can be partially predicted by changes in government policies and, in particular, by major changes in the partisan composition of the government. Spending flows are very sticky, but the evidence suggests that from time to time they can be shifted as a result of a major effort of political will. It also seems to be the case that nonexpenditure aspects of economic policy vary according to the partisan composition of the government. Relative dominance by right-wing governments, in particular, is associated with significant variations in key socioeconomic variables.

Does all of this mean that representative government makes a difference? The weight of evidence suggests that it does, at least in the economic sphere, which gives us all one important reason to get excited about the results of elections.

REFERENCES

Allan, James P., and Lyle Scruggs: "Political Partisanship and Welfare State Reform in Advanced Industrial Societies," *American Journal of Political Science,* vol. 48, no. 3, 2004, pp. 496–512.

Andeweg, R. B.: "Less than Nothing? Hidden Privatization of the Pseudo-Private Sector: The Dutch Case," *Western European Politics,* vol. 11, no. 4, 1988, pp. 117–28.

Armingeon, K.: "Determining the Level of Wages: The Role of Parties and Trade Unions," in F. Castles (ed.), *The Impact of Parties,* Sage, London, 1982.

Bauer, M.: "The Politics of State-Directed Privatization: The Case of France 1986–89," *West European Politics,* vol. 11, no. 4, 1988, pp. 49–60.

Bianchi, P., S. Cassese, and V. Della Sala: "Privatization in Italy: Aims and Constraints," *West European Politics,* vol. 11, no. 4, 1988, pp. 87–100.

Blais, Andre, Donald Blake, and Stephane Dion: "Do Parties Make a Difference? Parties and the Size of Government in Liberal Democracies," *American Journal of Political Science,* vol. 37, 1993, no. 1, pp. 40–62.

Boix, Charles: *Political Parties, Growth and Equality.* Cambridge University Press, Cambridge, 1998.

Budge, Ian, Hans-Dieter Klingemann, Andrea Volkens, Judith Bara, and Eric Tannenbaum, with Richard Fording, Derek Hearl, Hee Min Kim, Michael McDonald, and Silvia Mendes, *Mapping Policy Preferences: Parties, Electors and Governments, 1945–1998: Estimates for Parties, Electors and Governments, 1945–1998,* Oxford University Press, Oxford, 2001.

Budge, Ian, D. Robertson, and D. Hearl (eds.): *Ideology, Strategy and Party Change,* Cambridge University Press, Cambridge, 1987.

Castles, F.: "Explaining Public Education Expenditure in OECD Nations," *European Journal of Political Research,* vol. 17, no. 3, 1989, pp. 431–48.

Cerny, P. G.: "The Little Big Bang in Paris: Financial Market Deregulation in a *Dirigiste* System," *European Journal of Political Research,* vol. 17, no. 2, 1989, pp. 169–92.

Drumaux, A.: "Privatization in Belgium: The National and International Context," *West European Politics,* vol. 11, no. 4, 1988, pp. 74–86.

Esser, J.: "Symbolic Privatization: The Politics of Privatization in West Germany," *West European Politics,* vol. 11, no. 4, 1988, pp. 61–73.

Feigenbaum, Harvey, Jeffrey Henig, and Chris Hamnet: *Shrinking the State: The Political Underpinnings of Privatization,* Cambridge University Press, Cambridge, 1999.

Garrett, Geoffrey: *Partisan Politics in the Global Economy,* Cambridge University Press, Cambridge, 1998.

Heald, D.: "The United Kingdom: Privatization and Its Political Context," *West European Politics,* vol. 11, no. 4, 1988, pp. 31–48.

Hicks, Alexander, and Duane Swank: "Politics, Institutions, and Welfare Spending in Industrialised Democracies, 1960–1982," *American Political Science Review,* vol. 86, no. 4, 1992, pp. 658–74.

Hicks, Alexander, Duane Swank, and M. Ambuhl: "Welfare Expansion Revisited: Policy Routines and Their Mediation by Party, Class and Crisis, 1957–1982," *European Journal of Political Research,* vol. 17, no. 2, 1989, pp. 401–30.

Kalogeropoulou, E.: "Election Promises and Government Performance in Greece: PASOK's Fulfillment of Its 1981 Election Pledges," *European Journal of Political Research,* vol. 17, no. 2, 1989, pp. 289–311.

Kavanagh, D.: *Thatcherism and British Politics: The End of Consensus?* 2nd ed., Oxford University Press, Oxford, 1990.

Laver, Michael (ed.): *Estimating the Policy Positions of Political Actors,* Routledge, London, 2001.

Laver, M., and I. Budge (eds.): *Party Policy and Government Coalitions,* Macmillan, London, 1992.

Muller, E. N.: "Distribution of Income in Advanced Capitalist States: Political Parties, Labour Unions, and the International Economy," *European Journal of Political Research,* vol. 17, no. 2, 1989, pp. 367–400.

Müller, W.: "Privatizing in a Corporatist Economy: The Politics of Privatization in Austria," *West European Politics,* vol. 11, no. 4, 1988, pp. 101–16.

Notermans, Tom.: "Policy Continuity, Policy Change and the Political Power of Economic Ideas," *Acta Politica,* vol. 34, 1999, pp. 22–48.

Petry, François: "Fragile Mandate: Party Programmes and Public Expenditures in the French Fifth Republic," *European Journal of Political Research,* vol. 20, no. 1, 1991, pp. 149–72.

Pontusson, J.: "The Triumph of Pragmatism: Nationalisation and Privatization in Sweden," *West European Politics,* vol. 11, no. 4, 1988, pp. 129–40.

Rallings, C.: "The Influence of Election Programs: Britain and Canada, 1945–79," in Budge, Robertson, and Hearl (eds.).

Rose, Richard: *Do Parties Make a Difference?* Chatham House, Chatham (NJ), 1980.

Royed, T.: "Testing the Mandate Model in Britain and the United States: Evidence from the Reagan and Thatcher Eras," *British Journal of Political Science,* vol. 26, 1996, pp. 45–80.

Schmidt, Manfred: "When Parties Matter: A Review of the Possibilities and Limits of Partisan Influence on Public Policy," *European Journal of Political Research,* vol. 30, no. 1, 1996, pp. 155–83.

Stark, David, and Laszlo Bruszt: *Postsocialist Pathways: Transforming Politics in Property in East Central Europe,* Cambridge University Press, Cambridge, 1998.

Suzuki, Motoshi: "Domestic Political Determinants of Inflation," *European Journal of Political Research,* vol. 23, no. 2, 1993, pp. 245–60.

Thomson, Robert: *The Party Mandate: Election Pledges and Government Actions in the Netherlands, 1986–1998,* Thela-Thesis, Amsterdam, 1999.

Vickers, J., and V. Wright: "The Politics of Industrial Privatization in Western Europe: An Overview," *West European Politics,* vol. 11, no. 4, 1988, pp. 1–30.

Warwick, Paul: "Economic Trends and Government Survival in West European Parliamentary Democracies," *American Political Science Review,* vol. 86, 1992, no. 4, pp. 875–87.

Woldendorp, Jaap, Hans Keman, and Ian Budge (eds.): "Party Government in 20 Democracies: An Update (1990–1995)," *European Journal of Political Research,* vol. 33, 1998, pp. 125–164.

CHAPTER 14

POLITICS OUTSIDE PARLIAMENT

In most of this book we focus on what might be thought of as the "official" politics of representation in modern Europe. In the preceding chapters we deal with the national politics of choosing a legislature and an executive, the transnational politics of the European Union, as well as with the public policy outputs that emerge from these political processes. Although these are obviously central to politics in any European country, they are only part of the story. A large part of representative government in modern Europe takes place outside these formal structures, and there are some big differences between European countries in the ways in which this happens.

Political scientists have spent a lot of time thinking about differences between countries in how key social and economic interests play a part in public decision making. This research has led to two very different theoretical descriptions of the impact on the political process of a wide range of formal and informal social groups in what is often now described as "civil society." A model of group politics in which certain key groups are closely integrated into the formal political process is described by theorists as "corporatism" or "neocorporatism." An alternative model of group politics in which groups are seen to compete to put pressure on decision-making elites in a political "marketplace" outside formal political institutions has become known as "pluralism." Having come to regard these distinctions as too stark to capture the complexities of politics in most real countries, many authors also now talk in terms of notions such as "social partnership," "tripartism," and "policy networks," which blend elements of the pluralist and corporatist models.

In this chapter, we explore how well each of these approaches seems to describe the politics of economic policy making as well as the politics of decision making in some important noneconomic spheres of activity. Although policy making in any modern European state is a complex process that certainly does not conform to any simple model, it is nonetheless useful to describe the essential differences between pluralism and corporatism, and to illustrate the differences with brief discussions of group politics in Austria and in Britain, the former typically seen as the archetypal corporatist system, the latter as essentially pluralist. We then discuss the ways in which the notion of a "policy network" might capture a number of the insights of both the pluralist and the corporatist models of politics outside parliament.

✦ CORPORATISM

The Corporatist Model

Corporatism as we know it today has diverse sources in the political thought of the past hundred years or so. One important current that fed into modern theories of corporatist policy making was the fascism of the 1920s and 1930s. Fascist corporatism was a system of totalitarian state control of society based on an intimate interpretation of interest groups and the state. Domination of the major interest groups by the state was one of the main mechanisms of social control by the fascist one-party government, exemplified by Hitler's Germany, Mussolini's Italy, and Salazar's Portugal. Obviously, any form of thought even vaguely linked with fascism was totally discredited in Europe after World War II. This is the reason why postwar theories of corporatism severed any association with fascism before being relaunched as "neocorporatism" or "liberal corporatism."

A second intellectual source that flowed into modern corporatism was "Catholic Social Thought," especially influential during the early decades of the twentieth century. Catholic Church leaders became concerned that the role of the church was being undermined both by the growth of trade unionism and by what they saw as the relentless encroachment of the state into many aspects of social life. They mourned the passing of the medieval craft guilds and advocated an enhanced role for self-governing interest groups that constituted what they described as the "voluntary" sector. These groups would be intimately involved not only in the *planning* but also in the *provision* of major social services such as health care and education. What lay behind Catholic social thought was the belief that in a predominantly Catholic society these groups would be made up primarily of Catholics so that public policy would be sensitive to the teachings of the church, despite a formal separation of church and state. These ideas were taken up in the early postwar years by Christian democratic parties (see Chapter 8), whose electoral success gave corporatism additional political impetus.

A third factor that contributed to the rise of neocorporatism was the impulse for "national unity" that followed the destruction and trauma caused by World War II in many European countries. As we saw in Chapter 12, a number of states went through the immediate postwar period governed by coalitions of national unity encompassing both right and left. The sense that industry and labor had to work together in order to rebuild war-torn economies fostered tripartite cooperation in places such as Austria and Germany.

A fourth factor was the close relationship between the trade union movement and social democratic parties in several European countries (see Chapter 8). Many of these parties had grown out of the trade union movement and were still intimately connected with it. When social democratic parties were in power over long periods, notably in postwar Sweden and Norway, the relationship between trade unions and political parties became a relationship between trade unions and governments. Even in "pluralist" Britain, economic policy making came closest to being corporatist in style during the "Social Contract" between government and trade unions that was executed during the life of the 1974–79 Labour administration. Conversely, when social democratic parties move out of power, as they did in Sweden in the mid-1990s, the decision-making style can look a lot less corporatist.

One of the problems with the concept of corporatism is that many different people have used it in many different ways. Some authors have used the term to describe what is little more than a system of centralized wage bargaining in which government and the "social partners" of organized labor and business sit around a table and thrash out a national incomes policy. Others see corporatism as being rooted much more deeply in the policy-making system: as a set of institutional arrangements that entrench major social groups in the overall management of the national economy and much more besides.

In a recent and comprehensive review, which also provides an excellent bibliography for interested readers, Siaroff (pp.180–81) tabulates no less than twenty-four different working definitions related to corporatism used by authors writing between 1981 and 1997. (Wiarda also provides a recent review of this field. See also both Cawson and Lijphart.) On the basis of his review, Siaroff also offers a definition that he feels best captures the key ideas that most of these people are writing about. He feels that corporatism involves, "within an advanced industrial society and democratic polity, the coordinated, co-operative, and systematic management of the national economy by the state, centralized unions, and employers (these latter two co-operating directly in industry), presumably to the relative benefit of all three actors" (Siaroff, p. 177). Working from this general definition, Siaroff (pp. 177–79) breaks down the analysis of corporatist policy making into four general areas: the *structural* preconditions for corporatism; the *roles* within this structure fulfilled by key actors; the patterns of *behavior* that result; and the *contextual factors* that make corporatist policy making more likely to succeed.

Structural preconditions for corporatism are typically seen as the following:

- Most workers are organized into a small number of powerful unions.
- The business community is dominated by a small number of powerful firms organized into a powerful employers' federation.
- Wage bargaining between unions and employers is centralized.
- A powerful state is actively involved in the economy.

In a successful corporatist system, both employers and unions should have a formal institutional role not only in *making* policy but also in *implementing* it. The types of behavior by these "social partners" that are likely to make corporatism work include

- A consensus on broad social values shared by state, unions, and employers
- A preference for bargained solutions to problems, rather than solutions that either are imposed from above or are the outcomes of industrial conflict

The contextual factors argued to make corporatism work more smoothly include

- A long tradition of social democratic rule
- A small, open economy
- High expenditures on social programs and low expenditures on defense

The stress on policy *implementation* in this elaboration of the corporatist model is what sets corporatism fundamentally apart from other forms of political decision making that involve different socioeconomic groups. The implications of this are far-reaching. For any particular decision-making regime to be seen as "corporatist," interest groups must be comprehensive in their representation of particular sectors of society and must be able to *police* their members as well as *represent* their interests. This point is strongly emphasized by both Philippe Schmitter and Gerhard Lehmbruch, two of the most influential political scientists associated with discussions of corporatism: "Corporatism is more than a particular pattern of articulation of interests. Rather, it is an institutionalized pattern of policy-formation in which large interest organizations co-operate with each other and with public authorities not only in the articulation of interests, but . . . in the 'authoritative allocation of values' and in the implementation of such policies" (Lehmbruch, p. 150).

Many of the authors who have written about corporatism have gone on to produce rankings of countries in terms of how close they are to the idealized model of the corporatist state. Siaroff (p. 198) combined all of these into a single additive index of corporatism, the results of which are given in Table 14.1, with figures for the United States and Canada provided as a basis for comparison.

Table 14.1 groups countries crisply into three clusters. There are the "big three" corporatist countries (Austria, Norway, and Sweden), which are rated as being clearly more corporatist than all of the others. After these comes a group of countries that rank as moderately corporatist. The Netherlands, Germany, Denmark, and Switzerland are at the more corporatist end of this group; Luxembourg, Iceland, and Belgium are at the less corporatist end. Finally, there are countries that are hardly corporatist at all. In this group, Britain and Ireland (as well as the United States and Canada) are joined by the "Mediterranean" democracies: Portugal, Spain, Italy, Greece, and France. The parts of Europe that are neither English-speaking nor from the Catholic south are likely to be at least somewhat corporatist in their policy-making style.

TABLE 14.1

Corporatism Scores for European Democracies

Country	Corporatism Score	Social Democratic and Left Share of Cabinet Seats
Austria	5.00	60.7
Norway	4.86	73.1
Sweden	4.67	76.3
Netherlands	4.00	18.6
Denmark	3.55	50.7
Germany	3.54	24.8
Switzerland	3.38	23.8
Finland	3.30	33.6
Luxembourg	3.00	28.4
Iceland	3.00	31.7
Belgium	2.84	27.6
Ireland	2.00	9.7
France	1.67	24.5
United Kingdom	1.65	28.1
Portugal	1.50	5.7
Italy	1.48	12.4
Spain	1.25	26.0
Greece	1.00	19.7
United States	1.15	
Canada	1.15	

Sources: See sources for Table 13.1; Siaroff, p. 198.

Table 14.1 also repeats information from Table 13.1 on the extent of left or social democratic control of government over the postwar years, and it confirms the view that this is indeed conducive to the development of a more corporatist policy-making regime. Four of the five most corporatist countries—Austria, Norway, Sweden, and Denmark— were also the countries with the most extensive social democratic control of their postwar cabinets. The striking exception is the Netherlands. Christian democratic parties were dominant in the Dutch cabinet over much of the postwar era, yet the country exhibits strongly corporatist tendencies. In this sense, the Netherlands is more like some members of the group of more moderately corporatist countries, notably including Germany, Switzerland, and Belgium. In these, a tradition of "northern European" Christian democracy, combined with a need to reconcile fundamental religious or linguistic cleavages, has created an impetus to entrench extra-parliamentary groups in the policy-making system. (On corporatism in the Netherlands, see Woldendorp.)

As Table 14.1 indicates, most authors agree that of all western European countries, Austria exhibits the strongest form of corporatism. By looking in greater detail at the situation in Austria, therefore, we can gain some additional insight into what is involved in corporatist policy making.

"Corporatism" in Austria

Austria is usually taken as the classic case of a political system that is characterized by a very high level of corporatist policy making. Indeed, Marin has even argued that Austria is a "model-generator," one of a very few countries that theorists have in mind when they develop accounts of corporatism. This was possibly truer of the period up until the late 1980s than it is today, for the recent development of more confrontational party politics, combined with Austrian membership in the European Union, may have moved Austria somewhat closer to the European mainstream (Luther and Müller). Nonetheless, there can be little doubt that Austrian politics for most of the postwar period provided one of the main sources of ideas for those who have written at length about corporatism.

Perhaps the most striking and distinctive feature of Austrian politics in this regard has been the important role of the "chambers." These institutions were designed to provide formal representation for the interests, respectively, of labor, commerce, and agriculture. Although chambers (especially chambers of commerce) can be found elsewhere, the Austrian chambers traditionally have been much more important, given their statutory position and the vital role that they play in decision making. All working citizens in Austria are obliged by law to belong to the appropriate chamber. This rule requires the chambers to run their affairs in a manner that would withstand legal scrutiny—to make internal decisions and hold internal elections in a representative manner, for example. The chambers have the formal right to be consulted on and represented in a wide range of matters, as well as to nominate members to many other public bodies.

In addition to the statutory chambers, Austria has an extensive system of "voluntary" interest groups. These include a trade union movement organized under the auspices of the "peak" trade union organization, the ÖGB, and the League of Austrian Industrialists, the VÖI. The ÖGB, in particular, is a powerful independent actor in Austria, for a number of reasons. First, it is the main agency engaged in collective bargaining on behalf of its own members. The Chamber of Labor, by virtue of its statutory status, must also consider the "public interest" in its dealings. Second, the ÖGB is highly centralized. The member unions, legally speaking, are subdivisions of the ÖGB, rather than the ÖGB being a federation of autonomous unions. In addition, the level of trade union affiliation in Austria is relatively high, and unions tend to be organized on an industry-by-industry (rather than a craft-by-craft) basis.

Almost all observers agree that the three main chambers—the Chamber of Labor, of Commerce, and of Agriculture—and the ÖGB interact with one another as the four key players in the making and implementing of economic policy in Austria, in a system known as *Sozialpartnerschaft,* or "social partnership." This system operates in parallel with, rather than in opposition to, the formal parliamentary system. Although the key interest associations are quite distinct from the political parties, the obvious political affiliations of their respective memberships mean that each association tends to be dominated by supporters of one or another of the main parties. This gives interest group leaders a very strong position. As might be expected, the Chamber of Labor and the ÖGB are dominated by the Socialists (SPÖ), and the Chamber of Commerce and Chamber of Agriculture are dominated by the conservative Austrian People's Party (ÖVP). It is important, however, not to present relations between parties and interest groups in Austria as if they were in some sense exclusive entities. On the contrary, there has been an intimate interpenetration of interest groups and parliament, and this symbiosis has been identified by many as one of the strengths of Austrian corporatism. A steadily growing proportion of parliamentarians are also interest group representatives, and interest groups have played an important role in the selection of parliamentary candidates for the major Austrian parties.

The social partners in Austria traditionally have been concerned first and foremost with economic policy making, in particular with prices and incomes. The social partnership underpinning Austrian corporatism has thus involved both the negotiation and the implementation of policies on prices and incomes. This cooperation has been formalized in a powerful institution, the Joint Commission on Prices and Wages, representation on which has been governed by the principle of parity. Thus the representation of the Chamber of Labor and the ÖGB has equaled that of the Chamber of Commerce and Chamber of Agriculture, and the commission has often been referred to as the "Parity Commission." The concept of parity has been vital to the operation of Austrian corporatism, implying strictly equal membership for representatives of business and labor in all important economic policy-making bodies. The effect has been to compel groups that might otherwise be antagonistic to cooperate with one another, for no effective decisions can be made unless they do. Thus, many important decisions have been "bargained out" by the interest groups before the government becomes involved.

As a system of economic planning, Austrian corporatism has been judged, especially during the relatively affluent 1960s and 1970s, to have been an outstanding success. The Austrian economy enjoyed steady growth and a record on inflation and unemployment that was much better than the European norm. More remarkable, however, was Austria's record in preserving many aspects of corporatism during the recessionary 1980s and early 1990s, with an important social partnership agreement implemented in 1995. While other countries came to exhibit some of the more visible institutional features of corporatist decision making during the 1960s and 1970s, an effective corporatist system involves far more than mere institutions. It rests on a history and culture of collective accommodation that cannot simply be invented as the need arises. Thus, "Austrians have internalized attitudes and values of social partnership and apply them even when they appear to or do actually contradict their individual and immediate interests. Austrians even consider that, in the long term and overall, social partnership optimally realizes their individual preferences by collective regulation" (Gerlich et al., p. 218). Full-fledged corporatism, therefore, is a comprehensive and deep-rooted decision-making culture rather than just a transient collection of superficial institutions.

Tripartism and Social Partners

The theoretical notion of corporatism describes an ideal type of decision-making regime unlikely to be found in its pure form in any European country. The Austrian corporatist system that we just described is probably the fullest practical implementation in modern Europe, to the extent that, as we said, some authors have described it as a "model-generator." At the same time, as we indicate in Table 14.1, if we concentrate on the key area of economic policy, it is possible to classify European countries as being more, or less, corporatist in their decision-making ethos. To a large extent this classification depends on the "tripartite" integration of the two key social partners—trade unions and employers' associations—with government in the management of the economy. This in turn depends on the extent to which the social partners can speak and act authoritatively on behalf of those they represent.

Two of the key variables that affect the system of economic policy making are the level of trade union membership within the working population and the centralization of wage bargaining, or the extent to which the national peak organizations for labor and employers are involved in negotiations over wage levels. In general terms, European trade union membership is "densest" in Scandinavia, with membership rates of around 90 percent in Denmark, Finland, Norway, and Sweden. It is much lower than this in France, the Netherlands, Spain, and Switzerland. The centralization of wage bargaining is highest in Austria and Scandinavia and much lower in France, Switzerland, Britain, and Italy.

A highly unionized workforce combined with a centralized trade union movement, however, does not guarantee an effective system of corporatist decision making. Thus, although it is true that the Austrian trade union movement is highly centralized (nearly all trade unionists are members of the main trade union federation, the ÖGB), the level of trade union membership in the workforce is high but not especially high. Belgium, for example, has a much higher level of trade union membership and a moderately centralized trade union movement, but most people agree that it has a much lower level of corporatist decision making than Austria. The Netherlands, in contrast, which is generally held to be significantly more corporatist than Britain, has a much lower level of trade union membership.

Perhaps the most important condition for effective tripartite wage bargaining is that the social partners are able to rely on strong and effective peak organizations. In Germany, for example, the peak organization for the trade union movement is the German Federation of Trade Unions (DGB), which represents over 80 percent of all unionized workers. On the side of business and industry, there are three different peak organizations, but they do not compete with one another. The Federation of German Industries (BDI) concentrates on the political representation of business. The Confederation of German Employers' Associations (BDA) deals with social policy and the labor markets, including collective bargaining. The Association of German Chambers of Industry and Commerce (DIHT), representing nearly 3 million companies, all of which are obliged by law to affiliate, deals with trade and commerce. Thus, the three peak organizations representing the interests of capital coordinate their activities and often function as one. This division of the employers' peak organizations, however, as well as the fact that the DGB can negotiate on general prices and income strategy but cannot bind individual member unions in its negotiations, means that Germany is probably better thought of as an example of tripartism rather than full corporatism.

It is also the case that the institutions of tripartism can rise and fall in significance over a period of time, even in the absence of a more fundamental corporatist culture. In Ireland, for example, economic policy during the 1990s and early 2000s was based on a series of tripartite deals between government, employers, and unions—including the "Programme for Competitiveness and Work" and "Partnership 2000," the "Programme for Prosperity and Fairness" and "Sustaining Progress." These involved agreements on wage levels, productivity arrangements, aspects of employment conditions, and government policy in areas such as taxation, investment incentives, and the provision of certain social welfare benefits. Such deals were first negotiated at a time of economic crisis—the original deal in 1988 was called the "Programme for National Recovery." Public finances were then in disarray, inflation and unemployment were very high, and large numbers of young people were leaving Ireland to seek jobs elsewhere. The resulting national agreements between what are explicitly referred to in Ireland as the "social partners" contributed to a far more stable economic environment. There are doubtless many reasons to explain the remarkable growth of the Irish economy in the latter part of the 1990s and the early years of the new century. But the stable industrial relations environment produced by these partnership deals is certainly one factor that was used to explain the large inflows of foreign investment that fueled this growth. It has led successive Irish governments to go to great lengths to renegotiate partnership agreements between trade unions, business organizations, and the voluntary sector, creating a situation in which one of the central processes of economic policy making in Ireland takes place quite outside the formal political process. (For a comprehensive overview of the social partnership process in Ireland, see Murphy.)

Successful tripartite negotiations between the social partners can therefore generate a number of the effects attributed to a more comprehensive corporatist policy-making regime. Nonetheless, as we can see from the collapse of the 1970s "Social Contracts" in Britain, there is a real sense in which tripartism is only as good as its last deal. It is far less deeply rooted than the type of corporatist institutions that are grounded in more fundamental social attitudes about the institutional roles of the key social partners.

Tripartism in Eastern Europe

Creating a new system of relationships between government, business, and trade unions was not the very first thing on the agenda for the transition states of eastern Europe, but it nonetheless was a crucial matter on which important decisions had to be taken quickly. All postcommunist countries formed their first tripartite commissions and committees by the early 1990s. At that time, tripartism and neocorporatism seemed to be necessary and stabilizing features of the social and economic landscape. The perceived achievements of western European neocorporatism in moderating class antagonisms and coordinating the conflicting interests of labor and capital were often used as examples to justify new policies. Eastern European policy makers, by including representatives of labor in negotiations and decision making, hoped to ease the pains of economic transformation and generate mass support for liberal democracy.

Hungary formed its first National Interest Reconciliation Council in 1988–89, and Poland started its Round Table discussions in 1989. Soon, because of dramatic declines in earnings and living standards, these tripartite commissions started focusing on the economic concerns and demands of the general population. The Interest Reconciliation Council (IRC) was formed in Hungary in 1990 and included representatives of several national trade unions and employers' organizations. Critics suggest, however, that this body was largely a remnant of the communist past and failed to mobilize the working class to fight actively for its interests. They see the origins of tripartism in eastern Europe not in governments trying to mediate the conflicting interests of labor and capital but as a way to provide social support for government reform policies (Ost, p. 509). Even after the 1994 electoral campaign in Hungary, during which the concept of a "social pact" dominated almost all parties' electoral platforms, the situation did not radically change. Negotiations on a Social Economic Agreement (SEA) were long and highly contentious. By 1998, the IRC had been transformed into an informal "consultative" body, in a context where the government of Hungary was setting economic policy without much formal input from organized labor.

The Hungarian experience of tripartism was by no means unique across the region. The tripartite commissions in the Czech Republic and Poland were also quite weak in negotiating and implementing agreements, in defending workers' interests, and in negotiating with the employers' associations. This weak, or rather "symbolic" role of tripartism has even led to union boycotts in Poland, the Czech Republic, and Slovakia. In eastern Europe, the best that can be said is that tripartism means formal negotiations over very broad issues, with no guarantee that the agreements will become law or be respected by employers (Ost, p. 515). (See also Iankova; Stark and Bruzst.)

The Decline of Corporatism?

Views about the likely spread of corporatism were modified by the 1990s. The apparent decline of the institutions of corporatism in a number of countries during the preceding years of recession led to an increasing tendency to categorize corporatism as a "fair-weather" phenomenon: a form of concerted action that tends to fall apart when resources become scarcer and interest groups must bargain more competitively to divide up a pie that is fixed rather than one that is continually expanding (Keman and Whiteley).

Two other trends may be leading to a decline in the importance of "purer" forms of corporatism in modern Europe. The first has to do with the ever-expanding role of the European Union in major economic policy making, particularly after the Maastricht Treaty cemented an agreement to develop a common European monetary system. The need for a "convergence" of European economies to underpin a common European currency, the euro, implied the need for participating European governments to surrender some of the autonomy they had at least in theory traditionally employed to manipulate key instruments of macroeconomic policy, such as interest rates, exchange rates, and budget deficits. In addition, many other formerly national levers of economic policy have increasingly come under the auspices of the EU, including state supports to industry, competition policy, and regional policy.

As we saw when discussing EU decision making in Chapter 5, national governments remain very important in this process, through their role in the European Council. Thus, traditional economic groups still set out to influence economic policy making at the EU level, one stage removed, by influencing national governments. But the traditional institutionalized channels of influence used by such groups have been undermined to the extent that decision making is moved to EU institutions in Brussels. Interest groups, however, have not sat around twiddling their thumbs while this has happened, and many have set up very effective Brussels-based organizations designed to work directly on EU decision-making elites. Key groups may or may not have become more influential as a result of all of this, but the traditional corporatist model—entrenched as it is in what is essentially a national decision-making system—has undoubtedly been undermined (Adams).

A second important trend that may have weakened traditional corporatist arrangements has to do with the very steady shift in the sources of wealth generation in European economies toward the service sector, in line with trends in all affluent countries. This shift has been accompanied by a weakening of the power of the traditional trade union movement. Modern high-tech and service industries have created an increasingly white-collar workforce, a much more rapid turnover in employment histories, and new patterns of work, which have combined to undermine the industrial power of trade unions. (For an extended and very useful discussion of changing European labor markets, see Kitschelt et al.)

Notwithstanding these important trends, Siaroff's survey shows that even in the 1990s there were still big differences between European countries in the extent of institutionalized involvement by the main social partners—especially employers and trade unions—in the process of managing national economies. This is especially true in relation to the involvement of the social partners in policy *implementation,* as well as policy making, which is one of the key defining characteristics of corporatist systems.

✦ PLURALISM

Like corporatism, pluralism has tended to occupy an uneasy no-man's land between being a "normative" theory of how politics *ought* to be conducted and a "positive" theory of how groups *actually do* operate. As a normative theory, pluralism is one of the underpinnings of traditional liberal democracy, perhaps best summarized by Dahl (pp. 4–33). But this is not our main concern here. As a descriptive scheme, pluralism typically has been used to characterize interest group activity in systems such as Britain (and, for that matter, Canada and the United States), where groups put pressure on political elites in an uncoordinated and competitive manner. This is in contrast to the well-ordered and cooperative interaction between groups and elites that is implied under pure forms of corporatism.

Even though pluralism has been criticized for being a vague and incomplete theory of politics (Jordan, "Pluralism"), it does nonetheless have a set of striking features that allow us to regard it as a distinctive description of political decision making. Pluralism can be distinguished from corporatism in a number of respects. The most important is that pluralist interest groups have no formal institutional role in the allocation of resources and the implementation of policy. A second fundamental difference is that interest groups in a pluralist system are assumed to be self-generating and voluntary. This assumption implies the existence of a range of different groups, typically competing with one another to represent the interests of the same classes of people in a given sphere of economic or social activity. Another assumption in much of pluralist theory is that although not all groups have equal levels of power or resources, it is nonetheless relatively easy for people to form an interest group and thereby gain at least some access to the levers of political power (Smith, p. 309). This assumption suggests that many of the salient social interests in a pluralist system will be represented by the set of competing interest groups. New interests that might emerge, for one reason or another, can be represented in the political system as a result of the capacity of existing groups to adapt, or as a result of the relatively unhindered formation of new groups. (Good introductions to pluralist theory can be found in Jordan, "Sub-Governments"; Jordan, "Pluralism"; and Smith.)

The basic process by which pluralist theorists assume popular interests to be represented in decision making involves groups influencing the output of the executive branch of government by applying "pressure" on political elites. Different groups compete with one another for the ear of decision makers, who are pressed in many different directions at the same time. The groups that apply pressure most effectively (possibly because they have the most public support, but quite possibly also because they have the most resources or the most privileged access to elites) have the greatest success in bringing public policy closer to their own preferred positions.

Despite allegations made by some naive critics, few pluralists assume that the resources available to different groups are in any sense equal or that different groups have equivalent access to key political decision makers. Most pluralists accept that the market in political influence is far from perfect, containing actors with very different capacities to affect important political decisions. In particular, many pluralists accept that business interests are often in a highly privileged position and that the state is far from neutral, favoring business interests or, indeed, favoring the particular interests of the bureaucracy. A clear statement of this "neopluralist" position can be found in Charles Lindblom's influential book *Politics and Markets*. According to Lindblom, there are some "grand" issues that are effectively removed from public debate by the combined power of business interests and the state, and as a result, conventional pluralist politics operates most effectively in relation to what can be seen as "secondary" issues (Lindblom, p. 142). Even reconstructed pluralists are thus distinguished by their assumption that there is at least something important left to be contested in the accessible political arena and that such contests take the form of applying political pressure to decision-making elites.

Political pressure can be applied in a number of ways, although these ways are not always very clearly specified by those who write about pluralism. In the sphere of prices and income policy, however, the process is relatively clear-cut. Policy is set on the basis of bargaining between groups, backed up by the threat of the economic sanctions that each group has at its disposal. In the last analysis, trade unions get their way in a pluralistic system not because they are in some sense integrated into the political process but because they can go on strike and thereby inflict damage on the employers or the government with which they are dealing. Similarly, employers have power because they control the means of production and can inflict pain by engaging in firings, lockouts, and plant closures if they choose to do so.

Perhaps the single most distinctive feature of the pluralist account of decision making, therefore, is that it is characterized by conflict rather than consensus. Of course, conflict will not always manifest itself in the shape of strikes, lockouts, and so on. Rather, it is the *threat* of such sanctions, whether explicit or implicit, that underpins pluralist bargaining. Indeed, if the various actors are rational and equipped with perfect information, they will anticipate the outcome of any potential conflict and settle their differences before overt hostilities can begin. Actual observed conflicts—real-world strikes and lockouts—are, according to this view, the product of imperfect information. They are what happens when competing groups test each other's strengths and weaknesses. For all this, however, the outcome of political activity in a pluralist system is assumed to be the product of the balance of forces between the various groups involved. And this balance of forces is determined by the anticipated outcome of head-to-head confrontations over essential conflicts of interest.

Most people see pluralism and corporatism as being at opposite ends of a spectrum describing different types of group politics. For this reason, studies that describe different countries as being more, or less, corporatist are also making judgments about the extent of pluralist decision making. Thus Table 14.1 is also, in the minds of most authors, a ranking of European countries in terms of the extent to which they have a type of group politics that can be thought of as pluralist. As we already seen, a striking regularity in Table 14.1 is the tight cluster of the Mediterranean and English-speaking European democracies at the "pluralist" end of this spectrum. This group accounts for the seven countries reckoned by a large variety of authors to be the most pluralist. None of these countries has a long tradition of social democratic government in the postwar era, and all seem to be characterized by a more market-oriented style of interaction between the main social partners.

"Pluralism" in Britain

Table 14.1 shows us that Britain is a key member of the "pluralist" cluster of modern European countries. During the 1970s, when the interest of political scientists in corporatism was at its zenith, even Britain was diagnosed as moving toward the corporatist model. This prediction had much to do with the emergence of the "Social Contract" between the Labour government of the day; the main British trade union federation, the Trades Union Congress; and the main employers' federation, the Confederation of British Industry. This era was, however, short-lived. For most of the postwar era in Britain, "competitive" rather than "cooperative" has been the best way of describing interactions between the main social partners in Britain. Trade unions themselves have set great store by their right to "free collective bargaining," backed up by a right to strike that is regularly exercised. Even more than the unions, British employers have also been willing for the most part to take their chances in the rough-and-tumble of the labor market rather than getting involved in institutionalized collaboration with the unions.

This mode of economic policy making conforms closely to the model of a pluralist system based on a political market in which self-generating interest groups compete freely with one another to influence the flow of public policy. The argument that Britain is decidedly not a corporatist system thus rests on two important phenomena. The first is the general lack of integration of both unions and management into the policy-making process. The second is the apparent preference of both sides for confrontational methods of settling their differences.

The fragility of what appeared to be moves toward tripartite decision making in Britain, with the "Social Contract" of the mid-1970s, can be seen clearly from the speed with which confrontational bargaining was restored after the introduction of government-imposed wage ceilings in 1977. Equally striking is the success of the Conservative attack on trade union rights and privileges after Margaret Thatcher's election victory in May 1979. As early as July 1979, the Conservatives proposed a series of restrictions on trade union power. These included the banning of "secondary" picketing (that is, picketing away from the main scene of an industrial dispute); the restriction of closed shops (which oblige all who work in a particular employment to join a particular union); and the requirement that unions hold secret ballots of those involved before calling strikes. A series of laws restricting trade union power was passed shortly afterward. Confrontation between government and unions came to a head in a long and very bruising miners' strike that began in March 1984 and soured industrial relations in Britain for some time afterward. The Thatcherite approach to economic policy making in Britain was thus to use legislation to weaken the power of trade unions and then relegate them to the position of "mere" economic actors with no formal political role. These attacks on the trade unions were defended on the grounds that trade union power hinders the free play of market forces. A strong belief in the effectiveness of the market left no room for tripartite economic planning, involving agreements between government, employers, and unions.

In this regard, not a lot changed after the landslide election victories for Labour in 1997 and 2001. During the 1997 election campaign the Conservatives complained that Tony Blair's "New" Labour Party had "stolen" many aspects of Conservative economic policy, and research into the British party manifestos of 1997 confirms for the first time that Labour was no longer the most left-wing of the mainstream British parties and had moved sharply toward the Conservatives on economic policy (Laver and Garry). Over two full terms in office, from 1997 to 2005, Labour did not seek a dramatic rolling back of Thatcherite trade union legislation, made no conscious attempt to forge a new social contract between the social partners, and gave no real indication that Britain was likely to move away from an essentially pluralist form of interest group representation.

Pluralism in Action: The Women's Movement

The corporatist model of interest group politics explicitly refers to the management of the economy and to the role of unions and employers in the economy. The pluralist model, in contrast, is entirely open as to which particular interests might put pressure on the decision-making system. Indeed, one of the virtues claimed for pluralism by its champions is that a "free market" in influence can adapt to changes in society and allow new groups into the decision-making loop. Whether or not this claim is justified, changes both in the structure of society and in social attitudes do have the potential to change the focus of interest group politics. This effect can be seen quite clearly in the rise to prominence, toward the end of the twentieth century, of both the women's movement and the environmental movement.

As we saw in Chapter 11, women are systematically underrepresented at nearly every level of politics in nearly every European country. This underrepresentation arises not only within political parties and bureaucracies but also in the peak organizations of the social partners (there are relatively few women among senior trade unionists or business leaders) and in entrenched economic and professional interest groups such as churches, farmers, and doctors. The political underrepresentation of women arises even in Scandinavia, where the women's movement has made more progress than anywhere else. (For a comprehensive overview of the evolution of women's representation in the formal political system, see Leyenaar.)

It is not surprising, therefore, that groups promoting women's interests have often been forced to operate outside the traditional institutional structure. Of course, women's issues have also been pursued within existing organizations, be they trade unions or political parties (Leyenaar). Those promoting women's issues inside such organizations have often met with limited success, however. Women's activists have often found themselves in the role of activist groups within organizations, from which positions they have applied internal pressure for change with varying degrees of success. One of the best examples is the way in which many European trade unions have now been convinced—often not without a struggle—to campaign for equal pay and conditions for women who do the same jobs as men. Such intra-institutional campaigns for women's rights have had most success inside established public organizations in Scandinavia and the Netherlands.

However, campaigners for women's rights are also prominently involved outside traditional organizations, in single-issue pressure group politics of particular relevance to women. Obvious examples include abortion (Lovenduski and Outshoorn), divorce, domestic violence, and a range of equal rights causes (Dahlerup). A striking example was the important role played by the Women's Coalition as a mediating group during the early stages of the Northern Ireland peace process—although the same group was quickly sidelined by the traditional male-dominated political "players" once this process gained momentum. In almost all cases, however, women's groups have found themselves outside traditional institutional patterns of influence, and their "outsider" status has meant that they have had to fight very hard for every inch of ground won since the 1960s.

At the same time, however, activism by women's groups has probably forced at least the public face of many mainstream decision-making organizations to take women's issues more seriously than they did before. Indeed, the concept of "mainstreaming" gender issues in modern Europe—of building gender into the heart of public decision making, no matter who makes such decisions—has become central to the debate on the role of gender in the decision-making process (Beveridge, Nott and Stephen; Mazey, "Integrating"; Mazey, *Gender;* Rees). This approach rejects the notion of women as an "interest group" trying to influence public decisions-making from a position that is essentially outside the loop. Rather, women are seen as an integral part of the process. But the very existence and success of mainstreaming policies in a number of countries provides a good example of the way in which issues can be forced up the political agenda by interest group politics, to the extent that the entire decision-making system may come to take on some of the values that are being promoted.

Pluralism in Action: The Environmental Movement

The environmental movement in Europe has adopted a very different strategy in its attempt to have an impact on public policy. The effects of this strategy can be seen in the rise of Green parties in many European countries, a phenomenon discussed in Chapter 8. Green parties have tended to look quite unlike traditional political parties. Rather, they have shared many of the features of new social movements (described in the following section), having views that cut across traditional ideological lines, and members have had very ambivalent attitudes toward the need for strong party leadership. This tendency is reinforced by the fact that only one Green party has been in a position of sustained power at national level: German Greens took cabinet seats in a coalition with the Social Democrats following the 1998 election, a coalition that was sustained in office after it won a majority by the narrowest of margins in the 2002 election. With a few rare exceptions, Greens have had little real bargaining power in the formation of national governments, and the movement typically remains divided over even the merits of seeking power. The main impact of the Greens on environmental policy, therefore, has been indirect—in the "greening" of their main opponents, many of which have adopted more environmentalist policies once it became clear that Green politics could attract votes. Many European party programs have become "greener" in response to this potential challenge.

Notwithstanding the electoral role of the Green parties, there are many other active environmental groups in Europe, most of which use more direct political strategies. The Greenpeace organization, to take just one example, was formed in 1971 to oppose underground nuclear testing by (unsuccessfully in this case) attempting to sail a small ship into the nuclear test zone. Now based in Amsterdam, Greenpeace claims 2.8 million supporters worldwide in its 2004 annual report, with offices in over forty countries employing a substantial number of people (Greenpeace). Annual income net of fund-raising costs is listed in the audited accounts published in 2004 as being in excess of 120 million euros, while the organization's financial reserves amounted to 100 million euros. Since its formation, Greenpeace has engaged in a series of effective and headline-grabbing campaigns, blocking an outfall from the British nuclear reprocessing plant at Sellafield and placing Greenpeace members in rubber dinghies between whaling ships and whales in the Antarctic or in the way of ships dumping toxic wastes in the North Sea. One of its most famous campaigns, against French nuclear testing, culminated in 1985 with the sinking in New Zealand of its boat, *The Rainbow Warrior,* allegedly by the French Secret Service. Greenpeace now runs a fleet of four boats, spearheading its campaigns to put pressure on national governments, at a cost listed in its 2004 accounts as over 19 million euros a year. The most recent of these boats, the *Esperanza* relaunched in 2002, is a former Russian firefighting boat capable of withstanding heavy ice. Greenpeace is thus a very large and successful example of a classic "outsider" pressure group with a policy of "mass networking: enabling the people to act" and a view that "we cannot rely on governments, alone, to act and make change." Its philosophy is that "public opinion needs to be focused effectively if Greenpeace can direct public opinion to make a real difference" (Greenpeace).

Like Greenpeace, most other environmental groups have almost no institutionalized access to power and are forced to rely on more direct forms of pressure. When state environmental protection agencies are established, for example, prominent individuals associated with environmental causes may be selected for some role or other, but there are very few examples in Europe of environmentalist groups being given formal policy-making and implementation status, along neocorporatist lines. One reason may be that the most successful groups, such as Greenpeace, have deliberately distanced themselves from the political establishment. Another may be that established parties and other organizations have identified the politics of the environment as something that they can profitably annex for themselves, and they are therefore unwilling to allow environmental groups to use green politics to gain any sort of foothold within established political systems. (See both Carter and Rootes for comprehensive reviews of environmental politics.)

New Social Movements

The examples typically used to distinguish corporatist from pluralist decision-making systems tend to deal with the relations between the social partners representing organized labor and management. Major entrenched interest groups such as these are but a tiny fraction of the vast range of groups—women's and environmental groups provide only a few examples—that can be found in every European country. In particular, there is a cluster of groups and organizations, together with more loosely defined structures that we might think of as "movements," that appear to have a fair amount in common with one another. In addition to women's and environmental movements, almost all European countries now have active antiracist, antiwar, antiglobalization, anticolonialist, or pro–human rights groups, gay rights groups, animal rights and antinuclear groups, and groups promoting a range of more or less radical single-issue causes. Many of the groups share a number of features that, taken together, characterize them as what have been called "new social movements" by political scientists (Jahn; Kriesi et al.; Rucht; Schmitt-Beck). They are seen by some as "postmaterialist" or "postmodern" alternatives to traditional political parties and entrenched interest organizations.

The "membership" of a typical new social movement—though it may not be formally defined—tends to be rather fluid; people drift in and out of affiliation with a movement or cause on a rather casual basis. The "leadership"—though some of these groups are actively opposed to any notion of formal leadership—often has an intellectual lineage that can be traced to the period of student radicalism of the late 1960s and early 1970s. The views these movements represent tend to cut across traditional ideological lines. It is fair to say, however, that most of these groups can be seen as being aligned much more with the left than with the right of the traditional ideological spectrum, and that many such movements emerged as informal activist alternatives to more traditional and formal party political or trade union organizations representing the left.

Supporters of new social movements tend to strongly favor active participation and group democracy, rather than the more passive membership and hierarchical decision-making structures of a traditional political party, trade union, or interest group. Some new social movements, as we said, may even refuse to acknowledge that they have any "leadership" at all. When it comes to intervening in the political process, they tend to work outside traditional institutional channels. Demonstrations, boycotts, and other forms of direct action are preferred to lobbying, letter writing, petitions, and more conventional pressure tactics (Dalton). Direct action such as this serves a number of purposes for new social movements. It mobilizes and engages members who otherwise would be alienated from the political process; it forces new issues onto at least the media's political agenda; and it maintains the group's status as a radical outsider rather than as a co-opted part of the traditional establishment. Indeed, while mainstream politicians fret over the decline of popular participation in politics—measuring this decline as they do by looking at steadily falling levels of turnout at local, national, and European Parliament elections—others would say that the success of antiglobalization or antiwar groups at mobilizing people for large popular demonstrations shows that political participation is as vibrant as it ever was. It is just that people, especially younger people, are finding direct participation in the activities of various new social movements to be more fulfilling personally, and see it as potentially a more effective way to make a difference politically.

One very significant technological change underpinning a growing popular participation in various types of less conventional social movements has been the explosive growth and penetration of the Internet and World Wide Web. Certainly in modern Europe it is very easy for new movements and organizations to establish a significant presence on the Web, which is growing rapidly in importance as a source of information with the advent of powerful Internet search engines. Information on almost any issue is no more than a few mouse clicks away for large numbers of Europe's citizens, especially its younger citizens, and "information" can be found that is tailored to almost every social and political view. Email has made international person-to-person interaction cheap and effectively instantaneous. As a consequence, governments and other "official" organizations have seen their previously powerful roles as gatekeepers of information and communication greatly undermined. At the same time, forms of political organization that cut radically across traditional social and economic linkages have been greatly facilitated. All of this has had the effect of forcing people to reevaluate what they have in mind when they think of political participation, political communication, and group politics, recent changes in which have the potential to have far-reaching long-term effects. (For a widely cited, balanced, and ultimately somewhat skeptical review of this argument, see Bimber, "Internet." Bimber, *Information,* provides a book-length evaluation, though in an explicitly American context.)

For all these reasons, when all is said and done, new social movements fit more easily with a pluralist than with a corporatist view of the world of political decision making. Indeed, new social movements, particularly when they meet with some success, might even be considered as advertisements for the pluralist model, which holds the notion of an open and accessible market in political influence as one of its central normative justifications.

✦ THE NEW PLURALISM? POLICY NETWORKS

Political scientists increasingly have come to see the "pure" corporatist and pluralist models as being too simplistic to handle the complex ways in which the social actors of civil society influence decision making in modern Europe. The concepts that have emerged tend to blend aspects of the entrenched integration in policy making implied by corporatism, with aspects of the informality and practical power politics implied by pluralism.

Two very important and related political developments that are leading to changes in the ways that interest groups do their business derive from the general "globalization" of economic life and the continual accumulation of functions by the European Union. Both have the effect that key decisions are increasingly made—and thus must be influenced—at the supranational level. The European Union itself is a distinctive decision-making system, quite unlike any single national government and blending elements of pluralism and corporatism in its decision-making style. For many interest groups, it is very important to influence EU decisions, because they may weigh far more heavily on their interests than any decision taken by a national government. EU agricultural policy, for example, has a direct and vital bearing on how easy it is for every European farmer to earn a living.

One response to this development has been the growth in importance of European "peak" organizations, which reflect interests (of farmers, for example, or trade unions) at a supranational level. Because these peak organizations have direct access to EU decision-making elites, it is possible for a national interest group to bypass its national government completely and to attempt to influence EU decision making either directly or through its European peak organization. Alternatively, or indeed at the same time, a national interest group may put pressure on its national government in an attempt to influence EU policy through the government's role in the Council of Ministers. (For an analysis of the various channels open to those trying to influence EU agricultural policy, see Pappi and Henning, "Organization.")

This system of "multilevel" governance has created a complex environment for the exercise of group influence on key decisions. Many actors are trying to influence one another and are exploring different routes through a complicated system of interactions. One way of trying to make sense of such a complex system of links, whether within the EU or elsewhere, is to see them as a network. This approach has led to a distinctive way to study the paths that interest groups use to influence policy, which is to describe and analyze the entire system as a "policy network." David Knoke (p. 508) captures what most writers mean by a policy network as "a heterogeneous set of persons or organizations, linked by one or more relationships into an enduring social structure with the potential to influence public policy decisions of interest to the network's members."

The key relationships behind the idea of a policy network are those of mutual interdependence, and therefore of exchanges, between key actors in the policy-making system. These relationships are important because, as König and Bräuninger (p. 448) put it, "no one actor is capable of deciding public policies in western democracies." Since all policy influence involves interaction with others, when a public or private actor interacts over and over again with the same set of other actors, both sides steadily learn about each other and begin to develop well-defined mutual interactions. Thus, farmers' organizations these days deal repeatedly with their national Department of Agriculture, with farmers' organizations in other countries, with European "peak" organizations for farmers, and with particular offices of the European Commission. Each has information the other values. Each may be helpful to the other in some part of the process of either making or implementing policy. Thus, relationships between the various actors, including both private actors and agencies of national or supranational government, come to be conducted according to clearly understood informal rules of the game that can be as potent as formal institutions. This set of established interactions can be thought of as a policy network. (For thorough introductions to the literature on policy networks, see Thatcher; Pappi and Henning, "Policy." For a skeptical view, see Dowding.)

Policy networks differ from corporatist decision-making structures in the crucial sense that a network of relationships between key actors is not hierarchical (van Waarden). Corporatist decision structures are pyramid-shaped and are organized from the top down. Policy networks, in contrast, look like spiders' webs. The notion of a policy network might in this way seem to bridge the gap between pluralist and corporatist models of policy making. However, we still need to know which actors have the power to influence which decisions in which political arenas if we are to tell an accurate story about how any particular policy dispute is settled.

Policy Networks in Action: Doctors

Physicians are typically organized as members of a self-governing profession. This arrangement provides an important basis for the exercise of political power on behalf of sectional interests. The key powers associated with the professional status of physicians derive from the fact that health care is an expert service, one that cannot properly be evaluated by its consumers or even by nonspecialist political elites. Thus doctors have the more or less unchallenged ability to define and defend the professional standards of medical practice and to control medical training and licensing—and hence access to the profession. This control is typically exercised by a powerful guild-like medical association to which all licensed physicians must belong. The medical association typically also plays a vital policy implementation role, besides controlling professional ethics and standards (and thus practice), through a system of peer review. Politicians can make all the policies they want on health and medicine, but they cannot implement such policies effectively without the cooperation of the medical profession, organized by the medical association. This constraint gives the medical lobby a very powerful position in the policy process.

The control of highly specialized information by the profession, and the need for the cooperation of physicians in the effective implementation of policy, form the basis of an exchange relationship between physicians and decision-making elites that can very usefully be thought of as a policy network. In practice, European medical associations are incorporated into political decision making in ways that vary somewhat from country to country. In Germany, for example, the process of making health policy has taken on a decidedly corporatist flavor since the establishment of a Concerted Action organization in 1977. This has a sixty-member council, with representatives of medical associations, hospitals, insurers, and government, that makes annual recommendations on health care spending and doctors' pay (Altenstetter; Dohler). Thus the situation was that:

> Despite some attempts by governments to clip doctors' wings, the autonomy of German physicians remains unchallenged. ... On the macroeconomic level, their participation in a corporatist negotiating institution serves as a buffer against possible threats to professional autonomy, ... [facilitating] package deals between government and physicians, such as moderate fee increases in return for restricted access to medical schools. On the regional and local level the extensive self-governing authority, which is legally as well as structurally established, ... makes changes in the power structure extremely difficult to implement. (Dohler, pp. 186–88)

The situation in Sweden is rather different, despite the existence of the centralized Swedish Medical Association (SLF), which represents about 90 percent of all Swedish physicians (Dohler, p. 193). The SLF has monopoly bargaining rights in negotiations over pay and conditions, but the effectiveness of such an apparently powerful position was undermined by the decentralization of the responsibility for health care provision to Swedish local councils (Lane and Arvidson). What the Swedish example teaches us is that a powerful and hierarchical medical association can have a major impact on national policy making at an elite level, but its ability to influence a much larger set of local policy makers may be much weaker. At the local level of politics, the electoral concerns of politicians are more likely to prevail over sectional interests, and policy makers seem less likely to be co-opted into the received wisdom of what is good and bad about medical policy.

Overall, however, the Swedish case seems to be the exception to the European norm. When health policy is made at the national level, medical associations in Europe appear to be able to exploit with potent effect their ability to monopolize the market in expertise—a situation also found in the United States, given the political role of the American Medical Association. And the exercise of this monopoly inevitably gives medical associations both control over vital information and a key role in the implementation, as well as the making, of health care policy. This creates the type of mutual interdependency between decision makers and interest organizations that can fruitfully be seen as a policy network. (For an overview of the politics of health in Europe, see Freeman.)

Policy Networks in Action: Farmers

There is a strong tradition in Europe for farmers' groups to be very well integrated into the political system, wielding disproportionately more influence over policy makers than many other types of economic actor—such as the *consumers* of farm products, for example, or the unemployed. A succession of wars in Europe has led governments to cultivate indigenous food producers very carefully and set up a policy-making regime based on assumptions of mutual interdependence between decision makers and interest groups—in other words, to set up a policy network. As a result, there has been a long tradition of farm support programs, typically involving government intervention in agricultural markets at guaranteed prices, to protect the interests of farmers. For those countries in what has become the European Union (EU), this tradition was enshrined in the Common Agricultural Policy (CAP), with its system of intervention prices and consequent "mountains" of stored butter or grain and "lakes" of surplus wine or milk. Subsequent payoffs for farmers have been immense (see Chapter 5).

The very generous terms of the CAP were a testimony to the key role of the farmers' lobby in each of the member states over much of the postwar era. For a long time the CAP was perhaps the most important and expensive feature of EU economic policy, but its importance began to decline during the 1990s, a process that culminated in radical reforms of the CAP in 2003 and 2004. The reforms replaced the long-standing policy of price supports for agricultural produce with what was intended to be more transparent direct payments to farmers on specified public policy grounds. The reforms arose as a combined result of the enlargement of the EU to the east and ongoing north–south negotiations on world trade under the auspices of the World Trade Organization (WTO). In particular the enlargement of the EU brought in a number of eastern European countries with very substantial farming sectors. In almost all eastern European EU members, the proportion of the workforce engaged in agriculture far exceeded that of the western European member states. A total of 4 million additional farmers joined the 7 million already in the EU, and 38 million hectares (94 million acres) were added to the existing 130 million hectares (321 million acres) of land under agricultural production (europa.eu.int/comm/agriculture/publi/enlarge/text_en.pdf). Funding to the states under the CAP began to flow in October 2004, and it was widely perceived that the CAP in particular and EU finances more generally would simply have collapsed under the weight of its previous generous terms. The combined effect of the WTO negotiations and the economic and political realities of enlargement, therefore, meant that western European farmers' groups found their traditional ability to dictate the terms of agricultural policy significantly undermined.

Although the situation may thus change in the future, it is probably fair to say, looking back, that the prominence of the CAP from the early days of European integration has meant that agricultural policy making was one of the first policy arenas to involve a very explicit and effective policy network that operated at a supranational level. Farmers' organizations quickly learned that they needed to pile on the pressure in Brussels as well as in their national capitals, and they quickly adapted to do so. This tactic was made easier because the power of the farmers' lobby is usually exercised, even in pluralist systems such as Britain's, in a very institutionalized way. Farmers' organizations, such as the British National Farmers' Union, have traditionally had consultative status with Ministries of Agriculture on many matters. Farmers and civil servants have tended to settle matters between themselves and to exclude other interest groups if at all possible (Smith, p. 313). It has been quite common, furthermore, for farmers' groups to be involved in policy implementation, especially in relation to the distribution among individual farmers of the official national and regional production quotas for particular agricultural commodities. Above-market intervention prices typically lead to such quotas being introduced to avoid massive overproduction.

The political clout of farmers is not confined to the corridors of power, however, and farmers' groups have a long tradition of direct action, including large-scale demonstrations and blockades. An example can be found in skirmishes on the fringes of the 1999 "beef war" between Britain and France, provoked by France's continued refusal to import British beef after an international team of vets had decided that Britain's epidemic of "mad cow" disease was largely under control. Threats of reciprocal measures against French beef in Britain provoked a brief blockade of English Channel ports by tractor-driving French farmers. This was the latest in a series of disputes between Britain and France in which policy disagreements between politicians had quickly filtered down to local farmers' organizations and French farmers had taken direct action on the streets in support of policy objectives shared with the French decision-making elite.

France and Britain are by no means unique. The access of farmers' groups to policy-making elites is very good indeed in many European countries. This close cooperation between the farmers and the civil service might on the face of it look almost corporatist. However, the lack of any formal role in the political equation for any other "social partner" identifies this type of decision-making arrangement as being more like a closed policy network than an example of full-fledged corporatism.

→ CONCLUSION

Most recent developments in both the theory and the empirical analysis of interest representation imply that we are asking the wrong question if we ask whether a particular political system as a whole is characterized by corporatist or pluralist policy making. Political scientists these days concentrate much more on policy making within particular sectors. Corporatists see this as "sectoral" or "meso-" corporatism. Pluralists make a distinction between sectors characterized by particular "policy networks," which include some groups and exclude others, and sectors in which there is a more traditionally free-for-all pluralist competition between groups.

Even in a country such as Austria, the "model-generator" that all commentators agree has provided the clearest example of corporatist decision making in modern Europe, corporatism is concerned mainly with economic policy, especially with prices and income policy. A great many groups that represent important political interests have nothing to do with corporatist decision making. At the other end of the scale—even in Britain, cited by most as having a very clear-cut pluralist decision-making regime—there is an officially established state church, there are self-governing professions in the key areas of law and medicine, there is very close interaction between farmers' groups and the relevant government department, and there has been a major experiment with "contracts" between the social partners over prices and incomes.

The parallel development of the pluralist notion of a policy network and the notion of sectoral corporatism highlights the fact that as each approach has come to terms with the other's arguments, the two approaches have grown together. Nonetheless, given the vital importance of economic policy making and the role of employers and trade unions in this, it does still make some sense to classify countries by the extent to which the economic policy arena, at least, is characterized by corporatist or pluralist institutions. In some countries, the ones that we might think of as being more corporatist, a small number of powerful, authoritative, and centralized "peak" organizations monopolize the legitimate right to participate in the making and implementing of economic policy. In other countries, which we might think of as being more pluralist, trade union and employers' federations may well get their voices heard, but only if they make an explicit and often divisive political effort to do so. And these groups rarely participate in policy implementation.

In all countries, however, the only recourse for groups outside the political establishment—inevitably, the vast majority of groups anywhere—is the traditional portfolio of techniques that characterize pressure politics. In most European countries, we can find a range of groups sharing features of organization, membership, and strategy that identify them as new social movements. These groups provide a medium of interest representation quite distinct from traditional parties, unions, and interest organizations, and they do so in a way that has been significantly enhanced by the development of the Internet and the World Wide Web. In representing interests and opinions in this way, such groups are providing an alternative medium for political participation by citizens and in a sense are counterbalancing the long-term trend for declining citizen participation in more traditional forms of public decision making.

As the discussions in this chapter reveal, there have probably been more "mainstream" intellectual fashions and trends involved in the analysis of politics outside parliament than in any of the other subjects covered in this book. Perhaps this is because it is in this particular aspect of politics that we can see most clearly the impact of some of the major long-term trends that either have affected, or surely will affect in the future, the more general processes of representative government in modern Europe. We see a process of European integration that is transferring to the supranational level powers that used to be the cherished prerogatives of national governments. We see the rapid collapse of the former Soviet bloc and the radical political transformation of many eastern European countries. Almost inconceivably when viewed from the perspective of 1985 (and it must be said humbling for political scientists who are honest with themselves), a significant number of these countries are now members of the European Union—so that these supranation policy-making powers are now exercised in a large and complex environment. We see a process of globalization, associated with technological developments in information and communications technology, that is also likely to have a fundamental impact on the ways in which people try to influence political outcomes. In one sense governments have never before had so much technology at their disposal to gather, to process, and to act on information about their citizens, realizing the fears expressed in George Orwell's classic *1984*. In another sense, those same citizens have never before had so much technology at their disposal to gather their own information and to communicate and make common cause with like-minded others whom they have never met, others who might live in many different parts of the world. It is a plain fact that political campaigning and pressure group activity in most modern state these days make immense use of the Internet and the World Wide Web. We do not yet know how much and what kind of difference all of this will really make. But we should not be surprised to find that these differences are likely to be felt, in the first instance, in how people conduct politics outside parliament.

REFERENCES

Adams, Paul S.: "Corporatism and Comparative Politics: Is There a New Century of Corporatism?" in Howard J. Wiarda (ed.), *New Directions in Comparative Politics,* 3rd ed., Westview Press, Boulder (CO), 2002.

Altenstetter, C.: "Hospital Planners and Medical Professionals in the Federal Republic of Germany," in G. Freddi and J. W. Bjorkman (eds.), *Controlling Medical Professionals: The Comparative Politics of Health Governance,* Sage, London, 1989.

Beveridge, F., S. Nott, and K. Stephen: "Mainstreaming and the Engendering of Policy: A Means to an End?" *Journal of European Public Policy,* vol. 7, no. 3, 2000, pp. 385–405.

Bimber, Bruce: *Information and American Democracy: Technology in the Evolution of Political Power,* Cambridge University Press, Cambridge, 2003.

Bimber, Bruce: "The Internet and Political Transformation: Populism, Community, and Accelerated Pluralism," *Polity,* vol. 31, no. 1, 1998, pp. 133–60.

Carter, Neil: *The Politics of the Environment: Ideas, Activism, Policy,* Cambridge University Press, Cambridge, 2001.

Cawson, A.: *Corporatism and Political Theory,* Basil Blackwell, Oxford, 1986.

Dahl, R. A.: *A Preface to Democratic Theory,* University of Chicago Press, Chicago, 1956.

Dahlerup, D. (ed.): *The New Women's Movement: Feminism and Political Power in Europe and the USA,* Sage, London, 1986.

Dalton, Russell: *Citizen Politics,* 3rd ed., Chatham House, Chatham (NJ), 2002.

Dohler, M.: "Physicians' Professional Autonomy in the Welfare State: Endangered or Preserved?" in G. Freddi and J. W. Bjorkman (eds.), *Controlling Medical Professionals: The Comparative Politics of Health Governance,* Sage, London, 1989.

Dowding, Keith: "Model or Metaphor? A Critical Review of the Policy Network Approach," *Political Studies,* vol. 43, no. 1, 1995, pp. 136–58.

Freeman, Richard: *The Politics of Health in Europe,* Manchester University Press, Manchester, 2000.

Gerlich, P., E. Grande, and W. Müller: "Corporatism in Crisis: Stability and Change of Social Partnership in Austria," *Political Studies,* vol. 36, no. 2, 1988, pp. 209–23.

Greenpeace: *Annual Report 2004,* www.greenpeace.org

Iankova, Elena: "The Transformative Corporatism of Eastern Europe," *East European Politics and Society,* vol. 12, no. 2, 1998, pp. 222–64.

Jahn, D.: "The Rise and Decline of New Politics and the Greens in Sweden and Germany: Resource Dependence and New Social Cleavages," *European Journal of Political Research,* vol. 24, 1993, pp. 177–94.

Jordan, G.: "The Pluralism of Pluralism: An Anti-theory?" *Political Studies,* vol. 38, no. 2, 1990, pp. 286–301.

Jordan, G.: "Sub-Governments, Policy Communities and Networks: Refilling Old Bottles," *Journal of Theoretical Politics,* vol. 2, no. 3, 1990, pp. 319–38.

Kavanagh, D.: *British Politics: Continuities and Change,* 2nd ed., Oxford University Press, Oxford, 1990.

Keman, H., and P. Whiteley: "Coping with Crisis: Divergent Strategies and Outcomes," in H. Keman, H. Paloheimo, and P. Whiteley (eds.), *Coping with the Economic Crisis: Alternative Responses to Economic Recession in Advanced Industrial Societies,* Sage, London, 1987.

Kitschelt, Herbert, Peter Lange, Gary Marks, and John D. Stephens (eds.): *Continuity and Change in Contemporary Capitalism.* Cambridge University Press, Cambridge, 1999.

König, Thomas, and Thomas Bräuninger: "The Formation of Policy Networks: Preferences, Institutions and Actors' Choice," *Journal of Theoretical Politics,* vol. 10, no. 4, 1998, pp. 445–71.

Knoke, David: "Who Steals My Purse Steals Trash: The Structure of Organizational Influence Reputation," *Journal of Theoretical Politics,* vol. 10, no. 4, 1998, pp. 507–30.

Kriesi, H., R. Koopmans, J. W. Duyvendak, and M. G. Giugni: "New Social Movements and Political Opportunities in Western Europe," *European Journal of Political Research,* vol. 22, 1992, pp. 219–44.

Lane, J. -E., and S. Arvidson: "Health Professionals in the Swedish System," in G. Freddi and J. W. Bjorkman (eds.), *Controlling Medical Professionals: The Comparative Politics of Health Governance,* Sage, London, 1989.

Laver, Michael, and John Garry: "Estimating Policy Positions from Political Texts," *American Journal of Political Science,* vol. 44, 2000, pp. 619–34.

Lehmbruch, G.: "Liberal Corporatism and Party Government," in P. Schmitter and G. Lehmbruch (eds.), *Trends Towards Corporatist Intermediation,* Sage, London, 1979.

Leyenaar, Monique: *Political Empowerment of Women: The Netherlands and Other Countries,* Martinus Nijhoff, Leiden, 2004.

Lijphart, Arend: *Patterns of Democracy: Government Forms and Performance in Thirty-Six Countries,* Yale University Press, New Haven, 1999.

Lindblom, C.: *Politics and Markets,* Basic Books, New York, 1977.

Lovenduski, J., and J. Outshoorn: *The New Politics of Abortion,* Sage, London, 1986.

Luther, Richard, and Wolfgang Müller (eds.): *Politics in Austria: Still a Case of Consociationalism?* Frank Cass, London, 1992.

Marin, B.: "From Consociationalism to Technocorporatism: The Austrian Case as a Model-Generator?" in I. Scholten (ed.), *Political Stability and Neo-Corporatism: Corporatist Integration and Societal Cleavages in Western Europe,* Sage, London, 1987.

Mazey, Sonia: *Gender Mainstreaming in the EU: Principles and Practices,* Kogan Page, London, 2001.

Mazey, Sonia: "Integrating Gender—Intellectual and 'Real World' Mainstreaming," *Journal of European Public Policy,* vol. 7, no. 3, 2000, pp. 333–45.

Murphy, Gary: "Interest Groups in the Policy Making Process," in John Coakley and Michael Gallagher (eds.), *Politics in the Republic of Ireland,* 4th ed., Routledge, London, 2004, pp. 352–83.

Ost, David: "Illusory Corporatism in Eastern Europe: Neoliberal Tripartism and Postcommunist Class Identities," in *Politics & Society,* vol. 28, no. 4, 2000, pp. 503–30.

Pappi, Franz, and Christian Henning: "The Organization of Influence on the EC's Common Agricultural Policy: A Network Approach," *European Journal of Political Research,* vol. 36, 1999, pp. 257–81.

Pappi, Franz, and Christian Henning: "Policy Networks: More than a Metaphor," *Journal of Theoretical Politics,* vol. 10, no. 4, 1998, pp. 553–76.

Rees, T.: *Mainstreaming Equality in the European Union: Education, Training and Labour Market Policies,* Routledge, London, 1998.

Rootes, Christopher (ed.): *Environmental Protest in Western Europe,* Oxford University Press, Oxford, 2003.

Rucht, D. (ed.): *Research on Social Movements: The State of the Art in Western Europe and the USA,* Campus Verlag and Westview Press, Frankfurt and Boulder (CO), 1991.

Schmitt-Beck, R.: "A Myth Institutionalised: Theory and Research on New Social Movements in Germany," *European Journal of Political Research,* vol. 21, 1992, pp. 357–84.

Siaroff, Alan: "Corporatism in 24 Industrial Democracies: Meaning and Measurement," *European Journal of Political Research,* vol. 36, 1999, pp. 175–205.

Smith, M. J.: "Pluralism, Reformed Pluralism and Neopluralism: The Role of Pressure Groups in Policy-Making," *Political Studies,* vol. 38, no. 2, 1990, pp. 302–22.

Stark, David, and Laszlo Bruzst: *Postsocialist Pathways: Transforming Politics and Property in East Central Europe,* Cambridge University Press, Cambridge, 1998.

Thatcher, Mark: "The Development of Policy Network Analysis: From Modest Origins to Overarching Frameworks," *Journal of Theoretical Politics,* vol. 10, no. 4, 1998, pp. 389–416.

van Waarden, F.: "New Dimensions and Types of Policy Networks," *European Journal of Political Research,* vol. 21, 1992, pp. 29–52.

Wiarda, H. J.: *Corporatism and Comparative Politics,* M. E. Sharpe, New York, 1997.

Woldendorp, Jaap: "Neo-Corporatism as a Strategy for Conflict Regulation in the Netherlands," *Acta Politica,* vol. 30, 1995, pp. 121–51.

INDEX